NOTE ON THE COVER ILLUSTRATION

"Be on Guard!" by D. Moor (Dmitrii Orlov, 1883–1946), a poster issued in late 1921, depicts an outsized Red Army soldier standing astride western Russia, defending its borders. The central figure likely represents Leon Trotsky, then commissar of war, a veritable icon of revolutionary militancy. The image can appear as shorthand for centuries of Russia-centered imperial aggression, but at the time of its production, its message was precisely the opposite: the figure was intended to be seen as an anti-imperialist defender of the Revolution. Other meanings, far from those intended by the artist, can be read into the image as well. The variety of interpretations and the ways those interpretations are deployed illustrate both the multivalency and the power of images in history. See Laura Engelstein's essay in this volume, from which this note is adapted.

PICTURING RUSSIAN EMPIRE

pinxit.
Anno 1767
Comtesse
de Sa M.I.
Barbara
Dame d'honeur

PICTURING RUSSIAN EMPIRE

EDITED BY

Valerie Kivelson

UNIVERSITY OF MICHIGAN

Sergei Kozlov

UNIVERSITY OF TYUMEN

Joan Neuberger

UNIVERSITY OF TEXAS AT AUSTIN

OXFORD

UNIVERSITY PRESS

Oxford University Press is a department of the University of Oxford.
It furthers the University's objective of excellence in research, scholarship,
and education by publishing worldwide. Oxford is a registered trade mark
of Oxford University Press in the UK and in certain other countries.

Published in the United States of America by Oxford University Press
198 Madison Avenue, New York, NY 10016, United States of America.

For titles covered by Section 112 of the US Higher Education Opportunity
Act, please visit www.oup.com/us/he for the latest information about
pricing and alternate formats.

Library of Congress Cataloging-in-Publication Data

Names: Kivelson, Valerie A. (Valerie Ann), editor, author. | Kozlov,
Sergei, 1986– editor, author. | Neuberger, Joan, 1953– editor, author.
Title: Picturing Russian empire / edited by Valerie Kivelson, University of
Michigan, Sergei Kozlov, University of Tyumen, Joan Neuberger,
University of Texas at Austin.
Description: New York ; Oxford : Oxford University Press, [2024] | Includes
bibliographical references and index. | Summary: "Picturing Russian
Empire brings a fresh approach to both Russian and Imperial Studies by
centering the visual. In a series of short essays, focused on striking
images, the authors reexamine historical encounters and exchanges within
the shifting borders of the empire. The book not only offers
interpretations of the images but also shows the kinds of work that
images themselves can accomplish by changing or solidifying notions of
how the world is or should be organized. The book advances the idea of a
"pictosphere" in which images from the many visual cultures of the
empire interacted. The essays are lively and accessible, crafted to
engage the reader. Picturing Russian Empire also provides a historical
and visual approach to understanding present-day conflicts in Russia,
Eastern Europe, and Eurasia"—Provided by publisher.
Identifiers: LCCN 2022046974 (print) | LCCN 2022046975 (ebook) | ISBN
9780197600528 (paperback) | ISBN 9780197657065 (spiral bound) | ISBN
9780197600542 (epub) | ISBN 9780197600535 (ebook) | ISBN 9780197617304
Subjects: LCSH: Russia—History. | Soviet Union—History. | Russia
(Federation)—History. | Arts and history—Russia. | Arts and
history—Soviet Union. | Arts and history—Russia (Federation) | Arts,
Russian—History.
Classification: LCC DK42 .P53 2024 (print) | LCC DK42 (ebook) | DDC
947.084—dc23/eng/20221003
LC record available at https://lccn.loc.gov/2022046974
LC ebook record available at https://lccn.loc.gov/2022046975

Printed by Sheridan Books, Inc., United States of America

CONTENTS

LIST OF IMAGES

LIST OF MAPS

ABOUT THE CONTRIBUTORS

Gregory Afinogenov is Associate Professor of Imperial Russian History at Georgetown University. His first book, *Spies and Scholars: Chinese Secrets and Imperial Russia's Quest for World Power*, was published in 2020.

Mollie Arbuthnot is a Junior Research Fellow in History and Russian Studies at Jesus College, University of Cambridge. She specializes in visual and material culture in the Soviet Union—including mass media, propaganda, and theories of viewership—as well as the cultural history of the Soviet national republics, especially Uzbekistan. She received her PhD from the University of Manchester and taught in the history department at Durham University before joining Cambridge in 2021.

Sarah Badcock is Professor of Modern History at the University of Nottingham. Her research focuses on lived experience in late imperial and revolutionary Russia. She has published multiple articles and books, including *A Prison without Walls? Eastern Siberian Exile in the Last Years of Tsarism* and *Politics and the People in Revolutionary Russia: A Provincial History.*

Nick Baron is Associate Professor in History at the University of Nottingham. He has published two monographs, *Soviet Karelia. Politics, Planning and Terror in Stalin's Russia, 1920–1939* and *The King of Karelia: Colonel P. J. Woods and the British Intervention in North Russia 1918–1919*, as well as five edited volumes and numerous articles on the history and historical geography of Russia and Eastern Europe. He has also acted as consultant to three major exhibitions, at the Moscow Biennale (2013) and the British Library (2016 and 2017), and has co-curated a multisite exhibition on Displaced Persons in post-war Europe (2012–2023).

Maria Grazia Bartolini is Associate Professor of Medieval Slavic Culture at the University of Milan. She is the author of a monograph on Hryhorii Skovoroda and

Christian Neoplatonism (*Piznai samoho sebe. Neoplatonichni dzherela v tvorchosti H. S. Skovoroda*) and various articles on the religious culture of early modern Ukraine. Her research interests focus on the intersection between preaching and the visual arts in seventeenth-century Ukraine.

Nadja Berkovich is Teaching Assistant Professor of Russian at the University of Arkansas. Her current research is on the genre of literary ethnography, focusing on the ways in which Russian and Jewish writers represented the non-Christian ethnic subjects of the empire. She has published articles on Bogoraz's sketches about the Gomel pogrom of 1903 and on memory of the Holocaust in the works of the Russian Austrian writer Vladimir Vertlib.

Rosalind P. Blakesley is Professor of Russian and European Art and a Fellow of Pembroke College at the University of Cambridge. She has published widely on issues of artistic dialogue and differentiation across Europe, with particular interest in the visual culture of imperial Russia and the Baltic region and recent focus on portraiture, women artists, and the history of artistic education and professionalization. Her latest publications include *Women Artists in the Reign of Catherine the Great* (2022) and *The Russian Canvas: Painting in Imperial Russia 1757–1881* (2016).

Ekaterina Boltunova is Professor at National Research University Higher School of Economics (HSE; Moscow) and Head of HSE's International Laboratory "Russia's Regions in Historical Perspective." Her recent publications include the edited volume *Regioni Rossiiskoi Imperii: identichnost', reprezentatsiia, (na)znachenie* (coedited with Willard Sunderland) and the article "The Last King of Poland: Nicholas I's Warsaw Coronation and Russian-Polish Historical Memory" in *Kritika: Explorations in Russian and Eurasian History.*

Naomi Caffee is an Assistant Professor of Russian and Humanities at Reed College. Her research focuses on ethnic minority and transnational writing in Russian with a particular focus on authors from Central Asia, the Caucasus, Siberia, and the Russian Far North. Together with the Tbilisi-based scholar Robert Denis, she also manages "Beyond Caricature," a digital collection of early twentieth century political cartoons from the South Caucasus (schmerling.org).

Craig Campbell is currently working on the cultural history of an unbuilt hydroelectric dam in central Siberia, the weird time of a shadow, and the aesthetics of damaged, degraded, and manipulated photographs. In 2014, he published *Agitating Images: Photography Against History in Indigenous Siberia*, which explored, through archival photography, ethnography, and historical research, the history of contact between Bolshevik revolutionaries and Indigenous peoples in central Siberia.

Robert Denis is an independent researcher, writer, and translator based in Tbilisi, Georgia. His writing focuses on the history, politics, and cultures of the South Caucasus and Russia and has been published by Baku Research Institute, *Literratura*, and Freedom House. Along with Naomi Caffee, he created the site schmerling.org, dedicated to the graphic art of the founder of political caricature in the Caucasus, Oskar Schmerling (1863–1938).

Laura Engelstein is Henry S. NcNeil Professor Emerita of Russian History at Yale University and Professor Emerita of History at Princeton University. She is a member of the American Academy of Arts and Sciences, a corresponding member of the British Academy, and most recently the author of *Russia in Flames: War, Revolution, Civil War, 1914–1921*.

Catherine Evtuhov is a Professor of History at Columbia University and previously at Georgetown University. She is currently working on a book, *Russia in the Age of Empress Elizabeth, 1741–1761*. Her publications range in topic from the eighteenth to the early twentieth century and include *Portrait of a Russian Province: Economy, Society, and Civilization in Nineteenth-Century Nizhnii Novgorod*.

Joshua First is the Croft Associate Professor of History and International Studies at the University of Mississippi and specializes in the history of Russia and Ukraine in the twentieth and twenty-first centuries. He has published articles on Ukrainian cinema, Soviet film sociology, and the politics of melodrama. His book *Ukrainian Cinema: Belonging and Identity during the Soviet Thaw* appeared in 2014, and a follow-up volume on the Ukrainian film, *Shadows of Forgotten Ancestors*, came out in 2016. First's next book is about the idea of health as a socialist commodity in the period after Stalin.

Anna Graber is Assistant Professor of History of Science and Technology at the University of Minnesota, where she specializes in the history of earth science in early modern Russia and Europe. Her research focuses on the shifting meanings of the earth in the eighteenth century as Russians engaged with European and Indigenous knowledge traditions to build a rapidly developing mining industry.

Evgeny Grishin is a historian of Russia in the period of early modernity with particular interests in religion, language, and materiality. He received his BA and MA degrees from Russian universities and his PhD degree in history from the University of Kansas. In 2017–2020, Grishin was working at the School of Advanced Studies, University of Tyumen, Russia.

Helena Holzberger is a Lecturer in the program in Russian and Asian Studies at Ludwig-Maximilian University of Munich. Her first forthcoming monograph deals with popular photography in Central Asia, 1870-1940. Recently she started her second book project on the maritime history of the Soviet Union during the Cold War.

Valerie Kivelson teaches at the University of Michigan, where she is Thomas N. Tentler Collegiate Professor and Arthur F. Thurnau Professor of History. Her publications include *Russia's Empires*, coauthored with Ronald G. Suny; *Cartographies of Tsardom: The Land and Its Meanings in Seventeenth-Century Russia*; and most recently, *Witchcraft in Early Modern & Modern Russia and Ukraine: A Sourcebook*, translated and edited with Christine D. Worobec.

Nathaniel Knight is Professor and Chair of the History Department at Seton Hall University. He has published numerous articles on the history of Russian ethnography, Russian Orientalism, concepts of human diversity in Russian culture, Russian intellectual history, and the visual representation of ethnicity. His most recent article is "Faces of Russia's Empire: The Bergholtz Collection of Ethnographic Images" in *Baltic Worlds*.

Nancy S. Kollmann is William H. Bonsall Professor in History at Stanford University. Her works include *Kinship and Politics: The Making of the Muscovite Political System, 1345–1547; By Honor Bound: State and Society in Early Modern Russia; Crime and Punishment in Early Modern Russia, 1500–1725*); and *The Russian Empire 1450–1801*. She is currently working on visual images of Russia in early modern European print culture.

Irina Konovalova is the Chief Researcher and Head of the Department of Auxiliary Historical Disciplines at the Institute of World History of the Academy of Science in Moscow. She specializes in source study and the history of medieval Islamic geography and cartography, the history of connections of Ancient Rus and eastern Europe with the Islamic world, and also the history of the Carpathian lands and the Lower Danube region in the Middle Ages. Her most recent publications include *Ancient Rus in the System of Eurasian Communications (IX–X Centuries)*, coauthored with E. A. Mel'nikova (in Russian), and *The Riphean Mountains in Ancient and Medieval Geocartography*, coauthored with T. N. Jackson and A. V. Podosinov (in Russian).

Fedor Korandei is Senior Research Fellow in Laboratory of Historical Geography and Regionalistics at Tyumen State University. His recent research focuses on boosterism in the development of Siberia of the late Imperial and Soviet periods and practices of the literary imagination in the eastern expansion of the Russian Empire and the Soviet Union. Most recently, he published an article in *Novoe literaturnoe obozrenie* on state boosterism propaganda aimed at attracting workers to socialist development projects in late Soviet period.

Anna Kotomina is Senior Researcher at the Polytechnic Museum, Moscow. She is the program director of the annual conference, "History of Science and Technology in Russia and Soviet Union. Museum Studies," and curator and co-organizer of the museum exhibitions. In 2009–2019, she was a lecturer in the history and theory of media at the Russian State University for the Humanities, Moscow State University, and Higher School of Economics, and she has appeared as an expert on TV and radio broadcasts. She studies and publishes on the social history of Russian science, art, and technology.

Sergei Kozlov is Associate Professor and Head of the Laboratory for Historical Geography and Regionalistics at the University of Tyumen. His research centers on Byzantine relations with the Turkic-speaking nomads of eastern Europe and with the Rus from the late ninth to early thirteenth centuries. His recent publications include "'Svyatoslaviada,' or What is Common between the Knyaz Svyatoslav Igorevich and the Heroes of Poet Homer?" in *Studia Slavica et Balcanica Petropolitana*; "Leo the Deacon and Scylitzas' Narratives about the Battle of Svyatoslav near Dorostolon (971): A Fragment of the Lost Byzantine Epic?" in *Stratum Plus Journal*; and "More than Enemy: The Modes of Description of Pechenegs in the Byzantine Literature of the Early Comnene Epoch" in *Byzantinoslavica*.

Angelina Lucento is an assistant professor of history and art history at the National Research University–Higher School of Economics in Moscow. Trained as a social art historian, she studies the global histories of painting and photography with a specific focus on the contributions that artists from the former USSR made to those histories. Lucento is completing her first book, *The Socialist Surface: Painting as the Origin of Soviet Media Culture.*

Galina V. Lyubimova graduated from the Novosibirsk State University and the Moscow Institute of Ethnology and Anthropology of the Russian Academy of Sciences, where she studied the traditional culture and folk rituals of various groups of the Russian population of Siberia. Her interest in environmental and cultural landscape studies has continued while working as a senior research scholar at the Institute of Archeology and Ethnography, SB RAS, Novosibirsk, Russia. She is the author of the works, *The Symbolism of Age in the Calendar Holidays of Russian Siberians* and *Essays on the History of the Interaction of Rural Siberians with the Natural Environment (on the Materials of the Russian Agricultural Tradition)*, both in Russian.

Olga Maiorova is Associate Professor of Russian Literature and History at the University of Michigan. Her book *From the Shadow of Empire: Defining the Russian Nation through Cultural Mythology, 1855–1870* focuses on the intersections between literature, intellectual history, and nationalist discourses. She is the coeditor, with Deborah Martinsen, of *Dostoevsky in Context* and of several books published in Russia.

Evgeny Manzhurin is a researcher at the Karelian Institute, University of Eastern Finland. His research focuses on histories and geographies of space and place. His publications examine peripheral agency and local imaginaries of space, time, and order in Soviet cities. He currently works on spatial imaginaries in Soviet and post-Soviet Ukraine.

Erin McBurney teaches world history at Albuquerque Academy in Albuquerque, New Mexico.

Louise McReynolds is the Cary C. Boshamer Professor of History at the University of North Carolina, where she specializes in the cultural and intellectual movements of nineteenth-century Russia. She has published on the mass-circulation press, commercial culture, and sensational murder, consistently posing the broad question how Russians adapted to the changes associated with modernity by making it their own. The Guggenheim Foundation, National Endowment for the Humanities, Fulbright Scholar Program's Institute for Advanced Study, and National Humanities Center have supported her research.

Yulia Mikhailova is an associate professor of history at New Mexico Tech. She is the author of *Property, Power, and Authority in Rus and Latin Europe, ca. 1000–1236.*

Erika Monahan is the author of *The Merchants of Siberia: Trade in Early Modern Eurasia*. She has written two other articles analyzing Remezov's atlas: "Binding Siberia: Semen Remezov's *Khorograficheskaia kniga* in Time and Through Time," in *The Life Cycle of Russian Things: From Fish Guts to Fabergé*, and "Moving Pictures: Tobol'sk Travelling in Early Modern Texts," in *Canadian-American Slavic Studies*. She is an editor of *Kritika: Explorations in Russian and Eurasian Studies*, a 2023–2024 Alexander von Humboldt Foundation fellow at the University of Cologne, and associate professor at the University of New Mexico. Her current work deals with Nicolaas Witsen and the mapping of Eurasia.

Joan Neuberger is Earl E. Sheffield Regents Professor of History Emerita at the University of Texas at Austin. Her most recent book, *This Thing of Darkness: Eisenstein's Ivan the Terrible in Stalin's Russia*, won the American Historical Association's George L. Mosse Book Prize. Her current project is about Eisenstein and nature, the politics of landscape, and the evolution of montage.

Stephen M. Norris is the Walter E. Havighurst Professor of Russian History and the Director of the Havighurst Center for Russian and Post-Soviet Studies at Miami University, Ohio. He is the author of two books, *War of Images: Russian Popular Prints, Wartime Culture, and National Identity, 1812–1945* and *Blockbuster History in the New*

Russia: Movies, Memory, and Patriotism. He is currently writing a biography of Boris Efimov, the Soviet political caricaturist.

Karen Petrone is Professor of History at the University of Kentucky and the inaugural Director of the UK College of Arts & Sciences' Cooperative for the Humanities and Social Sciences. She is the author of *Life Has Become More Joyous, Comrades: Celebrations in the Time of Stalin* and *The Great War in Russian Memory* and is currently researching Russian and Soviet war memory in the twenty-first-century.

Bart Pushaw is an art historian at the University of Copenhagen in the projects "The Art of Nordic Colonialism: Writing Transcultural Histories" and "Indulgent Images: Indigenous Modernisms of the Colonial Arctic." His research and curatorial work examines issues of race, coloniality, and gender, especially in the Circumpolar North, the Baltic States, and Central America between 1750 and 1950.

Katherine M. H. Reischl has published extensively on Russian and Soviet photography, including her monograph *Photographic Literacy: Cameras in the Hands of Russian Authors*. Her work on the intersections of text, image, and materiality also includes publications on Soviet children's literature and Slavic digital humanities. She is currently working on a multimedia project dedicated to color technologies and color theories in late and post-Soviet spaces.

Alison Rowley is a professor in the Department of History at Concordia University, Montreal. She is the author of *Open Letters: Russian Popular Culture and the Picture Postcard, 1880–1922* and *Putin Kitsch in America* as well as many articles about Russian/Soviet visual culture and social history.

Oksana Sarkisova is Research Fellow at Blinken Open Society Archives, co-founder of Visual Studies Platform at Central European University, and Director of the Verzio Documentary Film Festival, Budapest. She teaches and writes on film, memory politics, and amateur photography. She coedited *Past for the Eyes: East European Representations of Communism in Cinema and Museums after 1989* and authored *Screening Soviet Nationalities: Kulturfilms from the Far North to Central Asia* and *In Visible Presence: Soviet Afterlives in Family Photos* (with Olga Shevchenko).

Erik R. Scott is an historian of the Soviet Union, the Caucasus, and the Cold War. An associate professor of history at the University of Kansas and the editor of *The Russian Review*, he is the author of *Familiar Strangers: The Georgian Diaspora and the Evolution of Soviet Empire* and is completing a second book that considers how disputes over Soviet defectors defined the borders of a globalized world in ways that outlasted the USSR.

Charles Shaw is Assistant Professor of History at Central European University, Vienna. He is at work on a book manuscript about Central Asia during World War II. His articles have appeared in *Central Asian Survey, Kritika: Explorations in Russian and Eurasian History*, and *The Russian Review*.

Olga Shevchenko Paul H. Hunn '55 Professor in Social Studies at Williams College, Massachusetts. She is the author of *Crisis and the Everyday in Postsocialist Moscow* and *In Visible Presence* (with Oksana Sarkisova). She is the editor of *Double Exposure: Memory and Photography*, as well as the author of a number of articles on post-Soviet political culture, consumption, memory, and photography.

Yana Skorobogatov is the Harriman Chair Assistant Professor of History at Columbia University. Her current book manuscript is a history of the death penalty and death penalty abolition in Russia and the Soviet Union. Her second book project looks at the transition from communism to capitalism on the island of Sakhalin, along Russia's Pacific coast.

Alison K. Smith is Professor of History at the University of Toronto. She has published widely on the social and cultural history of tsarist Russia, in particular on serfdom, social status, and food. Her most recent publications are *Cabbage and Caviar: A History of Food in Russia* and a volume coedited with Matthew Romaniello and Tricia Starks, *The Life Cycle of Russian Things: From Fish Guts to Fabergé.*

Willard Sunderland is Henry R. Winkler Professor of Modern History at the University of Cincinnati . His recent publications include *Regiony rossiiskoi imperii: identichnost', reprezentatsiia, (na)znachenie* [Russia's Imperial Regions: Identity, Representation, Meaning], co-edited with Ekaterina Boltunova; *Russia's Great War and Revolution in the Far East: Re-Imagining the Northeast Asian Theater, 1914–22,* co-edited with David Wolff and Yokote Shinji; and *The Baron's Cloak: A History of the Russian Empire in War and Revolution.*

Ronald Grigor Suny is William H. Sewell, Jr., Distinguished University Professor of History and Professor of Political Science at the University of Michigan and Emeritus Professor of Political Science and History at the University of Chicago. His most recent publications include *"They Can Live in the Desert But Nowhere Else": A History of the Armenian Genocide; Russia's Empires* (with Valerie A. Kivelson)*; Red Flag Unfurled: History, Historians, and the Russian Revolution; Red Flag Wounded: Stalinism and the Fate of the Soviet Experiment*; and *Stalin: Passage to Revolution*.

Maria Taroutina is Associate Professor of Art History at Yale–NUS College in Singapore and specializes in the art of imperial and early Soviet Russia. Her first book, *The*

Icon and the Square: Russian Modernism and the Russo-Byzantine Revival, was awarded the 2019 University of Southern California Book Prize in Literary and Cultural Studies. Taroutina has also coedited three volumes, *Byzantium/Modernism: The Byzantine as Method in Modernity*, *New Narratives of Russian and East European Art: Between Traditions and Revolutions*, and *Russian Orientalism in a Global Context: Hybridity, Encounter and Representation, 1740-1940*. She is currently working on two new book projects: a monograph on Mikhail Vrubel and a study of Russian imperial visual culture, tentatively titled *Exotic Aesthetics: Art, Race, and Representation in Russia in the Age of Empire.*

Nikolai Vakhtin is University Professor and head of the Center for Arctic Social Studies at the European University, St. Petersburg, Russia. He specializes in sociolinguistics and linguistic anthropology of the Indigenous minorities of the Arctic/Siberia. He has published extensively on Yupik Eskimo, Aleut, and Yukaghir endangered languages. His recent publications include a book (in Russian) about Yukaghir birch bark writings.

Olessia Vovina is Adjunct Professor of Anthropology at Seton Hall University and was previously a research associate at the Museum of Anthropology and Ethnography (Kunstkamera) of the Russian Academy of Sciences in St. Petersburg. She has written on the history of Russian anthropology and cultural revival movements among the peoples of the Middle Volga region. Her research interests include nationalism, ethnicity, religion, and anthropology of art.

Robert Weinberg is the Isaac H. Clothier Professor of History and International Relations at Swarthmore College, where he teaches European and Russian history. His research interests include antisemitism and the Jewish question in nineteenth- and twentieth-century Russia, and he has published books and articles on pogroms and the 1905 revolution, ritual murder and the trial of Mendel Beilis, Birobidzhan, and the communist campaign against Judaism.

Jessica Werneke is currently a Visiting Assistant Professor of European History at the University of Iowa, who specializes in Soviet photography and visual culture. Previously, she was an Assistant Professor of Comparative Humanities at Habib University in Karachi, a British Academy Newton Fellow at Loughborough University in the United Kingdom, and a Postdoctoral Fellow at the Higher School of Economics in Moscow. Her current research investigates the intersections of amateur culture, gender, and the history of photography in the former Soviet republics.

Monica White is Associate Professor of Russian and Slavonic Studies at the University of Nottingham. Her monograph *Military Saints in Byzantium and Rus, 900–1300* was published in 2013 and *Byzantium and the Viking World*, coedited with Fedir

Androshchuk and Jonathan Shepard, in 2016. She has published widely on various aspects of Orthodox sainthood and Byzantine-Rus relations in the high and late medieval periods.

Emma Widdis is Professor of Slavonic Studies in the University of Cambridge and a fellow of Trinity College. She has published widely on Soviet cinema. Her latest book is *Socialist Senses: Film, Feeling and the Soviet Subject*.

Erika Wolf is Professor in the School of Advanced Studies at the University of Tyumen, Russia. She is an art historian with particular interest in modernism and modernity, photography, propaganda, cross-cultural representation, and Soviet visual culture. She works closely with the "Ne boltai! Collection," a private archive of twentieth-century political art. She has completed two books that draw extensively from this collection: *Koretsky: The Soviet Photo Poster* and *Aleksandr Zhitomirsky: Photomontage as a Weapon of World War II and the Cold War.*

Elizabeth A. Wood is Professor of Russian History and Director of Russian Studies at MIT. Her books include *The Baba and the Comrade: Gender and Politics in Revolutionary Russia*; *Performing Justice: Agitation Trials in Early Soviet Russia*; and *Roots of Russia's War in Ukraine* (coauthored). Most recently, she has also published a number of articles on Russian President Vladimir Putin, political masculinity, and the performance of power.

Richard Wortman is James Bryce Professor of History Emeritus at Columbia University. His publications include *The Crisis of Russian Populism* and *The Development of a Russian Legal Consciousness*. The second volume of his *Scenarios of Power: Myth and Ceremony in Russian Monarchy* was awarded the George L. Mosse Prize of the American Historical Association, and the two volumes together were awarded the 2006 Efim Etkind prize. His most recent book is *The Power of Language and Rhetoric in Russian Political History: Charismatic Words from the 18 to the 21st Centuries*. In 2007, he received the American Association for the Advancement of Slavic Studies' award for Distinguished Contributions to the Field of Slavic Studies.

Ernest A. Zitser is Librarian for Slavic, Eurasian, and East European Studies and Adjunct Assistant Professor in the Department of Slavic and Eurasian Studies at Duke University. He is the co-founder and general editor of an open access, peer-reviewed, scholarly journal called *ВИВЛIОѲИКА: E-Journal of Eighteenth-Century Russian Studies* and the author of *The Transfigured Kingdom: Sacred Parody and Charismatic Authority at the Court of Peter the Great*.

ACKNOWLEDGMENTS

The editors would like to express their gratitude to their respective universities for supporting this project: the University of Michigan, the University of Texas at Austin, and the University of Tyumen. We are especially grateful to our editors at Oxford University Press, Charles Cavaliere, Danica Donovan, Amanda Brown, and Patricia Berube for their unflagging encouragement and wise advice. We would like to thank Wesley Morrison for scrupulous copyediting and Christopher Rose for his excellent maps. And we would like to thank all of our contributors for their brilliant work and their patience with us as we compiled and revised this multifaceted book.

We are also grateful for the critiques and helpful suggestions provided by both the readers of the original proposal and the reviewers of the initial draft of the manuscript. Their insights and feedback strengthened the project in myriad ways:

Audrey Altstadt, *University of Massachusetts*
Natalie Bayer, *Drake University*
Jeffrey Brooks, *Johns Hopkins University*
Marjorie Hilton, *Murray State University*
Shoshana Keller, *Hamilton College*
Nadieszda Kizenko, *University at Albany (SUNY)*
David McDonald, *University of Wisconsin–Madison*
Stephen B. Riegg, *Texas A&M University*
Mark Tauger, *West Virginia University*
Glennys Young, *University of Washington*

We have made every effort to identify, credit, and compensate the rights holders of the images reproduced in this book.

NOTE ON TRANSLITERATION

As a work covering over a millennium and with multinational and imperial subject matter, this collection draws on many languages and linguistic and orthographic traditions. Spelling, like everything else we discuss in this volume, carries weighty political implications and bears the ongoing burden of histories of imperial conflict, conquest, and control. People's sense of who they are and how they identify themselves within empire are inevitably layered and often hybrid, amalgams of multiple regional affiliations and ties, and consequently individuals themselves may adopt alternative spellings on different occasions, each with its own connotations. Conscious of the high stakes in decisions about spelling, we have generally adopted the following principles in presenting non–English language materials: When English names or terms have standard forms, we use those (so, Peter I instead of Petr Alekseevich, Semyon instead of Semën, Prokudin-Gorsky instead of Prokudin-Gorskii, or Moscow instead of Moskva). Otherwise, names and places are generally rendered in ways that remain true to their original presentation in the source materials, so, for instance, Estonian names are presented in their Estonian form. When multiple spellings compete, we list relevant alternatives. For example, in the case of the medieval Rus prince Volodimer, we note that his name is spelled Volodymyr in modern Ukrainian, Uładzimir in modern Belarusian, and Vladimir in modern Russian. Similarly, the Kazakh intellectual Cholkan Valikhanov was born Shoqan Shynghysuly Walikhanov.

For Russian-language terms, we follow a modified Library of Congress system. In the text, we have dropped soft signs for ease of reading, but we have preserved them where terms are provided in the original and in all endnote citations. For other languages, we defer to the transliteration choices of our contributors.

PICTURING RUSSIAN EMPIRE

INTRODUCTION

VALERIE KIVELSON, SERGEI KOZLOV,
AND JOAN NEUBERGER

PICTURE IN YOUR mind an imperial ruler—a tsar—holding a scepter topped with a double-headed eagle. Crowned with a cap of gold and sable, gowned in golden brocade, he sits on a throne of gold studded with turquoise. Follow that picture with a different one: rubble, the remains of a mountain village in the north Caucasus in the mid-nineteenth century, or of the city of Grozny, the capital of Chechnya, in the late twentieth century, both destroyed by invading Russian forces, though under very different circumstances. Or, summon yet another image to mind: a walrus tusk ornament, intricately carved by a reindeer herder above the Arctic Circle, far from the seats of power.

In this volume, we offer our readers a visual tour of the lands and peoples that constituted the Russian empire and those that confronted it, defied it, accommodated to it, and shaped it at various times over more than a millennium of history. Our project has multiple goals. We provide an overview of a long history by exploring the wealth of visual images produced in these regions. We also use images to delve into each of the weighty terms in our title: *Picturing Russian Empire*. Each of these terms—seemingly so straightforward—raises big historical questions and provokes lively debates. *Russia*, for instance, would seem to have self-evident meaning. But this is far from true. The volume begins in the tenth century, when Russia had not even been conceived as a country and when the people called the Rus barely registered in the ethnic or geographic imagination of their neighbors. Russia traces its historical roots back to the Rus and the territories they occupied, but Ukraine and Belarus do so as well, challenging the "Russianness" of the early chapters. When the word *Russia* (as opposed to the medieval term Rus) came into circulation in the fifteenth and sixteenth centuries, it was used in the names of other east Slavic lands, including White Russia (Belarus), Black Russia and Red Russia (now parts of Poland, Lithuania, and western Ukraine), and later, "Little Russia" (Ukraine). Only slowly did the name come to refer specifically to the place we now think of as Russia.

The stakes of these disputes over common medieval origins have become painfully evident as we write this introduction, three months into Russia's invasion of Ukraine. Selective, exaggerated or patently false reimaginings of that medieval past have been central to Russia's justification of its claims on its neighbor to the southwest. It has become more crucial than ever to bear in mind the entangled histories that developed out of ancient Kyiv and medieval Rus, and to remember the clearly imperial dynamics that, eventually, resulted in the piecemeal incorporation of the lands of present-day Ukraine into the Russian empire. Over the centuries, not only Ukraine but many neighboring non-Russian regions came under Russian rule through imperial conquest, annexation, and incorporation. Since our volume extends almost to the present day, we face the further complication of including the many parts of the former Russian empire that have thrown off their connection with Russia and become independent states, such as Ukraine, Kazakhstan, Georgia, and Estonia.

Russian imperialism confronts us with another problem, because non-Russian subjects of the Russian empire were often called Russians. Unlike English, the Russian language uses separate terms for these concepts: ethnic Russians and things concerning them are described as *russkie* (singular: *russkii*), while people and entities of broader empire, including those of non-Russian ethnicity, have been called *rossiiskie* (singular: *rossiiskii*). Because these labels were used unsystematically or even interchangeably at times in the past, their boundaries are unstable, and distinguishing them is tricky historically. Since the fall of the Soviet Union, however, their meanings have stabilized, and the terms have been used to signal the distinction between ethnic and imperial identities. We follow that usage here.

Empire is equally tricky to define consistently throughout the more than thousand-year history covered in this book. Russia began calling itself an empire under Peter the Great in the early eighteenth century, but this vast state had all the markings of empire since at least 1552, when Ivan the Terrible conquered and annexed the territory and non-Russian peoples of Kazan. During the Soviet period in the twentieth century, official ideology vehemently denounced imperialism and denied any characteristics of empire, but the Soviet Union held on to many of Russia's previously colonized regions and often exercised imperial-like powers over them. In post-Soviet spaces, the legacies of empire remain, but their traces are complex and cannot be simply assumed or asserted.

As this volume will show, neither *Russia*, nor *Empire*, is as clear a term as it initially appears. Their shifting and diverse meanings form one of the main themes that emerge from the essays presented here. Consequently, our volume seeks to avoid becoming yet another Russo-centric history of this complex, multinational empire. As the central, dominant power, the Russian presence weighs heavily, but at the same time, we seek to accentuate the voices and experiences of the empire's peoples. Their independent production and circulation of images, their interaction with other visual traditions, and their readings of Russian-produced images were often, but not always, shaped by being part of a Russian empire.

This book takes a new approach to understanding Russia and empire by centering images in our analysis, so our third term—*Picturing*—merits equal attention. Pictures, images, and the visual realm more generally have spawned their own field of academic analysis: Visual Studies. Alongside formal analysis of pictures, Visual Studies scholars explore the way the world is experienced through the eyes. So, in addition to examining the content, composition, genre, and implicit or explicit messages of an image, Visual Studies scholars, and many art historians, also examine the ways that various societies and cultures assess impressions received through sight. They focus on "ways of seeing," to cite the title of an important early contribution to the field.[1] Visual Studies situates visuality in its social as well as cultural and cognitive contexts by considering the production, class standing, position, imagination, goals, and technologies that go into the creation of images and the multiple ways that visual stimuli can be processed and understood. This approach is not hard to grasp: it situates the visual realm and experience of the eye in the living context of experience.

The authors in this volume present us with diverse models for thinking with images. Their analyses address key questions related to the intersection of visuality, empire, and Russia. How do images function and circulate in the world? To what extent do they work as active agents, effecting change or determining viewer response? How is empire configured by images? Do images have agency in producing empire, or in resisting it? Is there something particularly Russian—or particularly imperial—about the images produced in the Russian empire, or about the ways they were understood and circulated?

These are the central questions driving our collective endeavors in this volume. Bringing visuality together with empire and with Russianness in its slippery ethnic and imperial forms has led us to conceptualize our multifaceted subject in innovative ways. First, we offer a new way to frame visuality in historical, social, and political contexts, and for this, we advance a relatively new term, the *pictosphere*.

THE *PICTOSPHERE*

Google the term *pictosphere*, and you will find only a few sites, mostly art-sharing forums and open-access platforms for posting photographs and other images. It strikes us as appropriate that this invented term has popped up in the networked world of the internet. The circulation of images on the web and the ways that those images create virtual communities with their own realities have profound parallels with the ways that images functioned in the Russian empire, and continue to function in post-Soviet imperial space. These parallels reveal the power of a visual analysis that takes seriously the embedded social lives of images. The premise of this volume is that images shared in the networked space of the Russian empire made dynamic contributions to the creation and experience of that empire. Like the World Wide Web, empires are vast, their borders can be hazy and shifting, and they draw ever-growing numbers of people into their net. Proponents of the internet once gloried in its egalitarian horizontality, where anyone and everyone who can access the web can post freely. But today, the hidden hierarchies of power that structure life on the internet are impossible to ignore. Those sightings of *pictosphere* in a Google search, after all, are manifestations not of some self-evident logic but of Google's corporate algorithms. Where the power structures and hierarchies of the web are veiled, imperial power is often undisguised and explicit. And yet they create similarly interactive networks, facilitating linkages and channels of communication, as well as producing silences and amplifying conflicts, between people and peoples across vast spaces, political hierarchies, and social positions.

Within and across the boundaries of the Russian empire as it expanded and contracted, images circulated. Some were produced by the imperial regime with the explicit goal of announcing and fortifying the power and glory of rulers or ideologies. Others were produced as appeals to rulers and their regimes: for patronage or protection, status, or justice. But images could also arise in contexts unrelated to affairs of state. They could be drawn in private for beauty or laughs or commemoration, for scientific or spiritual or commercial reasons. They might draw on a common visual vocabulary that spanned and unified the empire, or they could work within aesthetic traditions forged apart from any engagement with or subjugation to Russian rule. Even when made "for the drawer," or for a small, private circle of viewers, or when made before modern mass reproduction and dissemination, images participate in larger interwoven spheres, because the hands and mentalities that produce them are shaped by communication with a world outside the individual self. It is this broad, and broadly defined, production and circulation of images within Russian imperial space that we are calling its pictosphere.

For the purposes of this collection, we define the pictosphere as the space of the visible world represented in images made by human hands or technologies. Visual experience naturally includes a far broader range of things to be seen—mountain goats, eggplants, oceans—but here, we stress the pictorial and the material objects on which pictures are found: coins, sketches, paintings, illustrated books, manuscripts, newspapers, maps, postcards, satirical cartoons, photographs, posters, films, children's books, embroidery, wine labels, dioramas, statues, paper, canvas, marble, steel, celluloid, and pixels on screens.

In dreaming up this key concept, we have adapted a term introduced by a prominent historian of Russia, Simon Franklin, in his work on the Russian graphosphere, which he defines as "the space of the visible word." "The graphosphere, or *a* graphosphere," he writes, "is formed wherever words are encoded, recorded, stored, disseminated and displayed through visible signs. The study of the graphosphere represents a holistic, non-hierarchical approach to the production, functions and dynamics of visible words in their environments."[2] Where Franklin's investigation explores visible words, ours substitutes pictures for letters and investigates images. The holistic, non-hierarchical approach allows us to consider the uses, dissemination, and meanings of images without privileging those produced at the center of power over works arising from the efforts of people in the territories of empire.

Thinking about images as embedded in the diverse, lived worlds of the Russian empire lets us see them not only as the creations of individuals, but as circulating among viewers in a variety of contexts, creating new impressions, meanings, and experiences as people of all kinds produce and encounter them in diverse contexts. The pictosphere, therefore, gives us an appreciation of one of the key features of the visual: its semantic malleability. Where some images seem to encourage single, fixed readings, others can challenge and complicate, or even thwart, intended meaning or reading. For example, in her essay in this volume, Maria Grazia Bartolini brings us book illustrations that use the multivalency of the visual to speak to spectators who have competing Russian and Ukrainian ecclesiastical loyalties and political interests. The images blur the differences in unexpected ways, making it possible for people on both sides see what they wanted or expected to see.

The non-verbal, non-narrative nature of images may also magnify their emotional impact, providing a powerful implicit or unconscious supplementary source of knowledge and connection to peoples and things of the world. Bringing awareness of these tensions to the interpretation of images shows them to be part of a dynamic social and political system such as the Russian empire, or any empire, where fixed intentions and dynamic responses are constantly interacting.

AN *IMPERIAL* PICTOSPHERE

What does the pictosphere tell us about empires that other treatments do not?

Most studies of empire still rely on a model of conquest and resistance (although allowing for various forms of hybridity and mediation at the margins). Traditionally, empires have been studied as a collection of two-way relationships between the center and a single colonial periphery, each in isolation. In such a scheme, visual production would be categorized as a tool of the colonizer or of the colonized, of appropriation or influence or of autonomy and pushback. Here, we join a recent trend in historical scholarship that expands that spoke-and-wheel model by attending to connections among colonies and movement through imperial space. The imperial context inherently defies neat division into Russian and non-Russian, and the people referred to as "Russians" often bore multiple, mixed identities that complicate the Russian/other divide.

An empire, by its nature, collects a diverse palette of peoples and polities under its aegis. That diversity is what maintains its imperial distinction. Not a unified state or tribe or religious community, an empire is, by definition, a sovereign power that holds multiple peoples, organized and administered in varying ways, under its command.[3] As Erika Monahan demonstrates in her article in this volume about symbols on late seventeenth-century maps, imperial space was so variegated that it might even include populations living in imperial space but not yet subject to the tsar's command.

The pictosphere illuminates those aspects of empire that define it as an ongoing creative process and an interactive, dynamic sphere that crosses conventional social and political boundaries. This framing, and the aspiration to examine a non-hierarchical, holistic visual plane, risks obscuring the inequalities of power and the sheer mass of material produced and preserved by, for, or in connection with the Russian state. Wherever and whenever it held sway, the Russian state attempted to assert its dominance, visually and otherwise. But along with the risks, the pictosphere approach illuminates aspects of imperial experience otherwise overlooked. By discussing the images in a broadly imperial frame, we can consider sketches by a Kazakh intellectual alongside official portraits of the empress, imported styles of noble portraiture with regional artisanal embroidery, or Tatar *shamails* (decorated prints and panels, usually featuring calligraphic excerpts from the Qur'an) with Bolshevik aesthetics. The pictosphere gives us a sense of the empire as a whole, both at specific times and across its long history. As Franklin describes the graphosphere, so, too, the pictosphere "can be imagined as a whole, as a physical entity or system with properties such as shape, borders, degrees of density and the like."[4]

The idea of "degrees of density" revealed by the pictosphere approach helps us understand some of the forms of diversity and unevenness within the empire as a whole. Most of the images discussed in this book do, in fact, engage in some way or another with the central authority and structures of empire, because those are the images that most densely populate the imperial pictosphere and dominate its collective archive. The Russian imperial state loomed over the shared visual space of the empire in many ways, including by means of administrative control or outright violence. Ethnic Russians also exercised a degree of cultural dominance, reinforcing their own sense of cultural superiority that paralleled the political imbalance of power. When artists or artisans from particular ethnonational groups created their works, they often did so not only in their guise as Estonians or Buryats or Uzbeks, or for that matter as ethnic Russians, but also, at the same time, as subjects of the empire and as members of the collective imperial population. In her essay in this volume, Helena Holzberger shows that when Jewish and Ukrainian photographers set out to document developments in Soviet Central Asia, they did so not only as Jews or Ukrainians, but also as Soviet photographers. In his essay, Willard Sunderland introduces us to Father Hyacinth, an Orthodox monk of Chuvash descent who represented the Russian Orthodox Mission in Beijing and dressed in his version of Chinese robes in St. Petersburg. Although he was a product of Russian imperial power, Father Hyacinth played on imperial and trans-imperial themes in his self-presentation and to situate himself as a scholar, a churchman, and an erudite man of the world.

The example of Father Hyacinth, with his investment in Chinese art and culture, reminds us that the physical boundaries of empire could not contain the variety of imagery contributing to the Russian imperial pictosphere. Collectors imported and commissioned works from abroad. Artists, techniques, and genres crossed political borders, and artistic production promiscuously drew on available influences or fashions, with little regard for the boundaries of empire. At the same time, some local visual traditions remained apart, undigested by a sweeping imperial pictosphere and underrepresented in its archive. As recent theorists point out, lack of uniformity remained a signature mark of empire,[5] and this diversity is evident even in the selective pictosphere with its skew toward the center that comes down to us and that our authors represent in their essays.

Especially interesting and typical of an imperial context is the degree to which various visual subcultures of empire intersect, how much they recognize each other, how much they share, and how much they appropriate or erase. The images that our authors study participate in an extensive imperial pictosphere, and to the extent that they represent the conventions of any alternative visual traditions, they show them in conversation with the imperial frame. An imperial pictosphere coalesces at the intersection of colonial and metropolitan visual cultures, and in the circulation of visual customs, not just in a two-way relationship but throughout imperial space. For example, in her essay in this volume, Mollie Arbuthnot looks at Soviet posters addressed to Muslim viewers that sought to blend regional visual styles with socialist messages to make state goals more legible and persuasive. Imperial images contain within themselves a mix of discourses and conventions that enable mixed interpretations.

Some of our authors explore dynamic exchanges between metropolitan visual practices and those of the empire's subject peoples. Anna Kotomina, for instance, highlights the productive relationship between a Russian artist and an Indigenous Nenets artist of Novaya Zemlya in the Arctic north. Nathaniel Knight shows how a regional headdress typical of the non-Slavic people of the Volga region entered the imperial pictosphere when it was depicted in a watercolor of Indigenous "types" for the ethnographic edification and viewing pleasure of a metropolitan audience—that is, for imperial purposes. Such emblematic representations, illustrations of "types," were intended to enhance and showcase imperial power by capturing the essential distinctiveness of its various subject peoples. An embroidered headdress, however, might have an entirely different meaning in an adjacent regional visual culture, a topic explored in Olessia Vovina's essay, which examines Chuvash embroidery from the perspective of Chuvash people of the Volga region. In these examples, we see the movement between metropolitan and local art forms. But a simple notion of binary exchange between the center and its colonized periphery is complicated in these instances when we discover, for instance, that the artists and ethnographers involved in sketching various headdresses were mostly German, and that their findings were published in illustrated compilations abroad. The imperial pictosphere creates imperial categories of people, forged in the common imperial space in which they moved, but without necessarily eradicating local and national identities. The people of empire encountered in this volume include not only educated Russian elites and colonized "others" residing in their titular regions—Kyrgyz in Kyrgyzstan, Poles in Poland, and Finns in Finland. They also include an ethnic German residing in the Caucasus, a Jewish cartoonist from Ukraine celebrated in Moscow for creating the satirical visual vocabulary for depicting the Cold War, a Kazakh intellectual trained in Russian schools making sketches of Kyrgyz customs, a Georgian Bolshevik (actually, Stalin) choosing to send a postcard bearing a symbol of Finnish national independence, and another Georgian introducing the delights of Georgian cuisine to diners in Moscow. And in her essay, Rosalind Polly Blakesley shows the ways that Vasily Surikov struggled with his hybrid Siberian-Russian identity as he sought to include the Siberian Tatar warriors in an epic historical painting celebrating their conquest by the Russians.

One of the characteristics of empire is that people don't stay still. They don't become a homogenous mass, and they don't remain in neat boxes, in their designated colonial space. Rather, they move, carried by the currents of imperial service or forced resettlement, opportunity, or marriage. This complexity defies attempts to tame imperial relations into bilateral ones between the center and a (singular) periphery. Movement between and among the peripheries contributes an important wild card, enriching the mix. This imperial dynamic, with its ambiguities, mixing, and shifting identities, finds its parallel in the overlapping, interactive, mutually formative visual dynamics that we are calling the imperial pictosphere.

A *RUSSIAN* IMPERIAL PICTOSPHERE

Do the images and articles in this book show that there is something especially *Russian*—in either sense, as *russkii* or *rossiiskii*—about the Russian imperial pictosphere? This is a hard question, and one that is haunted not only by overlapping terminology, but by centuries of speculation about Russia's uniqueness.

Slavophiles in the nineteenth century maintained that true Russians, by which they meant ethnically Russian peasants untouched by the blight of Western influence, were blessed with a simplicity and purity derived from their absolute faith in God and tsar. In their innate communalism and their absence of self-serving ego, peasants embodied what the Slavophiles identified as the true Russian "soul." This pious figure would stand as a bulwark against the dangers of European industrialization, urbanization, and crass individualism. Slavophiles drew on the most up-to-date European Romantic ideas about distinct nations with their most authentic nature embodied in their "folk." A countervailing trend met these claims with guffaws: the Russian peasant was backward, superstitious, ignorant, crude, and violent, and his (usually *his*, in this particular telling) barbarism was exacerbated by his chronic state of drunkenness. Only education and modern progress would knock the population out of its torpor and allow a true Russia to thrive.

These opposing narratives of Russian uniqueness left indelible traces in the ways that Russia has been discussed both at home and abroad, but at least in academic circles, both have been thoroughly debunked. The overly general characterizations of an entire people, the blatant moralizing, the claims about essential national types and something called "authenticity" have all been set aside by scholars who prefer to search for historical patterns based in the world of evidence.

A third grand theory, or set of stereotypes, is alive and well today in Russia in a political-philosophical movement known as Eurasianism, which posits Russia's special path in geographic terms. Because of its unique location between West and East, between Europe and Asia, Eurasianists imagine that Russia's epic destiny is to unite Eurasia and combine the supposedly essential characteristics of East and West into a single, natural force, superior to both. In order to grant Russia its special role in uniting the two, Eurasianist thinkers simplistically turn "Asia" into a timeless site of exoticism and despotism, and see Europe either as a site of "natural" democracy and freedom or, following the Slavophiles, as a demon's nest of urban blight, selfish ambition, and anomie.

Recently, the Putin administration has resurrected and revised another historical concept: the Russian World, or *Russkii mir.* Putin and others have used it to postulate a trans-national political entity of Russians and Russian speakers, wherever they might live. The expansive vision of a Russian World has been used to justify the annexation of Crimea and the invasion of Ukraine, ostensibly in defense of Russians and Russian speakers abroad. In her essay in this volume, Galina V. Lyubimova quotes one of the regime's ideologists as claiming that the "'natural and only possible state' of Russia—is to be 'a great, growing and land-gathering community of nations.'"[6] Olga Shevchenko, in her essay, shows how the state media use photographs of the multicultural, multimedia Victory Day parades known as the Immortal Regiment to create and disseminate representations of the Russian World.

Given the unsavory and unsatisfactory traditions of seeking a Russian *Sonderweg* (special path), we advance our own claims about what might be unique to the pictosphere of the Russian empire with some caution.

Our approach to thinking about the visual dimensions of the Russian imperial pictosphere is expressed in a concept we call *amidness.* Throughout these essays, we have found suggestions that Russianness—in both the narrow ethnic and the broader imperial sense—has been defined, felt, perceived, or signaled through an awareness of being amid, among, and in contact with multiple cultures. Writers and artists engaged in ongoing contemplation of the significance of their geocultural positioning, and they produced images based on that contemplation. Though superficially resonant with the discredited theories of Eurasianism, the Russianness born of amidness as we define it invokes no fixed polarities of East and West and presumes no essential cultural or national characters. Amidness is more than a reversal of center and periphery, and more than a multiplication of centers and peripheries. Rather, it captures a sense of cultural flow, contiguity, and exchange that is reflected in the source material and by the historical actors represented in this volume. Amidness connotes a recurrent and often self-aware consideration of the possibilities (and dangers) offered by being situated spatially among multiple neighboring cultures; of being a hybrid product of the integrated cultures of empire; of being constituted by ever-shifting, even opportunistic blends of borrowing and rejection. If, for example, painters borrowed the genre conventions of portraiture from western Europe, they might put them to work, as Alison K. Smith shows in her article, to contemplate and represent particular dynamics of power and subjugation within Russian empire. Her essay exposes the complexities of relationships generated by the circulation of people as they settled into newly forming hierarchies of status, gender, and race or ethnicity in a period of active imperial expansion.

We readily concede that *amidness* is a clunky and inelegant word, but no other existing term captures the condition we are proposing for identifying the visual experience of the Russian imperial pictosphere. Philosophers, geographers, and sociologists have all explored similar constructions of identity rooted in awareness of one's surroundings, or in a sense of place (or placelessness).[7] Historians have explored zones of interaction and accommodation, where new cultural forms develop at the margins or in the stateless spaces that Richard White labels "middle ground."[8] In the Russian field, too, scholars have deconstructed older binaries and traced the "entangled" nature of imperial history.[9] But none have proposed a term that conveys the particular, multilayered, multidirectional awareness of cultural connections and interactions among the peoples and places of the Russian empire that emerges from the essays in this book and that seems to define Russian imperial visual identity.

For example, at the beginning of our story, Monica White shows how the medieval Rus prince Volodimer (spelled Volodymyr in modern Ukrainian; Uładzimir in modern Belarusian; Vladimir in modern Russian) cobbled together images from surrounding empires to construct a display of power. Neighboring empires framed his sense of the world, and he drew on their models in assembling a political identity. Jumping far forward in time, in the late seventeenth century, the cartographer Semyon Remezov produced a manuscript atlas "of the entire interior of Siberia, . . . especially between the countries of Asia, Europe and America."[10] Visually, he showcased this amidness by featuring a two-hemisphere map, copied from a Dutch original, that depicts Russia stretching to fill the space defined by the surrounding continents.[11] Awareness of amidness, though not by that name, became more pronounced in the eighteenth and nineteenth centuries. The expansion of Russian imperial holdings coincided with increased reflection on geographic and, importantly, cultural consequences of sitting amid a profusion of surrounding cultures. Russia's preoccupation with "The West," which became pronounced in this period, is only one form of amidness. Armenian intellectuals, educated in Russian schools, celebrated the enlightenment brought to them by the empire but, when blocked from fully equal status, began to think in the more national terms that their European-style education inspired. The Baltic portrait photographers and their sitters in Bart Pushaw's essay used photography to construct new, assertive ideas about Estonian identity. The photographs presented that identity not only—and, indeed, not even primarily—in relation to the empire, although they did comply with requirements for acceptance into exhibitions in Moscow. More centrally, they mediated competing ideas of Estonianness among the old Baltic German elite and the newly emancipated Estonian peasantry, and translated into images the new social sciences and technologies originating all over Europe. In other words, they expressed an awareness of being situated amid multiple audiences and markets.

Amidness joined with visuality, then, gives us tools to rethink one persistent, nagging problem in reconstructing the history of Russia and its empire: figuring out its relations to western Europe. From the late seventeenth century, we see Russian images sharing a visual vocabulary with Europe. The debate about this cultural shift towards Europe, especially from the reign of Peter the Great on, is usually framed in binary terms: Is or is not Russia now Europeanized? This question then tends to be sliced and diced into the degree of Europeanization of various classes, genders, and ethnicities, as if one stratum existed divorced from the others. But the pictosphere found in our essays allows us to see the elite embrace of European cultures as only one thread among many interwoven in a multihued imperial tapestry. And it allows us to see that even when setting themselves apart, the most Europeanized Russians did so while immersed in the many visual cultures surrounding them. The dynamic of the pictosphere in the imperial context necessarily cuts across the binary terms that have so fundamentally structured debates about the construction of Russianness. While not dispensing with ideas of European or Western influence, the pictosphere situates those influences as one aspect, though admittedly an important one, in a richer, more multidirectional world of visual exchange. European art forms circulated amid other competing, combining, contextualizing visual cultures of the empire, and took on meanings in that larger pictosphere.

For the people of the Russian empire, then, and for those assessing them from all directions, the fact of being located amid other cultures—a nearly universal condition—morphed into a preoccupation with the Russian empire's category-spanning geographic position. At times, this hardened into a set of rigid stereotypes about Asians, Europeans, and the Russians who stood with a foot in more than one world. At times, it produced repressive language policies that asserted Russian cultural "greatness" over its imperial neighbors' cultural "inferiority." In other contexts, amidness opened artists and thinkers to creative multivalency. In some cases, dehumanizing stereotypes associated with otherness coexisted with a recognition of shared experiences and values. In her essay, for instance, Louise McReynolds looks at nineteenth-century artistic depictions of archeological finds. She shows how the artists used the ambiguity and emotional charge inherent in the visual not to exoticize the lands of the ancient Caucasus, nor to empty them out by turning them into untouched wilderness, but to make them feel familiar and inviting, as if their incorporation into the Russian empire were a natural occurrence. While smoothing the rough edges of imperial expansion for their viewers, the artists and archeologists also systematically erased all evidence of Islam, indicating what they felt could and could not be harmoniously incorporated into the imperial whole. The calculus of empire was always multifactorial.

Another key benefit that this notion of amidness confers is a way to untangle the knot of Orientalism in the Russian empire. Orientalism was a respected branch of European and Russian scholarship devoted to the study of a vast, ill-defined "East," including China, Japan, South Asia, the Middle East, and in the Russian context, Central Asia, but capable of expanding as convenient. With rigorous demands in terms of linguistic training, literary skills, and connoisseurship, Orientalism developed into one of the most impressive sites of European erudition in the eighteenth and nineteenth centuries. But its assessments were never neutral. As famously argued by Edward Said, Orientalism carried with it invidious ideas about the cultures of the mythical East that served European imperialist agendas. Russia to some extent "orientalized" its own colonies in the Caucasus, Asia, and Central Asia, just as the British did in India. Like European empires, it rated its own civilizational status highly and disparaged the perceived primitiveness, indolence, or barbarism of many of the people under its rule. Yet, looking over their shoulders to the west, educated people in the Russian empire understood that in the eyes of their European peers, they themselves might look barbaric, primitive, or "oriental." How these constructed notions of superiority and inferiority played out in visual terms is the crux of many of the articles in this collection. These essays offer a way to break through the encrusted binaries of the ongoing debate over Russian Orientalism. Our concept of amidness allows us to focus on the ways that Russians' own notion of their intermediary location and cultural standing fueled their sense of self and contributed to their evolving pictosphere. Our authors move us beyond questions of Russia and a phantom "West," or of Russia and a fictive "East," and compel us to think about the experience of the imperial pictosphere from the perspective of all the peoples of the empire. Encounters with others, both as experienced in life and as imagined, always took place in a messy, entangled world where everyone was geographically between, among, embedded, interacting with, and containing within itself many hybrid cultures and peoples.

Ultimately, the fate of the Russian empire did not rest on its straddling of two continents or on a binary division of East and West. In fact, as Martin W. Lewis and Kären Wigen point out, the continents themselves are a myth coined by geographers, who carved up the Afro-Eurasian landmass into separate theoretical units by drawing borders on maps.[12] Rather, as an empire, and as a state located in a world of movement, Russia was, and still is, situated amid a churning, dynamic, and sometimes destructive exchange of people, ideas, and practices. The Russian imperial pictosphere is a moving testament to the power, the beauty, and the creativity, as well as the terrible violence and oppression, that that exchange set loose.

NOTES

1. John Berger, *Ways of Seeing* (Harmondsworth: Penguin, 1972).
2. Simon Franklin, *The Russian Graphosphere, 1450–1850* (Cambridge: Cambridge University Press, 2019) 1.
3. Jane Burbank and Frederick Cooper, *Empires in World History: Power and the Politics of Difference* (Princeton: Princeton University Press, 2010); Valerie A. Kivelson and Ronald Grigor Suny, *Russia's Empires* (New York: Oxford University Press, 2016).
4. Franklin, *Graphosphere*, 1–2.
5. See Ilya Gerasimov et al., "New Imperial History and the Challenges of Empire," in *Empire Speaks Out: Languages of Rationalization and Self-Description in the Russian Empire*, edited by Ilya Gerasimov, Jan Kusber, and Alexander Semyonov (Leiden: Brill, 2009), 121–151. Recently, John LeDonne has published a work arguing the opposite position, as evident in his title: *Forging a Unitary State: Russia's Management of the Eurasian Space, 1650–1850* (Toronto: University of Toronto Press, 2020). We find the heterogeneity of the "imperial situation" more useful.
6. Lyubimova quotes Vladislav Surkov. *Dolgoe gosudarstvo Putina* (https://www.ng.ru/ideas/2019-02-11/5_7503_surkov.html).
7. For example, Martin Heidegger, *Being and Time* (Oxford: Blackwell, 1962 [orig. pub. 1927]); Yi-Fu Tuan, *Space and Place: The Perspective of Experience* (Minneapolis: University of Minnesota Press, 1977); Gilles Deleuze and Felix Guattari, *A Thousand Plateaus: Capitalism and Schizophrenia* (Minneapolis: University of Minnesota, 1987 [orig. pub. 1980]); Yuri Lotman, "The Semiosphere," in *The Universe of the Mind: A Semiotic Theory of Culture* (Bloomington: Indiana University Press, 1990 [orig. pub. 1984]), 123-214.
8. Richard White, *The Middle Ground: Indians, Empires, and Republics in the Great Lakes Region, 1650–1815* (Cambridge: Cambridge University Press, 1991). See also Edith Clowes, *Russia on the Edge: Imagined Geographies and Post-Soviet Identity* (Ithaca: Cornell University Press, 2011).
9. Among the first was Andreas Kapeller, *The Russian Empire: A Multiethnic History*, translated by Alfred Clayton (Harlow, England: Pearson Education, 2001). Other scholars further developed this in the pages of the journal *Ab imperio*. Thanks to our anonymous reviewer for this formulation.
10. Semen Remezov, "Working Sketchbook," *Rossiiskaia Natsional'naia Biblioteka*, St. Petersburg, *Ermitazhnoe sobranie* no. 237, *Sluzhebnaia chertezhnaia kniga Remezova*, l. 116 ob.
11. Harvard University, Houghton Library, Bagrow Collection, MS. Russ. 72, Remezov, *Khorograficheskaia sluzhebnaia kniga (Chorographic Sketchbook)*, 1697–1711, p. 2 verso. Remezov was familiar with Ortelius's atlas, which he studied during his time in Moscow. His atlas contains at least one map, the so-called Jenkinson Map of Tartary, copied from an Ortelius publication.
12. Martin W. Lewis and Kären E. Wigen, *The Myth of Continents: A Critique of Metageography* (Berkeley: University of California Press, 1997).

غانة للكفار
كوغه للكفار
سامه للكفار
بلد الحبشه
بلد الزنج
بلد المغرب
الجبال
فارس
كرمان
خوزستان
مفازة فارس
خراسان
الديلم
خوارزم
الخزر
خرخيز
التغزغز

PART

I

MEDIEVAL RUS AMONG THE EMPIRES

The East European or Russian Plain was never a part of the classical empires such as Assyria, Persia (Iran), Macedonia, or Rome. In texts of these great written cultures, the peoples of eastern Europe are referred to as "barbarians." The Assyrians, Persians, Greeks, and Romans considered themselves the only possessors of high culture and placed themselves at the center of an imaginary universe—the *oikumene*, or the "civilized world." They believed that the "barbarians" were wild men originating from the periphery of the inhabited world, where the climate was bad, order was absent, and dangers were numerous. In Homer's poem *The Odyssey*, the entrance to the Kingdom of the Dead was located north of the Black Sea, and the Greek historian Herodotus and other ancient authors wrote about the cruel and skillful nomadic warriors who lived there, "the invincible Scythians," whom none of the great empires of antiquity could conquer.

At the beginning of the Middle Ages, the East European Plain became an arena for great trans-Eurasian migrations of Turks, Slavs, and Scandinavian sailors in the "Viking Age." In the course of the eighth and ninth centuries, the Vikings passed to the south along the many branches of the river routes of eastern Europe to reach the Eurasian empires of Byzantium, Khazaria, and the Islamic Caliphate. In the Slavic chronicles, the Vikings were called *Varangians*, but they called themselves *Rus*, meaning, in the opinion of most historians today, "rowers." The Vikings controlled the key transit sites along the river routes of eastern Europe, the towns of Novgorod and Kyiv, where trade with the southern empires was centered. The first written and visual images of the Rus originated in the works of the surrounding empires, in which the Rus people are portrayed as cruel robbers, sailors, and merchants.

The earliest mention of a form of the term *Russia* is found in two Byzantine Greek treatises of the 950s. The Greek word Ῥωσία (*Rhosia*) was used to designate a territorial entity whose capital was Kyiv, where the descendants of a semilegendary Viking by the name of Rurik ruled. This political entity was not a state in a present-day sense of the word. It lacked a strong central government, ideology, codified law, and administration. Rus, a name that applied loosely to the territory, the people (or some of them), and the ruling dynasty, was rather a transnational corporation that controlled the transit of goods and people across the vast space between Scandinavia in the north and Byzantium, Khazaria, and the Caliphate in the south. By 1000 CE, the area claimed by Rus was large, covering as much as 1,330,000 square kilometers, twice as large as France. The head of that formation was the *kniaz'*, commonly translated as "prince," who exercised military and some judicial power. The Byzantines considered the Rus princes secondary rulers, subordinate to the Byzantine emperor (*autokrator*, "self-ruler").

In the tenth century, the Kyivan princes of the Rurikid dynasty—Oleg, Igor, and Sviatoslav—carried out military campaigns against Constantinople (*Tsar'grad* or the "Imperial City" of the Slavic chronicles), trying to win more profitable trade agreements with wealthy Byzantium. At the end of the tenth century, during the reign of

Prince Volodimer (Volodymyr in modern Ukrainian; Uładzimir in modern Belarusian; Vladimir in modern Russian), under the influence of Constantinople, Rus adopted Christianity in its Eastern Orthodox form. Orthodoxy differed in elements of doctrine, practice, and institutional organization from the western branch of Christianity taking shape in Rome. Unlike the Catholic Church, with its principle of Papal primacy, the Eastern Orthodox Church is organized into self-governing (autocephalous) jurisdictions or patriarchates along geographic, national, ethnic, or linguistic lines. Through the course of many centuries, assertions of legitimacy and jurisdiction were contested between the Moscow and Kyiv church leaders, and today, Orthodoxy itself has splintered into several mutually antagonistic branches.

In the ninth century, Byzantine missionary brothers Cyril and Methodius developed an alphabet for the previously unlettered Slavs. Known as the Old Slavonic writing system, it was forerunner of today's Cyrillic script. Orthodox monasteries, rich manuscript traditions, and a Christian visual culture with icons, architecture, mosaics, frescoes, jewelry, coins, and so on arose in the cities of Rus. In the early twelfth century, the oldest surviving Slavic chronicle, the *Tale of Bygone Years*, was created. In its pages, Rus was presented as belonging to the family of biblical peoples and described for the first time not as a periphery, but as a part of the Christian-imperial world.

In the thirteenth to fifteenth centuries, most of Rus fell into economic and political dependence on the Mongol Empire, the largest empire in history, stretching at its height from the Carpathian Mountains in the west to the Pacific Ocean in the east. During this period, the loose confederation of princes that had comprised the Rus lands unraveled. Some principalities spun into the Lithuanian or Polish political orbit, and others formed new affiliations to the north and east. The historical trajectories of these various regions would diverge sharply as they developed in profoundly different political and cultural milieus. At the same time, Rus continued to see itself as a part of the Christian-imperial *oikumene* on religious and symbolic grounds.

MAP 1 Medieval Rus among the Empires

CHAPTER 1

EARLY RUS: THE NEXUS OF EMPIRES

MONICA WHITE

THE EAST SLAVS did not always inhabit an empire. At the dawn of East Slavic history in the tenth century, human settlement in the forested zone of eastern Europe consisted of a collection of loosely connected, fortified towns known as Rus. Although a few, notably Kyiv and Novgorod, had grown to an impressive size by the standards of the day, Rus was hardly grand enough to deserve the title of "empire," and it would be more than half a millennium before anything on that scale emerged in that part of the world. Yet the appearance and early development of Rus took place at the nexus of three other empires, which profoundly influenced its religious, political, and economic systems. Much as the expansion of the Russian empire was later felt in far-flung corners of the globe, its medieval precursor was shaped by the trans-regional imperial polities of its own time.

These polities had been at the heart of Eurasian civilisation for centuries and had their own complex histories that predated the appearance of Rus. The Eastern Roman, or Byzantine, Empire, with its capital in Constantinople, was nearing a peak of size and power in the late tenth century. From its heartland in Asia Minor, it was steadily gaining territory in the Balkans and eastern Mediterranean under the leadership of the popular Macedonian dynasty. In the previous century, it had sent missionaries to the kingdom of Moravia in central Europe and overseen the conversion of neighboring Bulgaria to eastern-rite Christianity. To the east of Byzantium, the Khazar Khaganate had straddled the Caucasus and southern steppe since the seventh century. The Turkic rulers of this ethnically and linguistically diverse tribal federation had made the unusual choice to convert to Judaism at an uncertain date. From their capital in Itil on the southern Volga, they had gained territory and wealth by controlling lucrative north-south trade routes, although their power was in decline by the late tenth century. At the southern and eastern ends of some of these trade routes lay the Muslim world. The Abbasid Caliphate had enjoyed a period of rapid territorial expansion in the eighth century, when it threatened both Byzantium and Khazaria. By the late tenth century, it had been eclipsed by various successor states and no longer directly controlled much territory outside the Mesopotamian heartland, although its cultural and economic legacies continued to be felt across the region and beyond.

Each of these states had a different official religion and mix of ethnicities, languages, and economic structures, and each occupied far-flung territory across Eurasia. None of them shared a border with Rus, and even the northernmost, Khazaria, was separated from it by the steppe, which was often occupied by tribes hostile to both states. As trans-regional powers, all three empires had pressing concerns related to their own internal politics and immediate neighbors, and little interest in or desire for entanglements with a new, aggressive, and poorly understood entity far to the north. Yet through trade, diplomacy, and conflict, these empires made their mark on various aspects of the culture, economy, and society of Rus, contributing to its remarkable diversity at this early stage in its history.

The interlocking influences of Byzantium, Khazaria, and the Muslim world can be explored through the coins of Volodimer Sviatoslavich, the ruler of Rus from 980 to 1015. Volodimer's ancestors were among the group of eastern Vikings, known collectively as the Rus, who began migrating across the Baltic Sea in the eighth century to try their luck in the lucrative trade in fur, slaves, and forest products from eastern Europe. The network of settlements that they founded to facilitate these efforts eventually came to be known by the name of the settlers themselves, much as the name England is derived from that of Anglo-Saxon invaders. Over the course of the tenth century, Volodimer's ancestors consolidated most of the territory of Rus under their control. Volodimer continued and expanded this process, but his path to power was not straightforward: he was an illegitimate son and had to fight a number of battles with his half-brothers before taking control of the largest city, Kyiv, in 980. Even after he was able to exert his authority over the entire corridor from the Baltic to the mid-Dnipro River, he continued to reinforce his rule in various innovative ways. Some of these took physical form, such as waging war on neighboring tribes and founding new fortified outposts. Others were conceptual, including, from the mid-980s, flirting with monotheistic religions. Although chronicle accounts of Volodimer sending fact-finding missions to Muslims, Jews, and both western-rite and eastern-rite Christians, and receiving missionary delegations in return, are almost certainly legendary, they do reflect the multifaith environment of medieval eastern Europe and the diverse influences on early Rus.[1]

These influences did not disappear after Volodimer's eventual acceptance of eastern-rite Christianity in about 988. Indeed, they can be traced well into the next century through his issuance of the first native coinage, a medium with which he experimented between about the last decade of the tenth century and his death. In total, he issued one type of gold coin, or *zlatnik* (plural: *zlatniki*) (Image 1.1), and four types of silver coins, or *srebrenik* (plural: *srebreniki*) (Image 1.2). Over two hundred specimens of his coins have been discovered to date, mainly from hoards on the former territory of Rus.[2] Since they are the only surviving objects that can be linked directly to Volodimer, they provide extremely valuable information about his strategies for state-building, if not his economic policies.

IMAGE 1.1 *Zlatnik* of Volodimer. Obverse: bust portrait of Prince Volodimer; reverse: Christ Pantokrator, before 1015.

IMAGE 1.2 *Srebrenik* of Volodimer, type III. Obverse and reverse: portrait of prince on throne and *tamga*, before 1015.

Most scholars agree that the coins were essentially a "vanity project." Volodimer did not intend to introduce a monetary economy, which would have been unlikely to succeed even if he had. Rus was not organized enough to implement and oversee a monetary system and did not need one anyway, given its economic orientation toward the extraction and export of raw materials. The coins, however, had uses other than as a medium of exchange. Volodimer's numismatic project should instead be understood in the context of his other actions as a particularly bold effort to harness iconography in his consolidation of power. The circulation of coins made them an effective propaganda tool in a largely preliterate society in which other types of communication were limited, and Volodimer used them to send carefully composed messages to his own subjects and those of neighboring states. The symbolism of the coins reinforced his own authority and communicated his vision for the identity and future development of his rapidly growing state. Their imagery is extremely complex and varies considerably among the five types of coins that have been identified. Naturally, some aspects of the coins' iconography reflect domestic concerns beyond the scope of the present investigation to discuss. However, Volodimer also borrowed heavily from the traditions of powerful contemporary empires that were recognized and respected in his own territory. The prominent foreign influences on Volodimer's numismatic project serve to situate the coins, and Rus as a whole, on the receiving end of various pan-Eurasian cultural and economic processes.

The similarities between Volodimer's *zlatniki* and the gold *nomismata* of the contemporary Byzantine co-emperors Basil II and Constantine VIII have been most frequently noted (Image 1.3). Both feature on one side frontal portraits of the respective rulers holding full-length crosses. All of them are attired in courtly dress and wear the distinctive Byzantine crown surmounted by a cross and with hanging *prependoulia* on both sides. Circular inscriptions name the rulers: the *nomismata* give the names of Basil and Constantine in Latin letters, whereas the *zlatniki* feature Cyrillic inscriptions stating either "Volodimer and this is his gold" or "Volodimer on the throne." The other side of both coins features a type of portrait of Christ known as "all-sovereign" (Greek *Pantokrator*) holding a Gospel book, with circular inscriptions naming him.

The *nomisma* had been highly valued for its purity and stability since the emperor Constantine I introduced it in the fourth century. Given the coin's strong international reputation, it is not surprising that Volodimer chose to copy some of its

IMAGE 1.3 *Nomisma histamenon* of Basil II and Constantine VIII. Obverse and reverse: Christ Pantokrator and the emperors, dated 1005–1025.

features, which by the tenth century were traditional and well-established aspects of Byzantine numismatic iconography. Indeed, coinage was only one area in which Rus rulers looked to Byzantium as a model. The empire was the leading Christian power in the east with, at the time, a ruling dynasty of long standing, a powerful army, and vast wealth. Connections between Byzantium and Rus were well established. Volodimer's ancestors and other groups of eastern Vikings had been cultivating links of trade, diplomacy, and mercenary service with Byzantium for more than a century by Volodimer's time, in addition to engaging in occasional raids on the empire. Volodimer himself forged even stronger ties when he accepted baptism with Basil II as his godfather, and subsequently married Basil's sister Anna and established eastern-rite Christianity as the official religion of Rus. The presence on Volodimer's coins of distinctively Byzantine images, in particular the crown, cross, and portrait of Christ, was part of his postconversion effort to import many aspects of Byzantine culture, such as church architecture and decoration, texts, and moveable objects. The iconography of the *zlatniki* was clearly intended to reinforce the idea of Volodimer himself, and of Rus more generally, as up-and-coming Christian partners of Byzantium. An expanding territory and booming economy encouraged certain imperial pretensions in visual media, which Volodimer was eager to flaunt as widely as possible, even if this in no way reflected geopolitical reality.

Volodimer could thus only push his similarities with Byzantine rulers so far. In particular, it would have been obvious to contemporaries that the Byzantine crown featured on the *zlatnik* bore no resemblance to anything that Volodimer actually wore. It is clear, in fact, that the prince did not intend to produce exact copies of the Byzantine *nomisma*, despite a certain amount of iconographic overlap. The symbol above the prince's left shoulder provides evidence for cultural influences from other quarters. Known as a *tamga*, it was equivalent to a personal or family crest. Bident and trident versions were widely used among Turkic people of the steppe to the south and southeast of Rus, in particular the Khazars, and objects inscribed with a *tamga* began to appear in the territory of Rus in the late ninth to early tenth century.[3] Trade and diplomatic relations between Rus and Khazaria were intensifying at that time, since the Khazars controlled many of the north-south trade routes that the Rus used to transport their goods. The earliest Rus chronicle refers to Khazar rule over some East Slavic tribes in the territory that later became Rus, and various sources even address certain Rus princes by the Khazar title of *khagan*, showing that they coveted the prestige associated with these powerful rulers. As with Byzantium, there were also periodic hostilities between Rus and Khazaria, notably in the 960s, when Volodimer's father Sviatoslav inflicted a major defeat on the empire. Although Khazaria continued to exist into the next century, it never fully recovered from this incursion.

Perhaps not coincidentally, the earliest known use of the *tamga* among the rulers of Rus was on Sviatoslav's own seal. Despite having been appropriated from an enemy, the symbol must have been widely recognized and highly regarded across a large territory for Sviatoslav to use it as his official and public means of identifying himself. The prestige of the *tamga* remained high in subsequent generations as it continued to be used by Sviatoslav's son, and his descendants identified themselves with variations of it well into the thirteenth century. Indeed, even over the course of Volodimer's reign, the importance of the *tamga* seems to have increased. On his first, short-lived issue of gold coins, it was a small detail of the prince's self-portrait, but it grew to occupy an entire side of three out of the four subsequent issues of silver coins (Image 1.2). Interestingly, this rearrangement displaced the portrait of Christ, thus significantly changing the emphasis of the coins' iconography. Rather than his new affiliation with Christianity, Volodimer chose to display a means of self-identification that was borrowed from the symbolic vocabulary of a Turkic Jewish state.

The metal used in Volodimer's coins reveals another aspect of the cross-cultural influences in early Rus. The prince probably stopped minting *zlatniki* due to a lack of gold. There was no source of the metal in Rus, so other gold items had to be melted down in order to make the coins. However, he went on to mint four types of *srebreniki*, even though there was no source of silver on his territory, either. In fact, a large majority of the *srebreniki* that have been tested contain little or no actual silver, whereas the *zlatniki* have a relatively high purity of gold. If the coins were, indeed, a vanity project intended to showcase the entry of Volodimer and Rus onto the international stage, why did the prince bother to make fake silver when he had at least some real gold?

In all likelihood, it was because the prestige of silver was actually as great or greater than that of gold. This state of affairs, which is counterintuitive to modern assumptions, had arisen thanks to the *dirham*, a highly refined silver coin that began to be minted in the Abbasid Caliphate in the mid-eighth century. Desire for this silver, the purity of which could not be matched anywhere else in the known world, drove the Viking expansion into eastern Europe in order to reach Middle Eastern markets.[4] Despite the great distances separating the two groups, Arab geographers recorded vivid ethnographic accounts of eastern Vikings and described their efforts to obtain silver through raiding, trading, and mercenary service. Across northern Europe, archaeologists have discovered a staggering 400,000 *dirhams* buried individually or in hoards—one of few options for storing valuables in a time before banks or safes. Minted in the Abbasid Caliphate and its successor, the Samanid Empire of Central Asia, they far outnumber the finds of Byzantine silver *miliaresia* (some 1,250 coins), even though the source of the *dirhams* was much further away.[5] Demand was so high, however, that exhaustion of the mines caused the flow of silver to decrease sharply in the years before Volodimer's reign. This "silver crisis" severely disrupted the trade that had sprung up to satisfy the demand for *dirhams*, causing economic turmoil across eastern Europe.

But silver itself remained highly desirable, and the shortage of *dirhams* seems to have inspired Volodimer to fill this gap with a new coin, which made up in self-promotion for what it lacked in precious metal content. Like the *zlatniki*, the *srebreniki*, of which there are four types, feature a portrait of the prince wearing a Byzantine-style crown and holding a cross, and types II–IV give particular prominence to his throne. All four types feature an inscription analogous to that on the *zlatniki*: "Volodimer on the throne" and/or "Volodimer and this is his silver." Together with the self-portrait and the *tamga*, the inscription provided a third means of identifying the prince, calling attention to his status as a ruler and his power to issue silver or its reasonable facsimile. Volodimer was thus employing the standard established by the Abbasids to call attention to himself as a powerful leader with pretensions (if not actual resources) on a par with those of the Caliphate.

The history of Rus has too often been presented in a teleological way that emphasizes the triumph of eastern-rite Christianity and Byzantine culture more generally: the generations before Volodimer gradually entering into the Byzantine orbit and his successors sponsoring artistic, architectural, and literary pastiches of Byzantine forms. Such a reading smooths out or erases the many other roots of Rus culture and statehood, particularly from non-Christian parts of the world. But close readings of some of the earliest sources for the identity of Rus leaders reveal a more complex picture of influences from across western Eurasia, which they appropriated, modified, and rejected in turn. This study has focused on the evidence for Khazar and Arab traditions, as well as Byzantine ones, that were interwoven into Rus early model of leadership and statehood, but it could also have studied sources that betray influences from the steppe, the southern Caucasus, Viking strongholds in the north, or western Europe. Rather than understanding Rus simply as a linear recipient of one culture, this trans-regional and trans-cultural reading places the nascent principality firmly at a nexus of empires.

NOTES

1. Most of what is known about Volodimer's early career comes from the earliest East Slavic chronicle: *The Russian Primary Chronicle Laurentian Text*, translated by Samuel Hazzard Cross and Olgerd P. Sherbowitz-Wetzor (Cambridge, MA: The Medieval Academy of America, 1953), 91–119.
2. The classic study of these coins is M. P. Sotnikova and G. I. Spasskii, *Tysiacheletie drevneishikh monet Rossii: svodnyi katalog russkikh monet X–XI vekov* (Leningrad: Iskusstvo, 1983).
3. E. A. Mel'nikova, "K voprosu o proiskhozhdenii znakov Riurikovichei," in *Drevneishie gosudarstva vostochnoi Evropy*, edited by M. V. Bibikov et al. (Moscow: Indrik, 2008), 240–249.
4. Thomas S. Noonan, "Why the Vikings First Came to Russia," *Jahrbücher für Geschichte Osteuropas* 34, no. 3 (1986): 321–348.
5. Marek Jankowiak, "Byzantine Coins in Viking-Age Northern Lands," in *Byzantium and the Viking World*, edited by Fedir Androshchuk et al. (Uppsala: Uppsala Universitet, 2016), 117–139.

CHAPTER 2

PLACING RUS AMONG WORLD EMPIRES IN TENTH-CENTURY ARAB GEOGRAPHY

IRINA KONOVALOVA

WHAT WAS MEDIEVAL RUS, and where was it located? Did the term describe an ethnic group or a state? Was it part of the Byzantine Empire or a client state, only loosely falling in the Byzantine orbit? Or was it perhaps an independent polity, or not even a state with definable territory? This article considers the multiple, sometimes contradictory understandings of Rus, its location, and its political affiliation that appear in the earliest extant cartographic images of Rus as a state and a people.

These first cartographic representations were not produced by Rus people themselves, who would not draw maps for another 500 years, and not by the Byzantine Greeks or the peoples of what we now call Europe. They were products of the geographic scholarship that flourished in the Islamic world from the tenth century. This article investigates the depiction of Rus on the round world map of Ibn Ḥawqal, an Arab scholar of the second half of the tenth century. While the original map has not survived, a later copy is preserved in a 1086 manuscript, held in the Topkapi Museum in Istanbul (Image 2.1).[1] Analysis of Ibn Ḥawqal's maps and textual geographies in comparison with those of his predecessors and contemporaries will reveal the malleable image of the land of Rus and of its unfixed status in the world imperial order, from the perspective of a scientifically and culturally highly developed state for its time—the Islamic Caliphate, whose spiritual ruler, the Caliph from the Abbasid dynasty, had his residence in Baghdad.

Like most medieval Arabic maps, Ibn Ḥawqal's map is not a stand-alone product. It serves as an illustration to the textual description of the countries and peoples of the world in his book *Picture of the Earth* (*Kitāb ṣūrat al-arḍ*). Along with the world map, the cartographic part of this work includes twenty rectangular maps, depicting particular regions of the known world. The treatise's text gives a conceptual overview of the world system of empires, states, lands, and peoples, followed by a description of the maps. The three parts of the treatise—cartographic, conceptual, and descriptive—are usually

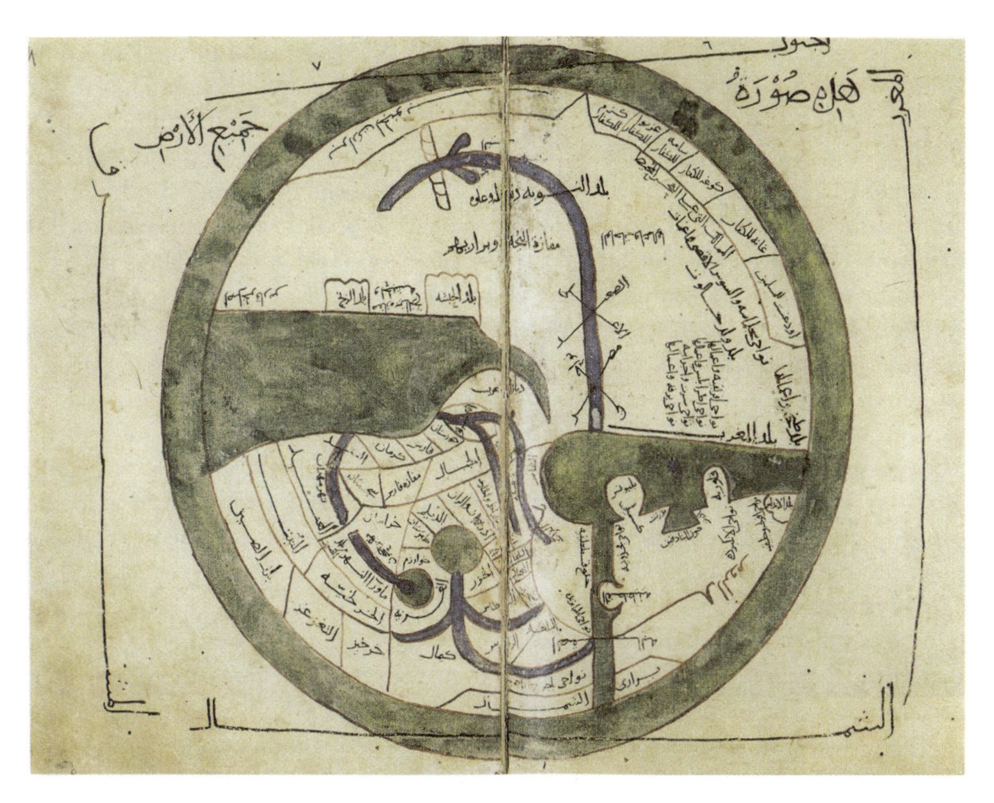

IMAGE 2.1 The world map of Ibn Ḥawqal, eleventh-century copy.

considered separately, even though they all characterize the same objects. I will show that Rus is depicted in ways that sometimes contradict each other. The contradictions showcase the various ways that Rus might be imagined in a fluid medieval system of shifting states and interconnected imperial systems.

Since Ibn Ḥawqal's book included a descriptive part as well as maps, we can compare different ways of presenting and conceptualizing the information about Rus that existed in the second half of the tenth century in the Islamic world. This is not only interesting for studying the history of medieval Rus, but also for considering the relationship between a map and a verbal description in ancient and medieval geographic sources. The compiler of the text and the cartographer used different methods of presenting information and producing new knowledge. Most pertinent to our themes of visuality and empire, authors of texts might designate the political affiliation or organization of Rus without assigning it a concrete geographic location. Mapmakers could not evade that task, but they could leave out questions of political sovereignty or allegiance.

To understand what was unique in Ibn Ḥawqal's presentation of the Rus in the world, we need to delve into the complex history of geographic scholarship in the medieval Islamic world. Ibn Ḥawqal created his book within the framework of the Balkhī school of geographers. Around 920, its founder, the Central Asian scholar al-Balkhī (d. 934), wrote *Pictures of the Regions* (*Ṣuwar al-aqālīm*), a collection of maps accompanied by a short explanatory text. Al-Balkhī's book has not survived to this day; however, it served as the basis for the works of other Islamic scholars.[2]

In the middle of the tenth century, al-Balkhī's book was reworked by a native of southern Iran, a geographer named al-Iṣṭakhrī, whose *Book of Routes and States* (*Kitāb al-Masālik wal-mamālik*) has come down to us.[3] Our author, Ibn Ḥawqal, was al-Iṣṭakhrī's successor. A native of the city of Nusaybin in Upper Mesopotamia, in present-day Turkey near the Syrian border, Ibn Ḥawqal began writing his treatise after meeting with al-Iṣṭakhrī. He conceived it a revised edition of the latter's work. However, during the prolonged process of writing his book (from the 950s to the 970s), he instead created a novel work, even if it still adhered to some of the basic practices of the earlier geographic tradition.[4]

For instance, like other geographers of the Balkhī school, Ibn Ḥawqal accompanied his maps with detailed textual commentary. He followed their custom of including a strictly prescribed number of maps, covering set areas and placed in a certain order. The maps are extremely schematic: there is no degree grid or scale on them, seas and islands are presented in the form of geometrically regular circles or ellipses, coastlines are shown without details, and rivers are drawn with straight lines.

Although the Balkhī school of geographers devoted their attention primarily to Islamic countries, al-Iṣṭakhrī and Ibn Ḥawqal also included some information about the countries and peoples of Europe and about non-Muslim regions of Asia and Africa. Most of this information appears in the introductions to their works, where they give a general description of the entire world as they knew it—countries, peoples, and seas—and set out their ideas about the structure of the world order.

Ibn Ḥawqal characterizes each state or people on three different scales: globally, as an integral part of one of the world empires; regionally, as a component of some historical and cultural region; and finally, by itself, on its own terms. The textual description of a state or people is complemented by its cartographic placement on the world map (and, for Islamic countries, on the relevant regional map). So, on the round world map, Rus is shown as one of the countries of the world; in the introduction to the book, it is described as part of Byzantine imperial space; and in the main part of the geographic text (in the section devoted to the description of the Caspian Sea), it is presented as an independent state, consisting of three regions.

As shown in this version of Ibn Ḥawqal's world map with English labels (Image 2.2), the entire Afro-Eurasian landmass is depicted as washed by the

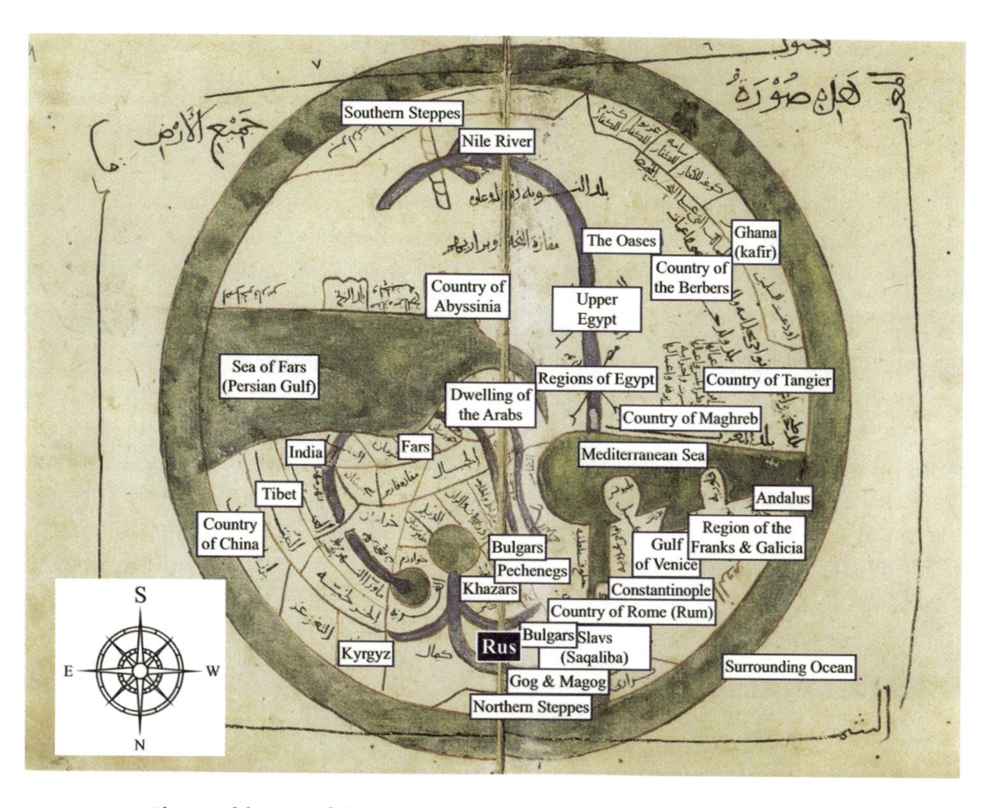

IMAGE 2.2 The world map of Ibn Ḥawqal with English translations.

Surrounding Sea (the unlabeled outer ring). The Mediterranean Sea and the Indian Ocean are shown as bays of this great ocean. The map is oriented to the south—that is, with the south at the top, as was often practiced by Islamic geographers. Three parts of the world—Europe, Asia, and Africa—are represented on the map, although their names are not indicated. Europe is depicted as an island on the bottom right, with annotations marking the lands reaching from "the country of Andalus" to Macedonia. The island of Europe is separated from Africa by the Mediterranean Sea and from Asia by the so-called "Gulf of Constantinople," which begins at Constantinople and reaches north to the Surrounding Sea, dividing the lands of the Slavs. This waterway metaphorically shows the set of river routes along which one can cross eastern Europe along a north-south axis. Another significant element of the map for us is the Caspian Sea. It is depicted as an isolated water basin, into which the Atil (Volga) River flows, connected in its upper reaches with other river routes of the region. The land of the Rus is shown in the Atil basin next to the Volga Bulgars and Slavs (bottom middle).

Ibn Ḥawqal himself described the location of Rus on his map as follows:

> In this part [of the map], behind the word 'North' is the country of Gog and Magog,[5] then, above—the Slavs (*al-Ṣaqāliba*) . . . Then behind them to the East—[Volga] Bulgars and Rus (*al-Rūs*). Then on the coast of the [Constantinople] Strait—the region of Trebizond, and over the river flowing nearby—[Volga] Bulgars, Rus, Bashkirs, Burtases,[6] Khazars, Pechenegs, another [group also known as] Bulgars [i.e., Danubian Bulgars], then the land of Sarir,[7] and above them—Inner and Outer Armenia. And to the left—Azerbaijan and Arran, and to the right of Armenia—the Tigris River.[8]

It is impossible to ignore the vocabulary that Ibn Ḥawqal uses to describe objects on the map—*behind, above, over, to the left, to the right*. All these terms are unusual for a modern person who determines the location of geographic points on the map using objective indicators—geographic coordinates and cardinal points. However, the spatial perception of the medieval geographer was not identical to ours. The fundamental feature of spatial perception in the Middle Ages was geographic egocentrism. With such a system of orientation in space, observers place themselves in the center of the world and perceive their surroundings in relation to themselves as to the central point. Despite the fact that Ibn Ḥawqal's map is oriented to the cardinal points (southward, as previously noted), it was the egocentric perception of space that determined those specific terms of orientation that Ibn Ḥawqal used.

In his verbal description, Ibn Ḥawqal establishes the position of Rus ethnographically, relative to other groups; that is, he uses the names of neighboring peoples to identify its location. The map's visual medium, by contrast, required the cartographer to place the Rus in a specific spot on the page. The name *Rūs* appears just above the Atil River, giving it a spatial location in addition to a place in a human geography. If the author of a geographic description—for example, Ibn Khurradādhbih (ninth century)—could hazily note that the Rus brought their goods "from the most remote outskirts of the country of the Slavs,"[9] then the cartographer who wanted to map information about the Rus had to find a well-defined place for them.

The cartographic imperative to assign the Rus a specific spot on the map sets Ibn Ḥawqal off from the textual geographers who came before him. The few geographers of the ninth and early tenth centuries who mentioned the Rus at all included only vague information on their location. Ibn Khurradādhbih, who made the first mention of the Rus in Islamic literature, spoke only of the routes they used to transport their goods to Byzantium and the Caliphate. He did not say anything about the country of the Rus or about any place of their residence.[10] That is, the Rus came to the international market, one might say, out of nowhere. The only part of the space marked by Ibn Khurradādhbih as "Russian," the only element of their existence that he found noteworthy, was the trade route they followed. Islamic writers also noted the presence of the Rus on the "River of the Slavs" (*nahr al-Ṣaqāliba*, actually a network of waterways rather than a single river), which allowed travel from the Rus lands to Khazaria and further along the Caspian Sea to the cities of the Caliphate. The emphasis on the river reinforces our sense that the geographers' interest was primarily piqued by trade, which pushed them to "put the Rus on the map."

At the same time, debate raged among the geographers about what exactly the term *Rus* meant. Where their predecessors assumed the Rus were a *people*, both al-Iṣṭakhrī and Ibn Ḥawqal argued that the term *al-Rūs* was the name of a *state*, not the name of a people, tribe, or city.[11] This statement was based on new information that had spread in the Islamic world by the middle of the tenth century. In particular, it became known that the state of Rus was not unitary, but had a complex composition, which included three distinct groups. Each group was territorially separated from the others and had its own urban center. The accounts attribute a clear hierarchy to these centers: *Kūyāba* (identified with Kyiv) is described as the most lively and well-known center; *Ṣalāwiya* (identified with a Slovenian tribe that lived near Lake Ilmen, near the city of Novgorod) as the second most famous city; and *Arsā* (the location of which is debatable) as an inaccessible territory connected with the outside world only through *Kūyāba*.[12]

Despite their updated information on the Rus and their new insight into their internal divisions, al-Iṣṭakhrī and Ibn Ḥawqal still did not provide any information about the geographic position of the Rus in relation to other peoples, or about the borders of the Rus. They knew only their centers of power. However, it is important here that they understood the Rus as a collective political entity. Since they were organized hierarchically relative to each other, they could be described as a whole, as a single territorial-political community with its own, internal subdivisions. Both al-Iṣṭakhrī and Ibn Ḥawqal open their sections on the Rus with the direct statement: "Rūs. There are three groups of them."[13]

Al-Iṣṭakhrī and Ibn Ḥawqal were the first in Islamic literature to show the place of Rus in the system of world empires (*mamlaka*), a system that included the Caliphate, Byzantium (*al-Rūm*), China (*al-Ṣīn*), and India (*al-Hind*).[14] In their conception of the world, these four empires corresponded to the civilizational areas formed on the basis of Islam, Christianity, Confucianism, and Hinduism. For example, they considered the diversity of the European political map insignificant in comparison with the shared Christian faith that, in their view, homogenized the region and even overrode differences between European and Greek realms: "As for the fact that we included the Franks, Galicians and other [peoples] in Byzantium, their language is different, however their religion and state are the same, just as in the state of Islam languages differ, and the ruler (*malik*) is only one."[15] In the same way, having data on the linguistic differences between the inhabitants of China and the surrounding Turkic tribes, al-Iṣṭakhrī and Ibn Ḥawqal nonetheless considered them all subjects of one sovereign—the ruler of China.

In this ideal model of an imperial world order, Rus was included in the sphere of influence of Byzantium. To some extent, this was done purely mechanically: "As for the state of Byzantium, to the east of it are the countries of Islam, to the west and south—the Surrounding Sea, and to the north—the borders of China region, since the lands of the Slavs and other peoples located between the Turks and the state of Byzantium, we included in the Byzantine state."[16] According to this logic, the Rus fell into the sphere of influence of Byzantium, because their lands lay between Byzantium and the Turks, whom al-Iṣṭakhrī and Ibn Ḥawqal assigned to the sphere of influence of China. At the same time, the Arab authors sometimes used religion rather than geographic proximity in explaining which groups belonged to which empires. Al-Iṣṭakhrī and Ibn Ḥawqal clarify that it was precisely the Christian peoples that were in the orbit of Byzantium's influence: "The state of Byzantium includes the borders of the Slavs and neighboring Rus, al-Sarir, Alans, Armenians and [other peoples], professing Christianity."[17] (Though the Rus had not yet officially converted to Christianity at this time, Al-Iṣṭakhrī and Ibn Ḥawqal would have known that at least some Rus merchants declared themselves Christians when trading in Baghdad, and consequently paid the tax set for non-Muslims.[18])

The novelty of information about Rus in the works of al-Iṣṭakhrī and Ibn Ḥawqal was associated with the interpretation of the term *al-Rūs* as a polity as well as an ethnonym, and also with the placement of Rus on the world map. Interweaving text and image, these two authors redefined the Rus within the Islamic scholarly tradition. Their innovations illuminate both of the interconnected themes of this volume. Conceiving of the Rus as a political entity rather than just a people, al-Iṣṭakhrī and Ibn Ḥawqal described power relations among the Rus themselves and attributed their links to the Byzantine Empire to religious ties. Imperial belonging, in their conceptualization, reflected religious spheres of influence more than any actual political sovereignty. Their tenth-century vision of imperial spheres of influence clarifies the meaning of one of our key terms, *empire*, as it was exercised in this early medieval time, when political claims were non-exclusive and overlapping and borders were not yet set. Equally, the introduction of Rus as a marked location on Ibn Ḥawqal's map reminds us of the power and demands of the visual. The imperatives of visual mapping required cartographers to make up their minds about the precise location of a people or state. A map resists any laziness in assigning location. It will not allow vague nods toward the banks of the Volga or poetic invocation of a chimerical "Island of the Rus." Nor will relative terms such as *to the left* or *behind* suffice on a map. Instead of such circumlocutions, Ibn Ḥawqal's pioneering map situates the Rus as a people and a polity with a place in the world.

NOTES

1. Istanbul, *Topkapı Sarayı Müzesi Kütüphanesi*, A. 3346.
2. Jerald R. Tibbets, "The Balkhī School of Geographers," in *History of Cartography*, Vol. 2, edited by John B. Harley and David Woodward (Chicago: The University of Chicago Press, 1992), 108–136.
3. Al-Iṣṭakhrī, Abū Isḥāq Ibrāhīm ibn Muḥammad al-Fārisī, *Kitāb al-Masālik wal-mamālik*, edited by Michael Jan de Goeje, Bibliotheca Geographorum Arabicorum 1 (Leiden: Brill, 1870).

4. Ibn Ḥauḳal, Abū'l-Ḳāsim Ibn Ḥauḳal al-Naṣībī, *Opus geographicum*, edited by Johannes H. Kramers (Leiden: Brill, 1938–1939), fasc. 1–2.
5. Gog and Magog (Arabic *Yajūj wa Majūj*)—monstrous creatures hostile to people living in the far east of the earth, mentioned in the Bible and in the Koran.
6. Burtases—tribal association of unclear ethnicity that lived in the Middle Volga region and mentioned in Arab sources since the ninth century.
7. Sarir—medieval state in mountainous Dagestan.
8. Ibn Ḥauḳal, *Opus geographicum*, 9.
9. Ibn Khurradādhbih, *Kitāb al-Masālik wal-mamālik*, edited by Michael Jan de Goeje, Bibliotheca Geographorum Arabicorum 6 (Leiden: Brill, 1889), 154.
10. Ibn Khurradādhbih, *Kitāb al-Masālik wal-mamālik*, 154.
11. Al-Iṣṭakhrī, *Kitāb al-Masālik wal-mamālik*, 223; Ibn Ḥauḳal, *Opus geographicum*, 394.
12. Al-Iṣṭakhrī, *Kitāb al-Masālik wal-mamālik*, 225–226; Ibn Ḥauḳal, *Opus geographicum*, 397–398.
13. Al-Iṣṭakhrī, *Kitāb al-Masālik wal-mamālik*, 225; Ibn Ḥauḳal, *Opus geographicum*, 397.
14. Al-Iṣṭakhrī, *Kitāb al-Masālik wal-mamālik*, 4; Ibn Ḥauḳal, *Opus geographicum*, 9.
15. Al-Iṣṭakhrī, *Kitāb al-Masālik wal-mamālik*, 9; Ibn Ḥauḳal, *Opus geographicum*, 14.
16. Al-Iṣṭakhrī, *Kitāb al-Masālik wal-mamālik*, 5; Ibn Ḥauḳal, *Opus geographicum*, 11.
17. Al-Iṣṭakhrī, *Kitāb al-Masālik wal-mamālik*, 4; Ibn Ḥauḳal, *Opus geographicum*, 9.
18. Ibn Khurradādhbih, *Kitāb al-Masālik wal-mamālik*, 154.

CHAPTER 3

THE "IMPERIAL MIRAGE" OF SVIATOSLAV (TWELFTH CENTURY)

SERGEI KOZLOV

IN THIS ESSAY, I will trace the ways medieval authors sought to define their political systems by delineating "national" entities within imperial space. My case study examines what I call the "imperial mirage" of the Kyivan prince Sviatoslav—that is, the mythologized, ahistorical image of the Rus prince and his military campaign against Byzantium as constructed in the narrative and visual sources of the tenth to fourteenth centuries. My study calls into question many modern certainties about the nature of empire and the definition of nation. Tracking the shimmering yet deceptive image of Sviatoslav as a rival to Byzantium and aspiring emperor in his own right, we find the image to be a carefully constructed mirage. Furthermore, digging under the surface, we find that the aspirations of nations, or rather of their proto-national antecedents, contributed to shaping the imperial mirage through their local epic traditions, and all this long before most modern scholars would acknowledge the existence of nations. Moreover, not only the two centrally involved parties, Byzantium and Rus, participated in shaping the myth of Sviatoslav. It was a collective effort, with contesting interpretations advanced by various medieval polities in the regions neighboring the Byzantine Empire. Neither empires nor nations, Kyivan Rus, the Norman kingdom of Sicily, and the Bulgarian tsardom, were, however, major regional powers in the Mediterranean and East European worlds. They all looked back to the Roman Empire as their inspiration and model.

The words *empire* and *emperor* are themselves of Roman origin. They derive from the Latin word *imperium*, which means "authority." During the period of the Roman Republic, the term *imperator* was a title that soldiers conferred on an honored commander who had won a significant victory. The first person to bear the title of *imperator* on a permanent basis was Julius Caesar. With time, *imperator* came to designate the head of the Roman state, and *empire* came to be understood as a state uniting a multitude of countries and peoples. After the fall of the Western Roman Empire in 476, the title of emperor was retained in the Eastern Roman Empire, later known as Byzantium or the Byzantine Empire, which lasted until 1453. In Byzantium, a new, Christian understanding of empire appeared. According to this new conception, the entire Christian world was to be unified under the authority of the Byzantine emperor, whose main responsibility was the defense of Orthodox Christians. The universal character of this Christian empire allowed for its expansion across the polities of the former Roman Empire and into territories and cities that had never been part of Rome.

Byzantium was not alone in drawing on the Roman legacy. The memory of the Roman Empire shaped the political imaginaries and aspirations of the many medieval rulers who dreamed of raising their capitals as the New Rome. The "barbarian" monarchies that conquered Roman cities and provinces expressed imperial ambitions, as did rulers who had never been part of the Roman World. These rulers transferred imperial ideas into their local, proto-national histories and ethnic mythologies. The Franks, Normans, Bulgars, and Rus defined themselves in relation to the Roman (and Byzantine) Empire. Their proto-national identity was defined through an imperial frame, the most attractive political discourse in the medieval Europe.

Today, the concept of the nation is closely associated with the French Revolution, when it came to mean, above all, a political body made up of ethnically or civically homogeneous citizens, who exercise popular sovereignty, with the goal of defense and cultivation of the common (national) good. But in the Middle Ages, the terms *natio*, *éthnos*, and *gens* had other meanings, combining the concepts of "people" (who were assumed to be multiethnic) with "troops." Their origin was not explained as a question of shared blood and kinship, but as shared, collective experience. As Herwig Wolfram observed, in the early Middle Ages the term *gens* meant nothing more than a union of diverse groups that rallied around a charismatic leader, or clans that traced their genealogical lineage back to gods and whose successes were fixed *in tradition*.[1] Whoever was connected to that tradition, whether by birth or as a result of experience, was part of the *gens*—that is, part of the collective, sharing a common origin not by blood but by collective memory. The "imperial mirage" connected with Sviatoslav was produced as part of the process of defining Rus in these proto-national and imperial terms.

Sviatoslav (ruled in Kyiv 945–972) was the last pagan (non-Christian) ruler of Rus and the first to announce territorial ambitions toward "New Rome" or Constantinople (now Istanbul), the capital of the Byzantine Empire. According to the early twelfth-century Rus chronicle *The Tale of Bygone Years*, Sviatoslav not only seized several Bulgarian towns that were part of Byzantium at the time, but also intended to move the capital of his realm from Kyiv to Pereiaslavets (Little Preslav = Nufăru?, Romania) on the Danube River, less than 455 miles from Constantinople. Sviatoslav stood on the outskirts of Constantinople and threatened the very existence of Byzantium.

The Rus assault on the greatest empire of the time impressed contemporaries and later generations of scholars. A number of competing versions of the conflict survive, but the pictures they present differ profoundly, depending on the author's allegiances. Byzantine historians declared that Byzantine emperor John Tzimiskes (ruled 969–976) was the victor, but the medieval Rus chronicler attributes victory to Sviatoslav. What can explain such contradictory images of Sviatoslav's campaign? Reading these divergent textual and visual sources closely, we discover that the figure of Sviatoslav came to occupy an important place in the evolving sense of collective identity of the peoples surrounding the Byzantine Empire. In historical memory, he became a productive site for expressing "nationalizing" impulses.

Both Byzantine and Rus chronicles about Sviatoslav's campaign are, in significant measure, literary constructions, derived from oral tales of a heroic-patriotic ilk that arose in the period of military confrontation between Byzantium and Rus. As Rakhil Lipets demonstrated, the passages about Sviatoslav in the Rus *Tale of Bygone Years* reflect Slavic epic songs that glorified the exploits of Rus princes and warriors.[2]

Many Byzantine historians wrote about Sviatoslav's campaign, but they all depend on Leo the Deacon (c. 950–992) and John Skylitzes (early 1040s–after 1101), who left the earliest and most detailed accounts about this campaign. In Deacon's and Skylitzes's chronicles, "the victory over Sviatoslav" also took on epic dimensions, becoming one of the symbols of the Byzantines' military genius and their status as "chosen by God." These texts were emotionally uplifting. Despite a fully historical basis, a significant number of the secondary details of these texts reflect not historical reality, but the fruit of popular storytelling. The names of real rulers and warriors were grafted onto epic heroes, the plots derived from folklore, and the situations fit into formulaic folk plotlines. Byzantine epic songs sung in praise of the martial accomplishments of the Greeks, in all likelihood, were repurposed by Byzantine historians in their descriptions of battle scenes with Sviatoslav.

They also bear some relation to popular Byzantine heroic-patriotic songs about wars with the Arabs. The Arabic Caliphate was a powerful state that was challenging Byzantium between seventh and twelfth centuries. It not only aimed to conquer the empire, but, in essence, offered an alternative view of the development of the Byzantine World. Byzantine victories (real and imagined) over the Arab threats established the basis of their epic tradition, expressed in works such as the Acritic songs. The most famous Acritic song was the so-called *Digenes Akritas*, often regarded as the only surviving epic song from the Byzantine Empire and considered by some to signal the beginnings of modern Greek literature. The epic details the life of the hero, Basil, whose epithet Digenes Akritas ("two-blood border lord") refers to his mixed Greek and Arab blood, and celebrates his exploits on the Arab-Byzantine border.

Sviatoslav's campaign against Byzantium fits easily into the Acritic schema. Although Sviatoslav apparently had no dreams of an "imperial project" of his own and his fundamental concern consisted of securing control of trade routes, he was viewed through this imperial lens by the Byzantines, and by the rest of the neighboring world. Sviatoslav's Byzantine campaign became part of an "imperial mirage," which recast border skirmishes and armed incursions as part of a great, epic clash of empires. The Rus-Byzantine conflict left a deep imprint on the cultural memory of medieval peoples and became the model among rivals of Byzantium—rivals as geographically dispersed as the Norman kingdom of Sicily and the Bulgarian tsardom—for leadership in the Mediterranean region after the Crusader capture of Constantinople in 1204.

Sviatoslav's campaign left an impression not only in the narrative texts, but also in visual form. In this connection, it is interesting to see how medieval artists depicted "national distinctiveness" in miniatures. Sviatoslav's campaign left its mark in the miniatures of two Byzantine illustrated histories: a manuscript known as the *Madrid Skylitzes*, a twelfth-century Greek codex (i.e., manuscript in book form) of John Skylitzes's chronicle that is now at the National Library of Spain in Madrid,[3] and a manuscript called the *Vatican Manasses*, a fourteenth-century Old Bulgarian (also known as Church Slavonic) codex of Constantine Manasses's chronicle (which, in turn, drew on the earlier chronicle of Skylitzes) that is now in the Vatican Apostolic Library.[4] These histories circulated widely in the Mediterranean world in manuscript form, but these particular copies are distinguished by the inclusion of colorful illustrations. The Byzantine chronicles had never been illustrated before in Europe, so these are some of the earliest examples of a new genre: the illuminated chronicle.

The *Madrid Skylitzes* was prepared by order of the Sicilian king Roger II (ruled 1130–1154), who was trying to assert Norman authority in South Italy. Episodes from the Rus-Byzantine war are illustrated on 21 of 574 miniatures of the Madrid manuscript. They include a few battle scenes, the siege of Preslav in Bulgaria, the meeting between Emperor Tzimiskes and Sviatoslav, the triumphal entry of Tzimiskes to Constantinople, and the killing of Sviatoslav by the Pechenegs. The *Vatican Manasses* was produced in 1331–1341 for the Bulgarian tsar Ivan Alexander (ruled 1331–1371). Two of 69 color miniatures in the Vatican manuscript are dedicated to Sviatoslav's campaign.

The places and circumstances of the manuscripts' production under the patronage of the Norman and Bulgarian rulers gave these "editions" of Byzantine chronicles an outsider skew, so they don't present an exclusively Byzantine view of events. Through close analysis of both manuscripts, Elena N. Boeck argues that Byzantine history was selectively reimagined to suit the interests of new powers of the Mediterranean region in the aftermath of the Crusades.[5] She demonstrates that the *Madrid Skylitzes* highlights wars and rebellions to subvert the divinely ordained image of order that Byzantine emperors preferred to project, while the Bulgarian version seen in the *Vatican Manasses* presents Byzantium as a platform for the accession of Ivan Alexander to the throne of the "Third Rome," the last and final world-empire.

Historians sometimes interpret the miniatures literally, taking their content at face value. They often use them as straightforward illustrations documenting Rus-Byzantine relations or to make a variety of historical claims, such as attempting to reconstruct the ethnographic appearance and military tactics of the peoples depicted. However, it turns out that building conclusions about ethnic distinction or identity on the basis of these medieval illustrations is more difficult than it might seem. Notably, ethnocultural distinctions, manifested in external appearance, costume, and weapons of the Byzantines and of various "Others" (Rus, Bulgars, Pechenegs, "Scyths"), were not relevant for the creators of these miniatures. Except for the fact that the Arabs (Muslims) were distinguished in the miniatures by their turbans, the troops of opposing sides were shown as identical to each other. Ethnic belonging was expressed only through captions on the drawings (Image 3.1).

IMAGE 3.1 The meeting of Tzimiskes and Sviatoslav, as depicted in Skylitzes's chronicle, first half of the twelfth century.

In the Madrid miniatures, Sviatoslav's troops are depicted without distinguishing ethnographic traits and are presented as unsuccessful in their challenges to the Byzantines. They suffer defeat, and either run away or perish. The battle scenes unfold in the dynamic visual form of a patriotic epic, reenforcing passages from Skylitzes's text. So, for instance, the miniature in folio 162r illustrates one passage with two battle scenes (Image 3.2). On the left, a Byzantine warlord, Constantine, is portrayed on horseback, as he attacks a Rus warrior with a mace. The Rus, holding a kite shield and lance, leans backwards to dodge the blow. In the right scene, Constantine has dismounted and, grasping the fallen Rus by the beard, raises his weapon to slay him. The visual and textual narratives of Skylitzes's chronicle are also supplemented by anonymous verses written in the margins of the Madrid manuscript. These verses celebrate the accomplishments of the Emperor John Tzimiskes and his miraculous triumph over the "Scyths," as the Rus were called in Skylitzes' chronicle.

It is possible, however, that we do have a representation of Sviatoslav's external appearance. Leo the Deacon described him in the following way:

> [Sviatoslav] was of moderate height, neither taller than average, nor particularly short; his eyebrows were thick; he had grey eyes and a snub nose; his beard was clean-shaven, but he let the hair grow abundantly on his upper lip where it was bushy and long; and he shaved his head completely, except for a lock of hair that hung down on one side, as a mark of the nobility of his ancestry; . . . on one ear was fastened a gold earring, adorned with two pearls with a red gemstone between them.[6]

According to Ihor Ševčenko, Leo the Deacon's description of Sviatoslav has an intriguing analogy in a mosaic of the Last Judgement in the Cathedral of Santa Maria Assunta on the island of Torcello near Venice, Italy, dating to the twelfth century (Image 3.3).[7] Torcello's mosaic was made by craftsmen from Constantinople. The central place in the composition is occupied by the Judge of the World, Christ. His mother and John the Forerunner (as John the Baptist is known in the Orthodox tradition) stand before him. On either side of them sit the apostles, and behind them are angels. Below the apostles, we see the four archangels. On the lowest tier are the people coming for Judgment: on Christ's right, the righteous; on his left, the sinners. The latter are depicted at the feet of Satan, who is portrayed with Judas upon his lap, and are divided into six groups according to the sins they committed. Among them is group of particular interest to us: the mustached and beardless head with an earring and with a lock of hair hanging over his forehead (Image 3.4).

According to Ševčenko, this image reflects Byzantine ideas about steppe nomads, including Sviatoslav. In developing this hypothesis, I want to pay attention to the possibility that this image embodied a stereotype that was widespread in Byzantium: of nomadic steppe peoples as "greedy Scyths." In their representational taxonomy of sins, these people came to represent the sin of avarice. Thus, if Ševčenko's identification of

IMAGE 3.2 Two battle scenes depicted in Skylitzes's chronicle, first half of the twelfth century.

IMAGE 3.3 *The Last Judgment*, mosaic from Torchello, near Venice, first half of the twelfth century.

IMAGE 3.4 Detail from *The Last Judgment*, mosaic from Torchello, near Venice, first half of the twelfth century: the sinners.

the figures is correct, the "avaricious" sinners in Torcello's mosaic provide an example of ethnic stereotyping by the Byzantines.

Thus, both contemporaries and successors regarded Sviatoslav's politics as expansionist and anti-Byzantine in their essence. Slotting the Rus prince into a ready-made understanding of "the greedy Scyth" and enemy of "God's chosen people," chroniclers and illustrators represented his attacks as part of an expansionist plan and assumed he pursued grand, anti-Byzantine imperial ambitions. Sviatoslav's campaign of cross-border raiding gave birth to a myth or an "imperial mirage," anticipating the imperial aspirations of the new leaders in the Byzantine region and, later, the Muscovite tsars.

This myth took root in the Russian collective memory to such an extent that it became one of the most enduring symbols of Slavic nationalism.[8] So, for instance, the nineteenth-century Russian historian Alexander Chertkov (1789–1858) fantasized about an alternative course of world history if the prince had triumphed over Emperor John Tzimiskes. He shaped his fantasy in the grandiose terms of nineteenth-century Russian Orientalism, with a tendency to view East and West as embodying essential civilizational qualities and a fascination with Russia's mediating status. To this vision, he added an imperial element, reflecting the beguiling influence of the "imperial mirage":

> In the tenth century Russia would have transformed from an almost Asian power to a European state during the reign of Sviatoslav and his heirs . . . A great Slavic empire would have occupied a big part of Europe, from the mouth of the Elbe, the border of

> Bavaria, Tyrol, Italy, the Adriatic, Morea, the Aegean Sea, the Bosporus, all the way to Kamchatka, America, and the Mongol and Kyrgyz steppes. The Roman colossus never occupied such space, but, most importantly, this vastness would have constituted one element, one language, and, probably, one faith.[9]

This grand, counterfactual vision of a history that never was drew on the same set of heroic tropes and entrenched ideas of clashing empires that shaped the image of the Rus in the Byzantine world.

In conclusion, in both text and image, Byzantine battles with Prince Sviatoslav drew on an ancient tradition of epic narrative, while also reflecting the dynamism and innovation that continuously shaped and reshaped that tradition. In Byzantium, the first epic elements appeared in the Acritic songs of the times of the Arab invasions; then were reinterpreted and integrated in the chronicles of Leo the Deacon and John Skylitzes to sculpt "the imperial mirage" of Sviatoslav. The Madrid manuscript introduced illustrations to the heroic representation of Byzantine history: visual supplements to the oral epic and proto-national visions of the Byzantine past. The "imperial mirage" of Sviatoslav was one of the inspirations of this impulse to depict those who challenged one imperial dream with another.

It is revealing that from the most ancient times, from the painted Attic vases of the archaic period to the reliefs on ancient Roman columns, the heroic epic was represented in visual media. And we see the same thing today; the heroic is visualized and mythologized around the globe: in Marvel Comics films, in propagandistic news programs, and most relevant to our story, in popular museum exhibits such as the over-the-top representation of Sviatoslav as heroic warrior and gallant protector of Rus, in the "Diorama of Sviatoslav's Last Battle" created in 1984 under Soviet auspices and still on display today in the Museum of Zaporizhzhian Cossacks in Zaporizhzhia, Ukraine (see Yulia Mikhailova's essay in this volume).

NOTES

1. Herwig Wolfram, *History of the Goths* (Berkeley: University of California Press, 1990), 5–6.
2. Rakhil Lipets, "Otrazhenie etnokul'turnykh sviazei Kievskoi Rusi v skazaniiakh o Sviatoslave Igoreviche (10 v.)," in *Etnicheskaia istoriia i fol'kor*, edited by Rakhil Lipets (Moscow: Nauka, 1977), 217 ff.
3. See the *Madrid Skylitzes*: http://bdh.bne.es/bnesearch/detalle/1754254
4. See the *Vatican Manasses*: https://digi.vatlib.it/view/MSS_Vat.slav.2
5. Elena N. Boeck, *Imagining the Byzantine Past: The Perception of History in the Illustrated Manuscripts of Skylitzes and Manasses* (Cambridge: Cambridge University Press, 2015).
6. *The History of Leo the Deacon: Byzantine Military Expansion in the Tenth Century*, introduction, translation, and annotation by Alice-Mary Talbot and Denis F. Sullivan, with the assistance of George T. Dennis and Stamatina McGrath (Washington, DC: Dumbarton Oaks, 2005), 199.
7. Ihor Ševčenko, "Sviatoslav in Byzantine and Slavic miniatures," *Slavic Review* 24, no. 4 (1965): 710–711.
8. See Viktor Aleksandrovich Schnirelmann, "Kniaz' Sviatoslav i politika pamiati," *Neprikosnovennyi zapas* vol. 112, no. 2 (2017): 35–50.
9. Aleksandr Chertkov, *Opisanie voiny velikogo kniazia Sviatoslava Igorevicha protiv bolgar i grekov v 967–971 godakh* (Moscow: Tipografiia Avgusta Semena, 1843), 245, 249–250.

PART

MUSCOVY AND THE EXPANSION OF EMPIRE

Muscovy is a conventional Latin name used for designating the united Russian state that formed around Moscow in the fifteenth century. In Moscow, the Hellenized (Greek) term *Rossia*, derived from *Rus*, was preferred to the Latin *Muscovia*, derived from *Moskva/Moscow*. In the early modern period, surprisingly, the right to the name Rossia was a bone of contention among the various realms that styled themselves as the heirs of Kyivan Rus: the Grand Duchy of Lithuania, the Kingdom of Poland, and the aspiring principality of Moscow. Wherever Orthodox East Slavs dwelled in significant numbers, the title of "Russia" and the historical inheritance of Rus could be, and was, claimed. The rival powers attempted to discredit Moscow's standing by actively promoting the name Muscovy and keeping the name Rossia, in various forms, for themselves. International, if not precisely interimperial, competition over the symbolic mantle of Rus thus set its imprint on Moscow's formation from the very start. The Muscovite label has remained standard in scholarship on Russia and its holdings in the early modern era, and we will use it here.

The Grand Prince of Moscow, Ivan III (ruled 1462–1505), nonetheless claimed for himself the legacy of Kyivan Rus and the role of unifier of the Russian lands. He benefited from the fragmentation of the former Mongol empire and the termination in 1480 of Mongol-Tatar demands for deference and tribute from Rus. He devised the title "Grand Prince of All Rus" after the annexation of the Novgorod Republic in 1478. By the conclusion of his forty-three-year reign, through negotiation, alliance, and on occasion, violent conquest, he had created a unified Muscovite state from the collection of scattered Rus principalities in eastern Europe. This new political entity represented itself as the heir of Kyivan Rus and sought to control the parts of the Grand Duchy of Lithuania that were inhabited by Orthodox East Slavs, people with historical, religious, linguistic, and perhaps, ethnic connections to Rus. During centuries of battles over these people and territories, the Grand Duchy and the emerging Muscovite realm rested their competing claims on particular readings of the historical past and what those ancient Rus connections implied.

To strengthen its international prestige, the Muscovite state also proclaimed itself the heir to the Byzantine (Eastern Roman) Empire. Within both the Church and the ruling circles of Moscow, legends arose that ascribed the origin of the Rurikid dynasty not to the Scandinavian Vikings, but to a brother of the Roman Caesar Augustus. The newly concocted legend claimed that the Cap of Monomakh, a gold, fur, and jewel-laden crown, had been presented to the Rus prince Volodymyr/Vladimir Monomakh by the Byzantine emperor, and that the White Cowl, a piece of religious regalia, could be traced back to the Byzantine ruler, Constantine I (the Great). These legends were reinforced by the dynastic marriage of Ivan III to the niece of the last Byzantine emperor, Sophia Palaiologina. His occasional appropriation of the title of Tsar, and his adoption of the Byzantine double-headed eagle as his coat of arms, further supported his claims. The ideological basis of power was expressed in references to other imperial centers, drawing on the greatness of the historical past and foreshadowing eschatological glory yet to come. Moscow styled itself "New Constantinople," or "New Jerusalem," or more rarely, "the Third Rome." These titles affirmed Moscow's claim to sole leadership in the Orthodox world after the capture of Constantinople by the Ottoman Turks in 1453. No longer content to be a second-rate ruler subordinate to the Byzantine emperor, or any other imperial overlord, the rulers of Moscow began to style themselves sovereign, answering to no overlord except their Orthodox god.

The heirs of Ivan III built on the foundation he established. Under his son Vasilii III and grandson Ivan IV (the Terrible), Muscovy developed many aspects of other early modern states: a nascent bureaucracy, a system for supporting military service, a series of law codes. The rulers worked closely with the Orthodox hierarchy to promote the regime's religious legitimacy. Orthodoxy played an outsized role in shaping Muscovite visual practices. In a largely illiterate society, the visual played a key role in spreading religious messages. Churches were filled with icons and their walls covered with frescoes that eloquently conveyed lessons about the rulers' piety and their God-given role in leading their people to salvation. An emphasis on sensory experience within Russian Orthodoxy imbued the very act of seeing with sacral potential. Within Orthodox Christianity, icons were venerated as contact points with the saintly figures they represented. Icons were not to be worshipped as idols, but venerated for the ineffable trace of the holy presence they carried. Perhaps for this reason, secular painting was frowned upon, and Muscovites developed little in the way of non-religious imagery—aside from purely decorative ornamentation—until the second half of the seventeenth century, when influences of the Baroque filtered into Russian circles.

The line of Ivan III, the Rurikid dynasty, died out after the brief reign of Ivan the Terrible's pious but feeble son Fedor. Fedor's brother-in-law, Boris Godunov, assumed the throne in 1598, but his legitimacy was contested from the start. As a non-dynastic ruler, he faced an uphill battle in establishing his right to the throne. Enticed by the weakness of the center, oppositional forces began to mass in the peripheries of the realm and to invade from across the borders. In a chaotic period known as the Time of Troubles, or *Smuta* (1605–1613), Muscovy was riven by competing forces: Cossacks from the south, Poles from the west, Swedes from the north. The most effective of these armies marched under the banners of a series of pretenders, claimants to the throne who falsely announced themselves to be the resurrected incarnations of dead sons of the last tsars. In 1605, the First False Dmitrii successfully took Moscow and was actually crowned as tsar, with Polish backing, until his assassination a year later. A few years after that, the Poles dispensed with the niceties of backing a pretender and took control of Moscow outright. Domination by Polish Catholic invaders did not sit well with Russia's Orthodox population. In an impressive turnaround, Russian forces mobilized in the absence of any tsar to command their service. Russian landholding elites, urban merchants, and Cossacks united to liberate Moscow, throw out the Poles, and select a new tsar. Sixteen-year-old Michael Romanov took the throne in 1613, the first of the dynasty that would hold the throne until the Revolution of 1917.

Romanov rule put its imprint on society both within ethnic Russian regions and in its imperial holdings. Within Russia, perhaps the most critical development, affecting the lives of the overwhelming majority of the population, was the legal codification of serfdom in 1649. The new legislation formalized relations of bondage that tied peasants to the land and subjected them to their landlords' will.

In the sixteenth to early-eighteenth centuries, the Muscovite state expanded significantly, annexing the Volga region, the northern Black Sea region, the Urals, and Siberia. After Ivan IV conquered the Khanates of Kazan and Astrakhan, former Mongol possessions, in the 1550s, the title of Tsar was adopted by Russian rulers. Compared to princes, Muscovite tsars commanded a significantly higher status in diplomatic relations with Europe. The title of Grand Prince was translated as "Grand Duke," while the title of Tsar (derived from the Latin *Caesar*) was equated in the monarchical hierarchy to the title of Emperor (Latin *Imperator*). The last "Tsar of All Rus" was Peter I (also known as Peter the Great), who accepted the title of Emperor of All Russia in 1721.

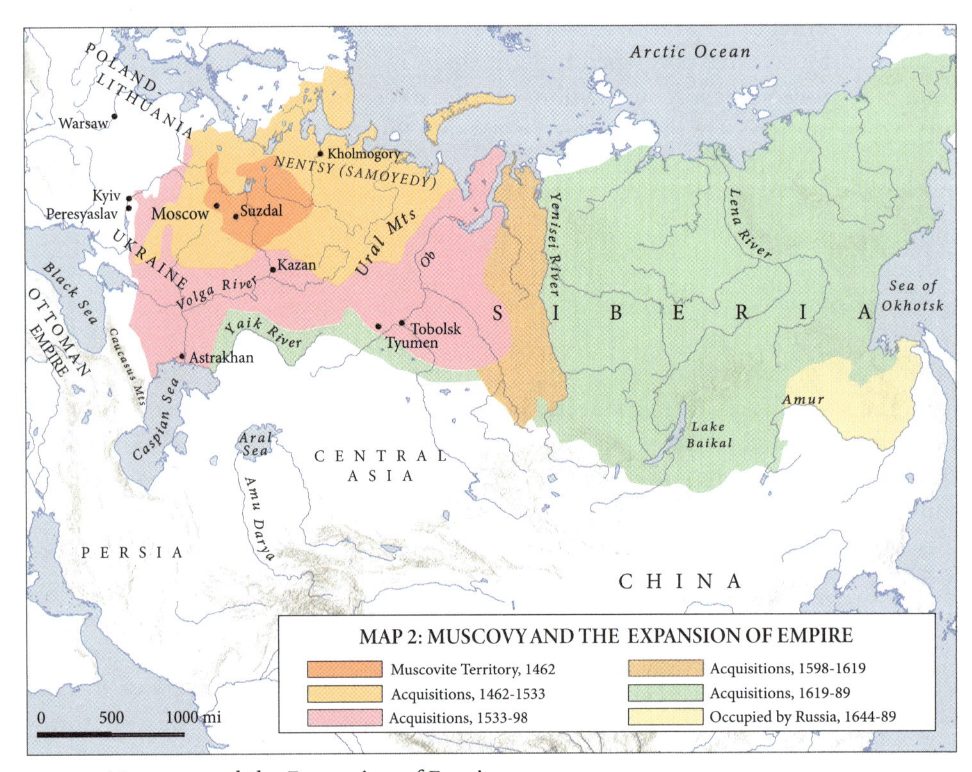

MAP 2 Muscovy and the Expansion of Empire

CHAPTER 4

EMPIRE AND CULTURE: THE SIXTEENTH-CENTURY ENGLISH ENCOUNTER THE SAMOYEDS

NANCY S. KOLLMANN

WHEN A SHIP full of Englishmen unexpectedly found themselves in St. Nicholas Bay in the White Sea while seeking a Northeast Passage to China through the Arctic, they set to work figuring out just what sort of polity and people they had encountered. Two ships of three that had set sail from London in May 1553 had shipwrecked, leaving only Richard Chancellor's *Edward Bonaventure* at safe haven near Kholmogory. Chancellor and his fellow seamen and merchants were fast learners. Informed that they were in the tsardom of Ivan IV and recognizing Muscovy as a sovereign state, if barely known to England, Chancellor headed to Moscow, letters from King Edward VI in hand. He proceeded to negotiate trade privileges between Russia and England, while the Russian court pushed for diplomatic ties. Merchants and explorers from the newly founded (1555) Muscovy Company soon streamed to Russia, some of whom explored the local area for trade possibilities. In the Russian North and along the Arctic coast of Siberia, they encountered the Samoyeds, nomadic reindeer herders. To make the Samoyeds "legible" in their reports back to London, Muscovy Company traders relied on familiar political categories and cultural tropes.

Native peoples of the Far North had been an object of fascination and fantasy since antiquity. Martin Waldseemüller reproduced many ancient views when he depicted savage peoples along the Arctic coast of western Siberia in his 1516 map of the world. He included a "Parosite" (who subsists on the steam from a bubbling pot), a "Cynocephalos" (a man with a dog's head), and a "Samoed." Of the three, only the Samoedy (or Samoyeds), whose proper name today is Nentsy, are real. Waldseemüller's description highlights characteristic features of their herding lifestyle: "The inhabitants live from hunting, and their clothes and tents are made of animal skins; they have a remarkable way of dealing with traders; they serve the Tartars [Tatars], and have no wheat."[1] Since he had no eyewitness reports of what the Samoyeds actually looked like, however, Waldseemüller depicted a "Wild Man," a bearded giant, chasing a rabbit with a club.[2] (In actuality, a Samoyed would fell it easily with bow and arrow.)

The first wave of Englishmen to Russia were intrepid, young explorers, curious about the world on its own terms. They reported back to the Company regularly and included ethnographic accounts of native peoples along with sketch maps and information on trade routes, local products, and potential demand for British goods. Educated in a basic humanist curriculum, many embraced their tasks with a capacious curiosity. Two—Stephen Borough and Richard Johnson—wrote extensively on the Samoyeds.

Stephen Borough (1525–1584) was an accomplished seaman and cartographer who served in 1553 as the main pilot of Chancellor's ship; in 1556, he returned to the White Sea to try (again unsuccessfully) for a Northeast Passage—that is, a northern sea route to China. He returned to London in May 1557. Richard Johnson was a seaman and small-scale merchant active with the Muscovy Company from at least 1553 to 1566. He accompanied Chancellor in 1553, Borough in 1556, and Anthony Jenkinson from 1557 to 1560 when Jenkinson traveled through Muscovy to Central Asia. Each made the effort to learn local languages: Stephen Borough published notes on the language of the Lapps, and he and Johnson mastered Russian to the point that Johnson noted of the Samoyeds, "they tooke me to be a Russian."[3]

When Anthony Jenkinson returned to London in 1560 from his sojourn through Russia to Central Asia, colleagues in the Muscovy Company collaborated with him to produce a map of his travels, amplifying his findings with the Muscovy Company's accumulated knowledge of Russia. Borough and Johnson were back in London at that time and might have talked with the mapmakers, or the latter might have read their reports from the field. Not surprisingly, Jenkinson's copiously illustrated map includes an image of a Samoyed (Image 4.1).

This little man swathed in fur hardly calls attention to himself. The text is not even as informative as Waldseemüller's: "The picture before you shows the clothing of inhabitants of this land who are called colloquially Samoides. They are idolaters, and they live in desolate places." But a fur-clad man would have piqued the English reader's curiosity. Wearing animal skins, rather than woven cloth, was one of the markers of "barbarity" that Europeans imbibed with a classical education. For millennia, settled people had looked down on nomads, but not simply because steppe nomads raid cities. Their whole nomadic way of life challenges settled existence. As long ago as Homer and Herodotus, nomads were dismissed as unproductive: they do not live in fixed houses, nor work the land, nor turn grain into bread; they do not brew ale or weave cloth. Their way of life was described, by commentators from settled societies, as passive: nomads live off their herds; they eat meat, drink mare's milk, dress in animal hides, and carrying tents made of skins, follow their herds as they graze. Wrapping the Samoyed in fur signaled to a European audience that this was an "uncivilized" people.

IMAGE 4.1 A Samoyed, on a 1562 map attributed to Anthony Jenkinson, *Nova Absolutaque Russiae Moscoviae et Tartariae descriptio.*

The implicit concept of civilization was central to the other critique here. By saying that nomadic people live in "desolate" places, the Englishmen are underscoring the importance they placed on living in society with others. The city, or *polis*, provided benefits not available to nomads living in small groups with no fixed residence: literacy, schools, libraries; established religion and fixed houses of worship; written laws and organized political life. Moving seasonally through steppe, forest, mountains, or tundra, nomads have no homeland.

Borough and Johnson readily fit the Samoyeds into these tropes, even as they also recognized them in contemporary political categories. They understood that the Samoyeds were imperial subjects of Moscow and participants, to some extent, in Russian culture. Johnson wrote "these Samoeds bee in subiection to the Emperour of Russia" and "the most part of them can speake the Russe tongue to bee understood."[4] They also saw them as trade partners, detailing where they customarily met for market. But they also saw the Samoyeds through the lens of their own cultural prejudices. In this, they were seconded by their Russian companions. Borough, for example, worked with a Russian guide, the seaman Loshak, who introduced him to myths and rites of the Samoyeds. Samoyed practices seemed as exotic to the Russian Loshak as to the English travelers. Imperial subjecthood notwithstanding, the Samoyeds were people of an entirely different culture.

Perhaps unable to resist lurid myths, Richard Johnson repeated a sensationalized tale of cannibalism and the Samoyeds, but took care to credit it to others. "As wee are tolde by the Russes," he noted in his 1556–1557 report, one group, the "wild Samoyeds" on the "great island," refused visitors on their shores: "they will kill them and eate them."[5] Even on his trip to Central Asia with Jenkinson a few years later, Johnson collected information on the Samoyeds, submitting a report allegedly written in Russian by "Pheodor Towtigin" of Kholmogory and translated by Johnson. It alleged that the Samoyed diet "is flesh of Olens, or Harts, and Fish, and [they] doe eate one another sometimes among themselves. And if any Marchants come unto them, then they kill one of their children for their sakes to feast them withall. And if a Marchant chance to die with them, they burie him not, but eate him, and so doe they eate them of their owne country likewise."[6] Cannibalism was all the rage in reports of the New World in the sixteenth century,[7] so Johnson was sure to please his audience. Meanwhile, it was easy for his Russian informants to attribute cannibalism to the Samoyeds because of the term's coincidental meaning in Russian. To Russian speakers, it seems to mean "people who eat themselves" (*samo* = self; *ed'* = to eat), while actually the term probably comes from a general name of Arctic Coast dwellers, the Saami.[8]

But Johnson couched such lurid tales as second-hand information. When he and Borough related what they actually saw, they were careful, even skeptical, observers. With eye-witness detail, Borough reported they "have no houses, but onely coverings made of Deersskins, set over them with stakes . . . their boates are made of Deers skins, and when they come on shoare they cary their boates with them upon their backes: for their cariages they have no other beastes to serve them, but Deere only. As for bread and corne they have none, except the Russes bring it to them: their knowledge is very base, for they know no letter."[9] Johnson reported similarly: "And they live in heards, and have all their carriages with deere, for they have no horses."[10] Both acknowledge that the Samoyeds are excellent hunters: "they are men expert in shooting" (Borough); "they shoot well in bowes" (Johnson).[11]

Perhaps most fascinating to Borough and Johnson was that the Samoyeds were "idolaters," worshipers of pagan images. Idolatry was a charged issue in the religious struggles that wracked England in this century, and Borough and Johnson were particularly attentive to Samoyed rites, priests, and idols. Loshak took Stephen Borough, for example, to a site of ritual sacrifice, where Borough describes a bloody altar, bloody deerskins, and "a heape of the Samoyds idols, which were in number above 300, the worst, and the most unartificial [poorly made] worke that ever I saw: the eyes and mouthes of sundry of them were bloudie, they had the shape of men, women and children, very grossly wrought, and that which they had made for other parts, was also sprinkled with bloud."[12] Broken sleds were also scattered about, suggesting on the model of modern-day Nentsy practice that this was a burial site.[13]

Richard Johnson describes an even more remarkable experience that would have resonated with his audience in England, where Protestantism had "stripped the altars" of ritual and mystery: he attended a shamanic séance.[14] Judging by its similarity to modern-day Siberian shamanism, he witnessed a ritual of prophesying, rather than healing.[15] For hours, Johnson sat among the people of the community (recall they took him "to be a Russian") and watched a shaman at work. "Hee that is most auncient is their Priest"; he plays "on a thing like to a sieve, with a skin on the one end like a drumme."[16] He wears on his head "a thing of white like a garlande, and his face is covered with a piece of a shirt of maile, with manie small ribbes, and teeth of fishes, and wilde beastes hanging on the same maile." He sings "as wee use heere in Englande to hallow, whope or showte at houndes," and everyone else answers him "Igha, Igha, Igha," and he replies and they answer back and forth until the priest "becommeth as it were madde, and falling downe as hee were dead." Johnson asked onlookers what he was doing, and they replied that their God shall "tell him what wee shall doe, and whither wee shall goe." Soon the shaman arose from his trance and resumed call-and-response chanting with the people.

Singing with the community all the while, "hee commaunded them to kill 5 Olens or great Deere." Then he took a long sword (Johnson reports its exact length, noting "I did mete it my selfe") and thrust it into his belly several times. But no wound appeared ("they continuing in their sweete song still"). The priest then heated the sword in the fire and thrust it through his own body. Doubting Thomas-like, Johnson reports, "the point being out of his shirt behind, I layde my finger upon it." Then the priest pulled out the sword and sat while they heated a kettle of water and built a sort of square chair. The priest removed his garland with its metal ornaments and his shirt and "sate down like a tailour" (cross-legged, perhaps) on the chair, singing in strong voice. They twisted a rope made of deerskin around his neck and chest, placed the kettle of boiling water in front of him, and covered him up. Then two men pulled the rope excruciatingly. Johnson heard something fall and asked "them that sate by me what it was that fell into the water." They replied that "it was his head, his shoulder and left arme," severed by the rope. "Then I rose up and would have looked whether it were so or not, but they laid hold on me, and said, that if they should see him with their bodily eye, they shoulde live no longer." He saw what he thought was the priest's fingers gesture from under the covering, but his neighbors assured him that the priest was still dead and that it was a beast, "but what beast they knew not nor would not tell." He concludes his account abruptly, leaving it to the reader to decide what to believe: "and then at the last the Priest lifted up his head with his shoulder and arme, and all his bodie, and came forth to the fire." This service took several hours. Afterwards, he asked a servant of the priest "what their God saide to him when he lay as dead," but the man answered that "his owne people doeth not know, neither is it for them to know, for they must be as he commanded." Appealing to the authenticity of eyewitness, Johnson concludes: "This I saw the fifth day of Januarie in the yere of our Lord 1556 [sic]."

These two curious Englishmen made sense of the Russian empire's variety of people and cultures in several ways. Richard Johnson applied a critical sensibility, insisting on measuring and touching the material reality of the pagan rite. But he and Stephen Borough also understood what they saw through the lens of established frameworks. Politically, they invoked empire, identifying local Russians and the Samoyeds as subjects of the great tsar in Moscow. Culturally, they understood the Russians as fellow Christians, while they saw the Samoyeds through stereotypes that ethnographers have been applying since Herodotus. These people had no political life, no formal religion, no productive labor. They were a different culture from English or Russian, and an inferior one.

Their accounts are not without value, however, despite the tropes. Stephen Borough and Richard Johnson were keen observers and faithful transcribers, like so many early modern travelers.[17] Johnson's description of a shamanic ritual, for example, conforms to modern-day Siberian practice. Their capacious curiosity about the tsar's subjects, and about the many new people and cultures they encountered between England, China, and Persia, provides us a window into the multiethnic, multireligious world of Ivan IV's empire.

NOTES

1. Chet van Duzer, *Martin Waldseemüller's "Carta marina" of 1516. Study and Transcription of the Long Legends* (Springer Open Access, 2020), 71–73. https://doi.org/10.1007/978-3-030-22703-6
2. On "Wild Man" imagery, see Stephanie Leitch, *Mapping Ethnography in Early Modern Germany: New Worlds in Print Culture* (New York: Palgrave Macmillan, 2010), chapter 3.
3. Borough on Lapps: Stephen Borough, "The voyage of the foresaid Mr. Stephen Burrough, an. 1557, from Colomogoro to Wardhouse . . . ," in Richard Hakluyt, *The Principal Nauigations, Voiages, Traffiques and Discoueries of the English Nation . . . ,* 3 vols. (London, 1598–1600), 1: 293. Johnson on Russian: "Certaine notes unperfectly written . . . with Steven Burrowe in the Serchthrift 1556 and afterward among the Samoedes, whose devilish rites here describeth," in Hakluyt, *The Principal Nauigations* 1 (1598): 285. Anne Pennington notes Stephen Borough's knowledge of Russian and calls his son Christopher an early "Slavist" for his expertise: "A Sixteenth-Century English Slavist," *The Modern Language Review* 62 (1967): 680–686.

4. Johnson, "Certaine notes unperfectly written," 284, 285.
5. Johnson, "Certaine notes unperfectly written," 284.
6. Richard Johnson, "Certaine notes gathered by Richard Johnson . . . of the reports of Russes and other straungers . . . [1560]," in Hakluyt, *The Principal Nauigations* 1 (1598): 337.
7. Cannibalism: Michiel van Groesen, *The Representations of the Overseas World in the De Bry Collection of Voyages (1590–1634)* (Leiden: Brill, 2008), 182–188.
8. Andrei V. Golovnev and Gail Osherenko, *Siberian Survival: The Nenets and Their Story* (Ithaca and London: Cornell University Press, 1999), 1–2.
9. Stephen Borough, "The Nauigation and discouerie toward the river of Ob . . . 1556," in Hakluyt, *The Principal Nauigations* 1 (1598): 280–281.
10. Johnson, "Certaine notes unperfectly written," 284.
11. Borough: "Nauigation and discouerie," 280; Johnson: "Certaine notes unperfectly written," 284.
12. Borough, "Nauigation and discouerie," 281.
13. Sleds in Nenets burials: James Forsyth, *A History of the Peoples of Siberia: Russia's North Asian Colony, 1581–1990* (Cambridge: Cambridge University Press, 1994), 18–19.
14. Johnson, "Certaine notes unperfectly written," 284–285.
15. Common elements include stabbing oneself with a knife, the wound not bleeding, singing, headgear, ecstatic trance, and bloodied idols: L. V. Khomič, "A Classification of Nenets Shamans," in *Shamanism in Siberia*, edited by Vilmos Diószegi and Mihály Hoppál (Budapest: Akadémiai Kiadó, 1978), 245–253; Å. Hultkrantz, "Ecological and Phenomenological Aspects of Shamanism," in *Shamanism in Siberia*, 27–58; Golovnev and Osherenko, *Siberian Survival*, 36.
16. This quote and those that follow are from Johnson, "Certaine notes unperfectly written," 284–285.
17. Joan Pau Rubiés, "Travel writing and ethnography," in *The Cambridge Companion to Travel Writing*, edited by Peter Hulme and Tim Youngs (New York: Cambridge University Press, 2002), 242–260.

CHAPTER 5

RACIAL IMAGINARY AND IMAGES OF MONGOLS AND TATARS IN EARLY MODERN RUSSIA (1560s–1690s)

VALERIE KIVELSON

EARLY MODERN RUSSIAN texts devote few words to describing the physical appearance of groups of people or attributing to them any collective physical or biological characteristics. Where Russian chronicles and tales from the sixteenth and seventeenth centuries showed no hesitation in labeling their enemies bloodthirsty heathens or denouncing them as pagans living in darkness and ignorance, they rarely described what these despicable beings looked like. Verbal records give us little basis for assessing whether, or in what way, Muscovites (early modern Russians) conceived of their steppe neighbors in what we might today understand as racial terms.

Visual sources supplement these taciturn texts, but they pose their own challenges. The painted image enjoyed exalted status among Russian Orthodox Christians. The Orthodox Church venerated icons—that is, religious images painted on wood. Few images were produced outside of religious settings, and even fewer survive. But the small number of such sources that do survive provide valuable information that reaches beyond the testimony of the written record. Beginning in the sixteenth century, as illuminated historical chronicles and illustrated saints' lives came into fashion, manuscript illustrators were forced to specify the looks of their subjects in ways that the chroniclers and hagiographers could easily sidestep.

Some working definition of *race* will be necessary as we start our inquiry. As it turns out, there is no simple definition available. Race has no stable, obvious, or natural contours or configuration, but instead expresses ideas developed by particular societies in particular times and places. Racial categories reflect, construct, and maintain power relations, conceptual and social hierarchies, and claims to superiority and inferiority. They intertwine and overlap with other divisive categories, such as religion, gender, or class. The working definition adopted here attends to markers of visible, physical, bodily difference as indicators of racial thinking. This is one of many possible definitions, and one with its own complexities and contradictions. Given the visual focus of this volume, however, it seems a reasonable way to anchor our analysis.

In Muscovite times, the vocabulary used to designate "others" pointed to multiple forms of diversity. Muscovite sources label groups as *inoiazychnye* (people of other languages), *inozemtsy* (people of other lands), *inovertsy* (people of other faiths), or they use slightly more specific terms such as "godless Tatars," *basurmany* (Muslims or non-Orthodox), or *iazychniki* (pagans). The closest to a racial category was the idea of *rod*, meaning kind, grouping, lineage, or maybe ethnicity, but textual sources make no mention of blood, appearance, or inherited characteristics. These elements, in some combination, would seem essential to even the most flexible definition of racial thought. Without dictating the specific content, most working definitions specify some concept of collective physical, biological, or phenotypical difference, usually with an inheritable aspect, as requisite to the term.

Still, race need not be explicitly identified as such in historical sources in order to serve as a useful conceptual category of analysis. If Muscovites did not express ideas about physical, biological difference in words, perhaps we can explore this question of Muscovite racial awareness by looking at visual depictions of people *we* might designate as racially distinct from Russians. In this regard, the Mongol and Turkic peoples of the Eurasian steppe offer a fruitful case to study. These Mongol-Tatar populations had a long, tense history of interaction with Russians, and these relations were amply described in Muscovite texts. The Mongols, with their Tatar allies, conquered the Rus in the early thirteenth century and ruled over them until the fifteenth century, when the tide began to turn. By the sixteenth century, Muscovites were ascendant and set on a course of conquering and subduing Tatars along the Volga, across Siberia, and in the territories to the south. In Muscovite usage, the term *Tatar* came to refer to a variety of shamanic or Muslim Asian and Turkic peoples, occupants of the Eurasian steppe.

For the sixteenth century, only a single major visual source survives to document those encounters with the steppe, but it is, to be honest, a doozy. The *Illustrated Historical Chronicle* (*Litsevoi letopisnyi svod*) is a massive, handwritten manuscript recording the entire history of the world, from Creation through the 1550s, in more than 20,000 pages, and illustrated with more than 17,000 (yes, that's 17,000!) miniatures. Most of the illustrations are drawn in ink and then colored in with paint. The grand history was compiled in the 1560s or 1570s, during the reign of Tsar Ivan IV, known as Ivan the Terrible. The chronicle's many illustrations of battles between Russian forces and Mongols or Tatars offer fruitful material on the question of Muscovite ideas, or absence of ideas, about race.

Approaching this question theoretically, we might expect that early modern Russians lived in a preracial world. According to most contemporary theorists, the concept of race is a relatively new one, a modern invention. Many race theorists see the beginnings of racial thinking in the fateful encounters of Europeans with Africans, with the rise of the transatlantic slave trade, and with white Europeans' efforts to invent moral justification of chattel slavery. Others situate the hardening of racial categories even more recently, with the development of spurious racial sciences in the late eighteenth, nineteenth, and twentieth centuries.

Scholars of medieval Europe sometimes push the origins of racial thinking back farther, to the mid-fifteenth century, when Iberian laws on *limpieza de sangre*, or cleanliness of blood, were introduced. These laws identified a physiological, heritable stain that purportedly flowed in the veins of Jews and Muslims. Many scholars see in these laws an early expression of racial thinking. The laws rested on a concept of essential, biological characteristics—in this case, the taint of corruption that passed in bloodlines through the generations even if individuals or their ancestors had converted to Christianity. Carried across the ocean along with other weapons and ideologies of imperial conquest, notions of blood and purity framed discussions of Blackness, Indigeneity, and racial mixing in colonial Latin America. If one defines race as having a bodily, physical element, however imaginary, and to be transmissible across generations, then *limpieza de sangre* would seem a clear early instance of racial thinking.

These two powerful narratives both approach the question of the origins of racial thinking from an Atlantic, or transatlantic, perspective. Here is where early modern Russia becomes relevant. What might we see if we examined the question from an altogether different vantage point, far from the frameworks of Europe, Africa, and the Americas? Will we find evidence of racial thinking at all, and if so, will it be substantially different from those other, better-studied racial imaginaries? Muscovy, and the early modern empire it dominated, give us just such an opportunity.

In the *Illustrated Historical Chronicle*, visible ethnic or racial distinction is little in evidence. The manuscript's pictorial conventions dictated that their subjects' rank, function (job description), age, and gender should be immediately recognizable. Using a stable visual code, the illustrators identified rank-and-file soldiers with pointy helmets, protective breastplates, and skirted armor. Rulers of imperial rank—that is, tsars or khans—were identifiable by their five-pointed crowns, and lesser figures were indicated by various distinctive kinds of headgear. This pattern is seen in an illustration of the famous "Stand on the Ugra River," a confrontation between the Muscovite forces of the Muscovite Grand Prince Ivan III and the Tatar leader of the Great Horde, Akhmet Khan (Image 5.1).[1] This inconclusive faceoff occurred in 1480, almost a century before it was commemorated by the chronicle illustrators. At first glance, it is impossible to tell who's who, since both teams look alike. They don't even wear different colors or carry distinctive banners. One might guess, given that this is a Russian version of history, that the imposing figure in the regal crown would be the Russian ruler. But that guess would be wrong. The Tatar khan, approaching the river from the right, is the one wearing the five-pointed crown of imperial office. The Russian grand prince leads the central regiment of archers attacking from the left. Shown in armor, he wears a rounded hat with a jaunty brim and protective side flap.

IMAGE 5.1 A confrontation between the forces of the Muscovite Grand Prince Ivan III and Akhmet Khan of the Great Horde. *Illustrated Historical Chronicle*, 1560s or 1570s.

The miniaturists also indicated age, showing beardless youths and bearded elders, but again omitting any signals about ethnic difference. A scene depicting negotiations between the twenty-six-year-old Tsar Ivan IV and the Tatar khan of Astrakhan in 1556 shows the young Russian clean-shaven, while the khan sports a magnificent, though unlikely, blond beard.[2] The visual coding stays constant across ethnic or racial divisions. It is hierarchical standing and function that mattered to the illustrators, while racial indicators mattered not in the least.

The evidence of the *Illustrated Historical Chronicle* supports the claim that Russians were race-blind in the sixteenth century. They might hate their Tatar foes, but they didn't imagine or depict them as physically distinct. Over the course of the following century, however, Muscovite illustrators increasingly attended to marks of physical and ethnographic differentiation, even as the accompanying texts remained mute on the subject.

By the second half of the seventeenth century, illustrators frequently drew steppe nomads as distinctive, alien, and even not quite human. Notably, it is well after the Tatar population had been conquered and incorporated into the tsarist empire that this imagined racial typing emerges. Russia conquered the Khanate of Kazan with its Tatar population in 1552. This victory was followed by the conquest of Astrakhan, at the mouth of the Volga at the Black Sea, in 1554, and the gradual incorporation of Siberia beginning in the 1580s. Physically distinctive depictions of Tatars show up over a century after those first imperial annexations. Late seventeenth-century copies of the *Tale of the Battle of Mamai* and *The Life of Evfrosiniia Suzdalskaia* offer particularly rich terrain for marking these changing visual patterns.

The epic *Tale of the Battle of Mamai* recounts the story of a battle between Russian troops, led by Grand Prince Dmitry Donskoi, and Mongol forces, under the command of their leader, Mamai. The battle occurred in 1380, and the tale was probably composed some thirty years later.[3] *The Life of Evfrosiniia Suzdalskaia* is a hagiographic tale—that is, an account of the life and miracles of a saint, Evfrosiniia, born around 1200 and active during the Mongol onslaught. Not written down until approximately 1560, the *Life* lauds her for her fervent prayers against the invaders.[4] Opposition to the Mongols lies at the heart of each of these literary works, and the poles of good and bad, Russian heroes and Mongol villains, are sharply delineated. Both tales survive in multiple manuscripts from the late sixteenth and seventeenth centuries, which testifies to their enduring, or even growing, popularity among readers. Many of the copies from the last third of the seventeenth century include illustrations that share a common approach to depicting the Mongol foe. It is an approach very different from the one we saw in the earlier *Illustrated Historical Chronicle*.

In these late manuscripts, Mongol-Tatar combatants are depicted as distinctly alien from the Russian protagonists. The differences are represented in both cultural terms and in the essential physiognomy of racial types. The enemy consistently show up with shaved heads adorned with a single sidelock of hair, a Tatar fashion in vogue during the seventeenth century and perhaps earlier, and with a wispy mustache that sometimes doubles as a mouth. Not all the enemy troops are shown this way, but at least one emblematic figure in a group will be identified by his shaving customs. Occasional Tatar figures are not only distinctively coifed but are also shown as physically misshapen, strange. An illustration of a duel between a Mongol champion, identified as a Pecheneg, a member of a steppe tribe (on the right), and the Russian hero, the giant warrior monk Peresvet (on the left), provides a good example (Image 5.2).

IMAGE 5.2 Duel between the Pecheneg (right) and Peresvet (left). Miniature from *Tale of the Battle of Mamai*, 1680s.

The Pecheneg wears the loose pants and leather armor of a steppe warrior, in contrast to the monastic robes of his Russian opponent. The Russian is bearded, while the Mongol is clean-shaven except for a thin mustache, again typical of the men of the steppe. More fundamentally, not a fashion choice but a part of his biological make-up, his face is oddly constructed. His eye is oriented in full-frontal view despite the fact that he is depicted in profile. This "side-eye" identifies the figure as a Mongol or Tatar. The same visual code is used to identify Mongol figures in a battle scene in the *Life* (Image 5.3). In this depiction of Baty Khan's attack on a Russian town, we can see the Mongol leaders' shaved heads, sidelocks, and sideways eyes, all elements of the emerging stock image of Mongol-Tatar enemies.

IMAGE 5.3 Tatar-Mongol attack. Miniature from the *Life of Evfrosiniia Suzdalskaia*, seventeenth-century manuscript.

What should we make of this evolving depiction of the men of the steppe as physically distinctive, alien? The most striking and stable indicator of Mongol-Tatar enemies is the sideways eye. The source of this element is clear in Orthodox iconography, where such eyes are associated with another much hated, greatly feared class of beings: demons. Depiction in profile alone is enough to raise suspicion of devilry in Orthodox iconographic tradition. Good guys are always shown with two eyes visible, usually in three-quarters view in scenes from life or facing directly forward if shown in postmortem sanctity. Demons, like Tatars, are shown in profile, and very often with the full-frontal eye (Image 5.4).

According to Dmitriy Antonov and Mikhail Mayzuls, who have studied demons in Russian iconography, the most consistent visual identifier of demons and sinners was not actually the sideways eye, though that was a common characteristic. It was their pointy hair. As we have already observed with Tatar sidelocks, hairstyle could have significant implications. Demons also display another interesting characteristic: dark skin, often blue. In texts, they can be called euphemistically Blue Ones, Dark Ones, or dark-visaged Ethiopians. Unusual hair, dark skin, and sideways eyes are commonly assigned to demons.[5] Demons appear as their own, supernatural species or race.

Skin color, however, is not used as an identifier in Muscovite depictions of the Muslims and shamanists of the Volga and the steppe. Faces and hands remain unpainted, the color of paper. What do persist in depictions of the religious other are the additional fantastical, hellish physiognomic markers: idiosyncratic haircuts, distorted heads, and more particularly, the sideways eyes of demons.

Does this list of features allow us to conclude that by the late seventeenth century Russians attributed particular, alien physical characteristics to their steppe opponents? Did they come to see, imagine, and draw race? The visual evidence demonstrates a trend toward imagining difference in corporeal form. So it seems fair to say that in depicting bodies as bearers of meaning, seventeenth-century artists did develop an understanding of physical appearance as a marker of meaningful distinction. But the concept of physical difference they expressed departed sharply from those that were forming in the Atlantic world. Their drawings identified Mongols and Tatars not with the attributes of their facial structure, but with the infernal allegiances that the artists could make visible. Just as a halo indicates sanctity, making the unseen quality of holiness visible, a sideways eye indicates iniquity and puts internal corruption on display. In their graphic shorthand, difference was manifested not in any "real" biological, physical markers, but in the visual equivalent of Orthodox dog-whistles.

Yet this observation still fails to capture the specificity of the miniaturists' work. Demonic eyes and nomadic hairstyles were not shown as attributes of all Tatars. When many Tatars mass together on a page, as in the scene of military assault shown in Image 5.3, just a few side-eyed, mustachioed warriors suffice to indicate the

IMAGE 5.4 Devils cast out of heaven. Detail from a Last Judgment Icon, second half of the sixteenth century.

demonic essence of the troops. Furthermore, demonic traits clung only to those actively endangering Russia or Russians. Corporeal difference reflected states of hostility or violent conflict, not immutable biological characteristics. In scenes showing peaceable encounters, demonic traits vanished. In such instances, racial imagining was apparently irrelevant to the illustrators' task. In other words, the caricatures of Tatars indicate moral, religious, and military hostility, not a notion of fixed, categorical physical distinctiveness. Interestingly, when the Tatars in question happen to be women, they remain untouched by the "othering" approaches so freely applied to men. Women could be easily absorbed into Russian society through bondage or marriage, so their gender eliminated the question of difference altogether in the eyes (and pens) of the illustrators.

In the seventeenth century, when Muscovy was becoming an empire and the tsardom faced the challenge of absorbing non-Russian populations into its body politic, this precise and limited form of racial imagination based on religious and political rather than on physical characteristics found echoes in imperial policy. Conquered and subdued populations were considered members of the realm, under the tsar's protection, so long as they accepted his overlordship. Even without conversion to Orthodox Christianity, the colonized could take their places within the complicated hierarchies of the realm.

Hatred comes in many shapes and forms. Muscovite images of the people of the steppe carried none of the particular prejudices or assumptions that racial distinction had in fifteenth-century Iberia, in the early modern Atlantic world, in the nineteenth-century slave societies of the Americas, or in the Jim Crow United States. Theirs was a theology of the body rooted in Orthodox Christianity and seasoned in historical conflict.

Did Muscovites think in racial terms? Our answer must be qualified. Their increasing tendency to project physical distinction on groups of people may partially satisfy some definitions of race, but race viewed through a distorting mirror, reflecting religion and partisanship rather than heritable biology, subject to change according to religious and political affiliation, and manifest only in the male line.

NOTES

1. *Litsevoi letopisnyi svod XVI veka. (LLS). Rus' 1483–1491 ot V.Kh.*, bk. 16 (Moscow: Akteon, 2022), 462. https://runivers.ru/upload/iblock/8ff/LLS16.pdf
2. *LLS*, bk. 22, 21. https://runivers.ru/upload/iblock/616/LLS22.pdf. Accessed 11-16-2022.
3. *Skazanie o Mamaevom poboishche*, edited by S. K. Shambinago (St. Petersburg: Tip. M.A. Aleksandrova, 1907). Dating of the tale is debated.
4. Iu. A. Gribov, "Litsevye spiski zhitiia Evfrosinii Suzdal'skoi XVII v. Sravnitel'nyi analyz miniatiur," in *Russkaia knizhnost': voprosy istochnikovedeniia i paleografii* (Moscow, 1998), 78–141.
5. Dmitriy Antonov and Mikhail Mayzuls, *Anatomy of Hell. Guide for Visual Demonology in Medieval Russia* (Moscow: Forum; Neolit, 2014), 33–41.

CHAPTER 6

VISUAL POLEMICS: THE TIME OF TROUBLES IN POLISH AND RUSSIAN HISTORICAL MEMORY (1611–1949)

EKATERINA BOLTUNOVA

IN 1730, a new book describing Warsaw and its environs was published in Dresden. Its author was Christian Erndtel, a botanist, meteorologist, and physician to Augustus II, King of Poland and Elector of Saxony. The book mostly covered Erndtel's research interests: the geography and botany of lands adjacent to the capital of Poland. However, history was featured there, too, and often appeared as a fascinating adventure story. In his section on the Warsaw castle, the royal physician describes the rich collection of paintings preserved there and mentions that the royal chambers once had two paintings by "Dolabella, the famous Italian painter: one showing the capture of Smolensk and the public act whereby . . . the famous Polish commander, Hetman (military commander) Zolkiewius, in the presence of senators, handed. . . . the imprisoned Grand Prince of Muscovy to the king (Sigismund III)." With a degree of sadness, the physician mentioned that the other painting "was taken by Tsar Peter of Russia . . . to Muscovy." Erndtel led readers to believe that this masterpiece was lost. He also mentioned that Peter "wanted to get rid of" the Sigismund III column, a monument to the victorious seventeenth-century king that had been erected in front of the Warsaw castle. Erndtel reported it was only the "tireless campaign that several senators led against this threat of desecration" that ultimately prevented the Tsar from destroying it.[1]

Erndtel got his facts right, except for one detail. In the late 1700s and early 1710s, Augustus II gave the Emperor of Russia not one, but both of the paintings he mentions. In terms of historical significance, his mistake was understandable: the painting the physician describes—Dolabella's *Stanisław Żółkiewski Brings the Captured Shuisky Kings to King Sigismund and Prince Władysław at the 1611 Sejm*—was the one that mattered. It left a significant mark on the Polish national memory, and it is the focus of this article (Image 6.1).

IMAGE 6.1 Tommaso Dolabella, *Stanisław Żółkiewski Brings the Captured Shuisky Kings to King Sigismund and Prince Władysław at the 1611 Sejm*, after 1611.

The new owner of the two historical paintings, Peter the Great of Russia, had a wide reputation as a collector of art and curios. A passionate man, he never failed to acquire an object he desired via a diplomatic gift or mutually profitable exchange, or simply by purchasing the item he craved. Yet Peter's reason for owning Dolabella's paintings was not their artistic merit. Peter never planned to feature them in his collection. By demanding that his Polish ally, Augustus II, hand over these pictures, Peter was serving an altogether different agenda, a strategic one. His goal was to subvert the Polish version of the historical past. King Augustus, dependent as he was on Peter's military support, could do nothing to prevent the tsar's effort to recast a key moment in Russian-Polish relations, the Time of Troubles, a century earlier.

The Time of Troubles was a prolonged political crisis that engulfed Russia at the beginning of the seventeenth century and culminated in massive military intervention by Poland and Sweden. The almost two decades of political instability and warfare (1598–1613) ended in the expulsion of the invaders by an all-Russian volunteer army and the rise of a new dynasty on the Russian throne, the Romanovs. During the crisis, the plan to invade Russia and seize political power was promoted by Sigismund III Vasa, the King of Poland. His military campaign led to the occupation of Moscow by the Polish army in 1610 and the election of his son Władysław as Tsar of Russia by a council of Russian aristocrats.

Tommaso Dolabella's painting, the one Christian Erndtel mentioned, depicted the humiliating aftermath of Russia's defeat. The dethroned Tsar Vasily Shuisky, together with his brothers, was handed over to Hetman Stanisław Żółkiewski, one of leaders of the Polish armed forces, who brought them to Poland. On October 29, 1611, in the capital city of Warsaw, the Shuisky brothers were forced to pledge allegiance to their former adversary, the King of Poland.

The ritual of surrender was staged in the most magnificent style. The oath swearing was elaborated down to the minutest detail, and all key members of the aristocratic elites took part. The nineteenth-century Russian historian Sergei Solovyov described the ceremony as follows:

> When the three Shuiskys were brought before the king [Sigismund III], they made a low bow, with their hats in their hands. Żółkiewski started a long speech on the mutability of fortune and glorified the king and his military feats, the capture of Smolensk and Moscow. He talked of the power of the Moscow tsars, the last of whom was now bowing before the King of Poland. At these words, Vasily took a deep bow, touched the ground with his right hand and kissed the king's hand. The second brother, Dmitry, bowed to the ground, and the third, Ivan, took three deep bows and started crying. The hetman continued his speech, saying that he was transferring the Shuiskys to the power of the king not as prisoners, but for the sake of human happiness and asked [him] to treat them kindly. The three brothers took another deep bow in silence. When the hetman ended his speech, the Shuiskys were allowed to kiss the royal hand. It was a grand, surprising, and pitiful spectacle, as contemporaries described it.[2]

The Shuiskys were then imprisoned in the Gostyn Castle, where they were kept in dire conditions. Vasily and his brother Dmitry soon died and were buried in the castle. The historian Ruslan Skrynnikov believed that the brothers might have been murdered and that their original burial place was underneath the castle gate.[3] If the latter was true, it was undeniably a form of symbolic humiliation of the former tsar.

The painting Peter the Great took to Moscow is now presumed lost, or maybe even intentionally destroyed. However, a copy that has survived among the collections of the Lviv Historical Museum can shed some light on what might have offended the Russian emperor enough to destroy it. In the center of the painting, we see Sigismund III and Prince Władysław towering over the dais. Although it was the son who was elected Tsar of Russia, the key figure is undeniably the father. Given that the thrones are of roughly equal height, he tops Władysław by half a head. They are dressed in ceremonial red, one of the Polish national colors, and thus easily stand out from the crowd. Sigismund and Władysław are shown listening to Żółkiewski's speech, the hetman appearing on the right side, draped in a red cloak and wielding a mace of power. All around the royal dais stand members of the Polish aristocracy, indicating the high status of the event.

The Shuisky brothers, who appear at the bottom of the canvas, also impress the viewer. Vasily, Dmitry, and Ivan are wearing rich and colorful *kaftans* (robes), with long sleeves in the old Moscow fashion and very high collars of a special design. It is clear that the artist took pains to show the intricate details, such as the ornament on the *kaftans* and the gemstones sewn onto the collars. The central figure must be Tsar Vasily, the tallest of the three people taking the oath of allegiance, and the one wearing the brightest and the richest clothes of gold color, with the big fur hat on his head. He is the only man in the painting turned away from the viewers. The Shuiskys form a clear opposition to the Polish aristocracy in the painting, with their clothes in stark contrast to the ceremonial robes worn by Sigismund, Władysław, Żółkiewski, and other Poles. The exotic manner Dolabella used to portray the Shuisky brothers is quite conspicuous and employed with the clear purpose of marking their belonging to a different cultural sphere.

This visual reminder of the humiliating oath sworn by Tsar Vasily Shuisky hung in a public chamber of the Warsaw castle. The painting must have left a deep impression on Peter the Great. Given that several generations of his ancestors had been at work to erase the memory of Polish victories over Moscow, this effect is unsurprising.

Efforts to shape historical memory played out actively in both Russia and Poland after the Time of Troubles. By the end of the 1610s, Polish dreams of exerting political power over Muscovy were growing increasingly unrealistic, while the need for symbolic fashioning of past Polish victories was becoming increasingly urgent. The Polish court staged celebrations commemorating military victories over Muscovy in addition to the capture and humiliation of the Shuisky brothers. In 1620, Sigismund III ordered the construction of what is known as the Moscow Chapel to hold the remains of the Shuiskys. The brothers' bodies were transferred to this new chapel, built to perpetuate the glorious memory of the king's triumph over Russia. The marble slab placed at the entrance had a Latin inscription glorifying Sigismund as a commander who "accepted the surrender of the capital city of Moscow" and who took prisoner "by right of war" Muscovite leaders (i.e., Shuisky and his brothers) who had "ruled unlawfully."[4] The chapel soon became a notable site and appeared on many maps of Warsaw from this period.

Almost two and a half decades later, a monument was erected in front of the Warsaw castle by order of King Władysław. This monument was the Sigismund III column, topped by a statue of the Polish king, in armor, leaning on a cross and wielding a saber. The western side of the pedestal featured an inscription in Latin listing the feats of the monarch: "Sigismund III, freely elected King of Poland and ancestral King of Sweden, the first among kings in his love of peace and glory, yielding to no one in war and victory, [who] captured the leaders of Muscovy, its capital and lands, defeated their armies, restored power over Smolensk . . . , reigned for 44 years, the 44th king, equal in glory to all [his predecessors] and fully glorified" (Image 6.2).

In the seventeenth century, Russian and Polish versions of historical memory of the Time of Troubles were in vigorous competition. In Russia, the first Romanovs opposed the Polish interpretation of the events and sought to dismantle the triumphant anti-Moscow commemorative landscape of Warsaw. The first of the Romanov tsars, Michael, succeeded in his demand to have the remains of the Shuiskys returned to Moscow, after which Vasily was reburied yet again, this time in the Cathedral of the Archangel, among the family tombs of Russian rulers. The tsar himself took part in the lavish funeral, and Vasily's new tombstone featured an epitaph describing his life and his death in Poland, as well as the final return of his body. Not a whit less active was Michael's son and successor, Tsar Aleksei Mikhailovich (Peter the Great's father). He demanded that the Poles take down the marble slab describing the humiliation of the Shuiskys and send it to Russia.

IMAGE 6.2 Sigismund III column, erected in 1644, rebuilt 1949.

The arrival of Peter the Great in Warsaw in the late 1700s marked a new stage in reworking the historical narrative. Peter is usually remembered as a figure who made a radical break with the Muscovite past, but his view of the history of Russian-Polish opposition was no different from those of his father and grandfather. His response to Dolabella's paintings shows that Peter the Great shared his predecessors' understanding of the Time of Troubles and openly worked to dismantle the Poles' competing vision.

Peter's efforts to reshape historical memory had to be carried out abroad, where his influence had its limits when Poland was still an independent state. How did the situation change after Russia annexed a part of Polish lands in the late eighteenth century, or, for that matter, when a nominally autonomous Kingdom of Poland (Congress Poland) was set up as part of the Russian Empire in the early nineteenth century? Did the Russian authorities try to completely erase the Polish interpretation of the Time of Troubles and promote the Russian national version of history in the Polish territories they had come to rule? And how were all of these processes influenced by the experience of interacting with the visual images of the past?

We must start by saying that the beginning of the nineteenth century marked a radical change in Russia's approach to Poland. Though stripped of its independence, Poland was still seen as an autonomous political entity. The recognition of these lands in 1815 as the Kingdom of Poland, with its own Constitutional Charter, within the Russian Empire had no precedent in terms of legal formalities. The coronation of Russian emperor Nicholas I as King of Poland in 1829 revealed a significant shift in Russian policy. Traveling to Warsaw for the ceremony, the Russian monarch found himself in the very space that symbolically marked the triumph of Poland over Moscow during the Time of Troubles (as Peter the Great had a century before). Unlike his ancestor, however, Nicholas did not attempt to destroy or symbolically recode this site. On the contrary, he made it his choice location for the coronation, which demonstrated his aim to achieve a political compromise. The ceremony took place in the Warsaw castle, and more specifically, in the same hall where the Shuiskys were forced to pledge allegiance to the King of Poland in 1611. When reciting the prayer, Nicholas knelt in front of the members of the Polish Parliament (*Sejm*) and Roman Catholic clergy who gathered in the hall, as the Shuiskys had done two centuries earlier. Polish subjects of the Russian emperor read this remarkable event (a Russian emperor voluntarily bowing before Polish elites!) through the lens of early seventeenth-century history, as their memoirs and other texts attest. In 1830, for example, Adam Gurowski, a Polish political writer, spoke in front of a huge crowd protesting Russian rule over Poland. Standing at the Sigismund III column and calling for overthrowing Nicholas I, he reminded his audience that they were gathered at the castle where "the Russian tsars were humiliated by Sigismund."[5] Two years later, the Polish poet Adam Mickiewicz, in his piece "The Redoubt of Ordon," called the Russian emperor "Vasily's son."[6] Undeniably, the coronation served to solidify the Poles' belief in their own significance.

In early nineteenth-century Russia, interest in the events of the Time of Troubles was exceptionally high. A new stage in shaping the historical memory of these events was starting, as can be seen from the publication of Nikolai Karamzin's *History of the Russian State* (1818–1829) or Alexander Pushkin's historical play *Boris Godunov* (1831). Another contributing factor was the unveiling of the famous monument (by Ivan Martos) to Kuzma Minin and Dmitry Pozharsky, heroes of the Russian resistance to the Poles during the Time of Troubles, in Moscow's Red Square in 1818. Sources show that Emperor Nicholas I himself took active interest in the history of seventeenth-century Russia and knew the events of the Time of Troubles quite well.

Despite this boom in patriotic commemoration of the Time of Troubles within Russia, official policy in Russian-dominated Poland adopted a tolerant strategy toward the Warsaw monuments. By ignoring rather than protesting the Polish commemorative topography of victories over Muscovy, Russia formed a political strategy of its own: submerging the memory of all previous wars and clashes between the two realms. It was this strategy, fostering a narrative that stressed historical amity between the two realms, that Russia was trying to bring to life in Poland.

This new political program soon led to the coexistence of two competing versions of history within the empire. The Polish interpretation was never officially prohibited (and was thus *de facto* sanctioned by the imperial authorities). For the moment, the Russian Empire granted Poland the right to shape its own national memory. And in the Polish historical narrative, the oath sworn by the Shuiskys was seen as a unifying symbolic event, or *lieu de mémoire* (locus of memory), to use Pierre Nora's term.[7]

Remarkably, this symbolic unification was powered by the visual. As time went by, visualization grew increasingly radical. In the late eighteenth and early nineteenth century, Polish painters followed Dolabella's formula—that is, they chose not to stress the Muscovites' humiliation. They showed them as standing erect rather than kneeling. With their ornate garb, they were shown as symbolically comparable to "barbarians" of the East, but their status as rulers was not denied. In this period, painters showed the Shuiskys appearing before the King and *Sejm* as conquered but not broken, standing with their heads bowed but not begging for mercy. In the latter 1820s and 1830s, however, after a shift in Russian policy toward Poland, the focus changes significantly. Polish artists Józef Peszka and Jan Kanty Szwedkowski show the Shuisky brothers genuflecting or even prostrate before Sigismund III. Peszka paints the main symbol of the dethroned power—the crown—being placed at the feet of the King of Poland.

The strategy of imperial erasure of past hostilities was adopted again over a century later in the foreign policy of the Soviet Union. In 1949, the capital of the Polish Republic, a state within the Soviet control zone, saw the reconstruction of the Sigismund III column, which had been destroyed by the Nazi occupiers during World War II. The column was ultimately restored in its original shape, with the inscription on the western side of the pedestal telling the story of the great king Sigismund, the capture of Vasily Shuisky, and the Polish occupation of Moscow. The restored Warsaw castle featured a great hall with paintings from 1892 by Jan Matejko, including one where Tsar Vasily Shuisky of Moscow is shown kneeling before the King of Poland. The Kremlin, often seen as totally in control of every aspect of power, evidently had nothing against the restoration of this paradigm of history, hostile to Moscow though it seemed to be.[8]

NOTES

1. Christian H. Erndtel, *Warsavia physice illustrata* (Dresdae, 1730) 22.
2. Sergei Solov'ev, *Sochineniia v 18 tomakh*. Vol. 8 (Moscow: Mysl', 1989), 623.
3. Ruslan Skrynnikov, *Vasilii Shuiskii* (Moscow: AST, 2006), 381–382.
4. *Russkaia starina*, Vol. 65, St. Petersburg, 1890, 91–92.
5. *Kurjer Warszawski*, 1831, no. 26. S. 134.
6. Adam Mickiewicz, *Izbrannie proizvedeniia v 2 tomakh*, Vol. 1 (Moscow: Gosdarstvennoe izdatel'stvo khudozhestvennoi literatury. 1955), 256.
7. Pierre Nora and Lawrence D. Kritzman, *Realms of Memory: Rethinking the French Past*, translated by Arthur Goldhammer (New York: Columbia University Press, 1996).
8. The book chapter was prepared within the framework of the Higher School of Economics University Basic Research Program.

CHAPTER 7

THE IMAGE OF THE GOOD ORTHODOX RULER BETWEEN KYIV AND MOSCOW (1660s)

MARIA GRAZIA BARTOLINI

THE SECOND HALF of the seventeenth century was a period of intense religious, social, and political turmoil for Ukraine. After the agreement of Pereyaslav (1654), which resulted in the political union of the Cossack-controlled territory of Ukraine with the Tsardom of Muscovy, the Kyiv Orthodox clergy faced the problem of preserving the rights and privileges of the Kyivan church in relation to the Moscow church while attempting to stabilize their position under the patronage of the Muscovite tsar. The Ukrainian lands were located between three imperial or quasi-imperial powers: Muscovy, the Ottoman Empire, and the Polish-Lithuanian Commonwealth. The region had belonged, at various times over the previous four centuries, to Lithuania and to Poland, with a brief period of independence immediately before its incorporation into the Muscovite tsardom. The agreement signed at Pereyaslav brought Ukraine into the sphere of influence of Moscow, starting the long, complex history of relations between Ukraine and Russia.

Two engravings produced in Kyiv in the mid-1660s shed important light on the modes of expression used by Kyiv Orthodox elites to describe their aspirations as they imagined their future under Muscovite rule. The engravings express their ideals of kingship, imperial hierarchies, political order, and church-state relations during this turbulent time. In approaching these images, it is important to understand that for Kyivan ecclesiastical authors, and for most of their contemporaries, political life was understood and represented in religious terms. In particular, in representing the authority of the tsar and his earthly mission, the author-artists drew on images and passages from the Book of Revelation, the biblical prediction of the apocalyptic clash between the forces of Orthodoxy and those of the Antichrist. This cosmic struggle took on specific geopolitical coloration in the 1660s, when these engravings where made. The city of Kyiv was transferred temporarily to the Tsardom of Muscovy in 1654, but its fate remained unclear until 1686, when it was incorporated permanently into Muscovite suzerainty. These years of uncertainty preoccupied both lay and clerical elites in Ukraine. The latter were strong supporters of the tsar's rule over Kyiv and celebrated him as the protector of Orthodoxy against other religions (Catholicism and Islam). At the same time, they were ardent defenders of the autonomy of the Kyivan Church. Centered in Kyiv, it was subordinate to the Patriarch in Constantinople—the head of the Eastern Orthodox Church, himself a subject of the Ottoman Sultan and of a Muslim imperial regime. In this complex situation, with overlapping claims that reached across imperial boundaries, the Kyivan Church had managed to remain largely autonomous. After the 1654 merger, the question arose: If Kyiv was to stay under tsarist rule, would its church maintain its cherished autonomy, or would it fall under the jurisdiction of Moscow, which had its own Patriarchate? Skillfully negotiating a dual message, the two images examined here addressed this issue in two ways at once. Their texts and images were subtly conceived to convey slightly different messages to viewers depending on the position they occupied in the new imperial relationships.

The first engraving is the frontispiece of Lazar Baranovych's sermon collection, *Spiritual Sword* (*Mech dukhovnyi)* (1666) (Image 7.1).[1] An alumnus of the Kyiv Mohyla College, the premier Orthodox seminary in the Slavic world, and of the Jesuit colleges of Vilnius and Kalisz, Lazar Baranovych (1620–1693) was a practical and ambitious personality, involved in many political intrigues. During the convulsive decades after the agreement of Pereyaslav, he acted as an intermediary between the Ukrainian clergy and the Moscow government. His *Spiritual Sword* was received favorably by Tsar Aleksei Mikhailovich, who allowed it to be sold in Muscovy. (Printing was closely controlled in Muscovy at the time.) The book's visual apparatus bears the stamp of Baranovych's efforts to strike a balance between local (Kyivan) and imperial concerns (the need to win the tsar's patronage).[2] Let us take a careful look at its frontispiece as we explore how it creates a mystique of the "good Orthodox ruler" for both Muscovite and Kyivan audiences, with their diverse but overlapping criteria.

On the lower, terrestrial level of this three-tiered image, the medieval Kyivan Prince Volodimer Sviatoslavich, the converter of Rus to Christianity in 988, is represented lying on the ground. Issuing from his head is a quotation from Psalm 1:3: "And he shall be like a tree planted by the rivers of water." From his side grows a vine, rising to the first of Aleksei Mikhailovich's sons, Simeon, whose figure carries the central axis of the tree up to his brothers Fedor and Aleksei and his parents Aleksei and Mariia Ilinichna, who occupy the topmost branches. The Romanov family tree, growing from a reclining Volodimer, is an adaptation of the motif of the Tree of Jesse, which is usually interpreted as representing the genealogical tree of Christ. This subject, which was common in the medieval art of western Europe and the Balkans, became popular in seventeenth-century Ukraine.[3] However, in the frontispiece of *Spiritual Sword*, Volodimer takes Jesse's place as the root from which the tsar-Christ grows. Such adaptations of the Tree of Jesse for the purposes of dynastic praise were

IMAGE 7.1 Lazar Baranovych, *Spiritual Sword* (*Mech dukhovnyi*), Frontispiece, 1666.

not infrequent in medieval and early modern Europe and passed to Muscovy, where the Tree of Jesse was used in the Kremlin Cathedral of the Annunciation as early as 1405.[4] Given its dynastic association, it is not surprising that Baranovych would use the Tree of Jesse iconography in conjunction with the Romanovs in a book designed as much for the Moscow market as for the Ukrainian one. This image establishes the Romanov line as a direct outgrowth of the dynasty beginning with Prince Volodimer in Kyiv. In other words, it establishes a direct link between the Kyivan and Muscovite lineages.

In the central tier of the image, two scenes, to the left and the right, depict a crowned eagle with its eaglets and a dragon-slaying horseman. A quotation from Psalm 17:38 accompanies these figures: "I have pursued mine enemies, and overtaken them." The Saint George–like equestrian has no halo, but has a crown strikingly reminiscent of that of the earthly rulers portrayed in the engraving. The message so far, linking the dynastic rulers of Kyiv and Moscow to holy figures fighting God's fight, is clear.

Surmounting the tree are images of Christ and Mary, surrounded by golden rays. Between Christ and the Virgin, and right above the tree, is the coat of arms of the Romanovs—a double-headed, triple-crowned eagle with a crescent under its feet. This image apparently refers to the Woman of the Apocalypse ("a woman clothed with the sun, and the moon under her feet"). A quotation from Revelation 12:1 in the banderole corroborates the reference, but the pronoun is modified to reinforce a militarized and political message ("and the moon under *his* feet"). The two-headed eagle has a representation of a dragon-slaying horseman on its breast, the same image that appears in the frontispiece of the 1661 Kyivan *Pateryk* or of the 1663 Moscow Bible (Image 7.2). Printed by the instruction of Tsar Aleksei, the Moscow Bible represents an officially sanctioned Muscovite picture of the proper earthly order. The figure on horseback is clearly meant to represent Aleksei himself as a pious warrior anointed by God. Above the eagle is a shining cross with the inscription "in this sign thou shall conquer," an allusion to the victory of the Roman emperor Constantine I at the Battle of the Milvian Bridge against pagan enemy forces, a victory that marked the beginning of Constantine's conversion to Christianity.

The identification of Aleksei Mikhailovich as a "new Constantine" was an important component of Muscovite political theology and court rhetoric.[5] Thus, the Baranovych engraving shown in Image 7.1 draws on this established parallel to connect three key figures: Constantine, the first Orthodox ruler, triumphant against the enemies of Christianity; Volodimer, the "second Constantine," who converted Rus to Christianity; and Aleksei, "the new Constantine." Tsar Aleksei's military power, symbolized by the dragon-slaying horseman and the eagle, both capped with a royal crown, is shown vanquishing the infidels just like his august predecessors. In a foreword addressed to the tsar himself, Baranovych explains that the moon under the eagle's feet represents the "barbarians," a term that includes the major "religious

IMAGE 7.2 *Moscow Bible* (*Bibliia*), Frontispiece, 1663.

others" of that time: Turks and Tatars.[6] The fight against the Turks was a unifying cause for Muscovy and a large part of the Ukrainian Orthodox clergy, who saw Turks and Tatars as a key foe. The eagle spreading its wings at the center of the frontispiece, a motif that was extremely popular among Kyivan intellectuals in the 1650s and 1660s, conveys their need for the tsar's protection in the face of growing anxiety over the Turkish and Tatar threat.[7]

Finally, on the upper, celestial level of the engraving, a heavenly hand bestows three crowns. As Baranovych explains in his Foreword to the tsar, God—who has "many crowns," as in Revelation 19:12 – gives his "earthly anointed" Aleksei Mikhailovich the three crowns in imitation of the Trinity.[8]

As we have seen from this description, the frontispiece of *Spiritual Sword* presents the princes of Moscow as divinely anointed and as branches of the tree originating with the Kyivan Prince Volodimer. However, we should keep in mind that *Spiritual Sword* circulated widely in both Muscovite Russia and Ukraine, and thus contributed to a conversation that took place between at least two different groups of readers and viewers. If, as art historian Michael Baxandall justly notes, every work of art is "the relic of a cooperation" between the author and the public,[9] then Baranovych moves in at least two directions. On the one hand, he uses a symbolic system that reflects the ideological constructs of seventeenth-century Muscovy. On the other hand, he infuses the work with contents that reflect the political and cultural tradition of the Kyiv clergy.

What message was Baranovych conveying to his Ukrainian colleagues as they came to terms with their new standing as members of the expanding Muscovite tsardom? In combining the Tree of Jesse with references to the Book of Revelation, he depicts Prince Volodimer and Tsar Aleksei Mikhailovich as actors in a sacred history that begins with Christ's Incarnation and culminates in his Second Coming at the Last Judgment. In the lower level of the frontispiece, the Tree of Jesse serves as an emblem of Christ's Nativity. The coming of the Messiah, foreshadowed by Volodimer/Jesse, is made explicit in the images of Christ and his mother, which mirror those of Tsar Aleksei and his wife on the topmost branches. On the upper level, the crescent under the eagle's feet and the accompanying reference to the Woman of the Apocalypse, who was usually interpreted by medieval commentaries as representing the Church as Christ's celestial bride, provide a reminder of the apocalyptic union to come between Christ and his faithful.

This sophisticated interplay of imagery associated with Christ and the Apocalypse in relation to the tsar can only be properly assessed if we consider the situations in Muscovy and in Ukraine. Concerns about the imminence of the Last Judgment and the appearance of the Antichrist were widespread during the seventeenth century. The Apocalypse was predicted in 1666, which, not incidentally, is also the year when *Spritual Sword* appeared in print.[10] In this respect, it is probably not surprising that specific apocalyptic ideas in relation to the tsar also resonate in the title page of the collection (Image 7.3). Here, the upper layer of the composition shows the same

Мечъ дх҃вный
еже есть гл҃ъ бж҃ій.
на помощь ц҃ркви воинствѹющей,
Или
Книга проповѣді слова бж҃го
юже сооружи
Лазаръ Барановичъ
Еп҃пъ Черниговскій Новгородскій и про.
Тѵпомъ издадеся въ ст҃ой великой
чѹдотворной Лаврѣ Печерской Кіевской.
В лѣто ѿ создания міра, ͵зро҃д.
ѿ рождества же Хв҃а, ͵ахѯ҃ѕ.

IMAGE 7.3 Lazar Baranovych, *Spiritual Sword* (*Mech dukhovnyi*), title page.

horseman of the frontispiece, capped with a crown—a possible symbol of Tsar Aleksei—and surrounded by a group of haloed figures riding white horses. The quotations in the banderoles—"and the armies that were in heaven followed him upon white horses" (Revelation 19:14); "and his name is called The Word of God" (Revelation 19:13)—are drawn from Chapter 19 of the Book of Revelation, which marks the culmination of the final battle between God and Satan, further stressing the link between Christ triumphant during his Second Coming and Tsar Aleksei. The lower level of the composition shows this cosmic battle as two ships facing each other, one headed by Christ and the Archangel Michael and the other by the Antichrist.

Thus, the three images examined here—the title page and frontispiece of *Spiritual Sword* and the frontispiece of the 1663 Moscow Bible—are part of a larger narrative that shows Christ's triumph in the contest against false Messiahs while praising the noble lineage of the defenders of Orthodoxy, a lineage that reaches from Constantine to Volodimer and Aleksei Mikhailovich.

In elaborating on this tradition, Baranovych stresses one of the tenets of Muscovite official ideology that was central for the Kyiv clergy as well—the role of the tsar as a patron of the Orthodox Church against the enemies of Christianity. The crescent and the dragon-slaying horseman reinforce this paradigm of sacred violence while pointing to the Muscovite tsardom as a universal monarchy that would lead to the establishment on earth of the Kingdom of God after the defeat of the Antichrist.

Educated Muscovite readers would have had the tools to interpret the iconographic program of *Spiritual Sword*. The political and visual vocabulary of the time would have equipped them to see the images as celebrations of their ruler as protector of the faith and champion of Orthodoxy against the forces of the Antichrist. But what might the reaction of the readers in Ukraine have been? Ukrainian churchmen would have viewed the Muscovite tsar from the vantage point of a territory only very recently, and not fully voluntarily, incorporated into the tsardom. Confronted with a continuous period of war and foreign invasion, and with uncertainty surrounding Kyiv's future, Ukrainian Orthodox clergy could have found spiritual comfort in the apocalyptic triumph of Tsar Aleksei. However, the support the Ukrainian clergy offered the Muscovite tsar was subject to certain conditions, which included the confirmation of the rights and freedom of the Kyiv Orthodox Church, and the guarantee that it remain under the jurisdiction of the Patriarchate of Constantinople.

For Baranovych, the welfare of the Church—and its independence from Moscow—were an overwhelming concern, one that shows itself in this frontispiece. Of central interest to my discussion is, again, the image of a tree sprouting from Prince Volodimer. If we look at tree imagery in other works by Baranovych, we will see that it is used to designate the Orthodox faith received by Prince Volodimer from Constantinople and the need to protect it from external threats. In the Foreword to the tsar, Baranovych writes that the tree in the frontispiece "was planted by the waters of the holy baptism of Volodimer." The Romanov eagle, he continues, has made its nest on this tree, which symbolizes the "triumphant faith."[11] The close association of the tree with the Christian (Orthodox) faith is further emphasized in the "Sermon on Volodimer" (1674), where Baranovych argues that, before baptism, Volodimer was like an "arid and infertile land." After he found the Orthodox faith "in Constantinople," a tree grew from that land, and the Kyivan Church found shelter in its branches. This tree, Baranovych continues, should be protected from "the axe [that] is laid unto the root," another reference to the sense of pending apocalypse.[12] Other Ukrainian works from this period similarly insist on Constantinople as the source of the Christianity brought to Kyiv by Volodimer, using the image of the "tree planted by the rivers of water" to represent the faith found by Volodimer "in Constantinople," and describing Volodimer as the "blessed root" that generated the Kyiv Orthodox community.[13]

Thus, for the Kyiv Orthodox hierarchies, the tree in this frontispiece might have symbolized the ancient and distinguished heritage of their own spiritual community, the Kyivan Church, which took its origins from Emperor Constantine and the Eastern Church in Constantinople through Prince Volodimer. The tsar, whom the frontispiece establishes as the champion of Orthodoxy, should protect this tree while preserving its continuing subordination to the patriarchate of Constantinople.

Far from unambiguously praising the tsar and the organic growth of his dynastic lineage, the frontispiece and title page of *Spiritual Sword* thus emerge as a site where ecclesiastical ideas about politics—and Orthodox political culture in particular—could flow between readers in both Kyiv and Moscow. What unifies the two engravings is an idea of kingship as a divinely ordained power, one that manifests itself historically through a series of "types of Christ" (Constantine-Volodimer-Aleksei Mikhailovich). Representations of the "good Orthodox ruler" mattered in both Kyiv and Moscow, but their meanings were not identical across imperial lines, allowing for subtle slippages of signification that contributed to the difference that distinguished Muscovite and Kyivan culture, even long after Ukraine's incorporation into the tsardom, as contemporary events continue to remind us.

NOTES

1. For a brief discussion of this frontispiece, see Serhii Plokhy, *Tsars and Cossacks: A Study in Iconography* (Cambridge, MA: Harvard University Press, 2002), 38.
2. On Baranovych's life and works, see Nikolai Sumtsov, *K istorii iuzhno-russkoi literatury semnadtsatago stoletiia. Lazar Baranovich* (Kharkiv: Tipografiia M. F. Zil'berberga, 1885).
3. Oksana Yurchyshyn-Smith and Nicholas Smith, "Dated Ukrainian Prints of the Seventeenth Century," *Print Quarterly* 18, no. 2 (June 2001): 190–200 (at 198).
4. I. Ia. Kachalova, N. A. Maiasova, and L. A. Shchennikova, *Blagoveshchenskii sobor Moskovskogo Kremlia. K 50-letiiu unikal'nogo pamiatnika Russkoi kul'tury* (Moscow: Iskusstvo, 1990), 38–40.
5. See Anthony Hippisley, *The Poetic Style of Simeon Polotsky* (Birmingham: University of Birmingham, 1985), 18.
6. Baranovych, *Mech dukhovnyi* (Kyiv, 1666), leaf iv of the Foreword to the tsar.
7. On the allegory of the eagle spreading its wings to protect its eaglets, see Plokhy, *Tsars and Cossacks*, 33–37.

8. Baranovych, *Mech dukhovnyi*, leaf 1r of the Foreword to the tsar.
9. Michael Baxandall, *Painting and Experience in Fifteenth-Century Italy* (Oxford: Oxford University Press, 1972), 48.
10. On apocalyptic ideas in seventeenth-century Muscovy, see Tat'iana Oparina, "Chislo 1666 v russkoi knizhnosti serediny-tret'ei chetverti XVII v.," in *Chelovek mezhdu Tsarstvom i Imperiei. Sbornik materialov mezhdunarodnoi konferentsii*, edited by Marina Kiseleva (Moscow: Institut cheloveka RAN, 2003), 287–318.
11. Baranovych, *Mech dukhovnyi*, 3r, 5v of the Foreword to the tsar.
12. Baranovych, *Truby sloves propovidnykh* (Kyiv, 1674), 245v–246r.
13. Antonii Radyvylovs'kyi, *Ohorodok Marii Bohoroditsy* (Kyiv, 1676), 235, 246.

CHAPTER 8

TENTS OR TOWNS: THE LIMITS OF SOVEREIGNTY IN THE RUSSIAN NORTH IN THE LATE SEVENTEENTH CENTURY

ERIKA MONAHAN

IN 1501, the grand prince of Moscow added the region known as Samoyedia on the Arctic coast to the list of lands that were subject to him.[1] In 1525, the grand prince issued a charter to the Samoyeds, the people who lived in this region, to mark the occasion of their accepting subjecthood.[2] In 1558, in a royal decree, Tsar Ivan IV declared himself "sovereign [over] all the northern coasts."[3] It would seem clear, if we take the rulers' claims at face value, that Russia had conquered and incorporated this Arctic region into its growing empire.

Almost one and a half centuries later, Semyon Remezov, a state servitor from the Russian empire's Siberian capital of Tobolsk, drew the first atlas of Siberia. Among the 150 maps in the atlas, he drew a map of this northern coastal area (Image 8.1). This map, depicting the mouth of the Ob River, which eventually empties into the Arctic Ocean, includes symbols of physical and human geography that reveal much about the Russian empire in the late seventeenth century. And even though the map was made by a servant, and we might say an advocate, of Russian state power, it inadvertently reflects the reality that despite the tsar's claims, he wasn't really sovereign over all the northern coasts. Samoyeds presented sustained resistance to Russian rule.

Ivan IV claimed sovereignty of "all the northern coasts," but this map and surviving documents suggest a different picture. This is significant, because when this map was made, Russia had claimed sovereignty over the territory depicted for more than a century, and its western European neighbors, with commercial interest in exploring a trade route to China, had long accepted that claim. Furthermore, like so many Indigenous histories, those of Samoyed resistance are undertold, less visible, but nonetheless sometimes revealed in unexpected ways.

IMAGE 8.1 Map near the mouth of the Ob River. Semyon Remezov, *Khorograficheskaia kniga* (Chorographical Sketch-book of Siberia).

Samoyed was the seventeenth-century appellation for the peoples of the Far North known in contemporary terms as Nenets, Elets, Nganasan, and Sel'kup. The earliest interactions between Russians and Samoyeds were not entirely hostile, but by the seventeenth century, conflict dominated their relations. Many Samoyeds proved uncooperative subjects, a dynamic that lasted long after the map we analyze here was supplanted by more modern cartography.

That this map shows Indigenous resistance to imperial rule is not immediately obvious. Like other pictures, maps invite, and often require, many levels of interpretation. Visual symbols, and the viewer's ability to understand their meaning, are essential to understanding all that the mapmakers meant to convey. The point here, then, stands in tension to the cliché that "a picture is worth a thousand words." The picture only gets us so far. With this map, and with maps more generally, we need additional apparatus to grasp the full meaning.

To be sure, anyone who's looked at a map can glean certain things merely by looking at its graphics. In Remezov's map, we readily recognize that we are looking at a river with various tributaries flowing into it. As the river approaches the left side of the page, we see several islands. It may not be immediately apparent to the modern viewer, but this represents the delta system, where the river, with streams created by annual flooding, empties into the sea. The Ob had a complicated delta. In 1616, a Russian merchant and soldier reported, "No one knows the mouth of the Ob. The river spills out into many places; there are often islands."[4] Remezov's map captures this complexity.

In the hinterland, we see a few clusters of trees—something that, above the Arctic Circle, can't be taken for granted. Then and now, along the northern Eurasian coast, the coniferous taiga (pine forest) sometimes gives way to treeless tundra before the land meets the ocean. Yet the large island in the center of this map has the label "Island of Larch." Larch is a coniferous tree plentiful in Siberia, so here the mapmaker indicates trees to us with words, where in other places on this same map he uses pictures. In a map of the northeast corner of Eurasia (Image 8.2), the mouth of the Ob is depicted as a decidedly more barren coast than the northern littoral farther to the east. In this map depicting the northern coastline at the other end of the continent, trees abound. We see rows of a fuller, deciduous-like trees contrasted with a narrower type of tree that tends to run along yellow lines, which indicate terrain changes.[5]

Returning to Image 8.1, in the lower part we see jagged figures in yellow, suggesting some sort of pronounced physical features. The longer yellow lines running parallel on either side of the main river indicate a sustained change in the height of land. Perhaps we are seeing the representation of a river valley or flood plain of

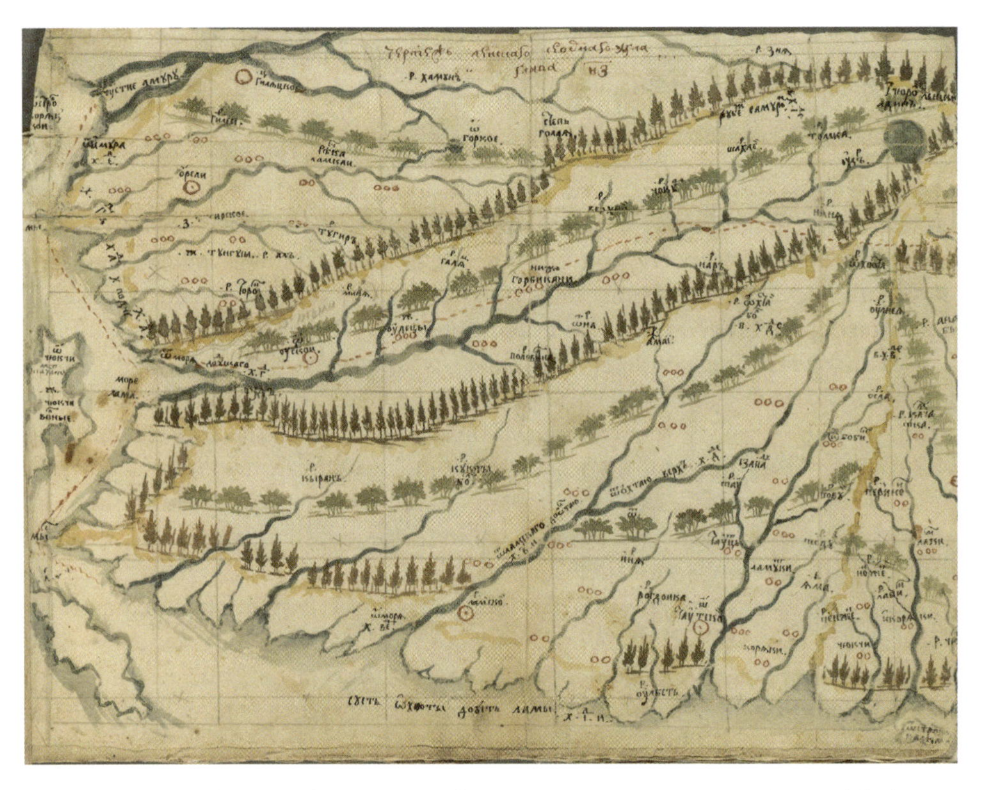

IMAGE 8.2 Map of the northeast corner of Eurasia. Semyon Remezov, *Khorograficheskaia kniga* (Chorographical Sketch-book of Siberia).

the river. Where the yellow line comes close to the blue river, we can imagine a high riverbank. And sure enough, the eighteenth-century explorer Peter Simon Pallas (1741–1811) described banks so steep on the lower Ob that sometimes chunks of earth would fall off so vast in size that they would break through the frozen sheet of ice, making a splash so great that it would throw unsuspecting fish up on shore.[6] At the mouth of the river, the dark blue gives way to light blue around the coastal edges. Given that this river empties into sea at the polar circle, we may see this as ice for much of the year. Thus, with a few strokes and shades, Remezov rendered paper a portal to an entire landscape.

These elements of physical geography we can see immediately. But if we know the symbols and can read the words, this map has even more to tell us. It depicts elements of human geography that reveal imperial structures and relations in this Arctic place. Two particular symbols, the town and the tents, offer insights into Russian imperial rule and its limits. Specifically, they convey clues of Samoyed resistance to Russian rule.

Let's begin at the top of the map just left of center. We see a cluster of buildings, a symbol frequently used by Remezov to indicate a town. Revealing a charming parsimony of Russian language, the words labelling the town read: "Town of the Sob [River] Samoyed people. They spring and autumn here, near the fish."[7] The Sob River, which is depicted on the next page of the atlas, is a tributary that flows into the Ob 322 kilometers upstream from its mouth.[8] The cluster of buildings gives an impression of permanence. That impression is confirmed by the other maps in Remezov's atlas of Siberia, in which our map of the Ob appears. In the whole atlas, there are thousands of other noted populations points (smaller, seasonal, etc.), but only dozens of these clusters of buildings, which suggests that such town diagrams designate more established, substantial towns—towns in which government administrators, for example, are stationed. This town, however, is labeled explicitly as Samoyed, not Russian, which may explain why historians have been unable to identify it with any certainty. Unlike most of the other towns indicated with the town diagram in Russia-claimed territory, this one may not have housed Russian officials. And yet it was significant enough to be depicted with a more substantive symbol.

Now let our eyes move down the map, across the river. We see more Samoyed settlements, but here, we see those settlements designated with five pointed tents in a blank space on a rise above the river plain. The labels differ slightly, too. The town diagram is labeled "the Samoyeds of the Sob [River]"; the tents are labeled "the Dorsk Samoyeds of the Sob [River]." That the names of Samoyed groups would differ is no surprise: Samoyeds organized their society as a set of extended clans, so it is common to encounter differently named Samoyed groups. Descriptors could indicate geography as well. Russian documents separated Samoyeds into "tundra" and "forest" Samoyeds, or associated them with nearby rivers (as here) and clan names.

As the tents on the map suggest, Samoyeds were exceedingly mobile. They fished along rivers in summer and retreated into woods in other seasons. Local conditions—when and where the fish run, the weather in a particular spot—could vary significantly. Eventually, trade also affected mobility patterns. It makes sense that all these dynamics contributed to various independent decisions for how groups of Samoyeds moved. When Russians and other early modern commentators refer to Samoyeds as willful and independent, they may well be referring to these uncoordinated patterns of mobility rather than deliberate political postures. The movements of discrete groups and their responses to local conditions could also heighten competition for resources and lead to conflict. The historian S. V. Bakhrushin asserted that Samoyeds were accustomed to fighting among themselves, which made them more experienced in warfare than other tribes in the vicinity, and thus more equipped to mount challenges to Russian encroachment.[9]

What is more puzzling than variations in naming, then, is the use of different symbols to designate different groups of Samoyeds. Why Remezov chose to represent Samoyeds with a town diagram on one side of the river and with tents on the other is not entirely clear, but based on his use of symbols throughout the atlas, we can assume the distinction is neither accidental nor random. Remezov, however, does not spell out the meaning for us. While the atlas includes keys to interpreting some of the symbols,[10] none explicitly defines what this tent symbol meant. His modern biographer, L. A. Gol'denberg, however, did. Gol'denberg defined the tent with the word *kochi,* short for *kochevye,* as in nomadic people.[11] We might conclude from this that Remezov is depicting some Samoyeds who are settled and some who are nomadic, and consider our curiosity satisfied. But not so fast. Recall that the map explicitly informs us that Samoyeds above on the other side of the river are migratory as well: "They spring and autumn here, near the fish." In the seventeenth century, there were no entirely sedentary Samoyed groups. Along the harsh, northern littoral, seasonal migration was necessary for survival—a dynamic that obtained not just for Indigenous peoples. The Russian town of Mangazeia came alive during the three summer months, but perhaps no one, not even the town governor, lived there year-round.[12] Since Remezov was well aware of these lifeways, the tents do not signal a group of nomads; they tell us that these Samoyeds did not accept Russian overlordship.

Early accounts reported that Samoyeds lived in tents with a circular footprint and a hole in the top for smoke egress, but Remezov chose to represent them with a stylized pointed tent.[13] Remezov had some precedent for choosing such a tent as a symbol. In western European maps of "Greater Tartary"—the blanket (and somewhat ambiguous) term applied to much of the territory of Eurasia—these stylized pointed tents often stood in as an iconic representation for the wild people of the steppe. They show up, for example, on one of the earliest known maps depicting Russia, a 1525 manuscript map drawn by an Italian cartographer. On that map, eight sharp-pointed tents and one seated ruler gazing westward are all that occupies the otherwise blank space of "Western Great Tartary."[14] Subsequent European atlases deployed this same symbology. Remezov, who had access to such atlases in Moscow, incorporated such symbols in his own work, with his own modifications.

Although some have argued persuasively that tents were used on maps to indicate "barbarous" or "uncivilized" peoples, I submit that Remezov's use of tents communicates an altogether different message, presenting us with a case of same form, different content. His tents denote groups that the state understands as not fully subordinated. This interpretation is suggested by Remezov's illustrated chronicle, where tents do not carry the civilizational connotations that they had for western Europeans. Around the year 1700, with the help of his sons, Remezov wrote the dramatic story of the Cossack Yermak's conquest of Siberia in the 1580s. In the chronicle, Yermak and Russian Cossacks battle against various Siberian Indigenous groups, most climactically against Kuchum, the khan of the Siberian khanate. The account of the conquest is illustrated with 154 images, making it, in a sense, an early example of "graphic history."[15] Various types of dwellings are shown. Remezov depicts both Kuchum and Yermak in solidly constructed buildings, and, when they are on campaign, in pointed tents.[16] Yermak is the hero of Remezov's chronicle, bringing Christian civilization to a land of infidels. Remezov describes him as "most courageous and shrewd, and humane, and well-favored and endowed with every kind of wisdom."[17] And yet he, the Christian hero, is depicted, while on campaign, in a stylized pointed tent, as is his rival, Kuchum. (Image 8.3)

We can return to the atlas for further evidence that Remezov's use of stylized tents was not governed by cultural chauvinism. Russians certainly perceived themselves to be on a civilizational level higher than that of Ostiaks (Khanty) and Voguls (Mansy), yet these groups are not represented by tents in the atlas. In fact, while the atlas represents a great variety of peoples, the use of tents is relatively meager.

Throughout the atlas, tents appear where the grip of Russian sovereignty was particularly illusory, or non-existent, at the northern and southern edges of the empire. In the entire atlas, amid over 4,000 population points, almost half of which indicate non-Russian population points, there are there are just 255 tents. These tents appear in the circumpolar north and in the southern borderlands. Given how different the climates are at these extremes, it is unlikely that the symbol is intended to provide a realistic image of housing. What the locations of tents do have in common, however, is that they come at the limits of territories where Russians claimed sovereignty. Siberia's great rivers that flow north into the Arctic Ocean originate in the depths of inner Eurasia, from mountain springs that flow into vast steppes. It is here, in lands that Kalmyks, Dzhungars, Mongols, and even Chinese frequented, that we encounter the majority of the tent symbols.[18] Although these places were mostly beyond territory Russia had claimed when Remezov worked, questions of who reigned supreme there were far from settled, and by the nineteenth century Russia would conquer most of the areas where Remezov drew tents. The other significant concentration of tents in the atlas—50—appears in Samoyed territory. Samoyeds' housing and lifeways differed drastically from those of Mongol-descended equestrian steppe warriors, but what these groups did share in common was the challenge

IMAGE 8.3 Yermak in a tent, from the Remezov Chronicle, c. 1700.

certain of them posed to Russian imperial expansion. And for that reason, on this map of Russian empire, they are represented by the same symbol of a pointed tent. That we see tents so clearly concentrated at the southern limits of empire, where expansion was checked by nomadic powers, and among the Samoyeds, a northern population hostile to Russian rule, suggests that these tents convey political information: they indicate a certain freedom from tsarist control.

From the perspective of the Russian state, Samoyed autonomy would have been evident in their refusal to pay tribute to the tsar's treasury, in the state's inability to force them to pay, and in coordinated attacks occasionally launched against Russians. While the Samoyeds likely did not conceive of themselves as constituting a sovereign entity in any political sense, annotations such as "unpeaceful Samoyeds," "[Russians] killed by Samoyeds," or "free Chukchi" (Image 8.2) sprinkled across Remezov's maps reveal that Siberia's northern Indigenous resisted many of the demands of the expanding imperial tsardom—Remezov's use of "free" in fact means a group that doesn't pay tribute in fur (*iasak*) [19]—and the state knew it. From the perspective of Remezov, cartographer for the Russian state, the deliberate use of the pointed tent symbol acknowledges that the group in question is on a different level of incorporation than other more acquiescent—even acquiescent Samoyed[20]—subjects. In identifying Samoyeds near the western shore of the Ob River with tents, Remezov indicates a group understood to be, if not wholly autonomous, not fully subordinate to Muscovite control.

Remezov's atlas of Siberia gives us valuable insight into imperial relations in the early modern Russian empire. Close examination of the symbols on this map reveals the contested and layered nature of Russian sovereignty around the mouth of the Ob River. Once we appreciate what is documented on this map, we can see it is a testament to the imperial reality that Russia was not truly "sovereign [over] all the northern coasts" as the eighteenth century dawned, despite its long-standing claims.

NOTES

1. Nicolaas Witsen, *Severnaia i Vostochnaia Tatariia, vkliuchaiushchaia oblasti, raspolozhennye v severnoi i vostochnoi chastiakh Evropy i Azii*, translated from Dutch by V. G. Trisman, 3 vols. (Amsterdam, 2010), 3:378.
2. *Obdorskii krai i Mangazeiia. Sbornik dokumentov*, edited by E. V. Vershinin et al. (Ekaterinburg: Tezis, 2004), no. 1 (April 2, 1524), 10–11.
3. G. F. Miller, *Istoriia Sibiri* (Moscow: Vostochnaia literatura RAN, 1999), 1:202.
4. S. V. Bakhrushin, "Puti v Sibir' v XVI-XVII vv.," in *Nauchnye trudy* (Moscow: Nauka, ANSSSR, 1952–1959), 31:115.
5. L. A. Gol'denberg, *Semen Ul'ianovich Remezov, sibirskii kartograf i geograf, 1642–posle 1720* (Moscow: Nauka, 1965), 183.
6. Peter Simon Pallas, *Puteshestvie po raznym provintsiiam rossiiskogo gosudarstva. Puteshestvie po Sibirii k vostoku lezhashchei dazhe i do samoi Daurii 1772 goda. Chast' tretiia.* (St. Petersburg: St. Petersburg Imperial Academy of Sciences, 1788), 18. https://www.vostlit.info/Texts/rus6/Pallas_5/text1.htm
7. Semen Ul'ianovich Remezov (1642-c. 1720), *Khorograficheskaya kniga [Chorographical Sketch-book of Siberia]*, MS Russ 72 (6), Houghton Library, Harvard University, Cambridge, Mass, f. 116 (hereafter cited as *KhK*). https://nrs.harvard.edu/urn-3:FHCL.HOUGH:4435676. In the text, the atlas of Siberia is used to refer to the *KhK*. I have not succeeded in identifying this place.
8. *KhK*, f. 117.
9. Bakhrushin, "Samoedy v XVII v.," in *Nauchnye trudy*, 3:6.
10. The *KhK* contains four keys. See *KhK*, ff. 9, 30, 79, 166v.
11. L. A. Gol'denberg, *Semen Ul'ianovich Remezov. Sibirskii kartograf i geograf* (Moscow: Nauka, 1965), 175.
12. Bakhrushin, "Legenda o Vasilii Mangazeiskom," in *Nauchnye trudy*, 3.1:333.

13. Witsen, *Noord und Oost Tartarye*, 2:1065; Corneille Le Brun, *Voyage par la Moscovie, en Perse et aux Indes orientales* (Amsterdam, 1718).
14. General Research Division, The New York Public Library, "Karta Rossii Batisty Agneze 1525g Tekst str.3," New York Public Library Digital Collections. https://digitalcollections.nypl.org/items/510d47e4-53d6-a3d9-e040-e00a18064a99
15. Nancy Shields Kollmann, "The *Litsevoi Svod* as Graphic Novel: Narrativity in Iconographic Style," *Kritika* 19, no. 1 (2018): 53–82.
16. Remezov Chronicle, in *Yermak's Campaign in Siberia*, translated from the Russian by Tatiana Minorsky and David Wileman, edited by Terence Armstrong (London: The Hakluyt Society, 1975). See Kuchum in buildings in Chapters 23 and 47. See Yermak in buildings in Chapters 84, 87, and 95. See Kuchum in tents in Chapters 24, 25, 26, 33, 34, 40, 55, and 66. See Yermak in tents in Chapters 10, 12, 13, 15, 29, 30, 31, 39, 95, and 96. The tent in Chapter 39 has a more rounded than pointed top.
17. Remezov Chronicle, in *Yermak's Campaign in Siberia*, Chapters 106, 208.
18. *KhK*, f. 129 has 43 tents; f. 141 has 21 tents; ff. 98 and 99 have 50 tents; f. 146 has 15 tents; ff. 148 and 150 have 44 tents.
19. *KhK*, ff. 93, 169, 115, 152. See Chukchi example at mouth of Lena River, *KhK*, f. 152.
20. For explicit indications of tribute-paying Samoyeds see *KhK*, ff. 132, 169.

CHAPTER 9

DIVINE CREATION AND RUSSIAN EXPLOITATION OF THE ENVIRONMENT IN SIBERIA (c. 1700)

EVGENY GRISHIN

SINCE THE MIDDLE AGES, Russians have been fascinated with Siberia's natural bounties. The desire to profit from them was the driving force behind the Russian imperial expansion eastward in the sixteenth and seventeenth centuries. The pioneers scouted the vast Siberian expanse for fertile arable lands, signs of precious metals, herbs and fruits, game, fowl, and fish. The most desirable of these commodities was the skins of Siberian furry animals. Exported primarily to European markets, the pelts fetched the silver currency necessary for the national economy.

During this period, Russian and native fur trappers in Siberia killed fur-bearing animals at a staggering rate. According to internal customs records, from 1620s to 1680s, sables alone were killed at the rate of about a hundred thousand a year, totaling more than seven million animals.[1] We can only wonder how many more animal skins were consumed within Siberia itself, or simply bypassed customs officers.

The detrimental effect of fur trapping became apparent early on to the Muscovites. Russian diplomat Grigorii Kotoshikhin testified in the 1660s that "in the regions closest to Moscow trapping of sables of the highest quality has fallen into decline, and sables of medium and poor quality are caught, because many animals have been frightened away (*otpuzhany*) and have decreased in number." That is why, he continued, "sables and other animals of the highest quality are obtained from the most distant regions of Siberia, on the Lena."[2] In other words, by that time the consequences of the intensive overhunting were felt even in Siberia, so the trappers had to move farther and farther east, chasing the disappearing animals. Internal customs records demonstrate the decline in the number of taxed skins starting in this period as well.[3]

Kotoshikhin and his contemporaries expressed no environmental concern over the disappearing populations of furbearers. In documents dealing with fur tribute collection and the fur trade in seventeenth-century Siberia, I found no evidence of environmental care anywhere; instead, profit seemed to be the driving force behind fur trapping in the area and, ultimately, of the rapidly expanding Muscovite empire. One vivid example from local documents is a decree from the 1680s addressing the collection of tribute (called *iasak*) in the town of Tyumen: "If they [tribute payers] claim that they cannot obtain furs anywhere and instead offer to pay the tribute with money . . ., refuse it, ordering them to purchase the [required number of] furs [elsewhere] and turn those over to the state treasury."[4] This and many other similar records demonstrate that the treasury's interests prevailed, despite the evident decrease in the number of fur-bearing animals.

Why would early modern Muscovites assume the furbearers were "frightened away," rather than extinguished? Why were they so unconcerned with the well-being of their fellow creatures, especially such highly valued ones? The answer is simple: their trust in the copiousness of the divinely created world precluded such concern. Human depredation, it seemed, could not eliminate animals placed on earth by God, and the Lord would always replenish his stores. More than that, the exploitative subjugation of the environment was an integral part of the Muscovite imperial vision. We can see this vision in two images that appear in the most spectacular literary source documenting Muscovy's conquest of Siberia, the illustrated *Siberian History* written around 1700.[5]

The *History's* author, Semyon Remezov (1642–c. 1720), was a historian, cartographer, and architect from the city of Tobolsk, in western Siberia. Fabulously illustrated by the author and his family members, the *History* presents an overtly religious story of Muscovy's subjugation of the vast western Siberian spaces and its local non-Christian population. The *History* demonstrates Russia's manifestly providential vision of Siberia's conquest, a religiously inflected vision that guided Russian frontiersmen in their venture.[6] The conquest of the natural environment was a vital part of that endeavor.

At first sight, the *History*'s text seems to be devoid of environmental observations, being focused primarily on the Cossacks' military campaign. Only once does the author remark, succinctly, that the Cossacks perceived the Siberian land to be "rich and abounding in all things."[7] Remezov, however, explained in one of his other contemporaneous works what kind of bounties Siberia possessed:

> The soil is fertile in grain, fruit and cattle, apart from honey and grapes, it is not lacking in anything. It is vaster and richer in priceless [furry] animals than any other part of the world, its marketplaces are overflowing with domestic and imported goods. Large rivers, backwaters, and lakes are countless; various fishes are plenty and catchable . . .[8]

Remezov draws a picture of the Siberian environment as plentiful and even inviting. The *History*'s visual narrative illustrates the stated abundance well and proves that the conquering of Siberian natural environment was, in fact, a vital part of the story. Throughout the work, we see images of the Cossacks navigating local rivers and lakes, passing through forests and hills. The skins of fur-bearing animals often come to sight as items of exchange, together with bunches of caught fish, but most frequently as trimming on hats and collars. Domestic animals, such as dogs, horses, camels, reindeer, sheep, and cattle, appear, too, as possessions of various Siberian peoples and Russian settlers alike.

The creatures of the Siberian environment come into view in the *History* as objects devoid of subjectivity, though: either as a mere terrestrial setting of divine and human actions or as commodities to be traded. This fact is especially vivid in the case of furbearers, who appear in the *History* almost exclusively in the commodified form of pelts, rather than as living beings.

Such portrayal of the natural environment is not simply an artistic convention, but a reflection of a set of assumptions the Muscovites had about the world. They assumed that the world had an omnipotent divine Creator, a Christian God, and natural resources that were inexhaustible; most importantly, they assumed that humans had a divinely sanctioned dominion over the natural world. These assumptions justified Muscovites' unrestrained consumption of animal life and natural resources in their imperial territories. Two images in the *History* speak about them candidly: Noah's sacrificial offering after the Flood, and the subordination of the animal kingdom to Adam in the Garden of Eden.

The first image (Article 138) (Image 9.1) seems unremarkable, as it looks like a conventional illustration of the well-known Biblical episode of Noah with his family, conducting the first postdiluvian animal sacrifice. The image is accompanied by an extended quote from the Book of Genesis calling on Noah "to replenish the earth and possess it" following the all-destroying catastrophe. Yet this image plays a vital role in the *History's* imperial message: God blessed the Muscovites to take over the Siberian environment.

The visual style of this portrait of Noah's animal sacrifice in Remezov's *History* is out of tune with the rest of its visual narrative. This discrepancy may be explained by the fact that Remezov seems to have reproduced a baroque-style frontispiece engraving from another book that he probably had at hand, namely Innokentii Gizel's *Synopsis*. The *Synopsis* (Kyiv, published in 1674, 1678, and 1680), was an account of the history of the East Slavs, immensely popular in Ukraine and Muscovy at the time. The engraving Remezov used can be found in editions from 1678 on and, in turn, was likely based on a western European original.[9]

The *Synopsis* illustration of the sacrifice (Image 9.2) depicts the inception of the nations of the earth from Noah's kin. The engraving portrays the humans kneeling before the sacrificial flames, the male figures having their names indicated—Noah, Shem, Ham, and Japheth. A calf, a ram, several sheep, and a hare graze peacefully before the humans, while a calf, a ram, and a griffin (!) calmly rest on the altar, enveloped in flames. In the background, we see the Sun with the tetragrammaton (the name of God—YHWH in Hebrew) inscribed on it, and an arch and a rainbow in

IMAGE 9.1 Noah's sacrificial offering after the Flood, from the Remezov Chronicle, c. 1700.

the clouds above the arch, signifying the renewed covenant between God and the humans. The text above the engraving explains the image by quoting the Book of Genesis: Noah erected an altar with an offering to the Lord (Genesis 8:20). In response, God blessed Noah and his kin and instructed them "to be fruitful and multiply" (Genesis 9:1). The text below the engraving, elucidates why Noah's sacrifice illustrates the history of the Slavic people. It quotes loosely from Chapters 9 and 10 of

IMAGE 9.2 Noah's sacrifice, from Innokentii Gizel, *Synopsis*, 1680 edition.

Genesis to demonstrate that all contemporary humans originate from Noah's sons Japheth, Shem, and Ham. Further in the book, the author of the *Synopsis* clarifies that Japheth was the forefather of all the Europeans, including the Slavs.

Remezov reproduced the *Synopsis* engraving and its text very closely, and yet with some strategic omissions and insertions. He effectively refashioned it visually, and especially textually, to complement his narrative of Muscovy's divinely sanctioned conquest of Siberia. The visual changes were rather minor. Remezov decided not to reproduce the ark and reduced the rainbow and the clouds to a set of lines, downplaying the themes of the Flood and the covenant. Also, unlike in the original, the heads of the Noah's sons' wives are expressly covered with headscarves, apparently to stress their Orthodox virtue.

The most important changes were in the text connected to Remezov's drawing. He chose to repeat the Biblical quotes accompanying the *Synopsis* engraving verbatim, but with some modifications. First, Remezov added a heading—"The Heavenly Blessing of Life for the Siberians"—which leaves no doubt that Noah and his family here metaphorically represent the new settlers in Siberia, the Orthodox Russians, who were destined to take over Siberia. Second, he replaced the initial quote regarding the erection of the altar (Genesis 8:20) with the phrase "Providence will be revealed in Siberia," to reinforce the heading's messages.

Finally, Remezov greatly expanded the passage concerning God's blessing to Noah's family "to be fruitful and multiply" (Genesis 9:1) by adding two other Genesis verses to it: verse 2 of Chapter 9 and verse 22 of Chapter 8. The former states that Noah and his kin received undisputed dominion over all living creatures: "upon every beast of the earth, and upon every fowl in the air, upon all that moveth upon the earth, and upon all the fishes of the sea." The latter affirms that Creation is a complete form that functions in a continuous cycle of regeneration: "I have created all the days, the seedtime and harvest, winter and heat, summer and autumn, day and night shall not cease," spoke God to Noah.[10] In other words, Remezov chose to stress human ascendancy over non-human animals and, at the same time, emphasize the natural equilibrium established by the divine Creator.

In Eastern Orthodox theological tradition, the premise of nature's cyclical regeneration led to an assumption that natural resources were practically inexhaustible. The compiler of the most popular Orthodox exegesis of the Book of Genesis, the tenth-century Bulgarian theologian John the Exarch, explained this using the rather dubious example of arable land. He insisted that time and again the earth has been "plowed, sown with seeds, planted [with plants], and its fruits harvested," and has endured rain, snow, and sun—all of it without turning "barren," without failing to provide for a man working it.[11] Remezov and his Muscovite contemporaries apparently shared this assumption.

The message of Remezov's drawing, therefore, comes into focus. Like Noah's family after the Flood received dominion over the living creatures of the air, water, and earth, so, too, Russian Siberians were to take control of the new land and the beings populating it. The new imperial possessions appeared to offer a limitless store of commodities that the Russian conquerors were destined, and even obliged, to benefit from.

The second image from Remezov's *History* examined in this essay (Article 151) (Image 9.3), also illustrates the Book of Genesis and continues the topic of

IMAGE 9.3 The subordination of animal kingdom to Adam in the Garden of Eden, from the Remezov Chronicle, c. 1700.

human-nature relationships. It is titled "Example of the pagan peoples' subjection to Christians" (*Primer o pokorenii iazyk khristianom*). The accompanying text consists of a mixture of quotes from the Book of Proverbs with a few original lines.[12]

The drawing presents an image of the Garden of Eden. A large tree dominates the landscape, and the second-largest figure is a man, Adam. A body of water full of fish and sea creatures lies under Adam's feet, while domestic and wild animals alongside creatures exotic for Siberia (peacocks, ostriches, a rhinoceros, an elephant, and others) as well as mythical animals (a unicorn and a viper) gather around the tree peacefully, some of them looking at Adam.

The image evidently illustrates the first chapter of the Book of Genesis, particularly the story of the creation of the world and the pinnacle of it—the human, Adam. The story goes that God created the first human in His own image and destined him to "fill the earth and master it" (Genesis 1:24–28). The dominion of Adam over "all the cattle and . . . the birds of the sky and . . . all the wild beasts" is reaffirmed in the act of giving them names (Genesis 2:18–21).

Unlike the illustration of Noah's sacrifice inspired by the *Synopsis* engraving, Remezov's Garden of Eden image does not seem to have one specific visual prototype, and it appears rather unusual for images of this type. Adam's female companion, Eve, is nowhere to be seen in the picture, while Adam himself is not naked, but modestly dressed in robes. Remezov's drawing celebrates Adam as a righteous master of nature, as the likeness of God, not as a soon-to-be sinner.

Compared with other contemporary illustrations of Paradise, the drawing reveals its highly conventional core. Deer, camels, elephants, peacocks, rhinos, vipers, and unicorns appear in the Russian sixteenth-century *Illustrated Historical Chronicle* (*Litsevoi letopisnyi svod*), in the fabulously illustrated Godunov *Psalter* from the early seventeenth century, and in the foreign printed editions of the Bible available to Muscovites, such as the Bible in Polish published in Krakow in 1577 or the seventeenth-century bestseller, Claes Visscher's *Theatrum Biblicum*, printed in Amsterdam numerous times throughout the century.

As in the illustration of Noah's sacrifices, the image of Adam in the Garden of Eden plays a specific role in Remezov's narrative of Siberia's conquest, making a case for the Muscovites' primacy over the humans of Siberia as well. The text that accompanies the drawing adds to the Biblical message of human dominion over nature an expression of what we might call Christian imperialism. The commentary is a mosaic of slightly reworked quotes from Chapter 11 of the Book of Proverbs. It directly states that what we see is the Tree of Life in the Garden of Eden and the first human, Adam, exercising his dominion over nature. Yet in this rendition, Remezov introduces a twist: the Garden signifies Siberia, the Tree of Life represents (Orthodox) Christianity, and Adam stands in for all Christian Russians. Animals symbolize the natural world of Siberia and, at the same time, the Indigenous populations: the human, non-Christian world of Siberia. "The tree of life grows from the fruit of truth for the

Siberians," the text proclaims, ". . . then like all creatures who submitted to Adam in Paradise, they [the pagan peoples (*iazyki*) of Siberia] would evidently submit to any Christian."[13] Thus, Remezov adds to the Bible-inspired hierarchy of creatures that separated humans from non-humans a ranking among the human creatures themselves: the pagan Siberians are presented as inferior to their Christian counterparts, and are expected to comply with such an order of things.

The two Remezov images analyzed here force the message of Christian imperialism in both ecological and ethnoreligious senses. The first one, Noah's sacrifice, acknowledges the Muscovites' mastery of the Siberian environment, while the second glorifies the Orthodox Russians' dominion over local non-Christian populations, in addition to their rightful mastery over the natural world. In other words, Siberia appears in Remezov's *History* as a playground for Muscovites, as they built their Christian empire. This imperial vision deliberately relegated non-human creatures, along with non-Christian humans, to a subordinate role. It confidently encouraged Muscovites to hunt and trade, to live and die, without taking responsibility for the well-being of the environment.

NOTES

1. P. N. Pavlov, *Pushnoi promysel v Sibiri v XVII v.* (Krasnoiarsk: KGPI, 1972), 106.
2. Grigorii Kotoshikhin, *Russia in the Reign of Aleksei Mikhailovich,* translated by Benjamin Phillip Uroff, edited by Marhsall Poe (Warsaw: De Gruyter Open, 2014), 105–106.
3. Pavlov, *Pushnoi promysel,* 106.
4. State Archive of Tyumen oblast', fond И-29, op. 1, no. 2, f. 9v.
5. *Remezovskaia letopis',* edited by E. I. Dergacheva-Skop et al., t. 2 (Tobolsk: Fond Vozrozhdenie Tobol'ska, 2006).
6. For more details, see Valerie Kivelson's pivotal work on Muscovite cartography that develops this argument: Valerie Kivelson, *Cartographies of Tsardom. The Land and Its Meanings in Seventeenth-Century Russia* (Ithaca: Cornell University Press, 2006), 133–161.
7. *Yermak's Campaign in Siberia,* translated from the Russian by Tatiana Minorsky and David Wileman, edited by Terence Armstrong (London: The Hakluyt Society, 1975), 108.
8. Semen Remezov, "Upodoblenie Sibirskiia strany," published in E. I. Dergacheva-Skop, "'Pokhvala' Sibiri S. U. Remezova," *Trudy otdela drevnerusskoi literatury* 21 (1965), 274.
9. Adapted from *Theatrum Biblicum* by Claes Visscher, also known by the Latin variant of the same name—Nicolas Piscator.
10. *Yermak's Campaign in Siberia,* 246.
11. G. S. Barankova and V. V. Mil'kov, *Shestodnev Ioanna ekzarkha Bolgarskogo* (St. Petersburg: Aleteiia, 2001), 307.
12. Translation is mine.
13. *Yermak's Campaign in Siberia,* 265.

PART

III

IMPERIAL RUSSIA

Between 1721 and 1917, Russia proudly called itself an empire in terms recognizable to its European counterparts, and its rulers, beginning with Peter I (also known as Peter the Great, ruled 1689–1725), called themselves emperors and empresses. In 1703, Peter transferred the capital of his new empire from Moscow to the city he ordered built, St. Petersburg. During this period, the terms *Russia* and *Russian Empire* were often used interchangeably.

Thanks to internal reforms and victory in the Northern War (1700–1721), fought against Sweden, Russia under Peter strengthened its international position and transformed itself into one of the Great Powers of Europe, playing an important role in European politics ever since. As a Great Power, Russia actively participated in colonization and the general European process of modernization, originating as well as borrowing and adapting modern administrative, military, ideological, and scholarly institutions to its own internal conditions. A major step in this direction was carried out during the thirty-four-year reign of Empress Catherine II (also known as Catherine the Great; reigned 1762–1796), who created an effective system for governing the vast, multinational Russian Empire as a more unified administrative and political space, based on the ideas of the European Enlightenment.

At the same time, Catherine and her successors adhered to time-honored imperial principles in governance. While expanding the uniformity and reach of their administrative system, the rulers continued to institute and maintain legal and cultural boundaries between diverse groups of people. Jews and Muslims, Bashkirs and Tatars, men and women, serfs and townspeople, and nobles of various ranks were assigned particular protections and privileges, restrictions and responsibilities, according to their ascribed collective identities. For instance, after incorporation of much of the former Polish-Lithuanian Commonwealth (a three-part process of partition carried out between 1772 and 1795) and the absorption of new territories to the west and south, Russia gained a large population of Jews for the first time. Rather than incorporate Jews into a uniform system of governance, Catherine allowed them to continue the traditional forms of self-administration they had enjoyed under the Polish Crown. She also created the Pale of Settlement, a region outside of Russia's historical borders to which her new subjects were confined. In other words, individuals were what society and state declared them to be, and one's life was prescribed accordingly. Homogeneity was antithetical to the imperial principle of ruling through difference and maintaining unequal, hierarchical relations between the metropole and its various peripheries, colonies, and subject populations. Managing diversity in an empire required that each subgroup received its own separate deal or distinctive arrangement, even as the imperial center continued its efforts to expand its reach and unify its control over its diverse lands.

Throughout this period, the Russian Empire continued to expand its borders. From the eighteenth to the twentieth century, it annexed neighboring lands in eastern Europe, the Black Sea region, the Caucasus, Central Asia, the Arctic, Siberia, the region called (from a Russian geographic perspective) the "Far East," and, reaching across the ocean, Alaska and California.

In the nineteenth century, the unified imperial administrative structure encouraged elements of empire-wide infrastructure in transportation (a system of postal routes and roads, the Trans-Siberian Railway); commerce (international and domestic trade, markets and trade fairs); spatial mobility (Siberian exile, peasant relocation); and social-cultural ventures (the Russian Geographical Society, other scholarly and scientific societies, ethnographic and cartographic expeditions, and literary publications).

At the same time, the diversity of the empire—ethnic, religious, economic, geographic—together with its location surrounded by neighbors and colonies in all directions helped produce a "Golden Age" of cultural flowering in the arts. Throughout the nineteenth century, the educated elite, drawing talent from across the empire, produced fiction, poetry, music, painting, and ballet that more than kept pace with the achievements of their peers in western Europe. As a result, Russia began to participate in global projects and discourses. All of these cultural activities, however, occurred under the watchful eye of the tsars and their censors. One might be arrested and exiled for perceived political criticism, and access to prestigious cultural schools and institutions remained out of reach for all but the most extraordinary members of the lower classes or ethnic minorities. In the late imperial period, artists in the Russian Empire began to excel in a number of new genres, including visual media. Journalism, photography, and film, alongside more traditional arts such as painting and theater, all produced extraordinary talents in realistic representation, as well as in formal experimentation.

In the 1860s and 1870s, Emperor Alexander II carried out what is known as the Great Reforms—large-scale transformation of the military, administrative, social, financial, and judicial systems. Chief among the reforms was the abolition of serfdom, which was greeted with hopes for genuine equality and opportunities for democratic political participation. These reforms hastened the process of modernization and the development of a government based on the rule of law, although many believed they did not go far enough. The shortcomings of the reforms were among the main reasons for the spread of discontent and radicalization within every sector of society. The last tsars continued economic modernization, but without alleviating poverty or sharing political power with members of society. Those failures, along with the stirring of independence movements among the non-Russian colonized populations, contributed to the rising discontent at the end of the nineteenth century.

Deep internal crisis, exacerbated by the First World War (1914–1918) and the radicalization of political movements, compelled Nicholas II to abdicate the throne in 1917. The Russian Empire was declared a republic.

MAP 3.1 Imperial Russia (Detail: Western Regions)

MAP 3.2 Imperial Russia

CHAPTER 10

RE-VISIONING EMPIRE UNDER PETER THE GREAT

ERNEST A. ZITSER

IT IS TEMPTING to treat the reign of Tsar Peter Alekseevich Romanov (1672–1725), or Peter I, as a sharp break with the past, but it is incorrect to do so. This is especially true in the sphere of foreign policy, where Tsar Peter, together with his advisers, confronted the same unresolved questions as their predecessors: What is the best way to communicate Muscovy's special role on the world stage? What distinguishes a dukedom or principality from an empire? Who gets to make such weighty political distinctions? And how could mere mortals dare to question the right of the Russian Orthodox tsar to the lofty title of emperor, of whom the Bible (Matthew 22:21; Romans 13:1) says there is no higher judge than God Himself?

The issue of Muscovy's imperial status was part of a long tradition of medieval and early modern Russian diplomacy. For almost two centuries, the Eastern Orthodox Christian rulers of this northern Eurasian principality sought recognition from their European counterparts—both Catholic and Protestant—for the imperial title that the grand princes of Muscovy had slowly but steadily appropriated for themselves. The issue became even more urgent after the defeat of the Eastern Roman (Byzantine) Empire by the Muslim rulers of the Ottoman Porte (1453), a seismic shift in geopolitics that left Muscovite Russia as the only independent, Eastern Orthodox realm in the world. The quest for recognition of the tsars' imperial pretensions was not a matter of Muscovites' particular vanity or Orthodox Christianity's supposedly undue attention to ceremony over substance. Muscovy displayed no more preoccupation with pomp and circumstance than any of its contemporaries. In a tradition-bound, hierarchical society like the medieval and early modern Christian commonwealth of nations, diplomats of all countries zealously guarded the honor of their sovereign and responded with alacrity to every perceived slight. They did so because even seemingly minor violations of diplomatic etiquette—especially the incorrect use of official titles and insignia—affected the precedence ranking of all Christian rulers. By seeking parity with the Holy Roman Emperor, the widely recognized heir of the Western Roman Empire, the supreme secular representative of the

Catholic Church, and by custom, the only monarch authorized to appoint kings, the tsars of Muscovite Russia were, in effect, destabilizing the international pecking order. And Muscovy, which was located on the fringes of Europe both geographically and in terms of its "schismatic" views on Christianity, was unlikely to be rewarded for trying to upset the traditional, divinely sanctioned political order.

Unlike all of his predecessors, Tsar Peter eventually succeeded, after more than two decades of continuous warfare and at tremendous social cost, in attaining international recognition of Muscovite Russia's status as an empire. One of the ways that he was able to accomplish this long-sought goal of Russian diplomacy was by reconceptualizing the notion of empire itself. That is, the tsar and his advisers reassessed and, when necessary, worked to revise the inherited image of Russia in a way that would bring this realm more closely in line with the political conceptions and self-presentations of contemporary Christian monarchs, but without abandoning his forebears' commitment to the idea of the "translation of empire" from Byzantium to Muscovy. The political significance of this new imagery explains why Tsar Peter commissioned the oil portrait and emblem book analyzed in this chapter. In turn, these two seemingly trivial, material objects reveal how "the visual" enacted the tsar's grandiose imperial claims.

For Tsar Peter, being a "modern" Russian Orthodox emperor meant, among other things, travelling abroad to recruit foreign and, if necessary, non-Orthodox Christian specialists to help train his army and build his navy. It also meant temporarily pausing his first and perhaps most significant foreign trip (1697–1698) just long enough to sit for a full-length portrait of himself by Sir Godfrey Kneller (1646–1723), a student of Rembrandt and the official court painter of the King of England (Image 10.1).[1]

It is important to note that the success of Kneller's portrait of Tsar Peter was predicated on much more than the German-born British artist's skill in creating what is, in fact, the first realistic rendering of the tsar's facial features. As is the case with other Kneller portraits, much of its value lay in the clarity of the political message that it communicated to its viewers on behalf of his royal client. This clarity was based, in large part, on the artist's and his audience's familiarity with the post-Renaissance, pan-European language of heraldry and emblems. The utilitarian, moralistic, and didactic purpose of Baroque portraiture helps to explain why Kneller depicted the Muscovite tsar as befits *European royalty*, sporting an ermine-lined mantle embroidered in gold and depicting the Russian coat of arms (a crowned, double-headed eagle, with a breast-shield showing St. George slaying the Dragon). At the same time, he dressed Tsar Peter in the by-then anachronistic, but still symbolically significant, metal armor of a *medieval knight*. Peter appears as the very embodiment of chivalry, lacking only the sash and star of a monarchical knightly order—like the one that appears in Kneller's series of portraits of the British Knights of the Order of the Garter, which provided the template for the portrait of his royal client. (The British Order inspired the tsar to create the Order of St. Andrew, Russia's very first order of chivalry, almost immediately upon his return to Moscow in 1698). In order to emphasize the

IMAGE 10.1 Sir Godfrey Kneller, *Petrus Alexeewitz Magnus Dominus Tzar et Magnus Dux Moscoviae*, 1698.

martial theme of the portrait, Kneller's Russian royal knight was shown holding a marshal's baton, symbolizing *military command*, rather than the more traditional scepter, such as the one in Kneller's portrait of King James II, the specific Garter portrait on which the tsar's painting was apparently modeled.[2] Finally, Kneller included a marine scene, depicting the naval maneuvers of armed sailing ships, the instruments of distinctly contemporary, rather than medieval, warfare. With these visual cues, the painter referred to the tsar's *passion for the sea* and his desire to obtain the latest military technology and expertise necessary to build his own *royal navy* and, in so doing, to transform his largely landlocked, continental realm into an international emporium, if not a colonial power of its own.

The key to Kneller's painting, however, is the crown that can be seen lying next to the sovereign's orb, on the cushion in the niche to the left of the chivalrous, sea-loving, Russian royal. Although it is in shadow, this piece of royal regalia was clearly painted to look like the type of ceremonial headdress worn by an eighteenth-century European monarch, and not at all like the Cap of Monomakh, the golden, fur-lined, and jewel-encrusted skullcap traditionally worn on formal occasions of state by the Russian Orthodox tsar in his role as the legitimate heir of the twelfth-century Byzantine emperor for whom it was named. Thus, although Kneller's Latin inscription still referred to Peter as "Great Lord, Tsar, and Grand Duke of Moscow,"[3] politically savvy, educated, contemporary viewers could not fail to see in the artist's work a portrait of the young Muscovite tsar as military commander, or *imperator*—the original meaning of the Latin word for Roman emperor. This may explain why the author of "one of the newsletters of the day" erroneously described Kneller's portrait of Peter as "drawn to the life at full length in a *Roman* habit."[4]

Tsar Peter was so pleased with Kneller's portrait and the pithy and clever way in which the allegorical language of Baroque portraiture allowed the artist to depict the tsar as an emperor in all but name, that he reused it in many different media productions. Kneller's image of the Muscovite tsar could be found, for example, on miniatures given away as tokens of esteem to visiting foreign dignitaries, as well as on engravings produced domestically and abroad. It was also featured prominently on the ornate, engraved frontispiece of Russia's first printed emblem book, *Symbola et emblemata*,[5] published in 1705, in accordance with the tsar's wishes, by a well-known Amsterdam-based bookseller and publisher named Hendrik Wetstein (1649–1726). This lavishly illustrated book provided the platform for Tsar Peter to make one of his first public statements regarding his pretensions to the imperial title, something that, until that point in time, he and his advisers had carefully avoided doing, for fear of alienating potential geopolitical allies.

The emblem book's elaborate frontispiece (Image 10.2), which was designed and etched by the renowned Dutch printmaker Joseph Mulder (1658–1742), constituted "a well-developed pictorial example of imperial Petrine propaganda."[6] The Dutch graphic artist relied on the allegorical, bimedial (i.e., combining both text and

IMAGE 10.2 Frontispiece of *Symbola et emblemata*, 1705.

image), and panegyrical language of devices and emblems to characterize Tsar Peter (the device holder), who is depicted in the large medallion at the center of the composition. The eight smaller medallions (devices) were organized sequentially, in clockwise order, around Mulder's etched version of Kneller's oil portrait. Among other things, they lauded the tsar's military virtues, like his Herculean strength of character (medallion 5) and rock-like steadfastness (medallion 3); insulted his enemies, who are represented (in medallion 6) as wild beasts at each other's throats; and referred to the divinely ordained nature of the monarch (medallion 1, depicting the rising sun) and his dynasty (medallion 2, showing an eagle and eaglet flying towards the sun). The latter, aquiline image, which extolled the principle of hereditary dynastic succession, was accompanied by a bilingual inscription that said as much about the ambitions of the Russian sovereign as about the true nature of his realm: "High is the hope of your Empire" (*Nadezhda vysoka G(osu)darstva tvoego/Imperii Spes alta Tui*). This emphasis on early modern matters of state—on the dynastic "sovereign realm" (in Rusian: *gosudarstvo*)/"empire" (in Latin: *imperia*) and, especially, on the question of war and peace—is not surprising, because at that very moment, Muscovite Russia was engaged in a military conflict over patrimonial lands claimed by both the Russian and the Swedish Crowns.

As was the case with Kneller's portrait, *Symbola et emblemata* depicted Peter primarily as a military leader/*imperator*. Unlike the British court painter, however, Mulder and Wetstein did not mince their words when it came to calling a spade a spade, or the tsar an emperor. Using a specially created type-block of Cyrillic letters, Wetstein printed a frontispiece that stated explicitly—literally in black-and-white—that this emblem book was published "by order" and "under the aegis" of none other than the "Muscovite Emperor" (in Russian: *Imperator Moskovskii*). The use of this unusual, never-before-mentioned, and never-to-be-used-again royal title—combining the adjectival form of the toponym "Moscow" with the Cyrillicized version of the Latin word for "emperor"—demonstrates that Tsar Peter and his advisers were still working on finding just the right wording for a title that, they hoped, would someday be recognized by the geopolitical powers-that-be. However, instead of simply waiting for that day to arrive, they employed two top-notch foreign experts and used the latest technological innovations in publishing to float various possibilities.

For those who could not decipher the Cyrillic alphabet, the Dutch publisher of *Symbola et emblemata* helpfully provided a Latin translation, which appeared on the title page proper, immediately after Mulder's allegorical frontispiece (Image 10.3). By employing alternating, colored letters of the Roman alphabet, Wetstein created a double text, which allowed for a dual reading—full and condensed versions—of the official title of both the emblem book and of the monarch who commissioned its publication. At the same time, the letters printed in red type stood out from the (more familiar) black-and-white text and served to highlight several key phrases, which emphasized the "Sacred Majesty" of the "Emperor of Muscovy" (in Latin: *Imperatoris Moschoviae*). This designation removed all doubt about the tsar's ultimate

SYMBOLA

ET

EMBLEMATA

Juſſu atque auſpiciis

SACERRIMÆ SUÆ MAJESTATIS

AUGUSTISSIMI AC SERENISSIMI

IMPERATORIS MOSCHOVIÆ

MAGNI DOMINI CZARIS, ET

MAGNI DUCIS

PETRI ALEXEIDIS,

totius Magnæ, Parvæ & Albæ ROSSIÆ, nec non aliarum multarum Poteſtatum atque Dominiorum

Orientalium, Occidentalium Aquilonariumque

SUPREMI MONARCHÆ,

excuſa.

AMSTELÆDAMI

Apud HENRICUM WETSTENIUM. Anno 1705.

IMAGE 10.3 Title page of *Symbola et emblemata*, 1705.

intentions, demonstrating his desire to assume the title of emperor in its Western—rather than its Eastern—Roman garb, while at the same time retaining his intimate connection to the divine source of all political authority on earth.

Kneller's portrait of the chivalrous Russian military commander (1698) and Mulder and Wetstein's emblematic panegyric to the Muscovite emperor (1705) preceded by many years the tsar's formal adoption of the imperial title. On October 22, 1721, at a solemn service of thanksgiving for the long-awaited peace with Sweden, during an acclamation ceremony that was explicitly modelled on that of ancient Rome, Peter acceded to the pleas of his grateful subjects and formally assumed the titles "All-Russian Emperor" (*Imperator Vserossiiskii*), "Father of the Fatherland," and "The Great." By means of this ceremonial act—rather than through any specific royal decrees, which would be drafted soon thereafter in order to specify the proper way of addressing members of the Romanov dynasty and describing their realm—Muscovite Russia formally became the "Russian Empire" (*Rossiiskaia imperiia*).

It took several decades before all the major powers followed Sweden's example and formally recognized Russia's imperial status. By then, however, European ruling elites had already embraced a new, more "Enlightened" definition of empire—one that did not rely on historical legends about the ruling dynasty's supposed genealogical and spiritual connections to ancient Rome, but rather on their own, rationally demonstrable superiority and their self-ascribed obligation to "civilize" the less-privileged and less-enlightened nations of the world. The fact that many of those "benighted peoples" happened to be of a different skin color, and to live in those parts of the globe that the political and economic elites of the imperial metropoles sought to colonize and exploit for their own benefit, only served to confirm their sense of moral and racial superiority, and to make empire-building and colonialism into the dirty words that they eventually, and quite deservedly, became in the twentieth century.

NOTES

1. Sir Godfrey Kneller, *Petrus Alexeewitz Magnus Dominus Tzar et Magnus Dux Moscoviae*. Signed and dated 1698. Oil on canvas. 241.7 × 145.6 cm. The Royal Collection Trust. Queen's Gallery, Kensington Palace. RCIN 405645. https://www.rct.uk/collection/405645/peter-the-great-tsar-of-russia-1672-1725
2. Sir Godfrey Kneller, *King James II*. Oil on canvas, 1684. 96¾ in. × 56¾ in. (2456 mm × 1441 mm) overall. National Portrait Gallery, Primary Collection, NPG 666. https://www.npg.org.uk/collections/search/portrait/mw03423/King-James-II
3. J. Douglas Stewart, *Sir Godfrey Kneller and the English Baroque Portrait* (Oxford: Clarendon Press; New York: Oxford University Press, 1983), 123.
4. Quoted in Anthony Cross, *Peter the Great through British Eyes: Perceptions and Representations of the Tsar since 1698* (Cambridge: Cambridge University Press, 2000), 142–143, italics mine.
5. *Symbola et emblemata* (Amsterdam, 1705) was based on Daniel de la Feuille's *Devises et emblems anciennes et moderns* (Amsterdam, 1691) and *Devises et emblems d'amour* (Amsterdam, 1696).
6. Endre Sashalmi, "The Frontispiece of Peter the Great's *Simvoly i emblemata* (1705): An Iconographical Analysis," *Canadian-American Slavic studies = Revue canadienne-américaine d'études slaves* 47, no. 4 (January 2013), 459–472; 462.

CHAPTER 11

DEPICTIONS OF CHINA FROM A CARAVAN JOURNAL (1736)

GREGORY AFINOGENOV

SPIES OFTEN USE images in the course of their work. Photographs of a military installation, blueprints, or mugshots can be vastly more valuable than verbal descriptions. It might be hard to imagine the same thing being true before the emergence of photography: How much detail could you really convey without a mechanical means for transmitting information? Could an oil painting really serve the same function as a snapshot? In the Russian Empire and elsewhere, it often could.

In 1807, a painter named Shchukin was attached to a Russian mission in Beijing. His role was both to seek out Chinese paints and painting techniques and to "unnoticeably" create paintings and drawings of noteworthy things he saw. But he was to make sure that "no Chinese servant was nearby" when he did so, and he needed to "conceal his knowledge and skill in painting" from his Chinese hosts. Just like any secret agent, Shchukin had to be careful about the images he produced, and their primary value was strategic rather than aesthetic.[1]

The images for this essay come from a similar assignment, but seven decades earlier. They were produced by the Russian secretary of a trade caravan who traveled to Qing-dynasty China every few years in the first half of the eighteenth century carrying furs from Russia to trade for porcelain, rhubarb, and other goods in Beijing. Image 11.1 depicts a pair of Great Wall fortresses, complete with terrain and fortifications. Image 11.2 shows a Buddhist shrine, two Chinese soldiers with their armaments, and a Korean merchant. (Actually, the "Chinese" soldiers were probably Manchus, part of the semi-nomadic northern people who had established the Qing dynasty.)[2]

The secretary's job was not only to keep the paperwork of the caravan—dealing with its staff and finances—but also to gather intelligence by means of journals like this one. A set of orders from a later caravan, explaining what keeping this journal was meant to entail, survives. Items of interest included "what people live there and what their numbers are, and where they obtain food and income, as well as where the rivers are, what they are called, and how distant they are from one another, and from

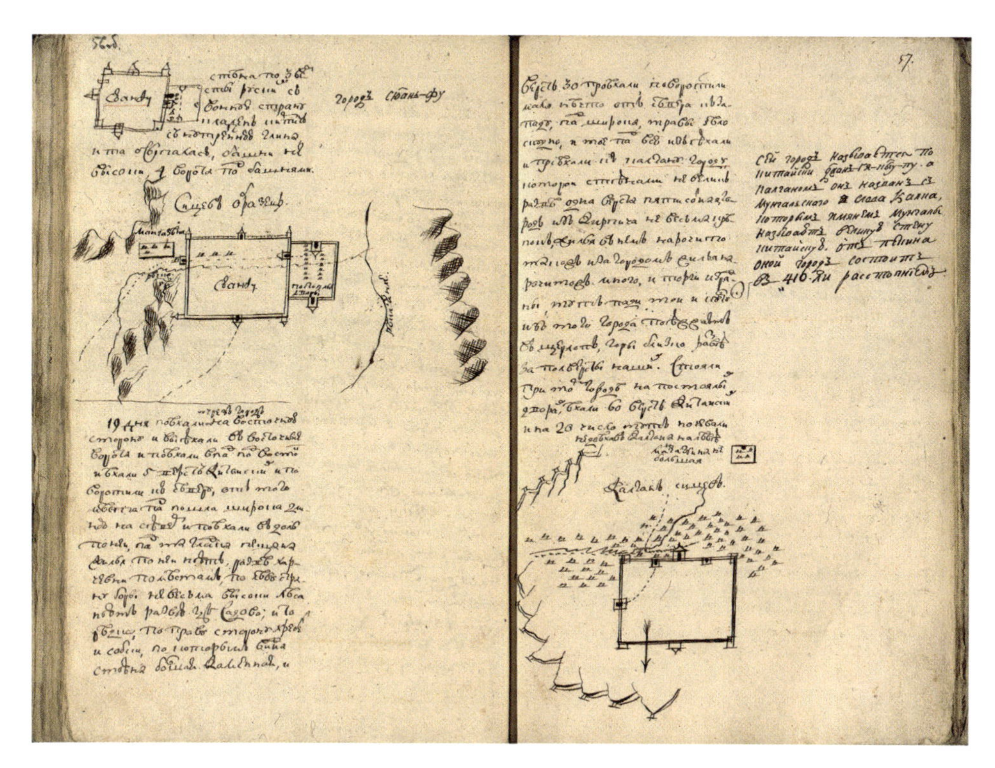

IMAGE 11.1 Sketch of Great Wall fortresses, 1736.

where and to where they flow, describe all this thoroughly and map it . . . While doing so this [he] is to conduct himself in an artful and secret fashion so that the Qing cannot discover or learn about this task from anyone or bear the slightest suspicion." Images like the ones here were part of a fabric of textual and visual information gathered in secret with an eye to strategic advantage. At the same time, the journal also included more miscellaneous information. For instance, alongside the images was a translation of a "Chinese song" about solitary geese, as well as details about fairs, hot springs, and religious institutions.[3]

Intelligence gathering was a common preoccupation for states in this era. It was important to know not only the military dispositions of competing powers, but also to delve into their political and social intricacies. In fact, one of the main roles of ambassadors across Europe was to make contact with local informants and recruit spies to collect information. Russia had no permanent ambassador in Beijing, but it did have students and missionaries, along with caravan employees, charged with these sorts of tasks.

Why was Russia so interested in Chinese secrets? Over the course of the seventeenth century, the borders of the Muscovite empire had grown eastward, from

IMAGE 11.2 Sketch of a Buddhist shrine, Chinese (or Manchu) soldiers, and a Korean merchant, 1736.

western Siberia to the Pacific Ocean. Although in some places Russian troops met fierce resistance from Indigenous people, there was no state capable of stalling the Russian advance—until Russian explorers burned and looted their way into what they called Dauria, a territory that would later be known as the Russian Far East. These lands adjoined the traditional heartland of the Qing dynasty in Manchuria, and the Russian incursions provoked armed response from the Manchus. After several rounds of bitter warfare, Russia renounced its claims to the region.

Eighteenth-century Russia hardly had any immediate intention of starting a new war with China. Siberia was too poor and too difficult to supply. Trying to field a substantial army there, given the difficulties of concentrating food and animals in sufficient quantities, was too onerous. Frontier administrators, however, believed that it was still important for the Russian Empire to keep tabs on its neighbor, and to be alert for opportunities to exploit ethnic tensions and other sources of weakness.

By the time these images were created, Russia and China had been at a standoff for years. In 1689, they signed the Treaty of Nerchinsk—the first such agreement China had ever signed with a European power. Gradually, trade developed, at first mostly through private merchants, and later through a state monopoly. Massive groups of officials, camels, and horses carried hundreds of thousands of pelts east through Siberia, south past the Mongolian border, and across the Great Wall to Beijing. There, they were exchanged—often at unfavorable rates—for tea, silk, tobacco, porcelain, rhubarb, and other commodities. (The rhubarb Russians bought from China wasn't the pie filling we know it as, but a very expensive root used to treat gout and similar diseases. The Russians sold most of their rhubarb onward to western Europe, where it was eagerly consumed by elite western Europeans in need of a purgative for their lavish diets.)

The main customers of Chinese luxuries were Russian rulers and courtiers. The imperial court had first pick of these products and often gave very specific instructions for what was to be purchased in the Qing capital. The custom of drinking tea out of porcelain cups, served with sugar (another imperial good), was a growing lifestyle habit of wealthy—and increasingly even middle-class—Europeans, and Russians were beginning to emulate them. They also decorated their palaces with "Chinese-style" art and artifacts, part of a European-wide trend known as chinoiserie. In other words, buying Chinese goods was paradoxically an emblem of the growing Westernization of Russian elites.

But the caravan wasn't just a source of commercial income. It also provided the Russian state with an opportunity to gather information about its rival. As the caravan made its way through Qing territory, members of its staff took careful note of the water sources, weather, terrain, and human geography of the lands through which they passed. In the event the Russians ever needed to invade China, this information would be enormously valuable for the logistics of moving and feeding an expeditionary force. That was where the plans of Great Wall forts fit in—once a potential army reached them, it would need to figure out how to lay siege to them, and images made the process much easier. Once the caravan arrived in Beijing, its members fanned out to gather information of all kinds, from buying the secret of porcelain-making to copying an important collection of imperial maps.

Including the Buddhist temple and the Korean merchant in these images was one way for the Russian intelligence-gatherers to signal that they were aware the Qing state was multiethnic. The Korean's image, for instance, is labeled "The Kou-li, who have their own lord, live under the protection of the Chinese [or rather Manchu] khan and come to Beijing to trade; this image is a true depiction of them, and they like to wear white." At this point, the Manchus had only held power in China for less than a century, but they had already put in place the foundations of the multiethnic order that would define the remainder of their time in power, which would end in 1911. Although members of the so-called Eight Banners—the Manchu bannermen—held privileged positions in the state hierarchy, Han Chinese, Mongol, Tibetan, and other non-Manchu elites were also highly influential in the empire.[4] The banners themselves incorporated non-Manchu elements, including the Albazinians, a community of Russian origin who had been captured and integrated into the system during the conflict of the 1680s. They were allowed, and even encouraged, to practice Orthodox Christianity; in fact, caring for their spiritual welfare was one of the pretexts that allowed Russia to maintain an Orthodox mission in Beijing. This was because the Qing emperor derived legitimacy from his patronage of different faiths: Buddhist, Daoist, and Muslim clergy also had important roles to play in the empire, as did Catholic missionaries.[5]

Russia itself was, of course, also a multiethnic state. The official personnel of the caravan included not just Russian speakers but also German and Swedish people, and in its long journey from Moscow, it relied on services from nomads like the Buryats (relatives of the Mongols) and Evenki (reindeer herders related to the Manchus), along with other frontier communities. This reflected the heterogeneity of Russia's ruling elite, which heavily relied on foreign experts and educated German-speaking nobles, as well as the diversity of its Siberian colony, where ethnic Russians were in the minority.

Each empire perceived its neighbor's diversity as a source of geopolitical advantage. Russians exploited the religious connections between the Russian-subject Buryats and the Qing-subject Mongols for the purposes of intelligence-gathering. By the middle of the eighteenth century, they would develop an extensive network of agents across northern Mongolia, including Buddhist lamas and monastery serfs. Meanwhile, Qing officials were in contact with frontier peoples that Russia also claimed as subjects.

These images are thus a reminder of the complexities of what we know as Orientalism, or the complex of ideas through which "the East" was constructed as the civilizational opposite of "the West"—backward where the latter was advanced, feminine where the latter was masculine, and so forth.[6] In the eighteenth century, Russians did not yet approach the Qing from a vantage point that emphasized civilizational inferiority, though they were certainly aware that they were looking at a different culture. Only later, in the nineteenth century, did they come to think of China as defined by its lack of Western civilization. Russian visual depictions of the Chinese became more similar to western European ones, and Russian scholars drew on British sources to argue that China had an inefficient economy and a decrepit state apparatus.

These differences come out starkly in comparing the caravan sketches to those produced by the painter and missionary A. M. Legashov in the mid-nineteenth century. Legashov, who achieved a degree of renown and whose paintings have been exhibited in the Russian Museum in St. Petersburg and other collections, produced a series of Chinese landscapes and portraits, such as this depiction of a "Chinese town" from 1864 (Image 11.3).[7] Although these images belong to different genres, we can point out what details the artists chose to focus on. Legashov's landscapes clearly draw inspiration from the ruined vistas of European painters like Hubert Robert, which depict common people herding animals in the ruins of vast classical structures. Legashov prominently features goats and donkeys cohabiting with people, and even this putatively urban environment is overgrown with vegetation.

IMAGE 11.3 A. M. Legashov, "Chinese town," 1864.

The only sign of China as a formidable military power are the unmanned battlements in the background; otherwise, it appears entirely unthreatening. Meanwhile, although Legashov's portraits are technically very precise, he pays little attention to the ethnic differences between Chinese, Manchus, and Mongols—all seem to wear the same outfits.

By contrast, the eighteenth-century caravan images clearly depict China as a military threat. Every detail of the soldiers' armor and weaponry is carefully picked out. One of the soldiers carries a gun, a bow, a sword, and a spear. His image is captioned "A Chinese soldier with all his weaponry, we saw regiments with this equipment in Beijing, where we witnessed them standing in formation." Likewise, although the journal notes the decrepit condition of some Chinese fortifications, they are clearly depicted as occupying strategically significant locations amid impassable mountains. Here, Chinese walls are objects of military concern rather than exotic background details.

Legashov and the artist of these sketches occupied structurally very similar positions—one was a missionary and the other a caravan official, but they were in China on roughly the same basis. Both were sent at least in part to gather intelligence. Thus, the shift from depicting China as a powerful military rival to seeing it as an exotic setting for a romanticized pastoral lifestyle is significant. It helps us understand how Orientalist ideas changed the terms on which the two empires encountered one another between the eighteenth and nineteenth centuries.

NOTES

1. Institute of Oriental Manuscripts, St. Petersburg, AO, fond 7, op. 1, d. 38, l. 37–38.
2. Russian State Archive of Ancient Documents (RGADA), Moscow, fond 199, op. 1, d. 349, ch. 2, l. 31–57.
3. RGADA, fond 248, op. 113, d. 485a, l. 109–111.
4. A good introduction to Qing history is William Rowe, *China's Last Empire: The Great Qing* (Cambridge, MA: Belknap Press, 2009).
5. See Eric Widmer, *The Russian Ecclesiastical Mission in Peking during the Eighteenth Century* (Cambridge, MA: Harvard University Press, 1976).
6. The term comes from Edward Said's classic *Orientalism,* first published in 1978.
7. N. A. Samoilov, "Kitai v proizvedeniiakh rossiiskikh khudozhnikov XVIII-XIX vekov," *Vestnik Rossiiskogo gumanitarnogo nauchnogo fonda* 82, no. 1 (2016). https://www.elibrary.ru/item.asp?id=26126255

CHAPTER 12

A "COMPLETE" ATLAS OF THE RUSSIAN EMPIRE (1745)

CATHERINE EVTUHOV

THE AUSTERE TITLE page of the 1745 *Atlas of the Russian Empire*—simple block letters in red and black—proclaimed an ambitious goal. Published in nineteen regional maps and a general map of "this great" empire (Image 12.1), the atlas promised to unite "geographical rules" and "new observations" to create a complete picture of the All-Russian Empire and contiguous lands.[1] The imprimatur of the Imperial Academy of Sciences imparted sufficient weight to make fancy illustrations and inscriptions unnecessary. Nonetheless, as the pages unfurl, we are greeted by the magnificent expanse of Eurasia from the Baltic Sea to the Pacific Ocean, adorned with the imperial seal, images of naval ships and whaling vessels, and, emphatically indicated, the newly discovered stretch of water separating Chukotka from Alaska. The regional maps depict Russia's districts (*uezdy*) and include the Kazan and Astrakhan khanates and the private domains of the Stroganov family. The hydrographic component—rivers, lakes, wetlands—is carefully represented; the six maps of Siberia are scaled smaller to accommodate the vast distances.

This Enlightenment-era atlas seems strikingly different from the tentative and geographically limited seventeenth-century sketches of Blaeu or Massa, or from Semyon Remezov's ebullient and ambitious *Map of All Siberia*.[2] The *Atlas of the Russian Empire* visually encapsulates the Enlightenment urge to scientific measurement and representation. The maps look different because their dominant concern is to arrange their materials around points whose exact location has been astronomically and geographically determined, and to bring the images on the flat paper maps into as close a relation as possible to the spheroid shape of the earth. Still, the cartographers preserved some of their Muscovite predecessors' fondness for pictorial detail, as evidenced, for example, by the trees, extravagant cityscapes, and fire-breathing mountains—all in miniature—that also grace the Atlas' pages.

The formation of the illustrious cartographic team coincided exactly with the early history of the Imperial Academy of Sciences, founded at St. Petersburg on the eve of Peter I's death in 1725. As in many spheres of European life during the eighteenth

IMAGE 12.1 "General Map of the Russian Empire," 1745.

century, expertise was valued above nationality, and the team brought together French, German, Dutch, and Russian explorers and cartographers. In this sense, the project reflected the spirit of Enlightenment cosmopolitanism. Invited by Peter in 1721, and finally arriving in March 1726, the talented French astronomer Joseph-Nicolas Delisle (1688–1768) was charged with establishing an observatory in St. Petersburg, and with crafting "a general map of the Russian Empire using the Delisle method of matching astronomical observations with measurements from travelers."[3] Delisle was soon joined by his older brother, Louis Delisle de la Croyère (1685–1741).[4] The brilliant Swiss mathematician Leonhard Euler (1707–1783), having received a coveted appointment to the Academy in 1726, would head in 1735 the newly created Geographical Department.[5] And the Atlas would not have been the same without venerable Senate clerk Ivan Kirilovich Kirilov (1689–1737), who, while not as sophisticated in mathematics or astronomy as the European specialists, brought practical expertise in navigation and surveying. His insistence on older mapmaking techniques, with rivers and roads as the foundation, proved productive for charting little-known territories.[6] Never a member of the Academy, Kirilov was appointed head of the Orenburg expedition by Empress Anna in 1734. He simultaneously launched a fantastically ambitious project of his own: a complete atlas of the empire in three volumes of 120 maps each. Just thirty-seven of these maps were published before his death in 1737.[7]

Contributing to the Atlas was a vast staff of trained geodesists (specialists in mathematical study of the shape of the earth), draftsmen, surveyors, and engravers.

Among them were the anonymous geodesists dispatched, two per province, throughout the empire in the late 1720s: thirty such specialists were trained in the early days of the Academy. While such initial efforts produced spotty results at best, the famous Kamchatka Expeditions, led by the Danish explorer Vitus Bering (1681–1741), were far more productive and mobilized up to 600 men at a given moment. De la Croyère, whose key astronomical observations during the Second Kamchatka Expedition (1733–1743) enabled the mapping of Siberia, traveled together with naturalist Johann Georg Gmelin (1709–1755) and ethnographer and historian Gerhard Friedrich Müller (1705–1783), as well as a team that included six students, an interpreter, five surveyors, and one instrumentmaker (all Russian), along with a painter and a draftsman (both German).[8]

Scientific and mathematical principles stood at the Atlas' core, with two scientific conversations particularly vital. The first was the determination of a sufficient number of latitudes and longitudes on the vast, literally uncharted territory, which was theoretically simple but practically challenging. Finding one's way on planet Earth has always been a function of the heavens: the North Star (or, in the southern hemisphere, the Southern Cross) operated as a stable point of reference for mariners and travelers. A simple triangulation, using a basic cross-staff or even just a piece of wood and a cord, sufficed to determine latitude. Longitude was more complicated. It required a comparison of local with standard time, based on a very accurate (and physically transportable) chronometer, or complex calculations of celestial events or magnetic variation. Italian Renaissance cartographers, working in the Mediterranean and drawing upon the maps of ancient Greeks and Egyptians, envisioned imaginary lines horizontally and vertically encircling the globe; in Russia in the early eighteenth century, despite the earlier exploration and conquest of Siberia, virtually no specific latitudes and longitudes had been measured.

The first thing Delisle did upon the completion of the observatory was to determine exactly the latitude and longitude of St. Petersburg. With its precise location now reliably fixed, St. Petersburg became ground zero, or the reference point for mapping the empire. The precise coordinates of Arkhangelsk followed.[9] When the Second Kamchatka Expedition concluded in 1743, the cartographers had complete data, based on new astronomical observations, for eight additional points: Kazan, Irkutsk, two Siberian log forts (*ostrogi*) at Kirensk and Olekminsk, Iakutsk, and the Petropavlovsk harbor near the southern tip of the Kamchatka peninsula. Latitudes, as mentioned, were easier. The Atlas boasted a table of sixty-two locations—towns, forts, or monasteries—whose latitudes were based on new measurements. The rest was a matter of geometry: locations on the map of Smolensk province and the surrounding region were based on the triangle of Kyiv, St. Petersburg, and Moscow; "Little Tataria" on Kyiv, Ochakov, and Azov; and for the Siberian map, on several overlapping triangles connecting Arkhangelsk, Kazan, Solikamsk, and Tobolsk.

The simplicity of the task, and the spare elegance of its representation on the map, belies the physical obstacles that needed to be overcome to accomplish it. De la Croyère's traveling partner, Gmelin, gives us a tactile sense of the daily adventures the scientists experienced in their decade-long voyage. It took the group several months to make it from St. Petersburg to Tver (about 300 miles), where they began their river trip to Kazan (about 600 miles). They managed to lose contact with the boat carrying their group and supplies, tracking it down only as they approached Kazan. Winter brought temperatures of −40° and lower, winds that froze their tea before they had time to lift the cup, and quarters in dark and windowless shacks. Summers were hot, and the mosquitoes and bugs made it impossible to write, even while fully hooded and wearing gloves. The cockroaches, which Gmelin can't help calling *Tarakanen* (using the Russian word) in acknowledgment of their fierceness, were ubiquitous. The travelers wended their way through nearly impenetrable forests and forded fast-flowing rivers. Local guides could get lost, and were sometimes unaware of recent changes in the landscape. Horses needed to be fed, and were sometimes so exhausted that they slowed the pace of the journey. On one occasion, Gmelin was forced to retrace his steps in loyalty to the dangerously ill Müller, losing a full ten days. The house he rented in Tomsk during the winter of 1741 burned to the ground, though he was able to salvage a small barrel of now smoky Rhine wine. As for de la Croyère, the Frenchman grew impatient with his colleagues' fascination with local industry and ethnography, and he left the group to press on to Tobolsk to take his astronomical measurements.[10] The struggle with nature, and the conquest of sheer technical difficulties, were hallmarks of mapping the empire's eastern expanses.

With longitudes and latitudes determined, how would they be drawn on paper? The second major scientific conversation embodied in the Atlas regards the shape of the earth. While its generally spherical nature was accepted, was it really more oval than strictly round, and were the poles somewhat flattened?[11] The strategy for the Atlas was highly conscious, and involved a philosophical understanding of the relation of parts to the whole. The maps do not all represent space in the same way. For the general map of the empire, Delisle adopted a modified conic projection, which had the advantage of preserving scale.[12] The empire's spread across Eurasia, from St. Petersburg to Kamchatka, was therefore a reasonable approximation of its shape on a globe—or in our day on Google Earth. In contrast, the maps of the European parts of the empire are drafted using a simple grid, where the meridians and parallels—the lines representing longitude and latitude, respectively—are presumed to be at right angles. This was a considered decision. In regional maps, where the area covered is not so great, a grid more clearly indicates distances and is therefore more useful for travel; the distortions are not significant. Finally, the six Siberian maps were distinguished not only by the difference in scale, but by their use, once more, of a conic projection. It is a remarkable illustration of the need to employ global mapping techniques for truly large spaces, and even more important, of the capacity to represent the Eurasian space in a way that could be integrated into a global map. The cartographers were obsessed with Siberia, where accurate new observations were necessary in order to draft any semblance of a map that could have meaning beyond the purely local.

An interesting clue in this regard is provided by the world map drafted by Guillaume Delisle, the brothers' father, at Paris in 1700. Eastern Siberia (as well as middle and western North America) is honestly and touchingly represented as a completely blank space. The Siberian expedition was the family's contribution to a complete map of the world.[13]

The mathematically clear lines of the final product conceal another major task. The Atlas team incorporated not only new scientific data, but also made a thorough study of preexisting regional maps. Sources included Chinese, Mongolian, and Jesuit maps; charts of the Don, Volga, and Siberian rivers; new maps of Livland and Kurland; maps of the Russian-Swedish and Russian-Ottoman borders; and so on.[14] These materials, originally drafted using a variety of techniques and with diverging ends in mind, were reconfigured to fit the mathematically calculated lines and curves of the meridians and parallels.

Yet scientific principles are not all that was reflected in these Enlightenment-era maps. The mapmakers seem loathe to abandon the pictorial richness of the Muscovite maps. They retain extremely reduced icons of important features, such as forests, villages, and monasteries, with a new, added attention to industrial sites, notably factories and key resources like ores or salt. And the Atlas inherited from the Muscovite tradition an obsession with one geographic feature: rivers, which occupy a special place in the cartographers' vision. This was mostly Kirilov's contribution. While he agreed with the ultimate goal of thorough astronomical observations, Kirilov believed that, pending the training of enough qualified geodesists, rivers and roads could provide the most reliable means of determining location. Rivers could be followed like natural roads or pathways. Kirilov specifically advocated carefully tracing the Volga, Oka, Kama, Dvina, Dnipro, and Don, as well as the great Siberian rivers.[15] The Atlas contains a separate map of the Volga from Iaroslavl to Tsaritsyn, with a whimsical inset depicting the river's pescatorial riches in the shape of a large sturgeon. The practical element is very present, with bridges, crossings, portages, shallows, visible rocks, and hidden rocks indicated in the legend. Rivers doubled as resources and as means of transportation, and were represented as such.

The Atlas also carefully depicted mountains, "fire-throwing mountains" (Kamchatka), the steppe, and forests. On the maps of the Urals region, for example, we see little trees, each of which casts a small shadow—the lush forests of Muscovite maps reduced to a minimum representation. The Atlas paid special attention to natural resources and factories, in keeping with the practical and commercial orientation at the time. We see salt mines and salt lakes, and the iron forges and foundries of the Urals region—just on the verge of the explosion of production that catapulted the Russian Empire into its position as the primary iron exporter in Europe.

The representation of places of human habitation deserves special attention, and prompts the reflection that it must be very difficult to get used to having one's environment reduced to a black dot on a map. The Atlas uses no fewer than twenty different icons for inhabited places, including capital cities, fortresses, castles, merchant cities, provincial towns, stone and wood towns, bishoprics, monasteries, villages, settlements, and even ruins. We can be sure, for example, that Tobolsk is an important place, because even on the full imperial map, it boasts multiple buildings topped by a cross; on the regional map, a flag completes the picture. Perhaps most intriguing is the special designation for "Mohammedan villages"—a circle topped by a crescent. While Gmelin in his travel notes describes the mosques and religious rituals of the Tatars of Kazan and Tomsk in abundant detail, I searched in vain for such villages on the regional map. My hunt proved more successful further south—across the southern steppe border, outside the empire, in "Little Tataria" or Crimea. The peninsula is studded with the little crescents, and very impressive Muslim centers in places like Bağçasaray, Qarasuvbazar, and Aqmescit (the future Simferopol). How should we read this? A possible explanation is that, on the eve of the Atlas' publication, the government had launched a campaign to destroy the mosques in the Kazan region; in this context their depiction would have been politically sensitive.[16] Once one is on the territory of the "other," however, it is fine to show the Muslim landmarks on the map. We can note, in addition, that the map's careful conformity with contemporary scientific principles fails outside the imperial borders. Presumably, the geodesists did not have the opportunity to travel to the Tatar khan's domains to establish landmarks in the Crimean peninsula. Instead, we have a misshapen agglomeration with only vaguely correct contours, with even Bağçasaray only approximately situated.

The *Atlas of the Russian Empire* was twenty years in the making—not such a long time for an excruciatingly difficult project—and proved trying to physical health. Euler, citing failing eyesight, was forced to leave the project prior to its completion. He soon left Russia, too, for the perceived stability of Frederick II's Prussia, returning only after the end of the Seven Years' War. His last years were very productive and included some of his key ideas on cartographic theory, although he was almost completely blind. Kirilov died in 1737, and de la Croyère died upon returning from Kamchatka in 1741. Prolonged absence could be dangerous as well: when Joseph-Nicolas Delisle went off to Obdorsk (at the estuary of the Ob River) in 1740 to observe the transit of Mercury, he found himself replaced on his return. Still, the final atlas was submitted in his name.

The "complete" Atlas embodies the Enlightenment vision of empire. The maps unite the simple scientific principle of precise measurement of latitude and longitude with an extremely trying and difficult immersion in the frozen and impenetrably forested landscapes of Siberia. The cartographers made full use of the scientific laboratory that was the expanse of Russia.[17] Science and precision also extended to the drafting process. The cartographers were acutely aware of the difficulties of bringing regional maps together into a whole, and of preserving physical contours while not losing accurate distances. The project fused the pinnacle of European science with the natural expanses of Eurasia. The maps further represent a synthesis of scientific principles with the representational tendencies of earlier Muscovite maps. The final product made the Russian Empire available to global cartographers, inscribing this difficult region into the Enlightenment map of the world. At the same time, this international scientific collaboration served the interests of its imperial sponsors magnificently. With rigorous cartographic accuracy, it presented to the world an imposing visual image of the Russian Empire stretching across a significant part of the globe.

NOTES

1. *Atlas Rossiiskii, sostoiashchii iz deviatnadtsati spetsial'nykh kart predstavliaiushchikh Vserossiiskuiu Imperiiu s pogranichnymi zemliami, sochinennoi po pravilam Geograficheskim i noveishim observatsiiam, s prilozhennoi pritom general'noi kartoi velikoi sei Imperii, staraniem i trudami Imperatorskoi akademii nauk* (SPb, 1745).
2. Valerie Kivelson, "Early Mapping: The Tsardom in Manuscript," in *Information and Empire: Mechanisms of Communication in Russia 1600–1850*, edited by Simon Franklin and Katherine Bowers (Cambridge: Open Book, 2017), 23–57; 25, 48.
3. Monique Pelletier, "Delisle Family," in *The History of Cartography*, Vol. 4: *Cartography in the European Enlightenment*, edited by Matthew Edney and Mary Pedley (Chicago: Chicago University Press, 2019), 338–342; 342.
4. Karl Svenske, *Materialy dlia istorii sostavleniia Atlasa Rossiiskoi Imperii, izdannogo imperatorskoi Akademiei Nauk v 1745 godu* (SPb: 1866), 6.
5. Gerhard Holzer, "Euler, Leonhard," in Edney and Pedley, *History of Cartography*, 400. See also Ronald S. Calinger, *Leonhard Euler: Mathematical Genius in the Enlightenment* (Princeton: Princeton University Press, 2016).
6. Alexey V. Postnikov, "Kirilov, Ivan Kirilovich," in Edney and Pedley, *History of Cartography*, 713.
7. I. K. Kirilov, *Atlas Vserossiiskoi Imperii* (SPb, 1722–1737).
8. Johann Georg Gmelin, *Reise durch Sibirien* (Göttingen, 1751), 4 vols., v. 1:1.
9. Svenske, *Materialy*, 6–7.
10. Gmelin, *Reise*, v. 1:8, 50, 104, 117, 389, 413; v. 2:168; v. 4:3-9.
11. Matthew H. Edney and Nicholas Dew, "Geodesy and the Size and Shape of the Earth," in Edney and Pedley, *History of Cartography*, 433–438; 437.
12. On conic projections, see Joel L. Morrison and Michael Winter, "Projections used for Geographical Maps," in Edney and Pedley, *History of Cartography*, 1119–1126; 1121. Euler improved the projection in the 1770s; its use became increasingly widespread by 1800.
13. For Guillaume Delisle's map, see Edney and Pedley, *History of Cartography*, 340.
14. Svenske, *Materialy*, v-xii passim; and esp. 20, 31.
15. Svenske, *Materialy*, 28.
16. The campaign, which took place in 1743 and 1744, is recounted in N.I. Barsov, "Maloizvestnye russkie propovedniki XVIII veka," *Khristianskoe chtenie* 1874 no. 2, 247–86; no. 4, 575-623; citation on p. 610-611.
17. See Hans Vermeulen, *Before Boas: The Genesis of Ethnography and Ethnology in the German Enlightenment* (Lincoln: University of Nebraska Press, 2015).

CHAPTER 13

WHAT'S IN A HAT? REPRESENTATIONS OF ETHNICITY AND GENDER IN EIGHTEENTH-CENTURY RUSSIA

NATHANIEL KNIGHT

THERE WAS A wedding in the Cheremis village when the Second Kamchatka Expedition of the Imperial Academy of Sciences passed through in December 1733 en route from Kazan to Tobolsk. The villagers were decked out in their festive attire, and spirits flowed freely, providing the expedition leaders, naturalist Johann Georg Gmelin and historian Gerhard Friedrich Müller, a unique opportunity to observe the community at an unguarded moment.[1]

Any number of things at the village wedding might have drawn the attention of the researchers, yet little of the nuptial pageantry found its way into their descriptions. Lacking knowledge of the language or local culture and traditions, they viewed the events with the detachment of outsiders. As such, their attention was drawn toward the externalities, the visual elements expressing most clearly the distinctiveness of the Cheremis people (now known as the Mari). In particular, they focused on the villagers' attire, though not all garments were of equal interest. Men's outfits were judged to be "in the Russian style" and therefore unworthy of note. Elderly women also wore non-descript clothes similar to the Russians. The dress of the younger women, on the other hand, was sufficiently unique to warrant special attention.[2] In particular, Gmelin and Müller were drawn to one item, an unusual piece of headgear. The leaders brought in the expedition's artists, Johann Christian Berckhan and Johann Wilhelm Lürsenius, and the image of the unusual hat, along with its wearer, was recorded for posterity.

The Cheremis woman, looking neither young nor old, with rounded face and large but even features, stares toward the horizon beyond and to the right of the artist with head slightly turned to show her right ear (Image 13.1). Her embroidered dress, visible only at the collar, neckline, and hem, is largely concealed under a long gray *kaftan*

IMAGE 13.1 Cheremis woman. Engraving from G. F. Müller, *Opisanie zhivushchikh v Kazanskoi gubernii iazycheskikh narodov* (Description of the pagan peoples living in Kazan province), 1791.

(robe), belted with a cloth sash and open to the waist. She wears a coral necklace with two large medallions alongside and a pair of crescent-shaped, brass earrings adorned with double hanging coral pendants. Yet the jewelry and clothing are of secondary importance: what draws the viewer's eye is the woman's headdress. A conical elongated cylinder, the hat stretches almost a foot above the woman's forehead. The headdress was secured by two bands, one running from below the chin to the top of the head and the other extending across the forehead and around the back of the head. The cap itself was made from a birch bark core covered with canvas or leather. From the rear of the cap, a long, tapered canvas tail, shown in a second drawing, extends down past the knee. All surfaces of the headdress both front and back are decorated with small coins, metal pieces, shells, corals, and ribbons arranged in ascending rows.

Müller identifies the headdress as a *shurka*, one of the oldest artifacts associated with the Mari. As early as the mid-seventeenth century, it had been mentioned by European travelers in the region.[3] Similar to the high headdresses of neighboring Finnic peoples, particularly the Udmurt *aishan* and the *pango* of the Erza-Mordva, the *shurka* was worn by women in their early years of marriage, especially during the transitional period between the wedding and the birth of a child. Ethnographer Nina Gagen-Torn, in her 1960 monograph on women's costume of the Volga region, suggests that the obligatory covering of married women's hair, common to all the peoples of the Volga region, served to protect the husband's clan from the disruptive magic of the alien in-laws. Yet the Mari *shurka* did not cover the hair completely: strands were visible in the front under the cap. Gagen-Torn sees this as a relic of an ancient matriarchal order surviving among the Mari and Udmurts (Votiaks), the most permissive of the Volga peoples in enforcing the prohibition on uncovered hair.[4]

The image of the Cheremis woman wearing the *shurka* is one of a set of eight drawings listed in an inventory of items sent by the Second Kamchatka Expedition from Tobolsk to St. Petersburg in 1734, an early installment in what would prove to be a remarkably productive and multifaceted undertaking that continued for the next ten years and extended to the farthest reaches of the Eurasian landmass.[5] Aside from offering insights into the representation of ethnicity, these drawings serve as a case study in the dissemination of visual information in eighteenth-century Russia. Given the available technology, the original field sketches by Berckhan and Lürsenius could not be reproduced directly. Only by rendering them as engravings could they be disseminated. Thus, copying and alteration were intrinsic to the spread of visual material. The eight images appeared as engravings in the 1791 Russian edition of Müller's study of the non-Christian peoples of the Middle Volga region. Müller had originally drafted his work in late 1733, while the expedition was in Kazan, and the eight drawings were prepared at the time as illustrations. Müller published the text of his study in Russian and German in the late 1750s, but the illustrations were included only in the 1791 edition.

There is evidence, however, that the drawings were circulating well before the engravings appeared in Müller's text. Most notably, eight watercolors almost identical to the engravings published in 1791 appear in an unpublished album of ethnographic images from the Russian Empire housed in the Swedish National Museum in Stockholm (Image 13.2). The album is associated with the courtier Friedrich Wilhelm Bergholtz, who served as tutor to the future Peter III in the early 1740s

IMAGE 13.2 A Cheremis woman's costume from Kazan Province.

before being expelled from the Empire in 1746 along with his friend and fellow tutor Count Otto von Brümmer, both victims of palace intrigue. Bergholtz likely assembled the album, drawing on materials available from the Academy of Sciences, then brought the collection out of Russia in 1746 and passed it on to the Swedish crown, perhaps in exchange for a Swedish pension.[6] The eight drawings published in the 1791 Müller volume appear in the Bergholtz collection in the same order and are largely identical in costumes, poses, and physical features, differing only in the backgrounds and colors, which are lost in the engravings.[7] Both the Bergholtz watercolors and the engravings in the 1791 volume were most likely copies of original drawings that are now lost. In addition to the eight drawings of the Volga peoples, the Bergholtz collection contains 28 drawings from the Second Kamchatka Expedition evidently assembled by Müller as illustrations for a study on the peoples of Siberia. Altogether, the Bergholtz collection includes some 209 images depicting peoples of the southern steppe regions, Ukraine, the Baltic region, and Russia proper, in addition to the inhabitants of the Volga region and Siberia encountered during the Second Kamchatka Expedition.

Certain images in the Bergholtz collection appeared in various other venues in the middle decades of the eighteenth century. The French artist, Jean Baptiste LePrince, who resided in Russia from 1758 to 1762, produced several sets of engravings depicting Russian soldiers, clergy, and scenes from everyday life that closely correspond to images in the Bergholtz collection. LePrince's use of these earlier images, however, did not extend to the images related to the Second Kamchatka Expedition, including the eight images printed in Müller's 1791 volume. The eight images, including that of the Cheremis woman, do appear, joined together in a fanciful pastoral scene, in a pair of unsigned engravings published in 1768 as illustrations to the French translation of Gmelin's account of the expedition (Image 13.3).[8] The engravings are reminiscent of LePrince in their style, but there is no evidence to support a firm attribution. What is clear, however, is that an artist in the 1760s had access to the drawings prepared for Müller's study of the Volga peoples, and used them as the basis for an idyllic scene featuring vaguely identified "women of Siberia" wearing Cheremis and Chuvash headdresses.

A more direct connection can be drawn between the Müller volume, the Bergholtz collection, and the engravings of Christopher Roth, published in Johann Gottlieb Georgi's *Description of all the Peoples Inhabiting the Russian Empire*, the most iconic collection of ethnographic images from eighteenth century Russia. Roth, to be sure, took liberties in converting the original drawings into finished, hand-colored engravings. The facial features in Roth's rendition of the Cheremis woman, for example, bear little resemblance to the original. But the *shurka* is fully depicted, and the costume details as well as the pose leave no doubt that Roth derived his image from Müller's original (Image 13.4).

IMAGE 13.3 "Various Costumes of the Women of Siberia." Illustration in J. G. Gmelin's *Voyage au Kamtschatka par la Sibérie (Journey through Siberia)*, 1768.

IMAGE 13.4 "Cheremis Woman from the Front." Illustration in J. G. Georgi, *Opisanie vsekh obitaiushchikh v rossiiskom gosudarstve narodov* (*Description of all the peoples living in the Russian state*) 1799.

In addition to the eight drawings mentioned in the 1734 inventory, Roth used other images of Siberian peoples appearing in the Bergholtz collection, supporting the supposition that he had access to the original drawings. Müller himself noticed the correspondence and, in a later account of the Kamchatka Expedition, wrote, "the copper engraver Roth has obtained my drawings, I do not know how, from the Academy."[9] Roth was, in fact, employed as a copyist and engraver for the Academy, and as such, he would likely have had access to the Academy's visual materials. But if Roth made use of Müller's drawings, he may have been the last to do so. After the publication of Georgi's ethnographic compendium, images traceable directly to Müller's originals cease to appear, and no sign has been found of the drawings in the Russian archives. Roth's engravings, on the other hand, were broadly disseminated and copied. Among other things, they served as models for the famous collection of porcelain figurines depicting the peoples of the Russian Empire produced by the Imperial Russian Porcelain Works for Catherine the Great. While the *shurka* itself gradually fell out of favor among the Cheremis in the nineteenth century, replaced by less extravagant headgear, the image survived. In short, at the moment in December 1733 when a group of traveling scientists happened upon a Cheremis wedding and ordered a drawing of a women wearing an unusual hat, an image was created that would serve as an emblematic representation, a kind of visual shorthand denoting Mari identity. The Cheremis *shurka* was instantly recognizable and utterly distinctive, making it an ideal marker of ethnicity.

The remaining six drawings from the Volga-Kama region published in the 1791 Müller volume show a remarkable consistency in style and subject matter. All portray women, and all highlight a distinctive piece of headwear. The image of the Votiak (Udmurt) woman, for example, shows the *aishan*, a tall headdress ending in two points on either side with a large, fringed shawl draped over the top. Like the Cheremis *shurka*, the *aishan* became an emblem of Votiak identity, continuing to appear in ethnographic depictions well into the nineteenth century. The Chuvash woman is shown in separate images from front and back wearing the traditional married woman's embroidered headscarf, the *surpan*. The remaining three images of Kazan Tatars show women wearing various forms of the *kashpau*, a round cap decorated with small coins and adorned in the rear with a cloth strip hanging past the waist.[10]

Why would Müller and his associates place such importance on depictions of women and their headgear? They might, after all, have chosen to highlight any number of items associated with the everyday life of the Volga peoples. The expedition did, in fact, collect artifacts—handicrafts, tools, weapons, articles of clothing, and so on—which were sent back to the Kunstkamera, the museum of the Academy of Sciences, for further study and preservation. As the expedition continued, a more diverse range of objects and individuals began to appear in the drawings. Yet women's costume retained its prominence. Of the images in the Bergholtz collection associated with the Second Kamchatka Expedition, more than half (22 out of 34) consist of full-length portraits of young women from front and back meticulously recording the details of attire, particularly headwear.

This disproportionate attention to women's headwear may have reflected the expedition leaders' broader sense of purpose. Trained in the emerging enlightenment methodologies of the natural sciences and philology, scholars like Gmelin and Müller viewed their research as a process of description, comparison, categorization, and classification, aimed at defining distinct collective units, analogous to species in the natural sciences, and situating them in relation to one another. When discussing human populations, "peoples" were the primary units of classification and analysis. Müller referred to this scholarly endeavor as *völkerbeschreibung*, the description of peoples.[11] Yet peoples, Müller understood, often shared more similarities than differences, and not all elements were of equal value in determining identity. In his research instructions to his fellow explorers, Müller delineated a broad range of cultural features worthy of observation, but placed special emphasis on language as the element denoting most clearly ethnic distinctiveness.[12] Initially, Müller relied on parallel translations of the Lord's Prayer as a framework for comparative linguistic analysis, but he soon turned to lists of core vocabulary compiled in various languages as a means for identifying and classifying distinct peoples.[13] Once grouped by language, peoples could then be subdivided on the basis of additional criteria, such as the distinction between sedentary and nomadic lifestyles. While traits common to various groups were noted, the emphasis on the distinctiveness of peoples remained paramount.[14]

Differences between peoples could be conveyed through textual description and linguistic analysis, but how could these distinctions be expressed visually? Physical traits were of limited use. Facial features and complexion might denote racial identity, distinguishing European from Asian peoples, for instance, but they lacked the specificity to distinguish between related ethnic groups, such as the Cheremis and Votiaks. Drawings from the Second Kamchatka Expedition depict individuals whose features cannot be readily generalized to entire groups. Roth, on the other hand, abandons the attempt to convey individuality entirely in favor of a kind of generic homogeneity. As Elena Vishlenkova points out, it was things, more than people, that signaled group identity in the ethnographic images of the eighteenth century.[15]

The drawings from the Second Kamchatka Expedition convey some information regarding lifestyle. In Müller's engravings and the Bergholtz watercolors, houses in the background are used to denote a sedentary lifestyle, while nomads are often shown on horseback or in front of yurts or chums (tipis). These symbolic representations, however, are of little help in identifying particular peoples. Clothing and accessories were a more effective means to express ethnic identity, but not all garments were distinctive. All eight figures in the Müller engravings wear long *kaftans*, colored brown and gray in the Bergholtz watercolors, that are largely indistinguishable. It was primarily the decorative elements of costume that ethnographers and artists turned to as accurate representations of ethnicity.

Women's headdresses were especially rich in such decorative elements. This aesthetic richness may reflect their symbolic and practical roles. If, as Gagen-Torn suggests, headdresses and the objects that adorned them served a protective function, then the role of coins, corals, and other ornaments as amulets may explain the lavishness and intricacy of the decoration. In addition, headwear marked the status of women, distinguishing between unmarried and married women of childbearing age, thus maintaining the stability of the patriarchal order. In the preindustrial era, when clothing of all sorts was produced in the home, traditions and techniques of decoration and design were elements of shared culture, practiced in common within linguistic communities and serving as emblems of collective belonging. Women who created and wore these distinctive articles of headwear, in accordance with their local traditions, became bearers of identity for the whole. Ethnicity, thus, had a gendered component that is often overlooked. Feminized representations of the nation, so familiar to scholars of modernity, may well have deeper historical roots in the material culture of peasant societies.

NOTES

1. I would like to thank Hee-Gwone Yoo, Senior Librarian for Reference at the New York Public Library, and the staff of the Swedish National Museum in Stockholm for invaluable assistance in attaining images. Han Vermeulen of the Max Planck Institute for Social Anthropology and Wieland Hintzsche of the University of Leipzig made available key sources, and Edward Kasinec set the entire project in motion.
2. J. G. Gmelin, *Reise durch Sibirien von dem Jahr 1733 bis 1743, Theil 1.* (Göttengen, 1751), 94–98, See also G. F. Miller, *Opisanie zhivushchikh v Kazanskoi gubernii iazycheskikh narodov . . .* (St. Petersburg: Imperial Academy of Sciences, 1791) 98–103.
3. Miller, *Opisanie,* 18.
4. Nina Ivanovna Gagen-Torn, *Zhenskaia odezhda narodov Povolzh'ia* (Cheboksary: Chuvashgosizdat, 1960), 144, 182–185, 197.
5. Wieland Hintzsche, ed., *Dokumente zur 2. Kamčatkaexpedition—Akademiegruppe; Quellen zur Geschichte Sibiriens und Alaskas aus russischen Archiven,* Bd. 5 (Halle: Franckesche Stiftungen, 2006), 281.
6. Björn H Hallström, *Russian Architectural Drawings in the National Museum* (Stockholm: Victor Pettersons Bokindustri AB, 1963).
7. Nathaniel Knight and Edward Kasinec, "Faces of Russia's Empire: The Bergholtz Collection of Ethnographic Images from the Early 18th Century at the Swedish National Museum," *Baltic Worlds* 14, no. 1–2 (April 2021): 86–97.
8. J. G. Gmelin, "Voyage au Kamtschatka par la Sibérie: Journal de M. Gmelin, traduit de l'Allemagne," in *Continuation de L'Histoire générale des voyages ou collection Nouvelles,* t. 18 (Paris: Chez Rozet, 1768), 100–103.
9. *Materialy dlia istorii Imperatorskoi Akademii Nauk.* (Sankt Petersburg, 1885-1900), t. 6, 409-410.
10. Gagen-Torn, *Zhenskaia odezhda,* 200–205.
11. Han Vermeulen, *Before Boas, The Genesis of Ethnography and Ethnology in the German Enlightenment* (Lincoln: University of Nebraska Press, 2015), 170.
12. Vermeulen, *Before Boas,* 169–170; Gudrun Bucher: "Von Beschreibung der Sitten und Gebräuche der Völcker," in *Die Instruktionen Gerhard Friedrich Müllers und ihre Bedeutung für die Geschichte der Ethnologie und der Geschichtswissenschaft* (Stuttgart: Franz Steiner Verlag, 2002), 106.
13. Müller, *Opisanie,* 81–101.
14. Vermeulen, *Beyond Boas,* 186–194. See also Yuri Slezkine, "Naturalists vs Nature: Eighteenth Century Russian Scholars Confront Ethnic Diversity," in *Russia's Orient* (Bloomington: Indiana University Press, 1997), 46–48.
15. Elena Vishlenkova, *Vizual'noe narodovedenie imperii, ili 'uvidet Russkogo dano ne kazhdomu'* (Moscow: Novoe Literaturnoe Obozrenie, 2011), 51–52.

CHAPTER 14

ANNUSHKA, THE KALMYK (c. 1767)

ALISON K. SMITH

THE FIGURE AT the center of the multilayered portrait *Annushka, the Kalmyk* immediately seizes the viewer's attention with her direct gaze and hint of a smile (Image 14.1). She is dressed at the heights of mid-eighteenth-century European fashion: the dramatic red of her stiff, boned bodice set off by intricate white lace at cuff and collar, the folds of a skirt bunched behind; more lace and blue velvet ribbon decorating a delicate bonnet, an earring set with a pale blue gem picking up the color; a jet bracelet around one wrist. She sits on a seat upholstered in a fine green fabric, a brocade or perhaps a patterned velvet. Her face is youthful, and her black hair is powdered. She is in every way a perfect example of eighteenth-century European high style. Of course, the figure also seizes the viewer's attention because of who she is. This exemplar of eighteenth-century style is evidently Asian. This portrait, therefore, also poses a series of questions: not only who she is, but also how did she come to be in such surroundings, in such clothing, in this place, and at this time?

The answers begin in the portrait within the portrait. The young woman holds a sheet of paper engraved with a second portrait, this one identified. The text tells us that this second woman is "the Countess Barbara Cheremettoff, Lady of Honor to her Majesty, Empress [of All the] Russias," and names an artist: "J. Argounow." The countess wears a pin on which the faint outlines of a third portrait, perhaps the empress, perhaps a family member, are just barely visible. Barbara Cheremettoff, or, rather, Varvara Alekseevna Sheremeteva, née Cherkasskaia, was the wealthiest noblewoman in the Russian empire, in part through her own inheritance and in part through that of her husband, Petr Borisovich Sheremetev. Their wealth was measured above all in the numbers of souls, or serfs, that they owned: thousands upon thousands, in villages large and small throughout European Russia. The painter, J. Argounow, more properly Ivan Argunov, was one of those serfs, educated as an artist, in demand as a portraitist, but living out his life in bondage.

All of this means that understanding this painting, and the figure at its center, requires grappling with the interconnected themes of serfdom, empire, and race. In contrast to histories of the Atlantic world, where slavery, race, and empire have been understood as tightly intertwined, these themes are rarely linked in studies of tsarist

IMAGE 14.1 *Annushka, the Kalmyk*, by Ivan Argunov, c. 1767.

Russia.[1] Serfdom is portrayed as something that happened to Russians, and although the wider imperial expanses of the tsarist state had their own stories of differential freedoms, they are rarely incorporated into the same narratives. Race, too, was long discounted in histories of tsarist Russia. "Foreign" nobles could become "Russian," the story went, if they converted to Orthodoxy, somehow proving the absence of racialized thinking in the Empire. In fact, that version of Russia's imperial story was part of Varvara Alekseevna's ancestry. Her great grandfather Uruskan was born into a leading Circassian family, one of the peoples of the North Caucasus. He took the name Iakov and converted to Orthodoxy upon entering the service of Tsar Mikhail Fedorovich in the seventeenth century. The tsar even served as his godfather, and later named him a boyar (noble).[2]

The story of Annushka, as the young woman in the portrait was known, could be read as part of this same story of race not really mattering and empire built on cooperation rather than violence. In fact, calling her Annushka, an affectionate version of the name Anna, is, in part, reading her story as exactly that, a story of family and love. This is the story that was told by later Sheremetevs, and those whose view of the past fell under their influence. In these versions of her story, she "lived in the count's home as a member of the family," and "she loved her adopted family, and they loved her."[3] This version, however, is incomplete. There probably was real affection in her story, but that affection does not negate, but rather complicates, the realities of unfreedom and inequality that also governed her life, just as they governed the lives of millions of subjects of the tsarist empire.

The painting first of all invites the viewer to ask how a figure like Annushka came to be in Moscow to be painted by Ivan Argunov, perhaps the greatest portraitist of eighteenth-century Russia. Her exact travels cannot be known, but some things can be guessed. Annushka was a Kalmyk, relative newcomers to the lands of the Russian Empire who first appeared on the southern Volga in the early seventeenth century. Tibetan Buddhists by belief, they were no pacifists, but instead posed a violent disruption to the lives of the Orthodox and Muslim inhabitants of the borderlands of Muscovy. They came to play a role in the machinations between powers vying for control over the steppe—Muscovy, Poland, Crimea—and to struggle with and against the groups trying to maintain a degree of autonomy there—Cossacks, Bashkirs, Nogais. Eventually, they entered into agreements with the Muscovite state, as subjects in the minds of Moscow's officials, but as allies in the minds of the Kalmyk elite. This was an unstable relationship, though, and these agreements shifted over the decades as other powers on the steppe waxed and waned.[4] The relationship changed even more in the eighteenth century as Muscovy became the Russian Empire and grew less willing to accept an uncontrolled borderland to its south. Increased fortifications and settlement pushing south into the steppe greatly disrupted the nomadic world of the Kalmyks by taking away their pasturelands bit by bit. When the Kalmyk khan Ayuki died in 1724, St. Petersburg began to take a more active role in Kalmyk affairs, promoting and supporting various candidates for khan, thereby dividing the Kalmyk elite.

When, precisely, Annushka was sent, taken, or fled from Kalmyk lands is unclear—and as this variety of verbs suggests, so, too, is the precise reason for her arrival in the Russian metropole. There was a longer history of Kalmyk "fugitives" seeking refuge in Russian towns—a treaty between Moscow and the Kalmyks in the middle of the seventeenth century included a clause promising to return such fugitives to the Kalmyks, assuming that they had not converted to Orthodoxy.[5] The profound disruptions of the 1730s and 1740s brought about by greater Russian interference also led to an exodus of Kalmyks from the region. Although some Kalmyks came to Moscow or St. Petersburg of their own volition, others were brought by force. In the middle of the eighteenth century, Cossacks regularly raided Kalmyk camps, taking money, livestock, rugs—and children. In one case from 1754, a baptized Kalmyk, Andrei Grigor'ev, complained to the sovereign about the ataman (leader) of the Don Cossacks, Stepan Efremov. According to Grigor'ev, the ataman had kidnapped his twelve-year-old daughter, Pelageia, the previous winter. When questioned about the case, Efremov had a simple answer to why he had taken Pelageia: "the court of Her Imperial Majesty has a need for boys and girls of Kalmyk origin."[6]

Indeed, starting in Empress Anna's reign, acquiring Kalmyk children for household service became fashionable in the Russian metropoles, perhaps as a symbol, conscious or not, of Russia's control over its wider empire. Records from elite noble households in the 1730s and 1740s show that Tatars and Kalmyks appeared regularly as household servants.[7] While some of them may have come to Moscow or St. Petersburg seeking service, others were brought to the capitals to be given as gifts or sold. In the 1760s, this practice received official approval when Pelageia's abduction from her family was pardoned "in light of the fact that these Kalmyk children were taken to the imperial court, and not for [the ataman's] own service."[8] Annushka was possibly one such Kalmyk child taken to the Russian court and given as a gift.

This is the general context in which Annushka arrived in the Russian metropole, but the portrait poses another question: Why was she painted in this particular way? The portrait suggests a loving relationship, Annushka carefully holding up the image of Varvara Alekseevna. Such a reading agrees with the way that Varvara Alekseevna's great-grandson wrote of their relationship. Rather than a story of abduction, in his telling Empress Elizabeth (ruled 1741–1761) "eagerly gave refuge to the daughters of elite Kalmyks seeking her protection," as did some of her leading statesmen like Varvara Alekseevna's father. He "gave refuge to two young Kalmyk girls, and assigned their education to his daughter." The girls, sometimes referred to as sisters, were baptized and named Anna Nikolaevna—Annushka—and Ekaterina Borisovna. According to his account, the two girls "grew up in total comfort; Countess Varvara Alekseevna took care of them with love … [They] grew up like children of the house, calling Varvara Alekseevna *babushka* (grandmother)."[9] The composition of the painting emphasizes this reading of their relationship: Annushka has the central role, and although the dark background makes the portrait she holds catch the eye, she is not necessarily an equal, but also not a servant. In fact, the painting is a curious inversion of many portraits from around the same time that foreground elite white subjects while placing servants of other races around the margins.[10]

The portrait may be an effort to de-emphasize the role that bondage played in Annushka's life. Accounts describe Annushka as having been "adopted" or being a "ward" of the Sheremetevs, but she also came into their lives at a time when Kalmyk children were regularly abducted, and when the subjects of the Russian Empire were being ever more strictly defined by a narrower range of legal statuses.[11] Were she and her sister officially household serfs, like Ivan Argunov, the serf artist who painted her portrait, or Praskovia Zhemchuzhina, the serf opera star whose life in the Sheremetev household overlapped with hers? In these cases, the legal structure of unfreedom was no impediment to affection, respect, or love, but neither did affection necessarily confer freedom. Was the same true for Annushka?

This uncertainty leads to a third question: Why was the portrait painted at this particular time? Even here, there is an ambiguity. The date on the portrait within the portrait is 1767, but that is the year of Varvara Alekseevna's death. In other words, the portrait may have been painted then or after that date as a memorial. In either case, the painting was presumably commissioned by Varvara Alekseevna's widower, Petr Borisovich. According to the Sheremetevs' great-grandson, Petr Borisovich and Annushka developed a close relationship in the years after Varvara Alekseevna's death. In his words, Annushka became "a necessity" for Petr Borisovich—she was "a connection with the past," a woman who was "cultivated and clever and could be a pleasant conversationalist." They became "inseparable," he writes.[12] When Petr Borisovich had to spend several weeks in St. Petersburg in the early 1780s, they exchanged letters almost daily. "*Dedushka* (grandfather), my dear!" wrote Annushka in one. "I am taking this occasion to explain to you how moved I am, having been parted from you, of my sincere affection for you, and my true, heart-felt thanks for all of your kindnesses to me." Petr Borisovich was more measured in his language, addressing her as Anna Nikolaevna, signing off as "your friend" (and using the informal pronoun *ty* to address her, while she used the formal *vy*).[13] Still, his letters are chatty and full of detail about his stay in the capital, even at one point about an attack of hemorrhoids that laid him low.

There is also a strong possibility that the two became something more, and that the portrait represents not only a past relationship between a mother figure and a daughter figure but also a later replacement of one by the other. In one of Petr Borisovich's early letters from his trip to St. Petersburg, almost as an aside, he asks Annushka to tell "the three little ones and Alena" about his travels so far. At the end of his stay, he sent presents, as well, to Annushka and to Nastin'ka, Iashin'ka, and Margaritushka.[14] These last three were the "three little ones": his children born out of wedlock between 1772 and 1779, all given the surname Remetev.[15] Although some sources describe their mother as unknown, others suggest—and these letters give some credence to the idea—that their mother was Annushka.[16] If so, the portrait may have emphasized Annushka's respect for Varvara Alekseevna in order to elicit approval of her new relationship with Petr Borisovich.

There was affection in this relationship, as their letters suggest, but that affection cannot be the whole story, particularly given that Annushka was likely only in her early teens when the first of the Remetevs were born.[17] Even if she was older, she lived in the household as at best a ward and at worst in bondage at the time their sexual relationship began. Neither alternative gave her a real option to leave it, or to object to the desires of her guardian or owner, but nor did they preclude her from finding a certain status through their long-standing relationship, one that seems to have lasted until Petr Borisovich's death in 1788.[18] Their three children were acknowledged even if their birth was not legitimized: the two daughters eventually married noblemen and were granted estates settled with serfs as their dowries, and the son was well educated and went into state service.[19] Annushka herself married (or was married off to) a minor nobleman from Kostroma Province after Petr Borisovich died, finally settling on her the status of a free woman—though one, of course, bound to her husband for status.

There is a final question posed by the portrait: What does it leave out? Not only does it obscure Annushka's own personal story, it also gives no vision of the world from which she came, a world that was about to be destroyed. In 1771, in response to a call from the Qing emperor, more than 150,000 Kalmyks headed east to Zungharia; fewer than a third of them survived the trek. Only 50,000 Kalmyks remained on the steppe, now incorporated completely into the Russian Empire.[20] It was a devastating event, and knowledge of it (at least later, Annushka was in contact with a Kalmyk man who called her sister, which suggests she still heard of goings on among the people of her birth) must have both underlined her dependency on the Sheremetevs and marked her as not simply a present other, but also as a relic of a past people.

Of course, this assumes that Annushka understood herself as racially or otherwise different. Varvara Alekseevna once wrote to her mentioning her "little black beetle-like eyes (*glazushki tvoi tarakashki*)," and it is hard to imagine that Annushka never heard other comments that focused on her physical appearance and the ways it did not conform to a Russian norm.[21] She almost certainly did not consider herself in terms of race according to modern understandings of the term, but likely did recognize her difference. In an odd way, in fact, Annushka's difference may be the thing that led to her immortalization in oil. There were many other women in bondage who gave birth to children of their lords, not only in the Sheremetev household but also throughout the world of Russian serfdom. It is a rare few whose portraits were painted. Annushka's otherness may have motivated the painting of her portrait, and the preservation and publication of her letters. And yet it is only a partial version of her life story that has been immortalized, one that leaves absent even her birth name, obscuring the realities of her experience even as it idealizes her life within this family.

NOTES

1. For one recent global history of empire that emphasizes race and bondage, see Kris Manjapra, *Colonialism in Global Perspective* (Cambridge: Cambridge University Press, 2020).
2. Vasilii Alekseevich Levshin, *Zhizn', anekdoty, voennye i politicheskie deianiia rossiiskogo general-fel'dmarshala grafa Borisa Petrovicha Sheremeteva liubimtsa Petra Velikogo i khrabrogo polkovodtsa* (St. Petersburg, 1808), 186–187.
3. N. G. Presnova and I. E. Lomize, *Argunovy, krepostnye khudozhniki Sheremetevykh: katalog vystavki* (Moscow: Gos. Tret'iakovskaia galereia, 2005), 49; Douglas Smith, *The Pearl: A True Tale of Forbidden Love in Catherine the Great's Russia* (New Haven: Yale University Press, 2008), 38.
4. Michael Khodarkovsky, *Russia's Steppe Frontier: The Making of a Colonial Empire, 1500–1800* (Bloomington: Indiana University Press, 2002), 133–139; M. M. Postnikova-Loseva, "Iz istorii sotsial'no-ekonomicheskikh otnoshenii na Donu v XVIII v.," *Istoricheskie zapiski* 60 (1957): 260.
5. Khodarkovsky, *Russia's Steppe Frontier*, 138.
6. Postnikova-Loseva, "Iz istorii," 261.
7. Iurii Aleksandrovich Tikhonov, *Mir veshchei v moskovskikh i peterburgskikh domakh sanovnogo dvorianstva: po novym istochnikam pervoi poloviny XVIII v.* (Moscow: Kuchkovo pole, 2008), 174, 216–217, 248.
8. Postnikova-Loseva, "Iz istorii," 261–262.
9. S. D. Sheremetev, "Dve Kalmychki," in *Otgoloski XVIII veka*, Vol. 6 (St. Petersburg, 1899), 2–3.
10. Thanks to Tamara Walker for this insight. See also her *Exquisite Slaves: Race, Clothing, and Status in Colonial Lima* (New York: Cambridge University Press, 2017) and Jennifer L. Palmer, "The Princess Served by Slaves: Making Race Visible through Portraiture in Eighteenth-Century France," *Gender & History* 26, no. 2 (2014): 242–262.
11. Alison K. Smith, *For the Common Good and Their Own Well-Being: Social Estates in Imperial Russia* (New York: Oxford University Press, 2014).
12. Sheremetev, "Dve Kalmychki," 100.
13. Sheremetev, "Dve Kalmychki," 27–28, 32–33.
14. Sheremetev, "Dve Kalmychki," 33, 94.
15. Alla Krasko, *Tri veka gorodskoi usad'by grafov Sheremetevykh. Liudi i sobytiia* (St. Petersburg: Tsentropoligraf, 2009).
16. Krasko does not identify their mother, but L. Starikova, *Teatral'naia zhizn' starinnoi Moskvy: epokha, byt, nravy* (Moscow: Iskusstvo, 1988), 209–210, does.
17. Several art historians date her birth to the late 1750s, including Presnova and Lomize, *Argunovy*, 49.
18. On similar tensions, see Brenda E. Stevenson, "What's Love Got to Do with It? Concubinage and Enslaved Women and Girls in the Antebellum South," in *Sexuality and Slavery: Reclaiming Intimate Histories in the Americas*, edited by Leslie M. Harris and Daina Ramey Berry, Athens, Georgia: University of Georgia Press, 2018), 159–188.
19. Krasko, *Tri veka gorodskoi usad'by*.
20. Peter C. Perdue, *China Marches West: The Qing Conquest of Central Eurasia* (Cambridge, MA: Harvard University Press, 2005), 292–299.
21. Sheremetev, "Dve Kalmychki," 3.

CHAPTER 15

"IF FATE HAD NOT GIVEN HER AN EMPIRE . . .": CATHERINE THE GREAT AND THE OPTICS OF POWER (1762–1787)

ERIN McBURNEY

CATHERINE II, also known as Catherine the Great, ruled Russia from her seizure of the throne in 1762 until her death in 1796. Her cultural, legislative, and military conquests, including the annexation of Crimea in 1783, continue, tragically, to influence policy in Russia and resonate in the wider world today. Catherine remains a challenging and complex historical figure. To her critics, she was a German outsider who stole the throne of Russia and sanctioned the murder of her husband, Tsar Peter III. For others, she saved Russia from the depredations of an unstable, anti-Russian martinet (Peter was himself half German and sought to model himself after Frederick II of Prussia). An unconsecrated usurper in 1762, within a decade Catherine was hailed at home as the "Mother of the Fatherland" and in Europe as the "Northern Semiramis" whose simultaneous military and cultural conquests seemed to recreate the legendary accomplishments of the ancient female ruler of Babylon.

Catherine was one of the most powerful monarchs of the eighteenth century, a singular woman who was able to transcend the limitations of her gender, assert legitimacy, and establish herself as an exemplar of absolute rule. She was a master politician and communicator whose strategic manipulation of the optics of power far exceeded that of her male contemporaries, such as the Hapsburg emperor Joseph II or Frederick II of Prussia. Unlike the French monarch, Louis XIV, who had an entire *department* devoted to burnishing his image, Catherine personally kept abreast of the latest trends in European art, art history, architecture, and literature through her extensive network of international correspondents. She composed seven different versions of her memoirs and commissioned at least fifteen official state portraits. Her coordination of textual and visual legacies provided Catherine with a means to negotiate the anomaly of female rule and adapt her ruling image to the exigencies of time and place.

Though her reign began under the literal and symbolic blight of usurpation and regicide, Catherine overcame negative and politically destabilizing associations by appropriating a masculine ethos of military and political command that reinforced her fitness to rule. Two portraits that were painted twenty-five years apart—in the immediate aftermath of Catherine's coup in 1762 and during her triumphant tour of Crimea in 1787—illustrate the continuity of her ruling scenario. In Vigilius Eriksen's 1762 *Catherine II Astride Brilliant* (Image 15.1) and Mikhail Shibanov's 1787 *Catherine II in Travelling Costume* (Image 15.2), the empress dispensed with standard representations of queens and empresses. For centuries, royal women were pictured as passive objects of beauty, and their status was signified by crown jewels, elaborate gowns, and ornate palace interiors. They were often surrounded by royal children and joined by a male figure, whether a father, spouse, or male heir. Many images of women rulers in the eighteenth century—such as the Russian empresses Catherine I and Elizabeth, or the Hapsburg empress Maria Theresa—featured these gendered representational conventions. In contrast, the 1762 and 1787 portraits of Catherine II appropriate markers of masculinity, physical courage, and military expertise. Moreover, they are devoid of any reference to a male relative.

Within weeks of Catherine's June 1762 coup d'etat, Vigilius Eriksen, a Swedish painter in the service of the Russian court, began the massive, twelve by twelve foot *Catherine II Astride Brilliant*, and it was sufficiently completed for her to view as she departed for her coronation in Moscow, in September 1762. The equestrian genre was an audacious choice for her first state portrait. Since the time of Alexander the Great, rulers pictured on horseback were associated with leading troops into battle and the celebration of military victory. Catherine chose to depict her seizure of the Russian throne as a military victory and an act of personal heroism. She had all other participants (and potential contestants) removed from the stage. Reading the portrait closely provides a visual corollary to Catherine's textual accounts of her coup.

Catherine usurped the symbolic order of representation just as she usurped the throne. Rather than presenting herself as the consecrated ruler of a European state or as regent and dowager empress, she chose to privilege a martial iconography to emphasize her triumphant conquest. The picture focuses on Catherine's heroic performance during her coup—she is in uniform, armed, and astride. The picture's scale and subject matter are deliberately hyperbolic but also suitable for such a dramatic subject. The portrait serves as a visual panegyric whose subject matter was echoed in contemporary Russian odes.

Catherine's equestrian persona displays her forceful control of horse and, by association, Russia. She sits easily astride (not in a more typically feminine sidesaddle), holding the reins of state in one hand and the sword of justice in the other, all the while spurring her mount (and, thus, her country) forward. Her hair is

IMAGE 15.1 Vigilius Eriksen, *Catherine II Astride Brilliant*, 1762.

unbound and unpowdered, reflecting both the haste with which the coup unfolded and the provocative nature of her personal leadership. Catherine's gaze is turned toward the viewer, and she maintains visual engagement with her audience. The composition combines serenity, strength, and beauty.

Eriksen's portrait also contains a symbolically important background. A tree, a conventional symbol of constancy and reliability, frames the left side of the painting. In one version of the painting, the date "28 June 1762" and Catherine's royal cipher are engraved on the trunk. Dark clouds overhead give way to blue skies, evoking a sun motif that would reappear not only at Catherine's coronation, but for years to come in textual (especially panegyric) and other visual media. Troop formations with their battle standards and rifles aloft reinforce the martial element of command. And beyond them, in the far distance, the golden cupolas of a large monastery complex are visible. The message is unambiguous: as Catherine II, a mounted warrior, leads her armies to victory, she simultaneously preserves the throne of Russia and protects the Russian Orthodox Church from its enemies.

The painting, however, presents an edited narrative of the coup. The young, virile figure is the same individual who a mere six months earlier stood in demure mourning at the bier of the Empress Elizabeth. Since then, she had given birth to Grigory Orlov's illegitimate son, plotted the coup, and moved swiftly to seize the throne in her own right, refusing to rule as regent for her legitimate son, the nine-year old tsarevich, Paul. Catherine spent much of the coup in a carriage rather than on horseback, because she had recently given birth. She was acclaimed by all three guards regiments and received at Kazan Cathedral while seated in an open carriage. She only donned the uniform of the Preobrazhenskii Guards, which had been founded by Peter the Great, and mounted her white charger on the third day, after her accession was assured.

Many smaller copies of this work were made, but the original was destined for Catherine's newly redesigned throne room at Peterhof, her least favorite suburban palace but one with dynastic significance, as it was linked closely with her predecessors Peter the Great and his daughter, the Empress Elizabeth. Eriksen's massive painting was placed on the wall directly behind her throne (where it remains to this day), a permanent symbol of her unique achievement. The placement of the painting also permitted Catherine to insert herself into a pantheon of Romanov rulers. The throne room contains a series of small, indistinct images of Catherine's predecessors, hung at ceiling height, but it is Catherine's equestrian image that dominates the scene. Catherine seized not just the throne of Russia, but total command of an empire. She would go on to experiment frequently with her official image on paper and on canvas, but this iconic picture constituted the foundational document of her visual archive.

Twenty-five years later, from January through July of 1787, the empress and a large entourage travelled four thousand miles from St. Petersburg to the Black Sea and back via Moscow. It was one of the most spectacular displays of command, control, and empire staged in Europe in the eighteenth century. The Crimean journey occurred at the apogee of Catherine's power, and it coincided with the twenty-fifth anniversary of her reign. She was confident enough in the stability of her government, and in the loyalty of her subalterns, to depart from her physical seat of power for an extended period of time. This voyage also underscored Catherine's personal bravery; she was visiting newly conquered territories that bordered directly on the Ottoman frontier and where outbreaks of bubonic plague occurred frequently.

She traversed distances that had never been attempted by a Russian ruler, at least not in peacetime. Ivan IV led troops into Kazan in 1552, while Peter I ventured as far as the Pruth River (in modern day Moldova) during his Persian campaign from 1722 to 1723. Only Catherine II was able to reach the Black Sea and convert imperial aspirations for a warm-water navy into reality. She and Prince Grigory Potemkin began planning a tour of Crimea a year later, but annual outbreaks of plague delayed Catherine's departure for several years. By 1787, text and image were coordinated to promulgate a coherent narrative out of seemingly contradictory impulses: Russia's conquest and subsequent militarization of the Crimean Peninsula *and* the introduction of European, "enlightened" civilization to the former Tatar khanate. The staging of the voyage was designed to connect the region's classical heritage to Russia's historical past, and to promote the singular role of the empress in this civilizing scenario. It was no coincidence that Catherine's *Notes Concerning Russian History* and her historical opera *The Foundation of Oleg's Reign* also were published in 1787. In both works, the empress strove to demonstrate the historical connections of the Crimean Peninsula (which she called by its ancient Greek name, Tauride) with Classical Greece, using Euripides's *Iphigenia in Tauris* as but one inspiration. Her playwriting became life-writing. Catherine presented herself as a modern-day Greek deity, traversing Crimea in a Homeric-style odyssey and visiting a series of new towns (and naval and military bases) with invented Greek names, such as Kherson, Sebastopol, and Odesa.

Nature and artifice were harnessed for maximum dramatic effect, and every aspect of the physical procession engendered its own theatrical display and splendor. At each stop along the route, costumed performers presented *tableaux vivants*, or "living pictures," that elevated and displayed the empress as the primary figure on a series of exotic stages. Although several artists accompanied the empress and her governor general, Prince Potemkin, to Crimea, no official state portrait was commissioned en route, though several retrospective images would be created after the empress returned to St. Petersburg.

Yet one of the most famous portraits of her entire reign, *Catherine the Great in Travelling Costume* (Image 15.2), was painted at the start of the journey by Mikhail Shibanov, a serf-artist who belonged to Potemkin. Shibanov painted Catherine in Kyiv as she waited for the ice on the Dnipro River to thaw, in the early spring of 1787, and it remains the only image of the empress created during the voyage. Catherine appears stern and imposing, yet visibly careworn. She was nearly fifty-eight years old, and this picture conveys the toll that years of ruling Russia had taken, as well as the physical hardship of the immediate journey, a fact rarely acknowledged in her correspondence.

Shibanov's portrait captured an exact likeness of the empress, according to many in her entourage. This is all the more extraordinary given the outsider status of the painter, who was unaccustomed to being in Catherine's august presence. We know that Catherine actually sat for Shibanov, perhaps the only instance in her reign when she posed for a native Russian painter. She is pictured in a red jacket decorated with brass buttons, gold braid, and the stars of the three major imperial orders: St. Andrew, St. George, and St. Vladimir, chivalric awards created by Peter the Great

IMAGE 15.2 Mikhail Shibanov, *Catherine the Great in Travelling Costume*, 1787.

(St. Andrew, 1698) and Catherine herself (St. George in 1769 and St. Vladimir in 1782). When worn together, the orders represented the highest personal decorations of the Russian Empire, signifying the wearer's military bravery and devotion to faith and fatherland. Catherine's "travelling costume" was, in fact, a military uniform. Despite repeated textual references to Iphigenia and other classical figures, Catherine was not travelling around Crimea in a toga. Instead, she often donned a regimental uniform to take formal review of troops and conduct inspections of new military installations. Although official rhetoric emphasized the peaceful annexation of Crimea, this portrait reveals the reality of a ruler on military maneuvers. Catherine was determined to display her country's military readiness, especially with regard to the Ottoman Porte. She wrote to Potemkin shortly before the trip: "There will not be any weak measures against him [the Sultan]; no words, only action is necessary in order to preserve our honor and our glory . . ."[1] In Shibanov's rendering, the Russian monarch appears battle-tested, resolute, and ready to engage her Turkish enemy without reference to or reliance on any divine or allegorical attributes.

Catherine chose to have herself portrayed in a manner similar to that of her closest ally, Holy Roman Emperor Joseph II, whose 1786 portrait (no longer extant) arrived in St. Petersburg weeks before the empress departed for Crimea. The picture was painted by Johann Baptist Lampi, official painter to the Viennese court. That Catherine may have been inspired by Joseph's portrait was underscored by her actions. After Joseph II's death in 1790, she hired Lampi to come to St. Petersburg, where he would serve as her official portraitist until her death in 1796.

In the Shibanov portrait and in Lampi's image of Joseph II, the enlightened absolutists display themselves not as peace-loving monarchs surrounded by symbols of their largesse and learning, but in literal battle mode, in simple military uniforms without crown, scepter, throne, or imperial backdrop. Joseph II, travelling incognito, joined Catherine in Crimea, where together they inspected new fortifications and ports on the Black Sea. They also confirmed their mutual assistance pact during this time: in the event of war, Austria would ally with Russia against the Ottomans, and Russia would support Austria in any military action against Prussia. This portrait of Catherine—especially when considered in conjunction with Joseph's own representation—serves as visual confirmation of their 1787 deliberations, and underscores the military and diplomatic missions embedded within the Crimean sojourn.

Shibanov's picture was quickly copied and then engraved that same year by James Walker, an English artist at the Russian court. Walker was instructed to place the following verse (in French) beneath the engraving:

> Recognized across the North as the magnet that attracts us
> This happy conqueror, profound legislator
> Amiable woman, great man and the envy of all who admire her

Who traverses her lands bringing Happiness
Master of the art of ruling, expert in the art of writing
Spreading light, removing errors;
If fate had not given her an Empire
She would always occupy a Throne in our hearts.[2]

It is certain that this inscription had the approval of the empress, and it may have been drafted by the Chevalier de Corberon, one of many foreign diplomats who accompanied her to Crimea. The verse offers a list of multiple, sometimes contradictory characteristics associated with Catherine's monarchial persona: happy conqueror and profound legislator, master of the arts of ruling and writing, and (to paraphrase) empress of both an empire and the people's hearts. Shibanov's portrait and the accompanying inscription convey Catherine's mature ruling persona and celebrate her twenty-five years ruling Russia. The text enumerates the vast scale of the Empress Catherine's enlightened rule, while the image embodies her resolute assumption of military command in defense of faith and fatherland. Despite the informal nature of the portrait's commission, the empress presented copies of the engraving to her close associates and had multiple copies (and miniatures) of the portrait made, several of which remained on display in Romanov palaces and galleries until the twentieth century.

Both the 1762 and the 1787 images of this "astounding princess, legislatrix and warrior" retain their power to inform and expand our understanding of Russia in the age of Catherine the Great.[3] At two critical junctures in her reign, the empress adopted masculine, military representational scenarios to transcend the political limitations of her gender, assert her fitness to command, and display the essential attributes of her unlimited rule. Though only a small part of Catherine II's extensive visual archive, these pictures underscore the agency and authority this empress exercised with regard to her own visual representation. Long before modern-day communications and public relations technology created synergy and symmetry between word and image, Catherine the Great fully exploited the optics of power.

NOTES

1. Unpublished letter of Catherine II to Potemkin, May 1, 1786, cited in Ol'ga Eliseeva, *Grigorii Potemkin* (Moscow: Molodaia Gvardiia, 2005), 378.
2. Walker's engraving of the portrait and this verse are reproduced in D. A. Rovinskii, *Podrobnyi Slovar' russkikh gravirovannykh portretov* (St. Petersburg: Imperatorskaia Akademiia Nauk, 1887), t. II, 807–808.
3. Quotation from Marie Daniel Bourrée de Corberon, *Un diplomat francais à la cour de Catherine II 1775–1780. Journal intime du Chevalier de Corberon*, Vol. I (Paris: Librairie Plon, 1901), 80.

CHAPTER 16

DEPICTING EXPERTISE AND MANAGING DIVERSITY IN THE URALS MINING INDUSTRY (1773–1818)

ANNA GRABER

THERE WERE FORTUNES to be made and careers to be advanced in the booming mining and metallurgy industry in the Urals during the eighteenth and early nineteenth centuries—if an ambitious mine owner or factory administrator could communicate his expertise in managing the Urals' natural and human resources to potential imperial patrons. The mining magnate Aleksei Turchaninov and the managers of the state-owned metallurgy and armaments factories in the southern Urals town of Zlatoust commissioned fine paintings of their good management in action as one means to advertise their skill in efficiently extracting and working the region's iron and copper ores.

Administering the Urals mining industry encompassed not just the shepherding of one of Imperial Russia's most essential industries, but included as well the delicate task of governing a multiethnic and restive workforce in a border region that otherwise knew little state presence. The mining industry was an imperial "contact zone," where the knowledge traditions and industrial practices of German experts, Indigenous Siberian prospectors, and noble Russian administrators coexisted, commingled, and conflicted.[1] Through painting, mine owners and factory managers selectively highlighted or obscured this diversity in the mining industry, moves calculated to best display their skillful management.

In the 1770s, Aleksei Fedorovich Turchaninov, owner of three highly profitable metallurgical plants, was absorbed in a campaign to win hereditary nobility for his family. Born a merchant, Turchaninov had acquired personal nobility in 1754, when Empress Elizabeth, impressed by a line of lavish copper dinnerware he had produced, granted him the service rank of titular councilor "for such zealous works for the profit of the fatherland."[2] From this date, he could enjoy the privileges of nobility, but he did not have a high enough rank to pass his noble status on to his children. Having gained his rank by demonstrating how his technical and entrepreneurial expertise furthered state economic policy, he endeavored to show how his sons similarly had the education and expertise to serve the empire as men of noble worth. In 1777, he commissioned the St. Petersburg Academy of Arts graduate Leontii Semenovich Stanishchevskii to paint oil portraits of his young sons Aleksei, Piotr, and Aleksandr. The younger boys are painted as guards officers, one way that young aristocrats commonly served the empire. The eldest son, 11-year-old Aleksei, is depicted at the entrance to the family's Gumashevskii copper mine, the richest copper mine in Russia, dressed handsomely in the uniform of a mining officer (Image 16.1). This portrait makes the case for Aleksei's nobility by virtue of the education he is receiving to prepare him to manage the family's mining empire.

Rich accessories make one kind of claim for Aleksei's exalted status. His lace cravat, sword, and powdered wig mark him as an elegant young gentleman of means. But a stronger case for Aleksei's nobility is made by his clothing. In his forest green pants and vest and his brilliant scarlet coat, Aleksei bears the uniform of a mining officer. As administrators in the imperial mining bureau, the College of Mines, mining officers managed state-owned mines and metallurgical plants and regulated the activities of the owners of privately held mine and factory systems. Mining officers in the 1770s had to have received an education in the mining sciences: mineralogy, chemistry, physics, mechanics, surveying, architecture, and hydraulics as applied to the problems of mining and metallurgy. This education identified mining officers as men with the systematic knowledge necessary to oversee the entire mining industry. The mining officers themselves saw their knowledge and expertise as setting them apart from workers and artisans. Crucially for the Turchaninov family, this education also drew the line between noble and non-noble, as graduates of the empire's mining schools were conferred a service rank of mining shift foreman and, with that rank, personal nobility.

The mining accessories that young Aleksei is portrayed with make further claims about his expertise and, hence, his nobility. He casually rests his hat on a brass theodolite, a piece of surveying equipment used to measure horizontal angles in plotting the course of ore veins and in building mine shafts. The theodolite suggests that Aleksei is receiving an education in geometry, trigonometry, and surveying, and that he possesses the mathematized understanding of nature essential to the work of mining officers. The theodolite also suggests that Aleksei and his family are not just maintaining the Gumashevskii mine, but actively expanding it by measuring the direction of new shafts. The pickaxe at Aleksei's feet suggests that in addition to his theoretical knowledge of mining, he also has the practical, hands-on experience to lead the work of expanding Gumashevskii from the very face of the mine.

The globe nestled between the legs of the theodolite is a curious artifact, as unlike the pickaxe and the theodolite, it is not a mining tool. Instead, the globe makes

IMAGE 16.1 Leontii Stanishchevskii, *Portrait of Aleksei Turchaninov*, 1777.

a claim about the importance of Gumashevskii. Though faint, it is possible to discern the outline of South America at the center of the globe. Here, Stanishchevskii is drawing a comparison between Gumashevskii and the famed silver mines of the Andes. The artist promises that Gumashevskii, with the expert and meritorious Turchaninov family carefully managing it, can deliver to Russia the wealth of New Spain. The globe also serves to connect young Aleksei to another famous son, Catherine II's heir Grand Duke Paul. In a 1766 portrait that Stanishchevskii, as a graduate of the Academy of Arts, surely would have been familiar with, Danish artist Vigilius Eriksen depicts a 12-year-old Paul in his classroom standing next to a large globe. The paintings of these two heirs in their classrooms—Paul in a palace, and Aleksei at the mine—present their subjects as the promising next generation of leaders in the process of acquiring the educations they need to govern their intended realms. In modeling Aleksei's portrait on Paul's, Turchaninov and Stanishchevskii make a powerful double claim about Aleksei's nobility—it is heritable from his prosperous and ennobled father, and it is merited through his training in the sciences that Catherine II and her government deemed necessary for the proper stewardship of the empire's mineral wealth. The portrait promised Catherine she could rest assured that, at Turchaninov's death, the empire's most important copper mine would pass into the hands of a young man equipped to fulfill her economic policy.

Young Aleksei sat for his portrait in St. Petersburg. The painting may have hung in the family's home there and been viewed by the capital's high society. We know that by the time of Aleksei's father's death in 1789, it was displayed in the Turchaninovs' principal home at the Sysert metallurgical plant near Ekaterinburg. The centerpiece of the family's extensive art collection, the painting would have impressed on visitors—imperial governors, mining officials, traveling scholars, and touring foreigners—the nobility and expertise of the Turchaninov family.

In 1783, six years after Stanishchevskii painted Aleksei's portrait, Catherine granted the Turchaninovs the patent of hereditary nobility that they had long desired. While the portrait made the case for young Aleksei's nobility to elite society, it obscures the very factor that persuaded Catherine to accede to the family's request: their firm governance of the workers pointedly absent from the painting.

In the 1770s, the Turchaninovs employed a large and varied workforce: 5,618 male prescribed peasants paid off their taxes through seasonal labor at Turchaninov's three metallurgical plants, 150 metallurgists and laborers processed Gumashevskii's copper ores at Polevskoi plant alone, while 200 miners, smiths, horse drivers, and carters worked year-round at Gumashevskii.[3] Italian stonework masters crafted Gumashevskii's finest malachites and colored stones from other Turchaninov mines into vases, sculptures, and carvings.

Like other mine owners, Turchaninov relied, in part, on Bashkirs, a seminomadic, Muslim, Turkic people, to prospect for surface-level ores. The entire southern Urals, including the Turchaninov land, had been Bashkir territory until the early eighteenth century. The Bashkirs had engaged in some copper mining and smelting of their own, and into the early nineteenth century, they constituted the main body of prospectors in the region. Though European mining practices provided the blueprint for expansion of the industry, both private mine owners and the state mining administration depended on the local knowledge and mining skill of the Bashkirs and other Indigenous groups. Over the course of the eighteenth century, Bashkirs led mine owners and administrators to hundreds of deposits, including Gumashevskii.

With such an ethnically, religiously, and culturally diverse population joined together in the pursuit of the mineral resources of the southern Urals, Turchaninov's enterprises were what historian Mary Louise Pratt has termed a *contact zone*. She defines this as a space in which people with different knowledge traditions worked—sometimes in cooperation, but often in spite of conflict born of hierarchical power structures—to create new bodies of knowledge capable of being mobilized by burgeoning capitalist interests and modernizing European empires. In just such a zone, Turchaninov deployed, mediated, and directed his workers' expertise—Russian and German metallurgy, Italian craft, and Bashkir knowledge of the products of their land—to considerable profit.

While economically fruitful for the Turchaninov family, this tremendous diversity made the mining industry a challenge to govern. Harsh conditions at the factories not infrequently led to riots among workers and prescribed peasants, and the Bashkirs twice mounted major insurrections against encroaching imperial power in the first half of the eighteenth century. The Urals erupted in rebellion from 1773 to 1774, when the mining industry's underclasses—laborers, peasants, and Bashkirs—flocked to the cause of the Cossack Emelian Pugachev. A deserter who claimed to be Catherine II's deposed and murdered husband, Emperor Peter III, Pugachev led the Iaik Cossacks stationed on the Orenburg Steppe in rebellion against the government's attempts to regularize them. Pugachev's promises of land, religious freedom, and freedom from certain taxes and service dues appealed to the Bashkirs and workers of the Urals, and the uprising quickly spread there as workers seized metallurgical plants and arms in the name of Peter III. In spring 1774, Pugachev moved westward, briefly capturing the major city of Kazan. He then retreated down the Volga, inciting serfs to slaughter their masters as his forces rampaged southward. While the rebellion was short-lived—Pugachev was captured after a year—it was the greatest mass uprising in the Russian Empire until the revolutions of the early twentieth century, and with seventy-four metallurgical plants damaged or destroyed, it was devastating to the Urals mining industry, yet brought the rebels little improvement in their conditions.

Turchaninov sagaciously perceived a threat to his metallurgical plants early in the course of the rebellion as copper plants 500 kilometers to the south were seized by the rebels. When rebels finally approached the Sysert plant in February 1774, he made sure his men were well armed and ready—a force of 300 "loyal" workers repelled

800 rebels.[4] Turchaninov was able to keep his workers from rebelling and to defend his three plants from further attacks. As the regional administration was overwhelmed by the scale of the rebellion, the successful defense of Turchaninov's plants, which protected the eastern approach to the city of Ekaterinburg, was a rallying point for beleaguered government and mining officials.

On the tenth anniversary of the start of the Pugachev Rebellion, Turchaninov received the patent of hereditary nobility. The text of the patent did not reference his nor his son's mining and metallurgical expertise, nor his good stewardship of the empire's mineral resources, but instead credited his defense of his plants in the rebellion.[5] Stanishchevskii's portrait of young Aleksei was executed in the wake of the rebellion and was meant to advertise the meritorious and expert service of the Turchaninov family, but it was Turchaninov's management of the diverse workers absent from the painting—his control over them such that they fought for his metallurgical plants and the crown—that ultimately convinced Catherine of the family's nobility.

In contrast to Stanishchevskii's portrait of the solitary Aleksei, a later painter of mining industry experts, Fedor Filippovich Cherniavskii, populates his watercolor with prospectors, swordmakers, and mining officers in a scene that emphasizes the ethnic and religious diversity of the Urals industry (Image 16.2). Cherniavskii was an employee of the Drafting Section of the Department of Mining and Salt-Making

IMAGE 16.2 Fedor Cherniavskii, *View from the Western Side of Zlatoust Plant and Arms Factory*, 1818.

Affairs. In 1818, four decades after Stanishchevskii completed his portraits, Cherniavskii traveled to the town of Zlatoust in the southern Urals to paint the town and its three state-owned factories. These included the Zlatoust Iron Plant, a second iron plant, and the Zlatoust Arms Factory, which was the empire's preeminent workshop for the production of damask steel swords and knives. The German-born founder of the arms factory had hired two dozen German, Danish, and Swedish metallurgists to staff the Zlatoust Iron Plant in 1809 and 1810, as well as 114 German and Alsatian weapons-making masters for the arms workshop. This colony of foreign, mostly German-speaking masters lived with their families in neat duplex homes constructed for them and arranged in rows along the aptly named Big and Little German Streets.

This German neighborhood is the setting for Cherniavskii's *View from the Western Side of Zlatoust Plant and Arms Factory*. Against a backdrop of wooded hills and German homes, factory workers gather with their families in the square abutting the factories to celebrate a holiday, presumably a Catholic or Lutheran one. At the center of the painting, a German couple dances. To the left side of the painting, similarly dressed German or Scandinavian families cluster around a table for card games and music.

Germans and other Europeans were not the only employees of the factories—in 1821, nearly a thousand Russians labored at the armaments factory alone. Cherniavskii included these Russian workers and their families in his scene. A group of Russian women is clearly identifiable on the right side of the painting, as they are dancing a folk circle dance, a *khorovod*. Unlike the European women, the Russian women wear *sarafans*, a long jumper dress. Family groups of Russians dot the painting—some masters wear flowing tunics and full-sleeved *rubakhas* (blouses), while others wear *kaftans* (robes) over trousers.

Remarkably for this post-Napoleonic period of increasing nationalist sentiment, Cherniavskii presents a harmonious, multiconfessional scene. Lutherans, Catholics, Orthodox, and even Muslims (a pair of mounted Muslim Bashkirs watch the central dancers) are seen here celebrating a Western Christian holiday. Cherniavskii's watercolor makes the case that this religious pluralism—and the expertise of the foreign workers—is not a cultural threat, because it is managed and directed toward the production of Russian arms and iron. In Zlatoust's workshops, European masters instructed 260 Russian masters and masters-in-training in German craft traditions and the latest metallurgical and swordmaking techniques. No blank slates, Russian masters arrived at Zlatoust from Tula and Olonets, centers of iron metallurgy and arm-smithing with traditions stretching back to the seventeenth century. Together, they crafted cavalry swords and other steel products of such quality that the visiting English geologist Robert Murchison hailed Zlatoust as the "Sheffield and Birmingham of Eastern Russia."[6]

Another neutralized threat is situated at the center of the painting—the Bashkir horsemen, identifiable by their spears, distinctive fur-trimmed hats, and characteristic long mustaches. Zlatoust was built on Bashkir lands, and in late 1773, Bashkirs rose in rebellion with Pugachev, reclaimed the town, and burned the metallurgical plant. But by 1818, this eighteenth-century history of unrest was long over—the suppression of the Pugachev Rebellion broke Bashkir power, and once the factories were rebuilt, local Bashkirs returned to military service and ore prospecting.

Cherniavskii counterbalances his Bashkirs with a pair of mining officers, who are dressed in navy coats with long tails, tight white breeches, black boots, and dark hats (the uniform had changed in 1804 from young Aleksei's red and green). They figuratively hold the horsemen in check. Formerly considered dangerous but necessary as prospectors, Bashkirs are tamed in the painting by figures who would govern them and, through their training in the mining sciences, render the Bashkirs' local knowledge of ores obsolete. As the mining corps swelled in the final decades of the eighteenth century with graduates from Russia's three mining schools, mining officers increasingly led prospecting expeditions informed by an academic mineralogy. By 1818, Cherniavskii's Bashkirs, now defanged and non-essential workers, appear in the painting to add a dash of exotic, eastern color to this scene.

The Urals industry of the eighteenth and early nineteenth centuries was of necessity a multiethnic enterprise, where mine owners and mining officials were obliged to rely on the heterogenous knowledge traditions—local, craft, theoretical—of nomads, peasants, workers, master craftsmen, and foreigners. While industry leaders in the period from the 1770s to the 1810s strove to increase profits and advance their careers through the scientific management of the industry, to state actors the most valuable skill a mine owner or factory administrator could possess was the ability to maintain order among this diverse workforce, as the paintings of Stanishchevskii and Cherniavskii demonstrate.

NOTES

1. I borrow this concept from Mary Louise Pratt, *Imperial Eyes: Travel Writing and Transculturation* (London: Routledge, 1992), and Kapil Raj, *Relocating Modern Science: Circulation and the Construction of Knowledge in South Asia and Europe, 1650–1900* (New York: Palgrave Macmillan, 2007).
2. E. P. Pirogova, E. G. Nekliudov, and M. B. Larionova, *Rod Turchaninovykh* (Ekaterinburg: Izdatel'stvo "Sokrat," 2008), 41.
3. Peter Simon Pallas, *Reise durch verschiedene Provinzen des Russischen Reichs* (Saint Petersburg, 1771–1776), 2:156.
4. Pirogova et al., *Rod Turchaninovykh*, 64.
5. Pirogova et al., *Rod Turchaninovykh*, 66.
6. Roderick Impey Murchison, Edouard de Verneuil, and Count Alexander von Keyserling, *The Geology of Russia in Europe and the Ural Mountains* (London: John Murray, 1845), 1:346–347.

CHAPTER 17

FATHER HYACINTH'S CHINESE PORTRAIT (EARLY NINETEENTH CENTURY)

WILLARD SUNDERLAND

WE ARE STANDING on the Palace Embankment in St. Petersburg, a stone's throw from the Winter Palace, the former residence of the tsars. Behind us is the Neva River, and directly in front of us is the elegant portico of another of the city's grand royal structures. We move through the doorway and enter an expansive foyer. A guard checks our passes. We turn to the right, moving through another door into another hall and then farther along, making our way to a broad stairway. We climb to the second floor, where we turn again down a long corridor lined with squeaky parquet until we reach an ordinary office door. After knocking, a scholar working inside ushers us into a high-ceilinged room lined with desks and books, and then we see it. In fact, we can't help but see it, because it's right there, hanging on the wall just across from us: the near life-sized portrait of a serious-looking man dressed in a flowing blue gown and a red, cone-shaped hat (Image 17.1).

We are in the New Michael Palace (*Novo-Mikhailovskii dvorets*), the former home of one of the children of Tsar Nicholas I and now the headquarters of the Institute of Oriental Manuscripts of the Russian Academy of Sciences, and the man in the canvas before us is Nikita Iakovlevich Bichurin (1777–1853), also known as Hyacinth (*Iakinf*), the name he took when he became a monk, or, more properly, Father Hyacinth, the greatest Russian sinologist of the nineteenth century.[1]

Visual reminders of the imperial past, both new and old, are everywhere in Russia today. Peter the Great appears on vodka bottles. Nineteenth-century statues loom over intersections.. Shiny new Orthodox churches go up in the Muscovite style. One effect of this saturation is a diminishment of the mystery of the past. Evocations of the old empire are so ordinary that they blur together, and as they become humdrum, we assume we understand them. In reality, however, every image of the past contains at least two sets of meanings, one more obvious, the other less so. The first is the meaning of the image itself, its physical shape and content. This is what we see

IMAGE 17.1 Father Hyacinth (*Iakinf*), self-portrait.

and assume we readily know. But the second is the historical meaning of the image, its signification as an artifact of the past, which is more elusive than the image itself, because we can't actually see the past. To uncover this order of meaning, we need to look beyond the image to probe the mystery behind it.

The same is true of this portrait. On the face of it, the painting is exactly what it appears to be: the representation of a single individual, a white European man, age thirty or so, dressed in Chinese fashion. But the meaning of it is more capacious and harder to grasp, for beyond being a portrait of Father Hyacinth, it's also the snapshot of a relationship—between Hyacinth and China in the first instance, but also between Russia and China more generally. To fully appreciate the painting, we need to examine it on each of these levels, decoding the image itself as well as its historical context.

The first thing worth mentioning before even getting to the painting is the appropriateness of the location. Hyacinth was one of the founders of Russian sinology, and his portrait hangs in one of the country's headquarters of Asian learning. As the heir to the old Asiatic Museum of the Imperial Academy of Sciences, the Institute of Oriental Manuscripts houses hundreds of thousands of rare books and documents in Asian and European languages, as well as the personal files of scores of Russian "Orientalists" (*vostokovedy*)—that is, scholars of Asian languages and cultures, like Hyacinth. Though the institute was founded after his time, this is very much his spiritual home.

But if the painting is in the right place, the image itself, at first glance, is surprising. We expect portraits of nineteenth-century Russian scholars, including esteemed scholars of Asia, to display their subjects in European rather than "Oriental" style. We also expect to see an Orthodox monk like Hyacinth dressed . . . like an Orthodox monk—in other words, in traditional Russian monkish garb, such as a black, flat-topped headdress and trailing veil, known as a *klobuk*, along with a body-length black cassock. In fact, he appears in exactly this guise in another portrait made shortly before departing for China in late 1807.[2] The hair and beard in our portrait shown in Image 17.1 are also not quite right. Russian monks in the early 1800s wore their hair long, with long beards, in keeping with the belief that to cut one's hair was to cast off God's power, as in the story of Samson in the Old Testament. Yet Hyacinth's head here is shaved, and his beard is a neatly trimmed goatee. He is thus at home in the institute, but in this painting at least, his appearance is unconventional.

The history around the painting helps to explain things. While there is no date or signature, it seems likely that Hyacinth painted the work himself during his service as the director of the Russian Spiritual Mission in Beijing (*Pekinskaia dukhovnaia missiia*) during the late 1810s or early 1820s.[3] As the only Russian presence in the Qing Empire at the time, the Spiritual Mission was an unusual institution. Though "spiritual" in one sense, it was a number of other things besides, which is also key to understanding the painting.

The Mission's avowed purpose was to tend to the religious needs of the Albazinians (*Albazintsy, Aerbajinren* 阿尔巴津人), a small community of Russian Orthodox believers whose history in the Chinese capital dated back to the late seventeenth century. This is why the Mission was headed by a monk and staffed by "priestmonks" (hieromonks) and deacons, as well as by a few seminary students sent to study Chinese and Manchu. Roughly every ten years, a new mission would arrive in Beijing to replace its predecessor. Hyacinth headed the Ninth Mission—that is, the ninth to reside in Beijing since the missions began in the early eighteenth century. There would be nine more, making eighteen in all, before the fall of the tsarist order.

At the same time, precisely because it was Russia's only toehold in China, the Mission also operated as a foreign trade office, supporting the Russian commercial caravans that periodically visited the city, as well as a diplomatic listening post, collecting and relaying sensitive information on China to the Ministry of Foreign Affairs in St. Petersburg.[4] (The Mission remained under the formal authority of the ministry until the 1860s.) Perhaps most curiously, the mission was not exactly "Russian" in a straightforward sense. The first Albazinians, all of whom resettled to Beijing from the region of the Amur River, included not only Russian Cossacks but also native Siberian Buryats and Tungus (Evenks), and by the early 1800s, the descendants of this mixed community—Russians and Siberians alike—had become, by all appearances, Chinese. Their everyday language was Chinese. They dressed in Chinese clothing and went by Chinese names. Albazinian men would braid their hair in queues in the Manchu fashion as required by Qing law. Even the church at the Mission had the look of a Chinese temple.

Hyacinth's presence in Beijing, thus, symbolized the Qing commitment to one of the long-standing practices of Eurasian empires, which was to ensure a certain cultural autonomy to their diverse subjects. In this case, this meant abiding by an understanding with the Russians that the latter would be able to uphold the Albazinians' Orthodox faith by assigning a small delegation of Russian religious personnel to maintain the mission church and perform Orthodox rites and services. In the interim, however, the Albazinians changed, becoming a more obviously Sinicized community—Russian in religion, Chinese in everything else—and yet this, too, was fairly ordinary imperial business.

In fact, for all the curiousness of "Russian Beijing" from the perspective of our highly national age, this milieu was *not* strange for its time. Empires inducted foreigners into their service, who then often adapted to the empires they served. Hyacinth's Chinese appearance isn't odd, either. During their time in Beijing, the members of the Mission received a stipend from the Qing government, including an allowance for clothing.[5] Hyacinth appears here in the plain summer robe (*chaofu* 朝服) and plaited bamboo hat (*liangguan* 涼冠) covered with strands of red-dyed silk typical of a low-level Qing official.[6] His parishioners were effectively Chinese. Like them, he dressed in Chinese fashion. In a basic sense, everything fits.

At the same time, the painting isn't just about the habits of Russian Beijing. It's also a personal document about Father Hyacinth. Not every Russian monk chose to be painted (or paint himself) in Chinese dress. That Hyacinth did so implies that this was how he wanted to appear. Unlike the Albazinians, Hyacinth was not a Sinicized Russian. Instead, it's more accurate to describe him as *Russianized*, given that he was not Russian by birth, but rather grew up in a Chuvash village in what is today the Chuvash Republic in central Russia. (The Chuvash speak a Turkic language completely different from Russian and other Indo-European languages.) Though his family was Orthodox, he likely spoke Chuvash at home and only gradually became more deeply culturally Russian, probably as a result of his religious schooling in Kazan. It was there that he took his monastic vows in 1800. After this, he served briefly as a monastery instructor and director in Siberia before being appointed to the Beijing mission in 1807. Following his return from China in 1822, he lived most of the rest of his life at the famous Alexander Nevsky monastery in St. Petersburg, while also working as a translator for the Asiatic Department of the Russian Ministry of Foreign Affairs. Yet even in St. Petersburg, he would occasionally wear Chinese dress. This Chinese "look," in effect, became part of his self-presentation.

In all, Hyacinth spent just fourteen years in China, but it was enough to change his life. In an autobiographical note completed a few years before his death, he recalls how he threw himself into studying Chinese "the day after [arriving] in Beijing," and he was noted both at the time and later (usually critically by his church superiors) for his apparently limitless passion for all things Chinese.[7] His time in China, in effect, laid the groundwork for everything that followed, since it was in Beijing that he learned Chinese (as well as some Manchu) and immersed himself in the cultural habits that allowed him to speak with authority about Chinese life. He also used his time in the Chinese capital to amass a vast collection of Chinese- and Manchu-language materials, leaving Beijing with some fifteen camel-loads of books, manuscripts, and maps.[8] He made his career as a Chinese expert by translating these works, sprinkling them with commentaries on Chinese culture and history, most of them infused with the idea that he—Hyacinth—was relaying valuable insider information, offering, in effect, the intimate view of a foreign land that only experience can provide.

Hyacinth's influence on Russian Sinology was immense. His works earned prizes and accolades in Russia and Europe, and Russian specialists on China still refer today to his time as the "Bichurin period" (*bichurinskii period*) of Russian Chinese Studies, seeing him as a kind of father of the field. It was also precisely in his time that the Russian Mission began a shift towards becoming a center for the Russian academic study of China.

But what of the painting? What does it tell us? Art always at once hides and reveals, and perhaps portraits and self-portraits especially. Everything about a portrait is constructed, planned, adjusted. What we're meant to see here is Hyacinth's depiction of himself as a Russian monk dressed in the uniform of a Qing official. We have no records describing the portrait, let alone what he might have had in mind when he painted it. But we can at least presume that he intended it as a true rendition. The painting is meant to be realistic. We feel this from the careful detail added to the face, the thin strap of the hat running beneath the chin, the buttons. That Hyacinth regularly wore Chinese dress during his time in Beijing is also true. According to the head of the Cossack escort that accompanied the Ninth Mission out of China, he remained in Chinese dress even after leaving Beijing, changing into his monk's robes only once the party reached Russian territory.[9]

Yet what the portrait doesn't reveal is the complex history of imperial encounters *behind* the painting: the borderland politics that led to the establishment of a small, mixed Russian-Buryat-Tungus Orthodox community in Beijing; the customs of imperial rule that laid the basis for the Russian Mission; and the cross-cultural dynamics that gradually changed the Albazinians and, in different ways, Hyacinth himself.

Though at first glance we might assume that this is a painting of a Russian pretending to be Chinese, it is, in fact, a portrait of a Russianized Chuvash serving in a tsarist imperial institution overseen by a Qing imperial institution whose practical function was to link the two empires. Rather than a Russian example of European-style Orientalist display, it's instead a small window on a lost but meaningful world of interimperial entanglement.

NOTES

1. See *"Pervyi al'bom" O. Iakinfa (N.Ia. Bichurina): issledovaniia i kommentarii*, edited and compiled by O. V. Vasil'eva (Saint Petersburg: Rossiiskaia natsional'naia biblioteka, 2010), 74; and *"Vtoroi" i "Tret'ii" al'bom O. Iakinfa (N.Ia. Bichurina)*, edited and compiled by O. V. Vasil'eva (Saint Petersburg: Rossiiskaia natsional'naia biblioteka, 2012), no page number indicated. For a brief overview of Father Hyacinth (Bichurin) in English, see David Schimmelpenninck van der Oye, *Russian Orientalism: Asia in the Russian Mind from Peter the Great to the Emigration* (New Haven: Yale University Press, 2010), 139–152.
2. Vladimir Terebenev, *Portrait of Bichurin as an Orthodox monk* (c. 1807). Reproduced in V. P. Zhuchkov, "Arkhivnye nakhodki o monakhe Iakinfe Bichurine," *Izvestiia Natsional'noi akademii nauk i iskusstv Chuvashskoi Respubliki*, 4 (2002): 44–51. http://www.nbchr.ru/virt_bichurin/pdf/page03/2.pdf
3. The back of the painting includes the inscription "Own portrait" (*Portret sobstv . . .*) in Hyacinth's hand, and we know that he was otherwise a talented artist. For evidence of Bichurin's talents as an artist, see the illustrations in the works cited in endnote 1. For more on the claim that the work is a self-portrait, see the following articles by Elena Nesterova: "Russkie khudozhniki dukhovnoi missii v Pekine," *Zarubezhnye khudozhniki i Rossiia* (St. Petersburg: Akademiia khudozhestv, Institut zhivopisi, skul'ptury i arkhitektury im. I. E. Repina, 1991), 4, no. 2 (1991): 24–30; "Avtoportret v kitaiskom kostiume," *Isskustvo Leningrada* 5 (1990): 58–63; and "K voprosu ob avtorstve portreta N.Ia. Bichurina," in *Pismennye pamiatniki i problem istorii kul'tury narodov vostoka: XXIII godichnaia nauchnaia sessiia LO IV AN SSSR (doklady i soobshcheniia) 1988* (Moscow: Nauka, 1990) pt. 1, 70–76.
4. Eric Widmer, *The Russian Ecclesiastical Mission in Peking during the Eighteenth Century* (Cambridge, MA: East Asian Research Center, distributed by Harvard University Press, 1976); Gregory Afinogenov, *Spies and Scholars: Chinese Secrets and Imperial Russia's Quest for World Power* (Cambridge, MA: Harvard University Press, 2020).

5. The Russian Mission fell under the legal authority of a special Qing office usually rendered in English as the Court of Colonial Affairs, though the Manchu name translates more directly as the Office for the Administration of Outlying Territories (Chinese: *Lifan Yuan* 理藩院; Manchu: *Tulergi golo be dasara jurgan*). On this institution, see the essays in Dittmar Schorkowitz and Ning Chia, eds., *Managing Frontiers in Qing China: The Lifanyuan and Libu Revisited* (Leiden: Brill, 2016). On the clothing allowance (*na plat'e*), see I.N.A. [Adoratskii], *Otets Iakinf Bichurin: istoricheskii etiud'* (Kazan: Tip. Imperatorskogo Universiteta, 1886), 44–45.
6. The red strands on Hyacinth's hat might be dyed horsehair rather than silk. For a description of Qing official garments in this period, see Valery Garrett, *Chinese Dress: From the Qing Dynasty to the Present Day* (Tokyo: Tuttle Publishing, 2019), 63–78.
7. For the reference to studying Chinese, see O. Iakinf Bichurin, *Avtobiograficheskaia zapiska* (Perepech. iz 3-ogo t. Uchen. Zapisok Imp. Akad. Nauk po Pervomu i Tret'emu otdeleniiam, 1855), 666.
8. S. A. Tokarev, *Istoriia russkoi etnografii (dooktiabrskii period)* (Moscow: Nauka, 1966), 160.
9. The clothing change occurred "in either Kiakhta or Irkutsk [Adoratskii]," *Otets Iakinf Bichurin*, 70.

CHAPTER 18

VIGNETTES OF EMPIRE: "ASIATIC PEOPLES" AT NINETEENTH-CENTURY IMPERIAL RUSSIAN CORONATIONS

RICHARD WORTMAN

NINETEENTH-CENTURY IMPERIAL Russian coronations gave visual expressions of the existence and meaning of empire at the outset of each reign. The expressions varied from reign to reign, revealing the changing concepts and goals of imperial rule through illustrations and sanctioned responses. The optics of the celebration transformed the immediate event into an elaboration of myth. Spectacle lifted observers above the ordinary and allowed them to behold, or imagine, an empire of vast reaches that comprised a multitude and variety of peoples, what Victor Zhivov described as "an ethnographic myth of empire."[1]

The words *Asiatic* and *exotic*, then, made these peoples appear foreign while they continued to be considered Russian subjects: "*poddannye rossiiskie*."[2] This made their presentation appear as masquerade—a different, more resplendent reality. At Alexander II's coronation ball in 1856, the poet Fedor Tiutchev felt that he was in the realm of a dream of Russia embracing the East. "Ah, how much dream there is in what belongs to reality," he wrote.[3]

The meaning of the spectacle, however, was not left to the imagination. Verbal texts and visual images elaborated both the significance of the event and the expected responses from the population as set forth in coronation albums and reported in the press. This chapter will focus on the presentation of the images of the Asian or Turkic "other" within the empire, both as revealed in the tsar's festive coronation procession and other events and as characterized by writers and illustrators who defined their meanings. Word and image joined to lend each coronation its special significance and aura, constituting an idiom of representation adopted by the ruler and his elite, here relating specifically to the presence within the empire of Asiatic peoples.

The imperial entry, as it evolved during the eighteenth and early nineteenth centuries, was a presentation of the governmental and military elite of empire in all their grandeur. It was a drama of conquest, as the highest officials of the state and court and the dashing figures of the leading regiments of the guard from the Europeanized capital, St. Petersburg, took symbolic possession of the more Russian "second capital," Moscow, and received its acclamation. The uniformity of their Western-style uniforms set the tone for a festive affirmation of the unity of an empire sharing a common culture and subordination to the emperor and his court. Few representatives of other national or social groups appeared, and when they did, their presence remained inconspicuous.

Nineteenth-century coronations, beginning with the crowning of Nicholas I in 1826, inaugurated a different theme. They incorporated non-Russians visibly in their ritual displays as evidence of imperial domination. The distinctive national character of the Russian empire was its command of the obedience of its subjects, whose number and diversity attested to the Russian emperor's sway. The non-Russian nationalities made their first appearance at Nicholas I's coronation as spectators of the entry procession to Moscow. They were included in the events surrounding and following the coronation as described in the semi-official account published by the artist and travel writer Pavel Svinin. They made the greatest impression at the coronation masquerade ball, which remained a symbolic venue for the display of the imperial domination of Eastern nationalities.

Viewing the scene from the balcony, the author saw the ladies' gowns sparkling in silver and gold. Svinin described "Asian ladies" who wore "sumptuous furs and valuable brocades," but he was more preoccupied by the dress of the Russian women "dressed in Russian *sarafans* [traditional long, colorful pinafores], with Russian *poviazki* [embroidered bands or ribbons] and *kokoshniki* [ornate headdresses] on their heads, bathed, one might say, in pearls and diamonds." As they danced the polonaise, their "patriotic attire" (*otechestvennyi nariad*) transported him back to the times "when Russians were not ashamed of their splendid dress, proper for the climate, having a national character, and incomparably more beautiful than foreign dress." To confirm the universal acceptance of this "truth," Svinin cited the opinion of an "enlightened foreigner," who preferred these ladies to those dressed in the latest European fashion.[4] The coronation album published in Paris in 1826 also presented the masquerade as an image of empire. The author, one Henry Graf, wrote, "It seemed to have reunited everything that Europe and Asia had to offer in beauty, wealth, and pomp."[5]

The coronation of Alexander II in 1856 marked a new phase in the optics of empire. The event celebrated the successes of imperial expansion in previous decades, compensating for a humiliating defeat in the Crimean War. The pomp and circumstance of the coronation were recorded in lithographs bound in massive commemorative volumes. The idiom is welcoming. In the context of Alexander's "scenario of love," the tone of the volumes is inclusive: nationalities were represented as if drawn into the mythical image of an empire adoring the sovereign.[6] The emphasis shifts from unity to the variety and esthetic brilliance of the Eastern nationalities. The emperor's coronation entry displayed the loyalty and devotion of the people Russian armies had succeeded in conquering in the Caucasus, Central Asia, and Middle Asia. For the first time, representatives of Asiatic peoples marched with the Russian elite.

The multinational character of Russian empire displayed at Alexander II's coronation entry played to an international audience and the many representatives of the Western press attending the event. The album, published in French as well as Russian, elaborated themes of incorporation: a cavalcade of empire, and a display of diversity, color, and extent, departing from the ordered reserve of previous coronations. Behind the horsemen of the "Black Sea Cossacks" rode those from "peoples subject to Russia," the coronation album noted. It then went on to enumerate those who "were distinguished by their picturesque attire." These "picturesque" peoples included Tatars and populations from the Caucasus: Gurians, Mingrelians, Kurds, Tatar elites (*beki*), and representatives of Cherkassian tribes. "The manly look of the riders and the rich saddles of the steeds drew special attention to this part of the procession."[7] The emphasis was on the colorful warriors, the empire as painting.

The plate in the coronation album presented the entry as a swirl of glimpses of parts of the procession as they passed by Moscow landmarks. A series of prints by the Baltic-German artist Vasily Timm in his illustrated journal *Russkii Khudozhestvennyi Listok* follow the model of eighteenth-century prints in showing the entire procession, without background, snaking back and forth on the page, but unlike the earlier prints depicting the tiny figures "from peoples under Russian power," these were depicted with distinguishable features.[8]

Vignettes of individual "Asiatics" encapsulated the changing attitudes to the imperial other elaborated in the texts. An inset in the album showed dashing figures of the Caucasian deputies to the coronation celebrating the event (Image 18.1). Another shows a Kyrgyz engaged in a hunt, displaying his skills at falconry. The tsar, on horseback in the background, looks on. (Image 18.2). The responses in the press were upbeat, savoring the vigor of empire, a counterweight to Russia's now diminished place in Europe. The reporters presented the dress and the manner of these horsemen as signs of the varied peoples of the empire, its vitality and vast reaches. Russian writers in the semi-official *Russkii Khudozhestvennyi Listok*; foreign correspondents from the Russian mouthpieces abroad, *L'Independance Belge* and *Le Nord*; and William Russell of the *Times of London*, reiterated these themes. *Russkii Khudozhestvennyi Listok* described the deputies of Asiatic peoples as "tangible proof of the vastness of our state, which some justly call a special kind of planet." Their appearance in procession "eloquently convinced all of the one whose power they recognize, whom they had come from their own lands to worship."[9]

IMAGE 18.1 Caucasian Deputies at the Coronation of Alexander II. Coronation Album of Emperor Alexander II and Empress Maria Alexandrovna (*Opisanie sviashchenneishago koronovaniia . . . imperatora Aleksandra Vtorago i imperatritsy Marii Aleksandrovny vsei Rossia*), 1856.

The spirit of imperial inclusion persisted in the first decades of Alexander II's reign, nurturing the expectation that the education of native elites would contribute to the unity and progress of the Russian Empire. Rather than an effort to subject all nationalities to the same laws and institutions, assimilation now would take the form of instilling a spirit of imperial citizenship (*grazhdanstvennost'*) in the populations of regions such as the Caucasus, Tatarstan, Bashkiria, and Turkestan.[10] Officials and generals sought to spread the ideas of citizenship to the Caucasus by introducing schools, opera houses, and the notion that the natives could be transformed into loyal servants of empire. This policy bore fruit, successfully producing a cohort of such native leaders. But the Imperial Russian state soon proved inhospitable to native leaders, who had their own ambitions and lacked the noble credentials and loyalties of earlier members of the elite.

The failure and unwillingness to integrate the national leaders into the Russian governing elite, as well as the refusal of Russian rulers to countenance public participation of any kind, resulted in a new national myth and a new ceremonial idiom.

IMAGE 18.2 Kyrgyz huntsman. Coronation Album of Alexander II (*Opisanie sviashchennei-shago koronovaniia*), 1856.

If Nicholas I's coronation unfolded as a display of domination over imperial subjects and Alexander II's coronation evoked a spirit of congeniality and acceptance, Alexander III's coronation, dominated by a spirit of hostility to the reform efforts of the previous decades, presented a third image of empire—Russia as colonial power. Following European and American examples, Russians began to cast themselves increasingly as a master race, bringing civilization to those they regarded as lesser peoples, particularly Asians.[11] The national myth, elaborated at the coronation, elevated a notion of an ethnic, Orthodox, ruling elite—as conquerors and, therefore, like other European powers, rulers of native peoples. The emperor appears in the illustrations of these events in the national dress he favored—Russian hat and boots.

The idiom was intimidating, reaffirming the motif of conquest, but in new imperial guise. While watching the entry into Moscow on May 10, 1883, the English correspondent, Charles Lowe, one of the forty-nine foreign correspondents invited at government expense to attend the festivities, felt he was witnessing a triumph from the time of imperial Rome. He caught sight of a "scarlet crowd" in the distance that looked like a British regiment. But it turned out to be the emperor's personal convoy, consisting of "three-squadrons of Circassians and Don Cossacks, all finely-made, handsome men, and bravely mounted." He cited the opening lines of Shakespeare's *Julius Caesar*:

> What conquests brings he home!
> What tributaries follow him to Rome
> To grace in captive bonds his chariot wheels!

Then came deputies from the numerous "Asiatic tribes" and "Cossack tribes." "All eyes turned on these picturesque strangers from the Far East," he wrote, "who pace along on their richly-caparisoned steeds. . . . On they ride before the mighty Monarch,"[12] confirming the Roman motif. The celebrations impressed Eastern deputies with the power and wealth of the Russian emperor. A delegation of chieftains from Turkestan invited to the coronation were so overwhelmed with the magnificence of the events and the shows of military might that they decided further resistance was hopeless. They formed a Russian party that petitioned for admission to the Russian empire in 1884.

The officially sponsored coronation descriptions no longer expressed a sense of admiration for the Eastern representatives in the entry procession. The "peoples ruled by Russia" are again mentioned in the coronation album, riding behind the Black Sea Cossacks, but without further comment.[13] A coronation volume published by the Pan-Slavist Vissarion Komarov expressed sentiments of national superiority and colonial disdain. The author depicted, without illustration, "a messy crowd, bumping into each other . . . a murderously funny procession of savages." They wore "the most motley robes," which were extraordinarily garish, and strange costumes in bright colors. "Some dress like women, others tightly like ballet dancers." One could not but "give a good laugh" at a Kalmyk mullah (on horseback wearing a wide red robe and a yellow cap, "like those worn by chorus girls in "Ruslan and Ludmilla" [a popular opera based on a Russian fairytale].[14]

The change in attitude reflected a broader shift in the conceptions of national identity reflected in both official and public discourse. As John Slocum and Paul Werth have demonstrated, in the mid-nineteenth century non-Russian nationalities began to be characterized in terms of ethnicity, rather than religion or simple backwardness. The change in discourse was reflected in the terminology for other nationalities, which shifted from *inovertsy* (peoples of other religions) to *inorodtsy* (people of other ethnic stock, or aliens). The new symbolic vocabulary increasingly precluded the possibility of transformation, either the religious hopes for conversion or the secular visions of enlightenment, that had been conflated in earlier visions of a multinational Russian empire.[15]

The album for Nicholas II's coronation in 1896 reveals the same condescension to subject peoples. After a detachment of gendarmes, the entry opened with the "Cossacks of the Emperor's own convoy." The album described these "dashing swarthy horsemen" in red Circassian coats and fur hats, brandishing their swords. "At their appearance, the admiration of the crowd burst forth into hurrahs and shouts of pleasure," the *New York Times* correspondent wrote. They led in a company of Cossacks of the Guard. The album described them as "Handsome fellows, their *papakhi* (wool hats) cocked to the side, holding frightening lances in their hands like feathers and merrily looking out at God's world." Then came the long line of "deputies of Asiatic peoples under the power of Russia"—representatives of Caucasian peoples, Turkmen, Tekintsy (a Turkmen group), Sarts (Uzbeks), and Kyrgyz. The description was not without a note of disdain: "original [*original'nye*; i.e. a bit odd] characteristic figures, quaint clothing, and ornate saddles of these eastern horsemen aroused the special interest of the people." The illustration or "vignette" by N. Samokish shows a group of disheveled and somewhat distracted horsemen[16] (Image 18.3).

The cantata performed at the coronation banquet, written by Alexander Glazunov and the popular playwright and chief of repertoire for the imperial theaters of

IMAGE 18.3 Deputies of "Asiatic peoples under the power of Russia." Coronation Album of Nicholas II (*Koronatsionnyi sbornik: Koronovanie v Moskve, 14 maia 1896*).

St. Petersburg, Victor Krylov, intoned rhetoric about the vast expanse of the empire and Russia's imperial destiny. The singers gave voice to the joy of the parts of the empire, North, South, East, and West, at the coronation of its sovereign. "Russia is united in a single feeling," the chorus sang. The mezzo-soprano, in the role of the South, sang of their forefathers' defeat of the Tatars. The basso, as the North, told how nature fell silent before the wondrous celebrations. The East, a soprano, announced that Russia was awakening Eastern nations, while the West, again the mezzo-soprano, told how Europe had shared enlightenment with Russia. Russia was the force of progress in the East:

> The Kamchatkian, the Kalmyk, and Sarmatian
> Leave their wretched hovels,
> And they greet the softening influence of morals,
> The mercy and kind impulses,
> Like sons, with open arms.

Then Russia, "conscious of its strength," turns in friendship to the West, in mutual love and accord, a reference to the image of Russian tsar as bringer of peace. The domination of empire was a national domination, personified in the ascendancy of Moscow, the demiurge, whom the chorus apostrophized to conclude the cantata:

> Moscow of the golden cupolas . . .
> In your walls was born the start,
> Of all these sovereign labors.[17]

NOTES

1. V. M. Zhivov, "Gosudarstvennyi mif v epokhu Prosveshcheniia i ego razrushenie v Rossii kontsa XVIII veka," in *Vek Prosveshcheniia. Rossiia i Frantsiia: materialy nauchnoi konferentsii "Vipperovskie chteniia – 1987,"* vyp. 20, edited by I. E. Danilova (Moscow: Gos. muzei izobrazitel'nykh iskusstv im. A. S. Pushkina, 1989), 154.
2. O. G. Ageeva, "Imperskii status Rossii: k istorii politicheskogo mentaliteta Russkogo obshchestva nachala XVIII veka," in *Tsar' i tsarstvo v russkom obshchestvennom soznanii* (Moscow: In-t rossiiskoi istorii RAN, 1999), 120, 123.
3. I. S. Aksakov, *Biografiia Fedora Ivanovicha Tiutcheva* (Moscow: M. G. Volchaninov, 1886), 262–263; "Lettres de Th. I. Tjutsheff a sa seconde epouse née Baronne de Pfeffel," *Starina i Novizna* XIX (1915): 160–161.
4. Pavel Svin'in, "Istoricheskoe opisanie Sviashchennogo Koronovaniia i Miropomazaniia ikh Imperatorskikh Velichestv Gosudaria Imperatora Nikolaia Pavlovicha i Gosudaryni Imperatritsy Aleksandry Feodorovny," *Otechestvennye Zapiski* 32 (1827): 26–34.
5. *Vues des cérémonies les plus intéressantes du couronnement de leurs majestés Impériales l'empereur Nicholas Ier et l'impératrice Alexandra à Moscou* (Paris: Didot,1828), 11.
6. On Alexander II's "scenario of love," that is, the messaging around his rule that presented him as loving member of a close family, and as beloved, benevolent father/ruler to his adoring subjects/children, see my *Scenarios of Power: Myth and Ceremony in Russian Monarchy. From Peter the Great to the Abdication of Nicholas II*, abridged edition (Princeton, NJ: Princeton University Press, 2006), 189-204.

7. *Opisanie sviashchenneishago koronovaniia Ikh Imperatorskikh Velichestv Gosudaria Imperatora Aleksandra Vtorago i Imperatritsy Marii Aleksandrovny Vseia Rossii* (St. Petersburg : Ak. Khudozhestv, 1856), 15.
8. *Russkii Khudozhestvennyi Listok* no. 29 (October 10, 1856), 1.
9. *Russkii Khudozhestvennyi Listok*, 1.
10. See Dov Yaroshevskii, "Empire and Citizenship," in *Russia's Orient: Imperial Borderlands and Peoples, 1800–1917*, edited by Daniel R. Brower and Edward J. Lazzerini (Bloomington: Indiana University Press, 1997), 69–71.
11. Andreas Kappeler, *The Russian Empire: A Multi-Ethnic History*,trans. by Alfred Clayton (NY: Routledge, 2001), 264–266; see also Austin Jersild, *Orientalism and Empire: North Caucasus Mountain Peoples and the Georgian Frontier* (Montreal: McGill-Queen's Press, 2002),126–144.
12. *The Times of London*, May 23, 1883, 5.
13. *Opisanie sviashchennogo koronovaniia*, 4–5.
14. V. Komarov, *V pamiat' sviashchennago koronovaniia Gosudaria Imperatora Aleksandra III i Gosudarynia Imperatritsy Marii Fedorovny* (St. Petersburg:, V. Komarov, 1883), 56–57.
15. See Paul Werth, "Changing Conceptions of Difference, Assimilation, and Faith in the Volga-Kama Region, 1740–1870," in *Russian Empire: Space, People, Power, 1700-1930*, edited by Jane Burbank, Mark Von Hagen, and Anatolyi Remnev (Bloomington, IN: Indiana University Press, 2007), 171–188; John W. Slocum, "Who, and When, Were the Inorodtsy? The Evolution of the Category of 'Aliens' in Imperial Russia," *Russian Review* 57 (1998): 173–190.
16. *Koronatsionnyi Sbornik: Koronovanie v Moskve; 14 maia 1896* (St. Petersburg: Eksped. Gos. Bumag, 1899), 1:209–210; *New York Times*, May 22, 1896, 7.
17. *Koronatsionnyi Sbornik*, 1:280–283.

CHAPTER 19

THE WOMEN OF EMPIRE STRIKE BACK (1856)

NADJA BERKOVICH

IN 1855, a well-educated young Kazakh officer, ethnographer, and explorer, Chokan Chingisovich Valikhanov (1835–1865), met the up-and-coming author Fyodor Dostoevsky. It was just a year after the writer had been released from the Omsk stockade in western Siberia, where he had been imprisoned for radical political activity. Each of the men would go on to produce accounts of their impressions of the non-Russian peoples of the empire, and they would become lifelong friends. At the time of their meeting, Dostoevsky was working on his novel, *Notes from the House of the Dead*, about his experience of imprisonment and of his first direct contact with the multilingual and multiethnic peoples of the empire. Valikhanov, too, was engaged in recording his impressions of non-Russians, in his case the peoples of Central Asia, and of areas not yet fully incorporated into the empire. While these two men both approached their subjects according to the quasi-documentary standards of colonial ethnography, they also, in some ways, challenged the imperious assumptions of the day. Instead of reducing colonial subjects (or soon-to-be-subjects) to a state of abject passivity, they both attributed a degree of active agency to the people they described in their writings—and in Valikhanov's case, in his drawings as well.

The comparison between Dostoevsky and Valikhanov proves interesting not only in the similarities it reveals, but also in the differences. As this article will show, the two men approached their material from very different positions within the empire. While Dostoevsky was a Russian, exiled from his home in St. Petersburg to Siberia, Valikhanov was Kazakh. His Kazakh name was Shoqan Shynghysuly Walikhanov. Though born and raised far from the metropolitan capitals of Petersburg and Moscow, he was highly educated in the prestigious Russian cadet school in Omsk and, later, at St. Petersburg University. His perspective gives us a rare double vision, that of insider and outsider, colonial official and colonized subject. His dual viewpoint is especially evident in his depictions and descriptions of Central Asian women. As a man of his times, he embraced the forms of male privilege and assumptions about women's passivity and sexual availability that typified imperial writings of the period, but he also allowed traces of female agency to slip into his work. Valikhanov, with his multivalent status within empire, produced a unique visual and textual corpus that complicates imperial attitudes to both ethnicity and gender.

Let us begin with a quick look at Dostoevsky's *Notes from the House of the Dead*. The work may be read as a quasi-documentary, colonial ethnography and investigation of prison conditions and the different categories of prisoners. In giving voice to a variety of characters with the status of colonial subjects, including Poles, Tatars, Lezgins, Chechens, and a solitary Jew, as well as Ukrainian and Russian peasants, Dostoevsky transforms the prisoners from voiceless objects into subjects who gain agency. Yet the main narrator of the *Notes*, Aleksandr Petrovich Gorianchikov, a Russian nobleman and an outsider among the criminal and political convicts, represents the subjects with a fixed ethnographic lens. Gorianchikov describes a "poor sooty yurt of some poor Kyrgyz . . . , a Kyrgyz woman who is occupied with her two sheep. All this is poor and wild, but free."[1] This exercise in imaginative ethnography repeats a standard Orientalist trope of presenting the Indigenous people as "poor and wild." In particular, Dostoevsky depicts Kyrgyz women (likely Kazakh, in current terminology) as being passive, obsequious, and subservient to their husbands.

Dostoevsky's fragmented depiction of a Kyrgyz family contrasts with Valikhanov's sympathetic description, revealing two opposite colonial visions. The fragmentation stems from the fact that Dostoevsky did not possess the linguistic skills and knowledge about Kazakh culture that Valikhanov had. In all of his works, Dostoevsky focused primarily on Russians rather than other ethnic groups. Significantly, Valikhanov was an ethnic Kazakh, according to the categories in use today, but his Russian contemporaries called him a Kyrgyz, as was customary at the time. Both Kazakhs and Kyrgyz were pastoral nomadic peoples at the time. They spoke Turkic languages, and most practiced Islam.

Born into an educated elite nomadic family, Valikhanov knew several Turkic languages, Chagatai, and Arabic, and he learned Russian at the imperial Omsk cadet school, from which his father had also graduated (though prior to its becoming a cadet school). His father, the sultan Chingis, spoke Russian well, and he served as a representative of the Kazakh people in Omsk. Growing up in a Kazakh family, Valikhanov was suited for imperial service because of his inside knowledge of the Kazakh and Kyrgyz people he was tasked to report on. He was an interesting example of double colonization. On the one hand, he was a colonial subject of the empire, an *inorodets* (an "other," non-Russian) according to imperial terminology. On the other hand, with his Russian education and his employment in the service of the state, he provided the regime with essential knowledge for further colonization. However, it is not clear whether the material that he collected was used by the tsarist regime for advancing the rights of the subjects he studied.

In 1856, at the age of twenty-one, Valikhanov set out on an expedition to Lake Issyk-Kul' (Lake Ysyk), situated in the northern Tian Shan mountains, in the northeastern corner of what is now Kyrgyzstan. The expedition was under the direction of Mikhail Khomentovskii (1820–1888). Even though the purpose of the expedition was political, to mediate between arguing tribes, Valikhanov utilized his ethnographic skills to explore ancient Kazakh stone sculptures and create topographic maps of the territory around Lake Issyk-Kul'. This mapping facilitated Russia's expansion into what is now Kazakhstan and Kyrgyzstan, which would later become part of the Russian Empire. On behalf of the Imperial Russian Geographical Society, he would later carry out reconnaissance in the Chinese Empire, collect ethnographic and folkloric material on the Kyrgyz, and record the national Kyrgyz epic poem, *Manas*. He would also make maps of the eastern Turkestan region of Central Asia and sketch drawings of its various ethnic peoples: Kazakhs, Kyrgyz, Uighurs, Chinese, and Kashgars, people who lived in the far western part of China.

Valikhanov served imperial interests dutifully. At the same time, however, he was capable of being critical of Russian governance and of his own culture alike. According to his classmate at the Omsk cadet school, Grigorii Nikolaevich Potanin (1835–1920), a famous ethnographer, geographer, and traveler to Central Asia, Mongolia, and Siberia, Valikhanov was a liberal thinker and not religious. He was also acquainted with many prominent intellectuals of his time, including the radical writer Nikolay Chernyshevsky and, of course, the politically suspect Dostoevsky.

Valikhanov's critical approach to Russian imperial governance, and his appreciation for the culture of the Indigenous people of the steppe, is also apparent in his "Notes on Judicial Reform," written in 1864, just before his early death at the age of thirty. In it, he discussed the judicial reforms aimed at the people of the steppe and the Turkestan region. He opposed the blanket application of the Russian judicial system and defended the traditional Kazakh system, with the tribal leaders (*bii*) at its center. He argued that the local institutions were more democratic and transparent than the new Russian ones. He pointed out that what was good for the Russian people might not work for the non-Russians (*inorodtsy*). Ultimately, he showed that in order to implement a new judicial system, one must first know and understand the everyday lives, beliefs, and cultures of the local peoples. His careful ethnographic work thus served a mixed agenda.

During approximately two months of travel with the 1856 expedition under Khomentovskii, Valikhanov wrote the "Diary of a Journey to Issyk-Kul'." The diary contained detailed descriptions of the region's landscape, hydrology, flora, and fauna. He also recorded folklore associated with specific places, and most relevant to the visual theme of this volume, he made sketches of the people he encountered. Valikhanov's drawings and the diary he kept during his travels to Lake Issyk-Kul' served the colonial ambitions of the Russian Empire to expand its eastern borders by visualizing future imperial subjects—that is, his own fellow Kyrgyz and Kazakh peoples. At the same time, his work subverted Orientalist perceptions of them as backwards and uneducated.

In its discussions of Kyrgyz women, and in drawings of those women that accompany the text, the diary exposed the Orientalist tropes and patriarchal perspective that Valikhanov brought to his work. Yet the diary also unexpectedly undermines its own positions. Including quotes from women, reporting interactions, and drawing their images on paper, the diary gives voice to the Kyrgyz women he encountered, by letting them speak. Valikhanov's diary, I argue, unintentionally exhibits a female alternative to the male gaze.

Together, the visual and textual inform and complement each other in empowering the female subjects, challenging the notion of their objectification. Troubling European Russians' tendency to imagine a passive "Orient," Valikhanov presents himself, a Kazakh, as an active viewer. Moreover, as a sort of insider, he enjoyed a kind of access to nomadic society that was inaccessible to Russians. He was able to see things that a Russian would not. He boasts of this privileged access, and in particular of his access to the sphere of women, in a way that elevates his masculine prowess. He shares a sexualized, androcentric view of steppe women with his male Russian colleagues, and titillates his readers with reports of his encounters. He states that "one could have a brief relation with them, if he had had the time."[2]

In these intimate encounters, however, he also, perhaps unintentionally, shows that Kyrgyz women were not at all the passive beings the Russian stereotypes anticipated. This is what sets him apart from Dostoevsky's depiction of the Kyrgyz people in *Notes*. Because of his dual Kazakh and Russian cultural identity, Valikhanov's representation is more nuanced than that of Dostoevsky, and hints at a somewhat critical stance toward empire. Valikhanov's depiction is more sympathetic, less judgmental and arrogant, in its assessment, and it gives his subjects a more humanizing treatment.

At the time of the expedition, Valikhanov was twenty-one years old and travelling in the company of other men. His diary suggests that he did not abstain from sexual encounters with Indigenous women. His Asian appearance and habit of occasionally dressing as a Kyrgyz may have made it easier for him to connect with the Kyrgyz women, and even to pursue dalliances with them. He describes his travels as "fruitful," due to the favorable disposition of women towards him and his entourage. The diary presents them as being "frivolous," though it also describes them as "witty."[3] He was not shying away from looking at them, and we can see that in his drawings (Images 19.1, 19.2, and 19.3). His access to the sphere of women may have been more limited than he admits, however. His drawings of women are rushed sketches in black and white, whereas the male leaders of different Kyrgyz tribes are presented in more detailed drawings, thoroughly developed, and often in color.

Valikhanov's drawings of women are executed in a simple, realistic manner representative of the ethnographic style of drawing of the time. His sketches were similar in style and composition to those of his teacher, A. Pomerantsev, and of other ethnographic illustrators during that period. Their works share elements of style,

IMAGE 19.1 Chokan Valikhanov, "Uch Aiach. Three Women," 1856.

IMAGE 19.2 Chokan Valikhanov, "Issyk-Kyl' Kyrgyz Women," 1856.

IMAGE 19.3 Chokan Valikhanov, "Nomadic Travels of the Kyrgyz from Issyk-Kul'," 1856.

technique, and ethnographic detail. They focused on the details of the head coverings and shoes, and they even standardized the way figures were positioned.

In Valikhanov's drawings of the Issyk-Kul' Kyrgyz, women's faces are not individualized, but their clothing is meticulously depicted, especially head coverings and hair arrangements, to signify differing social status. In his diary, Valikhanov stated that he assembled a collection of women's clothing, describing with great detail the attire of married and unmarried women of different tribes or ethnic groups. In the drawings, we see two types of head coverings and hair arrangements: the pointed hat (*fes*) with a small tassel, worn by unmarried women, and the two white scarves that wrapped around the head, worn by married women (Images 19.1 and 19.2). The married women braid their hair into two braids, decorating the endings with coins and other trinkets, whereas the unmarried girls do the opposite, displaying "braids that are [gradually] unplaited into multiple thin locks, decorated near the ears with pearls, coral, or beads, depending on their means. The length of hair is considered the foremost standard of beauty. That is why all women wear fake braids."[4] These elaborate depictions of hair indicate the marital status of the women, and also point out the intricate cultural markers that set apart one subculture from another.

The textual vignettes that make up his diary complement the drawings. Valikhanov goes against Russian expectations when he describes Kyrgyz women as assertive and outspoken, even in spaces dominated by men. Reading his diary, one sees these women objectified and, at the same time, exerting agency.

Whereas his illustrations emphasize ethnographic detail and realistic representation, his diary attests that he was fascinated by the Kyrgyz women and wanted to portray how they navigated their roles in their patriarchal societies. For example, he describes in passing the physical abuse of a teenage wife by her husband. The girl's ailments are attributed to her being possessed by demons, and the cure consists of being beaten. Having witnessed the violence, Valikhanov interferes, dismissing the claims of possession, criticizing the use of physical beatings as a way of healing her, and forbidding the husband to beat her. This scene illustrates Valikhanov's empathy. He could not bear to see the beatings, and he talked to the young girl in order to understand what was happening with her. But at the same time, his account reveals his certainty that his own rational, secular approach is the correct one, and that he, as an educated man in the service of the state, has the right to impose his enlightened understanding.

Elsewhere in the diary, Valikhanov stated that women feared him and his travel companions and avoided making appearances. In spite of their usual reticence, he reports that he inadvertently caught sight of a naked woman (*baba*), who "became extremely ashamed, but not completely. It was not normal that she, after having recovered from the first fright, began to berate me and berate me terribly . . ." He continues, describing his two-fold reaction to her diatribe with some humor: "On one hand, I was in grief; it was painful. On the other hand, I was glad that I managed at once to get acquainted with a sophisticated vocabulary of curse-words, but it was shameful that it was me who was listening to all of this from the mouth of a Kyrgyz beauty."[5] The first ellipsis here is also in the original. Valikhanov censors her sense of outrage with marks of omission, confirming the ultimately selective and androcentric character of his research. The woman in Valikhanov's account fiercely admonishes his voyeuristic gaze. She speaks back in a forceful way that contradicts Dostoevsky's depiction of Kyrgyz/Kazakh women, as submissive and obedient. Even though Valikhanov was rebuked, he shows that women were assertive, not only in their actions, but also with their foul language.

None of these insights into the lives of Kyrgyz women, none of the assertive speech, none of the sexual innuendoes, and no traces of the voyeuristic gaze are discernible in the drawings. They remain ethnographic, informational. Consulting the diary allows the viewer to see the drawings in a more nuanced way. For instance, the text explains that the beauty of the Kyrgyz women is in the "roundness and corpulence of the body, in her moon-shaped face and in the beauty of her cheeks."[6] Tipped off by this description, we notice these features in all of his drawings of women. By showing the Kyrgyz women in elaborate garments, whose designs indicate their social functions, Valikhanov emphasizes the richness and vitality of the local culture, bringing the eastern borderlands into the imperial center. Unlike Dostoevsky's Gorianchikov, who fails to see such differences, Valikhanov's drawings and diary show his ability to differentiate and appreciate elements of Kyrgyz women's lives.

I argue that while Valikhanov's ethnographic drawings served the empire by producing visual representations of its eastern borderlands, they also gave the colonial subjects a kind of visibility and, with this, disrupted the Russian imperial center. On the one hand, the drawings were an illustration of the empire's ethnic diversity that underscored otherness by depicting ethnic dress and traditional dwellings. Valikhanov indirectly challenged the notion of women of the steppe as being taciturn, and "poor and wild." Though the diary's language asserted colonial power and masculine agency, with an often sexually charged gaze objectifying women, it also gave them voice. In the early 1860s, back in St. Petersburg, Valikhanov gave lectures about his travels at the Imperial Russian Geographical Society, thus bringing his nuanced impressions of Central Asian society to educated Russians at the imperial center of power. The question remains, however, as to what extent his writings and drawings become a mediator between those living on the eastern borderlands and those in the Russian Empire's European region.

Through his diary and drawings, Valikhanov presented a nuanced, three-dimensional depiction of Kyrgyz women and men. In particular, he dismantled the stereotypical trope of women being submissive. In text and image, he empowered them and gave them voice, showing their actions, personality, and agency. Both mediums, the textual and the visual, exposed the empire's divisions, putting women on display as objects of the colonizing male gaze and desire, but also as tangible reminders that they can withstand that gaze and push back against colonial power.

NOTES

1. F. M. Dostoevskii, "Zapiski iz mertvogo doma," in *Polnoe sobranie sochinenii v tridtsati tomakh (Pss)* Vol. 4, edited by G. M. Fridlender et al. (Leningrad: Izdatel'stvo "Nauka," 1972–1990), 178. All translations into English are mine, unless otherwise indicated.
2. Ch. Ch. Valikhanov. "Dnevnik poezdki na Issyk-Kul'. 1856 g.," in *Sobranie sochinenii v piati tomakh*, Tom 1 (Alma-Ata: Izdatel'stvo Akademii Nauk Kazakhskoi SSR, 1961), 265.
3. Valikhanov, "Dnevnik," 265.
4. Valikhanov, "Dnevnik," 265–267.
5. Valikhanov, "Dnevnik," 263–265.
6. Valikhanov, "Dnevnik," 260.

CHAPTER 20

THE PEASANT AND THE PHOTOGRAPH: GENDER, RACE, AND THE SUNLIGHT PICTURE IN THE BALTIC PROVINCES (1866)

BART PUSHAW

THE INVENTION OF photography circa 1839 transformed how people understood truth in the nineteenth century. A careful manipulation of chemicals and exposure to light now created an image with a striking resemblance to reality. This resemblance, however, had an unintended consequence. If the photograph seemed to reproduce the real world, then the photographer as well as the photographed could shape, and even distort, the truth they sought to visualize. As new technologies demystified and simplified the science behind producing a photograph, the practice became cheaper and more accessible to a new range of clientele by the 1850s and 1860s. In Imperial Russia's three Baltic Provinces of Estland, Livland, and Kurland (today's Estonia and Latvia), photography became available precisely at the time when Estonians (and Latvians) were making unprecedented social, political, and cultural claims about the self. Overwhelmingly of peasant background, nineteenth-century Estonians understood photography, especially portraiture, as a powerful medium to materialize the change they desired while navigating the unequal structures of society.

If photography wielded the potential to visualize new truths, it also harbored the ability to reinforce old assumptions. Across Europe, the scientific origins of the photographic process categorized the camera lens not as a vehicle for aesthetic expression, but instead as an impartial tool of science. Therefore, photography's relationship with truth made the photograph a compelling kind of evidence from which viewers, especially scientists, could draw conclusions and claim to verify facts. For these reasons, the related fields of anthropology and ethnography—increasingly important in Imperial Russia since the 1860s—ascribed great value to the photograph, which could register the physiognomic markers that were thought to characterize a race or ethnicity. Indeed, the period's increasing reliance on race and ethnicity as fixed determinants of culture, civilization, and power would have a profound impact on image making in the nineteenth-century Baltic Provinces. A complicated history of conquest and subjugation created long-standing ethnic segregation between a wealthy Baltic German minority and an enserfed and impoverished Estonian peasantry. When the abolition of Baltic serfdom (1816–1820) threatened this Baltic German supremacy, photography appeared to offer the ruling group a tool for affirming Estonian ethnic inferiority and counteracting new Estonian claims of selfhood in the Russian Empire.

The nineteenth-century Baltic Provinces are an ideal place to investigate how the photograph could be an empowering as well as oppressive visual tool in picturing empire. In what follows, we will explore two photographs taken in 1866 that depict Estonian women in peasant garb. A close reading of these two photographs reveals how colonial conditions informed the limits and possibilities for Estonian women and their position within the Russian Empire.

DISPLAYING THE PEASANT: MARI WEINBERG AND THE ESTONIAN RACE

In 1866, Mari Weinberg traveled fourteen kilometers from her home in Jüri Parish to the hustle and bustle of Tallinn, the capital of Estland Province. Among the winding medieval streets of Tallinn's Old Town was the studio of the Baltic German photographer Charles Borchardt. Weinberg was responding to Borchardt's advertisement, which promised to pay sitters a small fee if they would serve as models for a series of photographs he needed to complete quickly. Borchardt himself was responding to a different call, one that circulated from the executive committee of the upcoming All-Russian Ethnographic Exhibition, to take place in Moscow the following year. The committee had published specific instructions regarding photographic commissions, wanting no fewer than fifty photographs per photographer that depicted "the most pronounced specimens of the various races" of the Russian Empire.[1] Mari Weinberg, it seemed, was one such specimen (Image 20.1).

When he photographed Weinberg in his studio, Borchardt was working under strict conditions. As the exhibition committee explained, "The portraits should be taken of every face in two positions, from the front and profile . . . When choosing a face to make a photographic portrait, one should be guided by the accuracy of type, understood as the person who is often encountered in a given tribe and in a given locality. In the case where the artist is in doubt in choosing a face, it would be desirable that he predominantly used the people of the peasant or merchant class."[2] This last missive, that subjects should preferably be peasants, meant that Borchardt's subjects would exclusively be Estonians. The social hierarchy of Baltic serfdom had secured ethnic segregation for so long in the Baltic Provinces that the notion of a Baltic German peasantry was an oxymoron. Portraying the Estonian face from the front as

IMAGE 20.1 Charles Borchardt, "Portrait of Mari Weinberg," 1866.

well as profile was an opportunity for Borchardt to engage his photographic practice with the latest scientific theories about race.

This photograph of Mari Weinberg is one of few surviving images from Borchardt's "Estonian Types" series that he submitted to the Moscow Ethnographic Exhibition. Draped in layers of multicolored striped cloth, Mari almost disappears under her clothing, staring stoically beyond the realm of the photograph, whose oval dimensions reinforce her conical shape. On the woman's lap is a small child, whose piercing eyes gaze directly at us. Tendrils of blonde hair frame the baby's chubby cheeks. However, the German inscription underneath the image ignores the child, reading: "Marri Weinberg, thirty-eight years old, Jüri Parish," for it is Weinberg's physiognomy that would be of greatest interest to the visitors of the exhibition.[3]

Why were exhibition organizers and visitors so interested in the face? In the eighteenth century, European science began to embrace the importance of classification in order to regulate knowledge and maintain order over the natural world. At first, this interest began with scientific nomenclature to identify different species of flora and fauna. Europeans soon applied this classificatory schema to humans, using visual difference as a way to categorize populations. When the scientist Johann Friedrich Blumenbach invented the racial category of Caucasian in 1795, he made clear that his vision of whiteness included all Europeans except the Sámi and "the true Finns," a group that included Estonians and whose origins archaeological evidence has traced to the Ural Mountains. These origins encouraged Blumenbach to argue that "the Finnish populations of the cold part of Europe" were racially "Asiatic," being "of a wheaten yellow, with scanty, straight black hair," and had "flat faces with laterally projecting cheekbones and narrowly slit eyelids."[4]

As the vast ethnic and linguistic diversity of the Russian Empire expanded in the 1860s, anthropology became essential to understanding this growing imperial population. When coupled with the presumed truth of photography, anthropologists claimed, pictures of a person's face provided irrefutable visual evidence of racial superiority or inferiority. In this context, Mari Weinberg's high cheekbones and dark brown eyes conformed to the characteristics of an Estonian racial identity that viewers expected in 1867. By emphasizing the appearance of Weinberg's face, Charles Borchardt visually activated this pseudoscientific discourse of Estonian inferiority.

Beyond its exhibition display, the photograph also functioned on a local Baltic level. With each shutter of the camera lens, Borchardt was able to recreate a truth that he was desperate to believe. As Borchardt created his "Estonian Types," a tsarist decree enacted the greatest threat to Baltic German supremacy since the original conquest of the region by Teutonic knights in the thirteenth century: the liberation of Estonian peasants from the custody of Baltic German manor lords. Though all Estonians were legally free by 1820, convoluted laws still bound them to landholdings and restricted their mobility until 1866. It was probably this decree that made it possible for Mari Weinberg to leave her parish and travel to Tallinn to be photographed in the first place.

We have little information about how Mari Weinberg herself navigated these ideas, or how she felt about being a photographic "specimen." Eager to earn money, she may have left Borchardt's studio as quickly as she arrived. However, we do have some insight into the responses of educated society to Borchardt's photographs. One review in the Estonian paper *Eesti Postimees* offers a surprising take:

> Readers have certainly heard that there was a great exhibition in Moscow this spring. Now we hear that the Tallinn photographer Ch. Borchardt has earned the prize of a silver medal for photographs he had taken of Estonian people and sent to the

ethnography exhibition. There, among 1,481 photographs taken of the other peoples living in Russia, were Borchardt's *figures of Estonian people* in front of a foreign viewer, who otherwise had never seen an Estonian person.[5]

Under the visual codes of imperial science, Borchardt's photographs of "Estonian Types" categorized and classified a disenfranchised population in order to uphold power imbalances that were newly threatened. Yet the premiere Estonian newspaper of the period valued Borchardt's silver medal for making Estonian people visible. The award revealed to Estonians that they could occupy a distinctive place among the various peoples of the Russian Empire. With her name prominently inscribed onto one of these photographs, Mari Weinberg could claim herself as a participant in realizing this change.

PLAYING THE PEASANT: LYDIA KOIDULA AND THE PROMISE OF *PÄEVAPILT*

While those in power used photography to prove the inferiority of others, many disenfranchised people embraced the ways sunlight revealed their humanity. The abolitionist and orator Frederick Douglass, the most photographed American of the nineteenth century, celebrated the fact that "simple but all-abounding sunlight" permitted "men of all conditions [to] see themselves as others see them."[6] For the once-enslaved Douglass, the ability to choose how to portray oneself through photography was an opportunity to counter racist stereotype and prejudice. Estonian newspapers also routinely emphasized the power of photographic visibility: "Poor people could see their face in a bucket of water, where they never stayed for long, if they even stood there at all. Now it is an entirely different story. The sun completes the picture and makes it in a moment, and your own face appears as created by God. The hand of a painter could also do this, but never as clearly and vividly as nature itself."[7]

The Estonian author and activist Lydia Koidula was keenly aware of the metaphorical power of sunlight. Koidula was a pen name, meaning "of the dawn" in Estonian. In the 1860s and 1870s, Carl Robert Jakobson's *Three Fatherland Speeches* (*Kolm isamaa kõnet*) deployed vivid language to explain Estonian history through three periods: before, during, and after serfdom. "Before" was "light," an ancient golden age, whereas serfdom—imposed through colonial conquest—was a "darkness," a "700-year-long night of slavery" (*700-aastat orjaööd*). The present era after abolition was the "dawn," brimming with hope and possibility. Jakobson's metaphors of light, darkness, and dawn emerged from the same cultural movement that encouraged Lydia Koidula to adopt her pen name. A photograph taken by Johannes Behse in Tartu reveals how Koidula manipulated the light of photography to envision herself (Image 20.2).

Koidula stands confidently, supported by a rake in one hand and grasping a small barrel in the other. She leans against an ornately carved wooden bannister. Since

IMAGE 20.2 Johannes Behse, "Lydia Koidula in Folk Costume," 1866.

posing for the camera lens required absolute stillness in 1866, the rake and bannister are necessary supports to maintain her posture. The black-and-white contrast of the photograph highlights crisp stripes in her skirt, geometric patterns on the belt cinching her waist as well as the pattern of her headpiece. Floral patterns embellished over her linen blouse also draw our attention. These details of her costume appear striking in comparison to the faded colors of the landscape of the painted backdrop behind her, a common device used in photography studios to enrich the sense of perspective and depth in an image.

Two elements of Koidula's dress reveal that her self-presentation did not correspond to her lived reality. Only married women would wear a white apron over a skirt. No more than twenty-four years old at the time of this photograph, Koidula would not marry for six more years. The other questionable element is the large silver medallion hanging from her neck, its reflection rendering it almost invisible. Silver medallions of such size, known as *sõled* in Estonian, are distinctive emblems of Seto culture. Long isolated at the southeastern borderland with Russia (near Pskov), Seto people developed a dialect, traditions, and even mythology different from other Estonians. Since Koidula's family hailed from Pärnumaa, the opposite side of Estonia, we know that Koidula could not claim any Seto heritage. If she was neither Seto, nor married, nor a peasant, why would Koidula actively construct this false image of herself?

Koidula's clothing and accessories—the hat, silver medallion, necklaces, and the details embroidered onto the sleeve—are typical attire of sacred peasant rituals, such as weddings or seasonal festivals. Yet she poses here with a rake and a barrel, suggesting instead labor in the field. With not a single speck of dirt soiling her clothes, Koidula does not embody the toiling peasant worker, oppressed under harsh conditions of labor. Instead, her portrait represents an idealized aesthetic of the generic Estonian peasant woman. Constructed and deliberate, her rural femininity is a motif more common in paintings than in photographs.

Carl Timoleon von Neff's 1839 oil painting *The Chicken Feeder* (Image 20.3) is exemplary of this tradition of peasant imagery. Neff has rendered each detail faithfully, if not obsessively: the woman's glistening, straw-colored hair; the intricate floral lace pattern of her blouse; the deep jewel tones of the majestic purple, navy blues, and crimson reds of the textiles. These exuberant colors and details conceal the strange contours of her body. Portrayed as graceful, her position is actually strained and awkward. Such representation glosses over the fact that this painted Estonian woman, like Koidula in her photograph, is unrealistically clean: she appears refined and immaculate as chickens kick dust into the air around her. Neff's vision of an Estonian peasant woman seamlessly blends the erotic and the exotic, reflecting how the Baltic German painter saw the gendered, ethnic, and class differences between himself and the Estonian subject as alluring. Produced under unequal power dynamics, Neff's painting projects a beauty that masks exploitation and concedes to colonial desire.

If Koidula's picture emerges from this fraught history of idealized imagery of Estonian peasant women, how does Koidula engage with that legacy in the photograph? The answer may be in the medium itself. Koidula often collaborated as an editor with her father, Johann Voldemar Jannsen, on the newspaper *Eesti Postimees*,

IMAGE 20.3 Carl Timoleon von Neff, *The Chicken Feeder*, 1839.

a known advocate of photography for its Estonian readership. As the social worlds of Estonians gradually changed in the decades after abolition, Jannsen invented new words in the Estonian language to account for new technologies and developments. One such invention was the word *päevapilt*, the new Estonian word for photograph.

An 1885 article entitled "The Ancestors of the Photographer" recalled the origins of this new word:

> You make your pictures with the help of light, and light comes from the sun, thus it is sensible that we christen your pictures with the name *päevapilt*. . . . Then, with proud lettering, *Postimees* declared to the Estonian people for the first time: "Every day in Tartu from nine in the morning to four in the evening, R. Sachker makes a *päevapilt* of people." . . . The beautiful word *päevapilt* had thus been found, the people had read it and partially understood, and the photographer dreamt how people flowed into his atelier to stand in front of his camera.[8]

Translated literally, the word *päevapilt* combines the words "day" (*päev*) and "picture" (*pilt*), while emphasizing the role of light (*valgus*) and the sun (*päike*) in photography. A better translation of *päevapilt* is "sunlight picture." Since Lydia Koidula and Carl Robert Jakobson connected sunlight metaphors to new possibilities after the abolition of serfdom, we can understand that the Estonian word for "photograph" encapsulated these new social ideals.

Through manipulating sunlight, Koidula visualized herself as a newly liberated peasant. In doing so, she demonstrated that Estonians could reject the history of exploitative aesthetics that Baltic German men had created, retooling the figure of the peasant from social backwardness into a bright beacon of both tradition and change in the Russian Empire. Ambitious and firm in her convictions, Lydia Koidula embodies the possibilities of new futures precisely in the year that the Estonian peasantry had been fully liberated.

CONCLUSION

As they posed for the camera in 1866, Mari Weinberg and Lydia Koidula found themselves on opposite ends of the changing colonial conditions of the Baltic Provinces of Imperial Russia. Weinberg seemed to be an ideal racial "type," her hindered social status key to her ethnographic authenticity for imperial audiences in Moscow. By contrast, Koidula revealed how the Estonian peasant woman could be an emancipatory figure, vital to envisioning new futures. Through the malleable truth of the "sunlight picture," Koidula retooled male-authored colonial ideas of aestheticized Estonian femininity into an aspirational ideal of increasing consequence. Pictured under precisely opposing politics, Mari Weinberg (or those who saw her image) could still find dignity and self-worth in her participation at the Moscow Ethnographic Exhibition of 1867, despite the racist views that propelled the creation of her portrait. As the old adage reminds us, the truth will come to light.

NOTES

1. "Die ethnographische Ausstellung in Moskau. I," *Rigasche Zeitung*, 22 May 1867.
2. *Etnograficheskaia vystavka 1867 goda. Izvestiia Imperatorskago obshchestva liubitelei estestvoznaniia antropologii i etnografii*, t. XXIX (Moscow: 1878), 5. I am grateful to Gleb Shuvalov for his help translating this source.

3. Mari is spelled with one R in Estonian and is archived that way; the double-R in the photograph is the German spelling.
4. Johann Friedrich Blumenbach, "Contributions to Natural History," in *The Anthropological Treatises of Blumenbach and Hunter* (London: The Anthropological Society of London, 1865), 277–340; 303.
5. "Ethnograhwia näitmine," *Eesti Postimees*, 18 October 1867.
6. Laura Wexler, "A More Perfect Likeness: Frederick Douglass and the Image of the Nation," in *Pictures and Progress: Early Photography and the Making of African American Identity*, edited by Maurice O. Wallace and Shawn Michelle Smith (Durham and London: Duke University Press, 2012), 18–40; 21.
7. "Pääwapildid," *Eesti Postimees*, July 12, 1867.
8. "Walguse imetegu. 1. Päewapiltniku esiwanemad," *Oleviku lisaleht*, 19 September 1885.

CHAPTER 21

SEVERED HEADS ON DISPLAY: VISUALIZING CENTRAL ASIA (1868–1872)

OLGA MAIOROVA

SHOCKING IMAGES OF "wild" Asian people cutting off human heads and putting their horrific trophies on public display began to circulate in Russia soon after the tsarist army embarked on its conquest of Central Asia. Spanning three decades (the 1860s to the 1880s), this colonial war—or, rather, a series of "small wars"—brought under Russia's control a vast and heterogeneous realm of predominantly Muslim populations. They ranged from pastoral nomads scattered across the steppes, deserts, and mountains (the Turkmen, Karakalpak, and Kyrgyz) to sedentary communities of farmers, artisans, and merchants (the Uzbeks, Tajiks, and many other ethnic groups) who inhabited the far-flung oases—the khanates of Bukhara, Khiva, and Kokand, vibrant centers of Islamic learning and international trade. With these territorial acquisitions, the Russian Empire, for the first time in its history, extended its reach up to the borders of Iran and Afghanistan, lengthened its existing borders with China, and solidified its power over the Kazakh steppe, the vast lands that the Romanovs had gradually annexed during the previous century. By projecting its power over Central Asia, Russia confidently signaled its parity with its western European counterparts, who were also expanding their colonial possessions. It was at exactly this historical moment, when imperial ambitions ran high across Europe, that the images of severed heads gained unprecedented prominence in representations of Central Asia. More intensely than ever before and in a wide range of media—art exhibitions, the illustrated press, travel accounts, and fictional narratives—these images spoke to the Russian public, offering up a symbolic marker of Asian menace, with all the scary traits usually ascribed to it: savagery, cruelty, brutality, vileness, and violence.

There was, of course, nothing unusual in a predator accusing its prey of aggression. Such role inversion was a standard rhetorical maneuver in the age of high imperialism, when the legitimacy of colonialism rested on the notion of a civilizing mission. Russia enthusiastically subscribed to this notion, seeing itself as a part of

Europe and, therefore, in the vanguard of historical progress, an agent in the humanitarian endeavor. And what could corroborate this self-serving construct more persuasively, and present it more graphically, than depicting "barbarous" Asians cutting off human heads?

The motif of the severed head emerged at the very first exhibition organized by the tsarist government in 1869 to introduce Turkestan, as the new colony was named, to the St. Petersburg public and the imperial elite, beginning with emperor Alexander II himself, who visited on the opening day. By showcasing its colonial engagement in public exhibit halls open to all, Russia made use of a West European model—or, more precisely, a British one—of celebrating imperialism, and did so to great acclaim from the press. "For most of us, Turkestan has existed so far only on paper, in dispatches from the theater of war," observed an anonymous reporter in the St. Petersburg journal *Messenger of Europe*, but with this exhibition, he concluded, the new colony "appears to us in the original, represented by its products."[1] The collections displayed at the exhibition—minerals, zoological samples, and various local artifacts—highlighted both the potential of the region and the glorious role that Russia could play in developing its rich natural resources and building modern industry. The journalists lamented only the limited coverage of the ethnography, ethnic types, and religious orientations of the Indigenous people. Just one portion of the exhibit responded to public curiosity on this score: a series of sketches, drawings, and paintings unanimously praised by the press for its quality, variety, and educational value. All these works were produced by a young Russian painter, soon to become a worldwide celebrity. Vasily Vereshchagin had accompanied the tsarist army in Turkestan in his capacity as the war's official artist, occasionally setting aside his brush and taking up a rifle as military circumstance dictated. Later, in his memoirs about this campaign, Vereshchagin recalled "the horrific bodies of the fallen Russian soldiers" beheaded by the locals.[2] In his visual representations of the war, he gave rein to his artistic imagination to depict the brutal business of beheading—an atrocity he never witnessed himself—and render it as a distinctive feature of the region, a bloody stamp on its "moral physiognomy." For the first time, and most forcefully, Vereshchagin presented this theme to the Russian public in his 1868 canvas *After Victory* (Image 21.1), which occupied an important place in the exhibition.

Designed to produce a chilling effect on the viewer, *After Victory* is doubly morbid. It not only foregrounds the severed head of a vanquished Russian, but also depicts two living natives taking gruesome pleasure in scrutinizing it. A master of visual narrative, Vereshchagin presents a blood-curdling story. Set on an abandoned battlefield, the canvas depicts a grim and yellowish expanse littered with the dead; vultures descend to feast on the ghastly remains. A Central Asian man holds his bloodied sword in one hand and grips with the other the hair of a head he appears to have severed a moment before. He lifts his shocking trophy to the sunlight, bringing it very close to his—and the viewers'—eyes, making it the focal point of the entire

IMAGE 21.1 Vasily Vereshchagin, *After Victory*, 1868.

composition. Another figure, also staring at the severed head, carries a sack that he is about to open. To hint at what the sack is for—and what it already contains—the painter depicts more corpses in the distance, freshly decapitated and all unmistakably Russian, as their uniforms betray. The entire scene is no chance encounter of foes, living and dead, on the field of battle. As Vereshchagin and many other Russians made a point of explaining in their accounts of this war, Central Asians collected these horrifying trophies in pursuit of gifts and honors promised to them in exchange by their khans. Within this context, we can understand why the two figures on the canvas are shown peering at the severed head so critically: to be a source of income or promotion, it has to be cut off perfectly.

Vereshchagin clearly regarded the beheading business as a quintessential symbol of Asian savagery. In his subsequent exhibitions, he displayed *After Victory* as part of a large series of canvases devoted to Turkestan that tells a fuller story of the severed heads' afterlife. Collected from the battlefield, these horrific trophies are brought to the feet of a powerful ruler who receives them in his palace (*They Present Trophies*, 1872). Later, they are placed atop tall spears, in the vast central square dominated by a madrasah (a school for Islamic instruction), where the Central Asian crowds celebrate their victory (*They Celebrate*, 1872). Taken together, all these paintings dramatize the long tradition of the decapitation in the secluded world of Central Asian cultures—a world now suddenly opened to outsiders. As Vereshchagin guides his spectators through this horrific journey, he demonstrates his passion for depicting the costumes, architecture, daily occupations, and social hierarchy of the Indigenous people. The painter embraced ethnographic accuracy as an artistic imperative, leading even the most skeptical art critics of his time to take his visual narratives—utterly judgmental and purely imaginary—as documentary evidence. It is the arresting ethnographic details that gave Vereshchagin's canvases an aura of professional expertise regarding Turkestan, even when he rendered scenes and situations that he could not possibly have witnessed firsthand.

As both a participant in the conquest of Central Asia and the artist who created the iconic images of the region, Vereshchagin would seem to be an archetypical Orientalist painter, whose works confirm Edward Said's famous argument about the linkage between knowledge production and imperial power. Vereshchagin's paintings of Turkestan echoed a wide range of European Orientalist artists, in particular the work of his French mentor, Jean-Léon Gérôme. As art historians have shown, Vereshchagin appropriated the iconographic motif of severed heads and its artistic treatment from Gérôme's canvas *Heads of the Rebel Beys at the Mosque-El Assaneyn* (1866), which depicts an imagined scene set in thirteenth-century Cairo, with a pile of severed heads on the mosque's steps and some of them suspended over the door. But artistic imports are always culturally transformed by domestication. Vereshchagin adapted the motif of severed heads for his own purposes, both artistic and ideological. In producing his own Orient, he addressed the key concerns of Imperial Russia.

When we think about imperial history, we tend to take for granted that a sharp line exists between colonizers and colonized. In Russia, however, the picture was far more complex, even confusing. Russia subjugated many peoples adjacent to its ethnic core, but prior to these conquests, it had cultivated centuries-old ties with almost every group that ultimately came under its sway. Shared trade networks, cultural exchanges, intermarriages, wars (not only against one another, but often in alliance against a common foe)—all these forms of interaction gave rise to reciprocal influences, which impeded the construction of an unquestionable divide between "us" and "them." The questions "Who are we?" and "Do we belong to Asia or Europe?" haunted the Russian self-perception.

Most historians agree, however, that the conquest of Turkestan enabled Russia to begin to demarcate itself from its new colony more consistently and self-confidently than ever before. The new Central Asian subjects—both sedentary and nomadic populations—were so distinct in their social composition, ethnographic traits, and religious orientations that Russians seemed to have no problem rendering them as the Other. And the image of severed heads cut off by "wild" Muslims proved instrumental in this respect. Though hardly unique to the Islamic world, decapitation as a form of execution and ultimate humiliation of the dead became a powerful marker of difference.

To draw a bright line between "us" and "them," Vereshchagin resorted to dramatic visual contrasts. In *After Victory,* the pale face of the fallen Russian stands out in stark relief beside the dark skin of the locals who have just severed his head. Vereshchagin couples *After Victory* with its mirror image, *After Defeat* (1868), in which a Russian soldier, surrounded by multiple Asian corpses, calmly smokes a pipe, expressing no interest in his fallen enemies. In this diptych, the brutal business of beheading is contrasted with aloof smoking after a fight. Vereshchagin organized his battle scenes to emphasize the disparities between the two armies. As a contemporary put it, "the wild hordes of Asia" represented a sharp contrast to the well-ordered Russian army, the "pioneers of the new culture."[3]

Such binary thinking pervaded the works of many Russians, and in all these representations, the beheading theme stood as the most powerful tool for othering Central Asians. In his novels and short stories, Nikolai Karazin, a painter, writer, and military officer who participated in the Turkestan campaign, repeatedly depicted natives busy with that horrific business. They decapitate captives, cut off the heads of the wounded, or dig up the graves of fallen Russians to mutilate the corpses and obtain the desired trophies. In his capacity as a journalist, Karazin also regularly offered the Russian public such rich fare, accompanying his verbal accounts with pictorial ones. Reporting about the death penalties in Bukhara, he added his own drawing (Image 21.2), where an impassive executioner slits the throats of helpless victims. In another drawing, showing severed heads on display (Image 21.3), Karazin added women to the local observers of the horrific trophies. As in Vereshchagin's works,

IMAGE 21.2 Nikolai Karazin, "Execution of Criminals in Bukhara," *Vsemirnaia Illiustratsiia*, 1872.

Выставка головъ военноплѣнныхъ. (Рис. Н. Каразинъ, грав. Ос. Май).

IMAGE 21.3 Nikolai Karazin, "Exhibition of War Captives' Heads," *Vsemirnaia Illiustratsiia*, 1872.

Karazin's writings and drawings used the beheading theme to draw a clear line between "us" and "them."

Yet the construct that seemed to be so persuasive and instrumental soon turned out to be fragile, ambiguous, and self-contradictory. When Vereshchagin began to show his canvases in England, Austria, and France, his visual narratives of Central Asia took on a new interpretation, one that does not sit comfortably within the Orientalist paradigm and, indeed, questions the demarcating line between colony and metropole.

An English art critic covering the London international art exhibition in 1872 bluntly declared Vereshchagin's work "an act of barbarism." Even though the Russian painter's "artistic powers" were indisputable, as all reviews of the exhibition acknowledged, this critic claimed that "the Russian Gérôme" lacked the aesthetic tact and refined style that made it possible for the French master to depict even the most monstrous violence without offending delicate modern sensibilities. Focusing on *After Victory* and *After Defeat*, the English critic found himself particularly unsettled by the latter, with its portrayal of a Russian soldier, who, standing close to "the blood-stained corpses in a heap," feels aloof and unflappable. He "looks like a butcher and lights his pipe with a grin, which is worthy of a Carib." The tsarist soldier—an agent of the European "civilizing mission," in the eyes of Russians—was relegated to the position of a colonized savage. Not only the protagonist on the canvas, but also the painter himself was filtered through notions of barbarism. Vereshchagin's skills, the English critic claimed, "are not sufficient to overcome the horror of humanity at such treatment of a vile theme."[4]

Today, we might simply dismiss this judgement as an expression of cultural (and perhaps political) prejudice were it not that Vereshchagin himself instantly embraced the criticism as a flattering recognition of his unique talent. Moreover, his friend Vladimir Stasov, the most influential Russian art critic of the time, dwelled on the argument about the painter's "barbarism." He translated and approvingly incorporated the English review into his own coverage of the London exhibition to imbue it with a new meaning. Vereshchagin's "barbarism," in Stasov's eyes, was a sign of true Realism, a refusal to sugarcoat brutal reality.[5] Later, after Vereshchagin exhibited his work in Vienna, Austrian newspapers also took note of his "barbarism" and drew attention to the "particular, Asian freshness" of his paintings.[6] Stasov, once again, enthusiastically embraced the point. For him, this "Asian freshness" signified the aesthetic breadth of Russian art, its openness to diverse cultural influences, Asian ones in particular—a quality Vereshchagin exemplified. A supporter of the tsarist imperial project, Stasov nevertheless questioned Russia's European identity and found aesthetic reasons to blur the line between metropole and colony.

Vereshchagin blurred that line on more general, existential grounds. Some of the paintings that he completed after the first Turkestan exhibition in St. Petersburg began to reveal ambiguities in the imperial vision. His *Apotheosis of War* (1871) palpably destabilizes the metropole/colony dualism that he had so vividly asserted previously. Featuring a pyramid of skulls set in a typical Central Asian space, vast and monotonous, the painting, as Vereshchagin himself explained, refers to Tamerlane, the ruthless Central Asian conqueror of the fourteenth century, and the devastating effect of his wars. But on the frame of the canvas, Vereshchagin inscribed a dedication, readily visible from any vantage point: "To all great conquerors, past, present and future." Conspicuously disregarding cultural boundaries, the phrase renders atrocities universal and refrains from ethnic distinctions, binding all conquerors through blood and violence. Employing the same pictorial motif of the severed head that he had presented as a defining feature of the Central Asian "moral physiognomy," Vereshchagin now strips it of any ethnographic traits. His mound of skulls is allegorical rather than real. With this dramatic shift in his rendering of the severed head theme, Vereshchagin expressed profound ambivalence toward the construction of civilizational boundaries between "us" and "them."

If Vereshchagin merely pointed out certain ambiguities of the imperial vision, his famous contemporary Leo Tolstoy, in his novella *Hadji Murat* (1896–1904), advanced a decidedly subversive (re)interpretation of Russian history and radically disrupted the conventional meaning of the beheading theme as a symbolic marker of the Muslim Other. Writing this novella soon after Russia completed its piecemeal conquest of Central Asia, with the memory of that war still fresh in the public mind, Tolstoy engaged with the Muslim world but depicted another colonial war—Russia's long fight to subjugate the North Caucasus (1817–1864), a war in which Tolstoy himself had taken part as a young military officer. Now an aging writer, he immersed himself in the study of the Caucasian campaign to revise its history, just as four decades earlier, in *War and Peace* (1863–1869), he had revised the history of Russia's war with Napoleon. This time, however, the revision was done with a fundamentally different goal in mind. Unlike *War and Peace*, *Hadji Murat* does not glorify the Russian victory. Quite the opposite. Now, Tolstoy produced what scholars have defined as "a guilt narrative," which he intended to serve as an anticolonial statement that would unite his Russian audience in a sense of complicity and repentance. The protagonist of the novella, Hadji Murat, is a historical figure, a hero of the anti-Russian resistance in the Caucasus, is depicted by Tolstoy as a relentlessly tragic character, caught up in a struggle between ruthless rulers. As a pious Muslim, Hadji Murat does not simply elicit the author's sympathy, he embodies what Tolstoy valued most: unadulterated and instinctive religiosity deeply embedded in the folk culture.

The killing of Hadji Murat—a tragic scene rendered by Tolstoy as a metaphor for the extinguishing of life itself—concludes with a tsarist soldier decapitating his corpse. As the narrator later recounts, Hadji Murat was killed after a long exchange of fire, whereupon one of his adversaries approached his dead body, "cut off the head with two blows and ... [and] rolled it away with his foot. Blood gushed scarlet from the arteries of the neck and black from the head, flooding the grass."[7] Tolstoy evokes the horror of beheading, depicting it with the gruesome details typical of Vereshchagin, Karazin, and many others. But in Tolstoy's novella, the distribution of roles among the actors is utterly reversed: This atrocity is committed by a tsarist soldier. And even though that soldier is a Caucasian Muslim, ethnically non-Russian, he serves in the Russian army and pursues Hadji Murat alongside the ethnically Russian characters, who approve the beheading. Moreover, it is the tsarist military authorities who, after the killing, dispatch an ethnic Russian military officer, a certain Kamenev, to travel from one Caucasian Muslim village to another, displaying Hadji Murat's head in each destination in order to instill fear in the locals. When Kamenev, on his way to the villages, encounters his Russian friends, he playfully offers: "Shall I show you a curiosity?"[8] The curiosity in question is the "object" he carries with him in a sack. When Kamenev reaches inside to pull out the head of Hadji Murat, it seems that Tolstoy is pointedly reminding his readers of the sack in which Vereshchagin's "wild" Muslims kept the heads of their enemies. As if to heighten the connection between the two works, Tolstoy's verbal narrative, just like Vereshchagin's visual one, holds the audience in uncanny suspense before it dawns on them what the sack is for. In this way, the severed head– a pictorial motif carefully crafted into a symbol of Asian menace—comes full circle to invert its initial message and present the Russian Empire itself as a ruthless savage devastating the lives of Indigenous peoples.

NOTES

1. "Khronika," *Vestnik Evropy*, no. 5 (May 1869): 373.
2. Vasily Vereshchagin, *Na voine v Azii i Evrope* (Moscow: I. N. Kushnerev, 1894), 33.
3. "Vystavka kartin Vereshchagina," *Niva*, March 25, 1874, 202.
4. "The London International Exhibition: Foreign Pictures," *The Athenaeum*, July 6, 1872, 21–23. https://search-proquest-com.proxy.lib.umich.edu/britishperiodicals/pubidlinkhandler/sng/pubtitle/The+Athenaeum/$N/2299/PagePdf/8698899/fulltextPDF/51205A9B81F34B6CPQ/1?accountid=14667
5. Vladimir Stasov, *Izbrannye sochineniia*, Vol. 1 (Moscow: Iskusstvo, 1952), 23, 231.
6. Vladimir Stasov, *Izbrannye sochineniia*, Vol. 2 (Moscow: Iskusstvo, 1952), 109.
7. Lev Tolstoy, *Polnoe sobranie sochinenii*, Vol. 35 (Moscow: Khudozhestvennaia literatura, 1950), 117.
8. Tolstoy, *Polnoe sobranie sochinenii*, 108.

CHAPTER 22

THE CAUTIOUS ONE: IDENTITY AND BELONGING IN LATE IMPERIAL RUSSIA (1877)

SARAH BADCOCK

ANTON CHEKHOV REGARDED Ilya Repin, alongside Leo Tolstoy and Pyotr Tchaikovsky, as epitomizing Russia's greatest artists. Repin's prolific output of extraordinary canvasses, spanning historical painting, state commissions, and portraits, captured a wide array of historical moments, and offer us a window into many aspects of late Imperial Russian life. In those portraits, it seems that no one escaped his gaze: the great and the good of the cultural and political worlds, musicians and artists, criminals and vagabonds, and of course, ordinary rural people. This chapter will consider one particular part of his extraordinary catalogue of work: those pictures that portrayed peasants, or lower-class rural Russians. We will explore a single image to ask two questions: First, what can Repin's painting of a single rural dweller tell us about Russian national and imperial identities? And second, how did Repin's lower-class social background and identity impact his depiction of peasants?

This essay focuses on the portrait sketch (a preliminary rough painting) *The Cautious One* (*Muzhichok iz robkikh*), which was completed in 1877 when Repin was thirty-three years old (Image 22.1). It was exhibited as a study (*etiud'*), rather than as a portrait, at the 1878 Sixth Travelling Art Exhibition, which visited St Petersburg, Moscow, Riga, Vilna, Kyiv, Odesa, and Kharkiv. It is currently exhibited by the Nizhnii Novgorod Art Museum. *The Cautious One* is a bleak and ultimately elusive study of a Russian rural dweller. Dominated by multiple shades of brown, the painting depicts a shabbily dressed older man with unkempt hair and an untrimmed beard, regarding the viewer with a sideways glance under hooded eyes, part of his face entirely obscured by shadow. Was he nervous, suspicious, fearful, resentful, or hostile? Characteristically, Repin offers us no clear answer, but rather sets up a series of challenges for the viewer—and for the historian.

Representations of Russian peasants right through the nineteenth century exposed significant anxieties for the Russian Empire. If it was to be an empire, was it

IMAGE 22.1 Ilya Repin, *The Cautious One*, 1877.

also a nation-state, with a homogeneous ethnic nation of Russians? Russian subjects could be identified by the state and by themselves using a range of markers, including religious faith, language, and cultural practices. While this was the case for any state, Russia's situation as an empire that inhabited a single contiguous land mass meant that Russian self-identity was more contested than in, for example, France or Britain, where geography, language, religious faith, and cultural practice, as well as elite constructions of race and ethnicity, provided clear markers of self and other that could be adopted when understanding the relationship between the polity and the empire. Peasants were an important part of national wrangling for self-identity in the Russian context. Romantic nationalism, which posited a unique, individual culture for each nation, often rooted in an invented past and an idealized view of peasant culture as the core of that past, is not uniquely Russian, but is a feature of nineteenth-century Russian nationalism.

Imperial Russian discourses about Russia's identity and historic pathways were highly contentious and divisive. One group, often described as Slavophiles, argued that Russia was unique, and that its political and economic development should follow a distinct path. The Slavophiles often drew on romantic nationalist ideas that presented Russia's peasants as resilient, pious, simple, hardworking, and the source of Russia's unique might. The Slavophiles' construction of Russian self and development was contested by those, often described as Westernizers, who argued that Russia needed to democratize and to reform in line with developments in western Europe (looking particularly at the models of Britain and France). The Westernizers were more likely to characterize Russia's peasant population as benighted, impoverished, oppressed, and in need of economic and social reform to enable them to transform their lives and contribute fully to state and society.

The Cautious One can be used to examine these competing visions. Did Russian peasants, despite their poverty and lack of education, embody an unsullied folk authenticity that the westernized, educated elites had lost? Or was the Russian peasant an incarnation of the "dark" and "un-European" nature of Russia: dirty, uneducated, irrational, poor, even rebellious and dangerous? This fundamental conflict strikes at the heart of Russia's identity crisis at the turn of the twentieth century. The Russian peasant in Repin's portrait was both romanticized and denigrated by commentators. Repin offers us an equivocal lens through which to simultaneously picture "Russianness" and "otherness." Was the Russian vision of empire subverted by this uncertain representation of the Russian self? *The Cautious One* functioned like a fairground mirror for the viewer. It allowed for multiple ways of seeing these uncertain Russian selves.

Repin's own life experience saw him transcend poverty and humble beginnings through skill, luck, and application to become financially secure and embedded among Russia's intellectual and social elites. For Repin, artistic training and success were prerequisites to social mobility and advancement. As the son of a military settler, a category only marginally higher than that of a serf, Repin's obligations to serve the state through tax and service were avoided by his own rise through the social ranks. He was born on July 24, 1844, to father Efim Vasilevich and mother Tatiana Stepanova, the second of four children, in a military settlement in Chuguev, a little town in Kharkiv Province, in Ukraine. Military settlements, established by the state in the early nineteenth century, required serving soldiers to take on agrarian as well as military service and aimed to reduce the cost of maintaining the standing army. Repin's father Efim was a low-ranking military settler who traded horses on the side. His literate and resourceful mother Tatiana taught the children to read and write. Repin was able to escape military service when he enrolled in the military topographical school at the age of ten. After apprenticeship with a local icon painter at the age of fourteen, he took on private commissions to fund his travel to St. Petersburg in 1863. With the support of a series of patrons and mentors, and through relentless hard work, he progressed through the Academy of Art and, in 1871, was awarded the Grand Gold Medal, the Academy's highest accolade.

Repin's social status and self-identity were complex. He identified as ethnically Russian, but he also sympathized with the Cossacks and Ukrainians he had grown up around. For much of his adult life, he was ensconced in materially comfortable environments, surrounded by people of education, wealth, and talent. Despite his adult identification with thoroughly bourgeois values and identities, viewers and critics continued to connect his artistic work with the impoverished rural milieu of his childhood. In a letter to the powerful art critic Vladimir Stasov, another celebrated portrait painter, Ivan Kramskoi, wrote that "Repin possesses the capacity to make the Russian *muzhik* [peasant] just as he is. I know many artists that represent *muzhiks*, some even well, but not one of them can come close to Repin."[1] This sentiment reflects Repin's extraordinary skill as a painter, but it also edges into a mystic conception of the "simple Russian person." Repin's humble background gave him an authority among his peers and his audience as a mediator between worlds. While there was great discussion in late Imperial Russia about the gulf that separated elites and ordinary Russians, the well-heeled audience attending art exhibitions were surrounded by rural people. The very prosperous had been raised by peasant nurses and servants. In the countryside, peasants were the main inhabitants of villages, husbanding crops and livestock, engaging in handicrafts and trade. In towns and cities, peasants drove cabs and sold flowers, labored in factories, shoed horses and mended stoves. Peasants filled the houses of the wealthy, serving as butlers and footmen, maids and cooks. Repin's art transformed these ubiquitous people who filled the streets and fields of Russia into picturesque snapshots, frozen in the moment, making them visible and remarkable to their audience—people to be considered, analyzed and discussed. His understanding and sympathy are evident in the warmth of his portraits, and in the empathy for his subjects that he invites. His humble origins did not, however, define his artistic vision, or his personal identity and values.

To understand our little sketch, we need to reflect on where Repin was in 1877. Repin's prominence and recognition, both in the art world and in the public sphere, had been cemented by the exhibition of his masterpiece *Barge Haulers on the Volga* (*Burlaki*) at the Academy of Arts in March and April of 1873 (Image 22.2). *Barge Haulers* was part of the collection chosen to represent Russia at the Vienna International Exhibit. This painting was composed over a period of three years, during which Repin spent two summers on the Volga making sketches of river workers and their world. The painting was an important development in Russian native realist art, because it represented working Russian men not as suffering husks, but as fleshed out, flawed, living individuals. Repin's work provoked angry hostility from some conservative voices, who saw the painting as a challenge to their notions of what art should be (a vehicle for beauty and deep thought), but also, more profoundly, to their idealized Slavophile vision of Russian peasants. Responses to *Barge Haulers* were not defined by political persuasion. The writer Fyodor Dostoevsky, who subscribed to

IMAGE 22.2 Ilya Repin, *Barge Haulers on the Volga*, 1873.

Slavophile ideas and was usually hostile to the radical left, admired *Barge Haulers* enormously as an "epic portrayal of the Russian people."[2]

Repin spent three years abroad between 1873 and 1876, mostly in Paris. These years were an integral part of his Imperial Academy fellowship, to learn from western European art. The works that he exhibited on his return delighted conservative viewers, but their turn from Russian subjects and their European style disappointed the liberal press. The art critic and close ally of Repin, Vladimir Stasov, was dismayed that Repin had foresworn the native, lower-class subjects that had made his name.

When Repin returned from Paris to Russia in 1876, he resolved to stay deep in the Russian countryside, in his hometown of Chuguev, where he lived from October 1876 until September 1877. Stasov was palpably relieved by Repin's return to Russia:

> During these three years [in Paris] Repin was in a milieu that was harmful . . . Somewhere inside Russia he will get rid of it and regain his powers—the full power of a realist, of a national artist . . . fully capable of creating and representing thoroughly national types and characters.[3]

Stasov, in these comments, perceived Repin as an "intuitive," "native" artist, whose skills needed the raw clay of Russian life as his medium. This construction of Repin as a wellspring of true Russianness suited Stasov's own politics and aesthetics, and it illustrates how Repin's works were imagined by many as "true" representations of rural Russians. Repin himself regarded his move to the provinces as a rediscovery of provincial Russia, though he never articulated a vision of himself as a national artist in the way that Stasov did. For Repin, the provinces were where an elusive "real" Russia could be found. In a letter to Stasov, he said, "I'm so glad I came here in winter: only in winter do the people live freely with all their interests, town, political and family."[4]

The Cautious One sits within a body of work produced while Repin was in Chuguev, where he concentrated particularly on peasant portraiture. He sought to explore the everyday internal life of Chuguev villagers. He used some of the sketches and inspirations from his Chuguev period to build one of his most contentious and best-known paintings, *Procession of the Cross in Kursk Province,* which was first exhibited in 1883. *The Cautious One* was not featured in this work, though we can see echoes of the subject in some faces in the crowd (Image 22.3).

The composer Modest Mussorgsky, a close friend of Repin's, was delighted by *The Cautious One*. He described its subject to Stasov as a "rascal/scoundrel, a peasant rioter . . . He'd kill ten men as soon as look at them!"[5] In his reply to Mussorgsky, Stasov gave a chilling account of the painting:

> To glance only at his glazed, unmoving, half-closed eyes, and your gaze is met coldly and fearfully; and you fall into some sort of hidden corner, where no help awaits you, and then you'll find out, what kind of "shy" he is.[6]

For Mussorgsky and Stasov, the painting was a vector for their own assumptions about the violent and suspicious nature of Russian peasants.

Scholars in the Soviet period, by contrast, had an entirely different perspective. They generally characterized Repin and his works as sympathetic to the peasantry,

IMAGE 22.3 Ilya Repin, *Procession of the Cross in Kursk Province,* 1883.

and to Russia's developing radical socialist movement. For instance, the Soviet art historian Dmitry Sarabyanov, writing in 1960, suggested that *The Cautious One* epitomized the ground-down, utterly impoverished, hopeless *muzhik*, and he made no reference to any malevolence.[7] While Repin's choice of subjects and sympathetic representation of lower-class Russians might give this impression, there is no clear evidence in his own writings to support this interpretation—or, in fact, any single interpretation. David Jackson, who wrote the definitive study of Repin in English, argued that *The Cautious One* sat at an awkward juncture between universal or national "type" and the subject's individual characteristics. Like Sarabyanov, Jackson says nothing about any incendiary potential of the subject.[8]

Repin himself did not leave written guidance on the meanings or intentions of his work, so there can be no definitive "knowing" of authorial intentions. Viewers infer their own meanings from the painting. The multiple interpretations of this single sketch exemplify the ways in which Repin's work invited diverse readings.

The ambiguity of Repin's sketch demands that we confront the process of not knowing, of acknowledging uncertainty. It cuts to the heart of our original questions: What does this single painting expose of Russia's existential identity crisis by the turn of the twentieth century? As both nation and empire, Russia was riven with uncertainties as to the wellspring of its identity. Unlike the maritime empires, which had the convenient means of seas and oceans to demarcate an essential "us" and "them," Russia's contiguous land mass empire lacked these most obvious markers of exclusion and belonging. Russian Orthodoxy served as one alternative marker of "us," as did Slavic ethnicity and Russian language. But even within these demarcations, uneasy tensions, particularly those distinctions of class, education, and culture, rankled. These tensions are writ large in *The Cautious One.* Our subject appears to be Slavic, probably Russian-speaking and of Russian Orthodox faith. He is apparently a simple rural person, who could epitomize the Russian person, the everyman hero of the Napoleonic conflicts, the harvester of Russia's crops, the loyal servant of the tsarist regime. Yet this image leaves us doubting. If this is the Russian everyman, his apparent poverty does not reflect well on the great Russian Empire. The simple Russian peasant is the bedrock of Russia's armed forces, but can we trust this fellow with a gun? Is the subject's expression one of deference, or fear, or suspicion, or concealment? If Repin sought to use the subject to present a "type" of Russian person with this picture, then what that type manifests is itself uncertain. It could be a portrait of poverty, of everyday rural life, or it could be as Mussorgsky suggests, a portrait of the rebellious peasant, who in 1905 would lead rural uprisings against local landowners, and leave the late imperial regime teetering on the brink. The ambiguities that Repin manifests in this one small sketch offer us a vision of late imperial uncertainties.

NOTES

1. Letter to Vladimir Stasov, December 1, 1876, in Ivan Nikolaevich Kramskoi, *I. N. Kramskoi. Pis'ma. Tom 2 (1876–1877)* (Moscow-Leningrad: Izogiz, 1937), 74.
2. Fyodor Dostoevsky, *Writer's Diary Volume 1: 1873–1876*, edited by Gary Saul Morson, translated by Kenneth Lantz (Evanston, IL: Northwestern University Press, 1997), 212–214.
3. Letter to Ivan Kramskoi, November 7, 1876, in Vladimir Vasil'evich Stasov, *Izbrannie sochineniia v trekh tomakh*, Vol. 1 (Moscow: Iskusstvo, 1952), 710.
4. Il'ia Efimovich Repin and Vladimir Vasilevich Stasov, *E. E. Repin i V.V. Stasov. Perepiska 1871–1906. Tom 1*, edited by Andrei Konstantinovich Lebedev and G. K. Burova (Moscow: Iskusstvo, 1948), 141.
5. Letter from Musorgsky to Stasov, 22 March 1878 in Nikolay Rimsky-Korsakov, *M. P. Musorgskii. Pis'ma i dokumenti*, edited by Varvara Dmitrievna Komarova (Leningrad: Gosudarstvennaia Publichnaia Biblioteka im. M.E . Saltykova-Shchedrina, 1932), 565.
6. Stasov, *Izbrannie sochineniia, Tom 1*, 303.
7. Dmitrii Vladimirovich Sarabyanov, *Ilya Repin*, edited by Dennis Ogden, translated by Xenia Danko (Moscow: Foreign Languages Publishing House, 1960), 19–20.
8. David Jackson, *The Russian Vision: The Art of Ilya Repin* (Woodbridge, Suffolk: ACC Art Books, 2015), 78.

CHAPTER 23

SIBERIAN TRAVELOGUES: IMAGES OF ASIATIC RUSSIA DURING THE TRANSPORT REVOLUTION (1860s–1890s)

FEDOR KORANDEI

IN THE SECOND half of the nineteenth century, readers and viewers across the globe came to know the landscape and population of Siberia and the Russian Far East through a flurry of publications, many of them illustrated. An examination of illustrated travel accounts from this period reveals that ideas about Russia's northern and eastern territories were shaped not only by the cultural and political currents of the age, but also, in fundamental ways, by the technologies of transportation and of print. By studying the images that accompanied travelogues, we can see the distortions and selectivity built into the accounts by the paths of rivers and by the iron structures of railroads, with little active choice or awareness on the part of the author and illustrators. The Russian Empire was shaped through its imprint on the pages of popular books throughout Russia, Europe, and America by structures that asserted their own kind of agency.

The number of travel accounts, both Russian and foreign, about the Siberian possessions of the Russian Empire reached its peak in the second half of the nineteenth century. The historical context for this rise was what is called New Imperialism—in particular, the clash of European interests in the Far East, and the competition between the Russian and British empires in Central Asia. These political rivalries took place against the background of a transport revolution in the region. In 1844, the first regular riverboat steamer service started between Tyumen and Tomsk in western Siberia, and in 1905, it was already possible to get from the shores of the Atlantic Ocean to the shores of the Pacific Ocean by railroad. Along with the growth of infrastructure that made it possible to reach the remotest parts of Russian Asia, interest in these territories grew. The American journalist George Kennan, who first came to Siberia in 1865 as an employee of the Russian-American company that intended to lay a telegraph cable from the United States to Russia through Alaska and the Bering Strait, was eager to share his experiences with readers back home. He subsequently wrote that lack of knowledge about Siberia among Americans prompted him to undertake a second expedition in 1885 to 1886, to study the Siberian exile system.

Complaints about Russians' own lack of knowledge regarding the eastern part of Russian Empire could also be heard from Russians themselves in the same period, and not only from those who lived in the capital of the Russian Empire, but also in Siberia itself.[1] Travelogues were often recognized as tools capable of filling the gap in popular geographic knowledge. A growing number of texts discussed travel through Tyumen, the westernmost city of the Siberian colonies and, during the period of interest, the main transit point between the river system of European Russia and the rivers of Asia. These accounts make visible the dynamics of literary colonization of the eastern part of the Russian Empire.

I have identified sixty-seven travel accounts describing voyages via Tyumen to or from Siberia that were published shortly after the voyage in question, between 1860 and 1900—that is, during the height of the transport revolution in this region. The number of travelogues rose partly as a consequence of increasing knowledge about Russian colonies in Asia and partly as a consequence of changes taking place in the publishing industry. Magazines and books became cheaper and readership was growing, both in the West and in Russia and its Siberian colony.[2] In the 1880s, newspapers began to be published in such Siberian cities as Irkutsk, Tomsk, and Ekaterinburg, and the first Siberian university was established in Tomsk in 1888.

The illustrations in travel books reflected, and prescribed, what would interest travelers who came to see the eastern parts of the Russian Empire. Most of these illustrations were various types of engraving and lithography, based on the sketches and photographs taken by the authors during their journey. Although the method of halftone printing, which made it possible to publish photographs in the pages of a book, was perfected in the 1880s, the first volumes illustrated with photographs appeared among the books under consideration only at the very end of the 1890s. Of those in our sample, only four Russian volumes include illustrations, and of these, three were published only at the end of the period, at the turn of the twentieth century. Almost all of the illustrated books of the 1860s to 1890s under consideration are Western in origin: English (nine), French (nine), German (three), American (three), Italian (one), and Danish (one).

What were these illustrations used for? What can they tell us? Illustrated travel books from this period were usually commercial projects requiring investment and intended for profit. They sought to attract a new, middle-class audience interested in remote lands for educational and entertainment purposes. In an effort to persuade readers to buy books, the authors tried to present themselves as authentic eyewitnesses.[3] Illustrations were one of the most important means to achieve that authenticity. For example, on the frontispiece of many books about Siberia, the reader found a portrait of a traveler wearing a fur coat that protected him from the legendary cold. The bulk of the 735 illustrations found in these travel books from the 1880s showed portraits, the built landscape, and natural landscapes.

Portraits included in these travel books most often depicted those who in the Russian colonial nomenclature were called *inorodtsy* (people of non-Russian lineage) and *inovertsy* (people of non-Orthodox faiths)—peoples who seemed exotic to the Western observer (20 percent of all 735 illustrations). Russians were portrayed in the travel books of 1880s much less often (6 percent). Another essential category of the population depicted in travel books was political exiles, who made up 4.5 percent of total illustrations. Siberian prisons were a topic of particular interest to the Western reader. In the 1880s and early 1890s, several books were published on the Siberian exile system, which associated Siberia with prisons in the Western imagination. The most crucial were the publications of George Kennan, who in 1885 and 1886 visited all the main Siberian penitentiaries of the empire.[4] Due to the popularity of this topic, depictions of prison convoys along rivers and prisoners in chains were found even in those books about Siberia whose authors did not visit any prisons.

Monuments and other built structures that could be found on the pages of illustrated travel books generally were not unique architectural landmarks, but ordinary objects reproduced in the book in order to confirm the authenticity of the travel. Most often, these objects were vehicles (5.7 percent); road infrastructure, such as post stations, pickets, caravanserais, and ferries (another 5.7 percent); as well as prisons (5.3 percent) and ordinary buildings, both Indigenous Asian and Russian (at least 4 percent of the total number of illustrations). It is noteworthy that hotel service of the European standard was so undeveloped that there were only two images of hotels. The Russian people, who did not particularly differ from Europeans in terms of their race and appearance, did not attract much attention of the authors of Western travel books, nor did the houses in which they lived and the carts in which they rode. The only exception was one kind of vehicle. Seven illustrations were dedicated to depicting a "tarantass." This type of springless carriage, which appeared in the first half of the nineteenth century, served the expansion of the Russian Empire into Asia until the beginning of the twentieth century, when the Trans-Siberian Railway was launched.

Although Russian readers usually were looking in books about Siberia to see exotic landscapes of the unfamiliar lands of the eastern empire,[5] the most popular places of Asiatic Russia illustrated in these Western books were the largest Russian cities of Siberia: Irkutsk (2.0 percent), Tobolsk (1.5 percent), Tomsk (1.4 percent) and Krasnoyarsk (1.1 percent). The taiga (dense boreal forest) and the beautiful Lake Baikal barely appeared among the illustrations. The natural beauty of the east was primarily represented by large rivers: Angara (1.6 percent), Ob (1.2 percent), and Yenisei (1.1 percent). These were not included *for* their beauty, however, but rather because they served as the most important transport channels before the construction of the

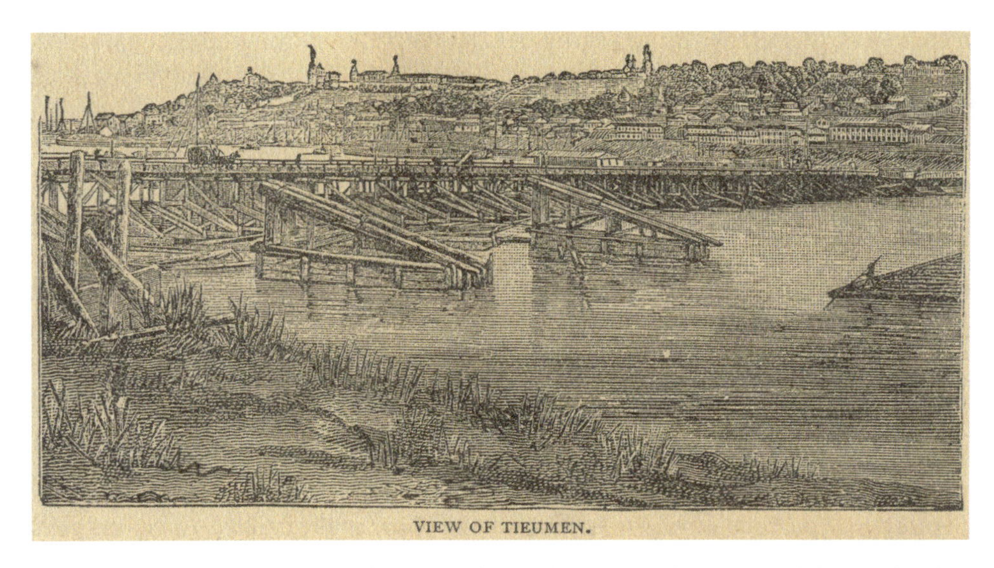

IMAGE 23.1 View purportedly of Tyumen, from James W. Buel, *Russian Nihilism and Exile Life in Siberia*,1883.

Trans-Siberian Railway. The making of illustrations for travel books was an elaborate and expensive process that usually required an artist or photographer to accompany the expeditions. Despite the fact that the number of visitors to Siberia was growing, not all authors could afford their own set of illustrations, so many made use of other people's work. Sometimes, however, attributions were omitted, and images were copied outright. In a book by the American traveler James Buel, who visited Siberia in the summer of 1882, one can see a view of Tyumen (Image 23.1), depicting, however, not Tyumen at all, but rather the pontoon fair bridge across the Oka River in Nizhnii Novgorod.[6] Whether the reader was deliberately misled or this was a technical error, we do not know. Buel's book was intended for an American audience, so the error may well have gone unnoticed.

Much odder was the case of a book by Harry De Windt, an English author who traveled to Siberia in 1891 under patronage of the tsarist government to refute the conclusions drawn by George Kennan, whose sensational articles on Siberian prisons and exile were released as a book the same year.[7] De Windt's voyage to Siberian prisons was shorter than that of his opponent. Unlike Kennan, who spent two years in Siberia and had an artist and a camera with him on the expedition, De Windt, who went only as far as Tomsk and spent only a couple of months traveling, traveled alone. The set of illustrations for De Windt's monograph reveals a number of borrowings from other books about Siberia. Most surprisingly, its publishers borrowed pictures from Kennan himself. For example, the image of a non-existent place in Tyumen (Image 23.2) turns out to be an edited view of Ekaterinburg from Kennan's book (Image 23.3).

A STREET IN TIUMEN.

IMAGE 23.2 View purportedly of Tyumen in Harry De Windt's *Siberia As It Is*, 1892

Let's sum up the discussion so far. According to the illustrated Western travelogues published during the era of the transport revolution in Siberia and the Russian Far East, the eastern part of the Russian Empire was a space with European-type infrastructure, inhabited by an exotic population. Portraying this population as predominantly exotic, the authors of these books may have deliberately or unintentionally contested the very fact of the successful settlement of Siberia by the Russians. An example of this trend was the prison issue, the most interesting to the Western audience. The atrocities of the tsarist government towards its subjects who were exiled to Siberia were one of the obvious political weaknesses of the Russian Empire. It was inevitably used against Russia in propaganda, for example, during the conflicts between the British and Russian empires. However, the fact that the prison system was difficult to hide was, paradoxically, a consequence of the increasing accessibility and visibility of Siberia at this time. The development of transport networks, and the political and economic evolution of the Russian Empire, made this period the time of the greatest openness of the region to the world. The travels of foreigners across the Russian colonies, which had been largely closed to them several decades before, were

IMAGE 23.3 View of a street in Ekaterinburg from George Kennan's *Siberia and the Exile System*, 1891, presumably the source for the non-existent view of Tyumen in Harry de Windt's book.

now not only possible, but also encouraged. Kennan, for example, was allowed to explore the territory of the empire completely legally. In the era of the nationalizing empire, primarily associated with the reign of Alexander III (1883–1894), the Russians began to compete with Europeans in the production and dissemination of popular geographic knowledge about these territories through the development of their own academic institutions and colonial journalism.

The heyday of publications that brought pictures of Siberia to the eyes of an international public was brief. It came to an end, surprisingly, with the completion of the Trans-Siberian Railway. The railway, as Wolfgang Shivelbusch wrote, annihilated the traditional space-time continuum that characterized the old transport technology: "On one hand, the railroad opened up new spaces that were not as easily accessible before; on the other, it did so by destroying space, namely the space between points."[8] This process can be demonstrated by the example of illustrations from travel books written by the first passengers of the Trans-Siberian Railway.

In May and June of 1900, the American pastor Francis Clark traveled from Vladivostok to Moscow. The lion's share of the space of his book (thirteen out of fifteen chapters, and fifty-six out of sixty-five photos) referred to the events experienced in Vladivostok, the starting point, and at the places of transfers: Khabarovsk, Blagoveshchensk, Sretensk, and Irkutsk.[9] After boarding the train in Irkutsk, he instantly, within one chapter, found himself on the Ural border, in Zlatoust, where he took only a couple of photographs. The cities between Irkutsk and Moscow, which were recently described in detail by travelers like Kennan, were now unworthy of interest:

> These places will be but names to most of my readers, and they will not be much the wiser if I tell them such facts as that Omsk has forty thousand inhabitants and Tschelabinsk has fifteen thousand. All these towns, and many smaller ones that I might mention, are places of no little importance in the districts of which they are the centres, but they do not as yet cut much of a figure on the world's maps.[10]

Of the thirty photographs that accompanied the book of another Trans-Siberian Railway traveler, Michael Shoemaker, in 1902, only four were dedicated to the Siberian part of the journey. These four were pictures of bears (they most likely served as a symbol of the region as a whole) on the frontispiece; the bridge over the Volga; a Mongol passenger, whom the author met during the voyage by train; and a typical Siberian railway station. The book, called *The Great Siberian Railway*, did not actually depict Siberia.[11]

NOTES

1. Fedor Korandei, "Opisaniia gorodov, ne imeiushchie dlia russkogo chitatelia osobogo interesa: kupiury v russkikh perevodakh inostrannykh puteshestvii po Sibiri (vtoraia polovina XIX v.) s tochki zreniia istorii populiarnogo geograficheskogo znaniia," *Ab Imperio* 4 (2014): 352.
2. Richard D. Altick, *The English Common Reader. A Social History of the Mass Reading Public, 1800–1900* (Columbus: Ohio State University Press, 1998), 306–307.
3. Beau Riffenburgh, *The Myth of the Explorer: The Press, Sensationalism, and Geographical Discovery* (London and New York: Belhaven Press, 1993); Dane Kennedy, ed., *Reinterpreting Exploration: The West in the World* (Oxford: Oxford University Press, 2014), esp. 80–108.
4. George Kennan, *Siberia and the Exile System*, 2 vols. (New York: The Century Co., 1891).
5. Korandei, "Opisaniia gorodov," 327–328.
6. James W. Buel, *Russian Nihilism and Exile Life in Siberia* (San Francisco: A. L. Bancroft & Company, 1883).
7. Harry De Windt, *Siberia as It Is* (London: Chapman and Hall, 1892); Kennan, *Siberia*.
8. Wolfgang Schivelbusch, *The Railway Journey: The Industrialization of Time and Space in the 19th Century* (Oakland: University of California Press, 1977), 37.
9. Francis. E. Clark, *The Great Siberian Railway: What I saw on My Journey* (London: S. W. Partridge and Co., 1904).
10. Clark, *Great Siberian Railway*, 183–184.
11. Michael M. Shoemaker, *The Great Siberian Railway from St. Petersburgh to Pekin* (New York and London: The Knickerbocker Press, 1903).

CHAPTER 24

"TO THE CAUCASUS": REPRESENTATIONS OF EMPIRE AT ABRAMTSEVO (1870s–1890s)

MARIA TAROUTINA

IN HIS EPIC poem *Demon: An Eastern Tale*, Mikhail Lermontov describes the Caucasus as a "land where splendor and contentment reign" and where "beauty bounteously flourishes."[1] Beginning with Russia's initial incursion into Caucasian territories in the early 1800s, fascination with this rugged, mountainous region continued to fuel the country's literary and artistic imagination throughout the long nineteenth century. The artists of the Abramtsevo artistic circle were no exception. The Abramtsevo estate was located sixty kilometers north of Moscow, in the Sergeievo-Posadskii district, and belonged to the wealthy industrialist Savva Mamontov. From the mid-1870s to the late-1890s, prominent Russian artists such as Konstantin Korovin, Vasily Polenov, Elena Polenova, Ilya Repin, Valentin Serov, Viktor Vasnetsov, and Mikhail Vrubel resided and worked on the estate.

Although traditionally associated with the ascendance of national romanticism, Slavic folklore, and the Neo-Russian style, the group's creative output drew on a diverse set of geographic, temporal, and cultural references. For example, Vasily Polenov executed a series of paintings on the Abramtsevo estate based on his travels in Egypt, Syria, Turkey, and Palestine. Similarly, Mikhail Vrubel's ceramic sculptures of *The Assyrian*, *The Egyptian Girl*, and *The Libyan Lion* (1890s), as well as his costumes and set designs for the theatrical productions *Judith* (1878), *Joseph* (1880), *The Black Turban* (1884), *King Saul* (1890), *To the Caucasus* (1891), and *Prisoner of the Caucasus* (1899), all betrayed an ongoing collective fascination with the so-called "Orient" and its multivalent relationship with Russia's historical past and present. As Lynn Garafola astutely observes, by the close of the nineteenth century, the very idea of "Russianness" itself increasingly "defied neat categories" and "even at Abramtsevo a fine line had divided nationalist material and exotica . . . the two inhabited similar compartments of the imagination."[2] In this context, the Caucasus occupied a particularly fraught discursive space, and was viewed as simultaneously sublime and barbaric, defiant and inferior, desirable and repellent, friend and foe. The present chapter will briefly discuss the Abramtsevo circle's interest in and exposure to the Caucasus, and will then focus closely on Vrubel's illustrations to Lermontov's *Demon* poem and their critical reception, all the while interrogating the various complex crosscurrents that informed and structured Russian aesthetic consciousness at the nexus of empire and modernity.

Various Abramtsevo members had undertaken multiple trips to the Caucasus. Mamontov himself had lived and traveled in the Caucasus, Central Asia, and Iran for nearly two years as a young man. In 1862, his father sent him on a trading mission to Baku, Shahrud, and Mashhad on behalf of the Trans-Caspian Trade Society. In his letters and diaries, Mamontov recorded memorable encounters with the historical sites, inhabitants, and customs of the region. He was impressed with the ancient architecture, melodious music, and "fiery eyes" of the local women.[3] These youthful experiences clearly made a lasting impact on Mamontov, who wrote two comedic plays dedicated to the region, *Black Turban* and *To the Caucasus,* both of which were staged at Abramtsevo several times. Ilya Repin, Konstantin Korovin, Valentin Serov, Elena Polenova, and both of the Vasnetsov brothers, Viktor and Apollinarii, had visited the Caucasus on a number of separate occasions, praising the region's "eternal snows, waterfalls, deserts . . . Eastern bazaars" and "impressive, fearsome highlanders."[4] They chronicled what they saw in a series of compelling watercolor studies and oil sketches, including Repin's *Street in Tiflis* (1881), Apollinarii Vasnetsov's *Kazbek* (1895-96) and Korovin's *In the Caucasus. Seated Mountaineers* (1889).

In an article from 1897, Repin described the Caucasus as the "monstrously-magnificent" land of the "languishing Prometheus."[5] Literary scholar Harsha Ram has termed such characterizations as the "imperial sublime," wherein the region was viewed as simultaneously majestic, mysterious, and "intoxicating," but also as frightening, assailing "the senses as an experience of grandeur" and "combining beauty with terror in such a way so as to induce rapture."[6] Sublime pictorial conventions included large scale, climactic lighting, deep space, and a precariously elevated or oblique perspective. Experientially, the sublime induced contemplation of the divine, the eternal, and the absolute. These qualities are palpably present in Polenov's striking stage set for Mamontov's play, *To the Caucasus.* In its breath-taking, sharp verticality, Polenov's *The Darial Gorge* (1891) (Image 24.1) capitalizes on the Caucasus' rocky, dramatic topography and presents a scenic alternative to what seemed at the time to be Russia's largely bland and monotonous "meagre" nature, characterized by winding, muddy roads, low horizons, and flat, open, and often dreary landscapes.[7]

Steep mountains are also ubiquitous in Vrubel's illustrations for Lermontov's *Hero of Our Time* and Caucasian poem cycle, as well as all of his portrayals of the Demon. Written between 1829 and 1839, Lermontov's *Demon: An Eastern Tale* recounts the story of a doomed love affair between a beautiful Georgian Princess named Tamara and Satan, or Demon. The action begins when the Demon sees Tamara

IMAGE 24.1 Vasily Polenov, *The Darial Gorge*, 1891.

dancing at her wedding feast. Driven by lust, he vows to possess her and surreptitiously murders her fiancé. Persecuted by his wooing, Tamara flees to a convent, but the Demon pursues her even there. When at last she submits to his advances, she is killed by his fiery kiss, and her soul is taken up to heaven by an angel sent by God.

This subject was especially popular at Abramtsevo. One of the first *tableaux vivants* to be staged at the estate in 1878 was *Demon and Tamara*, which was later elaborated into a full-length opera, *The Demon* (1896), and performed by the Mamontov Private Opera in Moscow and St. Petersburg.[8] When a jubilee edition of Lermontov's works was to be published in 1891, a number of the Abramtsevo artists were commissioned to create illustrations for it. Vrubel executed hundreds of images for the project, twenty-two of which were ultimately included in the publication. Besides the Abramtsevo group, a number of other artists, such as Mikhail Zichi, Konstantin Izenberg, and Konstantin Makovskii had also illustrated Lermontov's oeuvre. The vast majority of these illustrations fell into one of two antithetical categories: non-descript, abstract universality on the one hand and tantalizing Orientalist fantasy on the other. As such, they either portrayed the Demon as a handsome Romantic antihero with idealized European facial features and Tamara as an innocent and fair-skinned European beauty, or conversely, Tamara was depicted as a voluptuous Oriental odalisque with the Demon being shown as a loosely Asiatic despot. In some instances, an

Orientalized Tamara was paired with an Occidental-looking Demon, where, as Susan Layton argues, the Demon implicitly adopted the metaphorical identity of the European colonizer and/or western male reader-viewer.

In her analysis of Lermontov's poem, Layton contends that the poet's projection of the Georgian maiden as an emblem of the land continued the more general nineteenth-century Russian tendency to conceive of the Caucasus as a "virgin" territory of primeval forests, fertile valleys, and untapped mineral resources, thus intertwining sexual and imperial domination. In this scheme, Georgia's "Asiatic" alterity was consistently emphasized as a moral justification for Russian intrusion. Although the country was acknowledged to be a kindred Orthodox nation, and one that had converted to Christianity over six hundred years before Russia, it was nonetheless subjected to a systematic Orientalization, and even Islamicization, in Russian cultural and intellectual discourse throughout the course of the nineteenth century. For instance, in his 1837 poem "Hastening Northward from Afar," Lermontov described the Kazbek mountain as a white-turbaned "sentry of the Orient" and "Allah's eternal throne," which aspires to make spiritual "contact with the starry heavens."[9] Here, the Caucasian landscape is strikingly personified, as Lermontov invests it with spiritual, religious, and heroic qualities that he symbolically—but misleadingly—associates with Muslim warriors rather than the Christian people who actually populated it in reality.

As Leah Feldman contends, such direct associations between the sublime but harsh terrain of the Caucasus and the noble savagery of the region's freedom fighters would have simultaneously highlighted for Russian readers the necessity of the tsarist civilizing mission and the heroic, anti-authoritarian struggle of the Indigenous peoples, which undoubtedly resonated with the intelligentsia's own ongoing disavowal of Russia's oppressive, absolutist regime.[10] It is therefore hardly accidental that Lermontov chose to set the action of *Demon* specifically in the Caucasus, with Satan exemplifying the ultimate Romantic fallen hero and the first rebel against God's indisputable authority. This may also explain why Vrubel was especially drawn to this subject, producing close to a hundred pencil and watercolor studies, as well as standalone paintings, of the Demon. In a letter to his sister Anna, the artist explained that he was "a big admirer" of "the East" due to his "Tatar Basargin blood" and also viewed himself as a rebel against the conventional morality and entrenched artistic trends of his times.[11]

Unlike many of his predecessors and contemporaries, however, Vrubel downplayed any "Orientalizing" elements in his illustrations and was instead dedicated to a factually authentic rendition of the Caucasian setting of the poem and the Georgian ethnicity of its protagonists. Although he had never visited the Caucasus in person, he relied on period photographs of specific sites and landscapes, such as the Kazbek mountain, Darial gorge, and Terek River to inform his images. He also portrayed Tamara in traditional Georgian dress, surrounded by specifically Georgian folkloric ornament, tapestries, and musical instruments, such as the *chonguri*, a string instrument resembling a mandolin or lute. Vrubel likewise underscored Georgia's identity as an ancient Christian nation, populating his images with easily recognizable Christian symbols in the form of icons, Orthodox churches, and monasteries. Lastly, the restraint with which Vrubel chose to depict the climactic seduction scene at the end of the poem notably departed from steamier renditions. Instead of the charged eroticism and the tantalizing promise of sexual violence in earlier and later illustrations, Vrubel's version shows Tamara weeping on her bed with her face covered, while the Demon—rendered as a curiously feminized and androgynous figure—leans at her side (Image 24.2). The flat, geometric ornamentation envelops and almost dissolves the two figures in a riotous explosion of lines and angles. In contrast to other artists, who portrayed Tamara in enticingly form-hugging and translucent apparel, Vrubel deliberately obscured and de-emphasized the heroine's physique with the folds of her garments and surrounding fabrics. In both of Vrubel's versions of the seduction scene, the volumetric solidity of the figures' bodies is offset by a series of contrasting, interlocking planes and shifting angles that produce a peculiarly constructed, modernist effect.

Unlike his contemporaries' more naturalistic and legible treatment of form, Vrubel actively privileged the visual over the textual, and took numerous creative liberties with his illustrations. For this, he was vehemently criticized by a number of contemporary critics, who labeled his images "degenerate" and "repulsively decadent." The description that was published in the journal *Artist* was a typical response to these works:

> Mr. Vrubel . . . does not even feel that his figures do not resemble people, but rag dolls . . . In many drawings it is impossible to make out where the hands and legs are or the head, and one must admire only the play of several "artistic" dabs which, in Mr. Vrubel, replace drawing and plasticity and beauty. Apparently, Mr. Vrubel makes a pretense to "mood," but he forgets that where a neck is longer than a hand or an arm looks more like a leg, it is silly to look for mood, and without drawing there is no illustration.[12]

In addition to Vrubel's unconventional style, several contemporary reviewers found his geographic and ethnographic precision distasteful, and one commentator remarked with derision that in his attempt to create a "Caucasian Demon," Vrubel had made a grave error in departing from "the established canon," and that in his rendition, the Demon looks like "an ugly old Georgian woman with a hooked nose, thin, sunken lips, black, piercing eyes and wide black eyebrows."[13] In their Caucasian specificity and intrusive visual syntax, Vrubel's illustrations disrupted the pleasurable and voyeuristic delectation of a colorful, sensuous, seemingly realistically rendered but simultaneously comfortably distant and inchoate "Orient" to which nineteenth-century audiences had become so accustomed.

IMAGE 24.2 Mikhail Vrubel, *Demon and Tamara*, 1890–1891.

There were a few highly positive and appreciative responses to Vrubel's illustrations. For example, the contemporary artist Konstantin Bogaevskii insisted that out of all the artists who had illustrated Lermontov's poem, "only [Vrubel] had actually succeeded in capturing on canvas the majesty and grandeur of the Caucasus."[14] In fact, it was precisely the contradictions and tensions implicit in the critical response to Vrubel's illustrations that highlighted the larger problem of simultaneously visualizing the Caucasus as a friendly Christian—or potentially Christian—ally with its own venerable ancient past and as an Oriental foreign inferior in need of Russian admonition and enlightenment. This duality is aptly reflected in the commentary of the literary critic and art historian Sergei Durylin. Writing in the mid-twentieth century, he described Vrubel's illustrations in poetic, but overtly Orientalist, language. According to him, in *The Dance of Tamara* (Image 24.3), Vrubel

> extracted from the black watercolor captivatingly unexpected coloristic harmonies: the precious jet black of Chinese lacquer transitions into the playfulness of smoky topaz; antique ivory transforms into the dark orange or coffee matte finish of ancient bronze. In the figure of the dancing Tamara, in her light garments, in the rich Georgian costume of her stately partner . . . in the kaleidoscopic pattern of the carpet, there is something joyfully festive.[15]

These descriptive terms—*coffee, Chinese lacquer, antique ivory, ancient bronze, precious jewels, festive carpets*—conjured up by the sensuous dancing of an Eastern beauty invoke an inscrutable Orient that in the European imaginary stretched from Africa and the Middle East to India, Central Asia, and the Far East. In Durylin's description, Vrubel's image functions as a quintessentially Occidental construction of a desirable, elusive, and illusory "other" to the western—in this case, Russian—self.

And yet the same scholar insisted that although Vrubel's watercolors "shimmer and scintillate with all the colors of Lermontov's semilegendary Orient," they nonetheless do not submit to a "lush and extravagant Orientalism," or to a "self-satisfied exoticism."[16] Instead, Durylin contended that with their restrained monochromatic palette and laconic minimalism, Vrubel's images accorded a certain quiet dignity to their subject matter. The sharp, broken lines, shard-like forms, and striking black-and-white contrasts effectively communicate both the tragedy and action of the narrative, the dynamism and majesty of the terrain, and the inherent nobility and vitality of its populace without devolving into racial stereotypes, spectacle, or melodrama. To put it slightly differently: Vrubel's illustrations were certainly meant to portray a Caucasian alterity, but they nevertheless refrained from a fetishistic "Orientalization" and, in so doing, advanced an entirely different approach to and vision of the Caucasus.

It is important to emphasize that as a mass-produced, widely circulated printed medium, Vrubel's illustrations would have been readily available to thousands of people both in the metropolitan capital and in the colonial borderlands, thus

IMAGE 24.3 Mikhail Vrubel, *The Dance of Tamara*, 1890–1891.

directly contributing to the visual dialectics of empire, which, much like the Caucasian-themed plays and operas staged by Mamontov's Private Opera, mediated distant peripheries for audiences in Moscow and St. Petersburg. As such, the Abramtsevites actively participated in molding a broader imperial consciousness beyond their small, intimate circle of cultural practitioners. Perhaps even more importantly, rather than treating the Caucasus as a picturesque, remote, and impassive imperial outpost to be mined for content and creative inspiration, the Abramtsevo circle viewed it as an active cultural producer and important interlocutor in its own right. Mamontov was a great admirer of the Tiflis Opera House and hired some of his star performers and musicians directly from there, including the future star Fedor Chaliapin. The celebrated painter Ilya Repin insisted that a new school of art should be formed in Tiflis under local expertise, one that would fully embrace and reflect "the indigenous specificities of the region."[17]

To sum up, then, the divergences and dichotomies inherent in Vrubel's illustrations and the critical response to them, along with other Caucasian-themed works produced at Abramtsevo, clearly manifest how the Caucasus, as a physical and imaginary space, both embodied and reflected many of Russia's own inherently repressed dualities and, especially, the restive issue of its semi-Asian identity. After all, many members of the Russian aristocracy, military, and cultural elites such as the Usupovs, Sheremetevs, and the Bagrationi, had either Georgian, Armenian, or Tatar ancestry—like Vrubel himself—which further complicated the self/other binary. Consequently, rather than justifying and advancing imperial authority through essentializing and formulaic depictions, the visual semantics of multiple late nineteenth-century colonial representations, both at Abramtsevo and beyond, were inherently unstable and often became important discursive sites from which Russia's own political, social, and cultural shortcomings could be recognized and critiqued.

NOTES

1. Mikhail Lermontov, *Demon: Vostochnaia Povest'* (1839): Part I: IV.
2. Lynn Garafola, *Diaghilev's Ballets Russes* (Boston: Da Capo Press, 1998), 16.
3. Evgenii Arenzon, *Savva Mamontov* (Moscow: Russkaia kniga, 1995), 45–46.
4. Il'ia Repin, letter to Vladimir Stasov, June 9, 1888, in *Izbrannye pisma: 1867–1930*, Vol. 1, edited by I. A. Brodskii (Moscow: "Iskusstvo," 1969), 349.
5. Il'ia Repin, "Nuzhna li shkola iskusstv v Tiflise?" (1897), in *Vospominania, stat'i i pis'ma iz zagranitsy I. E. Repina*, edited by N. B. Severova (St. Petersburg, 1901), 253.
6. Harsha Ram, *The Imperial Sublime: A Russian Poetics of Empire* (Madison: University of Wisconsin Press, 2003), 91
7. In his discussion of Russian landscape painting, Christopher Ely contrasts Russia's "ugly" and "boring" nature to the sun-drenched shores of Italy and the imposing mountain peaks of Switzerland; see Ely, *This Meagre Nature: Landscape and National Identity in Imperial Russia* (DeKalb: Northern Illinois University Press, 2002).

8. *Tableau vivant* is a French term meaning "living picture" and was a popular pastime in Europe and Russia in the nineteenth century. During a *tableau vivant* performance, participants represented scenes from literature, art, history, or everyday life on a stage.
9. Susan Layton, *Russian Literature and Empire: Conquest of the Caucasus from Pushkin to Tolstoy* (Cambridge: Cambridge University Press, 2005), 64.
10. Leah Feldman, "Orientalism on the Threshold: Reorienting Heroism in Late Imperial Russia," *boundary 2* 39, no. 2 (2012): 170.
11. Vrubel's mother, Anna Grigorievna Basargina-Vrubel, came from the noble Basargin family, which had Tatar roots. Mikhail Vrubel. Letter to Anna Vrubel, October 1886, in *Vrubel': Perepiska, vospominaniia o khudozhnike,* edited by Eleonora Gomberg-Verzhbinskaia (Leningrad: Iskusstvo, 1976), 49.
12. *Artist,* no. 16 (1891): 133, quoted in Sergei Durylin, "Vrubel i Lermontov," *Literaturnoe Nasledstvo* 45–46 (1948): 580.
13. N. "Pis'ma ob iskusstve," *Russkii Vestnik* (June, 1893): 332, in Durylin, "Vrubel i Lermontov," 581–582.
14. Konstantin Bogaevskii, letter to Sergei Durylin, January 12, 1941.
15. Durylin, "Vrubel i Lermontov," 568.
16. Durylin, "Vrubel i Lermontov," 568.
17. Repin, "Nuzhna li shkola," 254.

CHAPTER 25

ARCHEOLOGICAL IMAGERY COLONIZES THE CAUCASUS

LOUISE MCREYNOLDS

ARCHEOLOGY AND THE art of representation have both been identified as active agents in the process of nineteenth-century colonization, but seldom discussed as co-conspirators. The connection between the two dates back to the mid-eighteenth century, when Johann Winkelmann transformed art history into the emergent discipline of archeology by comparing the minutiae of ancient Greek and Roman artistic styles in ways that allowed him to categorize and periodize distinctions between the two. His reliance upon descriptive detail made it possible to identify artifacts that would have otherwise been lost to the historical record, but words alone lacked the allure that had pulled Winkelmann to them in the first place.

Archeology collected material mementos of a distant past, objects that aroused a sensory connection to the present because they could be seen and touched. To secure their place in the popular imagination, though, these artifacts that linked past to present had to be made visible. Mediating between ancient cultures and contemporary viewers, archeological reproductions developed into a specific genre; enabling audiences to visualize realities, they encouraged them to further invest themselves emotionally in sentiments already felt for bygone years. This was the most pronounced power of these reproductions: to transform unfamiliar objects, distanced in both time and space, into "versions of a previously known thing."[1] That is, these visualizations inspired imaginary memories, affective connections across history that made the past accessible as the prelude to the present. Thus did this curated imagery help to delete the violence and displacement wrought by imperial expansion, playing an essential role in the strategy by which archeology satisfied colonizing objectives. Archeological reproductions served the imperializing state by converting the pasts of others into a form that its subjects could recognize and, hence, appropriate for themselves.

One of tsarist Russia's most successful colonizing endeavors in the nineteenth century was the incorporation of the South Caucasus into the imperial domain. For all the vastness of the Russian empire, no area captured the imperial imagination quite like the Caucasus. Sharing Christianity had smoothed the absorption of Georgia and Armenia, but ideological work remained to be done before these two ancient states could be thought of as belonging naturally within the empire. Georgia joined in 1801, followed by northern Armenia in 1828. Because a portion of Armenia remained in the Ottoman Empire, the annexed section was dubbed "Russian Armenia," the nomenclature easing colonization forward. Mikhail Vorontsov, Russia's Viceroy of the Caucasus from 1844 to 1853, was deeply committed to scientific ventures, and in 1850, in what was an initial foray into deploying archeology as an imperial practice, he sent Lt. Julius Kästner to explore Ani, the abandoned tenth-century capital of Armenia currently under Ottoman suzerainty. Kästner spent forty-four days sketching this unique collection of half-destroyed buildings, victimized by centuries of competing imperial powers and by an earthquake in 1319. Then, Vorontsov tasked Orientalist Marie-Félicité Brosset, who was trained in the languages of the Caucasus and was a member of the Russian Academy of Sciences, with making Ani accessible to those who could not travel across the Ottoman border.

Brosset first had to turn Ani into an artifact.[2] He collected and organized the multilingual travel reports, maps, and scientific descriptions of the ruins. Employing architect and lithographer Robert Mellin to make corrections that would assure the authenticity of the reproductions, he also invited an artist from the Academy of Arts to make adjustments to Kästner's sketches. The result was the two-volume *The Ruins of Ani* (*Les Ruines d'Ani*), a stunning selection of lithographs that accentuated the limits of descriptive language by highlighting the power of visual depictions. Known in its heyday as the "city of 1,000 churches," Ani became not just a collection of dilapidated buildings, but a Romantic ruin. It was recast as an evocation of the sublime, which, as "an emblem of transience, [could] abolish objective time by affording an imaginary repetition of the past with an intensity nearly identical to the original sensations."[3] Brosset's etchings (Image 25.1) forged the emotional bond that inspired the autocracy and its subjects to envision Ani as "previously known": both Christian and Russian. Designed initially for an elite audience of scholars and officials, these images smoothed the path forward for imperialist designs.

Brosset's lithographs rendered words unnecessary, because captions could not communicate what made the visuals so suggestive. The media of reproduction were themselves evolving, and in ways that would affect perception. Photography began coming into its own, sharing with archeology the promise of positivism, that nineteenth-century faith in rational, empirical knowledge. Photography assured a level of accuracy in reproduction that would revolutionize representation. English inventor William Fox Talbot himself made photography's first link with archeology when he used his calotype, a process that captured images on silver chloride in a camera obscura, to reproduce ancient scripts, thereby conserving many a text otherwise vulnerable to the elements. Moreover, photography was generating its own sort of imperialist gaze. Photographers were experimenting with ways to envision sceneries, from landscapes bereft of inhabitants to snapshots of ethnic "types,"

IMAGE 25.1 Marie-Félicité Brosset, "The Main Gate of Ani," from *Les Ruines d'Ani. Atlas Général*, 1861.

pictures of anonymous individuals posed to represent essentialized social and ethnic classifications.

The camera, though, faced numerous difficulties before it could become a weapon of colonization. Clunky equipment and a process that involved the use of chemicals to etch images on sensitive metal sheets, such as those used by both the fledgling calotype and its French equivalent, the daguerreotype, had kept photographers away from excavations during the early decades of archeology. The earliest illustrations produced by cameras for archeological use came by way of the photogravure, an advancement in printing that allowed photographic images to be first etched on metal plates and then refined in such a way that they softened the harsh contours of the earliest photographs. Able to retain some of the contemplative aesthetic of the lithograph while greatly enhancing accuracy and authenticity, the photogravure combined easily with the printing press, which meaningfully increased the circulation of visuals. But this reproductive process was also comparatively pricey, which meant that it required subsidization, primarily from autocratic coffers.

The first Russian enterprise in which archeology and photography imaginatively combined forces came in preparation for Russia's Sixth Archeological Congress, held in Odesa in 1884, and supported by Grand Prince Sergei Aleksandrovich. Youngest son of the recently assassinated Tsar Alexander II, he was the Romanov with the deepest interest in archeology. The grand prince backed Professor Nikodim Kondakov, a rising star in archeological and Byzantine circles, on an outing to Constantinople, where he would explore a number of Orthodox ruins in the Ottoman capital. Kondakov took a team of experts in reproduction with him: Iu. Raul, a French photographer who had relocated to Odesa and had made his reputation with photographs of Little Russian and Jewish "types"; draughtsman A. F. Krasovskii; and noted watercolorist E. S. Vile. The composition of the group signifies an assumption that archeology needed visuals, and in that same vein, these illustrators profited from archeology's capacity to infuse their work with scientific significance. The volume that appeared in 1887, ornamented with fifty full-page photogravures executed by the prestigious Moscow firm of Sherer and Nabgolts, displayed in full the creativity made possible by the collaborations. Kondakov's illustrators made the Orthodox religious past of the Ottoman capital palpable, in no small measure by keeping the Islamic presence invisible. By conjuring up images familiar from medieval chronicles while also erasing the Ottoman present, these extraordinary photos of places exercised the full force of archeological visualizations as a medium of imperialism.

Combined with his interpretive text, the Kondakov venture took a major archeological step forward in advancing the idea that the Russian Empire viewed itself as the successor of the fallen Byzantine Empire. At the crux of this lay the religious inheritance of Orthodoxy, which provided the cultural key to incorporating the South Caucasus into the Russian Empire. Enter Praskovia Uvarova, widow of the "father of Russian archeology," Alexei Uvarov, and whose personal acquaintances included Grand Prince Sergei Aleksandrovich. Having first traveled to Georgia in 1879 on an expedition with her husband, she became completely smitten with the region. Beginning in 1886, with tsarist sponsorship, she organized a series of archeological excursions throughout the Caucasus, which resulted in fourteen volumes under her editorship, published from 1888 to 1916. Uvarova's game plan was familiar: collect materials that had been written and reproduced by others, and then correct and expand upon previous efforts while also adding new analyses and pictures.

Both texts and images in these volumes ranged across the archeological spectrum: inscriptions, some photographed, others hand-copied; crumbling structures and kurgans (ancient burial mounds), with their random cornucopia of skulls, shards, tools, and weapons. Various types of images decorated the volumes' pages, from roughly drawn blueprints to phototypes. The fourth volume documented an excursion that Uvarova herself had undertaken, an expedition that produced the most magnificent illustrations. She had traveled through Abkhazia, itself a target of Georgia's colonizing ambitions, in search of "Christian monuments." Uvarova does not name her photographer, only that he was sometimes "too tired and too weak" to scale heights that did not daunt *her*.[4] Transformed into alluring photogravures, these reproductions of massive, abandoned stone buildings were photographed repeatedly from angles that obligate the viewer to defer to their dignity. They successfully revere both the obstinacy of the original structure and the force of the natural world intertwined with it. Making both time and space ethereal rather than absolute categories, these photogravures undercut the positivism that both archeology and photography had promised, forging emotional bonds in place of reasoned, empirical knowledge.

Uvarova's homage to the Christian Caucasus captured a spirituality that, while ostensibly softening her political agenda, made it all the more potent because of its emotive component. The image of the Safarskii (Sapara) Monastery (Image 25.2), a complex of churches dating from the tenth through the fifteenth centuries, positions the monastery precariously along a gorge, but unmolested by the surrounding forest. It evokes a turn-of-the-century sensibility of ruins, best articulated by Georg Simmel in 1907: "Although the ruin seems to signal the revenge of nature on the strivings of human agency, in reality the ruin returns us to the source of energy, to the core of our self." Uvarova's choice of visuals suggests, as Simmel also opines, that

IMAGE 25.2 Photogravure of the Safarskii Monastery, in Gr. P. S. Uvarova, ed., *Materialy po arkheologii Kavkaza* (*Archeological Materials of the Caucasus*), 1894.

"[p]aradoxically, the ruin is a window into the future, as it demonstrates that an object continues to exist and to develop even after it has been subjected to 'rape' when it was given a specific form by man."[5] Implicit in these Christian monuments was the notion that they had survived the onslaught of Russia's enemies, from Mongols to Ottoman Turks, Simmel's "rape." Therefore, the time had come for Russia to reclaim and restore these ruins.

The marvelously photogenic Caucasus, though, offered up more than monasteries for the imperializing imagination. Nikolai Marr, an obscure linguist who would one day become a personification of the perversions of Stalinist science, was sent to Armenia in 1891 to counterbalance the growing presence of western archeologists in the region. Ani, so memorable from Brosset's lithographs, had fallen into Russian territory as a result of the Russo-Turkish War of 1877. It captivated Marr much as the other Christian sites in the Caucasus had Uvarova, and he returned in 1904 with a vision for excavating it. His team included Armenian photographer Avram Vruyr. Marr's objective was to reconstruct the devastated city in situ, turning the dig site itself into a museum. Customarily, archeologists sent their finds back to the imperial Hermitage Museum, which enjoyed the authority to keep them for possible display. Marr interrupted this practice at the Ani site. He turned the lone mosque left standing into an exhibition hall for the display of artifacts, but the real museum was the city itself, which he intended to resuscitate.[6]

Vruyr's initial role was as documentarian, the chronicler of archeological activities. Using a before-and-after layout, what appeared in the first shot as an undistinguished hillock would in the second reveal a courtyard, remnants of those who had once lived there. Barely comprehensible, these grainy photos nonetheless celebrated the power of archeology to recover the past. Vruyr also captured the exoticism inherent in the buildings left in ruins; he successfully evoked the affective connections that Brosset established in his etchings, heightened now because of the authenticity inherent in photographs. These visuals helped Marr to solicit the private funding upon which he depended, because the meager government subsidy was hardly sufficient for his ambitions. Marr turned to the affluent Armenian diaspora for more generous support, and the photos proved to them that their money was being well spent. But these visuals also heralded a political problem: the bourgeoning contestation between Russian imperialism and Armenian nationalism. Ruing his monetary dependence on financiers with nationalist inclinations, Marr held fast to his idealized viewpoint of beneficent imperialism.

Precision photography aided Marr in expressing this ideal. Just as Fox had deployed his calotype to protect texts, so could a 1908 snapshot of an inscription on the wall of a mosque at Ani be salvaged, and when interpreted, it illustrated a tolerance for multiculturalism that Marr romanticized. A fourteenth-century directive from Persian ruler Abu Sa'id Bahadur Khan, written in Arabic, Georgian, and Armenian, declared to his multilingual, multiconfessional populace in Ani that he wanted them all to prosper, and that he would therefore defend them from ruinous extortions.[7]

Marr saw in this evidence that despite Muslim rule in medieval Ani, the city had been inhabited by "an international urban population right alongside the native Armenian trading class living peacefully with Persian-Muslim traders."[8]

The single most striking artifact that Marr unearthed was the discovery of a nearly seven-foot statue of King Gagik I (ruled 989–1020), found in 1906 (Image 25.3) and the solitary statue discovered at the excavation. Marr was particularly taken with

IMAGE 25.3 Photograph of the lost statue of King Gagik I, from N. Ia. Marr, *O raskopkakh i rabotakh v Ani letom 1906* (*On the excavations and work in Ani, summer 1906*), 1907.

Gagik's turban, which he interpreted as a Christian king wearing Moslem headgear, a practice that he considered common for the era and further evidence of benevolent multicultural imperialism. Rather than being sent to the Hermitage, Gagik was fastened sideways to a wall in the Ani Museum behind a glass case, and Vruyr's photo of him helped to lure the curious to Marr's city-museum. The photograph fashions a trace of Gagik's existence, generically exoticized and not tethered by either time or space. Gagik metamorphosed into a recognizable version of a tsar.

Vruyr's photo found a considerably more momentous historical role to play than even Marr had imagined. In 1918, when World War I began turning into a civil war in the Russian Empire, catastrophe struck the Ani artifacts. One of Marr's team loaded Gagik and other objects aboard a train bound for the newly established Archaeological Institute for the Caucasus in Tbilisi. The rail wagon vanished en route. Gagik, floating ephemerally in this photo, announces his presence there, and only there. Now, this photograph performs double duty, first as a testament to the necessity of photography to archeology, and second as a potential counterargument to those postcolonial theorists who would keep material artifacts strictly within the cultural milieu where they took shape. Should Gagik instead have been shipped to the Hermitage, where he could have stood safely under the gaze of all, even though that would have relocated an Armenian king to the capital of the empire that had absorbed his realm?

This artifact-cum-visual holds theoretical value beyond these rhetorical questions, because it addresses the concrete relationship of the object to its image. Walter Benjamin would have joined Marr with privileging the artifact. In his canonical "The Work of Art in the Age of Mechanical Reproduction," Benjamin argued that "the original preserved all of its authority; not so vis-à-vis technical reproduction . . . [and] since the historical testimony rests on authenticity, the former, too, is jeopardized by reproduction."[9] More than a century earlier, Immanuel Kant, in contrast, had put forward the notion of the "thing-in-itself": "we know not this thing as it is in itself, but only know its appearances."[10] Replicating artifacts transmuted the material into a different sort of object. From the moment it is reproduced, each bit of material culture generates a second self. Rather than looking for a lost authenticity, Kant suggests that it is more productive to seek out the affective and interpretive connections made possible by reproductions. As Gagik makes plain, the excavated artifact can lead a healthy metaphysical afterlife.[11] It also reminds that us the acclaimed positivism theoretically inherent in both photography and archeology is constantly being mediated by the discursive nature of realism, but whose reality? In the case of the Caucasus, it is that of the colonizing empire.

NOTES

1. Edward Said, *Orientalism* (New York: Vintage Books, 1979), 59.
2. Throughout this essay, I privilege the archeologist over the person who produced the reproductions, all of whom were also highly regarded professionals; I do this because the archeologist was the one who exercised control over the interpretation of the site.
3. Denis Diderot on "ruins," quoted in Andreas Schönle, *Architecture of Oblivion: Ruins and Historical Consciousness in Modern Russia* (DeKalb: Northern Illinois University Press, 2011), 12.
4. P. S. Uvarova, *Byloe, davno proshedshie schastlivye dni* (Moskva: Izd-vo im. Sabashnikovykh, 2005), 15.
5. Quoted in Schönle, *Architecture*, 14.
6. Louise McReynolds, "Nikolai Marr: Reconstructing Ani as the Imperial Ideal," *Ab Imperio* (May 2016): 102–124.
7. V. Bartol'd, "Aniiskaia seriia," no. 5 (St. Petersburg: Akademia Nauk, 1911), 3.
8. N. Ia. Marr, *Ani, Knizhnaia istoriia goroda i raskopki na meste gorodishcha* (Leningrad: Gos. sotsial'no-ekonomicheskoe izd-vo, 1934), 118.
9. Walter Benjamin, "The Work of Art in the Age of Mechanical Reproduction," in *Illuminations*, edited by H. Arendt (New York: Schocken, 1969), 217–251.
10. Immanuel Kant, *Prolegomena to Any Future Metaphysics that Will Be Able to Present Itself as a Science* (LaVergne, TN: Ingram Books, 1986), 32.
11. Jenny Newell discusses how artifacts removed from aboriginal sites can be "returned" through different modes of accessing them: "Old Objects, New Media: Historical Collections, Digitization and Affect," *Journal of Material Culture* 17, no. 3 (2012): 287–306.

CHAPTER 26

CHAINED TO A WHEELBARROW: HARD LABOR ON AN 1890S PICTURE POSTCARD FROM SIBERIA

ALISON ROWLEY

IN 1891, ALEKSEI Kirillovich Kuznetsov documented the working and living conditions of those condemned to hard labor in eastern Siberia. The seventy-four images that he included in an album entitled *Types and Views of Nerchinsk Hard Labor Camps,* which showed both prisoners and their surroundings, are interesting examples of fin-de-siècle ethnographic and landscape photographs.[1] But rather than focus on the album, here I consider a reworked version of one of the images and suggest that the resulting picture postcard—which had the potential to reach a far greater audience than the more elaborate and expensive album—provided viewers of the time with a number of avenues for imagining the people who inhabited this distant part of the Russian empire (Image 26.1).

Who was Aleksei Kuznetsov? The photographer, who took the picture seen in Image 26.1, was born into a wealthy merchant family in February 1845.[2] He received a good education. After finishing primary school in Kherson, in southern Ukraine, he enrolled at the Moscow Commercial College. He graduated in 1864 and then decided to pursue more advanced studies at the Petrovsky Agricultural and Forestry Academy, also in Moscow. There, he became part of Sergei Nechaev's group, something that dramatically changed the course of his life. Nechaev was a key figure in the revolutionary movement at the end of the 1860s. His "Catechism of a Revolutionary" outlined what he considered acceptable behavior in the fight against the government, and it provided a blueprint for creating a modern terrorist organization to do just that. When one member of the group objected to his rather chilling and immoral ideas, Nechaev arranged to have him killed. In his autobiography, Kuznetsov does not deny his involvement in the murder of his fellow student, Ivan Ivanovich Ivanov, but the sparse sentence he devotes to it is short on detail.

Kuznetsov was arrested on January 3, 1870, and housed in the Peter and Paul Fortress in St. Petersburg until his trial, which began the following July. Kuznetsov

IMAGE 26.1 A. Kuznetsov, "Nerchinsk Hard Labor Type. Chained to a Wheelbarrow." Chita, no date.

confessed and was convicted for his part in the murder of his comrade. He was deprived of all property rights and sentenced to ten years in prison—a sentence that was soon altered to hard labor and permanent exile in Siberia. He arrived at the Kara mines in eastern Siberia in June 1873 and spent the next six years laboring to fulfill his punishment.

In 1878, Kuznetsov was permitted to settle in Nerchinsk, on the Chinese border, and, like a number of other former political prisoners, turned to photography to make a living.[3] Despite the successes he had in his chosen field, Kuznetsov preferred to focus on his contributions to scholarship and public culture when he looked back upon his life. In his autobiography, Kuznetsov discussed his activities as a photographer in only a few sentences, while he spent half of the text outlining his scholarly work, showing how active he was in founding ethnographic museums and in organizing exhibitions concerning life in eastern Siberia. In this, he was also not alone, for as Sarah Badcock's research into the lives of political exiles at this time shows, other political exiles were similarly engaged in scholarly expedition and scientific work in Siberia.[4] These people spent countless days and weeks mapping the region, collecting plant specimens, and observing Indigenous populations. In other words, they continued to engage with the intellectual currents, and sometimes even with the scholarly institutions, of the European part of the empire from which they had been exiled, and they saw the region where they presently resided as a place in need of enlightenment.

Despite embracing commonly held tropes of empire in his scholarly activities, Kuznetsov refused to support the political regime that held the imperial structure together. Instead, during the 1905 Revolution, he was active in socialist-revolutionary circles in Chita, which led to his arrest in February 1906. The following month, Kuznetsov was sentenced to death, but after appeals by the Academy of Sciences and the Russian Geographical Society, his sentence was commuted to (another) ten-year stretch of hard labor. Again, the vagaries of the Siberian prison system were soon on display, for by June 1908, after only a short spell of hard labor at the Akatui prison, Kuznetsov had been sent to an agricultural settlement in the Yakutsk region. There, he occupied his time with gardening and organizing a free school for village children. And despite having been convicted twice for revolutionary activities, Kuznetsov was allowed by regional political authorities to continue his scholarly pursuits. For instance, over the next five years, he set up museums in Yakutsk and Chita. Kuznetsov continued to work in this field for the remainder of his life, and in the mid-1920s—in other words, a number of years after the Bolshevik Revolution brought a government Kuznetsov presumably considered more palatable to power—he was given a gold medal by the Central Russian Geographical Society in recognition of his contributions to ethnography. He died in 1928.

The postcard Kuznetsov had printed—likely to supplement his income, since many photographers did exactly that—quite literally embodied several possible visions of eastern Siberia. First, the postcard fits with long-expressed state desires to use prisoners as colonists for the distant regions of the Russian Empire, because the subject, as a prisoner, likely was not born in the region where he was forced to toil and was photographed. Next, the postcard fits into the popular "types" genre that categorized people by ethnicity or profession; its caption reads "Nerchinsk Hard Labor Type." Such postcards were an offshoot of the visual anthropological studies that began to be done across Europe in the 1860s and 1870s, and as someone who notably defined himself by his ethnographic work, it is not surprising to find Kuznetsov embracing its terminology in his photography as well. Previously, these "types" images had circulated on *cartes-de-visite* or as cabinet photographs. Picture postcards, however, cornered the market for cheap visual materials in the final two decades of the nineteenth century. "Types" photographs were employed as illustrations in public scientific lectures, collected by the libraries of learned institutions as well as individual scholars, and sold to tourists on postcards in photographers' shops. In these pictures, it was common to have a single individual stand in as the representative of an entire social group, and for that person to be anonymous, as is the case in our example. Indeed, giving a name to the subject in the caption would have undermined the entire idea of them serving as a "type," since individuality is quite incompatible with that notion. It also matters in this instance that Kuznetsov was presenting a "prisoner type," because prison regimes were by their very nature designed to rob those subjected to them of their individuality. In essence, the photograph used for this postcard shows a kind of double erasure: the man's identity has been stripped away first, by prison authorities, who clothed him in a uniform and who controlled his working life, and then by Kuznetsov, who labelled the man as a "type" in the caption instead of providing any kind of information—such as his name, precise place of incarceration, or sentence—that would have helped viewers to see the subject as a unique person. What we cannot determine, however, is the degree to which Kuznetsov may have sympathized with his subject, for what can be read as a dispassionate image classifying a prisoner according to contemporary scientific discourses, or suggesting that someone like this embodied a form of settler colonialism, may also be interpreted as a statement against the punishment being depicted and, possibly, even the entire exile system. As one of the editors of this volume noted, when she looked at the image, she saw "a decent man chained to a wheelbarrow, doing what looks like pointless hard labor in a grim and empty landscape."

Other elements of the postcard's composition further conform to the "types" genre. The man was depicted with props—in this case, the wheelbarrow full of rubble to which he was chained—and such items were intended to underscore the supposed authenticity of the scene, especially since at least some Russians would have known that being chained to a wheelbarrow for five or ten years was a punishment meted out to recidivists for much of the nineteenth century.[5] It is also important to note that Kuznetsov altered the original background of the photograph. As in many "types" pictures, a blank cloth or sheet was used as a backdrop, since, as Elizabeth Edwards notes, "the plain background accentuates physical characteristics and denies context. The meaning and 'reality' of the subject can be given only by those who interpret visual evidence."[6] In essence, the subject was turned into a specimen. Kuznetsov's tinkering with the background did nothing to alter that impression, but by substituting an outdoor backdrop for the sheet that was used in the original photograph, Kuznetsov implied that the photograph was an accurate depiction of a moment in this hard laborer's working day. His inclusion of the fetters did likewise, even though their use was, according to the memoirs of Petr Filippovich Iakubovich (who was arrested in 1884 and transferred to Akatui prison in the Nerchinsk complex in 1890), seen as obsolete by some local officials by then. As Iakubovich put it, "In eastern Siberia, where the administration isn't so pedantic as in Russia and prisoners wear fetters only as a formality, the rings are fixed directly to the boots so that under-chains and under-strains are never needed."[7] A quick glance at Kuznetsov's postcard shows that the positioning of the subject's fetters does not conform to the evolving norms that Iakubovich remembered; however, it is impossible to know precisely why.

Still, it is doubtful that most viewers of the postcard would have quibbled with the details, since the overall image conformed with contemporary imaginings of what Siberian exiles looked like. Modern viewers may find something disconcerting about the label being attached to the man in this picture, for it is difficult to conceive of "hard labor type" as a professional designation equivalent to, say, "coachman type" or "postman type." The man in the picture was not likely to have chosen his job—or even his incarceration, for that matter—yet this label now superseded any previous work-based identity that he may have had for himself.

At the same time, our "hard labor type" can be thought of as an agent of empire, because in the eyes of many Russian government officials, sending convicts to Siberia was not, to quote scholar Zhanna Popova, "purely an instrument for the punishment of convicts, for in itself the presence of exiles in the region assisted the Russian goal of colonization."[8] Indeed, ever since the first Russian subjects were exiled to Siberia at the end of the sixteenth century, those had been the paired goals of the penal system. Siberian exile rid the imperial metropole of dangerous criminals, while also ensuring a steady stream of settlers into peripheral regions.

As I have written earlier, however, Kuznetsov's postcard is similar to many visual sources in that it remains open to multiple interpretations. One reading certainly connects prison laborers with the settlement and continued economic development of eastern Siberia, even though the number of hard-labor convicts actually engaged in mining work had been declining since the mid-nineteenth century, owing to the gradual exhaustion of the Nerchinsk-area mines. On the other hand, it is possible to view the image in the context of fin-de-siècle discussions in Russia concerning the ideas of Italian criminologist Cesare Lombroso. Heavily influenced by Social

Darwinism as well as by nineteenth-century ideas concerning degeneration and physiognomy, Lombroso created a theory of anthropological criminology. The theory maintained that criminality was inherited, and that "born criminals" could be identified visually by physical (congenital) defects that marked them as savages or atavistic. Marina Mogilner's research has revealed that a broad swath of the Russian educated public—everyone from lawyers, politicians, and pedagogues to ethnographers, medical practitioners, and army officials—used the same vocabulary as Lombroso when discussing crimes and the people who commit them, even if they did not overtly indicate that they backed Lombroso's positions.[9] Kuznetsov's caption, "Nerchinsk Hard Labor Type," posits that such a distinct, biologically based, and visually identified group existed. The only difference between this particular postcard and others from the same era that purportedly depicted "Caucasian types," "Georgian types," and a host of other ethnic "types," was that the main marker of difference was not ethnicity, but innate criminality. In other words, the postcard offered another possible hierarchy that could be employed to categorize the inhabitants of the Russian Empire.

In the end, we are left with a postcard that represents its era, while also telling different stories to present-day viewers. The postcard exemplifies a widespread genre in one of the most important avenues of communication in popular culture during the final decade of the nineteenth century. It just so happens that this particular genre—the "types" postcard—also categorized and classified the people of the Russian Empire according to ethnicity, social class, or profession. Kuznetsov's photograph speaks to the role of prisoners and exiles in the settlement of eastern Siberia and ongoing perceptions of the region. The fact that this small piece of cardboard was made by Kuznetsov, whose revolutionary credentials were as strong as his scholarly ones, also shows that even hardened opponents of the tsarist regime were not immune to the visions of empire swirling through Russian society in the last years of the monarchy. And finally, the postcard contributes to our understanding of discussions concerning the nature of criminality, since it suggests that, in Kuznetsov's vision, a "prisoner type" existed, thereby conveying photographically the notion that at least some criminals were born rather than made by their environments. This idea found favor with many Russian scholars and theoreticians, who used the category to stigmatize particular social and ethnic groups when they thought about the nature of the empire they lived in at the end of the century.

NOTES

1. The entire volume can be viewed on the World Digital Library website. See "Views of the Nerchinsk Hard Labor Camps," https://www.wdl.org/en/item/18971/#collection=views-of-nerchinsk-hard-labor (accessed 20 July 2020).
2. Details about Kuznetsov's life are drawn from the account he wrote in February 1926. It has been published in *Deiateli SSSR i revoliutsionnogo dvizheniia Rossii—entsiklopedicheskii slovar' Granat* (Moscow: Sovetskaia entsiklopediia, 1989), 126–133.

3. Many of their stories are told in Tatiana Saburova, "Geographical Imagination, Anthropology, and Political Exiles: Photographers of Siberia in Late Imperial Russia," *Sibirica* 19 (2020): 57–84.
4. Sarah Badcock, *A Prison without Walls? Eastern Siberian Exile in the Last Years of Tsarism* (Oxford: Oxford University Press, 2016), 114.
5. Daniel Beer, *The House of the Dead: Siberian Exile under the Tsars* (New York: Vintage Books, 2016), 142, 281–282.
6. Elizabeth Edwards, "The Image as Anthropological Document—Photographic 'Types': The Pursuit of Method," *Visual Anthropology* 3 (1990), 241.
7. Petr Filippovich Iakubovich, *In the World of the Outcasts: Notes of a Former Penal Laborer*, Vol. I., translated by A. Gentes (London: Anthem Press, 2014), 7.
8. Zhanna Popova, "Exile as Imperial Practice: Western Siberia and the Russian Empire, 1879–1900," *International Review of Social History* 63 (2018), 135.
9. Marina Mogilner, "The Empire-Born Criminal: Atavism, Survivals, Irrational Instincts, and the Fate of Russian Imperial Modernity," in *Born to be Criminal: The Discourse on Criminality and the Practice of Punishment in Late Imperial Russia and Early Soviet Union. Interdisciplinary Approaches*, edited by R. Nicolosi and A. Hartmann (Bielefeld: Transcript Verlag, 2017), 37–38.

CHAPTER 27

SIBERIAN ROOTS IN AN IMPERIAL SPACE: *YERMAK'S CONQUEST OF SIBERIA* BY VASILY SURIKOV (1895)

ROSALIND P. BLAKESLEY

IN 1895, visitors to the twenty-third *Peredvizhnik* exhibition would have stopped in their tracks in front of one of the most ambitious history paintings yet exhibited at this prestigious annual event: Vasily Surikov's *Yermak's Conquest of Siberia* (Image 27.1), which I, like the artist, will refer to as *Yermak*. Depicting the Cossack leader Yermak Timofeevich's decisive engagement with Kuchum Khan's forces on the Irtysh River in 1582, Surikov's painting exemplifies the subjugating codes of colonialist discourse. A strong diagonal composition ensures that Yermak's troops are carefully articulated in the foreground, while the opposition, recessed behind the standards of the invading forces, is reduced in places to an amorphous, depersonalized mass. The background, too, is obfuscated, resisting identification of this as a civilized space.

IMAGE 27.1 Vasily Surikov, *Yermak's Conquest of Siberia*, 1895.

Purchased by Alexander III, the painting was a resounding success, winning Surikov the rank of Academician in the Imperial Academy of Arts.

Yet the artist's relationship with Siberia was complex and multifaceted. Born in Krasnoyarsk to a family who could apparently trace their ancestry back to Don Cossack recruits in Yermak's army, a grief-stricken Surikov had returned there from Moscow following the death of his wife in 1888 and raised his daughters in the Siberian town for over a year. Visiting remote settlements, he began preparatory work for *Yermak*, studying the material culture and customs of Indigenous people and producing sketches that depicted individual figures as well as the architectural skyline in considerable detail, even if much of this nuance was lost in the final work. Surikov's complicated trajectory towards *Yermak* can thus serve as a route to explore the intersection of empire, visuality, and nostalgia—an intersection that is inflected by Surikov's deeply personalized negotiation with Russia's colonial past.

Much has been made of Surikov's roots in Siberia, where he spent the first twenty years of his life. Born the son of a civil servant in 1848, he began his artistic career under the local artist Nikolai Grebnev, and was soon using the medium of watercolor to explore ways in which landscape could encapsulate both the prosaic and the sublime. His progress was sufficiently promising for the governor of Krasnoyarsk to send some of his drawings to the Academy of Arts to advocate for the young artist's admission. The Academy sent an encouraging response, whereupon Surikov set off for St Petersburg in December 1868, sponsored by the merchant and gold-mining industrialist Petr Kuznetsov, a notable Krasnoyarsk patron of the arts. Legend has it that the aspirant painter—a future colossus of the *Peredvizhniki*, Russia's most successful exhibition society in the closing decades of the nineteenth century—spent the first stage of his journey perched atop a wagon of fish. The presence of a generous and well-heeled sponsor casts doubt on this narrative, but its subtext of an underprivileged yet innately talented provincial artist overcoming adversity to triumph in the metropolis lent itself to the more ideologically charged of Soviet accounts.

In St Petersburg, Surikov was a dogged and resourceful student, responding to rejection by the Academy the first time he applied by studying at the school of the Society for the Encouragement of the Arts and auditing the Academy's classes before successfully matriculating in August 1870. Struck by the grandeur of St Petersburg, he produced his luminescent *Monument to Peter the Great on Senate Square in St Petersburg* (1870, Krasnoyarsk Regional Art Museum) as well as more informal, quotidian street scenes. Within a couple of years, Surikov was also developing the sort of history paintings that the Academy expected of its most ambitious students, with *Belshazzar's Feast* (1874, State Russian Museum, St Petersburg) winning first prize of 100 rubles in 1874.

In the summer of 1873, however, Surikov embarked on his first trip back to Siberia, which fueled a very different set of artistic and aesthetic concerns. Staying at Kuznetsov's estate in Khakassia, he returned to watercolor painting to test his responses to the expanse of the Minusinsk steppe and its native people. The fast-drying medium of watercolor is well suited to itinerancy. It is quick, portable, and unencumbered by the often weighty paraphernalia and long drying times that oil painting requires. For Surikov, it was the perfect tool with which to study the vast open spaces and cultural distinctions of his native land, with its yurts, barrows, and nomadic tents. His sketches of shamans, arquebuses on bipods, and local dress, among others, later provided useful material for *Yermak*. Surikov's attachment to the medium bore dividends in other respects, too, as the speed with which watercolor paints dry demands decisiveness and agility from the artist.

Surikov's reprisal of watercolor painting during his Siberian trip of 1873 confirms that he experienced his attachment to the place and landscape of his homeland in various ways. *Zaimka in Khakassia* (1862, Museum Estate of V. I. Surikov, Krasnoyarsk) and *Siberian Landscape in Torgashino* (1873, State Tretyakov Gallery, Moscow), for example, deploy the same palette and composition of modest vernacular buildings set against hills or mountains and cloudy skies, creating a notable continuity of effect. This is all the more striking in light of the decade that separates the two works, and of the life drawing classes, studies in perspective, and drive towards complex historical narratives that would have governed Surikov's life at the Academy by this time.

In contrast to this active recovery of previous visual practice, Surikov's verbal expressions of nostalgia for his Siberian haunts evince a sense of longing, but without a desire to restore earlier habits. This was particularly evident when, in 1877, he moved from St Petersburg to Moscow.

> Something strange stole over me here in Moscow. First of all, I felt much more at home here than in Petersburg. Moscow had something that was much more reminiscent of Krasnoyarsk for me, especially in winter. You would walk in the street at twilight, turn into a side street, and suddenly find something completely familiar and similar to what you see in Siberia. Like forgotten dreams, scenes of my childhood and then my youth came to mind more and more. I began to recall different types and costumes, and felt drawn to all of this as something native and indescribably dear.[1]

Surikov's experience of nostalgia during and after his trip home in 1873 therefore operates in different ways, with his visual responses requiring the restoration of an earlier practice (his watercolor landscapes), while his written utterances were reflexive and contemplative, rather than desiring the recuperation of a former world. This proves instructive as we consider the importance of associations with place in the development of *Yermak*.

By the time Surikov embarked on this landmark painting, he was a renowned history painter, having spent the best part of a decade working on a triumvirate of paintings that explore the intersection of political schism and individual punishment around the time of Peter the Great's reign: *The Morning of the Execution of the Streltsy* (1881), *Menshikov in Berezovo* (1883), and *Boyarina Morozova* (1887, all State

Tretyakov Gallery). This was a happy and productive time, with marriage to Elizaveta Charet, the birth of two daughters, a year travelling in western Europe (funded by the sale of *Menshikov in Berezovo* to Pavel Tretyakov in 1883), and a trip to Siberia with his family in 1887. This would be the first and last trip there for his wife, as Elizaveta died at the age of thirty on April 8, 1888. Consumed with grief, Surikov returned with his children to Krasnoyarsk in early summer 1889 and began work on *Yermak*.

Travelling widely both that year and during return visits to Siberia in four of the five subsequent summers, Surikov sketched landscapes and Indigenous people, including the Mansi, Khanty, Ket, and Samoyedic people (loosely referred to by Surikov and many of his painting's commentators as Tatars, Voguls, Samoyeds, and Ostiaks). No element of the painting was overlooked. Physiognomies were scrutinized. The Irtysh and Ob rivers were lovingly described. Potential combatants were visualized in saddle, in action, and in flight. From Tobolsk, Surikov wrote: "I am doing sketches in the museum and of local Tatars, as well as views of the Irtysh. . . . In a couple of days we go to Samarovo or Surgut, to draw the Ostiaks in the picture."[2] A month later, he was still doing "sketches of Tatars. I have painted a decent number. The air here is good."[3]

In the one summer during the first half of the 1890s that Surikov did not spend in Siberia, he went to the Don instead, thrilling in visiting Razdorskaia stanitsa, where Yermak had apparently set out for Siberia, and finding "several faces for the picture."[4] For Surikov, the painting provided an explicit and positive connection with his Cossack past. "I am painting 'Yermak,'" he wrote to his brother in April 1893. "I've read a history of the Don Cossacks. We Siberian Cossacks are descended from them. . . . I read and my soul rejoices that you and I come from good stock."[5] Nostalgia played a part as well, with Surikov seeing a strong resemblance between the Don and parts of Siberia, and believing that Yermak's Cossacks chose to settle in places that reminded them of their homeland.[6] These comments point to the complexities of Surikov's dual identity as a citizen of empire. Proud of his Siberian origins, he was quick to express admiration for its values, people, and landscapes, though with a colonialist tendency to generalize: "In Siberia, the people are different than in Russia: free, brave."[7] At the same time, he placed great store by his descent from Don Cossacks, and delighted in any evidence of connection to them, boasting that "I went riding with the Cossacks and the Cossacks praised my posture. 'Look,' they say, 'he has not served [in an army], yet he rides well.'"[8]

The ambivalent, shifting perspective on invading forces and subjugated territories alike is held in unresolved tension not only in Surikov's self-identity, but also in myriad studies for *Yermak*. At one moment, he revels in the local subject returning the invader's gaze in a forceful visual metaphor of fighting back (Image 27.2)—a dynamic that confirms how central the actual process of looking is to this painting. Indeed, a viewer of the final painting commented on the veristic individualization of members of Kuchum's forces and Surikov's reluctance to typologize. "The Siberians are not very typical and look more like photographs than types."[9]

IMAGE 27.2 Vasily Surikov, *Study for Yermak: Head of a Khakassian*, 1895.

Yet elsewhere, Surikov resorts to stereotypical hierarchies of the colonizer triumphant over the colonized. Yermak's men are depicted with care and attention, steadying arquebuses and cannons as they enter the fray, and their leader stands under the standard with the image of Christ that had served Ivan IV during his campaign against the Kazan Khanate. Surikov here invokes a glorious narrative of Russian battle against the Tatar yoke that resounded with apparent historical specificity. By contrast, while in his preparatory sketches he drew individuals in Kuchum's army in detail, they gradually become an indiscriminate cacophony, with just a tokenistic face, figure, or headdress standing out from the crowd.

Nowhere are these conflicted approaches more evident than in the compositional sketches for *Yermak*, which are many, varied, and revelatory. In an early sketch of 1891, Kuchum's forces barely figure, though the territory they are defending features as a civilized space, with a skyscape of elegant spires and buildings in the background. Semen Remezov's seventeenth-century account of Yermak similarly includes a vision of a Russian city with spires and domes at the meeting of the Irtysh and Tobol rivers. Published in 1880, this hugely influential text was almost certainly known to Surikov, and may well have been a source that he consulted while developing his work.

IMAGE 27.3 Vasily Surikov, *Yermak's Conquest of Siberia*. Sketch of the composition, 1891.

Another sketch of the same year gives the Siberian troops much more space and attention, and there is clear water between them and the Cossacks (Image 27.3). Over the next year, however, that expanse of water is reduced to bring the two armies into closer proximity, creating a claustrophobic effect that intensifies a sense of Kuchum's imminent defeat. Surikov seems to have been sufficiently satisfied with this arrangement to develop it in two increasingly detailed sketches in 1892. But other, undated sketches attest to his vacillations. In one, Kuchum's fighters are reduced in number but differentiated more clearly and painted on a slightly larger scale. In another, they are once more diminished and merged as a homogenous group. As late as 1895, the artist again extended the gap between the two opposing sides, before bringing them back together again in a congested and frenetic sketch that paved the way for the final painting, completed that same year. The horsemen on the clifftop and distant buildings similarly came in and out of focus over the five years, paralleling the waxing and waning of subjectivity and specificity among Kuchum's troops.

One way in which we might make sense of the indeterminate and non-linear progression of these images is to consider contemporary thinking about the individual versus the crowd. Surikov had strong views on this matter. Originally, he had intended to demarcate Yermak more clearly, sketching him full-length and elevated above his men. However, sheets of multiple drawings confirm Surikov's fascination with a range of figures in the painting, and he gradually merged Yermak with his neighbors, so much so that the Cossack leader is not immediately identifiable in the finished work. When working on *Boyarina Morozova*, Surikov had similarly considered intensifying the focus on the title character at the expense of the masses but decided against this, as it risked a loss of context: "I do not understand the actions of distinct historical figures without a people, without a crowd. I need to bring them into the light.[10] In this respect, his approach fed into wider debates in Russia, and in particular shifting attitudes towards the theory of Thomas Carlyle, an influential Scottish historian and philosopher, that great men were the drivers of history—an avowedly imperial text. Carlyle's work was well known in Russia by this time. The historian Mikhail Pogodin, among others, was influenced by Carlyle's views, and similarly conceived of history as a procession of outstanding biographies.

But other figures powering Russian intellectual and cultural debate fiercely opposed Carlyle's theory of exceptional men. Tolstoy, whom Surikov knew, had taken issue with this in *War and Peace*, and the war artist Vasily Vereshchagin published the sardonically titled *Illustrated Autobiographies of a Few Unremarkable Russian People* in 1895, the same year in which *Yermak* was complete. Surikov's ambivalence towards the protagonists and armies in *Yermak*—an ambivalence manifested time and again in their fluctuating positions and profiles in his preparatory sketches—thus maps in suggestive ways onto views concerning the relative importance of the individual and the crowd, and sees the visual serving to articulate an unsettled response to the often anonymized populations of a conquered land.

This irresolution did not escape commentators at the 1895 *Peredvizhnik* exhibition, even if they knew nothing of the many sketches and vacillations that had marked Surikov's tortured path to *Yermak*. One might have expected the heightened nationalism of the 1890s, tercentenary of colonizing Siberia, and start of the Trans-Siberian Railway (constructed 1891–1916) to fuel readings of imperial power in the painting. More often than not, however, there was comment instead on the contrived nature of Surikov's work. "The very composition of the author reveals in him a man completely unfamiliar with the methods of crossing a river under enemy fire, and even less conveys the mood of people entering a bloody, mortal battle."[11] For another reviewer, the painting seemed cold, "frozen" even, for all Surikov's firsthand study of landscapes, people, and artefacts. There was "too much rest in everything: these are not living, desperate people but some kind of machines, quietly sitting, standing or lying. . . . water is not water, air is not air, faces are not sufficiently alive."[12] These muted responses reflect *Yermak*'s unstable position at the intersection of vision and empire. It is undeniably a painting about imperial encounter. But Surikov's nostalgic and personal connection to both Siberia and its colonizers led to indecision and, ultimately, a certain paralysis, as these two reviewers identified.

Yet the very fluidity in Surikov's vantage point, born of his bifold identity as Cossack and Siberian, also lends *Yermak* its strength as a painting about the very act of looking. It is about the visual as much as the physical engagement between Yermak and Kuchum's forces as they eyeball each other across the Irtysh. Presaged by nostalgic images of Siberian landscapes and inhabitants, and developed through a welter of sketches in which the colonized crowd waxed and waned, *Yermak* compels us to consider how frameworks of empire might allow for different subjectivities and, in turn, how these enable questions of visual as much as political combat to take center stage.

NOTES

1. *Vasilii Ivanovich Surikov. Pis'ma. Vospominaniia o khudozhnike*, edited by N. A. Radzimovskaia et al. (Leningrad: Iskusstvo, 1977), 213–214.
2. Letter to P. F. and A. I. Surikov, June 1, 1892, in *Surikov. Pis'ma*, 87.
3. Letter to P. F. and A. I. Surikov, July 3, 1892, in *Surikov. Pis'ma*, 87.
4. Letter to P. F. and A. I. Surikov, June 4, 1893, in *Surikov. Pis'ma*, 90.
5. Letter to P. F. and A. I. Surikov, April 1893, in *Surikov. Pis'ma*, 89.
6. Letter to P. F. and A. I. Surikov, August 5, 1893, in *Surikov. Pis'ma*, 90.
7. *Surikov. Pis'ma*, 171.
8. Letter to P. F. and A. I. Surikov, August 5, 1893, in *Surikov. Pis'ma*, 91.
9. Rectus [P. P. Gnedich], "XXIII peredvizhnaia vystavka," *S.-Peterburgskie vedomosti* 51 (22 February 1895): 1.
10. V. S. Kemenov, *Vasilii Ivanovich Surikov* (Leningrad: Khudozhnik RSFSR, 1991), 50.
11. Rectus, "XXIII peredvizhnaia vystavka," 2.
12. O-shev, "XXIII peredvizhnaia vystavka," *Novoe vremia* 6816 (February 19, 1895).

CHAPTER 28

ALEXANDER BORISOV AND TYKO VILKA: TWO ARTISTS WHO MADE WORLDS OF THEIR OWN FROM THE ARCTIC WILDERNESS

ANNA KOTOMINA

THE TERRITORY OF Novaya Zemlya ("New Land," in English) consists of two islands in the Arctic Ocean divided by a channel. Located close to the mainland, the shores of the islands are rocky and generally ice-covered, even during the brief summer months. Good harbors are few; consequently, reaching the islands by ship as well as exploring the interior are difficult. There is little vegetation. The weather is often gloomy and changeable. The polar night lasts for many months. Yet despite being inhospitable to human settlement, Novaya Zemlya has long been home to a variety of birds and animals. Consequently, the few people who have ventured to the islands over the centuries have been outsiders: hunters, fishermen, wayfarers, travelers.

Tsarist officials began expressing an interest in the islands of Novaya Zemlya during the reign of Tsar Alexander II. During the summer of 1870, a naval ship under the command of Admiral Konstantin Poset visited the territory. Among his crew was the fourth son of the tsar, the young, lovesick Grand Duke Alexei Alexandrovich, who was serving as a lieutenant in the Russian navy at the time. Not long after Poset's visit, the navy established winter lodgings and a rescue station on the islands, which then allowed for visits by Russian hydrographers, who began composing coastal surveys and navigation charts.

Novaya Zemlya was then and remains today an overwhelmingly empty place. Landmarks are few, and most outside visitors have difficulty finding visual reference points. Private steamship service began from Arkhangelsk in 1880. Shortly thereafter. Governor of Arkhangelsk Province Alexander Engelgardt, a noted advocate for northern development, began settling Nenets families on the islands, in part to mark them as imperial territories. Known in tsarist times as Samoyeds, the Nenets are one of the native peoples of the Russian Arctic. Engelgardt offered free passage for the native settlers, along with tools and other supplies to assist them in starting their new life on the islands. For some of these Nenets, in particular those less fortunate families who had lost their reindeer herds on the mainland, the opportunity to start anew on the islands with government support must have seemed like a godsend. One of these seemingly fortunate settlers was the father of Tyko Vilka, a Nenets artist who is one of the heroes of this essay.

Curiously, for Russian artists trained in the academic traditions of the late imperial era, the featureless landscape of Novaya Zemlya provided an intriguing challenge, since capturing the emptiness of the islands seemed to require special skills of precise representation. Furthermore, reaching the islands was costly and time-consuming, while living there was even more difficult, given the generally harsh climactic conditions that were, to say the least, less than fully conducive to the creative process. Despite such challenges, however, one artistic outsider, the painter Alexander Borisov, who made his first trip to Novaya Zemlya at the age of thirty in 1896, developed an abiding passion for the region that would go on to leave a profound mark on his life and art.

The gifted son of a peasant family from Arkhangelsk Province in the Russian northwest, Borisov was singled out for his artistic talents as a teenager by monks at the Solovetskii Monastery and sent off to the Imperial Academy of the Arts in St. Petersburg at the age of twenty to further his artistic training. There, under the mentorship of aging luminaries of the famous Wanderers group (*Peredvizhniki*) such as Ivan Shishkin and Arkhip Kuindzhi, Borisov mastered not only the techniques of landscape painting but also his own intellectual style for expressing tonalities of light and color. The young novice was also tenacious, inventive, and affable, all of which helped him develop contacts with senior officials and other individuals of influence in the imperial capital, such as journalists and wealthy businessmen, especially those interested in promoting the development of transportation, trade, and industry in the Russian North. Not surprisingly, most of the funding he received for his work came from sponsors within these circles.

Borisov's paintings of Novaya Zemlya were displayed at numerous personal and collective exhibitions, and they proved quite popular with the Russian art-seeking public of the fin-de-siècle given the rising interest in the Arctic that characterized the era (Images 28.1 and 28.2). This was an age of active polar exploration, much of which was covered in the newspapers and documented in photographs, so in that sense, it was already quite familiar. But Borisov's paintings were different. The personal feel of his canvases appeared to convey a more intense authenticity than photographic images. His works were also physically large and imposing, so much so that he invariably completed them in his St. Petersburg studio, basing them on smaller-scale sketches that he brought home from his travels. In his studio, he had time to execute the works with the full deliberateness and skill that he had learned while a student at the Imperial Academy, and indeed, many of these paintings were produced for

IMAGE 28.1 "Novaya Zemlya. The Sailboat *Dream* (*Mechta*)." Magic lantern slide.

IMAGE 28.2 "Drinking tea with a Samoyed on Novaya Zemlya." Magic lantern slide.

official events and venues, such as the Academy's annual exhibitions and the Russian pavilion at the Paris Exposition of 1900. Yet curiously, though the large canvases are striking, the small oil sketches that Borisov based them on are arguably more powerful still. Painted on location under daunting Arctic conditions, the sketches communicate the full rawness and purity of Borisov's emotional encounter with the environment, and his complicated love-hate relationship with the islands.

After his first trip to Novaya Zemlya in 1896, Borisov made several return visits to the islands, passing his time there hunting polar bears and exploring the territory by dog sled. He even lived there through the winter of 1900–1901 in a wooden cabin that he constructed with one of his brothers. He transported all the lumber required to build the shelter from the mainland, and all the necessary supplies as well—lamps, lamp oil, the equipment he needed for his artist's workshop, food, even a cow and all its feed.

Borisov was more than just an artist of the Academic school. As the creator of his own vivid artistic world, he was also an active, if inadvertent, pioneer of imperial expansion. Together with his brothers, he built a sailboat, which he named *The Dream* (*Mechta*), that he used to investigate the largely unexplored coasts of the Northern Island of Novaya Zemlya. The boat was ultimately lost when it was crushed by pack ice, but during his travels, he named many of the land features he came across—mountains, bays, peninsulas—which he then mapped with the help of his team members. As a result of the wars and revolutions of the first half of the twentieth century, these names were retired or forgotten. In the 1960s, however, many of them were restored, and one can still see them today on official maps of the islands.

In all, Borisov took part in six northern expeditions, some of which he devised and outfitted himself. During these trips, he completed some three hundred paintings and sketches, which he then exhibited not only in Moscow and St. Petersburg but also in Vienna, Munich, Paris, and London. He once even exhibited his paintings in Washington, DC, where he made a private visit to the White House, the first and perhaps only occasion when an artist of the tsarist era met a US president in the American capital.

In addition to his art, Borisov also wrote a book and several articles about his travels in the Russian North, which he featured in presentations illustrated by colorful magic lantern slides. The magic lantern was an early slide projector, which shined light through small photographs printed on film so that they could be enlarged on a screen for a lecture audience. His entertaining lectures and high-quality slides, all of which he designed himself, helped make him a popular speaker with both Russian and foreign audiences, educating them about Russian colonial power in far-flung territories of the empire. After 1917, he threw himself—and his artistic creativity—into promoting the construction of a railway for the Far North. In the 1920s, he did the same for a plan to open a European-style therapeutic spa in his home village on the Northern Dvina River.

Many famous and lesser-known artists were inspired by Borisov to follow in his footsteps and make the voyage to Novaya Zemlya. Like him, they traveled there as touristic outsiders hoping for vivid impressions, though none of them ultimately made the turn that he did to recreating the wilderness of the islands as their own personal universe. The only exception in this regard was the Nenets Tyko Vilka. Vilka's father had been a day laborer who married a Russian woman upon moving to the islands. Vilka thus grew up in the Novaya Zemlya landscape, where he closely observed the natural world around him and became an adept hunter, apparently killing some hundred polar bears over the course of his lifetime. During Borisov's initial visit to the islands in 1896, he spent the night in the Vilka family's home. The following year, the Vilkas and their neighbors helped rescue Borisov and his crew after their boat became trapped in the pack ice. Following the rescue, the travelers then spent the winter not far from the Vilkas's settlement, which gave the boy Tyko, who was fourteen at the time, the chance to get to know Borisov and to watch him draw. Tyko remembered sitting by Borisov's side and watching in fascination as the Russian sketched his father's portrait with a coal pencil. This was the first time he had ever seen anyone draw such a likeness. The young boy had a keen eye and developed his own interest in drawing. Subsequent visitors would leave him pencils and paint, and he would stay in touch with them and sell them his sketches. One of these artistic visitors was Stepan Pisakhov, a Russian modernist and folklorist from Arkhangelsk who made frequent visits to Novaya Zemlya between the 1910s and the 1930s. Tyko once asked Pisakhov to give him art lessons, but the Russian refused, apparently telling the boy that his authenticity as a self-taught Nenets artist was too precious to risk being destroyed by exposure to formal artistic training.

Growing up as an experienced hunter, Tyko also became acquainted with the geographer Vladimir Rusanov, who had graduated from the Sorbonne and came to Novaya Zemlya as the member of an expedition researching Arctic wind and sea currents. Rusanov would ultimately perish on an expedition in the northern wilderness in 1915, but in 1913, he invited the young Tyko to Moscow, where Tyko initially felt as disoriented by the strange ways of the metropolis as Borisov had been in the midst of the icy wilds of Novaya Zemlya. But in the end, Tyko adapted, developing a passion for the opera and enjoying stepping out on the town in his stylish top hat. During his time in Moscow, he began to study art, though he was never interested in artistic theory or discussions of method. As he saw it, the natural world was not a separate realm to consider in aesthetic terms; instead, it was his living element, the world he inhabited. While the Arctic was harsh, its rigors were familiar to him, and in that sense, the environment seemed both approachable and tender. Tyko was prepared to sell his works to tourists, but he declined state commissions. His reputation and standing grew upon his return to Novaya Zemlya as his native neighbors treated him with the same reverence that Russians from the Russian interior treated polar explorers. After the Bolshevik Revolution, Tyko became the head of a reindeer collective farm on the islands, and became known locally as the "President of Novaya Zemlya."

Much like Borisov, he became the author of his own authentic universe, a world that he recreated as his own. In addition to his art, he also composed poems and songs and oversaw the administration of settlers on the islands.

In the 1960s, Tyko Vilka was forced to give up this world, as he and the rest of the Nenets population were removed from Novaya Zemlya as part of the Soviet government's remaking of the islands into a nuclear testing zone. He died in Arkhangelsk not long after his resettlement. Following his death, his fame grew beyond the Nenets community, as he became the subject of television specials and documentaries. His art began to be displayed in state museums. The poet Evgenii Evtushenko even wrote a poem about him.

Borisov and Vilka were both specialists in the production of visual images. The son of a Russian peasant family, Borisov earned a degree from an elite state institution—the Imperial Academy of Arts. By contrast, Vilka was a self-trained artist with no formal education, the son of a Russian mother and a Nenets father. Yet both drew their inspiration from their experience of the same far northern borderland of the empire. This frontier was remote and difficult to reach, yet at the same time alluring to outsiders because of its abundant natural resources, especially fish and furs. Both Borisov and Vilka, of course, were well aware of this, and both made use of their artistic experience of the north as a tool for communicating with members of the public as well as state officials.

It is also worth noting that each of the two men and their art managed to survive the upheavals of the first half of twentieth century. In contrast to so many other artists whose lives and works were destroyed by the events of the era, both Borisov and Vilka died of natural causes, in their own beds, in the presence of their families, and their paintings continue to hang today on the walls of state museums where we can see them as offering their own dualistic commentary on the enduring resonance of Russian imperial culture—a culture that included both art fashioned by central academic institutions as well as local art produced in far-off northern borderlands. The life experiences of these two creative individuals also underscore how this culture was shaped through the interactions between state and private interests, as well as by countless exchanges on multiple levels between the imperial center and its various peripheries.

Borisov and Vilka lived separate lives, but they knew each other and were curiously interconnected. Vilka the native islander was impressed and charmed by Borisov's ability to draw as well as his other life strategies, while Borisov the outsider relied on Vilka's family to rescue him from the ice. The images they created also seem to mirror each other. Borisov drew sketches and took photos of the Nenets, his guides to the icy wilderness, while Vilka drew sketches of the geographer Rusanov, his guide to the world of "civilization." Yet both Borisov and Vilka drew a similar inspiration from the world that they made for themselves in the north, sketching the residents of the islands in their traditional winter dress (*malitsa*) as well as the seals, polar bears, icy landscapes, and shimmering northern lights of Novaya Zemlya.

CHAPTER 29

YERMAK FROM YENISEI PROVINCE: A PEASANT PAINTING FROM THE EARLY TWENTIETH CENTURY

GALINA V. LYUBIMOVA

THE ORIGINAL IS LONG GONE, but an archival photo in the Russian Ethnographic Museum preserves a rare sample of peasant painting from the beginning of the twentieth century. The photo is utterly unique. There are no known analogues of this painting of Yermak made by a folk master (Image 29.1). The unknown folk artist depicted Yermak, the Cossack leader or ataman who is credited with conquering Siberia in the name of the tsar in the sixteenth century, standing upright and striking a Turkic warrior with a spear. The body of the latter is bending to the ground, and the right hand is pressing a bloody wound. The triumphant Yermak is represented as a Russian epic hero, a gallant warrior guarding the homeland, known as a *bogatyr*. The transformation of a Cossack Ataman into *bogatyr*—a recurrent figure in Russian folklore—reflects specific features of Russian historical memory. This folk version of Yermak resonates with and prefigures concepts formulated by modern Russia's official ideologists to justify the expansion of imperial borders in the historical past and ongoing territorial claims today.

Legends about Yermak as the "conqueror of Siberia" began to take shape in Russia soon after his death in the mid-1580s, but visual paradigms for depicting the hero began to coalesce much later. There were no portraits of Yermak made in his lifetime, since portraiture did not yet exist as a genre in Russia during the sixteenth century. The first visual images of Yermak, based on descriptions left by associates, appeared in the seventeenth century, long after his death. His image was reflected not only in official historical and professional artistic works, but was also embodied in various artifacts of folk culture, including visual and verbal ones.

The principles of portraying the historical hero changed from epoch to epoch and found reflection in both elite and folk art. The earliest of images of Yermak—the so-called *parsuna*, or portrait (from the Latin *persona*)—appeared in the late seventeenth century based on the works of foreign artists who worked in Russia. In this

IMAGE 29.1 Archival photograph of a peasant painting with the image of Yermak striking the enemy, Yenisei Province, 1906.

artistic style (a transitional genre from icon painting to secular portrait painting), Yermak is often portrayed without weapons and wearing western European clothes, as a peaceful Dutch or German burgher.

A second type of image of Yermak is marked by specific Cossack features. It is worth noting that historically the Cossacks declared themselves as a powerful force in the middle of the sixteenth century, during the time of Ivan the Terrible. Members of disadvantaged populations (runaway peasants and people from the urban lower classes) fled south to the lower reaches of the Don, the Volga, and other rivers, becoming free farmers and warriors. They were not afraid of clashes either with neighboring peoples or with tsarist armed forces. According to the popular version, the initiators of the campaign to Siberia were the Cossacks themselves, led by Yermak, who is remembered in Russian popular mythology as a wise and just historical figure dreaming of creating a free Cossack kingdom.

An early example of the Cossack-style representations of Yermak was published in the journal *Siberian Herald* (*Sibirskii Vestnik*) in the 1820s. The image of Yermak in a helmet, chain mail, and a sword on his left side was created by the painter Karl Bryullov and served as the basis for numerous images in book illustrations and popular prints (*lubok*). At the end of the nineteenth century, Bryullov's portrait became the inspiration for a sculpture of Yermak by Mark Antokolsky (1891) as well as the famous painting *Yermak's Conquest of Siberia* by Vasily Surikov (1895). These artists tried to convey Yermak as possessing what they considered the best features of the Russian national character—strength, courage, valor, and gallantry. According to contemporaries, there was no well-to-do house in Tobolsk Province at that time where a portrait of Yermak would not hang. The Siberians usually represented him as a broad-shouldered fellow with lively black eyes and a short black beard.

The peasant painting captured in the archival photograph is yet a third type. It represents Yermak as a *bogatyr* or Russian "epic hero." Let's take a closer look at it.

It's known that folk crafts production, known as "visual folklore," can be stylistically very close to folk icon painting, and this peasant painting follows that pattern. Folk artists embellished the surfaces and tools of daily life with their work. They were masters of decorative murals, and they painted the walls and ceilings of peasant dwellings, spinning wheels, chests, and other household utensils. Peasant dwellings were filled with color and decorative design. Beyond their decorative work, very often they also served as icon painters in peasant communities, since the demand for icons among the peasants usually exceeded the supply. For this reason, the stylistic features of folk icons and different forms of visual folklore were based on similar artistic principles, such as bright and intense color, lack of secondary figures, conventional silhouettes, and energetic linear contour.

All these features can be traced in the works of the famous Siberian icon painter Ivan Krestiannikov (1858–1941). His icon of the Savior (Image 29.2) is a good example of the way his work incorporated and expressed folk notions about God. Rewriting sacred history in their own terms and recreating it in their own artistic images, folk craftsmen placed sacred characters in familiar peasant environments, endowing them with recognizable features of peasant psychology. Such details brought the sacred characters closer and made them more understandable to the peasants. In the Krestiannikov icon, the Savior Almighty is dressed in a peasant shirt with floral decorative ornaments and holds the book of the Gospels in his left hand as a symbol of divine wisdom and universal justice. These details show him as a defender of the poor and a keeper of truth. His right hand is frozen in a gesture of blessing addressed to the disadvantaged and thus extending his protection over them.

In the peasant painting of Yermak, the unknown folk artist depicted Yermak standing straight and impaling his fallen Turkic opponent with a spear. The explanatory inscription in Russian notes that "Yermak Timofeevich has struck Sakpstar in the year of 1581." Well-known historical sources and works of folklore do not contain references to anyone with that name; however, the indication of the specific date of the event suggests that the figure depicted by the peasant artist is no ordinary warrior from the army of Kuchum Khan. In this case, most likely, one should have in mind not a proper name, but an erroneously copied expression, which should be read as "Yermak Timofeevich has struck the Siberian king." This formulation is often found

IMAGE 29.2 Icon of Savior the Almighty by folk artist Ivan Krestiannikov. Late nineteenth or early twentieth century.

in folklore texts about Yermak. The date of the event indicated next (1581) leaves little doubt that the author had in mind the ruler of the Siberian Khanate—Kuchum Khan himself. The inaccuracy of the inscription may suggest that the peasant artist was only marginally literate, or that the textual source from which he copied the label was itself garbled.

At the same time, there is an obvious paradox inherent in the whole composition. The placement of the defeated enemy indicates that this figure was added or drawn next to the main character at some point after Yermak was painted. Otherwise, the body of the Tatar warrior would have been located in the foreground—that is, in front of Yermak, not behind him.

Let's have a look at the clothes of the characters depicted. The garment of the Siberian ataman is a mixture of Cossack military attire and everyday peasant clothing. His headdress is shaped like a helmet, and his wide belt is covered with numerous small "scales" that are probably a remote hint of chain mail. These types of military and defensive armor were used by Russian warriors until the widespread introduction of firearms in the late seventeenth century.

The narrow cut of Yermak's trousers, clearly seen in the painting, also refers to historical realities of the era. In an illustrated chronicle from the late seventeenth or early eighteenth century by the Siberian historian and cartographer Semyon Remezov, all the warriors of the first Cossack campaign to Siberia are depicted in narrow, tight-fitting pants. At the same time, it is well known that an essential component of Cossack and peasant clothing at the beginning of the twentieth century, when the portrait was painted, were wide trousers. Evidently, the anonymous peasant artist went to some effort to depict his subject with historical accuracy. Yermak's upper garment, with its embroidery on the chest and the distinctive straight cut, closely resembles not armor, but an ordinary peasant shirt. Thus, a certain eclecticism of this image resists being pigeonholed into a specific epoch. On the other hand, the attire of the enemy defeated by Yermak (presumably the Kuchum Khan himself) reproduces quite accurately the traditional apparel of the Siberian Tatars, the Indigenous, Turkic-speaking peoples of western Siberia—the only Indigenous people in the region who had their own state (namely, the Siberian khanate) at the beginning of Russian colonization. The defeated Siberian in the peasant painting wears a loose tunic shirt without a belt, with long wide sleeves and a turban or ritual headdress.

It's highly possible that one of the inspirations or models for creating the whole composition could be the image of St. George in the Russian Orthodox icon-painting tradition. St. George, a Christian warrior, was conventionally depicted spearing a snake, the personification of Absolute Evil. In one such icon, St. George is depicted not on horseback (as usual), but "facing forward, in his full height" (Image 29.3). As the twentieth-century folklorist Vladimir Propp wrote of this kind of St. George icon: "He holds a spear in his right hand, and a sword in his left hand . . . This is a warrior guarding the homeland."[1] That is exactly what is presented in the peasant painting of Yermak. His image here resembles not an ordinary Cossack Ataman, but a *bogatyr*—an epic hero of the Russian folk tradition.

The famous painting of *bogatyrs* by Viktor Vasnetsov can be considered another source for peasant composition (Image 29.4). This suggestion is confirmed by common elements of the landscape in both paintings. Thus, a decorative tree and a nearby fir in peasant painting resemble small trees under the hooves of the horses of the Vasnetsov heroes.

IMAGE 29.3 Icon of St. George, Novgorod school, 1130–1140.

The tendency to endow Yermak with features of the epic hero manifests itself not only in visual, but also in verbal forms of folklore, such as historical songs and tales (*byliny*) from the late epic tradition that extended up to the seventeenth century. For example, a historical song called "Yermak Visiting Ivan the Terrible" describes a meeting of these historical characters that never really occurred. Epic features of

IMAGE 29.4 V. V. Vasnetsov, *Bogatyrs* (*The Epic Heroes*), 1898.

Yermak are expressed through formulaic verbal comparisons in the *byliny*, such as *silver speech* and *golden voice*. This tendency is amplified many times in late epic tradition, since "folk tradition firmly linked Yermak with previous eras and heroes of the past. His image organically entered the cycle of epics about early Rus: possessing supernatural power, Yermak acts as an epic hero against the invasion of the Tatars, being the nephew of Ilya Muromets (or Prince Vladimir himself)."[2] Ilya Muromets is the mostly legendary hero of medieval Rus epics. Prince Volodimer (Vladimir) was a historical prince of medieval Rus. These epics retrofit the sixteenth-century Yermak into these medieval tales, complete with a made-up genealogy.

The exaltation of the heroic Yermak had religious dimensions as well. Shortly after his death, attempts were made to canonize Yermak and his squad. According to Siberian chronicles and other religious and historical documents of those times, the subjugation of Siberia to the Russian state was viewed as an "act of God's will," and the Cossacks themselves were identified with the "chosen ones of divine providence."[3]

The trends toward turning Yermak into a Russian *bogatyr* were further developed in the twentieth century. In this regard, the story of the monument to Yermak in Kazakhstan is of particular interest. This monument was erected in 1965 in a young city built by participants in the development of the "virgin lands," a campaign championed by Soviet leader Nikita Khrushchev to open new lands to agriculture. Until 1995, the city bore the official name of Yermak. The inscription on the pedestal of the monument—"From the grateful descendants of participants in the development of virgin lands"—emphasized the connection between the image of Yermak and the idea of pioneering and developing new territory. For thirty years in Soviet Kazakhstan, the Cossack ataman "was embodied in the image of the Russian epic hero. In a helmet and chain mail, with his arms crossed on his chest, he gazed thoughtfully from his pedestal at the rapidly growing city (of the same name) of virgin lands."[4]

The *perestroika* years (1985–1991) were characterized by the desire to reclaim the historical past, which led to the creation of numerous competing versions of local history. After the collapse of the Soviet Union, the local Kazakh population decided to dismantle the monument as a symbol of their opposition to Russian domination in the region. On the one hand, the image of Yermak presented in the monument actualized the memory of the Cossack frontier of the times of the Russian Empire; on the other hand, it served as an unintentional reminder of the resistance of the Indigenous population to Russian colonization from the very start. The situation was aggravated by an assumption widely shared in Kazakh historiography, according to which Yermak's campaign to Siberia interrupted the Kazakh process of state formation. Yermak's luster had faded in Kazakhstan. In 1992, the city itself was renamed Aksu, and the monument to Yermak was dismantled. Later, however, some parts of the destroyed monument were secretly taken to the Altai territory, where more than ten years later, in 2006, with the support of the local Cossacks, the monument was restored and installed on a pedestal in honor of the 270th anniversary of the city of Zmeinogorsk. These events perfectly illustrate the idea that the installation of monuments to certain historical figures belongs to the sphere of historical politics, and is carried out with the aim of addressing urgent contemporary political problems.

The veneration of Yermak among Russian Siberians lasted through the twentieth century, and it continues in some circles even today. For example, the leaders of some new religious movements are again trying to canonize Yermak and revive his cult as a hero who unified Europe and Asia and opened the way to the East for Russians. In 1981 (the year of the official 400th anniversary of the incorporation of Siberia), the professional community of Soviet historians celebrated the Cossack campaign against the Siberian Tatars as the last link in the Russian's centuries-old struggle to eliminate the consequences of Chinggis Khan's rule in Asia and eastern Europe. The conqueror of Siberia himself was granted the paradoxical status of defender of the Motherland and, at the same time, a hero who expanded its borders. In true imperial fashion, "defense" of the homeland was equated with militant expansion of borders and annexation of new territories. Exactly the same rhetoric characterizes the ongoing Russian military invasion of Ukraine, which began in February 2022 – a new reality that few could have predicted three years ago when this essay was written.

The very fact of the transformation of a Cossack ataman into a Russian epic hero guarding his homeland can be considered a specific feature of Russian historical memory and one element of national identity that is close to present-day discourse of the so-called "Russian world"—a concept formulated by modern Russia's official ideologists to justify the historical expansion of imperial borders today. The Yermak mythology has important geopolitical applications in both imperial and present-day historical imagination.

The first time Vladimir Putin used the phrase "Russian World" was at the World Congress of Compatriots Living Abroad in 2001 in Moscow. According to the concept formulated on the website of the fund of the same name (russkiymir.ru), "the Russian World is not only Russians, not only citizens of Russia, not only our compatriots in the countries of near and far abroad, emigrants, immigrants from Russia and their descendants. They are also foreign citizens who speak Russian, study or teach it, all those who are sincerely interested in Russia, who are worried about its future." At the same time, the concept of the Russian World includes humanistic values declared by the scientific and educational journal of the same name. Regarding the collapse of the Soviet Union as "impossible, unnatural, and counter-historical," as well as recognizing the entire post-Soviet space as a sphere of Russian influence, the ideologists of the present-day Russian political regime are convinced that the "natural and only possible state" of Russia is to be "a great, growing and land-gathering community of nations."[5] Such ideas make it possible to justify territorial expansion under the veil of defending the broadly defined Russian World, both within and beyond the official borders of the Russian state. And this is exactly what we see in paradoxical interpretation of Yermak as an epic hero, or *bogatyr* and defender of his native lands.

NOTES

1. Vladimir Propp, "Zmeyeborstvo Georgiia v svete fol'klora," in *Fol'klor. Literatura. Istoriia. Sobranie trudov*, edited by V. F. Shevchenko (Moscow: Labirint, 2002), 96.
2. Boris Putilov, *Drevniaia Rus' v litsakh. Bogi, geroi, liudi* (St. Petersburg: Azbuka-klassika, 2001), 351.
3. Elena Dergacheva-Skop, ed., *Letopisi sibirskie* (Novosibirsk: Novosibirskoe knizhnoe izdatel'stvo, 1991), 248.
4. Michael Agapov, "Avatary Ermaka: monumental'nye formy reprezentatsii i aktualizatsii istoricheskoi pamiati," *Vestnik arkheologii, antropologii i etnografii* 32, no. 1 (2016): 145. https://doi.org/10.20874/2071-0437-2016-32-1-142-150
5. Vladislav Surkov, *Dolgoe gosudarstvo Putina*, https://www.ng.ru/ideas/2019-02-11/5_7503_surkov.html

CHAPTER 30

IMPERIAL COLOR IN THE PRESENT TENSE: THE PHOTOGRAPHY OF SERGEI PROKUDIN-GORSKY

KATHERINE M. H. REISCHL

THE ADVENT OF color photography in the mid-1930s was a global revelation for photographers and viewers alike. However, from the earliest days of photography, professional photographers and amateur practitioners had already embellished monochromatic prints with hand-added color.[1] Technologies for bringing fuller color to photography have evolved continuously until today. Now, in the twenty-first century, popular digital projects have sought to overcome the "distant" or "scratchy" look of historical black-and-white photography through colorization. In each iteration, these projects seek to bring photographs "to life" by adding color, because they assume that color makes their photographs appear to be more "true to life."[2] Color images of a world that we are used to seeing in black-and-white give us a jolt of recognition, but whether capturing the present or digitally altering captures of the past, photographs are always an imperfect and approximate representation of their subjects.[3]

The Russian chemist, journal editor, and photographer Sergei Prokudin-Gorsky (1864–1844) was a pioneering inventor who brought color to his photographic work remarkably early, at the start of the twentieth century. Prokudin-Gorsky's photographic survey of the Russian empire, undertaken from 1909 to 1915, on the eve of war and revolution, can be read as an "expression of imperial power, a confirmation of [that empire's] existence and a justification of its continued existence."[4] His photographs embodied Russia's ever-expanding reach, while also fixing the citizens, geography, industry, and beauty of the empire, as he put it, "in natural colors." Prokudin-Gorsky's belief in photography's affirmative, fixing power was fueled by the ever-growing technological imperative photography posed to picture everything. Prokudin-Gorsky's belief in the verisimilitude of color photography, shared across time and incorporated in present-day responses to his work, shows the complexity of the project that he undertook. An ambitious project of digital restoration of his color photographs, undertaken six decades after his work was completed, has been called a "trip in a time machine to a past rendered in color."[5] Consideration of Prokudin-Gorsky's imperial project—and of color representation more broadly—allows us to reframe the interplay between claims of enhanced realism and the lure of nostalgia in picturing a "lost" Russian Empire today.

MAKING THE CASE FOR COLOR

By the end of the first decade of the twentieth century, print editors and photographers in Russia, western Europe, and the United States offered a variety of answers to the then-pressing question of how best to represent the world as one sees it in "natural colors." In the pages of the journal he edited, *Amateur Photographer* (*Fotograf-liubitel'*), Prokudin-Gorsky published sustained and repeated claims to the importance of working in and towards natural colors. An article published in the journal in 1909 drew this desire for color in the grandest terms:

> Nature without colors would be nothing. It is impossible to imagine what the world would look like, made up of only white, gray, and black tones; in any case, such a world would have very little interest for an artist. Since the advent of photography, people recognized the inadequacies regarding the accurate reproduction of colors.[6]

This writer denies entirely the power of black-and-white photography in favor of a broadly defined use of color, but for Prokudin-Gorsky, not all colors or application of colors were equal. In the pages of *Amateur Photographer*, automatic rather than hand-added color processes were favored. One author conceded that "retouching" black-and-white photographs could be done well and "correctly," but that "photographs made over in this way cannot, strictly speaking, be considered works of color photography."[7] For Prokudin-Gorsky, as a photographer, chemist, and color photo evangelist, the chemical process of color photography positively filled the "contents" of its subjects, while monochromatic capture could only offer shape—an outline that demanded the fullness of color. The natural world, he believed, was best served by color photography.

Prokudin-Gorsky's own color technology was not the only color process on the market in that first decade of the twentieth century. A great number of his editorial features in *Amateur Photographer* were aimed at the shortcomings of the Autochrome, a patented technology of color photography invented in France by the Lumière Brothers and available in Russia after 1907. Prokudin-Gorsky's process, however, including camera, projection, and printing, was by no means uncomplicated. To form an image in "natural color," Prokudin-Gorsky began with the exposure of three negatives on one oblong plate through three different filters in rapid succession using the automated action of the camera. The resulting three images would be seen in color when projected through a triple-lens magic lantern (akin to an early slide projector). While the three glass plates were themselves black and white, the prism screens in red, green, and blue created the effect of natural colors. Here, in their projection onto a screen, color (made through the action of light on the screens) becomes part of the performance of viewing.

Amateur Photographer regularly featured reproductions from the editor's own color photographic enterprise. These reproductions, labeled as photographs "from nature," gave further opportunity for Prokudin-Gorsky to illustrate his color printing. Bucolic images of the Russian countryside or studio portraits were pasted onto special thick paper, set apart from the journal's black-and-white reproductions and articles. Prokudin-Gorsky describes the process of translating his photographs to the page through his mastery of "a typographical machine" using three colors and three different color plates in which the "nuances of colors, . . . a combination of blue, red and yellow dyes—testify to the faithfulness of [his] analysis of colored rays and synthesis of pigments."[8] In making his own strong assertions to "faithful" reproduction, Prokudin-Gorsky assumes, most basically, that we see the world in "natural colors" and, secondarily, that his process can provide an approximation of the sensory experience of color as perceived—all without drawing attention to the fact that the colors captured in his photographs are an approximation of the colors as we experience them in nature. Here, we see further support for Margaret Dikovitskaia's characterization of Prokudin-Gorsky as a "positivist," stating that he "went so far as to call the human eye 'a nature-given camera.'"[9] Prokudin-Gorsky's power lies in his ability to fix his readers' "nature-given cameras" onto those carefully curated images of Russia. No larger than a postcard, his picture of the Black River (Image 30.1), for instance, is an accessible and portable piece of the "traditional" Russian landscape. Moreover, the publication of images such as this in the journal—captioned as taken "from nature"—reinforces both appropriate choice of subject and manner of capture in this new color technology—intimating that Prokudin-Gorsky's invention provided a view identical to what we might see in life.

ARCHIVING AN EMPIRE

Prokudin-Gorsky's *Amateur Photographer* provided only part of the textual and visual argument for his colorized agenda. It was his truly remarkable survey of the empire, necessitating the personal approval of Tsar Nicholas II (himself an avid amateur photographer), that secured the photographer's legacy. The project was cut short by the outbreak of World War I and the subsequent Bolshevik Revolution, at which point many of his photographs were confiscated by Russian authorities.[10] In 1918, Prokudin-Gorsky emigrated to Paris with his remaining photographic negatives, photo-proofs, and albums. In relative obscurity, the collection went largely unseen for the next fifty years. Then, his photographs reappeared in public, first in a book published in the United States and then in digital form, published by the US Library of Congress.

IMAGE 30.1 Sergei Prokudin-Gorsky, "From Nature," *Fotograf-liubitel'* (*Amateur Photographer*), 1906.

In 1980, Robert Allshouse published a sensational selection of the photographs.[11] The images reproduced for the Allshouse volume were made through a laborious process that echoed Prokudin-Gorsky's printing process. The black-and-white contact prints and the glass-plate negatives were "translated" into color separations in yellow, red (magenta), and cyan. Allshouse notes that the "required manipulation" was necessary due to the delay between each of the three automatic exposures made by the camera, from color to color. In other words, digital tweaking was needed, because the three plates each recorded a slightly different moment, leading to blurry or misaligned images in the combined product. More manipulation was required to balance the color, and a final process in black gave the image "depth." Allshouse aptly asks, "Do the colors here accurately represent Prokudin-Gorsky's results? There is no way of telling. However, their soft, impressionistic glow is evocative of the bygone era Prokudin-Gorsky recorded, and one suspects he would be pleased."[12]

The Russian photographer and writer Vladimir Nikitin remembers his first "encounter" with the photographic collection in the late 1980s. Having heard about the book *Photographs for the Tsar*—a book that he had not yet seen—Nikitin told an incredulous friend that there had been color photography in Russia at the turn of the century. His friend, a collector, was finally able to obtain an elusive copy. Nikitin says that viewing the album for the first time "made a strange impression. There was this sensation as if something had broken in the ordinary world, as if you had suddenly seen a television report from the past. . . . [A]ll these images that were in black and white came to life in color."[13]

In the new digital age, Prokudin-Gorsky's photographs saw a "dual translation": conversion from analog to digital, and relocation to an altogether different environment—that is, the late twentieth-century American capital, rather than the prerevolutionary Russian Empire. In 1948, the US Library of Congress had purchased 1,800 of Prokudin-Gorsky's unique plates (including color and black-and-white) from the photographer's heirs. As his proprietary technology had fallen completely out of use by this time, the photographs were at first only accessible as black-and-white photo- proofs or as negatives. In the 2000s, the process of "correcting" the images in their digitized re-colorization was detailed in the American press. News articles crowed "Colors of a Lost Empire Are Reborn" and " Color Photographs of Imperial Russia Reveal a World Lost to History." At the same time, reporters lay bare the manifold problems of Prokudin-Gorsky's original image capture, including blurriness in the subjects due to plate changes.[14] If his subjects moved, "they produced colored ghosts. When children posing on a hillside twitched before the camera, one girl had a blue nose, another a pink chin."[15] (Look closely at the edges of the female tea workers in Image 30.2 for an example.) In the encounter with the past in the present, the process of digitizing and restoring Prokudin-Gorsky's body of work was featured in the *New York Times* in 2001 as "rebirth":

> The vertical and horizontal registration problems were easily corrected by cropping the images to eliminate the areas where the negatives did not overlap. The most troublesome problems came from the fact that the plate often moved between exposures. That led to blurriness and strange color patterns when the three-color versions of a photo were recombined. Using the standard image tools in Photoshop, [the restorer] learned to adjust the images. Eventually, he was able to correct the registration to an accuracy of one pixel at the center of the images.[16]

But while digitization of these photographs resolved some technological challenges, it raised another, complex set of representational issues. Contemporary documentary

IMAGE 30.2 Sergei Prokudin-Gorsky, group of workers harvesting tea, Greek women in Chakva on the Black Sea.

photographer and critic Fred Ritchin has written that the "date when the digital era came to photography," marking an end to photography as such, was 1982, just two years after the publication of Allshouse's book on Prokudin-Gorsky.[17] "It was then that *National Geographic's* staff modified a horizontal photograph of the pyramids of Giza and made it vertical, suitable for the magazine's February cover. They electronically moved a section of the photograph depicting one of the pyramids to a position partially behind another pyramid, rather than next to it." In so altering the image, the magazine's editor "opened the digital door."[18] Ritchin and his friend and fellow photographer Edouard Boubat expressed concern about manipulation of images. Their concern extended to tampering with color in particular. Boubat begged that such sacrilege not be perpetrated on the documentary sanctity of the black-and-white image, which had come to define "serious" photography in the latter half of the twentieth century.[19] The photographer and the critic understood that the digital alteration of a photograph could be easily concealed, and such doctoring could call into question the fundamental promise that photographs accurately represent the reality they depict.[20] Even when we that know that photographs are not exact reproductions of reality, we continue to believe that they are. The temptation to believe in the authenticity of photographic evidence afflicts photographers and lay viewers alike.

Digital reconstructions of Prokudin-Gorsky's images operate like photoshopped bodies, molded to fit expectations of what color photographs of the past should be, or what we—like Prokudin-Gorsky—believe they should be. While the Library of Congress intentionally exposes the imperfections of Prokudin-Gorsky's reproduction of the world around him in its display of the processing details and irregularities, on their website they also provide the "perfected-to-a-pixel" images for use. Another recent print volume dedicated to Prokudin-Gorsky's photographs, titled *Nostalgia*, purposefully retained imperfections in its reproductions of the "original" images. The pre-digital Allshouse volume includes a publisher's note on the dust jacket:

> Although great efforts were made to reproduce these remarkable photographs at the highest quality levels possible, there are imperfections visible in places. Time has taken its inevitable toll on some of the fragile glass photographic plates, causing flaws in prints. Also, the primitive techniques employed occasionally caused blurring in the original plates. Because of overriding historical interest, such factors were overlooked several times during the selection process.[21]

These variously "corrected" and curated images of a "lost past" capture what Svetlana Boym called the "ruin gaze." This gaze is "colored by nostalgia," the object of which "is forever elusive, and our way of making sense of this longing for home is also in constant flux."[22] This romantic appreciation for the imperfections of the photographs that confirm their location in an irretrievable past, however, coexists with a desire to revive that lost world through correcting and perfecting the images. However unstable our nostalgia and its objects may be, our fascination is still founded on a notion that these photographic images are fixed "in natural colors," in something real.

Prokudin-Gorsky's reconstructed image archive finds its home within the flux of the colorized ruin gaze that can be framed and reframed, often under the guise of continued recovery and rediscovery. In the contemporary public sphere, we see these contradictory impulses shaping responses to Prokudin-Gorsky's photographs. With their imperfections and fuzzy edges, they are often projected as an invitation to ruminate on the "lost" imperial past, while at the same time, the language of "bringing to life" through color prompts just the opposite: an encounter with something surprisingly contemporary. As the author Nikitin framed it, seeing color photographs from a period in history when we expect only static black-and-white or sepia sparked

IMAGE 30.3 Side-by-side juxtapositions of a photograph by Sergei Prokudin-Gorsky and a contemporary capture of the same location, Bol'shoe Chertovo Gorodishche (The Great Chertovo Settlement), by "S."

a vivid personal connection with that past. The practice of recreating these photographs today (Image 30.3) is further evidence that Prokudin-Gorsky's photographs are read through the lens of our twenty-first century media sphere, because they have become part of its technological construction. Viewed from this perspective, we might lose sight of the "lost empire," but regain a closer understanding of our fascination with the drive to fill in our experience with color.

NOTES

1. On the history of color photography, see *Color Rush: American Color Photography from Stieglitz to Sherman*, edited by Katherine Bussard and Lisa Hotsteler (New York: Aperture, 2013); on early Russian photography, see Elena Barkhatova, *Russkaia svetopis': pervyi vek fotoiskusstva*, 1839–1914 (St. Petersburg: Al'ians liki Rossii, 2009).
2. See "World War I—in Color" at https://www.history.com/news/wwi-color-photos and Peter Jackson's 2018 documentary film *They Shall Not Grow Old*. See also "Peter Jackson's Time Machine Back to the Trenches: They Shall Not Grow Old," British Film Institute, https://www2.bfi.org.uk/news-opinion/news-bfi/features/lff-62-they-shall-not-grow-old-peter-jackson
3. Robert H. Allshouse, *Photographs for the Tsar: The Pioneering Color Photography of Sergei Mikhailovich Prokudin-Gorsky* (New York: Dial Press, 1980), ix.
4. Estelle Blaschke, "The Russian Empire—Between Modernization and Decline," in *Nostalgia: The Russian Empire of Czar Nicholas II Captured in Color Photographs by Sergei Mikhailovich Prokudin-Gorsky*, edited by Robert Klanten (Berlin: Gestalten, 2012), 11.
5. Blaschke, "The Russian Empire," 1.
6. T. Thorne Baker, "Tsvetnaia fotografiia, Napisana dlia zhurn.," *Fotograf-liubitel'*, no. 5 (May, 1909): 146 (translated from English into Russian).
7. P. Shafranov, "Tsvetnaia fotografiia i zhivopis'," *Fotograf-liubitel'*, no. 5 (May, 1908): 143.

8. The clearest articulation of this testament comes in Prokudin-Gorsky's account of his capture of the famous author Leo Tolstoy "in natural colors from life." Michael A. Denner, Tolstoy Studies Website, http://sites.utoronto.ca/tolstoy/colorportrait.htm
9. Margaret Dikovitskaia, "Central Asia in Early Photographs: Russian Colonial Attitudes and Visual Culture," in *Empire, Islam, and Politics in Central Eurasia*, edited by Uyama Tomohiko (Sapporo: Slavic Research Center, 2007), 102.
10. Ian Austen, "Colors of a Lost Empire Are Reborn, Digitally," *New York Times*, June 14, 2001; Robert H. Allshouse, *Photographs for the Tsar*.
11. Austen, "Colors of a Lost Empire." See also Harold Leich, "The Prokudin-Gorsky Collection of Early 20th Century Color Photographs of Russia at the Library of Congress: Unexpected Consequences of the Digitization of the Collection, 2000–2017," *Slavic & East European Information Resources* 18, no.3/4 (Fall/Winter 2017): 223–230.
12. Allshouse, *Photographs for the Tsar*, 214.
13. Vladimir Nikitin, *Rasskazy o fotografakh i fotografiiakh* (Leningrad: Lenizdat, 1991), 48.
14. Quotations are taken from the titles of Ian Austen, "Colors of a Lost Empire Are Reborn, Digitally," *New York Times*, June 14, 2001, and *Smithsonian Magazine* (online), "Color Photographs of Imperial Russia Reveal a World Lost to History," March 26, 2014, https://www.smithsonianmag.com/travel/old-russian-empire-color-photos-180950229/
15. Pamela Kessler, "The Czar's Country, in Color," *Washington Post*, December 5, 1986.
16. Austen, "Colors of a Lost Empire." More detailed accounting of the process and the categories of reconstruction (including digital color composites and digital color renderings) are described on the Library of Congress website, https://www.loc.gov/pictures/collection/prok/method.html#composites
17. See also Michelle Henning, "Digital Encounters: Mythical Pasts and Electronic Presence," in *The Photographic Image in Digital Culture*, edited by Martin Lister (London and New York: Routledge, 1995), 218–219.
18. Fred Ritchin, *After Photography* (New York: W. W. Norton, 2009), 27.
19. Ritchen, *After Photography*, 27–28.
20. Henning, "Digital Encounters," 218.
21. "Publisher's Note," from Allshouse, *Photographs for the Tsar*, back jacket.
22. Svetlana Boym, "Tatlin or Ruinophilia," *Cabinet Magazine* (Winter 2007–2008), http://www.cabinetmagazine.org/issues/28/boym2.php

ԽԱԹԱԲԱԼԱ

ԳԻՆՆ Է 10 կ. ԳԱՒԱՌՆԵՐՈՒՄ 12 կ. 1906, Կիրակի. Հոկտեմբ. 14-ին ԹԻՖԼԻՍ. № 18.

Հրճուանք «[illegible]» ոչնչացման առթիւ

PART IV

THE REVOLUTIONARY ERA

The Russian Revolution of 1917, like other major revolutions, was one of the great watersheds in history. All over the world, whether they were for or against it, people were compelled to respond to the challenge of a government founded on radical socialist ideas. And those responses played a role in the historical development of the lands of the former Russian Empire for the rest of the twentieth century.

The Revolutionary era began somewhat earlier, in 1905, when people from all classes and beliefs came together to oppose the monarchy and call for democratic reforms. Many of the empire's non-Russian peoples participated in oppositional political activity, and the revolutionary movement unleashed a variety of anti-imperialist sentiments, which would continue to grow. The 1905 Revolution was suppressed, but not before Emperor Nicholas II was forced to issue a constitution that established an elected government (the Duma) and promised some constitutional rights. The hopes raised by these concessions were only partially fulfilled, however, and popular discontent simmered until the events of World War I (1914–1918) again created conditions for revolution. The unpopular war combined with food shortages and those long-simmering discontents produced massive demonstrations in the capital, Petrograd (as St. Petersburg was renamed at the start of World War I), in February 1917. As the situation in February spiraled out of control, protests and riots brought about the abdication of Nicholas II, the last Russian emperor. Russia was declared a republic, and a Provisional Government, made up of leading Duma deputies, took the reins of power. But the lower classes in Petrograd, the workers and soldiers, mistrustful of the upper and middle classes, elected their own representative organization known as the Soviet of Workers' and Soldiers' Deputies ("soviet" is the Russian word for council). Two centers of political authority faced each other.

The February revolution was a response to long-term domestic crises within the Russian Empire compounded by failures on the front. Those crises only worsened in the following months. During the course of 1917, increasing discontent with the new Provisional Government, which was unable to bring the war to a close, together with hopes for greater social and economic equality led to increasing support for socialism and socialist parties. Workers who wanted more control over their daily lives increasingly elected radical deputies to local soviets and factory committees, and peasants deserted the front in large numbers to return home to their villages and seize the land they had always believed was theirs. The Bolshevik Party, under the leadership of Vladimir Lenin, won their support by encouraging the most radical solutions to these problems. In October, government weakness, popular support for socialism, and Lenin's confidence allowed the Bolsheviks to seize power from the Provisional Government as well as to sideline the other socialist parties. Opposition to Bolshevik political extremism and radical socialism led to the bloody, destructive Russian Civil War, which ended with Bolshevik victory and the formation of the Soviet Union in 1922.

The new Union of Soviet Socialist Republics (USSR) was established according to Lenin's vision, rather than Joseph Stalin's competing proposal. Stalin wanted to incorporate the national republics on the former empire's territory into Soviet Russia (the Russian Soviet Federative Socialist Republic, or RSFSR) as autonomous regions rather than as independent republics. Lenin called for independent national republics to have the same *de jure* rights as Russia, including the right to voluntarily leave the USSR at any time. After the early years of Bolshevik rule, the right of voluntary secession was observed only on paper and not in practice, but it remained a formative element, and a ticking time bomb, in the legal and institutional structuring of the Soviet Union. In 1991, some of the Soviet republics declared their independence from Moscow, citing the Leninist principle, foreshadowing the peaceful collapse of the USSR in December of that year.

The 1917 Revolutions and the Civil War destroyed imperial institutions and provoked a chain reaction of national movements on the outskirts of the former Russian Empire. As a result, several new political formations arose on its territory, including Finland, Poland, Lithuania, Latvia, Estonia, Ukraine, and the Transcaucasian Republic. The chaos of imperial disintegration also saw an explosion of new national identities and visual political expressions. However, imperial fragmentation did not mark the end of the multinational state. By the end of the Civil War, the Bolsheviks had reconstructed most of the former empire's territory. Within 20 years, they would reclaim Bessarabia, Western Ukraine, Western Belarus, and the Baltic states for the Soviet Union—that is, all of its previous holdings except Poland, Finland, and lands in eastern Turkey. However, unrest continued in the North Caucasus and Central Asia into the 1930s, and as episodic expressions of anti-imperialist discontent demonstrate, nationalist sentiments were never completely stamped out. Rather, Leninist nationality policies favoring local cultures and literacy in local languages strengthened national cohesion and consciousness in several republics, like Armenia and Georgia. At the same time, efforts to repress nationalism, as in Ukraine and the Baltic republics, only encouraged separatist nationalism.

During the Revolutions of 1917 and the Civil War that followed, Soviet leaders and many sympathetic artists recognized the power of the visual as a tool for establishing Bolshevik legitimacy and promoting socialist ideas. They made use of the new technologies of mass media, such as cheap newspapers, illustrated magazines, posters, and cinema, to educate, to illustrate political conflicts, to model proper socialist behavior, and to unify the country across national borders, classes, and cultural differences.

CHAPTER 31

"GO BE RUSSIAN": POLITICAL CARICATURE, IDENTITY POLITICS, AND THE TBILISI PRESS AFTER THE 1905 REVOLUTION

NAOMI CAFFEE AND ROBERT DENIS

OUR STORY BEGINS in the South Caucasus, a mountainous and culturally diverse region flanked by the Black and Caspian Seas and bordered by Russia, Turkey, and Iran. Tbilisi, Georgia, might be best-known today as a picturesque tourist destination, but at the turn of the twentieth century, it was the site of paradigm-shifting intellectual activity and violent revolutionary agitation. At that time, the city served as the administrative center of the Transcaucasian Viceroyalty of the Russian Empire, a node in an extensive bureaucracy that managed the empire's power and influence across a vast territory populated by subjects of myriad languages and confessions. The Russian Empire's infrastructure connected Tbilisi to the Russian metropole—and beyond it, the world—via railways, telegraphs, steamships, and networks of highly mobile military and civil-service elites. Imperial power also facilitated the rise of industrialization in the region, which, coupled with natural resource extraction, created new wealth but also led to economic disenfranchisement and inflamed ethnic tensions. Meanwhile the empire's top-down efforts at cultural Russification led to the establishment of Russian-medium educational institutions, which, contrary to intent, produced a multicultural, multilingual generation of intellectuals who were attuned to European models of modernity, nationhood, and political self-determination. Inspired by these ideas, some turned towards increasingly radical means to realize them. In 1905, as the Russian Empire was consumed by revolution, life in Tbilisi would never be the same again.

Mass media was significantly altered by the events of 1905 in the way that information was created and circulated as well as in the scale of its influence and the diversity of its content. Tbilisi emerged as the center of a robust satirical press that reflected the cultural heterogeneity of the region and of the city itself, dominated by three local ethnic groups: Armenians, Azeris,[1] and Georgians. Satirical periodicals featured caricatures that were brightly drawn, expressive, irreverent, and—most important of all—hilarious. Yet caricature in the South Caucasus did not serve merely to entertain, or to provide a passive visual representation of current events. It also amplified the wide range of local responses to Russian imperialism and motivated its audience to political action. Moreover, because caricature provided a means of consuming media without requiring literacy, it rendered the satirical press—and with it, political discourse—accessible to broader swaths of the population. This set the stage for power struggles between the press and the imperial authorities, which grew in frequency and intensity as time went on. Thus, mass media, an innovation made possible by the conditions of Russian Empire, became increasingly critical of that empire and eventually hastened its demise.

SLINGSHOTS AND CARDBOARD SWORDS: THE CLASH OF PRESS AND IMPERIAL AUTHORITIES

The cover illustration of the October 14, 1906, edition of the Armenian journal *Calamity* (*Khat'abala*) depicts a rogue's gallery of the Russian Empire's most prominent bureaucrats, dressed in official regalia and dancing around a burning pile of progressive Russian newspapers and satirical journals, while representatives from conservative publications stand watch in the background (Image 31.1).[2] With the contorted body language of the officials, the enormous plumes of smoke rising from the fire, and the sinister, teeth-baring grimaces of the newspapermen, the scene recalls a pagan ritual or a witches' coven, and it is typical of the ghoulish depictions of Russia's top bureaucrats in caricatures of this period.[3] The caption reads: "Celebrating the destruction of rebellion." But what was the nature of this rebellion? And were the authorities celebrating too soon?

This image draws our attention to the chaotic mass media landscape following the 1905 Revolution, as well as the crisis of authority that both propelled it and formed its subject matter. Russian authorities had already begun to lose control of the press amid waves of violent unrest when, on October 17, 1905, Tsar Nicholas II delivered a decree known as the October Manifesto. In it, he promised unprecedented civil liberties, representative governance, and crucially, freedom of speech and of the press. This only poured fuel on the fire, however, emboldening radicals and sending the already disoriented censorship apparatus into a panic. In the words of one high-ranking censor, they "had to fight the revolution with cardboard swords" until the November Regulations, published just over a month later, provided a new legal framework for regulating the operations of the press.[4] But these new regulations were a mixed bag. By simplifying the bureaucratic process through which new periodicals could be launched, yet also streamlining the procedure for banning them, they led to a frenetic "press boom."[5]

Although the press boom in the South Caucasus was dominated by local ethnic groups and voices from the left, the conservative press had not gone away. As indicated by the leering newspapermen in the *Calamity* caricature, there was no shortage

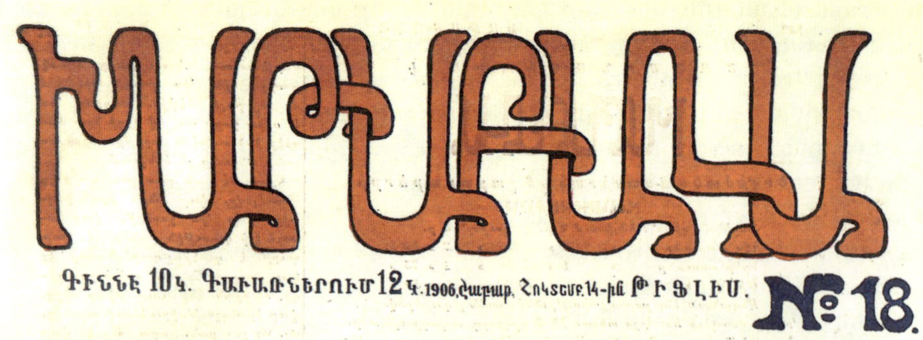

IMAGE 31.1 "Celebrating the destruction of rebellion," *Calamity* (*Khat'abala*), October 14, 1906.

of periodicals praising the monarchy and the Orthodox Church, espousing Great Russian patriotism, decrying revolutionaries, and denigrating Jews and Armenians.[6] Yet even arch-conservative monarchist publications could run afoul of government censorship, as was the case with *The Russian Caucasus* (*Russkii Kavkaz*), which was shut down in 1909 for its alleged "hostile editorial line."[7] This demonstrates how strictly the Russian state attempted to contain the press, censoring even the most loyal periodicals for minor critiques of state institutions. It also reminds us that the press, as a medium, had no inherent political bias and was used effectively by various rival ideological factions, leading to the further polarization of society.

"NO TRACE OF ENLIGHTENMENT": SATIRE AND MUSLIM SELF-CRITIQUE IN *MOLLA NÄSRÄDDIN*

In this much more subdued image from the April 14, 1906, issue of the Azeri journal *Molla Näsräddin*, the satire's "bite" lies not in grotesquely exaggerated visual messaging, but rather in the tension between the perspectives of the press and the communities that constituted its readership (Image 31.2). We see a newspaper seller offering his wares to a skeptical textile shop owner, while his assistant looks on passively in the background. A caption provides the shop owner's indignant retort: "Yes, today you come and say: 'Haji, buy a newspaper and read it.' Tomorrow, God willing, you'll come and say: 'Haji, get up and go be Russian.'" At first glance, the image and caption together seem to ridicule the conservative Muslim viewpoint that the press is something inherently alien to Muslim culture, and that the act of reading a newspaper, along with its prerequisites of literacy and engagement with current events, are tantamount to selling out, to Russification. The traditional Muslim dress of all three men, along with the absence of any markers of Russian culture in their environment, highlight the absurdity of the perceived exhortation to "go be Russian." Yet the journal's subject matter, and the lives of the Azeri intelligentsia who created and disseminated it, complicate the picture of who is ridiculing whom.

Both the shop owner's association of the press with "Russianness," and his conflation of Russianness with European discourses of modernity, has a basis in the history of Azeri print culture in the region. The first periodical to appear in the Azeri language was a translation of the official Russian newspaper, *Tiflisskie vedomosti* (1828–1833), founded by tsarist authorities who dictated that it should instill in the local Muslim population "a desire for European education and industry."[8] The relaxation of censorship in 1905 opened up new opportunities for the Azeri press, and the intelligentsia viewed it as a way of shaping local Muslim society and influencing public opinion. *Molla Näsräddin*'s editorial line, set primarily by co-founder and chief editor Cälil Mämmädquluzadä, stressed self-criticism of contemporary Muslim society, attacking local conservatives, and the clergy in particular, while promoting European-style cultural modernization. The language of *Molla Näsräddin* flagrantly ignored literary norms, communicating in a vernacular style well-suited to its

IMAGE 31.2 "'Yes, today you come and say: 'Haji, buy a newspaper and read it.' Tomorrow, God willing, you'll come and say: 'Haji, get up and go be Russian.'" *Molla Näsräddin*, April 14, 1906.

irreverent humor. Some of Mämmädquluzadä's acquaintances, put off or bewildered by the radical critique of their own community, predicted its failure.[9] But instead, the journal proved surprisingly popular among Azeris and the wider Muslim public, selling out the first issue almost immediately and, in 1908 and 1909, setting a sales record for Muslim periodicals in the Russian Empire.[10]

All the same, conservatives' fears that innovations such as the press would change their society or force them to "go be Russian" were not entirely unfounded. Mämmädquluzadä and his fellow multilingual, Europeanized Muslim intellectuals often expressed despair at the state of Muslim society and called urgently for its development along Western lines. This attitude is evident in Mämmädquluzadä's descripions of Muslim bazaars he had seen throughout the Caucasus and northern Iran: "dust and dirt, rubbish, . . . ruins, streets full of dogs and cats and bald-headed Muslim children . . . There is no trace of enlightenment, neatness, or decency here." Such observations, typical of *Molla Näsräddin's* progressive platform, provoked violent retaliation from the Muslim Azeri community.[11] Mämmädquluzadä notes in his memoirs that he was only able to publish such a paper because he lived in the ethnic Georgian section of Tbilisi, "out of the reach of Muslims."[12] Keeping this in mind as we return to the caricature, the shop owner's skeptical words seem to ricochet back at the same Azeri intelligentsia who are lampooning him. To some degree, it *was* necessary for them to "go be Russian" in order to critique their community from a safe distance. Ironically, this engagement with Russianness paved the way for a new vision of Azeri national unity that was to follow, unfolding—where else?—on the pages of the local press.

BEYOND "WRITERS, SCHOLARS, AND SMART PEOPLE"

Anticlerical messages were not limited to the Azeri satirical press, and the lines between progressive intelligentsia and reactionary religious communities were not as clearly drawn as Mämmädquluzadä would make it seem. A 1908 caricature from the Georgian journal *The Devil's Whip* shows a group of journalists trying to enter a meeting of Georgian Orthodox clergy, while armed priests stand guard in the foreground, repelling them at the point of a bayonet (Image 31.3). A Russian-language

IMAGE 31.3 "Congress of priests and press representatives," *The Devil's Whip*, January 1, 1908.

sign on the door reads: "Entry is strictly forbidden to writers, scholars, and all smart people." A smirking devil—the journal's titular figure—peers out from their midst. Reflecting the multilingual and multicultural press of Tbilisi at the time, the journalists' hats bear the titles of the Georgian, Armenian, and Russian-language newspapers they represent. As in the previous caricature from *Molla Näsräddin*, this image depicts a hostile relationship between the intelligentsia and the local population. However, in diving deeper, we will see that the Georgian clergy's role in the political upheavals of 1905 to 1908, as well as their stake in the ideological battles of the day, was more complicated.

This was a time of intense controversy over the status of the Georgian Orthodox church. In 1811, a decade after the Empire's formal annexation of Georgian lands, the local church was incorporated into the Russian church, and an Exarch (equivalent to a bishop) answerable to the Russian Holy Synod was appointed in place of the Catholicos (the patriarch or head of the Georgian church).[13] As a result, the Georgian church lost its de facto independence and was subjected to gradual Russification. On the other hand, in its new configuration, the previously fragmented Georgian church was united, and the new exarchate's authority was actually expanded to encompass all Georgian lands, and even beyond.[14]

Nevertheless, the Georgian clergy continued to pursue the restoration of its former independence (the ecclesiastical term is *autocephaly*), and in the revolutionary fervor that gripped the empire in 1905, they found a disparate group of allies—certainly among some of the revolutionary factions of the Georgian nationalist struggle, but also within the Russian church itself, where a movement for internal democratization was gaining strength.[15] The heady atmosphere also emboldened the autocephalists to employ ever more radical means against the antirevolutionary reaction. In June 1906, the Russian Holy Synod appointed a controversial new Exarch to the Georgian church, Nikon, who was a well-known opponent of autocephaly. Upon arrival in Tbilisi, he took fastidious measures to ensure his personal safety, wearing body armor and keeping armed guards outside his door at all times—echoing the siege mentality of the priests in the caricature shown in Image 31.3.[16] Nevertheless, in 1908, just five months after the caricature was published, Nikon was assassinated, purportedly by Georgian autocephalists.

As this short history demonstrates, Georgia's annexation into the Russian Empire reshaped its institutions and culture in complex ways, and by the twentieth century, both the church and the press had outgrown the subordinate roles envisioned for them by the authorities. Following the upheavals of 1905, they were able to pursue their new ambitions openly. This leads to a broader point about identity politics of the South Caucasus in the waning years of the Russian Empire: the dynamics cannot be reduced to a conflict between ethnic or religious communities, between colonizer and colonized, or between enlightened intelligentsia and backwards reactionaries. Certain factions of groups usually seen as opposed—Georgian nationalists and

Russians, clergy and revolutionaries—could sometimes unite for common causes. Revolution and modernity made for strange bedfellows indeed.

CONCLUSIONS

By studying political caricature in the South Caucasus during the "press boom" of 1905 to 1908, we get a close-up view of the diverse, and often unforeseen, outcomes of Russian imperialism, as well as the varieties of local engagement and resistance. The popularity and resonance of journals like *Calamity*, *Molla Näsräddin*, and *The Devil's Whip* reveal the central role of satire in depicting the contradictions of cultural and political life in the South Caucasus at this time. Irony, which presents the world from opposing sides, allows us to make sense of situations where expectations and realities, power and powerlessness, and officially sanctioned discourse and subversion coexist. We see this clash of meanings in the periodicals' written content, but it is especially visceral in the caricatures: the exaggerated features of the human body, the often grotesque depictions of power and authority, and the bold configurations of space, color, and perspective. As "expression by deviation," caricature goes hand in hand with two other artistic developments of the early twentieth century—modernist art and revolutionary propaganda, which similarly hinge on "deliberate violations of naturalistic standards" in order to depict a rapidly changing world.[17]

Further evidence of this paradigm shift is the fact that the press itself, and its impact on society, is a central feature of all three caricatures. Each one grapples with the implications of creating, disseminating, and consuming print media—or refusing to do so—and frames all of these acts as inherently political. In the South Caucasus during the final years of the Russian Empire, the press was more than just a means of "representing the kind of imagined community that is the nation."[18] It also actively eroded the authority of the imagined community that was the Russian Empire. What awaited the empire's Georgian, Azeri, and Armenian reading audiences in the ensuing years would be even more world-shattering: revolution, war, violent struggles for independence, and eventually, the emergence of Soviet national republics on the territory of the former Transcaucasian Viceroyalty.[19]

NOTES

1. The terms *Azeri* and *Azerbaijani* are anachronistic, insofar as they were not widely used in any language to identify the Turkic-speaking Muslim population of the Caucasus until the 1930s. At the time in question, a variety of other terms were used, most often *Tatars*, *Turks*, or simply *Muslims*, but a national identity had not yet fully formed and was secondary to religious and regional identities.
2. This image does not merely provide imaginative commentary on the state of the press, exaggerated for satirical effect: a few months prior, one such bonfire was organized by authorities in a cemetery in Kyiv. See V. Botsianovskii and E. Gollerbakh, *Russkaia satira pervoi revoliutsii, 1905–1906* (Leningrad: Gosudarstvennoe izdatel'stvo, 1925), 119.

3. Tobie Mathew, *Greetings from the Barricades: Revolutionary Postcards in Imperial Russia* (London: Four Corners Books, 2018), 140.
4. A. V. Bel'gard, *Vospominaniia* (Moscow: Novoe literaturnoe obozrenie 2009), 260.
5. Mathew, *Greetings from the Barricades*, 105–106.
6. Mathew, *Greetings from the Barricades*, 345.
7. National Archives of Georgia, fond 17, op. 1–1, no. 6578.
8. Enikolopov, "Pervaia tiurkskaia gazeta na Kavkaze," in *Kul'tura i pis'mennost' Vostoka*, kn. III, ed. Ia. A. Ratgauzer (Baku: V.Ts.K.N.T.A., 1928), 142.
9. Mämmädquluzadä, *Äsärläri 3*, 702.
10. Alexandre Bennigsen and Ch. Lemercier-Quelquejay, *La presse et le mouvement national chez les musulmans de Russie avant* 1920 (Paris: Mouton & Co., 1964), 124.
11. Mämmädquluzadä, *Äsärläri 3*, 705.
12. Mämmädquluzadä, *Äsärläri 3*, 704.
13. Paul Werth, "Georgian Autocephaly and the Ethnic Fragmentation of Orthodoxy," *Acta Slavica Iaponica*, no. 23 (2006): 76.
14. Werth, "Georgian Autocephaly," 83.
15. Abraham Ascher, *The Revolution of* 1905: *Authority Restored* (Stanford: Stanford University Press, 1992), 330.
16. Werth, "Georgian Autocephaly," 95.
17. Paul Klee, quoted in Rudolf Arnheim, "The Rationale of Deformation," *Art Journal* 43, no. 4 (1983): 319–320.
18. Benedict Anderson, *Imagined Communities: Reflections on the Origin and Spread of Nationalism* (London and New York: Verso, 2006), 31–35.
19. Research for this project was funded by Reed College and an NCEEER Title VIII Short-Term Travel Grant. The caricatures featured in this article were all drawn by the artist Oskar Schmerling (1863–1938). A broad selection of his graphic art, including the images featured here, can be found on our website "Beyond Caricature: The Oskar Schmerling Digital Archive" at https://schmerling.org

CHAPTER 32

IN THE CLAWS OF THE IMPERIAL EAGLE: FINLAND, GEORGIA, AND JOSEPH STALIN (1906)

RONALD GRIGOR SUNY

RETURNING FROM HIS first trip abroad in 1906, the young Joseph Stalin, then known to his friends and comrades as Koba, was already an emerging figure in the Bolshevik faction of the Russian Social Democratic Workers' Party. He had attended the Fourth Party Congress, the so-called "Unity Congress," in Stockholm that aimed to bring the rival Bolshevik and Menshevik factions of the Marxist party back into some kind of cooperation. Koba had made the journey from Tiflis (i.e., Tbilisi, the present-day capital of Georgia) through the empire, leaving by ship from semi-autonomous Finland. After the congress, he did not rush back to Tiflis, but wrote to a friend, Mikheil Monaselidze, on April 21, 1906, from Stockholm that he planned to visit his comrade and Mikheil's brother-in-law, Aleksandre Svanidze, in Germany.[1] The seemingly innocent postcard, written in Georgian, had more behind it than was immediately apparent (Image 32.1). Svanidze had earlier introduced Koba to his three sisters, the oldest of whom, Aleksandra, was married to Monaselidze. In 1905, Svanidze had asked Monaselidze if he could bring Koba to stay with them, and he agreed. He was not, however, to inform his sisters, who lived in the Monaselidze household, beforehand.

Already a revolutionary outlaw sought by the tsarist police, Koba holed up in the Monaseldizes' apartment in Tiflis, and various of his comrades visited regularly. At some point, one of the younger sisters, Ekaterine, caught his eye. Koba was soon smitten with Ekaterine Svanidze (1885–1907), known as Kato, and found surreptitious ways to visit her at Madame Hervieu's *atelier* where she worked as a seamstress. Despite the perils of married life for an underground revolutionary, Koba decided to wed Ekaterine. To please his mother, who approved of the quiet, pretty Kato, Koba agreed to a church wedding, a concession that ran counter to his revolutionary anti-religious convictions. Kato's brother-in-law, Mikheil Monaselidze, searched for a priest to marry the couple, but no one was willing to overlook Koba's illegal status.

IMAGE 32.1 Postcard written by Stalin to Mikheil Monaselidze, addressed in Russian, with text in Georgian.

Finally, a priest at St. David's Georgian Orthodox Church agreed to perform the service, but under two conditions: first, nothing would be said to the senior priest at the church, and second, the service would have to take place at one or two in the morning. Only a few could attend. In the early hours of July 16, 1906, Koba and Kato were wed, the ceremony witnessed by four Georgian friends and followed by a small traditional feast (*supra*) with Koba's Bolshevik mentor, Mikho Tskhakaia, as toastmaster (*tamada*).

The anodyne postcard sent from Europe had yet another message that could be read on the other side. It depicted a painting by a radical Finnish artist, Eetu Isto (1865–1905), *The Attack* (*Hyökkäys*), painted in 1899, and thousands of copies of the image were distributed through northern Europe (Image 32.2). An eagle, understood to represent Russia, was swooping down and ripping apart a large book labeled "Lex" (law) being defended by a blond maiden in the Finnish national colors, a white dress with a blue sash buckled with the coat of arms of Finland. Koba had chosen carefully an image that depicted the struggle between imperial power and a colonized periphery.

Parallels between Finland and Koba's native Georgia, two frontier regions of the Romanov empire, are easily drawn. In almost every way quite distinct and unique societies, Finland and Georgia actually shared certain commonalities in the nineteenth and early twentieth centuries. In both countries, the particular coincidence of

IMAGE 32.2 Postcard depicting the painting *The Attack* (*Hyökkäys*) by Eetu Isto, 1899.

class and nationality, of social status and ethnicity, produced particular forms of nationalism and national liberation movements. Instead of classic "bourgeois" nationalisms, both Finland and Georgia present pictures of national formation as a contest between rival visions of the nation and a socialist future. In Georgia, the principal movement of national liberation was socialist, even dedicatedly Marxist, rather than nationalist. In Finland, nationalism was complicated by the differences of two language communities: the Swedish-speaking Finns and the Finnish-speaking

Finns. Socialism was a latecomer to the political scene there, but when it appeared, and did so powerfully, in 1905, social democracy contested the nationalist visions of older generations of activists and intellectuals.

Both countries existed on the periphery of the Russian Empire; both were annexed by Imperial Russia in the first decade of the nineteenth century and achieved independence just over a century later; and both experienced the repressive policies of imperial domination, particularly at the end of the nineteenth century. At the same time, though denied by nationalists, both Georgia and Finland also benefitted from association with Russia in complex ways. The clash of cultures—Russian and Georgian, Russian and Finnish—was central to both the nationalist and imperial narratives of the nineteenth-century intelligentsias of both countries. In the story told by Georgian nationalists, an ancient people with a deeply embedded ethnoreligious culture confronts an emasculating imperial power determined to annihilate that culture and people through repression and assimilation. Yet the rediscovery of Georgianness was largely the project of Russian-educated Georgian intellectuals and political activists—the poets Rapiel Eristavi, Ilia Chavchavadze, and Akaki Tsereteli; the journalists Sergei Meskhi and Niko Nikoladze; and eventually, the Georgian Marxists—as well as dozens of lesser-known school teachers, librarians, booksellers, grammarians, and chorus directors. At the center of the national effort was a new respect for the Georgian language and the promotion of its literary culture. Committed to reviving and preserving what they took to be the essence of their culture, poets, scholars, and journalists selected from the chaotic past of traditions and symbols to inspire a new sense of nationhood.

Unlike many peoples of the Russian Empire, such as the Finns, Georgians were privileged to have a history of statehood that predated their incorporation into the empire, a recoverable record of heroic battles preserved in the royal chronicles, and glorious periods of art and architecture that were still physically present on the landscape. Consonant with the developing national consciousness of other peoples, the *tergdaleulni* (members of the Europeanized intelligentsia; literally, those who drank the waters of the Terek, the river that separated Caucasia from Russia proper) articulated a notion of nation based on the ethnic culture of the people, rather than primarily on religion, and emphasized harmony between nobles and peasants and development through education and economic growth.[2] The nobleman Ilia Chavchavadze (1837–1907), universally recognized as their most important nationalist writer and poet, urged Georgians to value their common culture. Rather than thinking of themselves as members of subgroups within Georgia—Kakhetians, Imeretians, Gurians, Svans, Mingrelians, or Kartvelians—or setting themselves apart from the peasants and dismissing them as uncultured, they should think as a coherent nation: "If Georgian is not their common name, then what is common to all of them? . . . if the people of the countryside are not Georgians, then who are they?"[3] What is most notable in his question is the fact that he had to ask it at all.

In contrast to the Georgians, Finns were not a "historic" nation able to claim the same kind of ancient origins in a cultural tradition and statehood that the Georgians so confidently and proudly celebrated. But in a way similar to Georgia, Finland's collective national identity was a construction of intellectuals in the nineteenth century. Largely peasants and workers, Finns had no native aristocracy, as the Georgians had, and no high culture of their own. But like the Georgians, they did not have much of a native bourgeoisie. Under Swedish dominion since the late thirteenth century, even after annexation by Russia in 1809, Finland was subject to the Swedish speakers, who made up the nobility, bureaucracy, and much of the middle class. Like Georgians, who coexisted with Russian rulers and an Armenian urban bourgeoisie, Finnish speakers were a subordinate people within a region where they composed the majority of the population. They had their own national Lutheran church and their own language, largely inaccessible to the ruling Russians and even to the Swedish-speaking elites living among them. And in the Finnish countryside, rather than a "feudal" structure of noble landlords and serfs, an independent landholding peasantry held sway, largely Finnish-speaking. The influence and power of the Swedish speakers came from their traditional social and cultural status and their position in the bureaucracy and administration of the Grand Duchy of Finland.

From the moment Russia took Finland from Sweden and incorporated it into the Russian Empire—a moment, it might be noted, of remarkable liberal tolerance unusual in Russian politics—Finland, which had never been an historic state, nevertheless was granted the status of an autonomous polity, with its own local Diet, a Senate at the apex of the bureaucracy, guarantees for the Lutheran religion, and the continuance of the Fundamental Laws of the Swedish period. The emperor Alexander I (ruled 1801–1825) not only declared himself Grand Duke of Finland and was formally recognized by the Diet, but also made himself head of the Lutheran Church in Finland and pledged to observe the constitution and laws of Finland. For the next eighty-odd years, Finland existed as a constitutional anomaly within the empire, a distinct country with its own army, legal system, currency, and taxation, separated from the rest of the empire by tariffs and a frontier. Within this autonomy, a sense of Finland as a country with its own identity developed.

Finland moved from being a geographic term to being a political designation, the Grand Duchy of Finland, while Georgia lost its political identity and its sovereignty, such as it was. It became submerged in geographic terms. Instead of preserving it as a geographic and political unit, the Imperial State officially designated the former Kingdoms of Georgia as provinces, primarily the Tiflis and Kutaisi provinces. Georgia ceased to be a political entity before the nationalist movement appeared, while Finland gained a political identity a few decades before the nationalist movement arose. Georgians would have to fight to recover some political autonomy, while Finns had to fight internal ethnolinguistic divisions within the country to protect its political autonomy from the threat of the ruling Russian authorities. Through the first eight decades of Russian rule, Finns pledged their allegiance to the tsar, served in the imperial army, and governed their local affairs in ways that no other part of the Russian Empire enjoyed. Nicholas I (ruled 1825–1855) is said to have remarked, "Leave the Finns in peace. That is the only province of my great realm that has caused me no anxiety or dissatisfaction throughout my reign."[4] But despite Nicholas's complacency, Finns of later generations increasingly chafed against both Russian imperial rule and the entrenchment of the Swedish-speaking bureaucracy. Growing discontent with the Swedish-speaking ruling groups led their rivals, many of them also Swedish speakers, including clerics and scholars, to promote Finnish language and culture in what in time became the nationalist movement. Most significantly, the Finnish physician Elias Lönnrot (1802–1884) compiled Karelian and Finnish folk poetry into the epic *Kalevala*, which soon was accepted as the Finnish national epic and a source of Finnish identity.

Opposed to the nationalist story of unrelenting oppression and forced Russification was the imperial story told by Russian officialdom and its supporters, a heroic tale of a great state, tolerant and caring of its constituent peoples, which then faces ungrateful and rebellious subjects subversive both to the civilizing mission of the empire and to a benevolent state. Here, repression, as with other imperial projects, is justified in the name of order and progress. Both stories are founded on clear lines of difference between ethnic cultures, on the one hand, and between empire and nation, on the other. What is largely lost in the nationalist narratives is the constitutive effects of imperial rule on the making of nations within the empire, as well as on the ways in which peoples shared, borrowed, and migrated between different cultures. Instead of static, fully formed, and clearly bounded cultures confronting one another, nineteenth-century Russians, Finns, and Georgians were simultaneously evolving, changing, and in many ways, affecting each other. Georgian and other non-Russian intellectuals spoke of the recovery of a primordial nationhood that the empire was determined to suppress. Yet restrictions on local language and culture by imperial authorities were haphazardly applied and served only to inspire affection among non-Russians for what was most intimately connected to family and home. Both Finnish and Swedish speakers resisted Nicholas II's attempts to curtail Finland's autonomy. Unwittingly, the empire, with its face turned toward Europe, aided the very process of nation-making by fostering education, social mobility, and the means of communication (railroads, roads, and telegraphs) by which isolated, illiterate villagers grew to imagine they were part of a larger community, the nation. The growth of cities, as well as the peace and security enforced by the imperial state, cultivated the ground from which nationalist and socialist intellectuals grew to become the most forceful voices of the nation.

The image that Koba chose to send to the family of the woman who would become his first wife was nationalist rather than socialist. But it expressed his emotional response to the plight of Georgia and, by extension, of other non-Russian peoples.

Liberation, in the view of Bolsheviks, was not conceived as one nation struggling against the empire, but rather as a coordinated, worker-led revolution of peoples stirred by shared economic, social, and political oppression. The Russian eagle tearing at Finland was the same one whose claws gripped Georgia. By 1905, the young revolutionary had decisively moved away from his earlier romantic affection for his native land and adopted, at least as a public political posture, the cosmopolitan perspective of Marxist internationalism. As a teenager, he had gloried in singing and writing nationalist poems about Georgia's salvation, but now, steeled by the fire of the First Russian Revolution, he had become much more pragmatic, manipulative, and calculating.

Even as he gravitated away from Georgia, abandoned his native land to the rival Menshevik faction, and moved in 1907 to the oil capital Baku, Koba, in his personal life, repeatedly turned to his Georgian friends and comrades, dependent on them as he was for his safety and support. He chose a traditional Georgian woman as his companion. Married and with an infant son, Koba engaged in the heady politics of the oil workers, running from meeting to meeting and avoiding the police and their spies. As the accepting, modest, attentive Georgian woman she had been brought up to be, Kato bore her fate without complaining. Koba cared for her in his own way, but he subordinated family to work. As his pal Giorgi Elisabedashvili put it, "Soso [here using Koba's childhood nickname] loved her very much, but if you didn't know Soso's character well, you would not understand his love. Wife, child, friend were good for him only if they were not hindering him in his work and if they shared his views."[5]

In the three months that she lived with her husband and son in Baku, Kato was largely alone. The heat and foul air of the city sickened her. Taken by her relatives back to Tiflis, she soon succumbed. Koba sank into despair. As he stood despondent at her bier, he took the arm of his boyhood companion and later enemy Ioseb Iremashvili, also known as Soso, and pointed to the corpse: "Soso, this creature softened my heart of stone; she has died, and with her my last warm feelings for people." Placing his right hand on his chest, he said, "Here it is so desolate, so indescribably empty."[6] What he felt for Kato, he did not extend to his son, Iakob. He left his child with Kato's mother and for years made little effort to see him. Grief, arguably the most powerful human emotion, consumed him. As a sign of remembrance of his lost wife, he adopted, for a while, the pen name "K. Kato."

NOTES

1. A. Ostrovskii, *Kto stoial za spinoi Stalina* (Saint Petersburg: Neva; Moscow: OLMA-PRESSA, 2002), 248; postcard to M. Monaselidze, RGASPI, fond 558, op. 1, d. 5095, l. 1; Ol'ga Edel'man, *Stalin: Biografiia v dokumentakh* (unpublished manuscript), 432–433. Aleksandre Svanidze (1886–1941), a Bolshevik who became Stalin's brother-in-law, served as a government official in Soviet Georgia and as a diplomat in Germany before he was accused of being a German spy, arrested in 1937, and shot, along with his sister, Mariko, in 1941.

2. For an extended treatment of the Georgian national movement, see Ronald Grigor Suny, *The Making of the Georgian Nation* (Bloomington: Indiana University Press, 1988, 1994), 113–143.
3. Il. Chavchavadze, "zogierti ram," *droeba*, no. 24, March 7, 1876; cited in Austin Jersild and Neli Melkadze, "The Dilemmas of Enlightenment in the Eastern Borderlands: The Theater and Library in Tbilisi," *Kritika* 3, 1 (2002): 38.
4. Quoted in Risto Alapuro, *State and Revolution in Finland* (Berkeley, Los Angeles, London: University of California Press), 265.
5. G. Elisabedashvili, "Vospominaniia," *i. v. stalinis sakhl-muzeumi* [Stalin House Museum, Gori], d. 1955/146, ll. 54–56.
6. Joseph Iremaschwili, *Stalin und die Tragödie Georgiens: Erinnerungen* (Berlin: Verfasser, 1932), 40.

CHAPTER 33

AGIT-EMPIRE: BOLSHEVIK CIVIL WAR ART

LAURA ENGELSTEIN

IN FEBRUARY 1917, the stress of World War I led to the collapse of the three-hundred-year-old Romanov dynasty, brought to its knees by widespread popular protests, mutiny in the armed forces, and defection of its loyal elites. The monarchy was replaced by a Provisional Government composed of moderate deputies to the imperial State Duma, or parliament. The Provisional Government was confronted by the newly constituted Soviet of Workers' and Soldiers' Deputies, an elected body under socialist leadership. The tension between cautious and radical visions of the revolution was played out in the realm of representation as well. In an orgy of physical iconoclasm, crowds destroyed imperial monuments and symbols of tsarist authority. The Provisional Government, while signaling its commitment to preserving the state, if in a form yet to be determined, still needed visual emblems to mark a break with the past. Portraits of generals and the imperial family were replaced by cameos of the new ministers; colorful posters continued to appeal for war loans, though now for a democratic Russia. A proliferation of illustrated handbills urged voters to choose party lists for elections to the many local soviets and to the anticipated Constituent Assembly that was to determine the character of the new regime.[1]

In this awkward transition, the status of the Russian Empire posed a special challenge. The autocratic embodiment of empire had been rejected, yet for Russia to retain its standing as a great nation, its imperial body had to be preserved. The new ministers granted equal rights of citizenship to ethnic and religious minorities, but maintained the principle of territorial integrity. Ruble bills, divested of the crowns or crests of subordinated regions, still bore an image of the double-headed tsarist eagle.[2] With the tsar gone, however, local elites began to press for cultural and administrative autonomy. In October 1917, when the Bolsheviks ousted the Provisional Government, such tentative demands escalated into full-fledged national movements. In 1918, Ukrainian leaders adopted the Trident (*Tryzub*) as their coat of arms, and Finland extricated its crowned lion from the imperial eagle's embrace.

Visual messages such as these played a key role in the Civil War that followed the October coup. Quick to institutionalize their claim to power, the Bolsheviks wasted no time establishing the fine arts on a centralized, administrative basis. They launched a program of "monumental propaganda" to redefine the urban landscape.[3] So-called agit-trains (from the word *agitatsiia*, meaning propaganda) sheathed in inspirational images toured the far-flung battlefields. The Russian Telegraph Agency, known as Rosta, was responsible not only for the printed word, but for the production and dissemination of political art. Posters, in particular, were officially lauded as "a new and powerful weapon of socialist propaganda."[4] Millions of them were turned out between 1918 and 1921. Hand-drawn or lithographed, stenciled or pasted onto walls, they hung in storefronts and on telephone poles. Observers talked of "poster fever" or "poster mania."[5] The "artistic front" was part of the general mobilization in defense of the revolution.

The anti-Bolshevik Whites also engaged in visual propaganda, creating an information agency of their own, which attracted artists from the same modernist stable out of which the Bolsheviks drew their talent, but the output and quality could not compete with the volume and energy manifested on behalf of the Soviet cause.[6] Representing the Russia-centric imperial model, the Whites issued currency that bore the double-headed eagle without its crown but retained other symbols of imperial majesty.[7] Another signature of the old regime preserved in White messaging was the motif of antisemitism. A flier featured Leon Trotsky, Vladimir Lenin's second in command, as a large spider, enmeshing all of Russia in its web. "Everyone to the defense of Siberia! Leiba Bronshtein (Trotsky), a spider sucking the blood of the Russian people," the image screamed.[8] Trotsky also dominated a White poster displaying him as a naked figure astride the Kremlin walls, its skin a devilish red, Star of David dangling from its neck, blood dripping from its bestial paws.[9]

In contrast to such crude exercises, many of the Soviet Civil War posters have become classics of political art. Initially, they served as calls to battle, identifying the enemy, arousing fear and anger, and countering rival appeals. As the tide of the Civil War turned in the Bolsheviks' favor, however, Soviet images began to anticipate the onset of a new kind of struggle, still directed against persistent enemies of the revolution, but now also focused on reconstruction and the reintegration of rebellious parts.[10] Creative and captivating, they ranged in style—from modernist photomontage, to playful abstractions, to comic-book style narratives, to symbolic tableaux—and were directed at visual consumers from the laboring ranks. The most accomplished of these productions combined the bite of political caricature with the vocabulary of the pseudo-folk block print known as the *lubok*.

The *lubok* had earlier offered a language for wartime appeals on behalf of the imperial regime. One of the style's most talented practitioners was the poet Vladimir Mayakovsky (1893–1930), who drafted patriotic postcards—first in support of imperial troops, then of the democratic republic, before transitioning to agitational broadsheets after 1918, all in the same exuberant spirit.[11] From late 1919 to the end of 1921, he was the dominant figure at Rosta, which developed a format known as Windows. These catchy images, inspired by caricaturist Mikhail Cheremnykh (1890–1962), were originally meant to fill now-empty shop windows, but were soon posted everywhere. The aesthetic was sophisticated, but the witty, simplified idiom was easy to grasp. Their purpose, Mayakovsky explained, was "to seize public attention, to compel a crowd of pedestrians, whether they want to or not, by whatever means, to stop in front of the slogans in front of which we want them to stop."[12]

Such punchy features coexisted with less easily readable ways to channel the spirit of the revolution. In the years leading up to World War I, avant-garde artists had been experimenting with forms of abstraction steeped in philosophical or spiritual meaning. These were the years of the artistic manifesto, the defiance of "bourgeois" taste and aesthetic convention. This high-brow iconoclasm, though remote from concrete political themes, suited the paradigm-changing character of the revolution. Some striking poster designs, most famously "Beat the Whites with the Red Wedge" (1920) by El Lissitzky (1890–1941), encapsulate the energy of pure motion.[13]

Such visionaries were enlisted to cloak the monuments and facades of public squares with improvised structures in jarring shapes and stark colors. Abstract but materially tangible, these displays telegraphed the revolution's dramatic shift in worldview, transforming the very texture of everyday life, the very process of seeing. Ilya Ehrenburg (1891–1967) remembered Moscow on May 1, 1918, covered in "demented squares [that] battled with rhomboids on the peeling facades of colonnaded Empire villas." Not everyone liked them.[14]

More effective with ordinary viewers were the colorful posters, among them the Rosta Windows, that communicated the message of radical transformation on a less exalted plane. These ubiquitous images focused primarily on the class enemy, but the Bolsheviks had inherited the ethnic diversity of the old empire, and the disruptive demon of nationalism (denounced as "bourgeois") was an important concern. Bolshevik rhetoric, and posters following suit, therefore aimed their shots in two opposite directions: on the one hand, against the dynastic empire, as a regime that had for centuries captured and oppressed subject peoples, and on the other hand, against the efforts of some of those same peoples to assert their independence in territorial and political terms against the new claimants to power.

The Bolsheviks could not ignore the drive for regional and national separation that threatened the integrity of the revolution's geographic core and provided a strategic foothold for its political enemies. Attempting to master what they could not suppress, they countered Woodrow Wilson's posture as the champion of nations—articulated most famously in his Fourteen Points of January 1918—with their own commitment to the principle of national self-determination. They thereby also positioned themselves in opposition to the neo-imperial Whites, who pledged to restore the map of the former autocratic state. The support the Whites received from Britain and France was perfectly consistent, in the Soviet view, with the Western democracies' own record as imperialist oppressors.

From the Bolshevik perspective, "empire" thus figured as the true face of the ideological enemy, both foreign and domestic. Yet the Bolsheviks could not afford to relinquish the ground they already occupied. They, too, had imperial ambitions. No less than their White challengers, they fought to preserve the contours of the old terrain. Moscow was to preside over a supranational confederation on the old footprint, but now under the aegis of proletarian power. As the revolution spread across the globe, nations in their bourgeois form would give way to proletarian nations, which would serve as stepping stones to the transcendence of nations altogether.

The opening move, therefore, was defensive. The first poster considered here presents a powerful image of Soviet territory threatened both by secession and incursion (Image 33.1). "Be on Guard!" by D. Moor (Dmitry Orlov, 1883–1946), issued in late 1921, depicts an outsized Red Army soldier standing astride European Russia, rifle in hand, defending its western borders. The central figure likely represents Leon Trotsky, then commissar of war, a veritable icon of revolutionary militancy. Finland, Estonia, and Latvia, recently freed from Imperial Russian domination, are represented by suited gentlemen—bourgeois icons. The center of attention, however, is the figure of Poland, shown in black tie and top hat, as the archetypal aristocrat. With a French general lurking behind his back, the figure straddles a portly, mustachioed character in a Polish Legionnaire's cap and tunic, whose outstretched fingers unleash miniature soldiers in the direction of burning peasant villages in western Ukraine.

The events depicted in this tableau came at the tail end of the Soviet battle to block the national aspirations of resurgent Poland and Ukraine. These two threats had combined in April 1920 when Józef Piłsudski, newly installed Polish head of state, and Symon Petliura, leader of the embryonic Ukrainian People's Republic, agreed to joint action against Soviet Russia. Full-scale war between Soviet and Polish forces broke out in May 1920. Through the year, Soviet poster workshops churned out images denouncing the Polish aristocracy not just as class oppressors and tools of Great Power imperialism, but also as imperialists in their own right, eager to revive the old Polish-Lithuanian Commonwealth.[15]

The Soviets were cocky. Caricaturist Boris Efimov (Boris Fridliand, 1900–2008), at the Ukrainian section of Rosta, prepared a poster captioned "Red Heroes have taken Warsaw!"[16] He was jumping the gun. In August, the Poles achieved a surprise victory at the Vistula River, thanks to conflicts within the Red Army command. By the Treaty of Riga (March 18, 1921), Poland recognized the Ukrainian Soviet Socialist Republic, installed by the Bolsheviks in March 1919. Piłsudski thereby ruptured the alliance with Petliura and netted for Poland much of western Ukraine. Moor's forceful poster is at once a general reflection on empire and a comment on events torn from the headlines. This, too, was war. Trotsky declared the artist "a hero of the pencil and the paintbrush."[17]

IMAGE 33.1 Poster by D. Moor, 1921: "Be on Guard!"

IMAGE 33.2 Poster (anonymous), 1921: "Look! The riches of the Soviet Republics await the exertions of labor! Comrade! To battle with devastation! With a mighty effort we will achieve a satisfying, plentiful life."

The second Soviet poster on the imperial theme considered here, also from 1921, has, by contrast, abandoned the mood of anxiety and belligerence (Image 33.2). "Look!" it beckons: "The riches of the Soviet Republics await the exertions of labor! Comrade! To battle with devastation! With a mighty effort we will achieve a satisfying, plentiful life." The work of an anonymous artist, published in Odesa under the aegis of the Ukrainian Soviet Socialist Republic, the poster affirms the unity of the consolidated Soviet map. The land embracing these republics is shown without internal borders, as a broad and natural expanse, ready for the hard work of the laboring peoples who are now its masters.

The poster presents this peaceful postwar landscape from the direction of the Ukrainian south, only recently subdued by force of arms and blocked in its struggle for sovereignty. Centered west of the Urals, the image is notable for its south-to-north orientation, unusual for maps, and for the exclusion of recently threatening zones. The proletarian on the left and Red Army soldier on the right, no longer in fighting mode, point toward the centers of power, urging the worker, seemingly in a posture of reluctance, to push up his sleeves and get to work. Though haystacks are everywhere, the fraternal peasant is nowhere to be seen—army and industry take the lead. The main point, however, is to offer a vision of harmony, in which the southern steppe merges seamlessly with the Russia-centered core. Indeed, in 1922, the Ukrainian Soviet Socialist Republic was formally incorporated into the officially constituted Union of Soviet Socialist Republics.

In this idyllic vision, power is secure, and economic development is the order of the day. It is an exhortation to undramatic toil. Soviet power is personified as the sum total of human effort. This is an empire with ships in its harbors, footholds in the Black and Caspian Seas, and control of the Caucasus, whose factories and broad wheatlands show no sign of the ravages of war. The tone of the poster—the warm yellow hue, the lazy meandering of the rivers, suggests that the danger is past, no enemy lurks, and it is time for cooperation. Empire has been appropriated and transformed into the Soviet nation. A vision of socialist empire as beyond empire—a socialist Garden of Eden.

In fact, the real picture of 1921 was considerably less rosy. This was the peak of the massive famine that left five million dead in the agricultural heartland. The humanitarian catastrophe was acknowledged in Moor's famous poster ("Help!") of the same year, depicting an emaciated peasant dressed in tatters, arms outstretched in desperate appeal. This tableau, by contrast, represents the future, not the present or the past. The vector points forward, toward reconstruction and unity. The republics are as one; the peoples toil together.

Soviet images of the world revolution in its transnational sweep typically emphasized the diversity of faces and costumes. During the Civil War, texts and images specifically targeted the peoples of the Caucasus and Central Asia, using native languages and cultural symbols, while instructing them in the principles of their new, Soviet identity. Here, by contrast, the Soviet landscape is inhabited by ethnically neutral abstractions, by emblems of class, not nation. Managing ethnic and national differences within the new postrevolutionary frame nevertheless remained a major challenge. The unresolved tensions of the Civil War were not easy to wish away.

These two images, one martial, the other bucolic, represent phases in the Bolsheviks' pacification of the territory of what is today independent Ukraine, which at the time was trying to free itself from imperial domination. From the Bolshevik perspective, the retention of these lands was essential to the survival of the revolution, which they understood as the triumph of the socialist ideal over the old class regime and its nationalist exponents, conveniently omitting the proclaimed socialism of Ukrainian leaders. Trotsky here is depicted, not as an agent of empire, but in the role of defender of the socialist homeland, an anti-imperialist champion of the Revolution.

From the perspective of 2022, as the Russian Federation, under Vladimir Putin's leadership, is waging a brutal war of conquest against an existing Ukrainian state, with the goal of destroying its sovereignty and distinctive culture, the Trotsky of 1921 might well be understood as the standard-bearer of a predatory crusade. Appearing on the cover, as an emblem of this volume as a whole, the image might appear as shorthand for centuries of Russia-centered imperial aggression. More controversial still, the figure of Trotsky (always identified by antisemites as "Bronstein," his original, recognizably Jewish, last name), looming over the border with Europe, might be understood to evoke the ominous mythology of a Judeo-Bolshevik conspiracy, with its lethal impact on European history. Clearly none of these were the messages the Soviet poster artist intended to covey.

Both nationalists and antisemites deploy belligerent stereotypes, which in the midst of actual war are difficult to counteract. From the perspective of the role of images in political life, it is useful to keep in mind the multivalent messages images can convey and how the repertory of interpretations can change with time and historical context. The diversity of images in this volume shows that a single one of them, however brilliant and captivating, cannot stand for the entire sweep of Russian history.

NOTES

1. *Veter Semnadtsatogo goda: Rossiiskii politicheskii plakat 1917*, edited by I. Ia. Velikanova (Moscow: GTsMSIR, 2017), 21, 23, 29, 31, 35.
2. Russian currency, 1905–1920: http://archives.dickinson.edu/russian-and-slavic-resources/imperial-and-civil-war-currency (accessed March 20, 2020).
3. *Revolution: Russian Art 1917–1932* (London: Royal Academy of Arts; New York: Harry N. Abrams, 2017), 42 (Otdel izobrazitel'nykh iskusstv, under Narkompros).
4. Stephen White, *The Bolshevik Poster* (New Haven: Yale University Press, 1988), 65–67, 112 (quote, October 6, 1918).
5. White, *The Bolshevik Poster*, 109–111.
6. White, *The Bolshevik Poster*, 114–115; Nikolaus Katzer, *Die weisse Bewegung in Russland: Herrschaftsbildung, praktische Politik und politische Programmatik im Bürgerkrieg* (Cologne: Böhlau Verlag, 1999), 317–324.
7. Russian currency, 1905–1920: http://archives.dickinson.edu/russian-and-slavic-resources/imperial-and-civil-war-currency (accessed March 20, 2020).
8. *Revoliutsiia i Grazhdanskaia voina v Rossii. 1917–1922 gg.: Fotoal'bom*, edited by R. G. Gagkuev et al. (Moscow: Dostoinstvo, 2016), 133.
9. Anonymous, "Mir i svoboda v Sovdepii" (Peace and freedom in *Sovdepia*) (Osvag, no date), in O. V. Budnitskii, *Rossiiskie evrei mezhdu krasnymi i belymi* (Moscow: ROSSPEN, 2005), plate insert following p. 320. See also Anonymous, "V zhertvu internatsionalu" (Victims of the International) (Osvag, no date), in Budnitskii, *Rossiiskie*, following p. 320.
10. White, *The Bolshevik Poster*, 92, 101.
11. *Veter Semnadtsatogo goda*, 149.
12. Quoted in White, *The Bolshevik Poster*, 111 (quote); also 67–68, 114.
13. Image available at Museum of Fine Arts, Boston: https://collections.mfa.org/download/314484;jsessionid=6F75E6D45BFA7459128F9E76A0C79B59 (accessed March 31, 2020).
14. White, *The Bolshevik Poster*, 109 (quote), 112.
15. White, *The Bolshevik Poster*, 90–91, 100. On Polish imperialism, see, e.g.,: Anonymous, "Belaia Pol'sha i Sovetskaia Rossiia" (White Poland and Soviet Russia) (1920/1), online at New York Public Library: https://digitalcollections.nypl.org/items/510d47de-83a9-a3d9-e040-e00a18064a99 (accessed March 23, 2020).
16. Laura Engelstein, *Russia in Flames: War, Revolution, and Civil War 1914–1921* (New York: Oxford University Press, 2018), 998.
17. White, *The Bolshevik Poster*, 112 (quote).

CHAPTER 34

BREAKFAST IN SUUK SU: THE RISE OF VISUAL "TATARISM" (1917–1923)

ANGELINA LUCENTO

AS THE MOMENTOUS events of the Russian Revolution unfolded in Petrograd, Konstantin Chebotarev, a young painter from the predominantly Muslim region of Bashkortostan, initiated a smaller-scale, cultural revolution in Kazan.[1] The city had long served as the cultural center for the Russian Empire's Volga-Ural Tatars, and the Kazan Art School was considered the best and most progressive in the region. As the son of impoverished peasants, Chebotarev had developed an interest in anti-imperial politics during his teens, and hoped to use art as a means for their realization. He applied to the Kazan Art School and was accepted in 1910. Once there, Chebotarev elected to study under Nikolai Feshin, a well-known modern painter. Feshin was continuing to develop the radical form of documentary realism designed to expose the harsh inequalities of everyday life in the Russian Empire that a group of painters known as the Wanderers (*Peredvizhniki*) had first introduced in the 1870s. While Chebotarev respected Feshin, he did not believe that documentary realist painting was visually or politically radical enough to help bring down an empire and establish an egalitarian, collectivist society in its place. Such a society, in Chebotarev's view, would not only require the most innovative and daring artistic methods, it would also have to be based upon a democratic theoretical framework that had effectively rid itself of imperialism's oppressive tendencies.

In 1923, Chebotarev helped found the Kazan Left Front of the Arts (KLEF), a group whose membership consisted of poets, playwrights, and visual artists. Inspired by Vladimir Mayakovsky's journal *Left Front of the Arts* (*LEF*), which published theoretical discussions about the role of modern proletarian art in the building of socialism, Chebotarev, as the acting leader of KLEF's visual arts section, sought to develop a radical modernist style that could unify the former Russian Empire's Slavic and Islamic groups as part of a broader effort to establish a socialist collective that was anti-imperialist as well.

Like Mayakovsky, Chebotarev aimed to create works that could intervene directly into everyday life by dissolving the boundary between art and all the other of forms of social and political existence. He studied carefully the formal techniques of the Russian Futurists, the avant-garde group Mayakovsky had helped found before the 1917 Revolutions whose members focused on creating a visual aesthetic that could shatter normative perceptions of reality. The Futurists were known for their emphasis on the flatness of their canvases, their interest in abstract forms, and their expansive use of vibrant colors, designed to shock viewers into thinking in new ways. Although Chebotarev took a keen interest in Futurist forms, he had no desire to appropriate their political theory. Many of the Futurists, including Mayakovsky, embraced the Bolshevik takeover as establishing the path to socialism and communism. Based on his pictures, however, it is clear that Chebortarev had serious doubts about the Bolshevik path, and that his exposure to the principles of Tatar Jadidism in Kazan ultimately led him to oppose the Bolshevik approach to revolution.

Jadidism was an early twentieth-century movement for pan-Turkic enlightenment and modernization that was particularly influential in Tatarstan. As part of their modernization campaign, the Tatar Jadids active in the Volga-Ural region during the first two decades of the twentieth century advocated social and educational reform that combined the study of secular subjects, such as mathematics, science, geography, and history, with Islamic jurisprudence. In particular, they were interested in developing the concept of *ijtihād*, the critical assessment of problems not explicitly covered in the Qur'an. While these Tatar Jadids condemned the Russian imperial state's discriminatory policies toward minority ethnicities, they also acknowledged that state as a powerful actor in global politics. They believed Tatars could become influential actors in international social, economic, and political spheres only if they integrated themselves into the legal organs of the Russian state, thereby using it as a vehicle for their own advancement.[2] Their commitment, therefore, was not to independence, but rather to attaining a political voice and autonomy within the state. The Tatar Jadids also advocated for a major shift in the state's power structure. With the exception of a few monarchists, most worked to transform Russia's imperial autocracy into a constitutional democracy through the modernization of its legal and parliamentary system and the diversification of its representatives.[3]

Most significantly for Chebotarev, the Jadids emphasized that Tatars were particularly well suited to integration due to the specific characteristics of "Tatarist" culture, which combined aspects of Russian secular culture with the practices and visual symbols of Tatar Islam.[4] Their unique Tatar characteristics would ensure easy communication and cooperation with their Russian counterparts as they worked together to transform the state. After the October Revolution in 1917, however, many Tatar Jadids voiced their opposition to the Bolsheviks' program of political self-determination for ethnic minorities, and instead sought national-cultural autonomy. The most left-leaning of the Tatar Jadids continued to promote social democracy instead of Bolshevik communism, but many were eventually forced to flee, while others joined the White Army as an act of protest.[5]

Chebotarev's 1917 Futurist painting *Red Army* (Image 34.1) can best be understood as both an expression of his dubiousness toward the Bolshevik project and as an attempt to establish the place of Tatarist culture in postrevolutionary society. Like his Futurist colleagues, the artist relied exclusively on vibrant colors and simple yet repetitive geometric forms to create a dynamic composition. The contrast between the severe red that

IMAGE 34.1 Konstantin Chebotarev, *Red Army*, 1917.

dominates most of the picture and the fluorescent green used to color the uniforms of the five rows of Bolshevik infantrymen who populate the picture's foreground gives the viewer a startling sense of the army men's physical power as they advance under a single communist flag. This power, however, appears to be a consequence of their homogeneity and mechanical rigidity. The contrasting reds and greens of each man's uniform bleed into the body of the figure next to him so that every unit appears not as a row of individuals marching in solidarity for an emancipatory cause, but as a single pyramid form that looks as though it could have been cast from an assembly line mold.

While *Red Army*'s energetic contrasts and simple, geometric forms fit squarely within the Russian Futurist lexicon, the picture's content stands out as unique. The artists in Mayakovsky's circle used their own laconic geometries and vibrant colors to disrupt standardized visions of everyday reality and to offer tragicomic interpretations of current events. Chebotarev's painting, however, is literally futurist; it provides a predictive vision of society under Bolshevik rule that twenty years later would turn out to be shockingly accurate. In 1917, for example, the Bolsheviks' ragtag mixture of militants did not yet have a proper name, nor were their numbers large or organized enough to form the aggressive, targeted columns that Chebotarev depicts. However, after the Council of People's Commissars officially established the

Red Army in early 1918, the institution's infantry acquired the kind of strength and discipline suggested in the painting.

The ultramodern steel, cement, and glass structures that appear to rise up behind the advancing Bolsheviks are also the result of Chebotarev's productive fantasy. In 1918, avant-garde Russian architects were eager to experiment with steel and cement, but the problem of how to form them into multistory towers had not yet been solved. Pressing as they do against the rows of pulsating infantrymen, the painter's fantastical architectural monoliths underscore the Bolsheviks' modernity and suggest that they will eventually be able to fulfill their plans for the new communist world order, an order that many Volga Tatars supported. Chebotarev acknowledges this fact through his depiction of the infantrymen. The deep reds that color the soldiers' uniforms signify not only their allegiance to the Bolshevik Party. In the Russian Empire, red mingled with green also symbolized Tatar culture. The artist's application of this Tatar color scheme to the uniforms of *Red Army's* foot soldiers, therefore, indicates that the figures advancing across the canvas are Tatar communists. Chebotarev suggests in the picture that while joining the Bolsheviks may well lead to integration of the Tatars into the Party's modern communist project, it might not lead to the type of cultural diversification and multiplicity of political voices that the Jadids defined as emancipatory.

The artist responded to this unsatisfactory situation in two very different ways. On an immediately practical level, Chebotarev, like many of the leftist Jadids he admired, joined the White Army. He also developed a Tatarist painterly aesthetic. In keeping with Mayakovsky's idea that radical modern art could directly influence political and social life, Chebotarev believed that this new visual style would help nudge the spectator toward a form of socialism based on the forms and ideas of Jadidism. *Breakfast in Suuk-Su* (Image 34.2) constituted the first manifestation of that aesthetic and provided a foundation for its further evolution.

Suuk-Su, a small resort village on the southern Crimean coast, is best known for its late-medieval Tatar cemetery. In his rendering of a group of diverse characters eating their morning meal in the ancient village, Chebotarev once again relies on the formal language of Russian Futurism. As in *Red Army*, the artist forms each individual figure from basic geometric shapes painted in pulsating colors. In contrast to *Red Army's* rigorous uniformity, however, *Breakfast in Suuk-Su* lacks a clear compositional order. Instead, Chebotarev presents a chaotic, all-over scene. In the picture's foreground, proletarians in workers' caps sit adjacent to Tatars in distinctive skull caps (*tubeteika*). A Bolshevik agitator dressed in red stands pumping his fist in the top right center of the painting, while bourgeois men in boating and bowler hats sit around the peripheral tables unhurriedly enjoying their breakfast. While the visual vibrancy of the characters' clothing is in keeping with the Futurist tradition, the artist's color palette is not. Here, Chebotarev bases his palette of electric reds, blues, greens, and yellows commonly used in early twentieth-century renderings of the Tatar *shamail* (Image 34.3).

The *shamail*, a widespread form of decorated scripture, constituted an important part of modern Islamic visual culture. Artisans developed its distinctive visual style from Arabic calligraphy. Each *shamail* usually contains a passage from the Qur'an.

IMAGE 34.2 Konstantin Chebotarev, *Breakfast in Suuk-Su*, 1918.

In the early twentieth century, Tatar artisans began painting *shamail* on glass and printing them as lithographs in order to maximize their visibility and availability. The Tatar *shamail*'s powerful color schemes and the rhythmic intonations of the sounds of their sacred expressions soon became part of everyday Volga-Ural visual culture. When the Jadids initiated their reforms, the *shamail* came to symbolize Tatarist cultural identity. By painting the figures in *Breakfast at Suuk-Su* in glowing, *shamail*-inspired colors, Chebotarev renders the café scene recognizably Tatarist.[6]

The artist presents and evaluates two competing postimperial political scenarios: Bolshevik communism versus a radical form of democracy based on Tatarism. For Chebotarev, the red fist-pumping figure at the center of the canvas represents the future of postimperial Russian politics under the Bolsheviks. Compared to the other café patrons, the Bolshevik appears bulky. His beefy biceps and energetic stance indicate both great strength and the capacity for physical confrontation. Yet despite the Bolshevik's impassioned gestures and fervent speech, his overall impact on the scene is minor. Only the patrons seated at the table in front of the Bolshevik offer him their undivided attention, perhaps because they both fear and admire his towering physique. Through his rendering, Chebotarev suggests that the Bolsheviks, despite vigor, vociferousness, and physical prowess, do not actually have the capacity to affect positive social change. According to the painting, however, they do possess both the ability and the intent to maintain one of empire's key features: the invocation of potential physical violence

IMAGE 34.3 Unknown artist, *Tatar Shamail on Glass*, early twentieth century (Qur'ranic text: "There is No God Except Allah and Mohammad, Who was Sent by Allah").

against anyone who challenges their progress toward power. Like the rows of advancing Bolshevik infantrymen in *Red Army*, the agitator in *Breakfast in Suuk-Su* appears primed and ready to fight anyone who might stand in the way of his cause.

In contrast to the bright red Bolshevik, the figures that Chebotarev colored with *shamail*-inspired blues, greens, yellows, and crimsons appear calm and even harmonious. Despite clear cultural and social differences, they have no difficulty peacefully coexisting in the same public space. The artist's particular depiction of figures from diverse backgrounds engaging in intense discussions around café tables recalls Jürgen Habermas's description of the coffeehouse as the origin of the public sphere in seventeenth-century Britain, where individuals first began to debate political matters outside of the private realm.[7] Chebotarev's café tables, however, are not sites for civil political debate. They represent a political alternative to Bolshevism. By covering his canvas from edge to edge in a *shamail*-inspired palette, the artist suggests that if Russia's postrevolutionary citizens take on or hone their Tatarist characteristics, as the figures in the painting appear to do, then the sheer prevalence and recognizability of Tatarist culture will open up a space for the creation of a radically democratic political system that allows for productive disagreement. Empire's hierarchical model of power will be replaced by a system based on lateral movement and constant transformation. As the rhythms of Chebotarev's palette suggest, the political effects of such a system will inevitably peak into red intensities, but the collective's overall egalitarianism will ensure that those peaks eventually ebb into calmer yellows and greens, without ever resulting in the capacity for physical or militaristic confrontation embodied by the Bolshevik figure in this painting and the soldiers in *Red Army*.

When the Bolsheviks eventually secured their victory over the White Army in the Volga region, Chebotarev returned to Kazan. He remained determined to resist through art what he understood as their neo-imperial impulses. When Chebotarev helped found KLEF in 1923 (later, Tatar Left Front of the Arts [TatLEF]), the activist art group based on Mayakovsky's and *LEF*'s theories about how to move art into life, it attracted other Kazan-based artists interested in Tatarist aesthetics, including the young Tatar printmaker Faik Tagirov. TatLEF served as a vehicle for the promotion and dissemination of Tatarist visual aesthetics and the radically democratic, Jadidism-inspired politics that went along with them. Chebotarev, Tagirov, and others moved to Moscow in the mid-1920s, where they hoped to continue to develop their work so that it might influence a much broader group of spectators.

Despite his ambitions, Chebotarev's plan for the proliferation of Tatarism within Soviet visual art never came to fruition. A stylistic dispute with two other politically engaged artists from Kazan, Pavel Radimov and Aleksandr Grigor'ev, both founding members of the influential, Moscow-based Association of Artists of Revolutionary Russia (AKhRR), helped ensure that Chebotarev was thwarted at every turn. AKhRR, whose artists favored more traditional forms of figurative realism, sought to quash not only Chebotarev, but any artist relying on Futurism or modernist abstraction. As a result, neither Chebotarev's visual Tatarism nor its radically democratic Tatarist politics became defining features of Soviet socialism. Since the fall of the Soviet Union, however, a newfound interest in his work has emerged among those seeking to understand the relationship between empire and visual culture, and in particular the ways in which artists and artisans proposed alternatives to empire's visual manifestations through their work.

NOTES

1. This essay is dedicated to the late Robert Bird. It was completed with support from the Higher School of Economics University Basic Research Program.
2. Galina M. Yémelianova, "Volga Tatars, Russians, and the Russian State at the Turn of the Nineteenth Century: Relationships and Perceptions," *The Slavonic and Eastern European Review* 77, no. 3 (July 1999): 467.
3. Yémelianova, "Volga Tatars," 470.
4. Galina M. Yémelianova, "The National Identity of the Volga Tatars at the Turn of the 19th Century: Tatarism, Turkism, and Islam," *Central Asian Survey* 16, no. 4 (1997): 545–546.
5. Galina M. Yémelianova, *Russia and Islam: A Historical Survey* (New York: Palgrave, 2002), 100.
6. The prominent Soviet art critic Yakov Tugendkhol'd first noted the influence of the *shamail* on the work of the Tatar avant-garde in his 1928 essay "The Fine Art of the People's of the USSR." See Yakov Tugendkhol'd, "Izobrazitel'noe iskusstvo narodov SSSR," *Iskusstvo narodov SSSR* (Moskva-Leningrad: 1930), 49.
7. Jürgen Habermas, *The Structural Transformation of the Public Sphere: An Inquiry into a Category of Bourgeois Society*, translated by Thomas Burger (Cambridge, MA: The MIT Press, 1991), 32–33.

شورا
ДАЙТЕ ШИРОКУЮ
ДОРОГУ ЖЕНЩИНАМ ПРИ
БАЮ, КУЛАКУ, ТОРГОВЦУ, И ШАНУ И ИХ ПРИХВ

PART

V

THE SOVIET UNION

The Soviet Union was one of a cluster of new states that appeared in the aftermath of the First World War (1914–1918), when modernization, the rise of nationalism, and military defeat exacerbated deep-seated crises in the major Eurasian empires: the Austro-Hungarian, the Ottoman, and the Russian. In the 1920s, the Soviet government cast itself as the leader of international socialism and proletarian revolution, as well as the avant-garde of a new culture that rejected imperialism and colonialism as vestiges of the old regimes. But while the new Soviet government denounced the injustices of empire, the Red Army battled separatists well into the 1930s.

In the 1920s, the Soviet leadership called for each region, each people, each former colony of the Russian Empire to achieve national self-determination while at the same time contributing their efforts to the building of Soviet socialism. Under Vladimir Lenin, the government made efforts to combat the imperial legacy and what he saw as the abuses of the old regime's Russian hegemony. He developed policies for supporting regional and national cultures, providing universal education, funding local cultural institutions, and developing alphabets and standardizing languages. But despite their anti-imperial goals, these projects meant that local autonomy was increasingly defined, regulated, and coerced by the central Soviet state.

After the Civil War, the Soviet Union faced multiple crises, the first of which was economic devastation after six years of war. Acknowledging its severity, Lenin adopted what was known as the New Economic Policy, which allowed for a limited degree of free-market exchange and individual profit. After Lenin died in 1924, his more gradual economic policies were replaced by a radical project under the leadership of Joseph Stalin. In an effort to combine pragmatic with utopian goals, the First Five Year Plan (1928–1932) sought to strengthen the industrial and military might of the USSR and transform it from an agrarian economy to an industrial one. These goals reflected a fundamentally different vision for the country than that of the former empire, a vision that promised a future free of the conflicts that characterized the old regime. Alongside industrial expansion and forced collectivization of the peasantry, the pictosphere developed new visual strategies for disseminating Soviet ideological propaganda and for developing Soviet citizens into people of the future. These social, economic, and cultural developments demolished the centuries-old institutions of Russian society and brought intense social upheaval.

From 1928 to 1953, the Soviet Union was also subject to the authoritarian regime of Joseph Stalin, as General Secretary of the Communist Party. Stalin's rule brought waves of arbitrary arrests and the imprisonment and execution of citizens. Millions of Soviet citizens, primarily Ukrainians and Kazakhs, died in the famine of 1932 to 1933, a tragedy resulting from deliberate policy decisions to prioritize feeding industrial cities over the lives of the agrarian producers. Many Russians and people of other nationalities fell victim to the famine as well. Hundreds of thousands perished during the Great Purges of the late 1930s, and many more suffered in Gulag prison camps. Entire peoples came under suspicion for treason and were arrested or exiled en masse. Koreans living in the Soviet Union, Crimean Tatars, Chechens, Ingushetians, and Volga Germans, among others, were rounded up and forcibly resettled in inhospitable regions far from their homes.

Political conformity was demanded, and the arts were closely scrutinized for any form of political criticism. At the same time, within these narrow limitations, artistic creativity was still possible, and Soviet film, music, literature, and ballet were all popular forms of enlightenment and entertainment.

World War II, known in the USSR as the Great Patriotic War, was won by the Soviet Union and its allies, but at a much greater cost in lives and physical destruction than that suffered by any of the other combatants. After the war, the USSR was able to extend its borders to encompass almost all of the former Russian Empire and establish its dominance over the countries of East Central Europe. Peace brought with it the Cold War competition with the United States, two hegemonic powers fighting to expand their influence around the world.

The aligned socialist countries of Eastern Europe that made up the Soviet bloc were not formally annexed into the USSR, but they were part of an external empire perceived by its critics as colonial. They were closely watched and controlled by Moscow, so their status as fully sovereign states was limited. They constituted a kind of quasi-imperial space, but in conformity with the mid-twentieth century's commitment to national self-determination, the official narrative emphasized their voluntary and friendly union with the Soviet people.

A similar rhetoric of harmonious union circulated within the Soviet Union as well. Under Stalin, ideology and, to some extent, practice promoted an image of the Union of Soviet Socialist Republics as a manifestation of the "Friendship of Peoples." Soviet ideology espoused an ideal of Union-wide egalitarianism, or at least near-egalitarianism, with Russia poised as "first among equals." The language of equality raised possibilities antithetical to the fundamental premises of empire. Decades of shared experience of Soviet rule brought incremental standardization of Soviet citizenship, law, and lived experience, though with glaring exceptions. Wide-scale arrests and executions of national leaders preceded the Russian purges of the late 1930s, and more subtle denigration of national cultures was officially sanctioned through campaigns of homogenization, as seen in Nikolai Vakhtin's article in this book on reading primers for schoolchildren in the Arctic region. At the same time, the anti-imperial aspirations of the 1920s diminished under Stalin with the increase of authoritarian power by the central government and the equation of Russian national culture with what was deemed patriotic and genuinely Soviet.

In 1956, the First Secretary of the Communist Party, Nikita Khrushchev, gave a speech that criticized Stalin and Stalinist authoritarianism. This ushered in the period known as the Thaw (1953–1968), which was a time of unprecedented cultural and economic improvement. This period saw the rapid economic development of some of the eastern territories of the USSR: Kazakhstan, Siberia, and what was called the Far East. These projects, some stamped with a distinctly colonial aspect, required massive recruitment of workers and volunteers, which the government encouraged by campaigns promoting a new, youthful enthusiasm for building socialism. The Khrushchev period also reopened questions about the role of national leaders, and of languages and cultures within the republics. In general, central policy dictated the advancement of local leaders and encouragement of the language of the "titular" population in each republic—Uzbek in Uzbekistan, Azeribaijani in Azerbaijan—though republic-level leaders were scrutinized and cut down to size if they moved too far toward "nationalism." Renewed attention to national cultures also invited some discussion of the status of "non-titular nationalities" within the republics. Small subgroups, such as the Ingiloi or the Lezgin, found their languages and practices silenced by the dominant republican cultures, thus replicating some kinds of imperial practices or what historian Krista Goff calls "nested nationalism."[1]

Leonid Brezhnev's rise to power in 1964 began a twenty-year period of economic and social stability, which some refer to as a period of "stagnation." In foreign affairs, this was a period of alternating "détente" and "escalation" of the Cold War. Domestically, this was a period of relative stability and growth for the post-war generation, During this time, regular openings in the "Iron Curtain" that separated the Soviet Union and its allies in Eastern Europe from the rest of the world allowed access to outside ideas and consumer goods, one of the causes of the crisis and collapse of the Soviet Union in 1991. The gap between an ideology that proclaimed the success of communism and the "Friendship of Peoples" and a reality of slow economic growth and increasing discontent could no longer constrain desires for change. The rise in nationalism led to movements for independence, most fervently in Armenia, Georgia, Moldova, and the Baltic states, and helped propel the Soviet Union towards collapse.

The Soviet Union is often associated with repressive cultural policies, but our essays show that even in the most dangerous times, artists, cartographers, illustrators, and other creators of images continued to engage in illuminating self-expression and vigorous discussion about the best ways to build socialism with images. Even with the rise of Russian nationalism in the 1930s, power in the Soviet Union remained in the hands of a multiethnic leadership, and the same held true for the contributors to the Soviet pictosphere. The suppression of ethnic autonomy under Stalin, and the slogan "national in form, socialist in content," narrowed the acceptable ways of representing the peoples of the Soviet empire, but it never eradicated the government's commitment to ethnic cultural expression, nor foreclosed the possibility of multiethnic contributions to Soviet culture as a whole.

NOTE

1. Krista A. Goff, *Nested Nationalism: Making and Unmaking Nations in the Soviet Caucasus* (Ithaca, NY: Cornell University Press, 2021).

MAP 4 The Soviet Union

CHAPTER 35

PROPAGANDA IN TRANSLATION: IMAGINED MUSLIM VIEWERS OF EARLY SOVIET POSTERS (C. 1926)

MOLLIE ARBUTHNOT

AROUND 1926, a young artist of Russian heritage, Maria Nesterova, designed a poster to promote local Soviet elections (Image 35.1). It was published in Samarqand, in the Soviet Republic of Uzbekistan, and it calls on its viewers to support the Soviets; to encourage women to participate in elections; to expel wealthy landowners, merchants, and kulaks (landowning peasants); and to strengthen the union of workers and peasants. So far, so unremarkable. But Nesterova's design is both striking and unusual, and it does not look much like a typical Soviet poster of the 1920s. The stock emblems of Soviet socialism are scarce—there are no hammer-and-sickles, for instance—and its organic curves and crowded composition owe little to the minimalist, geometric aesthetic that characterized many Soviet posters of this period. It is more detailed, busier, less laconic, and more ornamental than we might expect. Why?

To answer this question, we must first ask a few more. Who was its intended audience, and why do they matter? What effect was this image supposed to have? And what, then, can this poster tell us about how the state imagined its citizenry, and attempted to communicate with its vast and diverse population, during the formative early years of Soviet power?

Visual media played a substantial role in the Soviet enlightenment project, and posters were considered particularly useful because of their wide reach and potential for both public and domestic display. One commentator wrote in 1920 that "from the very beginning, Soviet power grasped the full significance of the poster in the field of agitation and placed it in a privileged and state-sponsored position among the fine arts."[1] Widespread illiteracy, especially among the peasantry, was often cited as a reason why posters (and other visual media) were necessary educational tools. However, it was by no means certain that images could convey political messages clearly and unambiguously across cultural and class boundaries, or between the literate and illiterate. Soviet propaganda theorists were concerned that some viewers

IMAGE 35.1 Maria Nesterova (aka Maria Nesterova-Berzina), untitled poster, 1926–1927.

may struggle to "read" images. Many in the 1920s argued that legibility, therefore, was vital to the success of a propaganda poster, and that artists must take their viewers into consideration when designing an image. Theorists argued that different types of viewer required different types of image. It was commonly stated that peasants, for example, would more readily accept and understand images that drew on familiar forms of folk art, such as the popular woodcut prints known as *lubok*, rather than on urban modernism. The art critic Janos Macza argued in 1931 that "we must take into account . . . the sphere for which the poster is intended. The village needs one poster, and the city another. Donbas requires a sort that is not needed in Moscow. The same goes for the national republics."[2]

In this context, and considering the vast cultural, linguistic, and ethnic diversity of the population that the Soviet Union had inherited from the Russian Empire, it's unsurprising that national differences were also taken into account by propaganda theorists. They argued that different groups of people had differing visual cultures—that they were used to creating and looking at different kinds of art—and that this fundamentally affected their ability to process images: the cultural identity of the viewer determined their way of seeing. We must note that this was a primarily Russophone, urban, elite discourse *about* rural, "backward" (in the terminology of the time), and non-Russian audiences. Its inherent biases are manifold. However, this is the context in which propaganda theory was developed and posters were produced in the Soviet Union during the 1920s, and so this discourse must frame our understanding of these images.

Theorists in this period, therefore, advocated a cultural-relativist approach to viewership. They argued that in order to convey the correct political message in a way that would be understood by the viewer, and in order to have the desired transformative effect on them, poster designs had to be targeted at a specific group of viewers and engage with their preexisting visual culture. An anonymous article published in Tashkent in 1922, for instance, alleged that "one must remember that the psychology of artistic perception and creation amongst the Muslim population is completely different from the European in its most basic principles."[3] One-size-fits-all images were criticized for being incomprehensible in the villages and non-Russian regions. (This also complemented Soviet nation-building policy at the time: logically, if the nascent Soviet nationalities required their own national literatures, languages, and governing elites, then so, too, did they require national artists, visual art, and propaganda.) Artists were encouraged to adapt elements of national or local art and craft traditions in their posters.

To return to Nesterova's poster, we might then assume that its composition and style are so unusual because this image was not intended for a Muscovite viewer, as many more famous posters were. But who exactly were the imagined viewers of this poster, and how were they imagined? By "imagined viewers" I do not mean actual people who may have seen this image at the time of its publication, but how poster producers—publishers and commissioners as well as artists—conceptualized their target audience. I suggest that the viewer of this poster was imagined through ideas about Islamic art and the prism of Muslimness as a quasi-national, as opposed to a strictly religious, category.

In particular, this poster seems to have been based on the printed Tatar *shamail*. The term *shamail* encompasses a wide range of decorative prints and panels, usually calligraphic, and primarily religious in content (often centered on quotations from the Qur'an or the Hadiths), which could be hand-painted on paper or glass or mass-printed as lithographs. These lithographic *shamails* are the ones that, in my view, served as a model for Nesterova's Soviet poster. Such mass-produced prints were widespread in the late nineteenth and early twentieth centuries and "can be regarded as a form of Islamic printed posters."[4] There were several established *shamail* painters in Kazan, and large numbers of lithographs for domestic display were produced there by local typographies, the most prolific of which was the Karimov Brothers' Printing House (1900–1919), which, alongside other printing houses, "issued enormous runs of *shamails* on paper, which were distributed widely, far beyond the regions inhabited by Tatars."[5] Private publishing and the sale of non-Bolshevik-printed material were severely limited by decrees of October 1917 and April–May 1919, making it unlikely that any *shamails* were printed after the October Revolution (it's unclear whether they continued to be made by hand). In any case, there was nothing to stop people from continuing to display prints they already owned. Ethnographer Nikolai Vorob'ev wrote in 1930 that, in the Middle Volga region, "at the present time . . . in the villages they are widespread from the middling-peasant upwards. Most often one sees a *shamail* above the entranceway, summoning peace and good fortune on the house."[6]

One notable feature of the *shamail* is its use of multiple framing devices: small pictures and framed blocks of text set within the larger composition. Often, this entailed having one central, focal image surrounded by a symmetrical arrangement of decorative borders and small, self-contained sections (pictographic or calligraphic). For example, one print depicts Mount Ararat within an oval in the center of the composition, beneath a scroll bearing the Shahadah (the creed "I bear witness that there is no deity but God, and that Muhammad is the messenger of God"), and surrounded by sections of poetry, Qur'anic quotes, and texts about Mount Ararat in the life of the Prophet Muhammed, each in a differently colored and shaped frame (Image 35.2). The same principles of symmetry and the use of multiple frames can be seen in the 1908 print *The Names of the Four Righteous Caliphs* (Image 35.3). Comparing the compositions of these images with our poster, we can see that Nesterova employed

IMAGE 35.2 Unknown artist, *Mount Ararat*, c. 1900–1920.

IMAGE 35.3 Unknown artist, *The Names of the Four Righteous Caliphs*, 1908.

similar structural elements, including the broad bands of color leading up to and framing the two figures standing in front of a building labelled "Soviet" (*sho'ro*), the central focal point.

This poster has an extremely crowded composition, far from the laconic minimalism recommended for urban posters, and the use of architectural motifs is also typical of *shamails*. The central Soviet building, with domed roof and pointed windows, looks not unlike some of the mosques and other buildings of religious significance depicted in Tatar prints. That the artist has depicted the Soviet building in this manner, rather than using European modernist architecture to connote the new, postrevolutionary world, suggests that she intentionally mimicked *shamail* tropes. In the upper corners are two cooperative buildings, one urban and one rural, connected by an illustration of the *smychka* (literally "connection" or "alliance," referring to the comradely partnership of proletariat and poor peasantry under the New Economic Policy). A procession of cart- and camel-loads of produce travel from village to factory, while tractors and goods trucks go in the opposite direction, all contained within a graceful, curved band of yellow: a bustle of industry and the onward march of progress—there is even an airplane gliding above. The visual similarity between this section and the curved scroll atop the Mount Ararat print is self-evident and suggests a conscious act of borrowing. In addition, a large part of the composition is taken up by text. This way of incorporating calligraphy into the design for decorative effect is also drawn from *shamail*, although Nesterova has Sovietized the Islamic associations of the visual language. The central slogans, in white lettering on a red background, are not written on a blank geometric space, nor on a ribbon or scroll, but on revolutionary red banners held up by the crowd underneath. This poster is, in my opinion, the most clear and complete example of an attempt to adapt the aesthetics of the *shamail* to the purposes of Soviet propaganda.

That Soviet poster artists took inspiration from an eclectic assortment of visual sources is well known, as is their appropriation of religious symbolism, particularly that of the Christian Orthodox icon. Bolshevik theorists were highly aware of the symbolic potency of icons, a power they consciously sought to harness. Art historian Aleksei Sidorov, for instance, in 1922 described the poster as a "contemporary icon."[7] Poster artists borrowed aspects of the visual language of Orthodox imagery, including color symbolism (particularly the holy connotations of red), images of the saints, and compositions familiar from well-known icons. Some examples, such as Vladimir Fidman's *All Hail the Red Army* (1920), demonstrate a direct and overt transfer of symbolic language from religious to political imagery.[8] The use of Islamic objects as models for posters has attracted less scholarly attention, but Nesterova's poster demonstrates that the *shamail* was used to produce propaganda images with an eye to legibility among a Muslim viewership in an analogous manner. Like the *lubok* and Orthodox icon, the *shamail* was intended for domestic display as an accessible devotional and decorative object for the masses of the faithful. Unlike many of the diverse—and often, in fact, secular—objects that Western (including Soviet) art historians have grouped together under the baggy category of "Islamic art," *shamails* are unambiguously religious. Their main subject was the text of the Qur'an or the Hadiths, and they were intended to confer blessing or aid prayer. The tradition of displaying *shamails* thus also served as an example of a significant object within the home, embodying a material connection between daily life and a higher meaning—a model that Soviet propagandists aimed to imitate. In this context, it is easy to see why they may have seemed an appealing template for Soviet propagandists and poster artists when addressing an imagined Muslim viewership.

It is not certain how popular printed Tatar *shamails* really were in early twentieth-century Uzbekistan. However, to appropriate the visual language of the *shamail* in order to make political posters for a Muslim viewership in Uzbekistan reveals how the Soviet state—or, perhaps, its Russophone administrators in Central Asia—conceptualized its non-Russian citizens. It reveals an assumption of commonality between the diverse Muslim populations of the former Russian Empire. Although "Muslim" was not an official Soviet nationality, Muslimness remained a point of reference for the Central Asian republics. Ethnographic studies at this time alleged that Islam was unusually deeply embedded in Central Asian life, and that art and handicraft traditions—themselves framed as Islamic—as well as religiosity were ingrained in the self-identity and cultural worldview of the Muslim population. Propagandists could justify using the Tatar *shamail*, associated with Kazan, as the model for a poster intended for the Samarqand region, several thousand kilometers away, on the basis that its visual language would apparently be legible and its religious connotations appealing to an Uzbek Muslim viewer, and could do so without overly concerning themselves with the specific origins or authenticity of the form. Images such as our poster point to a contradiction in the early Soviet period between the idea of a specifically Uzbek *national* art and an Orientalist assumption of a shared visual culture between disparate Muslim peoples. Islamic art, like national art, was a capacious and flexible category, and it was freely raided in the search for a new visual language.

Although posters for an imagined Muslim viewership appropriated various elements of Islamic art, they inevitably altered them in the process. The most obvious difference between the visual language of Nesterova's poster and *shamail* prints is the inclusion of human figures. Crowds of workers and peasants, men and women, file up symmetrical staircases towards the Soviet building, while the two central, outsized figures fling an assortment of enemies—wealthy landowners (*boylar*), merchants, kulaks, clerics, and their followers—into the abyss. No Tatar *shamail* depicts human figures. The discourse surrounding Islamic art in Soviet Central Asia in the 1920s was varied and contradictory, and while many argued that it must play a central role in the creation of new Soviet national cultures, aniconism—opposition to depicting living beings—was widely cited as one of the ways that cultish backwardness had directly impeded artistic development. With a heavy dose of Eurocentrism, Soviet commentators afforded figurative painting a privileged status and were near unanimous that *progress*, in Central Asian art, lay in the direction of figurativism. Few Soviet posters omit human figures. Thus, even while theorists argued that visual cultures and "ways of seeing" were culturally contingent, and artists accordingly appropriated elements of national artistic heritage for propaganda purposes, there were clear limits to Soviet cultural relativism.

In addition, considering this poster as a material object as opposed to merely an image gives us further clues to its function in the Soviet propaganda network and its place at the intercultural frontier of enlightenment projects in the Soviet periphery. The text is exclusively in Uzbek, but the example held at the State Archive of the Russian Federation, reproduced here, also has Russian translations handwritten on separate pieces of paper and stuck on to the poster surface. These are of uncertain date, and there is no space intentionally left for this in the design. However, it would be reasonable to surmise that they were put here soon after the poster's publication, when it was used in the 1926–1927 local election campaigns. This was one of the first substantive propaganda campaigns in Soviet Uzbekistan, and it entailed unprecedented cooperation between local party cells and central authorities, which was often hindered by miscommunication. The campaign organization even employed "explainers" to clarify the meaning of the posters to local viewers. In the Xorazm region, this was done by "members of Party and professional organizations," while in the Tashkent region, the role was taken by "members of the local intelligentsia."[9] The Russian captions, added as an afterthought to our poster, hint at the transcultural context in which it was first used.

A reading of Nesterova's poster thus reveals some of the complexities and contradictions of visual propaganda in the Soviet periphery. The dynamics of how religious, local, and transnational artistic traditions were included or excluded from the national culture of Soviet Uzbekistan, and how their forms were adapted, secularized, and appropriated for propaganda purposes, are too complex to be fully addressed in a short essay. However, this poster is a striking example of how preexisting visual art and handicraft traditions could constitute a usable past for constructing Soviet national cultures, and how such traditions could be instrumentalized to support Soviet political aims. It reveals, too, that the transcultural context of Soviet enlightenment projects had a significant impact on the development of early Soviet culture, in which we can see the roots of a tension between reinforcing (or creating) distinct national cultures and an attempt to create the pan-Soviet, socialist subject of the future.

NOTES

1. A. Vilenkin, "Vokrug iskusstva. K vystavke agitatsionnogo plakata," *Krasnyi mir* 231 (3 October 1920), 2. Cited in Klaus Waschik and Nina Baburina, *Real'nost' utopii: Iskusstvo russkogo plakata XX veka* (Moscow: Progress-Traditsiia, 2004), 84.
2. Janos Macza (aka Ivan Matsa), "Vstupitel'noe slovo," in *Za bol'shevistskii plakat: Zadachi izoiskusstva v sviazi s resheniem TsKVKP(b) o plakatnoi literature* (Moscow and Leningrad: Ogiz-Izogiz, 1932), 18.
3. "Zadachi khudozhestvennogo obrazovaniia v Turkestane," *Otkliki: zhurnal literatury i iskusstva (Organ khudozhestvennogo otdela Turkglavpolitprosveta)* 1 (January 1922): 11.
4. Igor Alekseev and Aidar Habutdinov, "Islam i ego mir v tatarskikh shamailiakh XIX–XXI vv.," in *Tatarskii shamail': traditsiia i sovremennost'*, edited by Maria Filatova and Igor Alekseev (Moscow: Mardjani, 2015), 9.
5. Nikolai Vorob'ev, *Material'naia kul'tura kazanskikh tatar (opyt etnograficheskogo issledovaniia)* (Kazan': Dom Tatarskoi kul'tury, 1930), 247.
6. Vorob'ev, *Material'naia kul'tura*, 247.
7. Aleksei Sidorov, "Iskusstvo plakata," *Gorn* 2 (1922): 125.
8. This poster can be viewed online via the digitized private collection of Sergo Grigorian, http://redavantgarde.com/collection/show-collection/1014-glory-to-the-red-army-.html?styleId=5
9. State Archive of the Russian Federation (GARF), Collection of the USSR Central Executive Committee and its Subordinate Institutions, fond P-3316, op. 48, no. 85, folios 7, 68.

CHAPTER 36

TWO LAWS: THE IMAGE OF THE TUNGUS IN SOVIET DREAMWORLDS (1920s)

CRAIG CAMPBELL

TUNGUS FROM THE KHENYCHAR is a silent fiction film produced in Soviet Siberia barely a decade after the 1917 Revolution (Image 36.1). The film was shot on location in 1928 around the village of Turukhansk at the confluence of the Lower Tunguska River and the great, north-flowing Yenisei River in an area occupied by Indigenous Evenki and Ket peoples. The cultural-historical importance of this film from the northern forests of central Siberia rests in its description of a very particular kind of encounter between the Soviet state and Indigenous peoples. The film constitutes one of the first examples of the state's efforts to construct a narrative about the socialist salvation of Indigenous peoples. This period in Soviet Siberia can be characterized as a time of great hope, development, change, terror, and trauma. In cities like Novosibirsk, rural villages like Turukhansk, and in the vast boreal forest known as the taiga, the force and presence of Soviet rule was rapidly increasing. The encroaching apparatus that generated a socialist way of looking at and representing the world was inescapable, even along the paths used by Indigenous Siberians to travel between one nomadic camp and another, located far away from Russian settlements or trading posts.

In the mid-2000s, while doing research on the postrevolutionary history of the central Siberian North, I came across a film script titled *Two Laws* (*Dva Zakona*) in the Novosibirsk State Archives. Alongside the script was a two-page protocol on the subject of "Filmmaking in the North." The document was originally prepared and presented in 1928 at a general meeting of a special committee tasked with developing socialism among Indigenous peoples in the arctic and subarctic regions of Siberia. *Two Laws* was tied to the film studio Kinosibir, which operated from 1925 to 1930.[1] It was touted by the writer M. A. Nikitin as the first professional film studio beyond the Urals.[2] In 1928, Manuel Bolshintsov, a young filmmaker trained in Rostov, was hired by Kinosibir. He turned his screenplay *Two Laws* into the film *Tungus from the Khenychar*. The film was a remarkable endeavor that followed the

IMAGE 36.1 A still from *Tungus from the Khenychar*, Studio Kinosibir, 1929.

preoccupations of Soviet socialism and state-building into the territory of the Siberian taiga. Under the direction of Bolshintsov, it projected a fantastical morality and hopeful futurity onto the bodies of the "Tungus" people. While Tungus in this film were named, they were also meant to stand in, in the cinematic imaginary, for all Indigenous peoples of the Soviet North. Across the Soviet Union there were more than forty Indigenous groups speaking different languages, with widely differing cultural practices, histories, and economies, but their generalized otherness to Russian and European modernity was mostly all that mattered. While "Tungus," in the context of the screenplay and film, referred to people who are now known as Evenkis, in many ways one Indigenous person could represent any of them in the dominant imaginary. Today, Evenkis, as well as other Indigenous peoples, continue to live and struggle for recognition and legal rights in the Russian Federation.

While *Tungus from the Khenychar* circulated internationally, there are no remaining copies, and it is assumed to be lost, like so many other films from this era. Nonetheless, the screenplay, along with a few reviews and descriptive accounts, gives us a good sense of the film. These impressions are augmented by a handful of photographic outtakes and journal illustrations. *Tungus from the Khenychar* played in Novosibirsk and Moscow, but it is not clear if this silent film was ever projected in the tent cinemas or newly built culture clubs of remote regions where it could have been seen by the so-called "native masses." Scattered accounts of the film were published in the journal *Soviet Screen* (*Sovetskii Ekran*) and elsewhere.[3]

The film was circulated in Germany as *The Law of the Taiga* (*Das Gesetz der Taiga*) and in France as *The Law that Rules* (*La Loi Qui Commande*). In the United States, *Tungus from the Khenychar* was reviewed in the *New York Times* as well as by *Time* magazine. In the socialist publication *New Masses*, Samuel Brody wrote of the film that

> its ethnographic and political implications are beyond criticism, while some very original mounting make it a film which holds you throughout its length. There is something which defies words of description in these Soviet films dealing with the formerly oppressed national minorities and the new relationships created by the Revolution. They are the epics of the rise of unknown peoples. They are immortal documents of Communism's struggle to restore backward and downtrodden sections of man-kind.[4]

The seven-act screenplay *Two Laws* begins with an evocative description of the northern forest, the taiga: "Century-old trees bend and sway. The treetops are swinging in the wind rhythmically." The drama opens with a failed shamanic healing ceremony in the taiga, far away from "civilization." An elderly Tungus man dies of his sickness, the unscrupulous Shaman nonetheless takes his payment from the impoverished, grieving family and leaves. A title card states: "THE TUNGUS GAVE ALMOST ALL HIS SAVINGS TO THE SHAMAN." The shaman, like the priest, rabbi, and imam, became one of the communists' great enemies. They were seen to be not only mystics, but also respected figures who commanded power threatening to the state's legitimacy.

The following action unfolds:

> The Shaman drives away from the yurt on a reindeer sled. The family stays outside the yurt.
>
> Three of them.
>
> The dead body looks out from the hollow of the tent.
>
> The Shaman is already far away. The wife and child are inside the yurt, but the Tungus stays and stares after the shaman.
>
> The face of the Tungus.
>
> He's deciding something,
>
> he enters the yurt quickly, approaches his wife, who is busy by the fireplace, and says to her:
>
> > WE NEED TO LEAVE THIS PLACE
> > IT'S NOT GOOD
>
> The wife looks at him. Bows her head obediently and gets up. They are facing one another, looking at each other, thinking about something.

In casual stage direction like this we see cultural impositions and the roots of ethnocultural ventriloquism. Were Evenki women "obedient" to men in this particular way? Certainly, this is not my experience as an ethnographer, though the gender dynamics of Evenki society in the 1920s were quite possibly different. The anthropologist Nikolai Ssorin-Chaikov offers a careful reading of Evenki gender relations as they were seen (and often misunderstood) throughout the Soviet and early post-Soviet era.[5] Nonetheless, this observation serves as an example of how the screenplay, authored by a Russian man with explicitly socialist politics, presents patterns of cultural behavior that Indigenous actors were then required to enact, turning themselves into cyphers for non-Indigenous expressions and ideologies.

In the second act, the family is confronted with an imposing and powerful fur trader, known in revolutionary parlance as a kulak. The kulak cheats them out of their last remaining stores and refuses to share his goods, even though the Tungus and his family are in need of food. We learn that the Tungus hero has a dream of Lenin and his redistributive laws. The Tungus later meets a group of Russians on a geological expedition. They befriend one another, and the Tungus expresses how he anticipates the coming of Lenin's law, hoping that these explorers will bestow on him "paper" that will give him hunting rights to the land he is on.

The geologists, who represent rationality and progress and an ideal of Russian intellectual masculinity, don't understand why the Tungus hunter doesn't help himself to food in an unguarded, raised cache belonging to the wealthy and selfish trader (who is identified in one review of the film as being ethnically Russian). The Tungus explains it is the "law of the taiga," and that he simply cannot take what is not his. Eventually, the geologists give him a piece of paper declaring that he has a right to the stores under "Lenin's law."[6] Armed with this new warrant, the Tungus crosses the legal boundary that is as invisible as it is tangible and takes the food to feed his family. In doing this, he undertakes a revolutionary act of redistribution. When the wealthy and greedy trader discovers this appropriation, he accuses the Tungus hero of theft and tries to kill him. Ultimately, the trader is not strong enough to overtake the Tungus hero, and decides to appeal to the head of the local outpost. After some tense moments where the Tungus hero is arrested, it is ultimately decided that the Tungus was legally entitled to take the stores and defend himself against the hunter. The film ends with a group of Evenki driving their reindeer down a path and singing:

> THE BIG TENT (*CHUM*)[7]
>
> IN THE TENT THE COURAGEOUS HERO (*BOGATYR*)[8] LENIN LIVES
>
> HE GIVES THE DEER TO THE POOR
>
> AND STAMPS HIS FOOT ON THE RICH

Two Laws, the screenplay, was based on a story by Mikhail A. Nikitin called *Khenychar River* (*Khenychar Reka*). Historians Tatiana Kuzmenko and Irina Maksimova (2019) have recently shown that Nikitin's original story of an encounter between Russians and Indigenous peoples relied on Russian representational conventions, and that it was not until the film's production that Indigenous people were able to insert some of their own agency into the project. The French film scholar Caroline Damiens has similarly noted how Indigenous participation in filmmaking needs to complicate how we understand authorship.[9] Nonetheless, as far as the screenplay is concerned, Evenkis only appear through representational practices and conventions of Russian authors.

Following the 1917 October Revolution, Bolsheviks—and others who fantasized about emancipatory politics, socialism, and change—organized rapidly to consolidate power and build durable institutions. While the violence of the Civil War flared across Siberia, the Bolsheviks demonstrated exceptional organization, appropriating the bureaucratic infrastructures of Imperial Russia and then transforming and reinvesting them with new purpose and direction. By the mid-1920s, with the Civil War successfully at an end and Soviet power firmly entrenched, local administrative outposts were established in most remote locations, and government inspectors were sent to report on the state of the postrevolutionary taiga. In this era of the New Economic Policy (1921–1928), Siberia was increasingly recognized as a vast bank of natural wealth, essential to the success and prosperity of the Soviet future.

Of particular concern for some socialist activists in the Siberian North was the state of the Indigenous minorities. Indigenous minorities of the North, Siberia, and the Russian Far East presented a uniquely challenging opportunity for Soviet socialism beyond simply "'reimagining' the former Russian Empire as a socialist federation of nationalities."[10] The Soviet Union aimed to actively create a new polity and a new, enlightened, socialist population, of which the Siberian Indigenous peoples were to be a part. One element of this process of invention was the classification of Soviet citizens according to reconfigured nationality labels and the production of a new category of Indigenous minorities ("Small Numbered Peoples of the North"). Under this configuration, for example, the ethnonyms Evenki and Eveni would replace the old name: Tungus. This is one of the ways in which the state's perception of the taiga was beginning to take shape, the way the state learned to see and the way it developed a grammar of rule. Walter Benjamin's concept of the "dreamworld" as developed by Susan Buck-Morss is a particularly useful analytic for appreciating the particularities of Soviet modernity and the expressions of a utopian desire for social arrangements that would transcend existing forms.[11]

What kind of reality did *Tungus from the Khenychar* mediate, and whose dreamworld did it work to support? The collective dream of Soviet socialism was increasingly forced upon all peoples in the USSR, including those in the Yenisei North. On the one hand, the screenplay *Two Laws* tells us about Soviet mentalities projected onto the bodies of Indigenous peoples—in particular about the kind of class consciousness and antagonism presumed necessary for building socialism. On the other, it allows us to speculate on the frames through which Evenkis and other Indigenous peoples were coming to know and negotiate the new, industrializing world of Soviet socialism. While it is possible that the film never was seen by Evenkis, that seems unlikely. It was, after all, an explicit aim of Soviet culture workers to expose Indigenous peoples to educational materials. There were Evenkis among the named actors, including the lead, Kevebul Kima.[12] The film had a clear antishaman, antikulak, pro-Soviet message for Indigenous peoples of Siberia. Quite likely, it was projected in newly built cultural clubs, schools, or itinerant agitational tent cinemas across Siberia. And yet there is an unfortunate silence around the Indigenous reception of this film. There are no memoirs from the Evenki actors, and no reviews from the perspective of Indigenous peoples.

Rather than being mere symbols of ethnic difference or people on the brink of disappearing (as they were treated in most of the Americas), Indigenous Siberians were declared by the state to be ethnic nations on the road to modernity.[13] The scripts for their becoming modern were largely manufactured by Soviet planners and bureaucrats.[14] As with all other nations in the Soviet Union, the Indigenous Small Numbered Peoples of the North were expected to participate in and submit to the Soviet project, to be seen and to see themselves being seen.

Two Laws describes a dreamworld of socialist encounter. Its realism is founded upon common parables that simplify a dualism of the oppressors and the oppressed. This narrative reproduces the Revolution's founding mythology and moral frame. In many ways, *Two Laws* is just another retelling of a well-developed socialist narrative with a thinly painted veneer of national culture. The expressed gratitude of oppressed peoples for their salvation or liberation by Lenin had become a manufactured trope of popular culture with clearly political goals. Each expression of gratitude helped to legitimize and burnish Soviet socialism as a truly multicultural and internationalist project. The moral ground of the revolutionary project is also that which most significantly complicates this story. It would be argued by Soviet philosophers and ethnographers that after the Revolution, with considerable help from their European comrades, Indigenous peoples in Siberia had bypassed capitalism and passed from the socio-evolutionary stage of "primitive communism" to "socialism."[15] In other words, there was baked into the liberation narrative another narrative about Indigeneity and alterity (difference).

The central problem presented by the film is the inadequacy of the law of the taiga to deliver justice. This was a problem for which Soviet socialism was presented as the solution. The *New York Times* reviewer wrote: "There is a bit of propaganda, if it may be called that, in favor of Russia's kindness toward her subjects. Some pictorial cheering shows that the Soviets are neglecting no corner of their immense domain."[16] The narrative of Indigenous liberation obscures Indigenous alterity. What the reviewer from the *Times* witnessed in the film was a dramatic theme, but it was a dramatic theme that relied on ventriloquism. Scholars need to look more carefully at the way the ventriloquism performs an erasure of Evenki alterity. This alterity is marked by ontological difference—that is, Evenkis had their own world view, their own way of understanding what the world is and what the world is about, of understanding social relations among not just humans but among a more-than-human world. Through *Two Laws'* ventriloquism, a sleight of hand is performed, and an erasure is enacted, prefiguring the great domestication of cultural difference in Stalin's nationalities policy.

NOTES

1. Liudmila Kuzmenkina, "Vzlet i padenie 'Kinosibiri,'" *Vechernii Novosibirsk*, January 11, 2007, https://vn.ru/news-83274
2. M. A. Nikitin quoted in Krasnoiarskaia Kraevaia nauchnaia biblioteka and Kraevushka, "2033. *Put' na sever vmeste s pisatelem Mikhailom Nikiktinim, ili s"emki kino v Turukhanske v 1928*" [Journey to the North Together with Writer Mikhail Nikitin, or Filming in Turukhansk in 1928] *LiveJournal*, May 2, 2016, https://kraevushka.livejournal.com/592752.html
3. *Sovetskii ekran* 1929: 12 and 23.
4. Samuel Brody, "*The Law of the Siberian Taiga*, A Kinosibir Production, USSR Shown at the Cameo Theatre, New York," *New Masses* 6, no. 4 (September 1930): 14.
5. Nikolai Ssorin-Chaikov, "Mothering Tradition: gender and governance among Siberian Evenki." *Max Planck Institute for Social Anthropology Working Papers* 45 (2002): 1–40.
6. T. A. Kuz'menko and I. E. Maksimova, "Kuda argishil 'Tungus s Khenychara': peripetii odnogo literaturnogo siuzheta," *Vestnik Tomskogo Gosudarstvennogo Universiteta. Kul'turologiia i Iskusstvovedeniia* 33 (2019): 253–273.
7. *Chum* is the Russian term for a conical tent. Often, the term *yurt* is used interchangeably (and incorrectly). Evenki peoples call their conical tents *diu*.
8. A *bogatyr* is a folkloric Slavic character who is a courageous hero. See Chapter 29 in this volume.
9. Caroline Damiens, "Incarnation de l'ethnicité à l'écran et politique du casting: l'exemple du cinéma soviétique," *Mise au point. Cahiers de l'association française des enseignants et chercheurs en cinéma et audiovisuel*, no. 12 (2019): 50–63.
10. Francine Hirsch, "The Soviet Union as a Work-in-Progress: Ethnographers and the Category Nationality in the 1926, 1937, and 1939 Censuses," *Slavic Review* 56, no. 2 (1997): 251–278.
11. Susan Buck-Morss, *Dreamworld and Catastrophe: The Passing of Mass Utopia in East and West* (Cambridge, MA: MIT Press, 2000).
12. Yuri Klitsenko, "Traditsii prazdnika Ikonipko v kino: iz istorii s"emok fil'ma «Mstitel'»," *Sibirskaia Zaimka*, 2012, http://zaimka.ru/klitsenko-ikonipko
13. Alexia Bloch, "Longing for the Kollektiv: Gender, Power, and Residential Schools in Central Siberia," *Cultural Anthropology* 20, no. 4 (2005): 534–569.
14. Craig A. R. Campbell, *Agitating Images: Photography against History in Indigenous Siberia*. (Minneapolis: University of Minnesota Press, 2014).
15. M. A. Sergeyev, "The Building of Socialism among the Peoples of Northern Siberia and the Soviet Far East," in *The Peoples of Siberia*, edited by L. P. Potapov and M. G. Levin (Chicago: University of Chicago Press, 1964) 487–510.
16. Anonymous. "A Tense Russian Drama: Kevebul-Kima Excels as Hero of 'Law of the Siberian Taiga,' Other Photoplays," *The New York Times*, July 28, 1930, sec. Archives.

CHAPTER 37

VIEWS FROM THE ROOF OF THE WORLD: 1920s SOVIET FILM EXPEDITIONS TO THE PAMIR MOUNTAINS

OKSANA SARKISOVA

BEGINNING IN THE MID-1920s, the newly established state film studios sent expeditions across the Soviet Union to record diverse territories and nationalities. The resulting films were often not financially profitable, but they were considered an important cultural and political tool for introducing the diversity of the new state, its peoples, and resources to audiences, as well as for strengthening viewers' sense of belonging, ownership, and loyalty to the new motherland.

The Soviet state was established as a multinational federation, imagined and propagated as a union of nationalities "breaking out" from the imperial "prison of nations." In addition to providing geographic and ethnographic knowledge about spaces and peoples, expedition films were expected to advocate that different nationalities "belong to" and "benefit from" being part of the Soviet Union. Shot on location, without props or professional actors, they were referred to as *kulturfilms* (culture films) at the time of their production. The Soviet film industry borrowed this notion from Germany, where the term stood for "edifying" cinematic representations and was widely used before the genre of "documentary" had been established. *Kulturfilms* aimed at supplying new knowledge and shaping the audience's ideas about the world. Today, some of these early Soviet *kulturfilms* can be found in the Russian State Documentary Film and Photo Film Archive, where they are classified first and foremost as documentaries and as such seen as authentic representations of pro-filmic social reality.[1] Analyzing them as visual sources, however, requires an awareness of the historical and ideological context of their production and the multiplicity of functions they performed.

Soviet filmmakers were commissioned to show diverse Soviet territories as part of a single political union, "conquering" space by cinematic means.[2] The first crews sent to the Pamir Mountains, also known as the "Roof of the World," came from the

Moscow-based film studios. The journey involved crossing not only many kilometers, but several newly established administrative units. The core of the Pamir Mountains lies primarily in the Gorno-Badakhshan Province of Tajikistan. In 1924, the Pamirs were made part of the Tajik Autonomous Republic, which was still part of the Uzbek Soviet Socialist Republic. In 1929, another administrative reform elevated Tajikistan to the standing of Republic in its own right.[3] As a result, the Pamirs constituted a true borderland space both within the Soviet state and also internationally, joining the Tian Shan Mountains along the Alay Valley (in the then Kyrgyz Autonomous Soviet Socialist Republic, at that point part of the Russian Soviet Federative Socialist Republic), stretching south to the Hindu Kush Mountains in Afghanistan, and extending to China's Kongur Tagh in the east.

With the creation of new administrative borders in Central Asia came ethnonational classifications, which were applied to people who did not necessarily define themselves in these categories. As Arne Haugen put it, "Even though the group labels 'Uzbek' and 'Tajik' were given priority in the 1920s and made the basis for the reorganization of Central Asia, they did not refer to groups that could easily be traced back in time, not even for a rather limited number of years."[4] The urban population of Central Asia was multilingual, and many people had mixed identities or identified themselves as Sarts (sedentary Turkic and Iranian speakers), a demographic category that was abandoned altogether in the 1926 Soviet census when those who identified as Sarts were mostly registered as Uzbeks. Soviet ethnographers remained divided, however, on how to define the Tajik: as "a non-nomadic Muslim, regardless of language," or as "a person who spoke a dialect of the Farsi language, regardless of religion."[5] The peoples of the Pamirs spoke various Iranian languages, and most were registered as Tajik in the Soviet classificatory system.[6]

Kulturfilms helped to visualize and naturalize the abstract categories of nationality and territorial belonging, and they did it in a variety of ways. To exemplify the workings of ideology in "non-fiction" visual works and to explore a range of visual and ideological conventions available to the filmmakers in the early Soviet period, I compare the two cinematic travelogues about the Pamir Mountains that were made in 1928. Released by Moscow studios as *Roof of the World* (Sovkino studio) and *At the Foothills of Death* (Mezhrabpomfilm studio), they were made by film crews external to and not familiar with the region they filmed. By comparing their representations of the Pamir Mountains, we can better understand how Soviet cinema framed culturally heterogeneous local communities, appropriating space both culturally and politically through visual means while preserving the illusion of impartial observation. The following analysis highlights points of convergence and divergence in the two works' narrative structure, camera work, and editing. The juxtaposition foregrounds alternative ways of representing ethnic diversity and highlights long-term imperial legacies in imagining the Pamirs as a borderland territory.

ROOF OF THE WORLD

In the summer of 1927, the Sovkino studio and the Geological Committee sent a joint expedition to the Pamirs. It was the first time that a Soviet film crew—director Vladimir Erofeev and cameraman Vasily Beliaev—had traversed this mountainous area close to Afghanistan, India, and China. The film crew travelled with a team of natural scientists who studied the area's resources. For Erofeev, who had made one compilation film before, it was his first "real" cine-expedition. This enthusiast of *kulturfilm* and promoter of expedition films had previously been a journalist, an active creator of the Association of Revolutionary Cinema, and a co-director of the montage travelogue *Beyond the Arctic Circle* (1927), which repurposed Fedor Bremer's footage from his 1913 travels to the Russian Far North.[7]

Given the paucity of knowledge about the region among people in the rest of the country, the *Roof of the World* presented an authoritative image of the Pamirs to its viewers. An animated map framed and guided the cinematic narrative, marking distances, geographic locations, and the expedition's progress. The film relied on this cartographic authority to orient the audience, emphasize the "documentary" status of the footage, and secure territorial rights. *Roof of the World* combined the motif of spatial exploration with attentive observation of ethnically defined cultural practices. It cut across culturally heterogeneous spaces and communities, showing their cultural practices as "archaic." The film introduced mountaineer Kyrgyz and sedentary Tajiks as the Pamir dwellers, divided by their lifestyles but contributing to a complex communication network in the borderland space. This is indicative of the official Soviet nationality policy, which, as Francine Hirsch has argued, "should be understood as a manifestation of the Soviet regime's attempts to define a new (and presumably non-imperialistic) model of colonization."[8]

The cinematic journey began in the town of Osh and proceeded across the Alay Valley to the Western Pamirs. While showing spectacular mountainous vistas, waterfalls, glaciers, gorges, and blooming valleys, *Roof of the World* emphasized a long history of connection and communication across a culturally heterogeneous space. Erofeev stressed the centuries-old human presence in the area by zooming in on ancient rock paintings, the ruins of an old fortress, and ancient pagan sanctuaries. Like the locals, the film crew made use of the shaky handmade hanging bridges and wooden ladders to cross the mountainous passages. They followed narrow, rocky paths to explore economic and cultural contacts across the Pamirs.

The camera combined topographic and cinematographic reconnaissance with a detailed examination of the lifestyles of the Kyrgyz and the Tajiks. Nomadic practices, such as tent construction, animal herding, the making of dairy products, and other gendered tasks were filmed in long and medium shots with occasional close-ups, utilizing ethnographic observation over dramatization. The expedition crew was filmed setting up a mobile medical station, and attributed endemic illnesses, such as trachoma and syphilis to a "wrong" lifestyle, thus advocating for state control over bodily hygiene—a prerequisite of the modern Soviet identity.[9] Filmed medical check-ups further served to demonstrate the benevolent care of the new authorities, and facilitated the claim of "civilizational superiority."

The crew also filmed the towns in the Pamirs. Among them was Murghob (then known as Murgab), established in the late nineteenth century as an imperial military outpost and described by the Swedish traveler Sven Hedin as a "little outlying fragment of mighty Russia."[10] *Roof of the World* avoided references to imperial military presence, and instead showed Murghob as a lively commercial center where the Pamiri people came into contact with merchants from Kashgar as well as the expanding Soviet network of cooperatives. Borderland trading practices included cross-border smuggling, and Erofeev re-enacted an episode of opium smoking, for which he paid a local smuggler to procure opium from Afghanistan.[11]

Unlike most Soviet expedition films, *Roof of the World* did not end with showing the Soviet-era changes, and even downplayed the motif of political transformation, which makes it stand out among the self-congratulatory cinematic accounts produced by the Soviet film studios. Rather, the film continued with a harvest festival in a Western Pamir village, where wrestling, a partridge fight, and local dances were recorded. Throughout the film, however, Erofeev's account visually unified the Tajiks into a single, sedentary *ethnie* within the Soviet classificatory system, reinforcing the new ethnographic and geopolitical designations.

The concluding episode of departure from Dushanbe, the capital of Tajikistan, is preceded by Erofeev's cameo appearance in a fleeting scene where the expedition horses are sold to a local merchant (Image 37.1). In an unusual departure from the filming conventions of the time, the director appears on camera to shake hands with the merchant, breaking with the presumed invisibility of the traveler and filmmaker, who is thus identified with the camera's gaze and, by extension, with the audience. For all its briefness, this uncredited appearance encapsulates and exposes the colonial hierarchy, and the ambiguity of the relationship of the observers and the observed. The former had come from the capital of the new state, equipped with modern technologies, to film their subjects, interlocutors, partners, and co-travelers, who by the very act of filming are being classified and "othered" as ethnically defined subjects without names or personalities.

Yet by entering the frame, Erofeev himself assumed the role of the filmed subject and, for a brief moment, abandoned the authorial position of "man with a movie camera." The scene exemplifies the ambivalence of screen "otherness." As a representative of the Soviet center, both within and beyond the frame, Erofeev exhibited the inherent tension within expedition filmmaking, which transformed recorded reality as well as the very world it "captured" on film. The performative agreement embodied in the handshake is an effective way to enhance the viewers' trust in the authenticity of the film, and to establish the Pamirs as a space of communication and contact, but at the same time a space of hierarchy and cultural otherness.

IMAGE 37.1 A still from *Roof of the World*, 1927.

AT THE FOOTHILLS OF DEATH

Less than a year after Erofeev and his crew boarded their plane back to the capital, Vladimir Shneiderov also headed towards the Pamir Mountains with a somewhat different film plan. Together with cameraman Ilya Tolchan, he accompanied and chronicled the journey of a Soviet-German expedition of scientists and alpinists who set off to explore the alleged "last blank spot" on the map of the Soviet Union (Image 37.2). Shneiderov was invited to document the expedition on the heels of his success with *The Great Flight* (1925), the first Soviet feature travelogue, which recorded the Moscow-Beijing flight, praised in the central daily *Pravda* as a "social epic" and "life as it is in all its real truth."[12]

The Soviet-German expedition came about through cooperation between the Association for the Emergency Funding of German Science (*Notgemeinschaft der Deutschen Wissenschaft*)—an organization aiming to overcome German international scientific isolation after World War I—and the Soviet Academy of Sciences, which

IMAGE 37.2 A still from *At the Foothills of Death*, 1928.

was eager to utilize German expertise and resources.[13] The Soviet contingent mixed scientists and state functionaries, such as Nikolai Krylenko, the Commissar for Justice and Prosecutor General of the Russian Soviet Federative Socialist Republic (RSFSR); his wife, Elena Rozmirovich, a former member of the revolutionary tribunal; Otto Shmidt, the Deputy Commissar of Statistics and later a renowned polar explorer; and Nikolai Gorbunov, Lenin's former secretary.[14]

The group set off from Osh with a caravan of 200 horses and 205 camels towards the Western Pamirs with the intention to create maps of the mountainous area, to collect information on its natural riches, and to practice mountain climbing. The film also marks the group's itinerary on an animated map, but this time it contains a "blank spot" with a large question mark hovering over it. The reconnaissance mission was thus to master and exert control over an "empty" space, while exploring its resources for future use. As one of the participants put it, they aimed to bring the "natural and cultural realms of the mountainous Pamirs within the system of coordinates of European science."[15]

Although the Soviet and German units spent most of their time apart from one another and kept separate agendas, the film depicts them as a single crew sharing the mission, equipment, a colonial attitude towards the explored space, as well as the self-appointed promoters of "science" which they believed constituted the ultimate borderline between East and West.

To make their film travelogue an engaging viewing experience, Shneiderov and Tolchan (Image 37.3) carefully planned each episode they filmed, organizing special "film ascents" (*kinovoskhozhdeniia*) with "photogenic" views.[16] Shneiderov later described *At the Foothills of Death* as a "documentary [that is] educational as well as captivating and exciting."[17] Tolchan's ingenious camera work, original compositions, attention to detail, and subjective camera angles provide the dramatic tension. The camera work and editing is more varied than in Erofeev's linear travelogue. The film combines panoramic shots with detail-rich close-ups, bird's-eye panoramas with subjective point-of-view shots, and reportage filming techniques to enter the thick of the dynamic action. Spectacular mountain panoramas not only confer a sense of the pristine beauty and sublime aesthetic to the viewer, but also visualize the emptiness of the space and its "unclaimed" status—facilitating its appropriation through discovery and exploration.

IMAGE 37.3 A still from *At the Foothills of Death*, 1928.

At the Foothills of Death expanded the conventions of the expedition film by showing "cine-conquest" not only by the physical advancement of the explorers, but on a symbolic level as well. While Erofeev exemplified the power relations between the observer and the observed by appearing on the screen, Shneiderov highlighted the role of media in spatial unification by visualizing radio transmission from the Pamir Mountains. As the Soviet expedition members recalled, one of their missions was to test the shortwave communication network.[18] Radio, along with cinema, was one of the most modern media technologies which transformed the cultural landscape in the 1920s. Radio transmission compressed time and unified space. The film visualizes radio waves as concentric, expanding black circles that cover the sky and cross mountains, lakes, and forests to make visible the invisible. These expanding waves stretch out from the Pamir plateau "connecting" it with Moscow and Berlin. In setting up the radio station, the expedition team brings the Pamirs into an expanding Soviet technological orbit and creates a media network unrestrained by physical boundaries. Altogether, the film's final scene enumerates the expedition's achievements: discoveries of glaciers, gold deposits, and other natural resources, as well as an ascent to the highest point in the Pamirs renamed as Lenin's Peak. The film, through exploration wrapped in a dramatized adventure, exudes its message of imperial appropriation and domination of space.

A comparison of *Roof of the World* and *At the Foothills of Death* reveals how established conventions of expedition films work towards symbolically appropriating and dominating the filmed space. The films follow a partially overlapping itinerary and rely on cartographic authority to enhance their claim to authenticity, but they each challenge the image of a single, monolithic Soviet filmmaking style. Erofeev used ethnographic optics, reduced narrative engagement, and emphasized an entanglement of the observers and the observed. He demonstrated the incongruity of cultural and political borders by focusing on communication and exchange, and on cultural plurality within Soviet-marked space. Shneiderov, on the other hand, relied on the authority of scientific vocabulary and the conventions of the natural sciences to classify and measure visible phenomena, downplaying existing cultural alternatives for dominating "empty" spaces. Both films brought the Pamir within the Soviet system of political coordinates and unambiguously connected and subordinated it to the imperial center.[19]

NOTES

1. For introductory discussion on documentary see Carl Plantinga, "What a Documentary is, after All?" in *Documentary* edited by Julian Stallabrass (Cambridge MA: MIT Press, 2013), 52-62. Robert Rosenstone, "Documentary" in Robert Rosenstone, *History on Film, Film on History* (Harlow: Longman/Pearson, 2006), 70-88. Bill Nichols, *Introduction to Documentary* (Bloomington: Indiana University Press, 2010).
2. The region of Pamir was at the core of the "Great Game," the imperial conflict between the British and Russian empires. Peter Hopkirk, *The Great Game: The Struggle for Empire in Central Asia* (New York: Kodansha International, 1992).

3. Arne Haugen, *The Establishment of National Republics in Soviet Central Asia* (Basingstoke, New York: Palgrave Macmillan, 2003).
4. Haugen, *Establishment of National Republics*, 34.
5. Francine Hirsch, *Empire of Nations: Ethnographic Knowledge and the Making of the Soviet Union* (Ithaca: Cornell University Press, 2005), 182.
6. Alisher Il'khamov, *Etnicheskii atlas Uzbekistana* (Tashkent: IOFSS-Uzbekistan, 2002), 198.
7. Oksana Sarkisova, "Arctic Travelogues: Conquering the Soviet North," in *Films on Ice: Cinemas of the Arctic*, edited by Scott MacKenzie and Anna Stenport (Edinburgh: Edinburgh University Press, 2015), 222–234.
8. Quoted in Marianne Kamp, *The New Woman in Uzbekistan: Islam, Modernity, and Unveiling under Communism* (Seattle: University of Washington Press, 2006), 63.
9. Paula Michaels, *Curative Powers: Medicine and Empire in Stalin's Central Asia* (Pittsburgh: University of Pittsburgh Press, 2003).
10. Sven Hedin, *Through Asia*, Vol. 1 (London: Methuen Publishing Ltd., 1898), 192.
11. Vladimir Erofeev, "U podnozhia Pamira," *Smena* 6 (1928): 12–14.
12. Vladimir Shneiderov, *Moi kinoputeshestvia* (Moscow: Soiuz kinematografistov SSSR, 1973), 16.
13. Franziska Torma, *Turkestan-Expeditionen. Zur Kulturgeschichte deutscher Forschungsreisen nach Mittelasien (1890–1930)* (Bielefeld: Transcript, 2011), 184.
14. A. Parkhomenko, "Akademik N. P. Gorbunov: vzlet i tragediia. Shtrikhi k biografii nepremennogo sekretaria Akademii Nauk SSSR," in *Repressirovannaia nauka* (Leningrad: Nauka, 1991), 408–423.
15. Torma, *Turkestan-Expeditionen*, 188.
16. Shneiderov, *Moi kinoputeshestviia*, 24.
17. Shneiderov, *Moi kinoputeshestviia*, 23.
18. Nikolai Krylenko, *Po neissledovannomu Pamiru* (Moscow: Gosizdat, 1929), 30, 35.
19. For further analysis of Soviet *kulturfilms* and representation of Soviet spaces and nationalities see Oksana Sarkisova, *Screening Soviet Nationalities: Kulturfilms from the Far North to Central Asia* (London: I.B.Tauris, 2017).

CHAPTER 38

A SHARED SOVIET SPACE: OVERCOMING DIFFERENCE IN FILMS OF THE CAUCASUS IN THE 1920s AND 1930s

EMMA WIDDIS

ONE OF THE KEY tasks facing the young Soviet state after the revolution of 1917 was the creation of a coherent and cohesive vision of the extended Soviet space. This was no mere luxury. A shared map was essential to the successful consolidation of Soviet power. Yet it was also not straightforward. The Bolsheviks inherited—and fought for—a vast and complex territory, inhabited by diverse peoples, and it was crucial that this new map be different from that of the prerevolutionary Russian Empire, even where it shared its geographic boundaries. What was needed was a fresh model of geopolitical organization. It must reflect the revolutionary newness of Soviet social economic structures, avoiding the center-periphery power structures of colonial empires. It had to find a way to celebrate national diversity while, at the same time, emphasizing cohesion.

In the eyes of Bolshevik ideologues, cinema could contribute to the creation of this new imagined map in two key ways. First, and most obviously, films could spread the Soviet message to people living in the non-Russian republics through visual images. Second, cinema could participate in the vital project of *discovering* (or even *creating*) the Soviet territory—producing and disseminating images of the Soviet world for the consumption of the wider population in a visual "mapping" of the territory. Cinema was uniquely placed to create networks of visuality that would bind together those diverse peoples, reflecting and refracting their diversity in order to find points crucially in common.

This essay will discuss some of the complexities of that project with regard to the area that, in shorthand, we can describe as the Soviet "East"—that is, the southern and eastern parts of the territory (the Caucasus and Central Asia in particular). This was a particularly important point of focus in the 1920s and early 1930s. After all, these areas had a history of native uprisings against colonial imperialism (both Russian and British), which could be easily appropriated to the Bolshevik propaganda narrative. The peoples of the so-called East could be reinvented as proto-revolutionaries. Producing the correct kind of films of, and for, the Soviet "East," however, was not straightforward, for it dealt with a number of imperial legacies. Still, in 1925, one Bolshevik official identified two "undesirable trends" present in existing films set in the "East":

> The first is perpetuating old traditions of portraying the Orient in the cinema with the creation of a stereotyped East through piquant fairytales in the style of *A Thousand and One Nights*. Such a vision of the East is just fine for Western city dwellers. But not for either Russian worker-peasants or Eastern audiences. . . . The other tendency is exaggerated, narrow propaganda.[1]

What was needed, instead, were films that would present images of "real everyday life," distinct from those Orientalized fantasies.[2] To create them, a new cadre of *native* film professionals would be needed, with "real" knowledge of the region.[3] Only they—with their eye from *within*—would make films that expressed a new, appropriately Soviet relationship with the spaces of this alternative, revolutionary Empire.

In the course of the 1920s, therefore, a major effort went into creating film production studios across the Soviet territory, and in particular in Caucasian and Central Asian Soviet republics. In some cases, this was a question of starting completely from scratch; in others, existing film companies were developed and expanded. Building on an existing prerevolutionary studio, for instance, a Georgian film production company (Goskinprom Gruzii) was set up in 1923, with established Armenian film actor Amo Bek-Nazarov at its head. In 1925, officials converted a mosque in Tashkent into a film studio, suggestively named "Stars of the East." Other republics followed suit. In all these cases, local film production was managed by people who had prior experience in cinema produced in the Russian empire or in the metropolitan centers of the Soviet space. Through the 1920s, there was frequent contact and much two-way travel between Moscow and St. Petersburg, the Caucasus, and the Central Asian republics. In 1927, for instance, leading leftists Viktor Shklovskii and Sergei Tretiakov spent a period of months in Tbilisi, working within Goskinprom Gruzii. And in 1928, a wave of Russian directors arrived in Central Asia. They were often responsible for on-the-ground training of local nationals, who began their careers as actors or production assistants but went on to direct films themselves.

As this new generation of native film professionals emerged, questions of *how* to represent the local space and peoples were much discussed. In the case of the Caucasus, this was particularly complex, for any representation of its dramatic mountain landscapes, or its peoples, had to navigate a powerful legacy. Long a site of Russian imperial cultural imaginings, particularly during the Romantic era, the mountains of the Caucasus had been appropriated by writers such as Mikhail Lermontov and Alexander Pushkin as emblematic of the Romantic sublime; its "exotic" peoples had been part of Russia's particular version of Orientalism. How, then, could Soviet films picture the Caucasus into lands transformed by socialist power (agriculture, technology) *without* losing their aesthetic power? How could they navigate the traps of pre-revolutionary imperialism in articulating an appropriately socialist form of empire? Was it possible to maintain the sublime, but reconfigure it to serve a socialist purpose? How could the people of the Caucasus be pictured as at once nationally specific yet also ideologically part of the Soviet collective?

The complexities of this project, and its evolution from the mid-1920s to the mid-1930s, are evident in two films produced by the Georgian film studio: *Eliso* (1928), directed by Nikoloz Shengelaia (from a screenplay adapted by Sergei Tretiakov), and *The Last Crusaders* (*Ukanashkneli jvarosnebi, Poslednie krestonostsi*, 1933) directed by Siko Dolidze. Both were made by young directors who formed part of the first wave of new native film professionals. Both films tell stories of two national-ethnic peoples living side-by-side in the North Caucasus mountains: Georgian Khevsur Christians and Muslim Chechens. They focus on the potential for interethnic brotherhood between these peoples, positing that their shared social "class"—and shared history of oppression by ruling classes—can form the basis for new, non-national bonds in the Soviet Union.

Set in 1864, *Eliso* recounts the forced resettlement of Muslim Chechens by tsarist forces. The Muslim Chechens and the Christian Khevsurs live peaceably side-by-side in mountaintop villages, but tsarist officers trick the Chechens into signing a letter approving their own deportation, after which they are "banished," rendered homeless and nomadic. Alongside this ethnic-political narrative, the film tells of an impossible love between a Chechen girl Eliso and a Khevsur Georgian Vazhia. Although doomed by the gulf between their religions, their romance signals a political alliance that can be formed between Georgians and Chechens. Vazhia works to overturn the deportation order that is carrying Eliso away. He is too late, but in overcoming of his ethnic allegiance, the film envisages a future in which oppressed peoples unite against their common imperialist oppressors.

Eliso's combination of crowd-pleasing love story and political narrative was well received, praised for its avoidance of "Eastern exoticism," and celebrated as a "new direction" for Goskinprom Gruzii. It was also praised for an ethnographic gaze. Images of the Khevsur and Chechen people avoided Orientalizing fantasy, focusing instead on the details of lived experience. In this film, as in many such films of the period, this ethnographic gaze dwelled in large part on hardship. The banished Chechens set up their tents in the middle of mountain plains, and feed their babies amidst the mud and debris of a life uprooted. As the camera lingers on the physical realities of survival, the gaze hovers uncomfortably between disgust and empathy, drawing the spectator into a sensory experience that has little in common with the visual pleasures of the exotic spectacle.

Eliso represents a key genre in early Soviet cinema about the Caucasus (and cinema about the Soviet "East" more broadly), which retold the history of the region as a narrative of nascent revolutionary energy. This is particularly evident in the figure of Vazhia, who was described by Viktor Shklovskii as "a type of Don Quixote, an individual of honor, standing up against the imperial politics of tsarist Russia"[4]

IMAGE 38.1 Vazhia. A still from *Eliso* (1928).

(Image 38.1). Vazhia is both proto-revolutionary and primitive epic hero. In this way, he represents an attempt to create a visual image of the ethnic "other" that would maintain—even emphasize—*difference* as a force for change, for the creation of a new brotherhood of the oppressed.

A similar combination is evident in the film's extraordinary funeral scene. A young mother falls ill and dies, and the community unites in a visceral rendering of grief. In the climactic montage, grief, pain, and anger are intercut with shots emphasizing raw physicality and energy in the face of death. The village elder begins the traditional dance, the *lezginka*. As other members of the community join him, their increasingly frenzied movement transforms grief into a release of latent power. The contemporary critic Adrian Piotrovskii identified these final sequences as an example of what he called "emotional" cinema:

The collective, elemental grief is exploded by the passionate, elemental dance of all the people together, amidst the clatter of tambourines and the blaring of horns.[5]

For Piotrovskii, this emotion prompted an affective response in the spectator. The visual spectacle harnesses the power of the ancient native ritual as a revolutionary call to action.

Like *Eliso*, the narrative of *The Last Crusaders* tells of class solidarity overcoming national difference. Here, though, the narrative takes place amidst the transformation of Georgia by Bolshevism. In the early 1930s, as Stalinist Socialist Realism took hold, filmmakers were called to picture the socialist world in the process of becoming reality: the transformation of the "backward" worlds of traditional culture into progressive socialist utopia. In this film's opening sequences, the grandiose, epic landscape of the Caucasian mountains is dotted with villages on the brink of ruin, held captive by patriarchal tradition—and in particular by the rivalry and bitter battles between Christian Khevsurs and Muslim Chechens. On both sides, it is the elders who stir age-old conflict, trying to maintain the status quo. By contrast the young represent a possible (Bolshevik) future in which ethnic divides are replaced by class solidarity. As the film begins, the Khevsurs have killed two Chechens. According to tradition, the Chechens must seek blood revenge. Instead, young Chechens arrive in the Khevsur community, bringing a milk separator as a peace-offering (Image 38.2). Technology and youth represent an optimistic route into the future.

IMAGE 38.2 The milk separator as peace offering. Still from *The Last Crusaders* (1933).

The main narrative of the film revolves around two young Khevsur brothers, Mgeliia and Torgvai. Mgeliia embraces the modern world, and communism. He has travelled away from his tribe. When he returns, he discovers his community still caught up in ethnic feuds. He sets out to broker a peace with the Chechens, in an attempt to create a new accord for the future. Faced with the enemy, he symbolically drops his sword and shield, picks up his flute, and plays a tune. Sharing no language, the young men (Mgeliia, Torgvai, and their nominal Chechen "enemy") have just one word in common: *Komsomol* (the name of the Young Communist League, or party youth organization). As they pronounce it, this word works magically across linguistic boundaries, and becomes their shared, joyous sign for peace. The village elders on both sides, however, resist the union of youth, and Mgeliia is killed. As a symbol of his new political understanding, his last word is *class*. The Khevsur elders manipulate his brother Torgvai, convincing him that *class* is a Chechen name, and that Mgeliia died with the name of his murderer on his lips. Torgvai goes to exact revenge for his brother's death, but is met by a young Chechen and learns the true meaning of the word *class*. Again, the young resolve to fight together against their common (bourgeois) enemy. Torgvai symbolically removes the cross that marks his brother's grave and replaces it with a non-religious monument, describing his brother as a *komsomolets*, or member of the Communist Youth League.

Foregrounding the potent agency of words (*class*, *Komsomol*), language has an active role to play in the narrative of *The Last Crusaders*, and its role makes clear the film's careful balance between sameness and difference as it presents the relationship between native peoples and Soviet brotherhood. Those political words—*Komsomol*, *class*—that eventually prompt interethnic understanding belong to a shared Soviet ideological framework. They exist alongside and amidst the native languages of the tribes. Such a combination of languages was echoed in the film itself. First produced as a silent film, *The Last Crusaders* had sound added postproduction.[6] The sound was added in Georgian, and the Russian titles were left. As Evgenii Margolit notes, this gives a powerful "heteroglossia" (the presence of multiple and diverse voices) to the film. It foregrounds national specificity while also making a case for cross-national solidarities. For the spectator—whether speaking Russian or Georgian—it creates a simultaneity of inclusion and exclusion. It makes difference felt, while arguing for commonality.

The visual track of the film treads a similarly careful line between sameness and difference: between sublime landscape, ethnographic material, and the celebration of modernization. Early sequences focus on the beauty of the landscape and the romance of a woman singing beside a waterfall, where her young beloved finds her. The scale of the mountains here, and the visual equation between landscape and emotional experience, situates the spectator firmly in a long-established context of Romantic visions of the Caucasus (Image 38.3). Elsewhere in the film, however, the film eye is more densely ethnographic: it insists on costume, and on the elaborate

IMAGE 38.3 The Caucasus as Romantic vision. Still from *The Last Crusaders* (1933).

visualization of local customs, such as a wedding feast. These two elements—the ethnographic and the romantic—sit in crucial relationship with a visual celebration of the transformations that technology—and Sovietization—will bring to this community. A striking scene at the local trade cooperative pictures a remarkable medley of national costumes, different ethnic faces, handmade products, and old traditions. The camera dwells on this cultural heterogeneity, drawing the spectator's eye firmly into the midst of the lived experience of the Khevsur tribes.

Alongside this insistence on ethnographic authenticity, the film is concerned also to picture a socialist future for the peoples of the mountains. Amidst those handmade products, we see new ideals. Torgvai—initially isolated from his community for rejecting his patriarchal duty of revenge—proudly displays the butter that he is able to make using the Chechen milk-separating machine. In this scene, Torgvai's compatriots' mistrust of technology turns into awe for his superior product and, eventually, into an admiration of the machinery itself. With its visual emphasis on the separator, gleaming amidst a world that seems at odds with it, *The Last Crusaders* used the visual track to enact a vital synthesis. This emphasis is consistent throughout the film: the milk separator is an odd but symbolically powerful image amidst visions of Caucasus tradition (Image 38.4). Such visual emphasis recalls the iconic scene in Sergei Eisenstein's *General Line* (1928), where a stunning montage of the gleaming, spinning parts of another milk separator, interspersed with close-ups of peasant faces, tracks a transformation from suspicion into awe, and sews together human subjects and technology. Similarly, the visual track of *The Last Crusaders* is one that overcomes difference. Just as those Soviet words shared between young Chechens and Khevsurs enable a new understanding, so technology also saves the day. The Khevsurs vow to create a dairy collective. Torgvai's "cowardice" is reconfigured as a new form of bravery, appropriate for the modern age. And an apparently timeless tale of ethnic rivalry is turned into a narrative of the birth of collective farming in the Georgian mountains.

IMAGE 38.4 The milk separator between past and future. Still from *The Last Crusaders* (1933).

In the first decades of Soviet power, cinema images were supposed to have agency. They were to encode new ways of looking—at the world, and at the other. More than that, they were to shape the *self-image* of communities and individuals. Their unique power lay in their capacity to capture lived reality and reflect it back transformed: to weave the disparate spaces and peoples of the Soviet state into a visually articulated collective. These films suggest, however, that this cannot be understood solely in terms of homogenization and modernization (as is common in existing accounts of Soviet Stalinist imperialism in the 1930s). Rather, *Eliso* and *The Last Crusaders*—produced *on the periphery* and *about the periphery*—exemplifies the particular complexity of the early models of Soviet "empire" as they changed into the Stalinist 1930s. The tensions in both *Eliso* and *The Last Crusaders* speak to tensions that run through cinema of this period—between the ideological call for the "flattening" of difference (the creation of a homogeneous Soviet subject), an aesthetic fascination with the cinematographic potential of the textures and surfaces of alterity, and the political imperative for a new model of Empire. A rhetoric of difference coexisted with the drive towards Soviet sameness. This fragile balance was not easy to achieve, however, and films about the Soviet East trod a careful line. They were marked, above all, by acute self-reflexivity, deeply aware of the power of the visual.

NOTES

1. A. Skachko, "Kino dlia vostoka," *Kino-zhurnal ARK* 10 (1925): 3, 4.
2. S. Bartenev, "Kino v srednei Azii," *Kino-zhurnal ARK* 10 (1925): 5–6; 5.
3. Skachko, "Kino dlia vostoka," 3.
4. V. Shklovskii, "Veter iz Tiflisa," *Kino* 35 (1927): 2.
5. A. Piotrovskii, "Khudozhestvennye techeniia v sovetskom kino," in Adrian Piotrovskii, *Khudozhestvennye techeniia v sovetskom kino* (Moscow: Teakinopechat', 1930). Reprinted in *Adrian Piotrovskii: Teatr. Kino. Zhizn'*, edited by A. A. Akimova (Leningrad: Iskusstvo Leningr. otd-nie, 1969), 232–256; 248.
6. See Evgenii Margolit, "The Problem of Heteroglossia in Early Soviet Sound Cinema (1930–35)," in *Sound, Speech, Music in Soviet and Post-Soviet Cinema*, edited by Lilya Kaganovsky and Masha Salazkina (Bloomington: Indiana University Press, 2014), 119–128 (124–125).

CHAPTER 39

SOCIALIST ORIENTALISM: PICTURING CENTRAL ASIA IN THE EARLY SOVIET UNION (1920s–1930s)

HELENA HOLZBERGER

IN THE EARLY SOVIET UNION, illustrated newspapers and magazines were important channels to communicate the new socialist ideology and the government's expectations for revolutionary social and cultural change. The new media that emerged in the 1920s from the devastation of revolution and civil war inspired a new generation of photojournalists aiming to serve socialist society and transform visual culture.

A new iconography emerged in the Russian illustrated press in the early 1920s that focused on the creation of New Men and New Women and, after 1928, on industrialization and collectivization. The photojournalists who contributed to Soviet mass media came from all over the former Russian Empire. The people and places in the new republics that were fashioned out of the former Russian colonies in Central Asia also became important subjects of Soviet photojournalism. How did these photographers represent the construction of socialism in Central Asia? And how did these photographers contribute to the paradoxes of Soviet policies that both opposed imperialism and carried it out? An analysis of photographs from Soviet Central Asia reveals that the image of the Soviet empire produced by photojournalists during this period was enormously influenced by cultural, political, and ideological developments in the imperial center. In short, images of the periphery reflect developments at the center of the empire, rather than simply or transparently representing their subjects in Central Asia. The development of these photographic conventions will be shown through the work of three Soviet photographers of the interwar period.

In this chapter, photographs of Central Asia will be considered part of the artistic genre of "Orientalism," which had accompanied imperial expansion since the nineteenth century. Long before cultural theorist Edward Said's groundbreaking work redefined the term *Orientalism* into a statement on the unequal power relations between Europe and the Islamic cultural area, it described an artistic style. This style was not characterized by a special artistic technique or method, but by its content. For art historians, Orientalist images include all depictions of people, landscapes, architecture, and animals of the Islamic cultural world. Ever since Said propounded his theory of Orientalism, historians and art historians have debated whether his claim that the Orient was imagined as the eternally inferior, stagnating antipode of the rational West is a valid interpretation.[1] The representation of the Soviet Socialist Republics in Central Asia does not fully conform to Said's theoretical framework. Soviet photographers and artists referenced canonical, "Orientalist" representations of colonized societies, but they also depicted the enormous dynamism that prevailed there in the 1920s and 1930s. Instead of conceiving such photographs merely as products of colonial power, this chapter focuses on the photographers' more complex interpretations of imperial space. The empire was characterized by a power differential between center and periphery that manifested itself in economic exploitation, but it also entailed a universalist program and symbolism that were intended to include political and cultural integration.[2]

During the first years of Soviet rule in Central Asia, local photographers of European descent produced most of the images of the region in Soviet mass media. After the revolution, in 1920 and 1921, all private photo studios were forced to close and hand their material over to the government for purposes of "agitation" and propaganda. The confiscation effected a *tabula rasa* for photographic production. Almost all the photographers who had established a vivid photographic presence in prerevolutionary Turkestan were gone. Meanwhile, the resurrection of photojournalism in the Soviet Union around 1925 produced considerable demand for pictures—both of the center and of the periphery—for Soviet mass media.

The first prominent photographer spanning the worlds of Central Asia and Moscow was Georgii Zelmanovich, who is now better known as Zelma, as he abandoned the suffix of his name. Born into a Jewish family in Tashkent during the Russian Civil War, Zelma moved with his family to Moscow, where he trained with the famous Abram Shterenberg to be a photographer. His origins in Tashkent helped him to obtain this position, as Shterenberg himself had worked in Tashkent during the revolution. After his training, Zelma returned to Tashkent in 1926 as a correspondent for the image agency TASS. Soon after his return, Zelma began to work in local photojournalism and became the leading photographer for the main local newspapers, *Pravda Vostoka* and *Kizil Ouzbekiston*. Zelma stayed in Uzbekistan until 1929 and produced many photographs.

With the beginning of Stalin's first Five Year Plan in 1928, photography gradually began to promote industrial and agricultural development. The years before 1928 were still strongly characterized by prerevolutionary iconography. At the same time, a new visual archive of the entire Soviet Union had to be created for the mass media to substitute for preexisting "bourgeois" imagery. The photographers were to

"Sovietize" earlier forms of imperial imagery in an effort to break with colonial patterns and to reinforce the Soviet Union's self-description as a decolonizing movement. Paradoxically, ethnographic photography became vital to the Soviet process of transforming the peoples of the former colonies into nominally independent nations. Serving as research material for ethnographers and other academics who contributed to this process, photographs helped to signify the individual "Eastern tribes" that would qualify to become nations. Soviets in Moscow and at the periphery regarded this as part of the decolonization process: it was supposed to underpin national self-determination under Soviet ideology, and it ultimately legitimated the socialist republics in Central Asia. The photographers' first task was to produce photographs able to impart ethnographic knowledge to the masses, especially in Soviet Russia.

The 1920s are special, because most of the imagery of Soviet Central Asia was produced by three photographers who had been residents of the region for many years: Zelma, Alexander Kapustyanskii, and Max Penson. All of them spoke Uzbek and were familiar with the place and the culture. All of them were also Jews, which meant that they were socially marginalized, yet they were not members of the colonized peoples of the East. Thus, their perspective is half-removed, despite identifying as supranational Soviets.[3] The result of their insider-outsider perspective and their adoption of modern photographic techniques from Moscow was a new ethnographic style that integrated new methods of photography and focused on Soviet motifs, like work, in a local context.

Zelma was a major contributor to the new Soviet language of picturing "types" in such photographs as his cotton spinner (Image 39.1), taken between 1926 and 1928. The cotton spinner had been an important and widespread motif in Russian representations of Central Asia ever since the conquest of the region. However, Zelma applied new photographic approaches to this classic subject matter.

The image is structured in three parts. The foreground shows the massive spinning wheel in active use. The spinning wheel is directly connected to the working woman in the middle ground through one string leading to her raised hand. The woman does not look into the camera; instead, her gaze concentrates on the string—controlling the work of the "machine." The areas of light and shadow in the background aestheticize the picture, which was also novel. It breaks with the practices of ethnographic photography in the studio and documenting ethnic populations on the street without any sense of aesthetic composition. By picturing an authentic moment of work as an aesthetic experience, Zelma's work reflects the state of contemporary photography in the Soviet Union. The documentary, ethnographic image became a worker's portrait and, thus, part of Soviet visual culture, in which work was an important site of identification with the new society. While in the Russian Empire before the revolution peoples of the East had been photographed because of their "difference," Soviet photographers in the 1920s also pictured them as integral

IMAGE 39.1 Georgii Zelmanovich, *Cotton Spinner, Uzbekistan*, between 1926 and 1928.

members of the Soviet working class by applying the newly developed visual styles to ethnographic iconography.

A new period in the history of photographic representation of Central Asia, and a new chapter in the reconfiguration of Orientalist tropes into the Soviet idiom, began around 1930 with two related developments. In 1929, the prestigious photographer Arkadii Shaikhet travelled to Soviet Central Asia with the aim of producing a photo essay. He was the first of many prominent Soviet photographers who found new themes in Central Asia for their artistic work. The Soviet state affirmed this project. In 1930 and 1931, all photojournalistic production was subsumed under the agency *Soiuzfoto* and their *Fotobiuro*, which directed propaganda and agitation campaigns for Soviet mass media, in Moscow. In 1931, these media campaigns valorized Soviet Central Asia and its transformation into a modern society.[4] Photographers were encouraged to travel to the Soviet "Orient"—that is, to Central Asia. One result was the well-known imagery of Central Asian peoples with modern objects like tractors, construction sites, schools, and new means of irrigation, which reproduced the work of local photographers. However, Soviet photographers still interpreted the genre of Orientalism according to their individual artistic dispositions.

The caravan of camels by photographer Eleazar Langman provides one example (Image 39.2). The camel motif belongs to the classical Orientalist canon and has symbolized "the East" since the first tales of the Silk Road, the trade routes that linked East Asia with Europe since ancient times. Langman used well-known iconography, yet he executed this picture according to his own aesthetic principles. The camel caravan is not depicted conventionally, in a row viewed from the side, but rather from a perspective along the line of camels. Langman captured a perfect moment, when the rear animals look forward into the camera, while the ones in front are in profile and

IMAGE 39.2 Eleazar Langman, *Camel Caravan, Kazakhstan*, 1934/1935.

seem to smile. Thus, the photographer's avant-garde principles of using unusual camera angles to distinguish the view of the camera from a natural view provides a unique perspective on caravans.

Langman was part of the *October* photographers' collective, which aimed to establish new aesthetic principles in Soviet visual culture. During the cultural revolution, which accompanied the restructuring of the state in the first Five Year Plan, Langman's photographs were often the target of public criticism. The important journal *Soviet Photo* (*Sovetskoe foto*, called *Proletarian Photo* [*Proletarskoe foto*] between 1931–1933), even dedicated an issue to criticizing Langman's "formalist" visual language, which, the critics asserted, did not serve the needs of the state. In 1934 and 1935, Langman redeemed himself with a photo essay on Soviet Kazakhstan for the journal *USSR in Construction (SSSR na stroike)*. Although cultural production in the Soviet Union had already entered the period of socialist realism, Langman's Orientalist photographs, most of which he took from uncommon angles and new perspectives, like the camel caravan, were well received by critics and extensively reproduced in the mass media.

Soviet Central Asia became a space of aesthetic freedom that attracted many important Soviet photographers. The production of photo essays from Soviet Central Asia peaked in 1934 and 1935, with the tenth anniversary celebrations of the Central Asian republics. Photographers who usually fought over the authority to interpret the proper content and style of socialist photography found common ground in the Soviet "Orient." Although the October photocollective, like all other artistic associations, had been dissolved by decree in 1932, its former members continued their visual representations of Soviet Central Asia. Some photographers, like Langman, travelled to the republics, while others, like the artists Varvara Stepanova and Alexander Rodchenko, used Central Asian images to design photobooks and special issues for the journal *USSR in Construction*. Their pictures did not critically reflect on classical Oriental iconography, but instead modernized it through new artistic principles like sharp angles and extreme close-ups. Their way of depicting empire was well-received, which implies that their interpretation of Orientalism was approved by the state.

The former members of the competing Russian Association of Proletarian Photography (ROPF) photocollective also photographed Central Asia extensively. They, too, produced special issues for *USSR in Construction* throughout the 1930s. In 1934, the journal *Ogonek* published a special issue with pictures of Soviet Uzbekistan and Tajikistan, implying that almost all ROPF photographers had travelled to the Central Asian republics. Artists like Arkadii Shaikhet, Max Alpert, and Elena Mikulina used an ethnographic approach to picture the Soviet empire, elaborating tendencies Zelma had begun eight years before. One photograph by Max Alpert that originated during his assignment for *USSR in Construction* and recorded the results of his time there in 1938 illustrates this approach particularly well (Image 39.3).

IMAGE 39.3 Max Alpert, *Kyrgyz Riders, Kyrgyzstan*, 1937.

The picture captures four riders in a mountainous landscape. The photograph focuses on a young Kyrgyz woman, Aini Bapaeva, in the front, visibly enjoying her horse's swiftness. The woman on the horse next to her wears a Kyrgyz headscarf called an *elechek*, a local symbol of married women. The national headgear signifies her particular ethnicity. In the background, two blurred male riders complete the feminist codification of Soviet Central Asia as a place that had empowered women thanks to Soviet policies. The emphasis on liberating the women of Central Asia was central to Soviet national policy. Yet in Kyrgyzstan, the women had never been veiled, so the photograph does not actually document any radical novelty. This portrait received much praise, especially in its cropped version where only the young woman is shown, when it was displayed at an important exhibition of Soviet photography in 1937. At the same time, critics condemned some of Alpert's other photographs in that series as appearing far too staged, especially one image of a rider wearing the *elechek*, Kadii Kokonbaeva, and her family sitting in a yurt surrounded by an unlikely cornucopia of Soviet objects, like Lenin's complete works, a gramophone, Russian wooden toys, and a little boy in a sailor suit.[5] With the staged modernity, Alpert tried to transfer the propagandistic messages of his famous ode to Soviet success—a photo essay depicting the Russian Fillipov family living an ideal, modern

Soviet life in Moscow—to the periphery. Yet as the critical responses to the images at the exhibition demonstrate, the overloaded composition failed to compel his contemporaries. They expected Orientalism to appear authentic and to satisfy their implicit standard of a photographic eyewitness account.

Political assessments of the acceptability of his imagery aside, Alpert's approach to ethnographic photography produced outstanding pictures of the Soviet empire. The Kyrgyz riders are beautiful people, and the picture is vivid and authentic. It is well composed in terms of lines and sharpness, embedded in a fascinating landscape. It is not Orientalist in Said's terms, because the woman leads: society changed with the destruction of patriarchy. Alpert was searching for something "typical," yet he managed to create a modern picture by applying principles of the modern photo essay to the ethnographic genre.

Throughout the late 1920s and 1930s, almost every important professional Soviet photographer produced a series in Central Asia.[6] These pictures received particularly good reviews and high reproduction rates through mass media, making a Central Asian assignment desirable for Soviet photojournalists. The spatial and cultural boundaries of the Soviet Union limited the range of the motifs available to the Soviet photographer. Instead of travelling the world or exploring hidden figures in their own society for new photo essays, Soviet photographers were tied to socialist realism and its repetitive motifs. In light of this, the peripheries of the Soviet empire offered them new topics. Modern ethnographic pictures were politically acceptable as long as they demonstrated national progress through socialism. Thus, for photographers like Zelma, Langman, and Alpert, ethnographic photography was an available field to explore new topics and styles. Soviet Central Asia became especially popular for such assignments, because it was relatively easy to reach and was surrounded by the "splendor of the Orient," which had deep roots in the European pictorial tradition.

These images were made in the context of the Soviet empire, so power relations inhered in them. While this observation applies to any image produced in any society, it was especially true of those images produced during the 1930s. From a critical postmodern perspective, immunizing the images of Soviet Central Asia against accusations of contributing to repression and stereotyping would be impossible. But Soviet photographers of the 1920s and 1930s did not see the camera solely as a weapon, and documentary photography, however limited, became also a way of producing artistic pictures. The Soviet version of Orientalist art became a subgenre that enabled artists to create new images. This socialist rediscovery of the Soviet East catalyzed exciting artistic innovations, just as the first artistic encounters of French artists with colonial topics inspired fauvist, primitivist, and other radically new approaches in the beginning of the nineteenth century.

Thus, not only Soviet nationality policy determined the picture of the Soviet empire; so, too, did developments and linkages in Soviet cultural policy in Moscow. Photographic images of Soviet Central Asia not only exemplify Soviet propaganda in the republics, but also mirror ideological imperatives and developments in visual culture in the Soviet center, making them a crucial part of the history of Soviet photography.

NOTES

1. For the debate, see Linda Nochlin, "The Imaginary Orient," in *The Politics of Vision: Essays on Nineteenth-century Art and Society* (New York: Harper & Row, 1989), 33–59; John M. MacKenzie, *Orientalism: History, Theory and the Arts* (Manchester: Manchester University Press, 1995).
2. Michael W. Doyle, *Empires* (Ithaca: Cornell University Press, 1986).
3. David Shneer, *Through Soviet Jewish Eyes: Photography, War, and the Holocaust* (New Brunswick: Rutgers University Press, 2011).
4. State Archive of the Russian Federation (GARF), R-4459, op. 11, no. 433, 16–17.
5. N. Kolli, "V chem sila izobratsitel'nosti fotoiskusstva," *Sovetskoe foto*, no. 3 (1938): 6–10.
6. V. G., "Litso nashei socialisticheskoi rodiny," *Sovetskoe Foto*, no. 1 (1938): 2–5.

CHAPTER 40

"FASCIST COLORS": STALINIST SPATIAL IDEOLOGY, CARTOGRAPHIC DESIGN, AND VISUAL LEARNING

NICK BARON

IN 1919, the Soviet government founded the Higher Geodetic Administration, subordinated to the central economic authorities. Its task was to survey and map state territory and produce maps and atlases for use in schools, political education, administration, and planning. It would conduct some work itself and coordinate other civilian organizations' cartographic activities. From the start, however, these rival organizations guarded their autonomy, refusing to cooperate with the new administration. For fifteen years, the Soviet government strove to overcome conflict and confusion through investigations, purges, and reorganizations. Finally, in 1935, the Politburo, the supreme policymaking body in the Central Committee of the Communist Party, centralized all civilian mapping under one agency, the Chief Administration of Geodesy, Surveying, and Cartography (GUGSK), which was subordinated to the People's Commissariat for Internal Affairs (NKVD), the political police.

Centralization did little to improve matters. Nor did the NKVD's tightening of controls over map production, which included strengthening the role and responsibilities of map editors, extending secrecy provisions and practices, intensifying censorship, and criminalizing the unauthorized creation and use of maps. Alongside the fact that precise surveys still covered barely a fifth of Soviet territory, the Party-state leadership was particularly concerned by the shortage of school maps and the perceived poor quality, in material, aesthetic, and ideological terms, of those that existed.

Pressure on cartographers intensified. In June 1937, the party newspaper *Pravda* published an article criticizing a political wall map of the world for primary schools produced the previous year. The newspaper decried the map's "wild absurdities," claiming that "the publication of this sort of geographical rubbish can only be called wrecking. A map that confuses all basic geographical concepts isn't just printers' 'waste'—it plants in the minds of pupils incorrect ideas about their country and the world."[1] One of the map's editors was arrested, and his name was removed from later amended editions of the map.[2]

In November 1937, the Soviet government issued a decree demanding that the GUGSK remedy the deficit in school cartography by producing a series of large-format wall maps, in a print run totaling 3.4 million, by the start of the next school year.[3] Immediately following this decree, the GUGSK launched a series of conferences bringing together officials, cartographers, pedagogical scholars, teachers, and school students, to discuss the design of these new wall maps. Over subsequent months, controversies erupted, positions were staked out, and compromises reluctantly reached. At the start, the only thing on which all participants agreed was that the maps should possess the quality of *nagliadnost'*.

Translated from the German *Anschaulichkeit*, and taken up by Russian pedagogues in the mid-nineteenth century, the notion of *nagliadnost'* encompassed various elements: the use of visual aids in teaching, the forms and attributes of visual representation that enable effective learning, and the mental processes that are stimulated through active, engaged contemplation.[4] It thus connoted both a particular quality that may be inherent in an image and the ways in which that image impresses itself on the observer.

The concept of *nagliadnost'* had fallen out of fashion in Soviet pedagogy after the revolution, but it reappeared in the 1930s with the reintroduction of more traditional curricula and teaching methods, involving greater use of illustrative material aids. For example, a May 1934 Party and government decree on "Teaching Geography in Primary and Secondary Schools" called on teachers to "reinforce in children's memory basic geographical names ... and solid knowledge of the geographical map, ... ensuring maximum *nagliadnost'*, accessibility, popularity, and engagement in its presentation."[5]

In terms of cartographic design, *nagliadnost'* implied that the map—as both image and artifact—should be alluring, legible, comprehensible, and compelling in a way that not merely stamped itself on the learner's passive mind, but stimulated their creative response. The Soviet map that conformed to all these principles would transcend didactics. It would contribute to developing an active, engaged visuality, constitutive of a new reality.[6] Cartography would create the New Soviet Person, and construct socialism.

The purpose of the GUGSK's consultations, then, was to determine how the design of their new maps might best realize cartography's transformative potential. In January 1938, GUGSK Director M. V. Nikitin and Head Map Editor L. Ia. Ziman travelled with colleagues to Leningrad for a meeting with teachers to discuss the "Political Map of Europe," currently being compiled under the editorship of V. V. Konovalov.[7]

At the start of the meeting, Konovalov presented five different drafts of the map. The main variations concerned color palette and choice of colors for individual countries, the depiction of internal and external borders, the form of city markers, and the scale, framing, and projection of the map. Delegates' interventions focused on specific design issues, but their arguments revealed more general divergences regarding cartographic form and function in relation to visual learning and the wider ideological project.

As regards scale, Konovalov had initially drafted this map at 1:3 million on six sheets. However, the need to accelerate production, plus concerns about paper shortages, had prompted him to reduce the scale to 1:3.5 million. That meant that the map could be printed on four sheets, while still incorporating both Greenland in the (otherwise empty) top left and the European colonial possessions in North Africa, with the strategically important (and therefore pedagogically relevant) Suez Canal at the bottom, lending the map equilibrium on both its vertical and horizontal axes (Image 40.1). Konovalov had also chosen to use a conformal conic projection that preserved territorial shapes

IMAGE 40.1 V. V. Konovalov, ed., "Political Map of Europe," (Scale: 1:3.5 million. GUGSK NKVD SSSR, 1938). Note that this illustration shows a revised version of the draft map discussed in the January meeting, incorporating some—though not all—of the changes recommended by delegates.

while progressively amplifying the size of regions to the north and south of a standard parallel running through central Europe. Thanks to both this reframing of the map's area of coverage and the scale distortion at higher latitudes, the vivid red monolith of Soviet territory now visually dominated the right-hand side of the map, looming massively over the narrowing patchwork peninsula of states to the west.

Regarding the map's coloring, Professor M. I. Silishchenskii, a prominent educational cartographer in the late tsarist period who remained active during the 1920s, but was now working (after a spell in prison) in an obscure role in the Tashkent Map Factory, declared that a "successful map" should have colors that are "more joyful and warmer." In some variants, he especially liked the blue of the sea and the subtle tones of green. These, he stated, had gained "a lot of admirers." The drafts that used brighter colors didn't tire his sight or weaken his concentration, as some of the cartographers claimed, but he still preferred those with calmer, more "true to life" tones. In designing school maps, he believed, "we must confront pupils with reality." His preference for gentler, more naturalistic coloring was shared by most of the mapmakers and opposed by most of the teachers, who demanded brighter hues to excite and impress the students.

A teacher named Elagin sought compromise. "Pedagogues don't believe that maps need to look like posters," he reassured his audience, "with the surface fully colored in." Teachers just wanted to ensure that all students in the classroom would be able to see the map's content, clearly and correctly. For this, firstly, pigments needed to be sufficiently transparent to render all base detail visible. He criticized one draft map on which France was shaded in a solid block of intense color that vividly delineated its territory but obscured its cities, railways, rivers, and labels. Albania's shading was also too opaque, he noted, "but it's an insignificant country, with few details you need for schools." Secondly, it was necessary to pay closer attention to color temperature, since students perceiving similar tones in different parts of the map would assume these elements were interrelated in some way. On one variant, Elagin complained, Greenland (dark pink) looked too much like the USSR (red). He recommended a more naturalistic shading: "in the North you shouldn't use such warm colors."

Another teacher, Kalantarov, declared that "the coloring of a state should be accorded a political character." As an example, he pointed to England. This bourgeois-democratic country, he said, should not be depicted in bright green, when green was also used for fascist Poland. England could instead be yellow, he suggested. Similarly, it was wrong that both Latvia and Austria were pale blue. They were both "fascist states," and as Germany was brown, they should be rendered in a shade of brown, too (Image 40.2). "You cartographers should know the colors of each state's national flag [and that] blue symbolizes freedom." He admonished them: "You cannot fail to realize that coloring is political."

Kalantarov was clearly throwing down a gauntlet to the cartographers. To be sure, Ziman had already stipulated that red should only be used for the USSR, as "this

IMAGE 40.2 "You cannot fail to realize that coloring is political." Detail of Central Europe and Soviet border, from Konovalov, ed., "Political Map of Europe," (Scale: 1:3.5 million, February 1938). In this revised draft, Germany and Hungary are depicted in different shades of "fascist" brown; Italy and Romania in visually and symbolically affinitive gray tones. Despite objections at the January meeting, the "fascist states" Latvia and Austria remain pale blue, in order to differentiate them more vividly from neighboring states. Poland's hue, however, has been changed from green to yellow, to preclude association with "bourgeois-democratic" England and relate it tonally to "fascist" brown. Poland's new coloring also creates a more vivid edge-contrast at the USSR's double-shaded external border and serves perceptually to foreground the more dominant red of Soviet territory.

color signifies freedom." Although the coloring of the USSR in red had never been in question, immediately after the November 1937 decree, the GUGSK had privately acknowledged that this could pose a problem. Soviet red dyes were of poor quality, someone had complained, more like "brick-dust than a color," lacking translucency and prone to fading.[8] Bozhenov, a map artist, now tried to explain some of the practical challenges regarding colors: "Concerning 'fascist colors'—this is very hard to show. The fact is that we need to find suitable colors to go next to one another, otherwise it becomes impossible to differentiate neighboring states." All Soviet political maps, he said, used green for Britain, since green could be printed in a wide range of tones, all of which retained good contrast. This made it easy to depict the metropolis in a darker, more solid green and its colonies and dominions in lighter tints of the same color. France, too, was commonly depicted using one color (pink) in different tones for the metropolis and its overseas territories.

At this point, GUGSK Director Nikitin, a career official in the political police, intervened to defuse tensions, knowing that Bozhenov's technical objections could readily be misinterpreted, deliberately or otherwise, as political naivety or error. Certainly, Nikitin responded, "it's entirely correct that on a political map of Europe we need to choose colors by political criteria." However, he couldn't ask artists to choose the colors of individual countries themselves; this needed to be resolved by an "appropriate person." Probably Nikitin meant by the Central Committee's Agitprop Department, which exercised ideological oversight over map production. In any case, this statement gave Kalantarov pause for thought.

Ziman chipped in. Of course, GUGSK artists had been instructed to ensure that "the USSR is sharply distinguished from the capitalist world, and the border between the two worlds makes itself distinctly felt." Partly for reasons of cost, other countries would be differentiated from each other solely by contrasting colors, with no shading of borderlines. The USSR's external state border, however, would be given a thick, dark-red edging to ensure it stood out—as soon as the GUGSK found a decent red pigment (Image 40.2). He agreed that countries' colors were important. Currently, he conceded, the fascist states did look "a little too similar to us."

Delegates also debated whether the map should delineate the Union republics, autonomous republics, and autonomous regions. Teachers were in favor, as it meant that they could use the map for teaching Soviet national-territorial structure. One teacher at this meeting, Prozorov, proposed depicting Soviet internal boundaries with lines of graduated thickness, widest for the Union republics. These should be prominent enough to be readily discernible (*nagliadnye*), while not obscuring underlying content. Another teacher, Orlov, preferred to differentiate Soviet national-territorial units by the use of varying shades of red, without borderlines.

Lederman, a specialist in one of the factories producing the new maps, rejected Orlov's idea on the grounds that it would be impossible to find nine different shades of red without some resembling the colors of foreign territories. This was impermissible. Moreover, he remarked, painting a patchwork of reds would mean that "the entire Union will not create the impression of an integrated whole." Instead, they needed to use borderlines, and these should be red, not green as at present, as green lines over red would look discordant in natural light.

Ziman agreed to include Soviet internal boundaries, so long as they didn't "upset the overall harmony of the map." They should be visible, he said, but only if you are looking for them. He proposed to use thinner red lines without a base layer. This would sufficiently convey to students "what our Union represents." Looking at the wall map, he said, a teacher could say that it shows thirty states: "the western half is capitalist, the eastern half is socialist with administrative subdivisions of various forms." Thus the map's division of the USSR into its constituent national-territorial entities, visually counterbalancing the division of capitalist Europe into its constituent states, would demonstrate to students that the USSR itself represented "an entire socialist world."

Discussions around the design of city markers concerned their size, color, and placement. As this was to be a political map, it was agreed that cities should be clearly visible, though Prozorov argued that only the markers needed to be given prominence, while their labels could be in the background. Orlov recommended that Union-republican capitals should be marked with symbols of the same size as those of foreign capital cities, according them equivalence in status and significance. Prozorov preferred to use red for all city markers, across the whole map, but, he grumbled, Ziman wanted "to monopolize [red] for the USSR." Nikitin expressed concern that on all drafts Moscow looked smaller than Berlin, Madrid, and other cities, even though its label and marker were, in fact, the same size. He ordered this to be corrected. Ziman agreed this was an error: Moscow's red star should be larger than all other city symbols. Nikitin also didn't like the use of white markers, which he said made the map look speckled, or as if it had holes in it. Bozhenov agreed; to him, the white dots looked like "peas scattered over the map." It was agreed that city markers should all be red.

Finally, the delegates at the meeting took a vote on the variants. The one with the most vivid colors, favored by teachers, received a majority. Nikitin promised to direct Konovalov to proceed with that draft, albeit incorporating some amendments proposed during the consultation. Although, to Nikitin's evident relief, the meeting ended amicably, it had revealed substantive differences of opinion about what constituted cartographic *nagliadnost'*.

In general, teachers had preferred starker color contrasts, bolder lines, and bigger features (even at the cost of informational content). They were preoccupied with the map's ideological correctness and the political-geographic inferences that viewers might draw from coloring, width of borderlines, or relative size of symbols. Their aim was to create a map-image that would stamp itself upon students' imaginations, stimulating their learning, instilling and rationalizing a worldview, and arousing their patriotism.

The cartographers had favored a more naturalistic, subtle, and harmonious style. They valued aesthetic appeal and precision above visual impact. Not surprisingly, they also harped on practical considerations, such as availability of paper, quality of ink dyes, and printing processes, which they warned would prevent them from implementing all the teachers' demands. Likely, they were also hoping to make the final map less ugly.

These design preferences reflected each group's professional expertise, priorities, and interests, as well as divergent notions of cartography's role in cultural development. For the teachers, the main purpose of classroom maps was to promote and facilitate the effective learning of geography and related subjects. For the cartographers, the main purpose of school maps was to teach the use and understanding of maps, to instill "cartographic culture," as a new way of seeing and conceiving reality: conventionalized, beautified, and ordered.[9]

As Nikitin, the NKVD officer in charge of the GUGSK, understood, the design consultation carried high stakes. During this time of mass arrests, a map deemed ideologically incorrect, in form or content, could cost lives. Politically, the teachers at the meeting were savvier, and the mapmakers were willing to make design compromises in return for their input and, tacitly, a sharing of risk.

In the end, all were reasonably satisfied that the "Political Map of Europe" appropriately represented and communicated the Stalinist vision of political space. It was both ideologically correct and pedagogically practical, and photographs of the map in use testify to its wide circulation and appeal (Image 40.3). Its geographical framing and projection demonstrated the USSR's formidable expanse. The map's coloring conveyed states' political character, alignments, and alliances, and emphasized Soviet separation, uniqueness, and self-sufficiency. The USSR's heavily shaded state border declared its closure and impregnability, and its lightly drawn internal boundaries and the large markers (in later drafts, embedded in mid-size red stars) used for Union-republican centers visualized its constitution as an "unbreakable union of

IMAGE 40.3 Alexander Ustinov, "Political Instructor G. S. Aksakalov conducts political training with young soldiers," 1940.

free republics" representing, as Ziman had pronounced, "an entire socialist world." Yet at the same time, the uniform red coloring of Soviet territory, and the huge red star marking Moscow, communicated spatial homogeneity, hierarchy, and centrality. In its depiction of the USSR, the map's great achievement was to reconcile both narratives—of internationalist integration and of imperial hegemony—in one commanding image.

NOTES

1. "'Chudesa' na geograficheskoi karte," *Pravda*, June 10, 1937, 16.
2. Russian State Archive of the Economy (RGAE), Soviet Geodetic-Cartographic Institutions, fond 8223, op. 1, no. 418, folio 50.
3. State Archive of the Russian Federation (GARF), Sovnarkom USSR Collection, fond 5446, op. 22a, no. 165, f. 72–70.
4. Waltraud Naumann-Beyer, "Anschauung," in *Ästhetische Grundbegriffe (ÄGB)*, Vol. 1, (Stuttgart: Metzler, 2000), 208–246. For late Soviet conceptions of *nagliadnost'*, see Sonja Luehrmann, *Secularism Soviet Style: Teaching Atheism and Religion in a Volga Republic* (Bloomington: Indiana University Press, 2011).
5. "O prepodavanii geografii v nachal'noi i srednei shkole SSSR" May 16 1934, *Pravda*, no. 133, p. 1.
6. Valerie A. Kivelson and Joan Neuberger discuss Russian/Soviet visual culture as a means of achieving transcendence and transformation, a practice that they term "seeing into being," in *Picturing Russia: Explorations in Visual Culture* (New Haven: Yale University Press, 2008), 6–8 and *passim*.
7. For the stenographic record of this meeting, see RGAE, fond 8223, op. 1, no. 512, f. 61–102.
8. RGAE, fond 8223, op. 1, no. 419, f. 44–47.
9. For Nikitin on "cartographic culture," see RGAE, fond 8223, op. 1, no. 426, f. 107–108.

CHAPTER 41

REPRESENTING JEWISHNESS IN THE RED ZION: THE JEWISH AUTONOMOUS REGION IN THE 1930s

ROBERT WEINBERG

JEWS WERE AN ANOMALY in the universe of tsarist and Soviet nationality policy, both because they lacked a historic national territory to call their own and because they tended to be subject to imperial control and domination differently than were many other ethnonational minorities. Even though the vast majority of Jews resided in the territory that was known as the Pale of Settlement after the partitions of the Polish-Lithuanian Commonwealth in the late eighteenth century, the concentration of Jews in the western borderlands of the tsarist empire did not render the Pale a Jewish national enclave in the way that Georgia and Armenia, for example, were treated as the territorial homelands of Georgians and Armenians. Nevertheless, like the Georgians and Armenians, Jews under tsars and communists can be viewed as a colonized people, inasmuch as they were subject to the rule of an imperial power that treated them as a collective unit and sought to limit their political and, at times, cultural autonomy.

Marxist theory stressed that the proletarian revolution would render national identities obsolete, blending all cultures into a common socialist one. Trying to bridge theory and practice, Joseph Stalin in 1913 wrote that a full-fledged nation in the multiethnic, multinational Russian Empire lived in its own territory, spoke its own language, and had a common culture.[1] Until such a time as socialism doomed to extinction all religious and national sentiments, loyalties, and attachments, the Kremlin would acknowledge the continued existence of national identity, so long as it was secular and committed to socialist principles.[2]

Soviet Jews, who numbered over 2.5 million at start of the 1920s and formed a significant minority in the country, posed a problem for the country's leadership. Being a diaspora people who lacked a territorial homeland, Jews were expected to easily integrate into Soviet society. And as religion disappeared under socialism, the secularization of Soviet Jewish society would, presumably, proceed apace and weaken obstacles to Jewish acculturation, and, eventually, assimilation. Just like other national minorities living in the Soviet Union, Soviet Jews were also entitled to exercise cultural autonomy so long as it conformed to the dictum "national in form, socialist in content" and followed the ideological dictates of the Kremlin. An integral part of the socialist project was the creation of a Jewish culture that embodied socialist, collectivist, and egalitarian principles.

During the early decades of communist rule, the Kremlin attempted to "normalize" the status of the Jews living in the Soviet Union as an ethnonational minority through territorialization. In 1928, the regime designated territory just west of Khabarovsk along the Chinese border and some five thousand miles from Moscow as the national homeland of Soviet Jewry and began to promote the settlement of this region as the center of a secular Jewish society and culture dedicated to the building of socialism. In 1934, the area known as the Biro-Bidzhanskii District was renamed the Jewish Autonomous Region, with the new town of Birobidzhan serving as the territory's capital.

The socialist transformation of Soviet society entailed more than changes in social and economic relations. The Kremlin relied on cultural production to promote the socialist agenda and depended on the creative impulses of artists, writers, and photographers. Deemed the national language of Jews, Yiddish (rather than Hebrew, which was considered the language of bourgeois Zionists, a class enemy) would play a crucial role in making Birobidzhan the new center of Soviet Jewish life. Written in the Hebrew alphabet, Yiddish developed about a thousand years ago and was the everyday language of most Jews in central and eastern Europe, including the Russian Empire. Yiddish would form the bedrock of the new Jewish, socialist society. In 1935, the government decreed that all official documents, including public notices, announcements, posters, and advertisements, had to appear in both Yiddish and Russia. In 1936, the government of the Jewish Autonomous Region issued a decree that elevated institutions devoted to the development and use of Yiddish in Birobidzhan to a preeminent position in the Soviet Union. In short, a "Jewish coloration" characterized social, cultural, and political life in the region.

Material culture ephemera, such as books, newspapers, and posters, along with photos of buildings and everyday life, reveal how the authorities presented Soviet Jewish culture and society to the populace of the Jewish Autonomous Region and beyond. In particular, they offer a visual representation of how aspects of life were coded both Jewish and Soviet as part of the Kremlin's approach toward Jews. The policy was a tactic of imperial management that demonstrates both the fissures and integrative qualities of life for all national minorities in the early Soviet period. It also underscores the fragile nature of these efforts, since socialism was slated, in the long run, to foster a *homo sovieticus* (a Soviet person) who would transcend national identity and embrace class-based internationalism.

Local officials, at the behest and support of ministries in Moscow, did not skimp on resources and energy in fostering a Soviet-Jewish culture in the new Jewish Autonomous Region. The main railway station in the region greeted visitors with "Birobidzhan" emblazoned in Yiddish and Russian, just as the name of the State Theater of the Jewish Autonomous Region appeared in both languages. A Yiddish newspaper (*Birobidzhaner shtern*) came out every day for many decades, and its publication continues to this day, albeit on a much-reduced level (Image 41.1). Street signs were also bilingual, and one of the city's main thoroughfares was named in honor of the prominent Jewish writer Sholem Aleichem. Even today, one can find bilingual signs of streets, markets, and other public buildings and spaces. Moreover, Yiddish was the language of instruction in some elementary and high schools, and textbooks were published to teach children how to read and write Yiddish. In keeping with the regime's commitment to instilling a communist ethos among the population, one such primer displayed a drawing of Vladimir Lenin, followed by this text:

> Vladimir Ilyich Lenin
> Lenin is our leader,
> Our teacher, Our friend
> We do as Lenin teaches us,
> All working people know and love Lenin.

Other markers highlighted the secular nature of Birobidzhan's Jewishness, and stressed how Jews were striving to jettison the religious elements of traditional Jewish

IMAGE 41.1 Man holding a copy of *Birobidzhaner shtern* (*The Birobidzhan Star*), 1931.

IMAGE 41.2 Soviet propaganda poster in Yiddish: "The pig is our main machine for producing meat in the near future," 1931.

life. The poster shown in Image 41.2, produced in 1931, illustrates the Soviet effort to promote a New Jewish Man and Woman who rejected both Judaism and capitalism and embraced the secular ethos of socialism. While the poster does not specifically target Jews in Birobidzhan, its message is one repeated in other depictions from Birobidzhan that underscore the visual ways the Kremlin addressed Jews. The breeding of pigs, the eating of which was taboo for religious Jews, underscored the secularization of Jews under communism. Elsewhere, Soviet propagandists publicized the extent to which Jews in Birobidzhan had left behind dietary strictures such as the eating of pork. The top line of the poster proclaims in Yiddish that "the pig is our main machine for producing meat in the near future," while the text at the bottom demands the organization of "agricultural councils and collective farms to raise pigs." In the background are the houses of collective farmers who raise the pigs in what appears to be modern facilities, evidence of the supposed material prosperity of Jews engaged in agriculture.

The poster shown in Image 41.3, produced in 1936, celebrates the effort to "turn the Jewish Autonomous Region into a flourishing area of the Far Eastern Territory." The photomontage depicts smiling, contented inhabitants of Birobidzhan—both young and old—engaged in a variety of work and leisure activities, along with the

IMAGE 41.3 Soviet propaganda poster in Russian: "Let's turn the Jewish Autonomous Region into a flourishing area of the Far-Eastern Territory," 1936.

achievements of the building of socialism. Also included is an excerpt from comments made by Joseph Stalin on the benefits of socialism.

In the 1930s, the emphasis on Yiddish in schools and in arts and culture, along with the public display of Yiddish on buildings, street signs, and official documents, undoubtedly generated excitement among those residents who believed Yiddish would play a leading role in Soviet Jewish society. I imagine that the emphasis on Yiddish fostered a sense of pride among those Jews who valued this language as the bedrock of the Jewish community. Itzak Prishkolnik, a Jewish teenager from Smolensk, felt the allure of Birobidzhan in the mid-1930s. He told me that he moved to Birobidzhan because of its status as the proclaimed center of Soviet Jewry. He recalled in the early 1990s how much he appreciated that "Yiddish was spoken everywhere," and how he welcomed what he called "the absence of antisemitism."[3] Another longtime resident of Birobidzhan, Fira Kofman, had been an enthusiastic member of the Young Communist League when she came to Birobidzhan in 1936 to help build a socialist homeland for Soviet Jewry. In the mid-1990s, she said Birobidzhan possessed a definite Jewish air: "Yiddish was heard on the streets. . . . We had Jewish schools, a Jewish theater, a Jewish restaurant where one could eat real Jewish food . . . One could feel the Jewish atmosphere. And why not? This is, after all, the Jewish Autonomous Region."[4] Both Prishkolnik and Kofman fondly remembered their years as young adults in Birobidzhan precisely because they believed that their hopes and dreams as young Jews committed to communism were realized by living in the Soviet Zion. As the lives of Prishkolnik and Kofman illustrate, the Kremlin's efforts to establish a Jewish homeland drew sustenance from such popular impulses.

Birobidzhan, however, never became the hub of a secular, Yiddishist culture. By the late 1930s, the intent of Soviet nationality policy toward Jews was, in fact, to efface religious identity as well as constrain secular national identity. Assimilation into the emerging Soviet way of life became an overriding goal of the Kremlin. The Soviet Union's leadership desired the fusion of all national cultures into a common socialist culture, with the Russian language and culture as the glue.

Efforts to promote new cultural forms using Yiddish and socialist values also failed. Novelists, short-story writers, journalists, and visual artists may have been serious about cultivating a new culture for Soviet Jews in Birobidzhan, but they were constrained by the ideological straitjacket imposed by the Stalinist regime in the 1930s. Regardless of the language, writers and artists essentially conveyed the same message, and emphasized the kind of socialist transformation determined by the Kremlin. The irony is that as Soviet Jewry achieved the semblance of national-cultural consolidation, little was left of the specifically Jewish content of the culture. The policy of "national in form, socialist in content" had reduced cultural and national identity to language, while imposing strict limits on content. For most government and party officials, however, the existence of a Jewish territorial enclave in the Soviet Union was sufficient evidence of a successful policy toward Soviet Jewry.

Jews remained , however, a distinct minority in the Jewish Autonomous Region. Of the approximately 109,000 inhabitants of the region at the end of the 1930s, fewer than 20,000 were Jews. Despite the government's concerted effort to tout Birobidzhan as the new center of Soviet Jewish life, most Jews were wary of moving to an unknown place where they had no historical roots. Even those committed to the building of socialism were understandably reluctant to move thousands of miles for a life on the land.

Yet even if the government had taken its commitment to Birobidzhan more seriously and had not withdrawn support by the end of the 1930s, it is likely that the effort to establish a Red Zion within the borders of the Soviet would have failed. As difficult as life in the former Pale of Settlement was, existence in Birobidzhan was even more challenging, thanks to deficiencies in the region's infrastructure, the difficulty of farming the marshy land, and the absence of an established Jewish community. Jews seeking escape from the dead-end world of the former Pale of Settlement had other avenues for social and economic advancement. Why would a young Jew from a shtetl (small town) in Belarus choose to move to Birobidzhan, some five thousand miles from Moscow, when a new life beckoned in the Soviet capital or cities like Leningrad, Kyiv, and Odesa that boasted rich educational and cultural offerings? Stalin's "revolution from above," with its emphasis on industrial and urban development, provided Jews with unprecedented opportunities. Moreover, opportunities existed in a variety of government and public organizations that focused on the development of a socialist Jewish culture. In 1952, prominent Yiddish writer Peretz Markish admitted, when he defended himself against charges of "Jewish nationalism" and "anti-Soviet activity," that as early as 1934 he "didn't think a smart Jew would go live in Birobidzhan when he already had everything [in Moscow]." As he confessed to his interrogators, Markish had rhetorically asked the American journalist Ben-Zion Goldberg, "What stupid Jew would give up Moscow for Birobidzhan?"[5]

Moreover, Yiddish limited the prospects for Soviet Jews, who nevertheless needed to learn Russian to succeed. Why attend Yiddish schools when Russian was the language necessary for professional success and advancement? Opportunities for upward mobility abounded in the 1930s, but Yiddish and Birobidzhan did not figure prominently in the minds of those seeking to get ahead. As one American observer noted in 1938, "If national culture is simply a linguistic variation of something that is called 'general Soviet culture,' then why does one have to have it? The young Jew is well able to learn Russian."[6] In other words, acculturation, integration, and even assimilation were virtually inevitable given government policy, personal preferences, and socioeconomic developments.

Despite the fact that Yiddish has been one of the region's two official languages since the 1930s, the public expression of Birobidzhan's Jewish nature became circumscribed after the heyday of Yiddish during the region's first decade of existence. True, the *Birobidzhaner shtern* still appeared on a daily basis, and Birobidzhan was still known as the Jewish Autonomous Region. But virtually all other markers of the region's status as the center of a Yiddish culture vanished. For example, postmarks from 1935 and 1947 were written in Yiddish and Russian, but by 1955, Yiddish postmarks had disappeared.

The purges of the 1930s also did irreparable damage to Birobidzhan, coming very close to destroying the project entirely. The inhabitants of Birobidzhan did not escape the bloodletting of the political terror between 1936 and 1938. In the greatest irony of all, during the purges the (Jewish) political leaders of Birobidzhan who had carried out Kremlin policy of developing the region were accused of furthering Jewish causes. The Communist Party leadership imprisoned or executed advocates of Birobidzhan, and it ended the concerted effort to encourage Jewish resettlement. The state closed all but two of the Yiddish schools in the region and, as it did elsewhere in the USSR, clamped down on cultural and educational institutions of national minorities. By the time World War II broke out, all efforts at the organized movement of Jews to Birobidzhan ended. The money dried up, and the commitment to Birobidzhan as the center of Soviet Jewry evaporated. Life for Jews in Birobidzhan fell victim to the new Russocentric policies of the Kremlin, which wielded its imperial power and control. By the end of the 1930s, Russification overshadowed Jewishness, despite the regime's stated commitment to promote Jewish culture and life. The experiment to settle Jews in Birobidzhan was an abject failure.

The fact that Jews accounted for just 16 percent of the region's population even at the height in 1939 is stark evidence of the government's inability to build a genuinely Jewish region in the Soviet Far East. Birobidzhan never became a center of Soviet Jewry embodying the aspirations of a secular Yiddishist culture. By the late 1930s, notwithstanding the lip service paid by officials and literary figures, the Kremlin intended to efface Jewish identity. Assimilation into the emerging Soviet way of life—the development of *homo sovieticus*—became the overriding goal of the Communist Party. The Kremlin, while not dismantling the structures dedicated to national consolidation, made clear that it desired to fuse all national cultures into a common socialist culture.

Ironically, as Soviet Jewry achieved the semblance of national and cultural consolidation, little was left of the specifically Jewish content of the culture in the territory. Soviet policy had stripped the region of all manifestations of traditional Jewish culture, which was heavily rooted in Judaism. In the words of Ezra Mendelsohn, "Soviet communism and Jewish nationalism were unable coexist."[7] By the end of the 1930s, the commitment to an autonomous national enclave for Soviet Jewry was, for the most part, over. In short, the socialist content became more important than the national (and religious) structures in which Jewish culture was expressed. The universalism of the Soviet experiment trumped the particularism of ethnic identity.

NOTES

1. Joseph Stalin, *Marxism and the National Question* (Moscow: Foreign Languages Publishing House, 1950), 16 and 64.
2. On Soviet nationality policy in the 1920s and 1930s, see Terry Martin, *The Affirmative Action Empire: Nations and Nationalism in the Soviet Union, 1923–1939* (Ithaca: Cornell University Press, 2001); Zvi Gitelman, *Jewish Nationality Policy and Soviet Politics: The Jewish Sections of the CPSU, 1917–1930* (Princeton: Princeton University Press, 1972); and Yuri Slezkine, *Arctic Mirrors: Russia and the Small Peoples of the North* (Ithaca: Cornell University Press, 1996).
3. Personal interview in February 1992.
4. Personal interview in October 1994.
5. Joshua Rubenstein and Vladimir Naumov, eds., *Stalin's Secret Pogrom: The Postwar Inquisition of the Jewish Anti-Fascist Committee* (New Haven: Yale University Press, 2001), 134.
6. Hayim Greenberg, "Why Not Biro-Bidjan?" in *Jewish Frontier Anthology, 1934–1944* (New York: Jewish Frontier Association, 1945), 32–33.
7. Ezra Mendelsohn, *On Modern Jewish Politics* (New York: Oxford University Press, 1993), 39.

CHAPTER 42

LOVE LETTERS TO O'G'ULXON: PHOTOGRAPHY AND IMPERIAL INTIMACY IN THE GREAT PATRIOTIC WAR

CHARLES SHAW

AS THE SOVIET ARMY marched through Eastern Europe in the winter and spring of 1945, a photograph of O'g'ulxon Qurbonova (Image 42.1) appeared in a number of Russian- and Uzbek-language army periodicals. As the short caption describes, she was a "Komsomolka Stakhanovka"—a "Stakhanovite," or exceptionally high-achieving member of the Communist youth organization. She worked at the Zarbdor *kolkhoz* (collective farm) in Uzbekistan, where she had harvested 18,000 kilograms of cotton in one season. For soldiers who could not read Russian, this information was brief enough that they could easily ask someone to translate. And if no translators were at hand, then at least they could see a young woman in familiar "national" dress and a patterned skullcap smiling back at them with a portrait's intimacy.

The photos of O'g'ulxon and other Central Asian *kolkhoz* heroines inspired thousands of letters from Soviet soldiers of diverse nationalities stationed in every theater of war. O'g'ulxon alone received over 3,000 letters, and as many as 106 in a single day.[1] Several hundred of these letters to her and to other Uzbek young women have been preserved, providing a rare opportunity to interpret how visual images were created and interpreted during wartime.

The inclusion of O'g'ulxon's photo in the frontline newspapers was calibrated with gender in mind, to inspire or even guilt young men at the front to match the home-front labors of such hardworking young women, or to reassure them that they had not been forgotten. But how, exactly, were this image and caption interpreted by their intended audience—Red Army soldiers from Uzbekistan and other Soviet republics?

World War II, known in the USSR as the Great Patriotic War, was a war of empires that paved the way for decolonization and the American civil rights movement as marginalized and subject peoples leveraged their wartime contributions to demand

IMAGE 42.1 Letters to O'g'ulxon with newspaper photographs attached. Caption to photo on the left: "Komsomolka Ogul'khon Kurbanova, from the collective farm Zarbdar, Izbaskentskii raion, Andizhanskoi oblast, having harvested 18,000 kilos of cotton this season." Handwritten text on the right: "Your picture Oglxan [sic] all the factory leadership knows of your Stakhanovite achievements."

civil rights and independence. The war also transformed the Soviet empire, most apparent in the conquest and occupation of Eastern Europe, but no less importantly by refashioning relations within the Soviet Union. The first universal Soviet military draft in 1938 ensured that the war became the first truly pan-Soviet military campaign, where Caucasian and Central Asian soldiers fought side-by-side with their Slavic, Siberian, and Baltic compatriots. The German invasion and devastation of the western Soviet Union led to the evacuation of millions of Soviet citizens and pushed the center of industrial war production east to the Urals, Siberia, and Central Asia, where diverse civilian populations intermingled for the first time. In 1943, the Soviet state won sympathy in rural Central Asia by reopening mosques and allowing local believers to reconcile their Islamic faith with Soviet patriotism. The war left the Soviet empire strengthened on its Central Asian periphery when veterans returned home and asserted their *frontovik* (frontline fighter) credentials, Russian-language aptitude, and cultural fluency to buttress the rural social order.

This Soviet patriotism did not congeal, however, without concerted efforts to overcome disastrous battlefield results, desertions, and ethnic tension in the first years of war. From October 1942, the Red Army ensured that non-Russian soldiers were supported by textual and visual materials, such as newspapers, that "indigenized" the goals and meaning of the Great Patriotic War into their own native languages.[2] Officers were instructed to introduce soldiers to the Red Army's epistolary culture by helping them to write letters home. Throughout the home front, young people adopted unknown soldiers as pen pals in order to ensure that no *frontovik* was without a correspondent.

The portrait of O'g'ulxon included her district and collective farm name, which was all the information needed to deliver mail. Her youth—she was born in 1925—and Stakhanovite accomplishment made her a logical choice for editors to include in celebrating the home-front contributions of Soviet civilians. Although these photos often portrayed women at work, O'g'ulxon's close-up hid her physical exertion. Her portrait was taken at eye level and with eye contact, creating an illusion of one-to-one intimacy that fostered a sense of romantic availability that was no less powerful even though it was artfully constructed.

For many, the emotional connection created by the photograph was strong. One soldier wrote that he had written six letters to her with no reply. Another thanked O'g'ulxon briefly and wrote simply: "You have left in me something unknown. I keep your photocard with me."

The photo and caption also bore an array of implicit messages. One group of writers could not get over the figure of 18,000 kilograms, assuring her that "as Uzbek soldiers, we understand how difficult it is to pick so much cotton." Another of the descriptors, "*Komsomolka*" (member of the Young Communist League), implied traits such as Party-mindedness, education, and patriotism to pan-Soviet audiences. It likely implied adherence to progressive social values and courtship practices in rural Central Asia as well. "Stakhanovka" encouraged the soldiers to engage in friendly competition with her, like the soldiers who promised to kill a German for each 1,000 kg of cotton harvested. And her "national dress" was suitably novel to most Russian and other soldiers to convey the promise of Soviet internationalism and its diverse patriots, while more assiduous readers from the region inferred romantic eligibility in the braids resting on her shoulders, which suggested unmarried status.

The soldiers who wrote to O'g'ulxon used a variety of languages and scripts, expressing gratitude, congratulations, desire for correspondence or a copy of her photo in higher quality, and frequently, romance. Some wrote on colorful army-issue postcards with caricatures of the enemy or pictures of the Kremlin. Others wrote on "trophy" stationery with German inscriptions. One lifted a sheet from a Russian-Japanese textbook. Some included original artwork, while many enclosed her cut-out newspaper portrait (like the photo included here) to explain how they had become acquainted with her. They wrote from throughout the Soviet home front, from Tbilisi to Khabarovsk, as well as newly "liberated" Eastern Europe, including Bulgaria, Budapest, and just outside Berlin. Although most letters formulaically

IMAGE 42.2 Postcard to O'g'ulxon Qurbonova with a picture of the Moscow Kremlin on the left and the text "Death to the German occupiers" at the top right. Addressed to Ogul'khon Kurbanova from Vasily Vasilevich Ivanov. The stamp in the middle says: "Read by military censor 17503."

recited the author's rank, medals, battle path, and the ideological language of victory, the great bulk of them reveal some human detail, even vulnerability, forged by the photograph's ability to create connection (Image 42.2).

War letters operated like diaries in which soldiers came to terms with their participation in war and experimented with self-fashioning—as Soviet *frontoviki* or, using the Soviet empire's ethnic clichés, as Uzbek *yigits* (horsemen) or Kyrgyz *batyrs* (heroes). Of course, they wrote in a supervised solitude, given that officers might read over their shoulders and military censors opened all mail; nevertheless, the girls' portraits could become almost devotional objects of inspiration, meditation, and obsession, unwitting agents in imperial transformation and cultural change among Central Asian men and the broader Soviet populace.

Nowhere is this cultural flux more evident than in the soldiers' participation in the burgeoning Red Army romantic culture and use of the Russian language. Military service required Russian as a language of command, but it also enabled the creation of a common *frontovik* culture. At the front, Central Asian men took Russian nicknames, modified Islamic prohibitions against alcohol and cigarettes, and became enmeshed in the front's increasingly permissive gender relations, sometimes courting or marrying their Slavic nurses. In Central Asia, the championing of companionate rather than arranged marriages had been a long-standing plank in Soviet cultural campaigns. By inviting O'g'ulxon into these courtship rituals, Central Asian soldiers—unwittingly or not—aligned themselves with the state's progressive agenda.

Cultural modes such as poetry could be adapted in this novel romantic culture predicated on visuality. For example, Umriy Kuziev wrote to O'g'ulxon, "if you are a Muslim girl, then reply as soon as you can." He offered a poem "I Wish to Love," which included his "desire to be inspired by the bud of [her] lips." By photographing Uzbek labor heroines in garden scenes, often with cotton bolls or grapevines, Soviet imagemakers reinforced clichéd motifs of classical Central Asian poetry, equipping would-be poets with a visual language that was suffused with new urgency and bluntness. A letter to different Uzbek home-front heroine included the lines: "My heart skipped a beat when I saw your photograph. I was enraptured by what I saw, by your smile like a flower, and I vowed to keep your photograph from the magazine forever." As evidence of the novelty of this form of courtship, Uzbek authors could signal their unease by apologizing for using the word *dear* or pleading that the addressee "not be offended" or "not get angry," whereas Slavic writers might simply acknowledge the strangeness of receiving letters from an unknown writer.

Even if they were not always aware, Slavic writers also engaged in novel transgressions of Central Asian cultural norms. Although the Soviet state had long championed interethnic romance, both to accelerate cultural change and as a symbol of anticolonialism, the usual iconography featured Slavic women coupling with Muslim men in recognition that Muslim women were, in practice, off-limits to conjugal attention from Europeans. Yet this truism of Central Asian rural life was lost on most Slavic men, who figured that Komsomolkas throughout the Soviet Union shared certain traits. Some Slavic writers inquired about "her" *rodina* (homeland), but others wrote to O'g'ulxon as a member of a common *rodina*. The term's elasticity illustrated the rapid pace of change in the multiethnic state. So it was not a stretch for Dmitry Bozhemovskii to address O'g'ulxon as a "leading daughter of the Soviet people" and inquire: "At the end of [my] service, if you are not yet taken, I hope to come and visit you at your *kolkhoz*. Please forgive me, dear Ogulkhon, but I can only dream about having a friend like you for myself. I beg of you don't refuse my request."

How had wartime experiences transformed Central Asian soldiers? In May 1945, O'g'ulxon received a request for correspondence from a soldier stationed in Ukraine who introduced himself as Mukhamed Ergashov, a native of her local region in Uzbekistan. He wrote: "If you can read Russian, then I will write in Russian, or if you can't I can write in our language. So long . . . with regards unknown, Mukhamed or Misha." He left his military return address as "Mikhail Ergashov." Although the dominant position of Russian at the front meant that the assigning of nicknames was not strictly voluntary, in Ergashov's case we see an embrace of his frontline pseudonym, which is confirmed by other cases of non-Russian soldiers employing their *frontovik* nicknames in various settings throughout their lives. But despite his comfort with the nickname, Ergashov left it to O'g'ulxon to decide how to address him. Ergashov's indecision captured the era of rapid flux in the Soviet empire. It suggested that for the *frontoviki* of this new Soviet community, ethnic divisions were not always clear, yet when and how to balance the component parts of one's national and Soviet identities was an ongoing dilemma of assimilation.

For O'g'ulxon and other young women whose photographs inspired such letters, their consent and awareness of the role played by their photos is far from certain. Ultimately, the gap between the agency of the images and the girls' own intents illustrates the suggestive power of photography as well as its inherent limits. It embodies the emotive rush with which a pan-Soviet identity was formed at war, as well as its contingent nature.

Cultural strictures prevented Central Asia's rural female patriots from going to the front as soldiers or nurses in significant numbers, yet they labored selflessly in support of the war. The Communist Party noted the necessity for female labor due to the departure of working men, as well as the political opportunity of women's mobilization in a region where some still wore veils and avoided public work. The Party resurrected its Women's Department (defunct since 1930), made efforts to support working mothers, and organized tractor classes for young women. However, the majority made their contributions via tireless physical exertion without relying on machinery.

Although it did not lie, the photo of O'g'ulxon hid a more complex story that emerges from the research of Uzbek historians immediately after the war, and from my 2014 interview with O'g'ulxon's sister, Imaxon (born 1927). The publication of the portrait severed O'g'ulxon from her family and social context and implied her labor was the result of one young woman's solo achievements. In fact, she was part of an ambitious team of six people (two men and four women). The team earned the nickname "the 100 centner" (a centner is a unit of weight, about 50 kg) for more than quadrupling the state's most ambitious harvest goals and was led by her father, Qurbon-ota Nurmatov.

A far different photo of O'g'ulxon and her father, by Max Penson, appeared in Soviet newspapers as early as August 1944 and does not seem to have launched a wave of epistolary sentiment. The two are depicted smiling, bent over in simulated labor.[3] By January 1945, word of Qurbon-ota's 115-centner cotton harvest spread, and the elderly man's photo appeared in a number of pan-Soviet newspapers, flanked by his two daughters, each holding a bounty of cotton bolls.[4] Qurbon-ota's supervisory presence could inspire a different sort of correspondence entirely. The handful of soldiers' letters that mention him by name are the most religiously forward—with writers describing themselves as fellow Muslims—and romantically subdued.

For a Union-wide audience, Moscow's *Izvestiia* newspaper devoted an entire article to Qurbon-ota in March 1945, mentioning a new detail—the loss of an adoptive son who fell at Stalingrad—but not a word about his daughters.[5] In later years, Imaxon maintained that her sister had begun the war married, and that her husband died at the front. It is possible that the *Izvestiia* journalist or her translator confused this "adoptive son" with a son-in-law. Either way, we must infer that the portrait in soldiers' newspapers depicted a married woman or war widow.

As O'g'ulxon's father and team leader, Qurbon-ota was partially responsible for his daughter's fame or, at least, gave consent to the TASS photographer Semyon Beznosov to create the portrait that fundamentally shifted O'g'ulxon's image and opened the gates to the flood of letters. Although Qurbon-ota was not opposed to celebrity more generally, it is doubtful he would have approved of the sudden attention from thousands of young men.

O'g'ulxon's own thoughts are elusive. She spoke no Russian and was illiterate, which broke the letters' imagined chain of sentiment. Imaxon recalled that a *kolkhoz* clerk read some of the letters aloud, but the majority may have gone unread. She also recalled that although O'g'ulxon was tickled by the offers she received, she did not take them seriously.

A researcher from the Uzbek Academy of Sciences visited O'g'ulxon in September 1945 and conducted a short interview that revealed an ascetic, driven young life. She had completed three grades of schooling before starting work in 1937, quickly proving to be a strong cotton harvester. O'g'ulxon herself could precisely list the kilograms of cotton she had picked in the preceding days. About her accomplishment, she said simply: "At the start of the Great Patriotic War . . . the young men left for the front . . . If I were a young man, I too would raise my hand to go to the front to fight the enemy." She added that producing cotton was another way to wage war. The notion of equivalent fronts for soldiers and rear workers was ideological orthodoxy by 1945, but her short remarks might also hint at her resignation toward the rural Uzbek gender strictures that left her pinned to her *kolkhoz*.

She explained to the visiting historian that her photo appeared in frontline newspapers, after which she began to receive thousands of letters: "They ask me to keep working hard and even more effectively. I am selflessly fulfilling the *frontoviks'* instructions." In the historian's interpretation, O'g'ulxon considered the letters to be simple reminders to work harder, betraying no knowledge of their intimate details.

The Soviet empire that withstood the war was more integrated and more durable, supported by rural labor heroes and *frontoviki* who considered themselves partners in Victory. Yet the postwar order saw efforts to redirect or bottle up the more egalitarian, boisterous iterations of pan-Soviet identity that threatened to unsettle imperial hierarchies. The wartime truce with religion also empowered cultural conservatives to reestablish community norms that had been unsettled. In Uzbekistan's definitive volume of frontline letters published in 1949, there were no traces of nicknames and ethnic transformations in the letters to O'g'ulxon and other young women, and Friendship of the Peoples became strictly chaste.

As early as May 1, 1945, Tashkent's *Pravda vostoka* newspaper provided its own authoritative narrative of the war letters in an article titled "Ogul'khon and Her Friends." In this version, an unnamed *frontovik* from the neighboring village visits the *kolkhoz* in the winter of 1945 in search of Qurbon-ota but is met by none other than O'g'ulxon, who informs him of her harvesting achievement. Amazed, the visitor snaps her picture and vows that they will meet again. Several months later, letters start arriving from all corners of the Soviet homeland from soldiers of various nationalities. Finally, she receives a letter from the man himself who, it turns out, was a war correspondent and had seeded the newspapers with her portrait. The article ends with O'g'ulxon late at night, having read a mountain of mail, composing a reply to her friend, the war correspondent, addressing the envelope "to Berlin."

NOTES

1. Arkhiv Akademii Nauk Respubliki Uzbekistana (AAN RUz), fond 54, op. 1, no. 16, f. 257. Direct quotations of all letters come from AAN RUz, fond 54, op. 1, no. 3 and 21.
2. Brandon Schechter, "'The People's Instructions': Indigenizing the Great Patriotic War Among 'Non-Russians,'" *Ab Imperio*, no. 3 (2012): 109–132.
3. "Izbaskentskie khlopkoroby (Uzbekskaia SSR) boriutsia za poluchenie 25 tsentnerov khlopka s gektara," *Zapoliarnyi trud*, August 3, 1944.
4. These included "115 tsentnerov s gektara," *Sotsialisticheskoe zemledelie*, January 30, 1945. Photo by V. Terekhov; *Komsomol'skaia pravda* (26 January and 10 February 1945); and *Qizil O'zbekiston* (precise date unknown).
5. Elena Bragantseva, "Vesna Kurban Ata," *Izvestiia*, March 30, 1945.

CHAPTER 43

FROM ETHNOGRAPHIC REALITY TO SOCIALIST REALISM: ILLUSTRATIONS IN SOVIET PRIMERS FOR THE INDIGENOUS MINORITIES OF THE NORTH

NIKOLAI VAKHTIN

A LOT HAS BEEN WRITTEN over the last twenty years about Soviet schoolbooks and their illustrations. I am unaware, however, of any publications that deal with the illustrations in the Soviet primers for the Indigenous minorities of the North.[1]

The first primers for Northern schoolchildren written in their own languages were printed in 1932. The development of alphabets and orthographies for the Indigenous minorities of the North started in 1929–1930, when the basis for the writing systems, the famous Integrated Northern Alphabet, was developed by the Research Association of the Institute for the Peoples of the North (RA IPN). The Integrated Northern Alphabet was based on the Roman alphabet and approved by the Academic Council of the RA IPN in 1930. This alphabet became the foundation for all writing systems of Indigenous Northern minorities.

The text and illustrations of the first primers in Indigenous languages were modeled on a Russian-language primer written by Professor Vladimir Bogoras and his student Sergei Stebnitskii to help the children of the Northern peoples to learn Russian.[2] Bogoras and Stebnitskii emphasized that they had tried to bring the text and, especially, the illustrations closer to the real life of the Northern children. In the introduction to the primer, they wrote:

> We aimed at making the drawings as artistic as possible, and at the same time making them clear for the indigenous Northern people. To achieve this, 30 drawings have been copied from indigenous originals . . . The rest were carefully checked and harmonized with the conditions of Northern life. Photographs, mostly unpublished, from various ethnographic collections served as originals for those drawings. Twenty-five drawings,

> mostly illustrating agriculture, urban life and political issues, have been borrowed from various publications.[3]

The main principle of the first primers was thus "realistic truth of the Northern life conditions." This can be illustrated by the Nenets language primer written by Georgii Prokofiev and published in 1932. (The Nenets were, and some still are, nomadic reindeer herders in northwestern Siberia.) The drawings for the primer were made by Prokofiev himself, an anthropologist who spent a long time living with the Nenets and was familiar with their life. Both pages shown in Image 43.1 depict women in a specific sitting posture: they are seated on the ground with their legs stretched forward. The cradle with the baby is drawn competently, as are the tools on the top left. The painter tried, and succeeded, in representing the people and objects familiar to the Nenets children who were supposed to use the primer.

The primers and other schoolbooks created by RA IPN for the Northern minorities in the early 1930s compared favorably with those printed for other ethnic groups of the Soviet Union. In an official review of the primers, the author analyzed primers intended for Karakalpak, Komi, Mordovian, and other minorities, and concluded

— 10 —

Harm tād! Məta sa həm.

Məta sam hamada tārā
Məta sam wətā tārā.

Əə Ss Ww

Harm tād! Məta sa həm.
Məta sam wətā tārā

— 25 —

Marja sawkam sədabi. Darja libtadm l,aŋgabta; libtadm tьrabta tara—ŋuliђ sa-ŋ,uj. Pıwam ŋobtar,em tьrabta tara.

N,ūd,ako Was,ka jebchana honь.
Jebcm manzabtad!
Jebcm janambowna manzabtad!

Cc

IMAGE 43.1 Georgii Prokofiev's Nenets primer, 1932.

that they contained "serious mistakes," especially as regards the illustrations. He accused the authors and the publishers of doing amateurish work instead of serious research: "The artists, who had never seen a Karakalpak in their life, who know nothing about the people's history, culture, or everyday life, who had no materials (such as photographs, illustrations, museum items etc.), who had no access to serious academic consultations, have chosen to follow the line of the least resistance and produced very rough, and often totally incorrect illustrations."[4] He continues:

> The work of the Leningrad branch of the State Pedagogical Publishing House was organized in a totally different way. The publisher contacted RA IPN and provided their illustrators with exact data and scholarly consultations, so the results were very different . . . the quality of the illustrations here is much higher than in the primers published by the Moscow branch. Precise knowledge of the material, of cultures, of everyday life forms the foundation for these illustrations . . . these primers should be considered as model ones.[5]

In other words, the official requirements at this time were to reproduce reality accurately. Children were supposed to recognize familiar things, animals, and themselves on the pages of the primer.

The illustrators of the 1920s and 1930s primers were professional artists and book illustrators. Many artists who worked for the publisher of the primers travelled to the North especially to see the life there. These included Irina Walter (1903–1993), who participated in many Arctic expeditions; Sergei Pervuninskii (??–1948), who was part of an ethnographic expedition to the Far East in 1939 and brought back an important collection of artifacts; and Nikolai Travin (1882–1950s), a graduate of the Ethnographic Department of Leningrad State University who took part in several Arctic expeditions in the 1930s as an official painter.[6]

This period of "ethnographic realism" in primer illustration, however, was short-lived. In February 1934, the Central Committee of the Communist Party published a decree, "On Schoolbooks for Primary and Secondary School." The decree pronounced the current policy of the People's Commissariat for Education wrong on the grounds that it aimed at decentralizing education. The decree demanded the standardization of schoolbooks for all schools and for all subjects. All schoolbooks were to be approved by the Commissariat, and all were to be published by the state publisher so that "no changes could be introduced without a special decision of the Commissariat." The decree also called for "standardization of school books as regards their technical form: format, binding, fonts, paper, stitching, cover, illustrations, etc."[7]

The mid-1930s also saw a sharp turn in the Soviet ideology. The policy of *socialist realism* was introduced as state-mandated guidelines that prescribed the form and content of all the arts. Socialist realism, both as state policy for the arts and as a discourse, sought to create socialist reality through narrative and representation. According to this approach, in the eyes of the authorities a socialist realist piece of art, be it a painting, a novel, or a film, must show life not as it is today but as it should become tomorrow.[8]

The requirements for schoolbook illustrations changed accordingly. The decree mentioned earlier stated that a schoolbook must be "cheerful and energetic, Bolshevik style," and must "call for struggle and victory." This cheerfulness and call for victory were repeated in the years that followed in all publications regarding schoolbooks. For example, in a 1934 publication on book illustrations, K. Kuzminskii wrote: "The illustrations . . . must inculcate the correct perception of reality, must incite the urge to strive actively for the goals set by the proletariat, radiating *cheerfulness and energy*."[9] In a critical article published soon after the decree was issued, A. Sukharev lists several "mistakes" in schoolbook illustrations. For example, he condemns a picture of a horse: "We need an *energetic and cheerful horse*, a bold steed (*bodryi kon'*). Children love this *energy and cheerfulness*. They appreciate pictures that encourage them and *call them to labor and victory*." He then turns to a picture of a chicken incubator: "[T]he drawing should show that the incubator yields many chickens," but in the drawing, there are just a few. "We are losing an important ideological point here: the incubator should produce chicken better than a hen does." He then discusses a drawing of a workers' town: the houses are shapeless, the streets are dirty—all this is wrong; no such drawings can be admitted into a schoolbook. He criticizes the depiction of gender roles: "The girl is wiping dust off the tables; the boy is opening the window. The painter draws just *as it is usually done*: all the dirty work is shifted onto the girl." But again, this is wrong: it doesn't matter what is "usually done," the painter must show how it should be, not how it is.[10]

Here is a quote from yet another article, by a different critic: "Take, for example, [the drawing of] the tractor factory: it is so ugly, so very much like old barracks; this shows quite clearly that the painters do not know *our new tractor factories*."[11] Clearly, the phrase "our new tractor factories" doesn't mean real factories; it means "factories that we will someday build." These critics understand, of course, that the drawings are realistic. But the ideology of socialist realism already "captured the masses," so one must draw not what is but what should be.

Let us now compare the illustrations in primers of the early and mid-1930s with those published in later periods for the Nanai (who were, and in some cases still are, hunters and fishers of the Russian Far East). Image 43.2 shows two double-page spreads from Nanai primers published in 1936 and 1956.[12] There are several interesting details in the 1936 primer. Note both women's typical sitting postures on the left page, but also the inevitable long and thin pipes that both Nanai men and women smoked constantly. The woman on the left-hand page is sewing; the man on the right-hand page is mending a fishing net. The woman at the bottom of the left-hand page seems to be simply talking to the boy; on the right-hand page, the boy is showing the man a bird's nest he apparently procured. The postures, the cloths, the situations are familiar to the children, and easily recognizable.

IMAGE 43.2 Comparison of illustrations in earlier and later primers, Nanai, 1936 and 1956.

The illustrations in the 1956 Nanai primer are quite different. On the left-hand page, we see a standard classroom with large windows, flowers on the windowsills, and standard furniture: desks, blackboard, abacus, a terrestrial globe. Nothing indicates that the classroom is Nanai. On the right-hand page, a man is holding two children by their hands: nothing in their posture or clothes shows they are Nanai.

The pipes and the special Far Eastern hats have disappeared. Only the hat of the smaller child vaguely resembles traditional design. In the 1950s, one could meet a man in such rubber boots and such quilted jacket anywhere in the Soviet Union.

The same is true for other primers, like earlier Saami (reindeer herders in the north of Sweden, Norway, Finland, and Russia) and the Sel'kup (hunters and fishers and living in northwestern Siberia). Early primers show mostly familiar scenes, in contrast with later primers in the same languages that show the inevitable classroom with large windows and flowers on the windowsills. I am not implying that after the 1934 decree all illustrations suddenly changed, but in general, there are more realistic illustrations in early 1930s and more socialist realistic ones in the later primers.

The reality of the actual classrooms was, of course, far from the pictures that the children saw in the revised primers. Here is a description of a classroom by Ekaterina Rubtsova, who taught in a Yupik Eskimo village, Sireniki, in southeastern Chukotka from 1930 to 1932:

> The first school was a small wooden house, American style, made of thin planks. Rich natives bought such houses from American merchants to keep hunting tools there . . . The house had two parts. The first was cold, with single-layer walls, the second was planked on both sides. Imagine a room four meters long and two meters wide, with a small iron stove in one corner and plank shelves instead of a bookcase in the opposite, and you will get the idea of the classroom that the local administration provided for me. A door led from the classroom to the second "room" if this is an adequate name for a cubicle the height of an average human, with room for one bed only. This was where I lived for some time until the Eskimos erected their winter tents.[13]

There were no modern desks, no large windows, no flowers on the windowsills. Real life quickly disappeared from the illustrations; the imagined life of the future took its place.

By the end of 1930s, and especially in the 1950s, a canon was formed for showing the North and the Northern life in schoolbooks that was totally different from what life really was. As Catriona Kelly wrote in an article on the primers for the Russian schools:

> In the consciousness of children, two different norms were present. On the one hand, children were aware of how [in reality] everyone lived . . . but on the other, they also regularly encountered "normal life" in the way it was represented in textbooks, where everyone lived in spacious apartments, every family had both a mother and a father, where people sat round every evening engaged in "worthwhile pastimes," where there was no such thing as a queue or shortages of food and essential goods.[14]

If this gulf between daily life and the lives represented in textbooks was evident to children in Leningrad and Moscow, it was all the more the case for the children of the North. While Northern children could recognize themselves and their life in the illustrations in the primers of the early 1930s, it was impossible to identify themselves in the idealized picture offered by the 1950s primers. For children, it was only possible to conclude that the primer demanded that they become like this, and that a "normal" classroom should look like this, and they prompted to think that "perhaps others children and other classrooms in other parts of the country are like this—but not me, not my school, and not my life."

IMAGE 43.3 Illustrations from late Soviet primers for Saami and Nentsi children, 1986.

I am convinced that these idealized and deceitful illustrations were perceived by the Northern children as an inaccessible ideal they were expected to attain. It is quite possible that this painted untruth was one of the causes of the social frustration that was characteristic of the Northern Indigenous minorities starting from late 1950s—that is, when the children who learned to read in the 1930s grew up. This is certainly not the only cause, but still . . .

The last picture (Image 43.3) shows pages of three late Soviet primers for Northern children. There is nothing Northern in these illustrations; they could be pages from any Soviet primer, in any language. There are no differences shown between children of different Indigenous peoples; some painters still try to imitate "indigenous" faces, others don't do even this.

A clear evolutionary line can thus be followed in the illustrations for the Northern primers between the 1930s and the 1980s. In the early 1930s, the illustrators were supposed to know the traditional culture of the people whose primer they were to illustrate. Realism and exactitude in showing the faces, clothes, utensils, and tools were valued. The children were supposed to recognize themselves and their lives in the pictures. After 1934, socialist realism took the upper hand. The pictures were supposed to show life as it was to become in the "bright future" that the Soviet people were building under the guidance of the Communist Party. This principle was in use till the end of the 1950s, and then gradually yielded to the pressure of a new canon. Late Soviet illustrations depicted an imaginary North and imaginary Northern children that had nothing to do with either the present or the future: these were just nice pictures.

The history of illustrations in Soviet primers for children of the North is a sad story of striving for exact and detailed knowledge that was erased under the steamroller of socialist realism and transformed into a conventional and false image of the "Far North" that was eventually accepted by everybody: the painters, the critics, the teachers—and the children.[15]

NOTES

1. In Russia, "Indigenous Minorities of the North" (*korennye malochislennye narody Severa*) is a legal term.
2. V. G. Bogoraz, and S. N. Stebnitskii, *Bukvar' dlia severnykh narodnostei* (Moscow: Tsentral'noe izdatel'stvo narodov SSSR, 1927).
3. Bogoraz and Stebnitskii, *Bukvar' dlia severnykh narodnostei'*, iv.
4. A. Reviakin. "O kachestve illustratsii natsuchebnikov [On the quality of illustrations for the ethnic school books]"; Kuz'minskii, K. S. *Illustrirovanie uchebnoi knigi*, 2nd ed., corrected and amended (Moscow: Gos. uch.-ped.giz. 1934), 98–112.
5. Ibid.
6. "Irina Vladimirovna Val'ter," https://artinvestment.ru/auctions/123950/biography.html; L. B. Stepanova, *Muzeinoe sobiratel'stvo v Rossii: Yakutskie etnograficheskie kollektsii* (Novosibirsk: Nauka, 2016), 79; and "Nikolai Antol'evich Travin," https://kennziffer.blogspot.com/2012/09/blog-post_18.html.
7. See https://istmat.org/node/58635

8. See Evgeny Dobrenko, *The Political Economy of Socialist Realism*, translated by Jesse M. Savage (New Haven: Yale University Press, 2007).
9. Kuz'minskii, *Illustrirovanie*, 115; italics added.
10. A. Sukharev, "Dat' uchebnikam khoroshie illiustratsii [Making good illustrations for schoolbooks]," *Prosveshcheniie Sibiri*, no. 5 (1933): 47–48; 47; italics added.
11. Reviakin, 102; italics added.
12. All primers cited in this article (as well as all other editions in minority languages of the former Soviet Union) are kept in the "Collection of Ethnic Literatures" of the Russian National Library in St. Petersburg.
13. *Teksty na iazykakh eskimosov Chukotki v zapisi E. S. Rubtsovoi* [*Texts in Yupik Languages of Chukotka recorded by E. S. Rubtsova*], compiled and edited by N. Vakhtin (St Petersburg: Art-Express, 2019), 9.
14. C. Kelly, "Papa edet v komandirovku: representatsiia obschestvennyh i lichnyh tsennostei v sovetskih bukvariah i knigah dlia chteniia," in *Uchebnyi tekst v sovetskoi shkole* (Moscow: Institut logiki, kognitologii i razvitiia lichnosti, 2008), 176.
15. The research for this article was funded by grant 2020-220-08-6030 from the Government of Russia for the project "Preservation of Linguistic and Cultural Diversity and Sustainable Development of the Arctic and Subarctic of the Russian Federation."

CHAPTER 44

THE STALINIST IMPERIAL BODY POLITIC IN A SOVIET PHOTO POSTER

ERIKA WOLF

THE 1951 SOVIET POLITICAL poster *Under the Leadership of the Great Stalin—Forward to Communism!* (Image 44.1) presents a striking synthetic image of the broad territory of the USSR, its diverse peoples, and its supreme leader. Combined, these three elements visually assert the imperial nature of the Soviet Union, with its unsurpassed sovereignty, expansive territories, and many peoples. Political posters such as this were a highly regulated form of representation that was under the control of the Central Committee of the Communist Party of the Soviet Union. Designed to clearly and persuasively communicate and propagate official ideology, this poster presents the USSR as a modern communist empire. This essay examines the broader political iconography that shapes this representation of empire, ranging from a statue of Roman Emperor Augustus to Thomas Hobbes's image of the body politic. This analysis reveals the poster's use of specific historical and current imagery of the body of the leader and of the body politic in publicity associated with the 1936 Constitution of the Soviet Union (or the "Stalin Constitution") and the nationality policy it framed.

Dominating the center of the poster, Stalin stands at a lectern, his arm raised in a gesture of oratory. Below and behind him, a veritable sea of Soviet peoples extends to the horizon, where the forms of buildings and industrial plants appear. To the left stands a new postwar Moscow skyscraper, with another massive building under construction next to it, while on the right, a row of electrical pylons leads off into the distance, rendered following the conventions of aerial perspective—with colors fading out and detail blurring as they go. Over this vast expanse, a map appears. Above the horizon, larger blue shapes double as both sky and water, and the map itself is curious. Instead of the conventional, direct mapping of land onto a two-dimensional surface, green orthogonal lines recede into the distance, creating the illusion of a three-dimensional projection of the vast expanses of the Soviet Union.

IMAGE 44.1 Boris Berezovskii and Mikhail Solovyov, "Under the Leadership of the Great Stalin—Forward to Communism!" Political poster, 1951.

While no borders are delineated, the locations of bodies of water, dams, hydroelectric projects, and a few cities are labeled. Instead of a unified, coherent space, the poster shows two distinct spaces—one filled with the populace of the Soviet Union and the other detailing planned developments for the country's territory. The central figure of Stalin cuts across and links these two spaces. With his left hand resting on the lectern, his right hand reaches up and points to the boundless Soviet space pictured by the map. Stalin's gesture is reinforced by the people assembled around him, a diverse mixture of ethnic and professional types. They all turn to focus on him, their smiling faces lifted to acknowledge his presence with admiration. With his back turned to them, the gazes of the vast mass of people extending to the horizon empower him. But instead of returning their gaze, he unifies and embodies all of their volition. He looks out to the broader world and points upwards, to the full realization of communism—as declared in the red text below the image: "Under the leadership of the great Stalin—forward to communism!"

The poster is the collaborative work of Mikhail Solovyov (1905–1990) and Boris Berezovskii (1910–1977), both of whom had prolific careers as Soviet political poster artists. Solovyov studied painting with Ilya Mashkov and Pavel Sokolov-Skalya at the art school of the Association of Artists of the Revolution (AKhR) and worked as a painter in the 1930s before taking up poster art during World War II. Originally from

Omsk, Siberia, Berezovskii undertook several years of informal art study during the 1920s and worked as a photo retoucher. It was only in the late 1940s that he began to publish posters with Iskusstvo (Art), the flagship publishing house for political posters. As a collaborative work, this poster combines the specific skills of the two artists to masterly effect. Berezovskii specialized in the photographic poster, creating socialist realist propaganda images that built upon the association of photography with evidentiary truth. This poster employs photography to persuade us about something in its becoming—a forward projection of state plans into reality. At the same time, the use of formal techniques from academic painting creates a highly structured image of a bright Soviet empire. In other drawn posters around this time, Solovyov employed similar compositions of Soviet peoples against backdrops of the land or maps.

The poster was first published in a large format (77 × 115 cm) at the start of 1951 and reissued in a smaller format (56 × 84 cm) the following year, with a combined print run of one million posters. A German variant of the basic design was used to promote the exhibition *Grossbauten des Kommunisum* (Grand Communist Construction Projects), which opened at the Grassi Museum in Leipzig in May 1952. The multiple editions and publication of a German variant indicate that this design was well received within the state propaganda apparatus.

The poster promotes several key Soviet initiatives of the era. Firstly, it celebrates the reconstruction of the country after the devastation of World War II, the rebuilding of cities and the restoration of vital infrastructure that lay in ruins. Secondly, it showcases the Great Stalin Plan for the Transformation of Nature, an initiative introduced in 1948 that envisioned the massive planting of forests in an effort to combat drought in the southern steppe, a scheme that has been identified as one of the first state-sponsored attempts to combat climate change.[1] Discontinued after Stalin's death, the plan included extensive forest belts that would protect the land from arid winds. The map in the upper half of the poster depicts the plan in the manner of an architectural projection. A modernist grid of green bands of forests crisscrosses the land and is interspersed with rivers, canals, and hydroelectric plants under construction.

In addition to this immediate postwar context, this poster may also be viewed as the culmination of various strands in the representation of Stalin as a political leader and the national politics that he implemented in the Soviet Union. As a photomontage image, this poster literally assembles an image of the Soviet body politic out of largely preexisting images and iconographies. Examination of these images and iconographies clarifies what the poster says visually about how the Soviet people would be guided by Stalin "forward to communism."

Ivan Shagin shot the source photograph of Stalin at the opening celebrations for the first line of the Moscow Metro on May 14, 1935, in the Columned Hall of the House of Unions. In the original photograph, Stalin stands next to Viacheslav

Molotov. This iconic image was widely used as a source for posters, paintings, and political graphics, usually without Molotov. Stalin addresses an unseen audience with his arm raised in an oratorical gesture that recalls the statue of Augustus of Prima Porta, a celebrated image of the first Roman emperor that was discovered in 1863 (Image 44.2). Clad in military garb, Augustus appears as a statesman, the commander of a victorious army (an *imperator*), and as an orator speaking to his troops.

IMAGE 44.2 *Augustus of Prima Porta*, first century.

The oratorical gesture, known as *adlocutio*, appeared widely in Roman statuary and coinage and is interpreted as a representation of the absolute power of the emperor. While Augustus appears in military regalia, this statue is also associated with the Pax Romana, two centuries of peaceful existence that was ushered in with his reign as emperor. This iconography was especially well suited to depicting the postwar Stalin, focused on rebuilding the country with the return to peace. Notably, Berezovskii first used Shagin's photograph of Stalin in a 1949 poster, the text of which asserts "We stand for peace and defend the cause of peace!"

In the twentieth century, the Augustus of Prima Porta became a key image in the iconography of political leadership, especially of the dictatorial kind. Augustus's *adlocutio* pose may be found in propaganda imagery of Mussolini, Hitler, Stalin, Mao, and others. Appearing with raised hands before the citizenry, these leaders are symbolically conferred the mandate—the authority to govern on behalf of the people. Raising his hand, Stalin both accepts the assent of the people gathered around him and embodies their will. He leads, guides, and drives them forward to communism.

The cropped body of a leader suspended over a landscape recalls another major landmark in the iconography of political leadership: the engraved frontispiece of the first edition of Thomas Hobbes's *Leviathan* in 1651 (Image 44.3). In this book, Hobbes proposes a model of government based on the social contract, in which the people surrender rights or freedoms to a sovereign authority in order to assure a well-functioning social order. In the upper part of the frontispiece, the crowned Leviathan of absolute monarchy rises above a landscape, holding a sword in one hand and a crosier in the other. The body of the monarch is comprised of his subjects, whose bodies turn to face him. Backs of heads are visible on his torso, while standing figures in profile gather along the arms. This is a visualization of the metaphor of the body politic—the state or nation is imagined as comprised of all the people of the realm purposively joining together, unified in direction and purpose.

The Soviet political poster employs a similar construction of the body politic. Like Leviathan, the gathered populace orients their bodies to face Stalin. Here, it becomes clear whom he is addressing—the unseen masses that radiate out before him. Viewers of the poster become part of this crowd that joins together from all directions to make up the Soviet body politic; they occupy a position comparable to the figures that appear on the front torso of Leviathan. Further similarities are evident in the larger scale of the leaders, the cropping of their bodies, and their superior vantage point in relation to the realm. In 1936, a new Soviet edition of *Leviathan* was published that featured a high-quality reproduction of the original frontispiece.[2] Perhaps inspired by the image from Hobbes's book, the iconography of Stalin as a kind of Leviathan was articulated in visual propaganda for the Stalin Constitution that came into effect in December that same year. Numerous posters and other propaganda images celebrating the new constitution depict diverse peoples of the USSR gathered together in a visual display of the new Soviet social contract under Stalin. Uniting together, they assent to the authority of the new, fundamental law and to

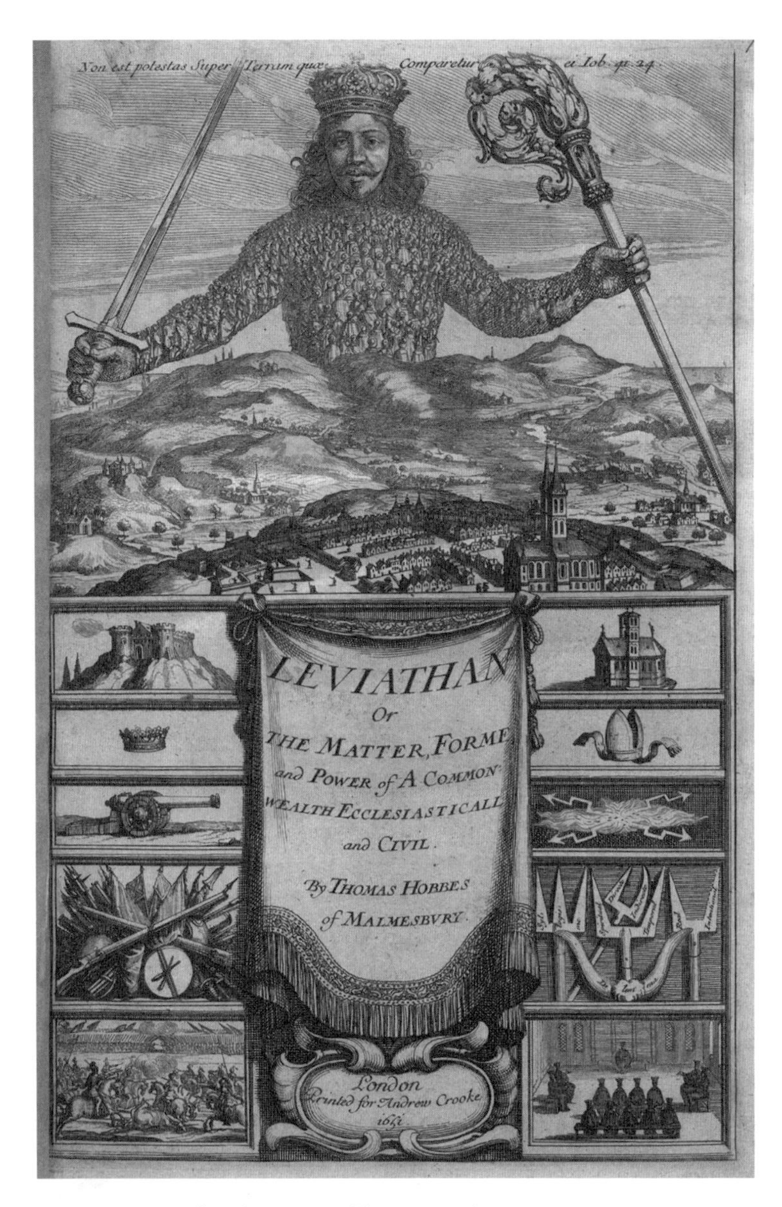

IMAGE 44.3 Frontispiece for Thomas Hobbes, *Leviathan*, 1651.

the absolute power of Stalin, who appears as a larger figure rising above the people. These images promote key aspects of the newly defined Soviet body politic: the harmonious unification of the peoples of the USSR and the leading role of the Communist Party.

Berezovskii and Solovyov's poster was informed by El Lissitzky's photomontages for a massive quadruple issue of the photographic propaganda magazine *USSR in*

Construction, dedicated to the Stalin Constitution that was published in 1937. Near the start of the issue, a foldout poster with Stalin in the pose of Augustus announces the first article of the constitution. The various Union-republics are joyously celebrated in four-page spreads that feature commentary on their transformation under Soviet rule, and montages that combine maps with photographs of local peoples, and technical and agricultural achievements. Many of these people reappear in one of the photomontage spreads, which depicts the new body politic enacted by the constitution (Image 44.4).

Stalin appears with other members of the Politburo, the supreme policy-making body in the Central Committee of the Communist Party. On either side of Stalin are key members of his inner circle: Lazar Kaganovich, Viacheslav Molotov, Kliment Voroshilov, and Mikhail Kalinin. Other members of the Politburo appear at smaller scale below them, and diverse peoples gather among banners in the background behind them. This photomontage illustrates Article 126, which guaranteed the right of citizens to unite in public organizations "in order to develop the organizational initiative and political activity of the masses" and for politically conscious citizens to join the ranks of the Communist Party. This image resonates strongly with the nationality policy enshrined in the new constitution, which gave the Russian nation a dominant role in the Soviet political order. In November 1936, Stalin delivered a speech at the

IMAGE 44.4 El Lissitzky, "Article 126," *SSSR na stroike* (*USSR in Construction*), 1937.

Extraordinary Eighth Congress of the Soviets that detailed the transformed relations of the peoples of the USSR: "The Constitution now in force, adopted in 1924, was the first Constitution of the USSR. That was the period when relations among the peoples had not yet been properly adjusted, when survivals of distrust towards the Great-Russians had not yet disappeared, and when centrifugal forces still continued to operate." Declaring victory in the task of building a multinational socialist state, Stalin described the transformed nature of relations between Russians and the former imperial others, noting that the political transformations "have brought about a radical change in the aspect of the peoples of the USSR; their feeling of mutual distrust has disappeared, a feeling of mutual friendship has developed among them, and thus real fraternal cooperation among the peoples has been established within the system of a single federated, multinational state."[3] The diverse Soviet citizenry gathered in both Lissitzky's photomontage and in the 1951 poster exude this "feeling of mutual friendship" and "fraternal cooperation" under the leadership of Stalin.

After the death of Stalin, Berezovskii employed a similar composition in 1959 for the poster *It Is the Responsibility of Every Citizen to Participate in the Soviet Census* (Image 44.5). At first glance, the two posters appear quite alike: both present expansive images of the Soviet populace made up of diverse ethnic types, with larger figures in the foreground that dissolve into massive crowds. Soviet imperial space is depicted

IMAGE 44.5 Boris Berezovskii, "It Is the Responsibility of Every Citizen to Complete the Census." Political poster, 1959.

in both posters—by means of the map in one and the flags of the Union-republics in the other. However, the construction of the body politic is radically different in the later poster. Promoting participation in the 1959 census, this composition suggests the forging of a new body politic based on the individual duties of Soviet citizenship. In the absence of Stalin, the all-powerful Leviathan who previously embodied and unified their volition, the gazes of the individual figures shift out to look towards the viewer, transforming them visually from subjects into active citizens.

In his posters, Berezovskii employed photomontage to intensify the impression of realism in his representations of the Soviet body politic. The photographs of actual peoples create persuasive images of the Soviet political order at different moments in time. However, comparative analysis unravels the truth claims of the photomontages, and exposes the highly constructed nature of these representations. On the lower right of the 1951 poster, a Turkmen couple appear: the woman is dressed in a folk costume with an elaborate headpiece and large metal necklace, and the mustachioed man wears a distinctive sheepskin hat. These two figures appear again in the later poster, but reversed and to the left. Remarkably, the Turkmen man appears twice in Lissitzky's photomontages for *USSR in Construction* in 1937—evidence that this issue of the magazine was a source for the 1951 poster. The man first appears in a four-page spread dedicated to the Turkmen Soviet Socialist Republic. Near the end of the issue, he appears again in the photomontage that illustrated Article 126 (Image 44.4), to the far left, just above Lazar Kaganovich. Several decades after their original appearance, Berezovskii once again deployed the couple alongside other Soviet citizens in a poster promoting the 1970 census.[4]

The repetitive deployment of the same photographs of the Turkmen man and woman across many decades points to their representation as unchanging, timeless, non-European Soviet subjects. While the clothing and hairstyles of their fellow citizens change across the decades, the Turkmen couple appears frozen in time. As "primitive" imperial others, they do not fully partake in modernity and the construction of socialism. Even in the 1959 poster, they do not turn out to look at the viewer, but seem to avert their gazes. A similar temporal freezing is evident in the repeated use of Shagin's photograph of Stalin across two decades. However, Stalin is not projected forward across the years—he is shown in historical time, as the lawgiver behind the Stalin Constitution—as the Leviathan at the moment of the signing of the social contract.

NOTES

1. Stephen Brain, "The Great Stalin Plan for the Transformation of Nature," *Environmental History* 15, no. 4 (2010): 670–700.
2. Thomas Hobbes, *Leviafan ili materiia, forma i vlast' gosudartsva tserkovnogo i grazhdanskogo,* translated by A. Guterman (Moscow: Sotsekgiz, 1936).
3. J. V. Stalin, "On the Draft Constitution of the USSR," in *Works* (London: Red Star Press, 1978), 1610.
4. Boris Berezovskii, *Pomogaite uspeshnomu provedeniiu perepisi!* [poster], 1969.

CHAPTER 45

CARICATURED EMPIRE: COLD WAR POLITICAL CARTOONS

STEPHEN M. NORRIS

ON JANUARY 27, 1965, the Soviet newspaper *Izvestiia* printed a political cartoon that addressed nuclear proliferation in Europe. The famous political caricaturist Boris Efimov drew the image. Several hands, representing members of the Warsaw Pact, clamp down on a NATO nuclear missile. Efimov's pithy text reads: "Put the multilateral nuclear scum in a vise!" (Image 45.1).

On the surface, the caricature effectively illustrates how Soviet propaganda presented the concept of empire during the Cold War. It split the world into two camps, one imperialist (the West) and the other anti-imperialist (the Soviet bloc), depicting a crucial component of Soviet Cold War culture. Here, the anti-imperialists, symbolized by the unified hands of the socialist world, contained the imperialist world, symbolized by the angry missile branded with "NATO." The cartoon captures what images can do well—namely, clearly define and interpret complex phenomena.

Efimov's caricature characterized NATO as an aggressive empire, seeking to plant missiles everywhere. The members of the Warsaw Pact are ready to contain the threat, their unity and equality an indication that the Soviet bloc is not an empire. Yet the USSR and its bloc was an empire, albeit a strange one.[1] In the wake of the Great War, as World War I was known at the time, and its imperial cataclysm, the Bolsheviks sought to transform the peoples of the former Russian Empire into socialist nations that could eventually merge together to create the utopia of communism. To achieve this goal, the state encouraged its peoples to think of themselves first as nations living among other nations. Eventually, it was thought, the peoples of the former empire would evolve to become "Soviet."[2] Conceived originally as an anti-empire, the USSR under Stalin became more and more imperial, particularly when the state increasingly promoted Russianness in the 1930s. Yet Soviet leaders still insisted the peoples it ruled over were configured in a brotherhood of nations. After World War II, the regime established a bloc of "friendly" socialist states in Eastern Europe, an arrangement best understood as an imperial space where power and identities had to be negotiated.[3] Officially, the policy of a "friendship of peoples" held sway in

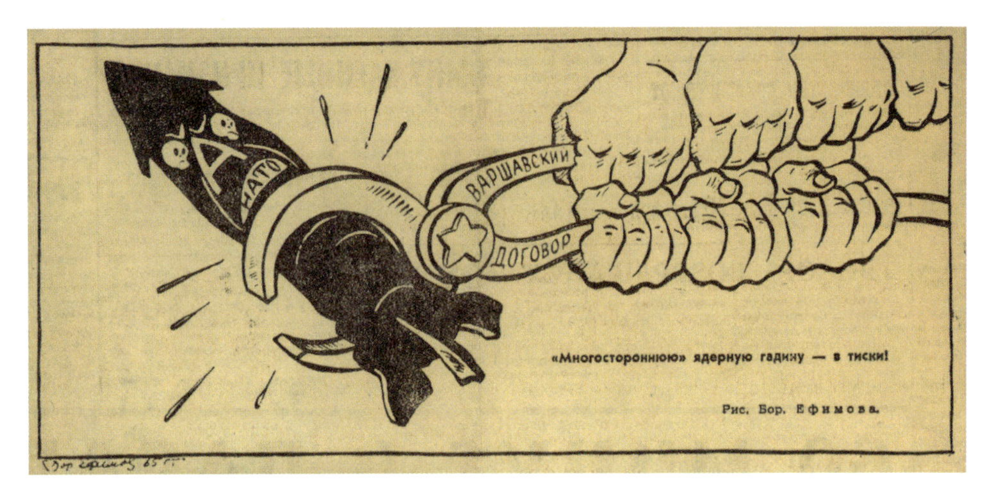

IMAGE 45.1 Boris Efimov, "Clamping Down on Cold War Enemies," *Izvestiia*, 1965.

both the Soviet Union proper and its bloc. But it functioned like an empire both internally and externally, in that governing the USSR and the Eastern Bloc involved exercising power over diverse territories and diverse peoples. Soviet leaders, however, always insisted it was not an empire.

Efimov's 1965 cartoon provides a coded visual representation of these contradictions. It blends traditional elements of Soviet visual satire with the specific contexts of the time. Four years before the cartoon appeared, the Communist Party passed the "moral code of the builder of communism" at the Twenty-Second Party Congress held in October 1961. Among the principles all good communists pledged to uphold—and those that informed Efimov's caricatures—were "friendship and brotherhood of the peoples of the USSR, intolerance toward national and racial hatred," as well as "intolerance toward the enemies of communism, peace, and freedom of nations."

Efimov followed up by authoring an article in 1962 connecting the role of visual satire to the proclamations of the Party Congress. He urged his fellow propagandists to "think about how our weapons—fiery words, sharp pens, brushes, and chisels—can take an active part in the education of people in communist consciousness, and to help them quickly remove the power of bourgeois ideology, narrow-mindedness, individualism, and careerism."[4] Tapping into a long history that proclaimed Soviet satire as a "weapon" in the fight to build communism, Efimov affirmed that the role of the caricaturist remained vital. Good visual satirists constantly wielded, and constantly sharpened, the weapons in their arsenal, for a well-aimed satirical arrow such as a political cartoon "can be as powerful and persuasive, as intelligible and popular, as a detailed, solid article."[5] The Cold War brought new challenges, Efimov concluded, but Soviet satirists were up to the task. "The traditions of worldwide satirical art not only did not lose their force," he wrote, "they acquired particular significance today in our aspirations to help formulate the most important moral principles in the people of a communist society." Unfortunately, "the enemies of peace and socialism" still lurk, but fortunately remain easy targets for the "lashings given by satirical works."[6]

Efimov had delivered these lashings for years. Caricatures revealed the ugly side of enemies and cut through their rhetoric like a surgical scalpel. By exposing the enemy's "true" nature in an easy-to-comprehend image, the satirical cartoon, at least in the official language used to interpret it (including Efimov's own), could destroy the attempts to sabotage the Soviet effort to build socialism. Over the years, Soviet critics and commentators regularly referred to Efimov and his cartoons as weapons. His entry in the second edition of the *Great Soviet Encyclopedia* summarized this interpretative language well: "His sharp lashes delivered in his satire are directed against fascism, against reaction, and against warmongers."[7] As the entry also noted: "He masterfully chooses material from newspaper reports for his drawings and brilliantly makes use of sharp words," and "Efimov works through the help of simple, precise drawings, unpretentious and clear, almost without shadows or unnecessary nuance."[8]

Born in Kyiv in 1900, Efimov taught himself the art of political caricature by studying satirical journals from Germany and those produced after the Russian Revolution of 1905. He joined the Bolshevik cause in 1918 and began to produce cartoons for journals and newspapers based in Ukraine. In 1922, he moved to Moscow and was named principal political caricaturist for *Izvestiia*, the Soviet government's official newspaper. The paper expanded over the years, serving as one of the two most-influential print media papers in the USSR (the other being *Pravda*, the official newspaper of the Soviet Communist Party). By the time Efimov's 1965 cartoon appeared, *Izvestiia* had a circulation of 8.5 million. It cost 2 kopecks in 1965, making the paper and its contents accessible to all.

Efimov had developed certain visual themes and motifs in his cartoons, ensuring that he could slot whatever event dominated that day's headline into a reassuring pattern. In this particular cartoon, Efimov has visualized two competing postwar empires: NATO and the Warsaw Pact. The former is weak, the famous cartoonist suggests, because its cause is aggressive, fueled by the anger the missile itself exudes. The latter will prove victorious, the cartoon confides, because its cause is just, its members work together to contain NATO's threat (and, therefore, it is not really an empire, at least in this imagining). The hands of the Warsaw Pact member countries are indistinguishable: Bulgarians, Czechoslovaks, East Germans, Hungarians, Poles, Romanians, and Soviet grip alike. And all grip firmly.

The American missile depicted in this 1965 cartoon had become a recurrent character in Efimov's works from the late 1950s on. A 1959 caricature introduced Soviet viewers to the newly developed Polaris, a two-stage, nuclear-armed, submarine-launched ballistic missile. First designed in 1956, and first launched successfully in 1960, the Polaris missile became the centerpiece of the United States' updated nuclear weapons arsenal between 1961 and 1966. Efimov's simple yet effective cartoon casts Polaris as a human-like figure with a grinning skull for a face. The missile is at a bar, with "beer" and "whisky" signs behind a smiling bartender who eagerly accepts the missile's dollars for a glass of beer. The bartender—as stand-in for European leaders—is thus allowing the deadly weapon to be part of his world (Image 45.2).

A second 1959 cartoon ("Down with the Pirate Flag!") has the missile aboard a small ship emblazoned with the word "aggression" on it. Two men accompany the missile aboard: a generic American general with a dollar sign on his helmet

IMAGE 45.2 Boris Efimov, "A Polaris Missile Walks into a Bar," *Izvestiia*, 1959.

(a recurring character in a host of Efimov's cartoons) and a West German general with a swastika on his (another regular in Efimov's caricatured world). They fly under a skull-and-bones flag that also has "NATO" written on it. Fortunately, a large hand (yet another Efimov visual trope, always signifying the combined will of all the Soviet people) blocks their way.

The black Polaris missile became a familiar sight to Soviet viewers of Efimov's *Izvestiia* cartoons throughout the early 1960s. Typically drawn with a skull or "made in the USA" written on it, Efimov used it as a visual shorthand for continued American and NATO aggression directed against the peaceful Soviet world. West German leaders, West German generals, British lions, NATO leaders, Spanish fascists, and American capitalists: Efimov drew them and more bearing Polaris missiles, all threatening the peace-loving USSR. Fortunately, as Efimov illustrated again and again, either the bumbling foolishness of Western leaders or the steady hands of the Soviet people and their allies consistently foiled the missile's harmful intentions (even if it did get a glass of beer).

Together, these caricatures present a visual narrative of empires in the era of the Cold War. The NATO countries are dominated by American militarists, capitalists, and Nazis trying to disguise themselves (they also have beer-drinking, angry Polaris missiles). They are frightening foes to be sure, yet the visual satirist's well-aimed weapon could expose them. Efimov reveals and then mocks the impurity of their cause, rendering it powerless. Meanwhile, the united forces and united peoples of the Soviet Union and the members of the Warsaw Pact are there to thwart the warlike plans of NATO imperialists.

This, then, is how an empire that does not want to be seen as an empire uses visual sources as a form of discursive power. A Moscow-based cartoonist working for a Moscow-based newspaper consistently crafts the United States and NATO as imperial entities. In the cartoon that opens this essay (as well as others), he draws the Soviet Union and its Warsaw Pact allies as equals, working together to ensure the survival of socialism.

Of course, careful observers of the January 1965 cartoon might have known that Romania's leader, Gheorghe Gheorghiu-Dej, was sick (he would die in March). Or that Czechoslovakia was already experiencing the internal problems that would lead to a revolution in 1968. Or that many Poles continued to chafe at their satellite status within the Soviet empire. Or that leaders in Poland and East Germany had engaged in their own Cold War within the Soviet bloc (East German leaders privately referred to their Polish comrades derogatively as "Polacks"). Or that the new Brezhnev-led state was dealing with dissent. And so on. The unity of the Warsaw Pact countries expressed in Efimov's cartoons belied many grumblings on the ground.[9] Teodor Zhivkov, the Bulgarian communist leader, may have declared that his country and the USSR "breathed with the same lungs, and the same blood flows in our veins," but Warsaw Pact countries in the 1960s huffed and puffed in different ways.

Efimov's 1965 drawing and the words he used in it produced a flurry of letters sent to the *Izvestiia* office in Moscow. Careful viewers, perhaps ironically, perhaps sincerely, seized on one flaw in the cartoon to suggest how "dangerous" and potentially "counter-revolutionary" the caricature was. The great cartoonist, it seemed, had let his visual weapon dull a bit, and had allowed in unnecessary nuance. One of these letters, from an engineer living in Kramatorsk, deserves to be quoted in full:

> Dear Editors!
>
> Out of feelings of goodwill toward your newspaper, I consider it necessary to give you my comments about an unsuccessful caricature printed in your newspaper on January 27 of this year.
>
> The caricature, despite the fact that its author is a recognized master, is unsuccessful in all respects, moreover, it can even be "read" in the opposite meaning, which of course is undesirable.
>
> The problems are as follows:
>
> 1. The text says "in a vise," but it actually depicts tongs (this is not so important).
> 2. The nuclear missile, by design, should be clamped, but in fact it is not clamped and can fly freely.
> 3. Truly—as can be seen from the figure—we must understand that the participants in the Warsaw Pact will not be able to hold the rocket with their hands clasped together on the handles.
>
> Now it's not difficult to guess that an idea for a good caricature, if executed incorrectly, provokes an undesirable, opposite interpretation, namely, that because of the clash of interests of the Warsaw Pact parties, it will not be possible to put forward the adventurous plans for the creation of multilateral nuclear forces.
>
> Of course, I am far from thinking or suspecting the author of a deliberate distortion of meaning, but objectively it turns out that way. Therefore, the placement of such ambiguous cartoons in a leading, central newspaper is certainly unacceptable.
>
> Reader, engineer Bivul, A. G.
> Kramatorsk, Donets oblast', Lenin St., House 6 Apartment 6[10]

Several other readers clipped the cartoon, noted the tension created by the gripping hands was off, corrected it, and sent it back. An "engineer Kostrov" from Perm noted the handles on the tongs should be spaced further apart and sent a helpful correction that "this is better." Most of the letter writers, following Bivul, pointed out the fact that the clamps were open, which implied the Warsaw Pact countries could not, in fact, grip very well at all. A typical response, echoing that of Bivul, was to express horror that a leading Soviet newspaper printed a cartoon that clearly revealed cracks in the foundations of socialist cooperation.

One reader, another engineer, named Natalia Nikolaevna Sokolova from Leningrad, sent a letter that expressed how much she usually enjoyed Efimov's cartoons and how disappointed she was in the one from January 1965. She also clipped the cartoon from her paper, drew on it to indicate the flaw, and sent it back (Image 45.3).

Efimov's replies to these complaints and reader outrage contained over-the-top apologetics. To Engineer Bivul he claimed "I indisputably allowed an unfortunate and unforgivable mistake in this work" and thanked Bivul for his "reading attention." Engineer Sokolova received the following reply:

> Dear Natalia Nikolaevna!
>
> Your criticisms of my drawing in *Izvestiia* are completely fair and correct.
>
> For my annoying oversights, I give to the readers of *Izvestiia*, including to you personally, my most sincere apologies.
>
> The technical mistakes of the ill-fated caricature have already been fixed in a color poster that I made on the same topic.
>
> When this poster comes out, I'll send you a copy, if you like.
>
> 8 February 1965

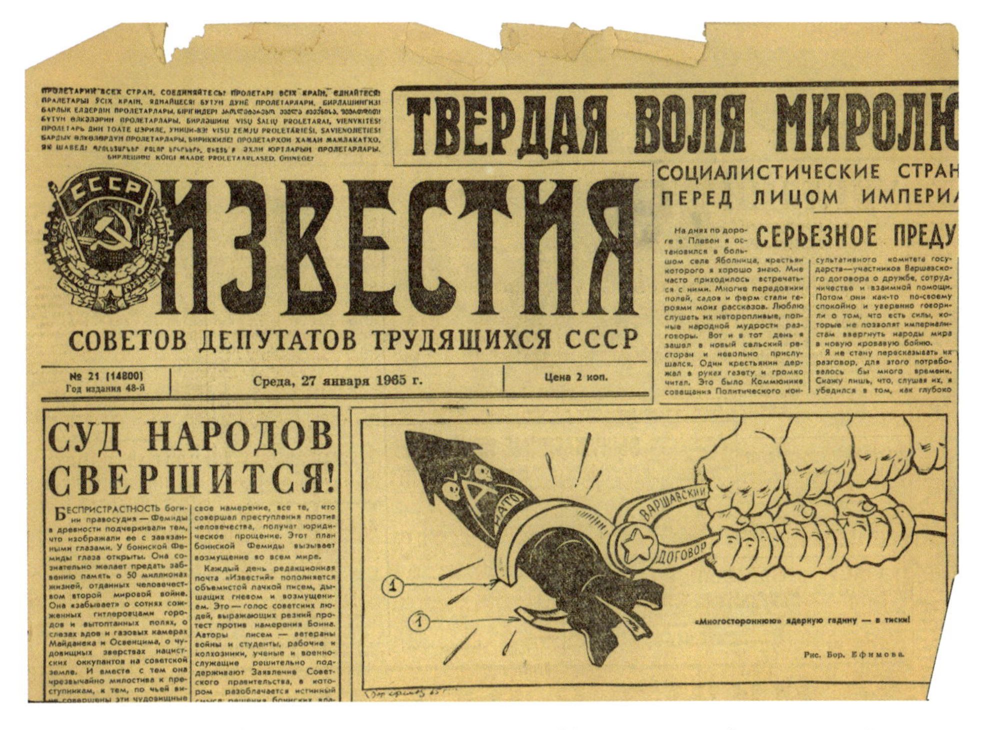

ПРОЛЕТАРИИ ВСЕХ СТРАН, СОЕДИНЯЙТЕСЬ! ПРОЛЕТАРІ ВСІХ КРАЇН, ЄДНАЙТЕСЯ! ПРАЛЕТАРЫІ ЎСІХ КРАІН, ЯДНАЙЦЕСЯ! БУТУН ДУНЁ ПРОЛЕТАРЛАРИ, БИРЛАШИНГИЗ! БАРЛЫҚ ЕЛДЕРДІҢ ПРОЛЕТАРЛАРЫ, БІРІГІҢДЕР! БУТУН ӨЛКӘЛӘРИН ПРОЛЕТАРЛАРЫ, БИРЛӘШИН! VISŲ ŠALIŲ PROLETARAI, VIENYKITĖS! ПРОЛЕТАРЬ ДИН ТОАТЕ ЦЭРИЛЕ, УНИЦИ-ВЭ! VISU ZEMJU PROLETĀRIEŠI, SAVIENOJIETIES! БАРДЫК ӨЛКӨЛӨРДҮН ПРОЛЕТАРДАРЫ, БИРИККИЛЕ! ПРОЛЕТАРХОИ ХАМАИ МАМЛАКАТХО, ЯК ШАВЕД! ЭХЛИ ЮРТЛАРЫҢ ПРОЛЕТАРЛАРЫ, БИРЛЕШИҢ! KÕIGI MAADE PROLETAARLASED, ÜHINEGE!

ТВЕРДАЯ ВОЛЯ МИРОЛЮ

ИЗВЕСТИЯ

СОВЕТОВ ДЕПУТАТОВ ТРУДЯЩИХСЯ СССР

№ 21 (14800) Год издания 48-й | Среда, 27 января 1965 г. | Цена 2 коп.

СОЦИАЛИСТИЧЕСКИЕ СТРАН ПЕРЕД ЛИЦОМ ИМПЕРИА

СЕРЬЕЗНОЕ ПРЕДУ

На днях по дороге в Плевен я остановился в большом селе Яболница, крестьян которого я хорошо знаю. Мне часто приходилось встречаться с ними. Многие передовики полей, садов и ферм стали героями моих рассказов. Люблю слушать их неторопливые, полные народной мудрости разговоры. Вот и в тот день я зашел в новый сельский ресторан и невольно прислушался. Один крестьянин держал в руках газету и громко читал. Это было Коммюнике совещания Политического консультативного комитета государств—участников Варшавского договора о дружбе, сотрудничестве и взаимной помощи. Потом они как-то по-своему спокойно и уверенно говорили о том, что есть силы, которые не позволят империалистам ввергнуть народы мира в новую кровавую бойню.

Я не стану пересказывать их разговор, для этого потребовалось бы много времени. Скажу лишь, что, слушая их, я убедился в том, как глубоко

СУД НАРОДОВ СВЕРШИТСЯ!

Беспристрастность богини правосудия — Фемиды в древности подчеркивали тем, что изображали ее с завязанными глазами. У боннской Фемиды глаза открыты. Она сознательно желает предать забвению память о 50 миллионах жизней, отданных человечеством второй мировой войне. Она «забывает» о сотнях сожженных гитлеровцами городов и вытоптанных полях, о слезах вдов и газовых камерах Майданека и Освенцима, о чудовищных зверствах нацистских оккупантов на советской земле. И вместе с тем она чрезвычайно милостива к преступникам, к тем, по чьей вине совершены эти чудовищные свое намерение, все те, кто совершал преступления против человечества, получат юридическое прощение. Этот план боннской Фемиды вызывает возмущение во всем мире.

Каждый день редакционная почта «Известий» пополняется объемистой пачкой писем, дышащих гневом и возмущением. Это — голос советских людей, выражающих резкий протест против намерения Бонна. Авторы писем — ветераны войны и студенты, рабочие и колхозники, ученые и военнослужащие решительно поддерживают Заявление Советского правительства, в котором разоблачается истинный

«Многостороннюю» ядерную гадину — в тиски!

Рис. Бор. Ефимова.

IMAGE 45.3 Boris Efimov, "Clamping Down on Cold War Enemies," *Izvestiia*, with corrections by a concerned reader.

He did, in fact, make good on this promise and eventually sent her the poster, with its major problem corrected. Sokolova wrote back, thanked Efimov for his response, and expressed surprise that he would take the time to answer her complaint. It made her happy, she wrote, to receive the letter and the poster. This time, the Warsaw Pact members gripped better, and the clamps closed around the nuclear missile. Because of the rhyming pattern, however, Efimov still called them a "vise," but like Comrade Engineer Bivul admitted, this was not so important.

Efimov continued to sling his satirical arrows and did not give up depicting missiles, hands, or unified Warsaw Pact actions in his cartoons. In 1968, as events in Vietnam and Czechoslovakia heated up (the two events that dominated his caricatures that year), he drew a cartoon titled "Double Pincers Tactic in Action" that illustrates the Tet Offensive of 1968, when the Vietnam People's Army and National Front for the Liberation of South Vietnam coordinated to launch a surprise offensive against US forces. Efimov drew an American general holding his clamps apart, failing to clamp down on the South Vietnamese countryside (the so-called "double pincers" tactic referred to in the title). The clamps around the general's head are marked "Liberation Army." Much like those in the 1965 cartoon, they have not closed entirely.

In an untitled Efimov caricature from that same year, five hands from Warsaw Pact countries block NATO and West German revanchist aims in Czechoslovakia (Image 45.4). In the spring of 1968, NATO forces held maneuvers in West Germany near the Czechoslovakian border, actions the Soviet press deemed as provocations to further destabilize Czechoslovakia during the so-called Prague Spring (a term used to denote the reform efforts of Czechoslovakian leader Alexander Dubcek). The Czechoslovakian flag flies above, supported by Soviet, Polish, East German, and Hungarian hands. Careful viewers would certainly realize these hands contained one fewer than 1965: Romania's new leader, Nicolae Ceauşescu, refused to participate in the Warsaw Pact invasion of Czechoslovakia in August. Here, again, the unity of the Soviet empire, which was not an empire as depicted by Boris Efimov, proves to be elusive. No doubt dedicated viewers in the mold of Comrades Bivul and Sokolova pointed out the faults of this caricatured empire as well.

NOTES

1. I borrow "strange empire" from Valerie Kivelson and Ronald Grigor Suny, *Russia's Empires* (Oxford: Oxford University Press, 2017), 337–340.
2. Francine Hirsch, *Empire of Nations: Ethnographic Knowledge and the Making of the Soviet Union* (Ithaca: Cornell University Press, 2005).
3. I take this basic idea from Patryk Babiracki, "Interfacing the Soviet Bloc: Recent Literature and New Paradigms" *Ab Imperio* 4 (2011): 381.
4. Boris Efimov, "Oruzhie smekha" *Voprosy literatury* no. 1 (1962), 22.
5. Efimov, "Oruzhie smekha," 22.
6. Efimov, "Oruzhie smekha," 22.

IMAGE 45.4 Boris Efimov, "Hands Off Czechoslovakia" *Izvestiia*, 1968.

7. "Efimov, Boris Efimovich," in *Bol'shaia Sovetskaia Entsiklopediia*, 2nd ed., Vol. 15, edited by B. A. Vvedenskii (Moscow: Iz-vo BSE, 1952), 566–567.
8. "Efimov, Boris Efimovich," 566–567.
9. For the dynamics of the socialist bloc in the 1960s, see John Connelly, *From People into Nations: A History of Eastern Europe* (Princeton: Princeton University Press, 2020), 590–621.
10. This letter and the others quoted are located at the The Ne boltai! Collection.

CHAPTER 46

"WHERE THE SUN BEGINS ITS PATH OVER OUR SOIL": SOVIET RUSSIAN EMPIRE IN ELDAR RIAZANOV'S *SAKHALIN ISLAND* (1954)

YANA SKOROBOGATOV

JUST A YEAR AFTER STALIN DIED, and two decades before Soviet filmmaker Eldar Riazanov's satirical comedies made him a household name, Riazanov co-directed with Vasily Katanyan a short documentary film titled *Sakhalin Island* (*Ostrov Sakhalin*, 1954). A travelogue at its core, the documentary introduced viewers to Sakhalin, a sturgeon-shaped island in the Sea of Okhost, just south of the Kamchatka peninsula and just north of Japan. In the middle of the nineteenth century, Imperial Russia made its first foray onto Sakhalin, and in 1875, Alexander III's government transformed the island into a penal colony. Both Anton Chekhov and journalist Vlas Doroshevich wrote popular accounts of their journeys to the island for Russian readers in the 1890s.

Since the thirteenth century, Sakhalin had been claimed by multiple imperial governments: by the Mongols, China, Japan, Russia, and the Soviet Union. Throughout this history, members of various Indigenous communities—including the Nivkh, Ainu, and Orok—called the island home. After its defeat in the Russo-Japanese War in 1905, Russia forfeited southern Sakhalin to Imperial Japan. The Japanese government renamed the territory Karafuto Prefecture and ruled it as a colony for the next three decades. Between 1907 and 1945, the population of Karafuto ballooned from about 10,000 to about 400,000 citizens. Ethnic Japanese and ethnic Korean settlers made up the vast majority of Karafuto's population. Meanwhile, northern Sakhalin remained under Imperial Russian and, after 1917, Soviet control. By the early 1930s, northern Sakhalin's agriculture (mainly fishing and reindeer herding) was collectivized, and mining and oil industries dramatically increased production as part of Stalin's industrial drive. And it remained ethnically diverse. In 1931, Northern Sakhalin was home to 30,419 ethnic Slavs (Russians, Ukrainians, and Belarusians), 2,998

Chinese and Koreans, and 2,000 members of various Indigenous groups.[1] Yet one ethnic group predominated. The number of ethnic Russians clocked in at 26,780, or 76 percent, of Northern Sakhalin's total population that same year, making Sakhalin, with its divided government and relatively new status as a Russian colonial possession, at once one of the most and one of the least Russified parts of the Soviet empire.

In 1945, after the fall of Imperial Japan and the end of the Second World War, the Soviet Union annexed Karafuto. Between December 1946 and July 1950, the defeated Japanese government repatriated 279,356 Japanese subjects to Japan. No sooner did Japanese citizens evacuate than the Kremlin began to populate the island with Soviet citizens, motivated by a desire to "Sovietize" formerly fascist enemy territory. But some Soviet citizens were deemed more suitable for Sakhalin settlement than others. Which citizens were those? The answer to this question can be found in Riazanov's *Sakhalin Island*.

SAKHALIN ISLAND AND EARLY THAW FILM

In the last years of Stalin's regime (1950–1953), strict censorship severely reduced the number of completed films. The few films that were released skewed towards the apolitical, conflict-free, and hyper-realist. Documentary films turned out to be especially adaptable to this new environment, because they took on subject matter that was politically safe but also new. Documentaries could embrace topographical subjects through travel narratives that emphasized the geographic vastness and greatness of the Soviet Union. Didactic films like *A Tale of the Caspian Sea Oil Workers* (1953) and *The First Spring* (1954) offered viewers a "spatial orientation" to the empire they called home.[2] They heeded state calls to depict Soviet reality as it was and at its best, all while embracing new camera technology, film techniques, settings, and narrative devices. It was in this context that Eldar Riazanov produced *Sakhalin Island*.

Sakhalin Island takes cues from long-standing visual traditions of imagining and depicting Russian imperial territories. Historically, remote regions on the fringes of the Russian empire have been presented as ideal places of conquest and test cases for imperial civilizing missions.[3] Early in *Sakhalin Island*, one of the narrators describes Sakhalin as the Soviet Union's easternmost region, "where the sun begins its path over our soil." Like the aphorism "the sun never sets on the British Empire," the expression conveys the Soviet Union's territorial vastness as an imperial power, with Sakhalin occupying a crucial place in its imperial geography.

Riazanov depicted the island as a *tabula rasa* awaiting its encounter with Soviet modernity. This approach can be gleaned from the film's first scene, which begins on the deck of a passenger ship sailing across an open ocean (Image 46.1). Viewers are introduced to a group of young women and men, neatly dressed in crisp button-down shirts, ironed slacks, and casual but full skirts. Many smoke cigarettes on the ship's deck. All appear ethnically Slavic and gaze out at the sea in front of them like modern-day conquistadores. The film's two narrators—a young woman and a young

IMAGE 46.1 A still from *Sakhalin Island* depicts Russian-speaking, Moscow-trained scientists traveling by boat to Sakhalin.

man, both speaking perfect Russian—introduce those on board as oil specialists, geologists, and fishery specialists who "had recently married, received their university degrees in Moscow, and now set out to build their lives on Sakhalin." Ironically, this introduction to the island of Sakhalin and the people who lived there begins with people who were neither from nor on the island. Yet the narrative choice reflects the film's larger goal of depicting Sakhalin as a place ready for, and perhaps in need of, the kind of development that only a group of Moscow-trained scientists could provide.

In the same opening scene, the young scientists sail across calm ocean waters before arriving at the port of Korsakov, Sakhalin's southernmost port. But where did the scientists begin their boat trip? The film does not say, but presumably, they boarded the ship in Vladivostok, Russia's easternmost port city, 9,000 kilometers east of Moscow. The trip from Moscow to Vladivostok alone would have involved a grueling multileg and multiday journey by plane or train. But viewers are spared from watching their protagonists endure this arduous itinerary. And all for the better. Omissions like these persist throughout *Sakhalin Island*, and allow Riazanov to cast

Sakhalin as a place little more than a boat ride away from the Soviet capital. The film's distorted depiction of the island's geographic location relative to mainland Russia portray the task of bringing modernity to Sakhalin as not just necessary, but logistically easy to accomplish.

YUZHNO-SAKHALINSK, THE MOSCOW OF THE FAR EAST

Once the scientists reach Sakhalin, the real tour of the island begins. The documentary's next scene takes place in Yuzhno-Sakhalinsk, the island's administrative capital. Before the Second World War, Yuzhno-Sakhalinsk went by Toyohara, located as it was in the island's southern, Japanese-controlled half. But no sooner did the Japanese forfeit control over the island than Soviet Russia gave the city a Soviet makeover, one that *Sakhalin Island* showcases in full. Unlike other formerly fascist-controlled cities earmarked to be razed to the ground and rebuilt as industrial centers and agricultural "breadbaskets," Yuzhno-Sakhalinsk was remodeled as a "Moscow of the Far East," a site not of Russian exploitation but of Russian settlement.[4] To that end, the Soviet government made a concerted effort to provide citizens who settled in Southern Sakhalin with better accommodations and a higher standard of living than their counterparts in other newly conquered territories.

Without making any mention of Yuzhno-Sakhalinsk's Japanese history, the film's narrators take viewers on a fast-paced sight-seeing tour of the city's main attractions. "Here, Soviet people live like they do everywhere else," one of the film's narrators states, further underscoring Sakhalin's proximity to the rest of the Soviet Union (Image 46.2). Viewers encounter newly built neoclassical buildings standing alongside wide city boulevards reminiscent of Moscow's Garden Ring. The sequence includes a newly opened branch of the Soviet Academy of Science and a majestic post office building reminiscent of Moscow's Central Telegraph Building. The camera then moves to a visibly upscale grocery store, where the film's narrator announces that city residents could find the same, if not more, products as they would in a fashionable store on the mainland. The film destabilizes any assumptions that a viewer might have had about the capital of Sakhalin as wild and undeveloped, and therefore the very opposite of a typical postwar socialist city. Life in Yuzhno-Sakhalinsk looked just like life in Moscow, Leningrad, or other major Russian cities, and perhaps even better.

Riazanov's Yuzhno-Sakhalinsk, however, lacks the ethnic diversity found in the Soviet capital. Slavs make up the vast majority of the people seen in the film, suggesting they are Yuzhno-Sakhalinsk's single predominant ethnic group. Here, the film departs significantly from reality. In 1954, Yuzhno-Sakhalinsk was far from homogenous. While the vast majority of residents were ethnically Russian, the city had a sizable Indigenous and Korean population, but the film suggests that Slavic people represented not only Yuzhno-Sakhalinsk's past, but also its future. Several shots feature young women of European background cradling infants or pushing young

IMAGE 46.2 A still from *Sakhalin Island* shows an ethnically Slavic settler holding a newborn on a balcony overlooking a main street in the modern, newly Sovietized city of Yuzhno-Sakhalinsk.

children in strollers, conveying the sense that Yuzhno-Sakhalinsk was not only an ideal place to live and work, but one to have and raise children as well, and Slavic children in particular.

Moscow is mentioned no fewer than twelve times in the short film, and always to create an illusion of Sakhalin's proximity to the capital, both literal and figurative. Take, for example, one of the film's earlier scenes, where cameras guide viewers inside a bustling post office in Yuzhno-Sakhalinsk. "Perhaps some mail awaits us?" the film's female narrator playfully asks her male co-narrator? "It's quite possible," he responds. "Even though we travelled so far from Moscow, it's highly likely that the airmail beat us here a long time ago." The remark highlights two things at once: Sakhalin's close ties to Moscow and the technological sophistication of the Soviet postal system, capable of surpassing human travel in speed and efficiency. "When it's this easy to stay connected to the ones you love, it's easy to forget about the great distances that separate you," the narrator adds.

Viewers who might have worried about what life in distant Sakhalin would mean for their access to Moscow's cultural offerings would be pleasantly surprised to learn that they would have access to cultural outlets on this island in the North Pacific. Once they leave the post office, the camera zooms in on a white-columned building that resembles Moscow's Bolshoi Theater. The male narrator introduces the building as the city's main theater, where "residents of this far away island can see the same performances that residents of our capital city see on the historic stage of the Bolshoi Theater," presumably as a stop on a tour outside the capital. To travel to Yuzhno-Sakhalinsk was not to travel to a different and unique city, replete with its local cultural sights and institutions. Rather, it was tantamount to living in a replica of a familiar city, tailored to reflect the cultural tastes of its most recent colonial settlers.

OUTSIDE THE CITY, FAR FROM MOSCOW

The film's emphasis on Sakhalin's resemblance and proximity to Moscow has the peculiar effect of magnifying their differences. These differences become apparent once the cameras leave Yuzhno-Sakhalinsk and embark on a tour of Sakhalin's less developed parts. In typical travel narrative fashion, these scenes highlight the island's unusual collection of flora and fauna in a whimsical, almost seductive way. Cameras move over dense conifer taiga in bloom, gurgling river, imposing oceanside cliffs, and icy tundra enduring a ferocious blizzard. Reindeer herds, iron mines, and oil rigs occupy landscapes that look more lunar than terrestrial to the Russian urban eye.

Yet even here, Riazanov tries to tame Sakhalin for viewers to make it more inviting, rather than making it alluringly exotic. Take, for instance, the moments in the film when two of the island's most vicious predators, a sea lion and a grizzly bear, make appearances. Rather than depict these animals as dangerous adults, viewers encounter a sea lion pup and a grizzly bear cub—miniature, less intimidating versions of their mature selves. When they appear, they do so not in their natural habitat, but in a contrived environment. The baby sea pup rests alone on a thick sheet of sea ice with no defensive mother in sight, a setting safe enough to allow a group of ice-breakers to approach and stroke the pup while posing for the cameras. Viewers meet the grizzly bear cub perched aboard a ship—an even less natural environment. Here, Riazanov stages a scene so undeniably artificial, it might as well have been shot in a film studio in Moscow. Approachable, adorable, and nearly domesticated, the animal wildlife that make cameos in *Sakhalin Island* offer a dramatic counterweight to an exotic landscape that no amount of editing could tame.

If the places Riazanov depicts might have appeared foreign, the people inhabiting them would have looked surprisingly familiar to Russian audiences. And here we get the answer to the question of who, exactly, postwar Sakhalin was for. Those on the front lines of development in Sakhalin were, for the most part, people of Slavic descent. None of the people cast in the role of "Soviet modernizer" could claim Sakhalin as their native land. Like the young specialists introduced on the boat sailing to Sakhalin in the opening scene, the people performing the labor to develop the island came from somewhere far away from Sakhalin's shores. The future of Russia's newest colonial addition was, according to the film, being built not by Native Sakhaliners—people of Chinese, Korean, Nivkh, Ainu, and Orok descent, who had been the island's longtime stewards—but by ethnic Slavs from the Russian mainland.

The single instance when *Sakhalin Island* does acknowledge the presence of non-Slavic peoples only bolsters the film's depictions of it as a place for Slavic settlement. Partway into the film, a scene unfolds with a young postal worker riding a reindeer to deliver copies of the newspaper *Trud* (*Labor*) and a pile of letters to an Orok family of reindeer herders living in the thick taiga somewhere on the island's northern tip (Image 46.3). The family consists of two matriarchs, an elderly woman and her adult daughter, and a pair of young girls (Image 46.4). The film's narrators explain that the letters came from Leningrad, where the family's eldest sons are attending university. The two matriarchs greet the delivery boy with delight and have difficulty containing their excitement as they open the letters and begin to read about what how their sons and grandsons are living on the mainland, eight time zones away. The narrators use the moment to reflect on the benefits that Soviet modernity has bestowed upon this one Orok family. "The Orok people have been illiterate for such a long time, it's a

IMAGE 46.3 A still from *Sakhalin Island* shows a postal worker delivering a stack of letters and a Russian-language newspaper to a smiling Orok woman.

IMAGE 46.4 A still from *Sakhalin Island* depicts two young Orok children near their home in the forested Northern Sakhalin region.

miracle how they have survived," one of the narrators exclaims, as the camera zooms in on one of the women, her face beaming as she read her son's letter. "And now, they are able to receive and read letters, connecting them to places all over the world."

This scene throws into sharp relief the imperial paradigm from which *Sakhalin Island* was born. Unlike the Slavic-looking residents of Yuzhno-Sakhalinsk picking up their mail, reading copies of the Moscow daily newspaper, and working the iron and oil fields, the Orok women and children exist in the film as recipients, not agents, of the kind of development that the Soviet state sought to bring to Sakhalin. As peaceful bystanders, they compel viewers, and especially viewers based in Moscow, to imagine Sakhalin as a place where they would be welcomed as surrogates for Soviet modernity, and where their cultural superiority would be celebrated as opposed to threatened. In this way, Riazanov's film reveals Russian Sakhalin as a space that existed neither for Native Sakhaliners nor for Soviets, but rather for Slavs.

This type of erasure of Indigenous agency is far from uncommon in traditional visual representations of empire. Colonial states from the British to the French to the American have, throughout their histories, presented themselves as agents of modernity, bringing "civilization" to "backward" colonized peoples. The Soviet

Union repudiated this sort of imperial narrative in its official rhetoric. Instead of fashioning itself as an exporter of civilization from the Russian center to a non-Russian periphery, the Soviet state sought to promote socialism as an ideology of empowerment that could lift people along the periphery to become agents of their own development. According to the Bolsheviks, socialism's arrival in Sakhalin, as well as in the South Caucasus, Ukraine, Central Asia, and other regions within the vast Soviet empire, would motivate their native populations to "civilize" themselves. Soviet propaganda and policymakers celebrated the "development" of the union's non-Russian republics by routinely placing people of non-Russian descent front and center, showcasing them as agents of their own uplift.

But *Sakhalin Island* broke from this tradition. In the film, Sakhalin's native population—both the Indigenous people who had lived on the island for hundreds of years prior to Russian arrival, as well as relative newcomers, notably ethnic Chinese and Koreans—appear as bystanders rather than architects of Soviet modernization. In the early 1950s, Soviet visual representations of empire had come to have much in common with visual representations of empire advanced by the capitalist colonial governments that the architects of Soviet nationalities policy had originally excoriated.

NOTES

1. Taisho Nakayama, "Japanese Society on Karafuto," in *Voices from the Shifting Russo-Japanese Border: Karafuto/Sakhalin*, edited by Svetlana Paichadze and Philip A. Seaton (London: Routledge, 2015), 24, Figure 1.2. As Nakayama reports, Karafuto distinguished itself from other Japanese colonies for its majority ethnic Japanese population (90%).
2. Raisa Sidenova, "From Pravda to Vérité: Soviet Documentary Film and Television, 1950–1985 (Ph.D. Diss., Yale University, 2016), 43.
3. Mark Bassin, *Imperial Visions: Nationalist Imagination and Geographical Expansion in the Russian Far East* (New York: Cambridge University Press, 1999).
4. Tarik Cyril Amar, *The Paradox of Ukrainian Lviv: A Borderlands City between Stalinists, Nazis, and Nationalists* (Ithaca: Cornell University Press, 2015); Franziska Exeler, "Reckoning with Occupation: Soviet Power, Local Communities, and the Ghosts of Wartime Behavior in Post-1944 Belorussia (Ph.D. Dissertation, Princeton University, 2013); Inna Penkhvaena Kim, "Razvitie territorri, prisoedinennykh k SSSR posle vtoroi mirovoi voiny (Vostochnaia Prussiia, Iuzhnyi Sakhalin, Kuril'skie ostrova), 1945-pervaia polovina 1949 gg.," synopsis of Iuzhno-Sakhalinsk University dissertation (2010).

CHAPTER 47

CRAFTING THE ART OF TRADITION: CHUVASH EMBROIDERY REFRAMED

OLESSIA VOVINA

A PASSENGER ON a cruise along the middle stretches of the Volga River will likely visit Cheboksary, the capital city of the Chuvash Republic. Walking along the waterfront, with its churches, monuments, bridges, and fountains, the traveler is drawn into the history of this land and its people. Here, one can see the Chuvash National Museum and Chuvash Theater of Drama, and sample authentic national cuisine in a restaurant decorated with Chuvash artifacts. There is even a Museum of Beer, highlighting the traditions of cultivating hops and brewing. Nearby, artists sell handicrafts and expound on local culture. Every year in late June, the people of Cheboksary celebrate the Day of the Republic, and the capital is transformed into a colorful tapestry. Decorated with national flags and billboards, the waterfront overflows with revelers. The noise of the crowd mingles with folk music performed by Chuvash ensembles—singers and dancers in national costumes on the brightly lit stage in front of the theatre.

Amidst this celebration of ethnic identity, certain images are noticeably prevalent—recurring patterns and combinations of colors and shapes that seem to communicate at a glance the idea of being Chuvash. Much of this visual language of ethnicity can be traced back to the tradition of embroidery as reframed and reformulated by Soviet era artists and designers.

Scholars have long studied the Chuvash art of embroidery. Ethnographers and linguists have examined its origin, its semantics, and the typology of its patterns. Historians have treated it as a primary document, shedding light on ethnic roots, ancient migrations, and cultural contacts. Above and beyond these academic interests, embroidery exemplifies a Chuvash tradition that has survived to become a conspicuous element of contemporary life.

In this essay, I will examine how Chuvash embroidery has been preserved, transformed, and reconceptualized in Soviet and post-Soviet times, serving as a source for the creation of new symbols of Chuvash ethnicity. As illustration, I will focus on two related objects: the traditional female headdress known as the *surpan*, and the work of the famous Chuvash artist Ekaterina Efremova, who pioneered the study of embroidery and its reconfiguration in contemporary life. Artists and intellectuals like Efremova, I argue, helped to sustain a distinctive form of folk art, and participated in reshaping Chuvash national culture as part of the broader Soviet nationality project. In the present day, embroidery patterns, reframed as symbols marking social space, continue to play an essential role in the visualization of national heritage.

The Chuvash tradition of embroidery and decorative ornamentation is on full display in downtown Cheboksary at the Museum of Embroidery, a branch of the Chuvash National Museum. The exhibits reveal not only the artistry with which the artifacts were crafted, but also their integral role in the ritual life of the Chuvash and their communicative function. In the original context, the costumes and headdresses would have conveyed essential information about the wearer's age, marital status, and identity in relation to the three ethnic subgroups of the Chuvash people—the Vir'ial (upper), the Anatri (lower) and the Anat Enchi (mid-lower).

Among all groups, the status of a married woman was marked by a special headdress consisting of several items, the main element of which was the *surpan*, a long strip of decorated cloth. *Surpans* of the Vir'ial were made of thin fabric with a red border along both sides. Geometric patterns were embroidered in rows, with fringes and colorful beads embellishing the ends. An embroidered headband known as a *masmak* was fastened to the *surpan*, as an integral part of the costume (Image 47.1). *Surpans* among the Anatri were originally narrow and short, but later, they became long and wide, with a red hem and multicolored patterns at the ends (Image 47.2).[1] Before the early twentieth century, the *surpan* was worn along with the *khushpu*, the married woman's headdress, decorated with coins, beads, and cowrie shells. Later, the *khushpu* came to be used only in the wedding ceremony.[2]

A number of rituals are associated with the *surpan* and similarly embroidered cloths. Religious leaders wore them during communal prayers at sacred groves, and participants often left these items on tree branches as offerings to ancestral spirits and guardians of sacred sites. Long white cloths were also left on graves and tied to special poles (*iupa*) as markers for the spirits of the deceased.[3]

The *surpan* and similar items had special significance in wedding rituals. A bride would embroider kerchiefs and shawls for the guests, groom, father-in-law, and matchmaker to be worn during the ceremony. Even the horse on which the bride was taken from her home was led with a bridle made from embroidered cloth.[4] But the culminating event was the *puș syrni* or *surpan syrni*, in which the maiden's headdress was replaced with the *surpan* and the full women's headdress. As a farewell ritual, it marked a girl's separation from her family, symbolizing her new status as a married woman. Even when couples eloped to avoid the expense of a wedding or to circumvent parental disapproval, a *surpan* was given to the groom as a sign of the bride's agreement. This ritual was reflected in a wedding song: "If you want to marry very much, take your *surpan-masmak*, go outside your village, and we will take you away."[5]

IMAGE 47.1 A woman wearing a *surpan* of the Vir'ial (upper) group of the Chuvash (early twentieth century).

IMAGE 47.2 *Surpans* of the Anatri (lower) group of the Chuvash (late nineteenth century).

After marriage, the *surpan* became an obligatory element of a woman's attire. For a wife to appear with an uncovered head, especially in the presence of her male in-laws, was considered a serious transgression that would lead to misfortune.

The *surpan* symbolized not only the union between spouses, but also divorce. According to Chuvash customary law, a marriage was dissolved when the husband tore the *surpan* into two parts, leaving one to himself and giving the other to his rejected spouse.[6]

Toward the end of the nineteenth century, women's headdresses and *surpans* began to change, incorporating polychromic pattern weaving and lace. As city fashions penetrated the villages, scarves and shawls began to appear alongside the usual headwear. Ethnographers, observing these transformations in the early twentieth century, reported that holiday attire in particular was often made from bought material (chintz and satin) rather than homespun linen.[7] The perceived loss of ethnic heritage led to a wave of "salvage ethnography," as both professional scholars and local enthusiasts rushed to preserve artifacts of "vanishing" culture for future generations. Yet the *surpan* was not relegated solely to museum display cases and the dowry chests of old women.

The first decades of the Soviet power brought dramatic changes in Chuvash life, including the destruction of prerevolutionary institutions, rituals, and material culture. In the 1920s, activists promoting the emancipation of women condemned the wearing of the *surpan*, accelerating its decline in daily life as required attire for wives. Traditional costumes continued to disappear in this period as factory-made clothing rapidly took hold in the villages.[8]

While losing its significance in ordinary life, however, embroidery attained a new role in the emerging Soviet culture. In 1920, in connection with the early Soviet policy on national self-determination, a Chuvash Autonomous District was formed, later reorganized into the Chuvash Autonomous Republic. As a recognized nation with its own designated administrative-territorial unit, the Chuvash were involved in the broader Soviet nationality project, participating in the building of socialism and all major cultural initiatives. One such program was the development of handicraft production, integrating the rural population into the workforce and contributing to the creation of national forms of art. Chuvash women were active participants in this process, working in specially organized labor cooperatives (artels) and bringing their skills in embroidery. Several of these artels, originally formed to provide work during the Volga famine from 1921 to 1922, grew into specialized companies. One such group in the village of Al'geshevo, which in 1929 took on the name *Pakha Těrě* ("beautiful pattern" in Chuvash), played a central role in preserving and reshaping the art of the Chuvash embroidery, producing items with a more functional emphasis oriented toward interior design.

The symbolic role of the *surpan* in gift-giving and award ceremonies was retained in Soviet times, albeit with a new meaning. Now presented during official holidays, the *surpan* highlighted contributions to the achievements of the Soviet state. For example, this change can be seen in the use of *surpans* during the Chuvash celebration of spring. In the nineteenth century, special *surpans* called *sělkě*, embroidered with a tree of life, a sky, and stars, were awarded to the winners of various competitions at the spring holiday, *Akatui*, signifying the wedding of the earth and the plow. During the Soviet *Red Akatui*, redefined as a socialist holiday "free from backward religious superstitions" and "national in form, proletarian in content," leading collective farmers received *surpans* in recognition of their contributions.[9] As symbols marking achievements in the socialist construction of rural life, works of embroidery became integral components of new state rituals.

Gifts of embroidery also became a form of ideological expression, commemorating important political events, anniversaries of the October Revolution, creation of the Chuvash Autonomous Republic, and meetings of the Communist Party. In 1922, a delegation of Chuvash women traveled to the Kremlin in Moscow and presented Klara Tsetkin, the famous international communist leader and women's rights activist, with a large, embroidered cloth. One of the first works of the *Pakha Tĕrĕ* artel in Al'geshevo was a *surpan* made in honor of the 1927 Cheboksary Communist Party district conference. Ornamentation from traditional artifacts, such as wedding kerchiefs, was used to create the first flag and the emblem of the Chuvash Autonomous Republic.[10]

A new stage began in 1933 with the establishment of the export company Chuvash Embroidery. Created by professionally trained artists and designers, its early work glorified the economic and social achievements of Soviet society. Traditional patterns of embroidery were often combined with images of airplanes, tractors, and ears of wheat, symbolizing modernization and the new socialist life.[11] Increasingly, these forms were oriented toward interior design. Once vanished from women's heads, *surpans* made their way into people's homes. Apartments were decorated with embroidered pillowcases, table runners, towels, curtains, lamp shades, and later, coverings for TV sets, retaining the ornamentation of ritual objects and the resulting connection with traditional culture. In the postwar period, embroidery began to influence clothing design. Women's dresses, men's shirts, handbags, and so on were embellished with simplified patterns, reflecting Chuvash identity. Objects of material culture, denoting the progress and prosperity of modernity, were thus marked with ethnic symbolism, expressing the distinctiveness of Soviet life.

It was in this context that the designer Ekaterina I. Efremova (1914–2000) began her professional career, first in the Chuvash Embroidery company after graduating in 1936 from the Moscow Industrial School of Art, and then at the *Pakha Tĕrĕ* factory after completing a degree from the Moscow Institute of Applied and Decorative Arts in 1948.[12] From that time on, Efremova played a key role in rediscovering and reconceptualizing Chuvash ornamental art. Her works were shown in major exhibits, acquired by museums, displayed in more than 60 countries, and presented in cities such as Brussels, Montreal, Osaka, and New York. In Chuvashia, she was honored with high awards, including the title "People's Artist of the Chuvash Republic."

Efremova's embroidery designs drew on ethnographic research in the Chuvash countryside, study in archives and museums, and collaboration with scholars. She uncovered secrets of the village masters, collected patterns, and composed a handbook on techniques, gradually building a canon used by generations of embroiderers. Efremova's reinvention of tradition laid the foundation for a professional craft of embroidery, thus giving new life to ornamentation from *surpans* and Chuvash costumes. A photograph of the artist in her studio depicts the process of creation from initial sketches of patterns derived from the *surpan, masmak,* and *keske* (embroidered woman's shirt front) to the finished decorative objects (Image 47.3).

IMAGE 47.3 Chuvash artist and designer E. I. Efremova in her studio.

One of Efremova's designs that illustrates the appeal of her work is a table runner that replicates in its ornamentation the Chuvash female headdress. The runner combines embroidery motifs from both the Vir'ial and Anatri groups in a freestyle composition. It includes symbols of large and small horses standing next to the world tree, evoking the idea of the continuity of life. Similar items created by Efremova (tablecloths, curtains, etc.) include other cosmogonic elements from Chuvash mythology (birds, sky, stars, etc.). The design is easily recognizable as Chuvash by the technique, composition, combination of colors, and symbolism. No longer tied to gender roles, social status, or religious rituals, it nevertheless resonates with native identity.

During the entire postwar period and into the post-Soviet era, Efremova's work came to occupy public and private spaces throughout the Chuvash Republic, serving as a marker of national culture. Administrative centers such as the Registrar of Civic Acts and the House of Soviets, offices in large factories, education institutions, and museums were decorated with her designs. The language of Chuvash embroidery, which she formulated and popularized, evoked a broad response, becoming an integral component in a national revival.

On an official level, this process was guided by policies that took hold in many areas of life from the 1960s onward, aimed at sustaining and developing ethnic traditions. Embroidery skills were taught in schools and were revived in rural areas, where celebrations of weddings and holidays in national dress became more common. The growing interest in national costumes and embroidery extended throughout the arts as well, encompassing Chuvash literature, theater, and folklore. Not only did embroidery travel to international exhibitions, Chuvash professional song and dance ensembles in the 1960s and 1970s performed throughout the Soviet Union and abroad in costumes designed by Efremova, spreading knowledge about the Chuvash beyond the borders of the Republic.

Along with artists, writers, and musicians, scholars actively participated in the rediscovery of embroidery, seeking to uncover deeper meanings in national costume design. Ethnographers sought to shed light on ethnic origins (ethnogenesis), claiming to find evidence of cultural migrations and historical contacts. Some scholars traced links between the Chuvash female costume, including the *surpan*, and that of the Danube Bolgars, revealing common Turkic roots.[13] Other researchers, relying on embroidery patterns, searched for more ancient Chuvash origins, extending back to the Near East and the civilizations of Mesopotamia, Sumeria, and Indo-Iranian traditions of Zoroastrianism.[14] More recently, Chuvash scholars have detected in Chuvash embroidery ancient pictographic writings and runic symbols, the mythology and meaning of which they have tried to decode. But how do these theories about the language of ornamentation resonate with public perceptions and contemporary life?

Today, symbols from embroidery and *surpans* have multifaceted significance in relation to Chuvash ethnicity. While tourists buy embroidered tablecloths in the souvenir shops of downtown Cheboksary, participants in the movement for the revival of the traditional religion perform ceremonial prayers wearing ornamented costumes created by Chuvash designers.[15] Whether used in a religious or a secular context, symbols from embroidery, and the *surpan* in particular, have become a national brand, a constant reminder of the distinctiveness of Chuvash culture.

On the Volga embankment in Cheboksary, the continuing relevance and vitality of such symbols can be readily observed. The space around the waterfront is dominated by a large monument, forty-six meters in height, devoted to the mother of the Chuvash nation—*Anne*. Representing all Chuvash women, the figure wears a national costume and a headdress—the *khushpu* and *surpan*. According to its creators, the site evokes the ancestral past, connecting it with living ethnic traditions. A continuation of this visual manifestation of the Chuvash cultural heritage can be seen in another monument recently unveiled at the harbor—a stone with engraved runic signs, pictograms called "symbols of wisdom" derived from embroidery motifs that, in the eyes of its creators, express the core values of the Chuvash ethnos, the spirit of the entire nation.

Over the past century, the patterns of Chuvash embroidery have been infused with diverse meanings and called upon to serve various purposes. But the persistence of these forms of artistic expression suggests a deeper resonance. As long as the Chuvash retain awareness of their identity as a people, they will continue to seek ways to express their distinctiveness in visual form, and the tradition of embroidery embodied in the *surpan* will pass down to future generations.

NOTES

1. *Chuvashskoe narodnoe iskusstvo* (Cheboksary: Chuvashskoe knizhnoe izdatel'stvo, 1981), 48; *Chuvashskii kostium ot drevnosti do sovremennosti* (Moskva, Cheboksary, Orenburg: Nauchno-khudozhestvennoe izdanie, 2002), 345.
2. P. V. Denisov, *Etno-kul'turnye paralleli Dunaiskikh Bolgar i Chuvashei* (Cheboksary: Chuvashskoe knizhnoe izdatel'stvo, 1969), 47, 53.
3. N. I. Gagen-Torn, "Obriadovye polotentsa u narodnostei Povolzh'ia," *Etnograficheskoe Obozrenie* 6 (2000): 103, 105–106.
4. G. I. Komissarov, "Chuvashi Kazanskogo Zavolzh'ia," in *O Chuvashakh: Issledovaniia. Vospominaniia. Dnevniki. Pis'ma* (Cheboksary: Izdatel'stvo Chuvashskogo Universiteta, 2003), 51, 59.
5. P. V. Denisov, *Etno-kul'turnye paralleli*, 52–53.
6. I. G. Georgi, *Opisanie vsekh v Rossiiskom gosudarstve obitaiushchikh narodov* (SPb, 1799), Vol. 1, 41; N. I. Gagen-Torn, *Zhenskaia odezhda narodov Povolzh'ia* (Cheboksary: Chuvashskoe gosudarstvennoe izdatel'stvo, 1960), 150.
7. *Chuvashi. Etnograficheskoe issledovanie. Material'naia kul'tura*, vol. 1 (Cheboksary: Chuvashskoe gosudarstvennoe izdatel'stvo, 1956), 299, 313; *Chuvashi. Istoriia i kul'tura*, vol. 1 (Cheboksary: Chuvashskoe knizhnoe izdatel'stvo, 2009), 374.
8. *Chuvashi. Istoriia i kul'tura*, 374.
9. K. V. Elle, *Akatui* (Cheboksary: Chuvashskoe gosudarstvennoe izdatel'stvo, 1935), 23.
10. A. A. Trofimov, *Problemy narodnogo iskusstva Chuvashii* (Cheboksary: Chuvashskoe knizhnoe izdatel'stvo, 1985), 16, 17.
11. A. A. Trofimov, *Ornament Chuvashskoi narodnoi vyshivki* (Cheboksary: Chuvashskoe knizhnoe izdatel'stvo, 1977), 102.
12. *Chuvashskoe narodnoe iskusstvo*, 240.
13. N. I. Gagen-Torn, *Zhenskaia odezhda narodov Povolzh'ia*, 175–177, 226–227; P. V. Denisov, *Etno-kul'turnye paralleli*, 47–51.
14. A. A. Trofimov, "Antropomorfizatsiia modeli mira i narodnyi zhenskii kostium Chuvashei," in *Iskusstvo: Izbrannye trudy. Sbornik statei* (Cheboksary: CHGIGN, 2005), 344–346.
15. O. P. Vovina,"Chuvashskaia *kiremet'*: traditsii i simvoly v osvoenii sakral'nogo prostranstva," *Etnograficheskoe obozrenie* 4 (2002): 39–65.

CHAPTER 48

THE IMPERIAL ICONOGRAPHY OF THE GEORGIAN TABLE (1900–1980s)

ERIK R. SCOTT

THE SOVIET UNION was not simply a Russian empire. Although Russians made up a slight majority of the population and the Russian language served as its lingua franca, the state was expressly multiethnic and shaped by the diverse populations within its borders. While the USSR was centered in Moscow, the Russian city was reinvented as a socialist metropolis open to all nationalities. The Soviet capital's stages hosted song and dance ensembles from Ukraine and Uzbekistan, its markets teemed with goods and traders from the Caucasus, and its restaurants served national dishes rendered for a Soviet-wide public. The state sought to manage the terms of national difference within the Soviet Union, showcasing the ideologically useful contributions of non-Russians even as it suppressed dissenting forms of national culture. Yet non-Russians were not merely pawns in the state's efforts; some took advantage of the state's promotion of difference for their own purposes.

Although they hailed from a distant republic on the southern periphery, Georgians became prominent among the state's political elite, with Joseph Stalin (born Ioseb Jughashvili) the most famous representative of a group of Bolsheviks from the Caucasus who came to power in the late 1920s. Georgians also became fixtures on Soviet stage and screen, and profited by selling fruits and vegetables from their temperate republic in Moscow's markets. Perhaps most of all, Georgians were renowned for their cuisine, which was featured in Soviet cookbooks, served in Moscow's top restaurants, and accompanied by distinctive rituals of toasting that became a fixture at Soviet-wide celebrations.

Georgian cuisine offered a feast for the eyes as well as the palate. The Georgian table was immediately recognizable, with its dishes served all at once and piled high with long skewers of meat, vibrantly colored vegetables, and oversized loaves of bread. In the Soviet context, its iconography offered a visual representation of the socialist promise of abundance as well as a manifestation of the multiethnic "friendship of the peoples" celebrated in official ideology.

Yet a closer inspection of the imagery of the Georgian table reveals the tensions inherent in a minority population's participation in the broader Soviet empire. Although state patronage created opportunities for Georgian chefs and winemakers, it required that dining practices, recipes, and winemaking traditions be altered to meet the needs of pan-Soviet consumption. For these reasons, Soviet Georgian cuisine was an imperial creation that turned national distinctiveness into a marketable commodity. Catering to Soviet tastes promised prominence to culinary entrepreneurs from Georgia, but also left some Georgians feeling that their culture was being appropriated by an imperial state.

In visual representations, tensions between the Georgian periphery and the predominantly Russian center are expressed as an interplay at the dinner table between tradition and modernity, as well as between authenticity and dilution. However, the extent of Georgia's integration into the center's political, cultural, and culinary networks makes it difficult to place the figures and objects represented on just one side or the other of these binary pairs. The privileged status of Georgian culinary institutions in Moscow blurred the boundary between colony and metropole; Georgian dining practices depicted as traditional were in flux even before they reached the center; and idealized appeals to an authentic Georgian cuisine were complicated by its long-standing history as an imperial hybrid.

As the early twentieth-century painting, by the renowned Georgian artist Niko Pirosmani, shown in (Image 48.1) reveals, such tensions were not new. In fact, Georgian dining practices, along with Georgian culture more generally, had developed in a Russian imperial context long before the establishment of the Soviet Union. Following the Russian Empire's annexation of Georgian territories in the early nineteenth century, some Georgians rebelled against tsarist rule, while others saw Russia as a pathway to European modernity. Modern Georgian culture developed in dialogue with Russian culture; its literature, music, and perhaps even its toasting practices were distinctive, but also significantly influenced by Russian authors, composers, and poets. The Georgian capital of Tbilisi was physically transformed under Russian rule, with the wide boulevards constructed by imperial planners offering a sharp contrast to the winding streets of its older neighborhoods. The city also changed in less planned ways, its population altered by the arrival of rural Georgian migrants uprooted by industrialization and its intellectual life shaped by political currents sweeping the Russian Empire as a whole.

Pirosmani's life and career were representative of these changes. Born in 1862, he came to Tbilisi as a rural migrant, moving there from his native village in eastern Georgia and, eventually, earning money painting signboards for the city's growing network of restaurants, which gathered and popularized regional dishes from across Georgia to forge a more unified "national cuisine," served to a predominantly male clientele with the money to consume it. A self-taught artist who lived on the margins of Georgia's artistic establishment, Pirosmani's deceptively simple style of painting

IMAGE 48.1 Niko Pirosmani, *The Feast of Tbilisi Merchants with a Gramophone,* undated, probably 1900s–1910s.

imbued everyday scenes with an expressive, almost magical lyricism. His "primitivist" approach was at once traditional and modern. It was rooted in folkloric sensibilities, yet celebrated for its bold aesthetic vision by leading members of Russia's avant-garde. To many observers, he captured the essential vitality of Georgian culture, even as he documented a rapidly changing society.

The Georgian table was one of Pirosmani's main preoccupations. While some of his paintings showed Georgians gathered outside for a traditional feast arrayed on a long blanket laid on the ground, *The Feast of Tbilisi Merchants with a Gramophone* (Image 48.1) reveals the Georgian feast's transition indoors and the changing practices unfolding around the Georgian table. In the painting, the *tamada*, or toastmaster, standing at the head of the table to the left and holding a traditional *qantsi*, or drinking horn, speaks to the scene's recognizably national elements. Georgian feasts were typically structured around a series of lengthy toasts that followed a prescribed order. National distinctiveness is also evoked by the rich array of dishes on the table; the long, crescent-shaped loaf of bread; the giant wineskin on the floor; and the man in the traditional coat, or *chokha*, seated at the center of the table. The painting also presents, in a wry and melancholy fashion, the changes wrought by modernity that were readily adopted by the city's upwardly mobile merchant class. The most obvious is the gramophone in the painting's foreground: it has visibly displaced the traditional Georgian instruments that now hang as mere decorations on the wall. One imagines the gramophone's sounds, amplified by the bright brass horn, drowning out the toastmaster's words. The man holding the gramophone wears what appears to be an English-style boater hat, a counterpoint to the heavy wool hat, or *papakha*, worn by the traditionally dressed man at the center. Far from conjuring a festive mood, the man with the gramophone appears distracted from his company and his surroundings. There is also the suggestion that he may be drunk: blood-red wine stains begin near his area of the table and streak downward, pointing to an overturned cup on the floor. The waiter, a boy, looks on impassively, his thoughts inaccessible to the viewer. What at first might appear to be a joyful celebration is destabilized by these dissonant notes, all of them betraying a profound ambivalence with the social and economic changes extending outward from the metropole and transforming Georgia.

The next image, a photograph taken about five decades later in 1965, reveals the Georgian table's transposition to the heart of the Soviet empire and the acceleration of some of the modernizing trends observed by Pirosmani (Image 48.2). The photograph documents a sumptuous banquet table at the Aragvi restaurant in Moscow laden with Georgian dishes and wines. The Aragvi, first opened in 1940, was the Soviet Union's first and most famous "national" restaurant, serving Georgian dishes to well-connected residents of the Soviet capital. Thanks to the patronage of Stalin and fellow Georgian Lavrenti Beria, who arrived in Moscow in 1938 to serve as Stalin's spy chief, the Aragvi represented the height of Soviet fine dining, with its twelve-page menu offering grilled and stewed meats; dishes seasoned with corriander, saffron, and other rare spices; and subtle sauces combining sweet and savory flavors with the taste of pomegranates and walnuts. Located just a short walk from the Kremlin, the restaurant transported visitors to a lavish reproduction of Soviet Georgia, with frescoes conveying the southern republic's agricultural abundance, an

IMAGE 48.2 A banquet table is set at Moscow's Aragvi restaurant, 1965.

Eastern Hall decorated with Georigan national motifs, and an ornate Marble Hall that could be reserved for special occasions. Even more exclusive were the restaurant's private rooms, including one frequented by Beria himself. In a city characterized by drab dining halls and chronic shortages of basic ingredients, there was simply no other place like it.

In the Stalinist era, eating out at the Argavi promised proximity to the Kremlin's leadership and gave diners a taste of the Georgian food known to be favored by Stalin and his circle. The restaurant's first director had previously worked as Stalin's personal cook, and its wines, cheese, meat, vegetables, mineral water, herbs, and spices were all shipped directly from Georgia. Its establishment created an opening for Georgian culinary entrepreneurs: Georgian food and wine producers secured lucrative agreements to supply the showpiece restaurant, and a team of chefs arrived from

Georgia to run its kitchen. The most prominent among them was Nikolai Kiknadze, who perfected the restaurant's most famous menu item, chicken *tabaka*, a dish in which a young chicken was flattened and fried under a heavy weight. Adapting the recipe to Russian tastes, Kiknadze spared the hot pepper used in his native western Georgia and served the dish with *tqemali*, a Georgian sour plum sauce, rather than a more traditional Georgian garlic sauce.

After Stalin's death, the restaurant's luxurious setting helped it remain an elite space popular among enterprise managers, artists, and curious foreign visitors. It continued to offer an expressly Georgian dining experience, and diners were still serenaded by Georgian musicians and treated to performances by Georgian dance ensembles. Yet by 1965, when this picture was taken, the restaurant's original connections to Georgia had been severed. In the late 1950s and early 1960s, control of its operations was transferred from the Georgian Ministry of Trade to a restaurant organization based in the Soviet capital, its ingredients were supplied by facilities in the Moscow region, and its original team of Georgian chefs, including Kiknadze, had retired, replaced by a Russian cohort of chefs they had helped train.

The photograph reveals the extent to which the Georgian dining experience promoted by the restaurant was a product of Soviet empire. The dishes on the table show the items favored by Russian diners, such as grilled meat *shashlyk* (known as *mtsvadi* in Georgian), over the more complex flavors of other Georgian dishes composed of stewed meats cooked with fresh herbs, spicy peppers, and tangy fruit. The table setting also suggests the ways that dining at the Aragvi served as a domestically produced Soviet substitute for the French-style fine dining that had once been offered in Russia's top restaurants but had fallen out of favor after the revolution. While the dishes have been served at once, in a Georgian style, the fine china, crystal glasses, and elaborate napkin arrangements convey a Soviet attempt at cosmopolitan European elegance. The table is arrayed with Georgian wines and brandy, but it also features a bottle of Soviet Champagne, another domestic substitute for an unavailable foreign good, being chilled in an ice bucket. The arrangement of the dishes, along with the elaborate fruit display that augments the table's sense of abundance, looks like it may have been modeled after a similar image in a major Soviet cookbook. However, it is difficult to tell which way the influence flowed in this regard: Kiknadze, the restaurant's former head chef, had supplied many of the Georgian recipes for the most popular Soviet cookbooks, the *Book about Delicious and Healthy Food* and the lavishly illustrated *Culinaria*. It is likely that the man arranging the lavash-style bread on the table, dressed in the manner of a French chef and wearing a Soviet-manufactured dress watch, is one of Kiknadze's Russian apprentices. Pirosmani, who had cast a critical eye on the erosion of custom at the Georgian table a half-century earlier, would have been bewildered by the scene, which mixed Georgian goods with Soviet ones and mobilized Georgian cusine to meet Soviet aspirations of European-style fine dining.

Perhaps the most recognizably Georgian items on the Aragvi's table were the wine bottles labeled in Georgian script. The labels combine the markings of Georgian national distinctiveness with pan-Soviet systems of classification, demonstrating how the Georgian "brand" was conveyed across the Soviet empire (Image 48.3).

Visually, the element that first strikes the viewer is the name of the wine, Kindzmarauli, written in the Georgian alphabet in bright red at the label's center. The Georgian script was indecipherable to the vast majority of Soviet citizens, but it was recognizably distinct and marked the wine as authentically Georgian. Georgian letters are also clustered together in the red seal affixed to the grape leaves at the top of

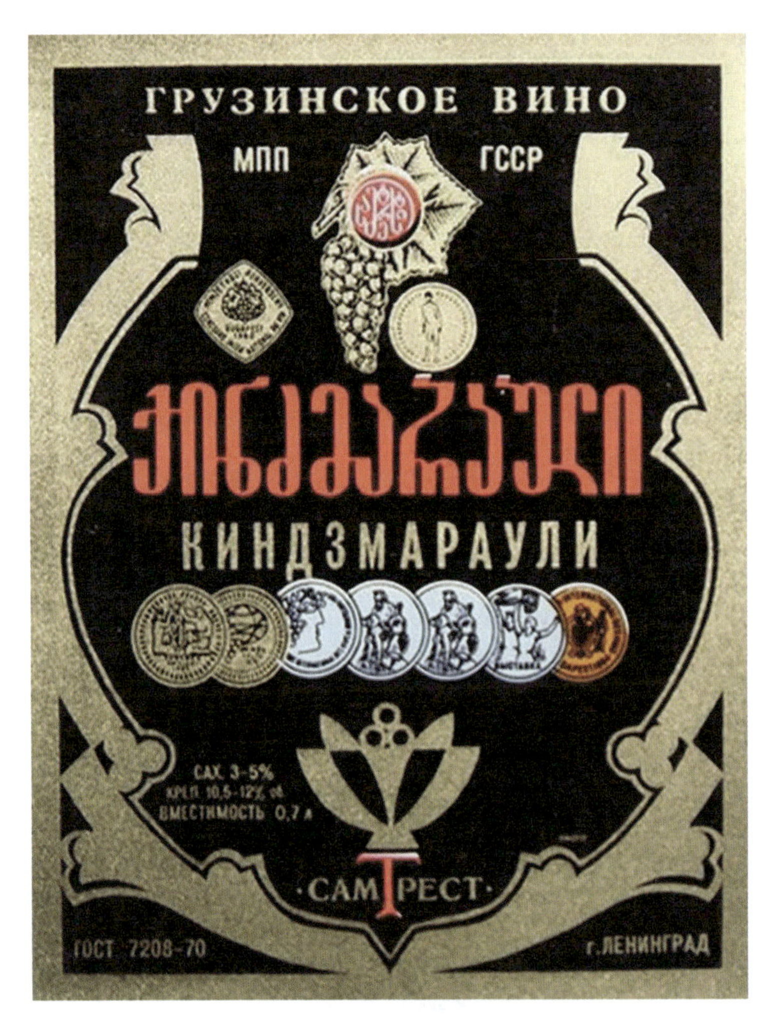

IMAGE 48.3 Label for the Georgian wine Kindzmarauli, bottled in Leningrad in the 1980s.

the label; these spell out "Samtrest," the wine producer's union that operated under Georgia's Ministry of Food Production and was responsible for producing, distributing, and marketing Georgian wine in the USSR. For each of these elements, there is a Russian-language analogue. The wine's name is written in easy-to-read capital letters below its name in Georgian, and the name of Georgia's union of wine producers is also spelled out at the bottom, the "T" in Samtrest forming a table for the goblet in which geometrically rendered grapes are transformed into wine. To reinforce the product's essential Georgianness, block letters at the top label it (in Russian) as "Georgian wine." The final national element is the stylized earthenware vessel, or *kvevri*, that rings the edges, embracing the design's central features and evoking the traditional methods of Georgian wine production.

Dark red in color and semisweet in taste, Kindzmarauli was among the most popular Georgian wines in the Soviet Union. Like the Aragvi, it had its origins in the Stalinist era: it was first introduced to Soviet consumers in 1942, with the Soviet leader's blessing. Rumors about which Georgian wine was Stalin's favorite—Kindzmarauli or Khvanchkara (another semisweet red)—added to the drink's appeal, but Kindzmarauli remained a luxury good that was difficult for most Soviets to obtain. According to official guidelines, it was supposed to be made from Saperavi grapes grown in the Kvareli microregion of eastern Georgia, in the foothills of the Caucasus Mountains. Its sweetness was supposed to come from the naturally occurring sugar content in the grapes, and its finest batches were aged in traditional earthenware *kvevri*.

While patronage in Moscow helped connect Georgian wine producers to eager consumers, it also put a distinctly Soviet stamp on the way Georgian wine was marketed and produced. In the Stalinist period, wines were labeled according to a numerical system of classification. Kindzmarauli was frequently referred to by its assigned number: 22. As the popularity of Georgian wine further expanded after Stalin's death, these numbers were gradually removed from labels, since marketing wines under exotic-sounding appellations conveyed a greater sense of authenticity while also mirroring the practice of French winemakers. Although Georgian wine was virtually unknown outside the Soviet Union, it was sold to Soviet consumers as a product with international cachet. The label for Kindzmarauli features an array of gold, silver, and bronze medals. These were indeed won at international exhibitions, but the overwhelming majority of these events took place in allied socialist countries.

This particular label dates from the early 1980s, when Soviet Georgian wine production was at its peak. Millions of bottles were produced each year, and in 1981, a new wine appellation named in honor of Pirosmani was introduced, featuring the painter's artwork on the label. Yet Georgian winemakers struggled to keep up with demand, and their product was figuratively, and sometimes literally, diluted even as marketers went to new lengths to emphasize its national authenticity. The bottom right corner of the label, reading "Leningrad," bears evidence of ramped-up production levels: the grapes for this wine may have been grown in Georgia's wine country, but it was bottled in a Russian city on the Baltic Sea. Soviet wine connoisseurs believed that wine bottled in Russia was inferior to its Georgian-bottled counterpart. Shipping the bulk wine north by railroad disrupted the aging process, raised the risk that it might spoil, and increased the possibility that it would be blended with other wines or finished with added sugar before bottling. Although it was considered to be one of the Soviet Union's premium wines, the product hardly lived up to the promise of traditional earthenware aging suggested by its label.

Evolving over time but illuminating some unresolved tensions, the iconography of the Georgian table was an imperial creation that drew upon and reframed nationally accented elements, just as Georgian dishes and wines merged local recipes and ingredients with mass production and marketing techniques to satisfy Soviet tastes. The Soviet-wide prominence accorded to Georgian food and drink created lucrative opportunities for Georgian culinary specialists operating out of the southern republic, but it came at a cost, undermining the authenticity and the perceived quality of Georgian goods. By the late Soviet period, Georgians and other national minorities in the Soviet Union came to question more broadly the ways that their cultures had been adapted, altered, and appropriated to meet the needs of Soviet empire.

CHAPTER 49

REPRESENTATIONS OF WOMEN IN THE SOVIET PERIPHERY: TARTU PHOTOGRAPHY EXHIBITIONS IN THE 1980s

JESSICA WERNEKE

IN 1983 AND 1986, the Photo Club in Tartu, Estonia, hosted two international, interclub exhibitions entitled *Women in Photo Art* (*Zhenshina v fotoiskusstve*). Contrary to what one might expect, these were not exhibitions featuring the work of women photographers, but artistic photographs of women. Women photographers hardly participated in the exhibitions at all. In 1983, only 6 of the 112 artists chosen by the selection jury, or roughly one in twenty, were women.[1] In 1986, the number of women participants rose to 15 out of 216, or just under 7 percent.[2] Women photographers were always a minority in Soviet photography clubs, and these skewed numbers invite an investigation into the gender imbalance within Soviet photography, both amateur and professional. In the comparatively liberal space of the Tartu photography club, the limitations on representations of women in the 1980s retracted, but not in ways that helped them achieve gender parity. This was, in part, due to Estonia's peripheral yet exceptional location within the Soviet empire, which expanded representational possibilities in ways that elevated the male perspective. Similarly, however, the general gender disparity present in Soviet photography clubs meant that there were few women to challenge these patriarchal depictions.

The growth in the popularity of photography clubs in the Soviet Union occurred roughly a decade after the integration of the Baltic Republics of Estonia, Latvia, and Lithuania into the USSR. The reconstruction of the Soviet economy after World War II, coupled with First Secretary Nikita Khrushchev's reorientation of Soviet industry towards consumer products in the mid-1950s, allowed for the production of cameras, equipment, and development chemicals for personal use. Photography as a documentary medium flourished in the relatively relaxed environment of Khrushchev's Thaw, when "a concern with 'truth,'" as opposed to the "'fallacies' of the Stalin cult, characterized the culture of the Thaw as a whole."[3] As photojournalists began to expose Stalinist lies, citizen photojournalists, with their newly purchased cameras, were galvanized to document how the new regime became more invested in the material well-being of its citizens. Amateur photographers went out to capture the changing landscape of cities transformed by mass housing and privately owned automobiles. Amateur photography became a popular leisurely pursuit in the 1950s, and amateurs founded photography clubs across the whole of the Soviet Union.

The relatively late incorporation (or annexation) of the Baltic Republics into the USSR had a profound impact on the trajectory of cultural institutions within these republics. Geographically peripheral to the seat of Soviet power, the formerly independent state of Estonia was formally reestablished as the Estonian Soviet Socialist Republic in 1940. Nevertheless, the new Estonian SSR continued to orient itself to some degree towards northern and western Europe, with which it maintained significant contact and cultural cross-pollination.[4] Further emphasizing this exceptional, geographically peripheral status of Estonia was its higher material standard of living relative to the rest of the USSR. Given its location abutting the West, together with continuing shortages of valuable consumer commodities, both local and All-Union officials were willing to overlook certain black market activities, as long as Estonians maintained political stability in the region. The Baltic republics in general, and Estonia in particular, became a sort of "Western Oasis" [and a] . . . showcase of 'progressive' Soviet culture."[5] And yet despite Tartu's status as a university town in perhaps the most liberal of the republics in the late Soviet period, this "progressivism" is almost completely absent in the representation of women at the Tartu club photography exhibitions.

Many historians have commented on the double burden faced by women in the Soviet Union and Eastern Europe, where both work and domesticity were expected of nearly all women. Even taking this into account, however, the number of women who pursued careers in photography or participated in photography clubs is exceedingly low, making both professional and amateur photography extremely male-gendered environments. Though there were a handful of prominent women in the Soviet photographic industry, when interviewed they remarked that one of the biggest issues they confronted was not lack of ambition, interest, or drive, but simply the lack of female role models and access to positions as photojournalists.[6] Those who did "make it" ascribed their career successes to happenstance, and credited their breakthrough opportunities largely to the mentorship of male press photographers.

Amateur photography clubs were as male-dominated as professional circles and not particularly hospitable towards women's photographs even in the more progressive Baltic republics. Latvian photographer and artist Zenta Dzividzinska found photography clubs to be hostile environments, especially for photographers who chose to depict the female form in ways that confronted masculine ideals of beauty. According to Dzividzinska's daughter, art historian Alise Tifentale, this was one of the reasons her mother's foray into art photography in the Riga Camera Club in the 1960s was short-lived. These realities of the club environment help explain the lack of gender diversity among the photographers at the Tartu exhibitions.

The photographs featured in the exhibition also lacked variety and largely conformed to conventional stereotypes typical of the male gaze. In Laura Mulvey's concept of the male gaze, women exist as passive subjects in the visual arts of patriarchal societies, and operate as signifiers of the heterosexual male other, through which men can enact, reenact, and impose their fantasies onto the silent image. The woman is thus the bearer, not the maker, of meaning, and the male viewer can ascribe to her whatever role or significance he desires.[7]

The female subjects depicted in the exhibition photographs fall roughly into four age groups. The first are young girls aged about seven to ten, and the second are adolescents and young women in their late teens to mid-twenties, who were either coquettishly dressed (by the standards of the day) or photographed nude or seminude. The third group is smiling mothers with infants, and the fourth group includes a handful of photographs of elderly women, or *babushki*. Images of seminude young women or women as mothers far outnumber the images of girls and elderly women, and correspond to Mulvey's assertions about the scopophilia (pleasure in looking) inherent in the male gaze.

By depicting women as sensuous objects of desire or prototypical, doting mothers, nearly all images of women in the exhibition defied ideological visual norms of productive citizenry and realistic experiences of women's everyday lives. While a handful of photographs depict women at work, they are far outnumbered by images of nudes and mothers, none of which showcase women as industrious, dynamic, or constructive citizens outside of their (potential) reproductive capacity. In the early 1980s, however, women made up 51 percent of the workforce. After 1960, 80 percent of women who were of working age were employed full-time, and a further 7.5 percent were employed part-time because they were enrolled in higher education.[8] The Tartu photographs not only defied the existing realities of workforce participation and of women's lives, they also did not engage with Soviet narratives celebrating universal commitment to labor. This propagandistic rhetoric may have become hackneyed by the 1980s, but it is nonetheless striking that the photos do not even gesture toward an official image of society, in which every able individual, regardless of age or sex, was obligated to participate in the building of socialism through physical or intellectual labor.[9]

The exhibited photographs also run contrary to the common understanding of the purpose of photography in the Soviet Union. After the Stalin era, when visibly doctored photographs were the norm, both professional and amateur photographs were expected to include a measure of "truth" in representation, and this emphasis remained in place until the collapse of the USSR. "Art for art's sake" did not exist in late-Soviet theoretical conceptions of art; therefore, overly aestheticized images still required some basis in reality. While some photographers were bucking this trend, they did so not through progressive or liberating means, but with decidedly conservative and heteronormative depictions of women. If the Tartu photographs represent a rejection of traditional Soviet understandings of photography, it is not by means of emancipating women in visual images, or allowing women the parity to represent themselves and their bodies.

MOTHERHOOD

The Tartu exhibition photographs are indicative of how male photographers chose to depict women, and how the selection committee wanted the exhibitions to represent women *given the available options* (to my knowledge, there is no comprehensive list of entries to the exhibitions, and only the successful applicants were included in the catalogues). In the photographs presented in the catalogue, there is a strong emphasis on youth. The nude and seminude images of young women reinforce the importance of youthful vitality, and what emerges is a chronology of male preoccupation with a limited number of phases in women's lives—childhood, sexual maturity, maternity—with little deviation. Elderly women, along with women engaged in active labor, are almost altogether absent.

The introductions to the exhibition catalogues provide insight on the selection committee, its logic, and its frustrations with submissions. In the introduction to the 1983 catalogue, selection committee member V. Parkhomenko expounded on the success of the exhibition and the talent of those selected to participate. Parkhomenko complained, however, that despite the large number of submitted images, many photographers "did not pay sufficient attention to the local and national features related to the life and activity of women in the republics, regions, and oblasts, etc." Although the exhibition was originally meant to be organized according to the categories of "Portrait" and "Act" photos, a third, unofficial category—"Women-Mothers"—was incorporated because so many of the submissions, primarily from amateur photographers, depicted women and their families. "After all," he justified, "it is this image to which the highest aspirations—family, love and fatherland—are directly related."[10] While photographer V. Zuev was awarded first prize in the "Portrait" category, no award was even issued for the initial "Act" theme.[11] In this way, amateur (male) photographers were able to substantially alter the exhibition program.

Parkhomenko also noted that "the exhibition [was] dominated by the poetic theme of women's beauty," associating beauty not only with reproduction and motherhood, but also with youth, conforming to male-dominated ideas about what constitutes "beauty" and "value."[12] This is reflected in the majority of the photographs that show young mothers contentedly cradling their children, seemingly ignorant of the camera's presence, directing all their maternal joy and attention to their children. T. Noorits's grand prize photograph, *Madonna-85*, featured on the cover of the 1986 exhibition catalogue, shows the mother and child superimposed against the cover's black void, smiling at one another, oblivious to the world around them (Image 49.1). The excising of extraneous background detail further highlights the emphasis on maternity and the bond between the infant and its mother. The viewer is permitted to participate voyeuristically in this happy moment from an implicitly male perspective: as part of this picturesque scene, but also outside the normative bond between the woman and her baby.

Motherhood by Y. Lun'kova (Image 49.2), one of the exhibition's few woman photographers, stands in stark contrast to the depiction of maternity in Noorits's

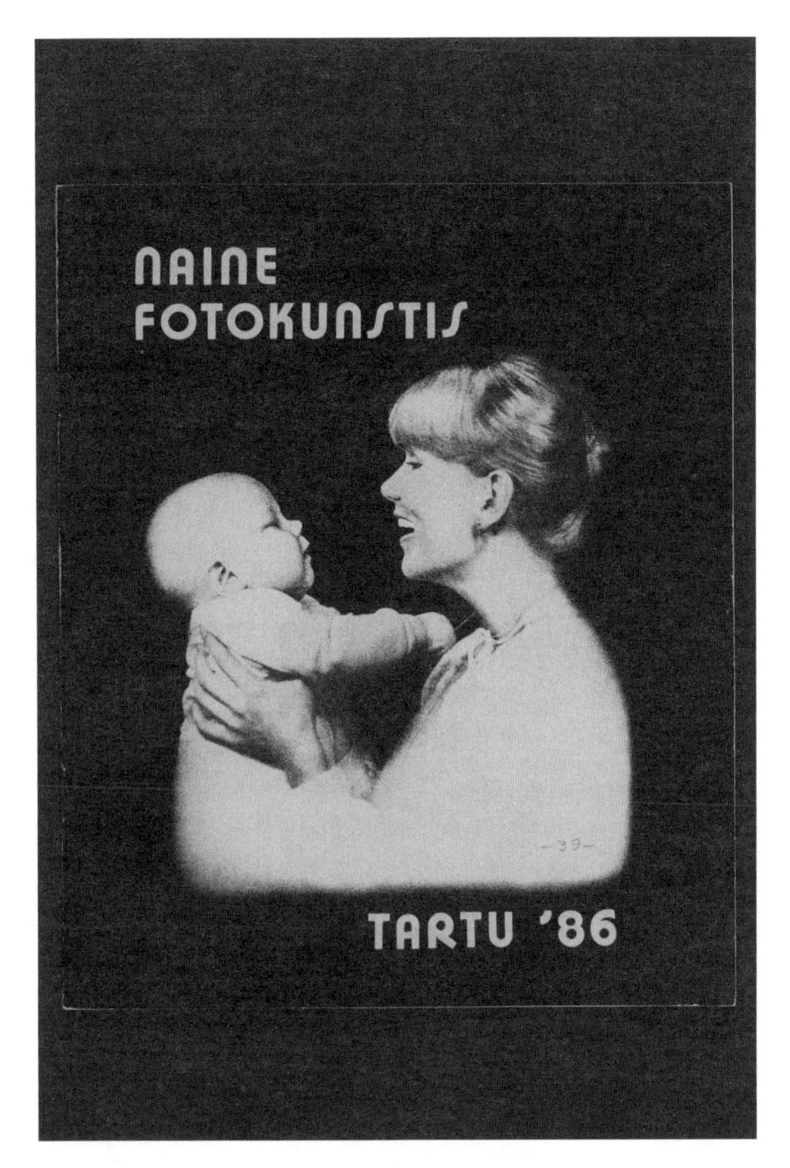

IMAGE 49.1 T Noorits, *Madonna-85*, *Zhenshchina v fotoiskusstve* (Women in Photographic Art), exhibition catalog cover, 1986.

Madonna-85. Lun'kova's photograph of a mother breastfeeding her child challenges the romanticized and disconnected portrayal of motherhood in *Madonna-85* with a confrontational and active depiction that disrupts the viewer's voyeuristic tendency. It is the viewer who is unable to escape *her* gaze as she scrutinizes us watching her and her child, inverting and nullifying the objectifying male gaze. Lun'kova's *Motherhood* is one of the only photographs in either exhibition where a seminude or nude

IMAGE 49.2 Y. Lun'kova, *Motherhood. Zhenshchina v fotoiskusstve* (Women in Photographic Art), exhibition catalog, 1986.

woman looks at the viewer. While Lun'kova's photograph wrests back some control over women's representation, the majority of nude or seminude images featured in the exhibition succumb to the gaze of the male photographer and viewer.

NUDES

A startling number of the images in the exhibition feature entirely or partially nude women. The nude images that appeared in the Tartu exhibitions were, in some cases, abstracted or obscured by light or shadow, but many contained erotic elements highlighting the breasts and genitalia while obscuring recognizable facial features. A. Tenno's *No. 17* (Image 49.3) features the nude torso of a woman lying prone, a single breast visible, her genitals covered by a translucent cloth. Her head and limbs are entirely absent, displaying the parts of her body least useful for socialist production, though necessary for reproduction and objectification. C. Pokaliyakin's *Portrait I* similarly features a truncated female body and single breast, while the majority of all other features are shrouded in shadow. In such photographs, even in the titles of the works themselves, the women subjects are deprived of an identity apart from their naked bodies.

It is noteworthy that the majority of images featured in the exhibitions are not identifiably Soviet in any way. If anything, they are more representative of Western historical heteronormative male depictions of women, a tradition that had been temporarily replaced by socialist realist depictions of strong working men and women in the Baltic region after it was incorporated into the Soviet Union. Socialist realism favored active subjects (both men and women) in contrast to the prone, passive, and often nude female muse so commonly found in Western art.

Yet as early as the late 1960s, Soviet attitudes towards nudity and erotica were changing. Less stringent anti-obscenity laws reduced penalties for distributing "pornography" from prison time to a modest fine. The depiction of the sexualized nude body was never fully developed as a genre in Russian photography before the revolutions of 1917, and while there was some experimentation with nudity in photography during the Soviet Union's New Economic Policy (1921–1928), generally photographers of the period were uninterested in the prospects of nudity, as it had little to do with the revolutionary agenda of their work. After Stalin's consolidation of power in 1928 and the institutionalization of socialist realism in the 1930s, nudity became all but banned and, when it was present, devoid of sensuality.[13] But while nudity remained a contentious issue even after the 1950s, it slowly began to appear more frequently, particularly in the Baltics, which did not have decades of institutional memory treating the nude as taboo. Simultaneously, "amateur photography in the USSR especially in postwar times, was actively channeled to . . . areas of intimate life," according to Ekaterina Degot. "Thus, the Soviet authorities unknowingly stimulated erotic photography."[14]

While there were still limits on what could be shown, nudity in photography was more or less accepted by the 1970s, especially in the peripheral Baltic republics and

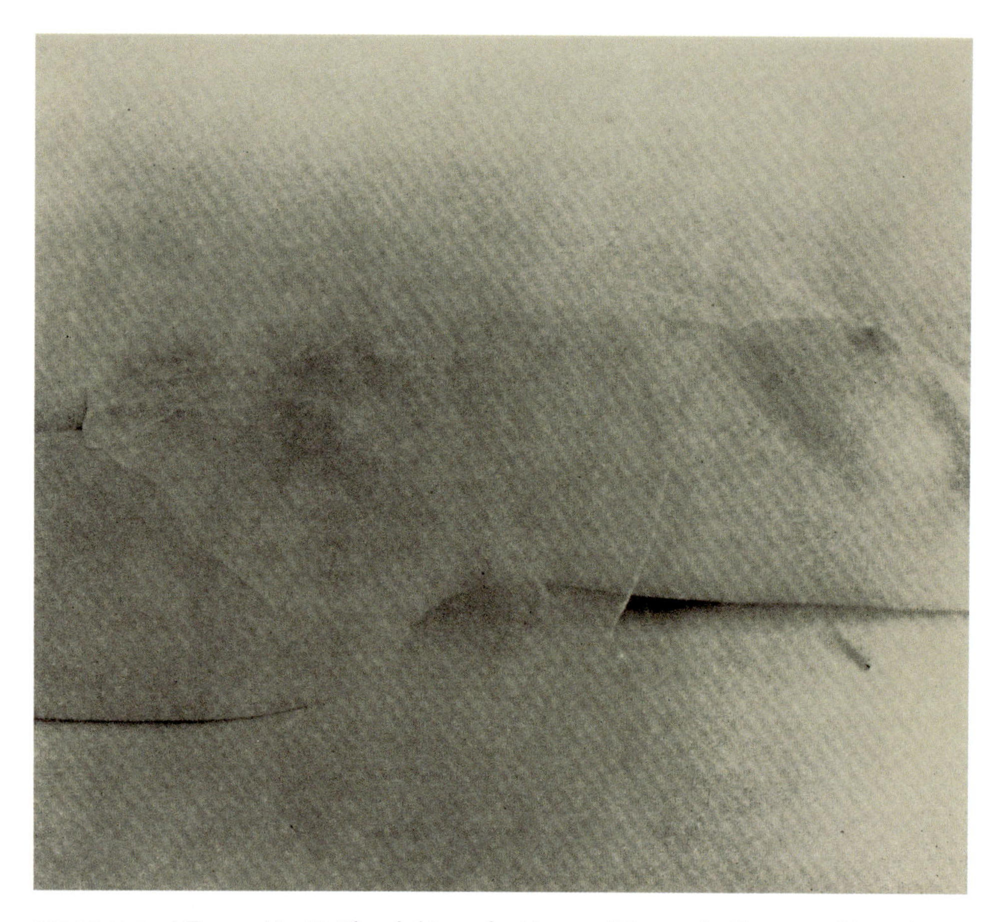

IMAGE 49.3 A Tenno, *No. 17. Zhenshchina v fotoiskusstve* (Women in Photographic Art), exhibition catalog, 1986.

Eastern Europe. Lithuanian photographer Rimtautas Dichavicius's nude photographs of women set against Baltic landscape were well-known and published in the Lithuanian press.[15] Yet Dichavicius's photographs and the Tartu images were not private, as Degot suggests. They were published, publicly displayed, and replicated in the exhibition catalogues. The Tartu exhibitions indicate the acceptance of the nude as a genre in photography, but this genre could exist publicly only because of the Estonian Soviet Socialist Republic's exceptional place within the Soviet empire and informal contract with central authorities in Moscow. No equivalent display of nude photographs was exhibited elsewhere in the Soviet Union outside of the Baltic republics. For example, Ukrainian photographer Boris Mikhailov's *Superimpositions* and *Black Archive* series were preserved on slides and only shown surreptitiously to small groups of fellow artists until after the Soviet Union collapsed.[16]

CONCLUSIONS

Was this erasure of the reality of most women's experiences a conscious rejection of Soviet values, a representational shift that can be explained within the late-Soviet Baltic context, or a combination of these factors? Based on this short inquiry into the Tartu exhibitions, the answer appears to be both. In the Soviet 1980s, as the acceptable means of portraying the female body expanded in some ways, it contracted in others: male ideas about femininity, beauty, and even functionality and purpose remained largely static. However peripheral and progressive Estonia may have appeared to the late-Soviet era tourist, the representations of women included in the *Women in Photo Art* exhibitions hardly offered a dynamic reinterpretation of women's roles in Estonia. The inclusion of more female participants in the Tartu exhibitions might, or might not, have changed or challenged male depictions of women, though Lun'kova's *Motherhood* suggests that it was certainly possible this could be the case. Yet applying our current standards about equal (or semi-equal) representation ignores the context and regime in which these photographs of mothers and nude women were produced. The images were a product of their era, demonstrating progressivism within the USSR while simultaneously consolidating traditional representations of women.

NOTES

1. The National Archives of Estonia (NAE), fond t-483, op. 1, no. 896, f. 37, exhibition catalogue.
2. NAE, fond t-438, op. 1, no. 896, f. 39.
3. Susan E. Reid, "Photography and the Thaw," *Art Journal* 53, no. 2 (Summer 1994): 33.
4. Olaf Mertelsmann, "Western Influence in Soviet Estonia," Art and Political Reality Conference, October 26–27, 2012, Kumu Art Museum, Tallinn, Estonia.
5. Eva Näripea, "East Meets West: Tallinn Old Town and Soviet Estonian Pop Music," in *Relocating Popular Music: Pop Music, Culture and Identity*, edited by E. Mazierska and G. Gregory (London: Palgrave Macmillan, 2015): 148.
6. A. Sergeev and N. Parlashkevich, "*'Za kruglym stolom'—zhenshchiny-reportery: o professii i o sebe*" *Sovetskoe foto* no. 3 (March 1974): 11.
7. Laura Mulvey, "Visual Pleasure and Narrative Cinema," in *Film Theory and Criticism: Introductory Readings* edited by Leo Braudy and Marshall Cohen (London: Oxford University Press, 1999): 834.
8. Mary Buckley, "Women in the Soviet Union," *Feminist Review*, no. 8 (Summer 1981): 80.
9. Katerina Katz, "Gender, Wages and Discrimination in the USSR: A Study of a Russian Industrial Town," *Cambridge Journal of Economics* 21, no. 4 (July 1997): 431.
10. Katz, "Gender," 431.
11. Katz, "Gender," 431.
12. Katz, "Gender," 431.
13. Alexander Borovsky, "Closer to the Body," in *Beyond Memory: Soviet Non-conformist Photography and Photo-related Works of Art*, edited by Diane Neumaier (London: Rutgers University Press, 2004): 80.
14. Ekaterina Degot, "The Copy Is the Crime: Unofficial Art and the Appropriation of Official Photography," in *Beyond Memory: Soviet Non-conformist Photography and Photo-related Works of Art*, edited by Diane Neumaier (London: Rutgers University Press, 2004): 113.
15. Elena Barkhatova, "Soviet Policy on Photography," in *Beyond Memory: Soviet Non-conformist Photography and Photo-related Works of Art*, edited by Diane Neumaier (London: Rutgers University Press, 2004): 57.
16. Berlinische Galerie, "Boris Mikhailov: Time Is Out of Joint. Photography 1966–2011," exhibition catalogue, June 15, 2021, https://berlinischegalerie.de/assets/downloads/presse/Pressetexte/Pressearchiv/2012/Press-kit_Boris-Mikhailov_23.2.12_Berlinische-Galerie.pdf

PART

VI

THE POST-SOVIET ERA

In December 1991, the first and last President of the USSR, Mikhail Gorbachev, submitted his resignation, and the Supreme Soviet of the USSR (the highest representative and legislative organ of the country) ratified the termination of the Soviet Union. The USSR officially ceased to exist. In its place appeared 15 independent countries: Armenia, Azerbaijan, Belarus, Estonia, Georgia, Kazakhstan, Kyrgyzstan, Latvia, Lithuania, Moldova, Russia, Tajikistan, Turkmenistan, Ukraine, and Uzbekistan. The peaceful dissolution of the USSR also put an end to the Cold War.

The 1990s was a period of considerable turmoil as post-Soviet states sought to transition to capitalist economies and democratic (sometimes quasi-democratic) governments. In post-Soviet states, the weakness of new democratic institutions compounded social and economic crises. Russian citizens, and those of other post-Soviet countries, adopted diverse political and ideological positions as they tried to adapt to the rapidly changing landscape. History was invoked by all sides to justify and guide their vision of post-Soviet transition.

In 1999, due to failing health and his inability to curb social and economy turmoil, Russian President Boris Yeltsin (1991–1999) stepped down and appointed Prime Minister Vladimir Putin to succeed him as president. In 2000, Putin was elected to the presidency. The first two terms of his presidency (2000–2008) coincided with an advantageous conjunction of international markets that allowed for economic stabilization and growth. As president, Putin carried out fundamental political and economic reforms: centralizing power, expanding energy extraction and exports, and blocking the political participation of economic elites, focusing especially on the so-called "oligarchs," who had exploited the policies of the 1980s and 1990s to accumulate vast stores of personal wealth. This exclusion from politics was part of a larger policy to delegitimize political participation generally in order to promote Putin's own monopoly on power and policymaking.

Policies and actions redolent of former imperial relations continued to shape Russia's relations with its non-Russian regions, and also surfaced in the policies of the now independent post-Soviet states. Russia fought two wars against a Chechen separatist movement in the North Caucasus to reassert its power in Chechnya (1994–1996 and 1999–2000, with sporadic fighting until 2009). Attempts by some post-Soviet countries to reorient themselves to the West met with determined, military rebuffs from Russia—for example, in wars with Georgia in 2008 and in Ukraine after 2014.

Putin's policies have been interpreted in a number of ways: as a response to NATO expansion, as a resurrection of earlier forms of tsarist Russian imperialism, as an expression of Eurasianism (See Introduction, pp. 9–10), and as protection for the Russian-speaking population in the former Soviet republics. After the collapse of the USSR, 25 million ethnic Russians ended up outside the Russian Federation. In some post-Soviet countries, particularly in Estonia and Latvia, where Russians had long been viewed as oppressors of local populations, the newly empowered nations subjected ethnic Russians within their borders to political discrimination and popular prejudice. Protection for the Russian population in post-Soviet space has become one of the principles of the Putin government's foreign policy. Even before the invasion of Ukraine in February 2022, he spoke about the urgency of combatting what he described as Russophobia abroad, and he advocated the recognition of a *Russkii mir*, or Russian World. The concept of the Russian World is based on the idea that ethnic Russians and Russian speakers, wherever they might live, collectively form a dispersed nation of sorts, "a transnational space populated by Russians," as Olga Shevchenko writes in her essay in this volume (see Chapter 55). The connections between the Russian diaspora and the Russian Federation were used to justify Russia's annexation of Crimea in 2014, as well as its invasions of Georgia and Ukraine.

At the same time, new post-Soviet governments outside Russia have rejected Soviet ideology and symbols of Russian power, and have sought to use historical memory to create new national narratives and new visual vocabularies. Some local authorities have reintroduced early modern and pre-Soviet imagery to minimize the prominence of the Soviet period in their longer national histories and to fashion new, post-Soviet identities. Historical figures who fought for independence from Russian or Soviet dominion have been elevated as new national heroes. In some post-Soviet states, such as Ukraine and the Baltic states, monuments that had celebrated unified Soviet efforts have been taken down or reconfigured, as discussed in essays by Karen Petrone and Joshua First in this volume. In others, such as Belarus and Kazakhstan, monuments marking the shared sacrifices of the Second World War continue to serve as sites of collective memory.

In the Russian Federation, as the successor to the USSR and the Russian Empire, history has been used differently than in other post-Soviet states: to celebrate imperial unity rather than national independence. Putin called the collapse of the Soviet Union "the greatest geopolitical catastrophe of the twentieth century." The politicization of history has crystallized around The Great Patriotic War (World War II), and is manifested in the popular Immortal Regiment processions held each year on May 9, the day in 1945 when the victory over the Nazis was signed. More recently, historical memory of the war has been weaponized in Putin's justifications for invading Ukraine.

The internet has contributed novel twists to these developments, and to protests over these developments, and, in the process, has transformed the Russian imperial pictosphere. New state-sponsored and grassroots, independent visual regimes have been shaped not only by reactions to the past, but by technologies of the present. Despite government control of radio, television, and newspapers in Russia and other post-Soviet states, the internet continues to facilitate communication, and YouTube in particular has made possible new forms of visual communication, propaganda, satire, and independent media. In the 1920s, the great Soviet cinema pioneer Dziga Vertov called for the universal distribution of film cameras to ordinary people: YouTube, phone cameras, and now TikTok have made that wish an ever-evolving reality.

Independent new media have fueled opposition to the reassertion of authoritarian power and pervasiveness of corruption across post-Soviet space. In some post-Soviet states, such as Belarus and Kazakhstan, when political opposition has been met by police crackdowns and outside Russian interference, detailed exposés immediately circulate on social media, both in the countries where protest is occurring and across borders in other post-Soviet states. While some of these images are approved and manipulated by authoritarian governments, the power unleashed by the internet and circulated in the pictosphere enables the production of multiple new narratives and identities beyond the control of the state. Even in wartime Ukraine, even under occupation, images and stories leak out, providing means of moral support and shaping international narratives as Joan Neuberger discusses in her photo essay.

The new imperial pictosphere has become an international arena for the dissemination of images of power, visual assertions of defiance, and everything in between. In 2022, when the Russian government eradicated all independent media outlets to prevent criticism of the war against Ukraine, potent images of the war and of protest and repression inside Russia circulated in the region and beyond, mobilizing local and global reactions to the tragic events transpiring as we write this. The power of the visual to evoke feeling, to summon responses, and to shape narratives is evident in the contesting elements of today's war-torn pictosphere.

MAP 5 The Post-Soviet Era

CHAPTER 50

COMPETING NATIONALISMS IN IMPERIAL AND POSTIMPERIAL SPACE: SVIATOSLAV OF KYIV AND THE DIORAMA OF HIS LAST BATTLE

YULIA MIKHAILOVA

THIS PAPER, WRITTEN IN 2020*, is a relic from a different historical era. I was working on it at a time when apparently no one—and certainly not me—could imagine the horror that would start on February 24, 2022. Wars are not caused by falsifications of medieval history, but such falsifications do help those who wish to start a war. Conversely, setting the historical record straight does not prevent wars, but it is more difficult to start them in a world where intellectuals are not engaged in nationalistic twisting of the past. One day, the current war will end, and the time will come when two free and democratic countries, Russia and Ukraine, will engage in forging a better Eastern Europe, and historians of Rus will participate in this process by dispelling nationalistic myths. After much hesitation and soul-searching, I decided to publish this paper as it was written, in the anticipation of this time to come.*

What do most people do when they want to find information about the early history of their country? We all know the answer: they Google it. If the people in question are Russians, Ukrainians, or Belarusians, they will find websites about Rus, the early medieval realm ruled by a dynasty based in Kyiv. They will read about early Kyivan princes and their struggle with the Pechenegs, the nomads who occupied the steppes to the south of Kyiv. The most up-to-date sites will not only tell stories of warfare, but also of cultural interaction and mutual influence. All the sites, however, will mention Prince Sviatoslav, who died in battle against the Pechenegs in 972 and whose son Volodimer is famous for his conversion to Christianity and the baptism of Rus.

Among the most popular illustrations found on websites about Rus history are reproductions of the diorama "Sviatoslav's Last Battle," built in 1985 for the Museum of Zaporizhzhian Cossacks in Zaporizhzhia, Ukraine (Image 50.1). Dioramas, three-dimensional exhibits seeking to create an illusion of reality, were often used in Soviet

IMAGE 50.1 Diorama by Nikolai Ovechkin, "Sviatoslav's Last Battle," 1985. Ovechkin was a Soviet artist who received many awards from the government for his works that ideologically supported the government.

museums. The genre as a whole saw its popularity peak during the first half of the nineteenth century. It is interesting, then, that "Sviatoslav's Last Battle" did not become irrelevant in the digital age, but found new life on the internet.

In fact, there are some unexpected affinities between the digital age and the old-fashioned diorama. In the nineteenth century, large-scale dioramas were built by entrepreneurs who advertised them as a way to experience what otherwise would only have been possible by traveling through space and time. Popular subjects included famous cities, landscapes, and historical events. The diorama's most praised quality was meticulously realistic representation, ostensibly showing Paris "as it is," or the Waterloo battle "as it was." Dioramas were thus early attempts at virtual reality.[1] Apparently, the creators of historical websites also perceive the Sviatoslav diorama as a realistic depiction of history. Online photographs of it are often presented without attribution, and the captions read simply "Prince Sviatoslav" or "Sviatoslav Fighting the Pechenegs." On some websites, these images may serve no further goal than livening up the text, but the creators of Russian and Ukrainian nationalistic propaganda use "Sviatoslav's Last Battle" for political purposes, such as promoting pseudo-historical narratives about the "eternal" existential struggle between civilized European Slavs and savage Asiatic nomads. In Russia, these narratives proliferated in the late 1990s and early 2000s, the period of increased tension between ethnic Russians and people from the Caucasus and Central Asia, deemed "Blacks" by virulent nationalists. The number of such websites subsequently decreased, but as late as 2020, they were still present on the Russian internet.

It is easy to see why far-right Ukrainian and Russian nationalists are fond of images that show Nordic-looking, blond good guys fighting against Asiatic-looking, swarthy bad guys. Representing Sviatoslav as blond may be historically accurate: the Byzantine author Leo the Deacon, who relied on eyewitness accounts, described Sviatoslav's eyes as "blue" or "gray." However, the diorama contradicts historical truth in representing all Sviatoslav's men as blond and all their enemies as dark. In reality, Sviatoslav's multiethnic troops included Turkic nomadic allies.[2] Moreover, there was little, if any, difference between the physical look of the people on opposite sides of the border between Rus and the steppe. The *Primary Chronicle* compiled in Kyiv during the early twelfth century tells the story of a youth who escaped the besieged city by passing for a Pecheneg. Apparently, for the chronicler and his readers, there were no clear visual distinctions between the Pechenegs and the Kyivans. The same is true of medieval artistic representations of Sviatoslav's battle, where the Rus and the opposing troops look exactly the same (Image 50.2). The 1985 diorama, however, depicts the two forces as looking drastically different, associating one side with light, whiteness, and goodness and the other with darkness, blackness, and evil. The pagan priest praying for Sviatoslav is highlighted so that he looks whitish-bluish. The traditional Slavic idol is shown here in white with a blue highlight, visually connecting the praying scene with

IMAGE 50.2 A miniature from the fifteenth-century *Radziwill Chronicle*. There are no contemporary visual representations of the Pechenegs. This late medieval illustration to a story about a single combat between champions from the Rus and the Pecheneg troops depicts Sviatoslav's son Volodimer I of Kiev and the Pecheneg leader with their men discussing the terms of the combat.

the white figure of the fighting Sviatoslav and the blue-white river glimmering on the left side of the diorama, where his blond warriors are concentrated. The popular perception of the resulting effect is reflected in the description of the panorama on the website created by a group of Zaporizhzhian citizens describing their town's attractions: "The composition saturated with expressive colors" shows "Sviatoslav on the white horse fighting treacherous nomads" coming "from the black rock."[3]

Such symbolism is typical of the artistic tradition that grew out of European racist discourse of the late nineteenth and early twentieth centuries. For example, the 1880 painting *Siegfried Kills the Dragon*, by the German artist Wilhelm Hauschild, highlights the blond Nordic hero fighting the dark-skinned, African-looking evil creature (Image 50.3). This kind of racism was condemned by Soviet ideology, which claimed that racial and ethnic problems existed only under capitalism, while the Soviet Union enjoyed the "friendship of peoples." Soviet visual art, however, sent a more complicated message. Contemporary people of various races and ethnicities were depicted as friendly and equal, but popular history books, school texts, and museum exhibitions often included representations of blond Slavs fighting swarthy savages.

Such illustrations bring to the fore the tension present in Soviet ideology, which proclaimed that all Soviet peoples were equal and brotherly, but also that ethnic Russians were "big brothers."[4] The "big brother" metaphor, with its implications of seniority and superiority, was part of the effort to reconcile Marxism-Leninism, an explicitly anti-imperial ideology, with prerevolutionary imperial discourse. This discourse, reflected in the Sviatoslav diorama, goes back to classic nineteenth-century historiography, in particular to the great Russian historian Sergei Solovyov.

Solovyov's work is representative of European historical scholarship of his time. The nineteenth-century scholars established the tenets of modern, source-based historical research, but also created grand narratives of their countries' pasts shaped by nationalism and other ideological agendas of the time. Twentieth- and twenty-first-century medievalists have spent much effort liberating their field from these agendas and changing the paradigms established by nineteenth-century historiography.

For Rus historians, this process was complicated by the ideological constraints that characterized Soviet intellectual life. Some ideas of Solovyov and other nineteenth-century historians made it into the Soviet canon, but their authorship was largely unacknowledged and their assumptions unexamined. After the end of the Soviet era, prerevolutionary historians were widely published and celebrated as part of the cultural heritage that had been suppressed and now returned in triumph, a situation not conducive to a critical reexamination of their legacy, which has only started recently.

An important part of this legacy is Solovyov's representation of relations between Rus and the steppe as implacable hostility between "civilized" European agriculturalists and "barbarian" Asiatic nomads. In fact, medieval sources contain plenty of information about alliances, intermarriages, and mutual cultural influence between

IMAGE 50.3 Wilhelm Hauschild. *Siegfried Kills the Dragon*, 1880.

Rus and its steppe neighbors. Solovyov, however, interpreted this information as evidence not of productive interaction between the two societies, but of southern Rus as the frontier of European civilization being overwhelmed by Asiatic barbarians. His account of the conflicts with the steppe conflated medieval Rus with the later Russian state, and presented this anachronistic "Russia" as part of civilized Europe fighting against the dark forces of Asia.

Such a view of "us," the enlightened West, and "them," the barbarous Orient, was prevalent in western Europe, but not necessarily in Russia, at the time. Solovyov and his contemporaries operated within an imperial framework in which ethnic Russians and other Slavs cohabited with subjects of the Russian Empire of other ethnicities. Unlike English or German identities, Russian identity had to be forged with an awareness that Russia encompassed a profusion of peoples.

In the 1860s and 1870s, when Solovyov was publishing his magisterial works on Rus and Russian history, Russian elite culture did not have a single, dominant narrative of identity, or a single sense of who their essential "other" might be. For example, the ideas about "us" and "them" in Leo Tolstoy's greatest novel *War and Peace* (1869) are very different from Solovyov's. In *War and Peace*, people of Slavic and Asian descent share a supra-ethnic Russian identity, from which Russian subjects of German and Polish ancestry are excluded. The mother of the Rostov family, which embodies "Russianness" in the novel, has "an oriental type of face." While describing General Bagration, an ethnic Georgian, Tolstoy emphasizes his "brown face" and "oriental accent."[5] Regardless of these non-European and non-Slavic features, Tolstoy's Bagration is a true Russian patriot, in contrast with the characters descending from the regions to the west of the Russian heartland. These "Germans" may have been born and raised in the Russian Empire, but they are represented as aliens, underscoring Tolstoy's construction of "us" in opposition to Europe rather than to Asia. Solovyov's view of the barbarous Orient as Russia's eternal opposite only became a dominant strain in Russian thought in the later nineteenth century, but even then, "barbarism" was not generally associated with race or skin color.

Arguably, a view of Asians as the inferior "other" emerged among the Russian elite in connection with Russian conquest of Central Asia during the second half of the nineteenth century. However, when Solovyov addressed the contemporary implications of his interpretation of medieval history, he mentioned Central Asia only in passing. His real focus was Ukraine and the Cossacks.

The Cossacks were inhabitants of the Eurasian steppe who "combined their freebooting with fishing, hunting, and foraging," and later with farming. In the late medieval period, when they first emerged as a distinct cultural group, the Cossacks "recognized no state jurisdiction."[6] Eventually, most of them were incorporated into the Russian Empire, where they had a semi-autonomous status. However, the Zaporizhzhian community, one particular Cossack group located in modern-day Ukraine and famous for fighting the Ottomans, was disbanded by the imperial government in the eighteenth century.

The Museum of Zaporizhzhian Cossacks, where the Sviatoslav diorama is located, reflects the significance of Cossack heritage for Ukrainian culture. The heroic exploits of the freedom-loving Zaporizhzhians are the stuff of Ukrainian folklore. Nineteenth-century nationalists assigned to the Cossacks a central role in the formation of Ukrainian ethnic identity. Russian antimonarchist intellectuals of the same period also had a highly positive view of the Cossacks, arguing that their social organization was a harbinger of liberty and equality. It is these two groups, the Ukrainian nationalists and Russian left-wing intelligentsia, who were the primary target of Solovyov's account of the relations between Rus and the steppe. A key part of this account is the notion of a moving frontier between "civilized" peoples, organized into states, and stateless "barbarians." Contact between them may result in two different outcomes. Some barbarians exposed to civilization learn its ways. As soon as they become civilized, they either join an existing state structure or form their own state. The frontier then moves to the area of contact with the next barbarian group.

Some barbarians, however, are not capable of being civilized because of their inner nature. After the Germanic tribes became civilized Germans, the frontier moved to the area of their contact with the Slavic barbarians. Since the Slavs belonged to the same "richly endowed Aryan branch" as the Germans, they, in turn, could be civilized. West Slavs became part of civilization after they were absorbed by the German Empire, while East Slavs evolved into civilized Russians by creating their own state of Rus/Russia. After absorbing the Slavs, however, European civilization came into contact with the barbarians who could not be civilized—the steppe nomads. This new contact zone was located in the Rus southwestern borderland, the population of which came to be known as Ukrainians. Solovyov argues that as an ethnic designation, the term is misleading: the Ukrainians were simply frontier Russians, and all their culturally distinct features were not really distinct, but typical of any frontier society.

In Ukraine—or "southwestern Rus," as Solovyov prefers to call it—these features may have endured longer than in other frontier zones, creating an illusion of permanency; however, the reason for this longevity was the presumed nature of the barbarians who were in contact with the Slavs in this particular borderland. The steppe nomads could not be civilized and hindered the process of state-building in Rus not only by raiding, but also by strengthening antisocial elements within the budding East Slavic civilization. In the Russian heartland, such elements were successfully suppressed or expelled, but they became a permanent presence in the southwest, where riffraff and outlaws of all sorts flocked under the pretense of fighting the nomads. Solovyov argues that in reality these elements were attracted by the lawless life in the steppe, where they fell under the influence of the nomads whom they nominally were fighting. In the end, they themselves turned into nomadic enemies of civilization and came to be known as Cossacks.

This anti-Cossack message lies at the heart of Solovyov's narrative of the relations between Rus and the steppe. By tracing the Cossacks' origins to the influence of the steppe nomads, represented as incorrigible savages bent on the destruction of any civilized society within their reach, Solovyov counters both the romanticized image of the Cossacks and Ukrainian claims to a distinct ethnic identity.[7] It is the height of irony, then, that a Ukrainian Cossack museum proudly displays a diorama reflecting Solovyov's narrative of the steppe. In a strange twist, this narrative ended up exerting a strong influence on Ukrainian nationalists. They adopted Solovyov's legacy selectively, accepting the idea of the existential struggle with the steppe, but representing the Cossacks not as a rabble, locked into barbarism by the influence of their nomadic foes, but as Slavic defenders of civilization from Turkic nomadic savages. In this respect, Ukrainian nationalistic ideology is similar to Soviet historiography, an eclectic assortment of diverse strands that combined Solovyov's dark view of the steppe with the positive image of the Cossacks promoted by Solovyov's ideological opponents.

This combination is reflected in the diorama, where Sviatoslav's figure draws on the popular image of a Cossack, masterfully fighting on horseback, wearing a white shirt, and most characteristically, displaying a shaved head with a single hairlock. Scholars agree that Sviatoslav, and later the Cossacks, borrowed this hairstyle from the steppe Turks, but the general public is largely unaware of this fact. In the diorama, the Pechenegs are wearing helmets, and Sviatoslav is the only one displaying a hairlock, a signature Cossack feature.

Ukrainian nationalists claim Sviatoslav as one of their own. They argue that their pure Slavic country is the exclusive heir of medieval Rus, while the Russians, who also claim descent from Rus, originate from the savage Finnic tribes that lived in the forests to the east of Rus and mixed with some Slavic exiles and outcasts. Russians, Ukrainian nationalists argue, have nothing to do with the glories of Rus. In this context, the representation of Sviatoslav as a proto-Cossack makes him a purely Ukrainian hero who can be employed to counter Russian claims to the Kyivan Rus legacy. One nationalistic outlet excitedly reported that Sviatoslav, "who looked like a Zaporizhzhian Cossack," became the mascot of Kyivan soccer fans, exemplifying what some concerned Ukrainian journalists described as a growing cult of Sviatoslav.[8] Interestingly, Russian nationalists are also fond of Sviatoslav and use the same diorama image on websites that deny Ukrainian nationhood. For them, Sviatoslav is a pure Russian, representing the glory of the ancestral Russian realm, Kyivan Rus. In their telling, the southwestern part of Rus became Ukraine after it was corrupted by pernicious alien influences, from steppe nomads to Catholics, and lost its original pure Slavic character. They argue that Ukraine needs to shed these corrupting influences, return to its true roots, and become one with Russia.[9]

Thus, both sides use the Sviatoslav myth to stake national and territorial claims in the aftermath of the collapse of the Soviet Union. Both sides argue that the other one is corrupted by an uncivilized, non-Slavic influence, whether steppe Turkic savages or forest Finnic savages. They employ the same image to promote their competing interpretations of history, which go back to ideas about Rus and the steppe typical of the late nineteenth-century imperial discourse. These ideas have become influential among the general public not least because of widespread visual representations of noble-looking blond Slavs fighting dark and evil nomadic savages.

Writing this paper in 2020, I ended it with a conclusion full of misguided optimism:

It appears that things are finally changing. Recent school textbooks and some new educational websites illustrate their accounts of relations between Rus and the steppe with images from medieval chronicles, and do not reproduce late twentieth-century art based on nineteenth-century imperialist discourse. Hopefully, this new trend signifies a break with the long and toxic tradition of which the Sviatoslav diorama is a part.

This hope, of course, was not realized. The equivalence of the two opposing nationalistic interpretations of the Rus history discussed in this paper ended when one side became a party to a military aggression against the homeland of the other one. The toxic nationalistic tradition reached a horrifying new level when it became part of wartime propaganda that uses twisted narratives of the past to justify crimes committed in the present.

NOTES

1. Barbara Maria Stafford et al., *Devices of Wonder: From the World in a Box to Images on a Screen* (Los Angeles: Getty Publications, 2001), 315–330; Erkki Huhtamo and Jussi Parikka, *Media Archaeology: Approaches, Applications, and Implications* (Los Angeles, University of California Press: 2011).
2. Simon Franklin and Jonathan Shepard, *The Emergence of Rus: 750–1200* (London: Routledge, 2014), 143–146.
3. "Posledniaia bitva Sviatoslava: Rasskaz ob odnoi diorame muzeia zaporozhskogo kazachestva." July 8, 2012, http://retro.zp.ua/attraction/museum/320-dioramabitva-svyatoslava-u-dneprovskih-porogov-v-972-godu.html
4. See Ronald Grigor Suny, "The Contradictions of Identity: Being Soviet and National in the USSR and After," in *Soviet and Post-Soviet Identities*, edited by Mark Bassin and Catriona Kelly (Cambridge: Cambridge University Press, 2012), 17–36.
5. Leo Tolstoy, *Voina i mir*. Tom I—II (Moscow: Eksmo, 2013), 65, 259–60.
6. Serhii Plokhy, *The Cossack Myth: History and Nationhood in the Age of Empires* (Cambridge: Cambridge University Press, 2012), 31, 33.
7. S. M. Solovyov, *Nabliudeniia nad istoricheskoi zhizn'iu narodov* (Moscow: Astrel, 2003), available as an electronic text at http://dugward.ru/library/solovyev_s_m/solovyev_s_m_nabludeniya_nad_istorich.html#narod; Solovyov, *Istoriia Rossii s drevneishikh vremen*, Vol. 2 (Moscow: Mysl': 1988), 639, 647–648, 463, 466, 481, 648.
8. Roman Grivinskii, "V poiskakh velichiia," *Den'*, August 19, 2016, https://day.kyiv.ua/ru/article/obshchestvo/v-poiskah-velichiya; Vasil' Iavir, "Nevdalyi heroi: pro kul't kniazia Sviatoslava v Ukraini," *Spil'ne*, July 25, 2016, https://commons.com.ua/ru/nevdalij-geroj-pro-kult-knyazya-svyatoslava-v-ukrayini/
9. T. V. Chernikova, "Sviatoslav," *Rossiiskoe voenno-istoricheskoe obshchestvo*, n.d., http://100.histrf.ru/commanders/svyatoslav-knyaz/; "Ukraintsy—eto tiurki?" *Velikoross*, October 22, 2016, http://www.velykoross.ru/actual/all_8/article_2910/ (the author, unusually, acknowledges a Turkic influence on Sviatoslav); Petr Akopov, "Iskonno russkaia Ukraina ne smozhet otrech'sia ot svoei istorii," *Vzgliad*, December 23, 2019, https://vz.ru/politics/2019/12/23/1014800.html

CHAPTER 51

RETURN OF THE SABLES: THE SYMBOL OF IMPERIAL SIBERIA FROM THE SEVENTEENTH CENTURY TO TODAY

EVGENY MANZHURIN

FROM ITS EARLIEST DAYS, heraldry in Russia was at the service of the nascent empire. The use of coats of arms or emblems to represent towns and cities was institutionalized with the creation of the Herald's Office (*Geroldiia*) in 1722. Its task was to establish heraldry as the official visual and symbolic language of the state. In the spirit of Peter the Great's modernization, the Herald's Office was intended to transfer contemporary European practices to the Russian Empire. This was ensured through the hiring of a foreign expert, Francisco de Santi.[1] From that moment until the fall of the empire in 1917, heraldic symbols for Russia's lands and cities were designed in the imperial capital and personally approved by the monarch.

Santi had artists trained to follow the European style of painting heraldic images, and his designs followed the combinations of colors and forms established in western Europe. This stylistic consistency did not mean that all emblems were cast in the same symbolic language. Rather, in the imperial logic of managed diversity—that is, the recognition of the empire's diverse cultures, ethnicities, and topographies, all under the power of the tsar—Santi's symbolic catalogue of imperial holdings combined new and old, borrowed and original, abstract and utilitarian, descriptive and programmatic emblems. The newly incorporated western provinces had used European-style abstract emblems, and these received approval from the tsar without alterations. Traditional emblems of ancient Tver, Novgorod, and a few other western Russian cities were approved with minor corrections, in spite of the fact that they included visual symbols with strong local histories and projected power and meanings developed when they were still independent political centers, prior to unification with Russia. The empire was thus incorporating territories with diverse histories, populations, and cultures into a complex symbolic landscape where the supremacy of the center was ensured through imposition of a uniform visual style and a special distinction of the emblem of its capital.

While many of new emblems designed by Santi were utilitarian, the symbol of the imperial capital St. Petersburg "spoke" a symbolic language of supremacy charged with imperial ideology. It featured two symbols of the emperor's authority, the scepter and the crown looming over two crossed anchors. The composition with two crossed elements and a symbol of power at the top was borrowed from the emblem of the Holy See in Rome, the archetype of an imperial capital and, like St. Petersburg, the city of Saint Peter.

Once the design of territorial emblems was standardized and centralized in St. Petersburg, a distinct Russian style of symbol-making gradually developed. The imperial gaze from the center onto the periphery singled out key features, goods, or resources of local places in terms of their contribution to the center's prosperity, security, or imperial diversity, and then asserted them as territorial symbols.

By the time of the reign of Catherine II, this utilitarian imperialism had become dominant in the symbolic language of emblems. This period also saw a change in Russian territorial heraldry that emphasizes its role as a top-down imperial symbolic catalogue of images: from the 1770s, the symbol of the regional capital was to appear in the upper half of any emblems newly created for cities under its jurisdiction. A reform of territorial heraldry initiated by Nicholas I in the early nineteenth century created decorations denoting a city's status, its main industries, and its merits, adding further detail and distinction to the symbolic catalogue of imperial holdings. Thus, while in Europe the city's heraldic symbol was a sign of its rights and privileges, in the Russian Empire it asserted the city's subordination to the center.

All these developments point to the role allocated to heraldry in the Russian Empire: local distinction was rendered through a uniform symbolic language that was created and dictated by the imperial center. Starting with Peter the Great, new territorial emblems portrayed local sites according to their distinct features in the imperial context, as seen from St. Petersburg. However, the discriminating and ordering gaze, associated with the empire, was present before the period of the Russian Empire, and its visual heritage lives on to this day, long after its demise. To demonstrate that, I will trace the history of one visual motif, the so-called Siberian sables, in symbol-making from the late Muscovite period in the seventeenth century to the present day.

SIBERIAN SABLES FROM THE SEVENTEENTH CENTURY TO THE FALL OF RUSSIAN EMPIRE

The use of the sable as a central element of the official symbol of Siberia is in line with the utilitarian approach characteristic of the imperial heraldry, because it reflects the key resource Siberia provided to the center: sable fur. The key imperial function of Siberian outposts was to collect fur tax from the Indigenous population, so it is not surprising that as many as twenty-two Siberian towns used fur-bearing animals on their seals. Almost half of those fur-bearing animals were sables.[2] The iconography of the state's symbolic presence suggests that the scarce infrastructure of remote outposts was about fur, fur, and more fur for the center. This visibly demonstrates the fundamentally colonial nature of Russia's expansion into Siberia, when local peoples were subjugated by Russian military force and were incorporated into the Russian state as tributaries paying tax in fur, preferably sable.

One of Santi's sources on Russian heraldic symbols was the 1672 *Tituliarnik* (a reference book for the Ambassadorial Chancellery). It contained emblems of thirty-three territories ruled over by the tsar. Some of these emblems were based on medieval symbols of formerly independent principalities, but many were invented in imitation of the European tradition. Among them was the emblem of the Siberian Tsardom, which featured two sables standing upright and holding a crown, a bow, and two crossed arrows, a composition known as "The Siberian Sables" (Image 51.1).

The 1696 seal of the Siberian Tsardom codified the *Tituliarnik* version of the Siberian emblem, which eventually replaced other alternatives. Finally, in the 1698 state seal, the wings of the double-headed Russian eagle were decorated with emblems of key imperial holdings, including the Siberian Tsardom. The seal's structure imitated the coat of arms of the Holy Roman Empire, and the emblem of Siberia was now a part of the visual representation of Petrine imperial ambitions.

The value of its resources gave Siberia a special place in the catalogue of the empire's riches, while the status of a "tsardom" gave it a prominent place in the imperial coat of arms. The imperial vision of Siberia projected through its heraldic symbol is that of a unique, higher-status periphery, but one whose importance was based on its natural resources that fed the imperial treasury. Designation as a tsardom highlighted the distinctness of this vast territory in the typology of imperial holdings, recognizing and proudly displaying its pre-Russian history as an independent khanate, a vestige of the powerful Mongol Empire. The emblem of the Siberian Tsardom expressed an imperial vision that simultaneously downgraded Siberia to a source of raw material and raised its status to the same level as formerly independent polities of Kazan, Astrakhan, and Poland.

The sable itself, however, was more than just a symbol of the Siberian Tsardom; in the late seventeeth and early eighteenth centuries, a pair of sables was engraved on the seals of Siberian Chancellery and the large administrative unit of the Siberian governorate. Its image was also used in emblems of smaller administrative and territorial units. When in 1724 two new subdivisions were created within the Siberian governorate, both of them received symbols featuring sable. Irkutsk was represented by a tiger carrying a sable, and Yeniseisk by two standing sables with an arrow between them.

In the eighteenth century, the image of the sable began to be used to brand other valuable Siberian products. When mandatory iron branding was introduced in 1722,

IMAGE 51.1 The emblem of the Siberian Tsardom from the 1672 *Tituliarnik*, displaying two sables standing upright and holding a crown, a bow, and two crossed arrows, a composition known as "The Siberian Sables."

the Demidov Ironworks in the Urals adopted the word *Siberia* (*СИБИРЬ*) with a sable silhouette as its trademark.[3] Between 1763 and 1781, Siberia was allowed to mint its own coins featuring the Siberian sables motif (Image 51.2). This further popularized the sable as a symbol of Siberia, and the history of local coinage remains a source of pride to Siberians to this day.

IMAGE 51.2 A five-kopek coin minted in Siberia in the late eighteenth century with Siberian sables.

Until 1917, the emblem of the Siberian Tsardom continued to occupy an honorable place in the imperial coat of arms. Sables remained on emblems of the Irkutsk governorate, Yakutsk province, as well as the towns of Irkutsk, Yakutsk, Yeniseisk, and Verkhoturye. All these were discontinued after the establishment of Bolshevik rule in Russia.

SABLES IN SOVIET AND POST-SOVIET SYMBOLIC DISCOURSE

In the early Soviet Union, the territorial emblems of the Russian Empire were rejected, and new ones were only created for major political units such as Soviet and autonomous republics. Lower-level territories and cities were left without heraldic symbols. Although Vladimir Lenin's 1918 Decree on Monuments of the Republic called for the creation of new city symbols, its only result was a clumsy 1924 emblem of Moscow that was soon forgotten[4]. However, the imperial tradition of regulating the symbolic landscape from the center returned to Soviet practices in the late 1920s, when Moscow began censoring and standardizing republic emblems. Under Joseph Stalin's Constitution of 1936, only the emblems of Soviet republics retained some originality in their visual language, although their composition and style were becoming more and more uniform. Smaller entities, including regions, districts, and cities, had no local symbols whatsoever. However, it was precisely the absence of local symbols, together with the lack of regulation, that eventually made it easier for local actors to fill the void and to develop new heraldic emblems in cities across the Soviet Union.

Unplanned and unsupported by the party leadership, the discourse calling for new city heraldry, which I call the Soviet heraldic revival, was shaped during a unique window of opportunity made available by the period of cultural "Thaw" initiated by Nikita Khrushchev.[5] Between 1959 and 1965, three well-known writers, Daniil Granin, Evgenii Dolmatovskii, and Vasily Peskov, independently called for creation of city symbols in leading Soviet newspapers. The idea gained popularity, and the press continued to describe local competitions and new adoptions, while the party leadership remained displeased but largely passive. As a result, in the 1960s, the idea came to be perceived as legitimate, and by 1967, more than thirty cities formally adopted new symbols. By the fall of the USSR in 1991, no less than four hundred cities had locally adopted emblems.

Apart from popularizing new symbols, the press familiarized its readers with local heraldic history. This information was in great demand, as the few books on Russian heraldry that existed were not widely available. Moreover, apart from the western periphery, by the 1960s there were no artists and just a handful of historians familiar with heraldic design in the Soviet Union. Nevertheless, already the first new urban symbols of the mid-1960s contained cautious references to the imperial heraldic heritage. The revival of symbols from the imperial period meant that the creators of new emblems had studied the imperial heraldry of their cities and made conscious decisions to reference it in their new, Soviet-era symbols. It also meant that they had developed arguments that persuaded the gatekeepers in local Communist Party committees to allow images derived from the prerevolutionary imperial period. During the heraldic revival, its protagonists pounced on the opportunity opened by the Thaw to use the press to introduce new topics into the public domain. City emblems were created locally to produce locally relevant visions of space and time, and to replace the Stalin-era monolithic symbolic landscape regurgitated by the center. New city emblems became tools for spatial socialization on the local level that supported identification with the city, region, or Siberia as a whole.

In the Soviet period, the sable appeared in official symbols of three urban locales. A visual reference to the Demidov sable (the eighteenth-century ironworks trademark) was adopted in 1973 for the emblem of the city of Sverdlovsk (formerly, and now again, Ekaterinburg) and in 1982 for Gari, a small town in the same region. The composition of the Sverdlovsk emblem simultaneously referenced the original image of Siberian sables, with two standing animals. A similar overlap was also present in the emblem of Gari. Its description read: "the image of the 'Demidov' sable symbolizes fur procurement in the Urals taiga."[6] In the 1981 emblem of Ust-Ilimsk, an imperial-period sable emblem was used as a "citation" in accordance with late imperial heraldic convention. In 1977, novel sable iconography appeared on the unofficial emblem of Megion, in which a black sable represented natural wealth and oil extraction.[7] In these examples of Soviet-period uses of the imperial heraldic heritage, the sable remained a symbol of natural resources and received a new meaning of a symbolic link to pre-Soviet history.

The association of the sable with Siberian natural wealth and history continued in the post-Soviet period. Since the beginning of the heraldic revival, fifty-three regions and municipalities in Asian Russia have adopted an image of the sable as their symbol, and twenty of these include a reference to the original Siberian sables motif.[8] Imperial-period symbols received a boost from the reestablishment in 1992 of the state office for heraldry, the Heraldic Council, which has set out to revive and promote heraldry of the imperial period both in form and in spirit. The heraldic symbols adopted in post-Soviet Russia continued the trends that first appeared in the late Soviet period. These include references to imperial-period emblems, use of the sable across Siberia, and broadening of its meaning to include all kinds of natural wealth. Where mining is fundamental to the local economy, the historic allusion to wealth in pelts is used to represent oil, gas, or whatever metal is locally mined. Other emblems broaden the meaning further, using the sable as a symbol of all the local resources provided by nature. In official emblem descriptions, the association of the Siberian sables motif with resource extraction remains celebratory and untouched by environmentalist regret.

Lack of other uncontested symbols of Siberianness made the sable an easy choice for new emblems across the region, in places like Lesosibirsk, Tashtagol, Ust-Kut, Zalari, and many more. The pan-Siberian nature of contemporary sable symbolism is apparent in the use of sables in the emblems of organizations aiming to represent the whole region: the Siberian Accord (a governors' association) and several organizations of Siberian regionalists (*oblastniki*).

A novel post-Soviet function of the Siberian sables is to revive the historical precedent that conferred special status on the Siberian Tsardom and celebrated its standing within the empire. This interpretation is suggested by the motif's iconography: the sables are positioned to uphold the claim to Siberia's elevated status thanks to their holding up the (imaginary) Siberian crown. This intention is visible in the post-Soviet emblems of Ekaterinburg (1995), Novosibirsk (1993), and Tyumenskaia *oblast* (2008), where the sables are moved outside of the heraldic shield to the position of shield supporters. In heraldry, such supporters denote special distinction, or the ancestors of the symbol's owner, ideally rooted as deeply in the mythical past as possible. In these examples, where sables have been moved outside the shield itself and situated to hold the shield aloft, a key resource that drew Russians into Siberia appears metaphorically as the ancient forebears of contemporary Siberians.

Even without specialist heraldic knowledge, the move of the sables to the role of shield supporters is open to a purely visual interpretation. As in the Russian national coat of arms, the eagle representing Russia visually serves as the background to the central shield representing the capital, Moscow. So, too, on the emblems of Ekaterinburg and Novosibirsk, the sables, when moved to the sides, form a background to the shield they hold. Spatially, the sables then represent Siberia, and the central shield its most important locality. Thus, Novosibirsk, with sables on both sides of the city symbol, presents itself as a capital of Siberia (Image 51.3), while Ekaterinburg has replaced one of the sables with a (Russian) bear to emphasize its aspiration to be the

IMAGE 51.3 A monument in Novosibirsk with sables holding up the city symbol.

capital of the Urals, where the "old" European Russia meets its more recent Siberian expanses.

The fact that territorial emblems are now created and adopted locally rather than imposed from the imperial center redeems the heraldic image of the Siberian sables from its original colonial connotations. The imperial heraldic language has been internalized and stripped of negative associations. Now, it's not the central imperial administration but Siberians themselves that proudly represent their land as primarily a source of natural resources. What previously could be read as a symbol of imperial oppression through coerced extraction of Siberian pelts has been reclaimed and repurposed as a symbol of local wealth and pride. Even the recent restoration of the imperial symbol of the capital of the Yakut republic—a sable being captured by an eagle—has not caused concern over its potential interpretations of colonialist oppression in a place with a strong sense of ethnic identity. These emblems employ imperial-period visual tropes featuring the sable as a symbol of renewed connection with the past and its traditional association with colonial extraction, along with a contemporary pride in local natural resources and prosperity that they bring to local communities. Whether the shift in the meaning of heraldic sable from top-down imperial coercion to bottom-up local pride will have an impact on actual resource-extracting practices and prove any less destructive to the Siberian environment, or to the sables themselves, remains an open question.

NOTES

1. In what follows, *emblem* denotes both preheraldic and heraldic territorial symbols. The term *coat of arms* is only used for official symbols of the Russian Empire.
2. Irina Kurennaia, "Zveri iadomye, snednye, pushnye i tainstvennye," *Sibirskie ogni*, no. 2 (2016): 170.
3. Aleksandr Zaimogov, *Siniachikhinskie zhelezodelatel'nye zavody*. (Ekaterinburg: Grachev i partnery, 2011), 21.
4. "Dekret O pamiatnikakh respubliki," *Dekrety sovetskoi vlasti*, tom II: 17 marta—10 iiulia 1918 (Moscow: Gosudarstvennoe izdatel'stvo politicheskoi literatury, 1959), 95–96.
5. Nikita Balagurov and Evgeny Manzhurin, "Gorod bez gerba? Sovetskii Vyborg v poiskakh simvola," *Stranitsy Vyborgskoi istorii: sbornik statei*, Vol. IV (Vyborg: Vyborg Museum-Preserve, 2020), 380–401; Evgeny Manzhurin, "Voobrazhaemaia preemstvennost': dorevoliutsionnoe geral'dicheskoe nasledie v sovetskoi gorodskoi simvolike (1953–1991)," *Vestnik Permskogo universiteta. Seriia: Istoria* 30, no. 3 (Summer 2015): 116–122.
6. Viktor Melikaev and Vladimir Serzhan, *Katalog sovremennykh gerbov gorodov, poselkov i sel SSSR*, Part III (Minsk, 1989).
7. Igor Mukhamadeev, "Gerby Tiumenskogo Severa," *Vestnik geraldista*, no. 8 (1995).
8. A similar, if not greater, increase is seen in the number of emblems with the squirrel, the chipmunk, the capercaillie (a large Eurasian grouse), and the moose. However, these do not appear in (supra-)regional emblems, and thus do not challenge the sable as a symbol of Asian Russia.

CHAPTER 52

SOVIET WAR MEMORIALS IN POST-SOVIET SPACES

KAREN PETRONE

WHEN THE SOVIET UNION collapsed in 1991, Eastern European and post-Soviet states had to confront not only the political and economic legacies of the Soviet Union, but also its physical landscape of monuments and memorials. Immediately after the Second World War ended in 1945, the Soviet Union built grandiose monuments in Berlin, Vienna, Prague, and Warsaw as imposing visual reminders that Red Army soldiers had sacrificed their lives liberating these territories from Nazi rule. East Germany, Czechoslovakia, and Poland first became symbolically indebted to the Soviets for their liberation, and then became semicolonial "satellite" socialist states under strong Soviet influence, though not under direct Soviet territorial control.

In the Soviet Union, monuments commemorated "The Great Patriotic War," which began when the Nazi army invaded the Soviet Union on June 22, 1941. This chronology conveniently omitted the previous two years of war. In September of 1939, the Soviet Union and Nazi Germany, carrying out the secret protocols of the Hitler-Stalin pact, split Poland between them, and the Soviet Union forcibly occupied the Baltic states of Estonia, Latvia, and Lithuania. In 1944, the Soviets reconquered these territories and reintegrated them into the Soviet Union, placing them once again under direct Soviet imperial rule. All Soviet war memorials projected Soviet influence and bolstered the legitimacy of socialist rule in Eastern Europe. Memorials within Soviet republics also redefined previously contested territories as officially Soviet spaces. This essay explores the fate of two of the latter monuments, in Estonia and Ukraine, to understand the contexts in which these monuments were built, and what their post-Soviet existences tell us about anti-imperial struggles in post-Soviet space.

Both memorials are located on territory first annexed to the Soviet Union in 1939 and 1940. "The Bronze Soldier" in Tallinn, Estonia, was created in 1947. The "Monument to the War Glory of the Soviet Armed Forces," or "The Glory Monument," in Lviv, Ukraine, was erected in 1970. The twenty-three-year difference in the timing of the two monuments is significant, as are their different locations, the different time-frames they depict, and their different political contexts.

The monument in Tallinn commemorated the third anniversary of the Soviet "liberation" of the city from the Nazis in 1944 and was placed at the gravesite of thirteen Soviet soldiers and officers, underscoring the loss of Soviet life in securing the territory (Image 52.1). While the monument celebrated the Soviet liberation of Tallinn, most Estonians understood this event as a reoccupation. In 1946, two Estonian teenage girls had destroyed the original wooden marker on the gravesite, an anti-imperial act "in revenge for the demolition of the monuments of the [Estonian] Independence War." The girls were imprisoned in the Soviet Gulag, and likely provoked the building of a grander and more permanent monument on this site in the city center of Tallinn, on Tõnismägi (or St. Anthony's Hill), which Soviet authorities had renamed "Liberators' Square" in 1945.[1] The Soviets claimed this central space in Tallinn as theirs and as sacred, due to the buried corpses of the Red Army soldiers martyred for the "freedom" of the Estonians. From the very outset, pro- and anti-Soviet residents of Tallinn perceived the location and the monument itself in

IMAGE 52.1 "The Bronze Soldier" on Tõnismägi, April 24, 2007, three days before being moved to the Defense Forces Cemetery of Tallinn. Photograph by Liilia Moroz.

radically different ways and contested the monument's meaning within frameworks of Estonian nationalism and Soviet imperialism.

Compared to the contemporaneous monuments in Germany and Austria that sport towering, classically inspired columns, the Bronze Soldier in Tallinn is relatively modest. He stands in full uniform, slightly larger than life-sized, with no weapon visible, a bowed head, and an extremely somber expression. He holds his helmet in one hand as he pays respect to the dead, mourning for the comrades who are buried around him. His other hand is clenched at his side, showing his anger at this loss. In 1964, an "eternal flame" was added to the site, reflecting new post-Stalin commemorative practices that made war memorials even more explicitly sacred spaces by using the ancient symbol of fire to denote immortality. On each side of the Bronze Soldier is a plaque that now reads, in Estonian on one side and Russian on the other, "To the Fallen in the Second World War." In Soviet times, the inscription read "Eternal Glory for the Heroes who Have Fallen for the Liberation and the Sovereignty of our Country."[2] This post-Soviet broadening of the inscription underscores the contested nature of virtually every aspect of remembrance of the Second World War in Estonia.

The Glory Monument in Lviv appeared under significantly different circumstances (Image 52.2). While Soviet monument-building in Eastern Europe flourished during the first few years after the war, such monuments were rarer in the Soviet Union proper. Early plans for monuments commemorating the heroic siege of Leningrad and other significant wartime events were put on hold in the Stalin era, due in large part to Stalin's antipathy to acknowledging the deaths of tens of millions of Soviet citizens. While the Tallinn monument fit into the earlier trend of monument-building to assert Soviet imperial influence over a newly conquered territory, the Lviv monument was built during the Brezhnev period, when Communist Party leaders sought to reinvigorate a Soviet patriotic identity that had been shaken by de-Stalinization. As a result, victory in the Great Patriotic War took on a very significant role as a unifying cultural moment for all Soviets, buttressed by previously suppressed grassroots efforts at commemoration as well as by support from the Communist leadership.

Lviv's Glory Monument was much more imposing than the Bronze Soldier. It was located at a busy intersection near the entrance to Bohdan Khmelnytskyi Park, adjacent to Lviv's military academy and museum. The monument celebrated the achievements of the Soviet military beginning in 1918, twenty-one years before Lviv became Soviet. The historical narrative sculpted onto six chronological panels used the glorious Soviet victory in the Second World War to tie the history of Lviv to that of the Soviet Union. In addition to a high wall containing the six striking panels of bronze reliefs, there was a sculptural composition of two massive figures and a ninety-foot red granite pillar. The two giant figures depicted a Red Army soldier holding a sword in his outstretched hands and an ageless female figure, representing Ukraine or the

IMAGE 52.2 "Monument to the War Glory of the Soviet Armed Forces," Lviv, Ukraine, 1970 (detail).

Soviet motherland, with one arm held straight out in front of her and the other resting on the soldier's sword. The motherland is both blessing the soldier and receiving his oath. The ninety-foot pillar towered above the statues, punctuated with five bronze friezes depicting various types of military forces in martial stances. In 1992, Ukrainian officials changed the monument's inscription from "To the Military Glory of the Soviet Armed Forces," to "To the Victors over Nazism."

The style of the Glory Monument's statues, reliefs, and friezes is clearly recognizable as socialist realism, with blocky figures and typical Soviet visual tropes of vigilant armed and uniformed soldiers, male workers in their factory aprons, and female agricultural workers in traditional Ukrainian national clothing. Even though most of the figures are purportedly clothed, the male figures' arms and legs are sculpted as if they are naked. The brawny musculature of their shoulders, their straining back muscles, their powerful thighs, and their bare knees are visible through their clothing. This rendering of the male body is also used for the subjugated Whites cowering and being killed in the Russian Civil War panel. In depicting the female bodies of the motherland and of the women on the panels, the sculptors emphasized women's erect breasts, with nipples visible through diaphanous clothing.

The sculpting of female bodies to emphasize women's ideal status as mothers is most evident in the panel depicting "Liberation of Western Ukraine." A woman in Ukrainian national costume presents a Soviet soldier with a loaf of bread in the traditional gesture of welcome, while another Soviet soldier greets a worker, his wife, and their newborn child.[3] The new mother is naked from the waist up, with her breasts and nipples very clearly defined, as if she has been interrupted in the act of breastfeeding her child. This scene of "liberation" connects the fertility of Ukraine's land and people with traditional images of hospitality to convey the political message that Western Ukrainians welcomed Soviet annexation in 1939.

After the fall of the Soviet Union in 1991, the physical presence of these monuments gained new meanings and became a focal point for conflicts between imperial and national ideas in both Estonia and Ukraine. The monuments came to symbolize contemporaries' relationship with the Soviet past, with lingering and developing interethnic tensions, and with the rising threat of Russian dominance in the region. The Bronze Soldier itself caused tensions between Estonia and Russia. The Estonian decision to remove it from central Tallinn in 2007 precipitated a cyberattack on Estonia, presumably carried out by Russia. In Ukraine, armed hostilities, including the 2014 annexation of Crimea and the ongoing border war in Eastern Ukraine from 2014 through 2021, led to escalating attacks on the Glory Monument. The changed inscriptions on the monuments also reflect the two states' different post-independence priorities. The new Estonian inscription "to the fallen in the Second World War" included Estonians who fought on both the Nazi and Soviet sides, preventing the exclusion of any Estonians from the nation. The new Ukrainian inscription excised the reference to the Soviet Armed Forces, but still recognized only those who fought against the Nazis. The more inclusive Estonian monument remains standing, though not at its original site, while the Ukrainian monument has been dismantled.

After Estonians gained independence from the Soviet Union, new Estonian national narratives lamented the dilution of the Estonian nation by genocidal deportations during the Stalin years, the tragedy of Estonian emigration to flee Soviet authorities in 1944, and the Moscow-imposed immigration of hundreds of thousands of non-Estonian Russian speakers between 1945 and 1991. The post-Soviet Estonian state required a rigorous Estonian-language examination before post-1940 immigrants could apply for citizenship. This stringent requirement caused the disenfranchisement of and provoked the resentment of Russian-speaking Estonians.

During this time, the Bronze Soldier became a symbolic site for contemporaries to work out these conflicts. While Russian speakers in Tallinn (at times egged on by Russian politicians and protesters sent from Moscow) saw the Bronze Soldier as a source of Russian pride, Estonian speakers viewed the monument as a reminder of the hated Soviet occupation and continuing Russian threat to the Estonian nation, and they targeted the statue with vandalism.

There were numerous physical changes to the Bronze Soldier site after 1991. The Estonian government extinguished the eternal flame, asserting that Tallinn was no longer part of Soviet memory space.[4] Between 1991 and 2007, authorities took down a bronze plate with the names of the thirteen soldiers buried there and put up a granite sign that read "to the unknown soldiers," obscuring the Soviet and Russian identities of the dead. In 1995, a competition was held to redesign the monument completely. Some Estonians derogatorily called the monument the "Unknown Rapist," desacralizing the space and questioning the honor of all Soviet soldiers and the legitimacy of the Bronze Soldier as an Estonian symbol.[5]

The Bronze Soldier became a rallying point for Russian speakers living in Estonia, and they organized demonstrations against their disenfranchisement at this physical location symbolically connected to Soviet claims of legitimate rule over Estonia. They continued to celebrate Victory Day there on May 9, keeping alive the Soviet-era commemoration of the capitulation of the Nazis. The Russian-speaking population saw the Bronze Soldier as their representative—both in terms of his identity as a Russian speaker and because he represented the "liberation" of Estonians from the Nazis. Both he and they legitimately belonged in Estonia thanks to the Red Army's service to and sacrifice for the Estonian nation.

Estonian-speaking residents of Tallinn resented that a monument they saw as a symbol of Soviet oppression was still allowed to stand while a nationalist statue at Lihula portraying an Estonian soldier in German uniform was removed by the government in 2004.[6] They feared the power of the site as a location for demonstrations of disaffected Russians, especially after clashes there on Victory Day in 2006.[7] Estonian authorities sought to, quite literally, decenter the remnants of the Soviet/Russian presence and the focal point of Russocentric Great Patriotic War rituals by relocating the statue. When they did so, in April 2007, there were two nights of rioting and looting led by Russian speakers from inside and outside of Estonia, the so-called "Bronze Nights." The Russian government in Moscow equated the removal of the statue with "fascism." According to this interpretation, the Soviets/Russians had stood up against fascism, while Estonians had collaborated with fascism in the 1940s and continued to do so in the present. The statue and some of the graves were relocated to the Defense Forces Cemetery of Tallinn. After the removal of the monument from the city center, the Estonians experienced cyberattacks from Russian IP addresses.[8] These crises led Estonian authorities to strengthen their efforts to integrate Russian speakers into the Estonian polity.

As of late 2022, the statue is fully accessible to all those who wish to see it. To pay the Bronze Soldier homage, however, requires traveling to a military cemetery on the outskirts of town. The statue has been granted a place of respect, but has been made much less visible due to its distance from the capital city's central civic landscape and its relegation to a place for the dead. The Bronze Soldier remains a focus of contestation between pro- and anti-Russian Estonians. It was vandalized in April 2022 as a protest against Russia's February 2022 invasion of Ukraine, and one of the Soviet military medals on the chest of the Bronze Soldier was damaged.[9]

The post-Soviet fate of the Glory Monument in Lviv is markedly different. Between 1991 and 2014, the memorial site stood as before but suffered from neglect, as funding for upkeep was not forthcoming from the city. Neglect gave way to calls to dismantle the monument in light of the Russian annexation of Crimea in 2014 and the ongoing border war in Donetsk and Luhansk. In 2015, the Ukrainian government passed an anticommunist law, making it possible to demolish Soviet symbols. Lviv's City Council rejected the Glory Monument as a symbol of communist totalitarianism and began to discuss removal. Then, Ukrainian nationalists repeatedly defaced the monument, rejecting the idea that the Soviet Armed Forces had "liberated" Lviv in 1939 and 1944 by forcibly altering the visual messages that the monument conveyed. On June 2, 2017, for instance, vandals splashed the monument with blood-red paint and scrawled "occupation" in white under the inscription.[10] By early 2018, protestors regularly attacked the monument with hammers, destroying its stone facing and inscription.[11] Vandals struck, for example, on June 22, 2018, the anniversary of the Nazi invasion of the Soviet Union. A telling act of defacement targeted the "Liberation of Western Ukraine" panel in particular. Protestors painted the bottom half of the panel yellow and the top half blue, superimposing the Ukrainian flag over the image of "liberation." A representation of Soviet legitimacy was negated by the display of the Ukrainian national colors.

The Lviv City Council fenced off the Glory Monument site, because, ostensibly, it feared that the plinths might fall off the ninety-foot pillar. Graffiti appeared on the fence around the monument declaring "Glory to the Ukrainian Insurgent Army," partisans who fought for Ukrainian independence during and after the Second World War. In February 2018, the Lviv City Council passed a resolution to take down the pillar, and it was demolished in March 2019 "in order to prevent accidents," though it seems clear that the decision had political as well as practical origins (Image 52.3). In 2021, the six bronze panels and the statues of the soldier and the motherland were also removed. These are to be displayed at an anticommunist museum called "The Territory of Terror" along with the friezes from the pillar.[12] A commission is planning a contest to create a new memorial on the site.

In Tallinn and Lviv, the continued visual presence of the monuments challenged Estonian and Ukrainian sovereignty, respectively, by revealing divisions among their populations. In Tallinn, the monument mobilized pro-Russian elements that sought to regain the dominant places they had held in the Soviet hierarchy and to push Estonia back toward the Russian orbit. In Ukraine, the monument became a visceral symbol of the division between pro-Russian and anti-Russian Ukrainians, a division that has led to years of war. By destroying the hated Soviet symbol, the residents of Lviv struck a blow against the Russian occupation of Ukraine. The solution in both cases has been for local governments to make the monument less visible—either neutralizing its rallying power by displacing it, or asserting its space as definitively Ukrainian by reimagining the geography of the entire site.

IMAGE 52.3 The destruction of the "Glory Monument" in 2021.

These cases demonstrate the ways that the visual presence of Soviet-era monuments engendered civic conflict about national identities in postimperial societies. While the Soviet war memorials of 1945 still stand in Germany and Austria, states that are more confident in their ability to resist contemporary Russian influence, memorials have been moved or taken down in postimperial states that are struggling to withstand Russian ambitions in the region. The more danger the country is in from Russian aggression, the worse the fate of Soviet war memorials. The Estonians have sought to counter potential Russian influence by making Russian-speaking Estonians more welcome, while simultaneously displacing symbols of Soviet/Russian power. The Ukrainians, existentially threatened by Russia, have outlawed, attacked, and dismantled Soviet symbols.

NOTES

1. Martin Ehala, "The Bronze Soldier: Identity Threat and Maintenance in Estonia, "*Journal of Baltic Studies* 40, no. 1 (March 2009), 139-158, quote at 140; James V. Wertsch, "Collective Memory and Narrative Templates," *Social Research* 75, no. 1 (Spring 2008), 138.
2. Ehala, "The Bronze Soldier," 141.
3. See https://lia.lvivcenter.org/en/objects/monument-slavy/
4. "Den' Pobedy bez pobeditelia: Tallin brosil vyzov istorii," *RIA Novosti*, April 27, 2007, updated June 7, 2008, https://ria.ru/20070427/64549323.html
5. Wertsch, "Collective Memory," 135–136.
6. Ehala, "The Bronze Soldier," 142.

7. "Estonia: Defense Minister Says Bronze Soldier Had To Go," May 9, 2007, https://www.rferl.org/a/1076363.html
8. Damien McGuinness, "How a Cyber Attack Transformed Estonia," April 27, 2017, https://www.bbc.com/news/39655415
9. "Photos: Bronze Soldier Monument in Tallinn Vandalized," *ERR News*, 18 April 2022, https://news.err.ee/1608568171/photos-bronze-soldier-monument-in-tallinn-vandalized
10. See https://galinfo.com.ua/news/u_lvovi_vidchyshchayut_vid_chervonoi_farby_monument_slavy_261202.html
11. See https://dyvys.info/2018/02/16/monument-slavy-u-lvovi-pam-yatnyk-bezdiyalnosti-miskoyi-vlady/
12. "Vo L'vove okonchatel'no demontirovali sovetskii monument slavy," *Ukrainskaia Pravda*, July 23, 2021, https://www.pravda.com.ua/rus/news/2021/07/23/7301564/; https://museumterror.com/en/home-2/.

CHAPTER 53

CRIMEA IN MY HEART: VISUALIZING PUTIN'S RESURGENT EMPIRE IN 2014

ELIZABETH A. WOOD

ON MARCH 18, 2014, Russian President Vladimir Putin appeared at a victory concert celebrating the illegal annexation of Crimea. Standing under a heart in the national colors of white, blue, and red (Image 53.1), he proclaimed Crimea to be an integral part of Russia "in the people's hearts and minds."[1] Why would this macho leader, who until then assiduously cultivated an image of raw masculinity, choose instead a heart-centered rhetoric and visual imagery?

This performance, I argue, was carefully crafted to give an appearance of Putin's imperial care for the Russian people and the territories of the Russian land. Borrowing from visual images related to Grand Prince Volodimer (ruled 980–1015) and Empress Catherine II (ruled 1762–1796), both of whom were given the title "Great," Putin and his media team justified Russia's geopolitical expansion as an expression of emotional ties that supposedly united ruler and people through history. (Note that in this essay, I use the medieval spelling for the historical Grand Prince Volodimer and the Russian spelling when his name is invoked by Putin. Modern Ukrainians use a third variant: Volodymyr.)

Putin and his advisors faced a legitimacy problem in taking Crimea, and they knew it. The Crimean Peninsula, which juts into the Black Sea, was originally incorporated into the Russian Empire when the armies of Catherine the Great won it from the nominally independent Crimean Khanate in 1783. It was officially declared a part of the Ukrainian Soviet Socialist Republic in 1954, a status that was affirmed in 1991 when Ukraine gained its statehood. International observers were shocked, therefore, when Putin ordered the seizure of Crimea for Russia in February 2014 and announced the annexation that March. It was a brazen attack on administrative and international law. For this reason, once they had secured the province militarily, the Russian government rapidly moved to hold a referendum on Crimean status (March 16), declare Crimea an independent state (March 17), and sign a so-called "treaty" between Russia and Crimea "admitting" the latter (March 18).[2] At every turn, this

IMAGE 53.1 "Crimea in My Heart," Vladimir Putin celebrating the annexation of Crimea, March 18, 2014.

"recognition" of Crimea, first as a "a sovereign and independent state" and then as a Russian geographic unit, depended on what Putin called the "will of the people expressed voluntarily." He assumed that the world would accept a sham referendum at gunpoint as voluntary accession.

March 18, 2014, was a long day for the Russian president. In the morning, he informed the government and Parliament of the "admission" of Crimea into the Russian Federation. In the afternoon, he gave an hour-long speech centering on his claim to answer the will of the Crimean people. Multiple times he spoke of Russians' "hearts and minds," of "truth and justice," and of the Russian conviction that Crimea had always been an "inseparable part of Russia." In the breakup of the USSR, he said, "Russia felt that she had not only been robbed; she had been plundered." Not to have responded to Crimean residents' "plea for help" would have been a "betrayal." In short, he explained, the people of Crimea had overwhelmingly shown that they wanted to be "with Russia." The Russian president then proceeded to sign a "treaty" with three individual Crimean accessories to the takeover: Crimean Prime Minister Sergei Aksyonov, who had seized power at gunpoint in Parliament on February 27, the day before Russian troops massively began taking over the peninsula; Crimean Parliament Speaker Vladimir Konstantinov, in place since 2010; and Alexei Chaly, Sevastopol's self-appointed mayor from February 25.

In the evening, Putin appeared at the celebratory concert with the white, blue, and red colors of the Russian flag in the form a heart. In his three-minute speech, he welcomed Crimea and its most famous city, Sevastopol, back into their "native harbor" and "homeport" of Russia. He thanked the citizens of Crimea and Sevastopol for their "clearly expressed will to be with Russia," for their "courage and persistence." Russia, in his words, "gave them its warmth, turned towards them, and opened its whole heart to them, its whole soul." Russians, he noted, were "worried" about them and gravely concerned about developments in Eastern Ukraine. The choice of heart in word and image brazenly expressed the ruler's concern for his loyal subjects and his conviction that he and Russia as a whole were opening their hearts to the Crimean people and welcoming their return as members of the imperial family of Russian peoples.

Putin's emotional language vividly evokes that of Empress Catherine the Great, who issued a special decree on the first Russian accession of Crimea in 1783, an act of conquest after prolonged warfare. In Catherine's words, out of her generous concern for her subjects, the monarch "accepted" Crimea as the Taurida Province—she did not annex it, though this is what later sources would call it. The Tatars who made up the majority population of Crimea had "bowed to foreign indoctrination," her decree claimed, but now they are "happy in their transformation from rebellion and disorder to peace, quiet and lawful order." Her language reflects the emphasis on maternal love that she would show again two years later in her Charter to the Nobility (1785) where she listed one of her dozens of titles as "Tsaritsa of Khersones-Tauride [Crimea]."[3]

Why would President Putin use emotional language and visual images similar to those of Catherine the Great? Putin did not, in fact, invent the references to Catherine or the heart imagery. The glorification of Catherine's Crimean annexation began in the early 1990s, when Moscow Mayor Yuri Luzhkov poured money from his city coffers into the Ukrainian peninsula in order to foster Russian nationalist ideas there. This fostering of Russian ideas in neighboring Ukraine was not subtle. Starting in 1996 (eighteen years before its reannexation), the Russian Community of Crimea (itself founded in 1994) began celebrating April 19 each year as the anniversary of Catherine the Great's decree, calling it "The Day of the Unification of Crimea with Russia."[4] The Russian Community met annually at the steps of what they hoped would be a monument to Catherine the Great in Simferopol (the capital). The base of that monument was finally installed in 2007 but vociferously opposed by both the Crimean Tatar and Ukrainian communities because of its implied message about the proposed Russian annexation of Crimea.

A little visual forensics reveals that Putin's concert title "Crimea in My Heart," first appeared in an art exhibit in Simferopol in 2010.[5] Three years later, the same title, "Crimea in My Heart," was used in materials for a competition of schoolchildren's performances across the peninsula. The state educational TV channel trumpeted the contest with an image of the Crimean peninsula wrapped in a blue, white, and red heart (the Russian colors).[6] Winners of the contest received certificates from the Ministry of Education and Science of the Autonomous Republic of Crimea, a branch of the *Ukrainian* government, sporting the same image of a heart in Russian colors.[7] Although the colors in the 2013 certificates do not appear in the same order as those at the victory concert attended by President Putin in 2014 (his are white, blue, and red), the style, shape, and significance of the heart are identical.

The success of the emotional appeal of Putin's heart imagery in March 2014 depended on a constant assertion of the "bloodless" nature of the Russian takeover of Crimea in the weeks before. These assertions were accompanied by emphasis on the role of Crimean "self-defense" forces (set up from Moscow by pro-Moscow paramilitary groups) and the involvement of those whom Putin called "polite people" (invading masked troops with no identifying military insignia). This, too, was a Catherinian move, emphasizing what Kelly O'Neill has called the latter's "quiet conquest."[8] In September 2014, a Russian parliamentary deputy proposed a special "Day of Polite People" to mark the "quiet victory" of the masked people.[9] Although later on the day was set for February 27, the original proposal was for it to be on October 7, Putin's birthday.

In addition to the pre-made heart image, the president's narrative of Crimea as "ours" (Russia's) also relied on three historical myths—invitation, baptism, and military glory—each deliberately selected to emphasize a long tradition of voluntary, ostensibly loving bonds between Russia's rulers and their devoted people. The Crimeans' fabricated plea to Russia in 2014 to rescue them resonated with the first, founding myth of the medieval Rus people, who, it was said, invited the Varangians (Vikings) to rule over them in the ninth century. To justify Russia's claim to Crimea, Putin evoked a second myth, the story of Prince Vladimir's adoption of Orthodox Christianity and baptism of Rus in 988. Finally, Putin's speech situated the Crimean annexation in a long, supposedly peaceable history of territorial expansion by invoking a third myth of the "gathering of the lands" of Russia by the tsars who added new territories through the centuries.

To justify the annexation, Putin and his media team echoed the medieval invitation to the Varangians to come and rule over Russia. In March 2014, Putin claimed, in his most important speech, that the Crimeans "turned to Russia for help in defending their rights and lives." In another parallel to Catherine, Putin represented himself as the wise ruler who was rescuing the region from barbarians, this time from alleged "fascists" in Kyiv (as some Russians referred to the Euromaidan revolutionaries) who threatened the Crimeans' safety and their Russian language. Not to have helped the Crimeans in their hour of need, Putin said, would have been base treachery on Russia's part.

Immediately, Russian Internet memes, t-shirts, and billboards proliferated with the phrase "We don't abandon our own," often with the President's picture. "Crimea is ours" (*Krym nash*) went so viral, both in images and in words, that it was designated "word of the year" in 2014. Putin himself was shown in t-shirts as "the politest of people."[10] Occasional memes even showed Putin juxtaposed with Catherine the Great (Image 53.2).[11]

In December 2014, during his annual address to the General Assembly, Putin brought in the christening of medieval Rus by Grand Prince Vladimir (using the Russian spelling of Volodimer) in 988, which he viewed as a "powerful, spiritually unifying force." Despite the fact that the medieval chronicles offer multiple versions of Vladimir's conversion story, Putin chose the Crimean one, set in Khersones at the southern tip of the peninsula. He further designated Crimea, Khersones, and Sevastopol as having "invaluable civilizational and even sacral importance for Russia, like the Temple Mount in Jerusalem for the followers of Islam and Judaism." Emphasizing this as a timeless and, hence, sacred claim, he said, "That is how we will relate to this now and forever more."

Eight months later, on July 28, 2015, on "The Day of Rus's Christening," Putin held a Kremlin reception for church and secular leaders where he referred five times to the baptism of Rus in Crimea, calling it the "lead turning point in all of Russian history, in Russian statehood and in our culture." In reading his speech, Putin particularly emphasized the word *statehood*. He also spoke of the thousand-year elevation of Vladimir to sainthood as showing "the grandeur of his personality" as a "great

IMAGE 53.2 Internet meme juxtaposing Putin with Catherine the Great.

creator of Rus."[12] In this Kremlin reception with more than five hundred attendees, Patriarch Kirill (leader of the Russian Orthodox Church) addressed Putin as "your excellency" (*vashe prevoskhoditel'stvo*), a tsarist-era honorific for those of the third and fourth ranks in the Table of Ranks (which were abolished by the Bolsheviks in 1917), and congratulated him for his connection to the saint: "I would like to particularly congratulate those who carry the name of the holy prince, including our President. Today is your double name day—through your name and the name of your father." He stressed the Grand Prince's blameless life (a quality most historians would dispute given Volodimer's many wives and concubines), and particularly his virtues: "the Russian Orthodox ideals of loyalty, valor, sacrifice, and love for the Motherland and the Church." By linking Crimean annexation with foundational religious events of the past, the patriarch and the president made this a sacred event.

Putin as the warrior-saint was further incarnated a year later with the erection of a fifty-six-foot, three-hundred-ton statue of "Vladimir the Great" in the center of Moscow. At the dedication on November 4, 2016, Putin referred to Vladimir as a "unifier [literally, gatherer] and defender of the Russian lands and a far-sighted politician who created the foundations of a strong, unified, centralized state."[13] Here, he drew on the Russian state tradition of "great" rulers who "gathered the Russian lands" through military conquest, a conquest subsumed under the euphemism "gathering" as if one were gathering flowers. At the same time, he rode roughshod over Ukrainians' claim to Vladimir (whom they call Volodymyr) as the founder of their Kyivan Rus.

On January 19, 2018, Putin submerged himself in the icy waters of Lake Seliger, site of a patriotic camp for Russian youth northwest of Moscow, to celebrate Jesus's baptism by John the Baptist (Image 53.3).[14] Visually, this immersion gave him an opportunity to once again display his bare torso, emphasizing his imperviousness to cold and his quintessential Russianness (he wore felt boots before he entered the

IMAGE 53.3 Vladimir Putin before and during his plunge into an ice-hole in a traditional celebration of the Orthodox feast of Epiphany at St. Nilus Stolobensky Monastery on Lake Seliger, January 19, 2018. Photo by Alexei Druzhinin.

water and a prominent cross on his neck). This ritual dip also identified him personally with Vladimir the Great, whose baptism had historically signaled the founding of the Russian empire, with Christianity as its civilizing mission, though critics claimed that the water was actually warm since no steam rose from it when Putin entered the waters.

The taking of Crimea has thus served mythically and intuitively to enhance the image of Russia as an empire and Putin as Russia's savior. Like his namesake Vladimir the Great, Putin has claimed success in "Christianizing" Rus, this time returning it from godless Soviet atheism to the path of Orthodox Christianity.[15] He has responded to the Crimeans' "invitation", bringing them "back into the Motherland" and showing off his martial prowess as hero and unifier of Russia. Glorying in others' exploits, Putin has referred to Vladimir's christening of Rus as a "spiritual feat," to Russian troops' defense of Sevastopol in the Crimean War (1853–1856) as an "immortal feat," and to the Soviet defeat of fascists in World War II as "the feat of generations."

While underlining a monolithic unity between the empire and the ruler, Putin has portrayed the ruled, by contrast, as heterogeneous. Crimea, in Putin's 2014 formulation, is the "spiritual source of the formation of the multifaceted, yet monolithic Russian nation and the centralized Russian government." Like Catherine the Great, Putin lists the diverse place names—reflecting Greek, Turkic, and Russian origins—as themselves proof of Crimea's place in the Russian empire, focusing on battle sites from the Crimean War and World War II, while claiming that Crimea is a "unique alloy" of cultures and traditions, just like "big Russia." The formal dedication of the statue of Vladimir the Great in 2016 likewise created a visual image of this multisided Russia, since leaders of all the faiths in Russia were shown on Russian television wearing their ceremonial robes for the occasion.

In the end, Putin's reference to Crimea "in the hearts and minds" of the Russian people makes an emotional claim to a spiritual state of belonging and to a Russian civilizational unity. The Russian president today draws on archaic, imagined concepts of oneness as a means to unite an empire that is conceived of as multiple and heterogeneous. Standing under the white, blue, and red heart, Putin claims to personify the words "Crimea in my heart." Crimea is in Putin's heart because he, as emperor, demonstrates his feelings for, and his defense of, his diverse peoples. Through his selective use of historical imagery, Putin presents himself as uniting the tsarist and Soviet pasts, creating a timeless and sacred unity of the whole under Russian rule. The stakes of this reading of history have become even clearer since Putin extended the narrative of historical unity from Crimea to the entirety of Ukraine. It should be stressed that these claims have been disputed by citizens of the Ukrainian nation and most of the world.

NOTES

1. Putin's speeches can be found on the official Kremlin website: http://www.kremlin.ru/news/20603; http://www.kremlin.ru/events/president/news/20600; http://kremlin.ru/events/president/news/20626; https://www.youtube.com/watch?v=QMAVnAvWv2k; http://kremlin.ru/events/president/news/47173; http://kremlin.ru/events/president/news/53211. For the English translations, see http://www.en.kremlin.ru (e.g., http://www.en.kremlin.ru/events/president/news/20603).
2. For discussion of the elaborate military involved in the takeover, see Colby Howard and Ruslan Pukhov, eds., *Brothers Armed: Military Aspects of the Crisis in Ukraine* (Minneapolis: East View Press, 2014).
3. *Manifest o priniatii poluostrova Krymskogo, ostrova Tamana i vsei Kubanskoi storony pod Rossiiskuiu Derzhavu*, https://histrf.ru/lenta-vremeni/event/view/dien-priniatiia-kryma-v-sostav-rossii; "Manifest Velikoi Imperatritsy Ekateriny II," https://krym.rusarchives.ru/dokumenty/manifest-imperatricy-ekateriny-ii-o-prisoedinenii-kryma-i-kubani-k-rossii; "Gramota na prava, vol'nosti i preimushchestva blagorodnogo rossiiskogo dvorianstva" (April 21, 1785), http://www.hist.msu.ru/ER/Etext/dv_gram.htm. On Catherine's maternal love, see Richard Wortman, *Scenarios of Power: Myth and Ceremony in Russian Monarchy*, Vol. 1 (Princeton University Press, 1995), 110–146.
4. Natal'ia Pupkova, "Pod derzhavu Nashu," *Krymskaia pravda*, April 20, 2012, https://dlib-eastview-com.ezp-prod1.hul.harvard.edu/browse/doc/27067498; Aleksandr Shevtsov, "19 aprelia—Den' Priniatiia Kryma Pod Derzhavu Rossiiskuiu," *Portal russkogo naroda Kryma—Russkaia obshchina Kryma*, April 19, 2020. http://www.ruscrimea.ru/2020/04/19/19-aprelya-den-prinyatiya-kryma-pod-derzhavu-rossijskuyu.htm
5. Liudmila Milina, "Krym v moem serdtse," *Krymskaia pravda*, November 27, 2010; https://dlib-eastview-com.ezp-prod1.hul.harvard.edu/browse/doc/22990864
6. "2013—Luchshii god detstva moego," November 27, 2013, https://www.youtube.com/watch?v=Ff__1931xoM; image at 2:33.
7. "2013/2014 uchebnyi god," https://28-школа.рф/nashi-dostijeniya-13-14
8. *Claiming Crimea: A History of Catherine the Great's Southern Empire* (New Haven: Yale University Press, 2017).
9. Alena Sivkova, "7 Oktiabria predlagaiut uchredit' Den' vezhlivykh liudei," *Izvestiia*, September 12, 2014, https://iz.ru/news/576558; on the February 27 celebration, see https://drakonit.livejournal.com/454839.html
10. See https://files.voenpro.ru/products/futbolka-samyj-vezhlivyj-10_1.1600x1600.jpg
11. "Ekaterina 2 i Putin, chto obshchego," https://zen.yandex.ru/media/vse_je_dostalo/ekaterina-2-i-putin-chto-obscego-5d20d95fd5299900add2adfc
12. "Priëm po sluchaiu tysiacheletia prestavlenia sviatogo ravnoapostol'nogo kniazia Vladimira," July 28, 2015, http://kremlin.ru/events/president/news/50068
13. "V Den' narodonogo edinstva v Moskve otkryt pamiatnik kniaziu Vladimiru," http://kremlin.ru/events/president/news/53211
14. "Putin nyrnul na Seligere," *Gazeta*, January 19, 2018, https://www.gazeta.ru/social/2018/01/19/11617922.shtml
15. Mikhail Suslov credits the Russian Orthodox Patriarch with supplying an "army of metaphors" about Crimea to Putin in his "'Crimea Is Ours!' Russian Popular Geopolitics in the New Media Age," *Eurasian Geography and Economics* 55, no. 6 (2014): 588–609.

CHAPTER 54

THE MAIDAN: ANTI-IMPERIAL MODES OF MYTHMAKING IN DOCUMENTARY FILM (2014–2015)

JOSHUA FIRST

UKRAINE'S CAPITAL, Kyiv (Kiev in Russian), has held a dual significance in the history of the Russian and Ukrainian peoples. On the one hand, Kyiv was understood as the birthplace of Russian civilization, the first Russian state. During the nineteenth century, the city developed rapidly as an integral part of the Russian Empire. The architectural style of the city mimicked the classicism of the imperial capital of St. Petersburg. On the other hand, Kyiv also emerged during this time as a center of a specifically Ukrainian cultural activism that sought to distinguish these imperial borderlands as a nation distinct from Russia. Some of the city's urban monuments commemorate events from the Ukrainian past that can be read in either of these ways, or even both at once. Ambiguous in their lessons, they may celebrate either imperial accomplishments or moments in the history of independent Ukraine. The 1888 statue of Cossack leader Bohdan Khmel'nyts'kyi on Sofia Square, for example, is at once a symbol of Ukrainian sovereignty rooted in the independent seventeenth-century Cossack Hetmanate, and a representation of the subordination of a proto-Ukraine to Muscovy when Khmel'nyts'kyi signed the Treaty of Pereyaslav in 1654. During the Soviet period, statues to the nineteenth-century poet Taras Shevchenko and eighteenth-century philosopher Hryhorii Skovoroda, both symbols of Ukrainian exceptionality, coexisted with the massive Motherland Monument celebrating an all-Soviet victory in the Great Patriotic War, and the Arch of Friendship of Peoples, with imagery accentuating Ukraine's status as Russia's "little brother."

Kyiv's central square epitomizes these tensions. During the Soviet period, it was called October Revolution Square, named after the 1917 Revolution that ultimately reestablished Russian hegemony over Ukraine. Later, it became Independence Square—in Ukrainian, *Maidan Nezalezhnosti*, or simply "the Maidan." After the collapse of the Soviet Union, Ukrainian authorities took down monuments to the Soviet empire, and in the early 2000s, a new symbol appeared: a massive column with the ancient Slavic earth goddess, a winged Berehynia, standing on top replaced a dismantled monument of Lenin.

As a space that fits tens of thousands of people, and now understood as a site of national significance untainted by imperial or Soviet memorial objects, the Maidan became the battleground for two moments of political upheaval in post-Soviet independent Ukraine. First, during the Orange Revolution in 2004, Ukrainians protested and overturned a fraudulent election, and second, a decade later, protesters toppled the autocratic government of President Viktor Yanukovych, months after he refused to sign a free trade agreement with the European Union. Because of the heightened violence that left over a hundred Ukrainians dead, along with the forceful toppling of a legitimate government, the Maidan protests of 2013 and 2014 have justifiably been labelled a revolution by scholars, journalists, and many Ukrainians. And the word for the square in Ukrainian, *Maidan*, became associated with this revolutionary movement.

The second Maidan in 2014 also coincided with the explosion of smartphone technology and affordable digital cameras with video capabilities that allowed participants and amateur videographers to record the protests. An emblematic image of the 2014 revolution in Kyiv saw crowds hoisting their smartphones above their heads to capture and "share" their participation in the historic events that brought down the Yanukovych regime.

In addition to the thousands of YouTube videos about the events, Ukraine's "Euromaidan" of 2013–2014 provided the subject for several feature-length documentaries shortly after the events themselves occurred. Three of the most significant examples included the Babylon '13 filmmaking collective's *Heavenly Company*, part of a documentary series about the Maidan broadcast on the Ukrainian television channel 1+1; Sergei Loznitsa's film festival favorite, *Maidan*; and Evgeny Afineevsky's *Winter on Fire: Ukraine's Fight for Freedom*, released on Netflix in the fall of 2015. Although the films are quite different aesthetically and ideologically, they are similar in how they structure and use the urban landscape of the revolution's central location, the Maidan. In each of these films, Kyiv emerges as a postimperial city with few remnants of its past recognizable. Symbols of Soviet and Russian imperial power exist only on the margins of these films, and history itself rarely appears on the urban landscape. Instead, symbols of global capitalism exist in harmony on the Maidan with a mythologized Ukrainian present.

These three films establish different postimperial modes for understanding the Maidan. By *mode*, I mean to suggest that the films' formal and aesthetic properties work in tandem with the ideological and narrative goals of the filmmakers. The first mode is a nationalist one, where the filmmakers identify and celebrate heroes and martyrs of the Revolution and mobilize symbols of the nation to heighten the conflict between the revolutionaries and the Yanukovych regime. In this mode, the filmmakers (through their on-screen surrogates) tell us directly what meaning the

Maidan should have for us. Although present to some degree in all three examples, this is most evident in Babylon '13's *Heavenly Company*. The second mode of understanding the Maidan is an observational one, which reveals an aesthetic of detachment. It looks for meaning not at the height of conflict, but in the everyday activities behind the scenes. Films made in the observational mode refrain from imposing a grand narrative on the events, and instead seek to understand the participants' daily life in the Maidan during the months-long protests. There are elements of this mode in each of the three films, too, but Loznitsa's *Maidan* best embodies this observational mode. The final mode in this revolutionary trilogy is the liberal mode of representation, which emphasizes individual agency and democratic values. Here, the filmmakers focus on the lives and ideas of ordinary protestors, not necessarily the heroes and leaders, but regular people who decided to become agents of change. This mode is most evident in Afineevsky's Oscar- and Emmy-nominated *Winter on Fire*. This film became most accessible to an international audience, because it also strove to provide context and clarity about the events more generally.

THE NATIONALIST MODE OF *HEAVENLY COMPANY*

The filmmaking collective Babylon '13 formed on the eve of the initial Maidan protest in November 2013 and started a YouTube channel on December 2 to circulate their short videos.[1] Joanna Nowosad writes that the collective initially understood the Maidan through the lens of something akin to what I am calling the observational mode, arguing that "their main conceptual aim . . . is to create a base of documentary sources, without any commentary . . . open for the viewers' own interpretations."[2] Later, however, Babylon '13 expressed a more nationalistic and, indeed, militaristic perspective when it began filming the conflict between the Ukrainian government and Russia-supported separatists. *Heavenly Company* was made in the middle of this transition from an observational mode toward a nationalistic mode.

In addressing the fate of the more than a hundred protesters killed in early 2014, *Heavenly Company* mobilizes memory and transforms it into a modern-day mythology of the nation in revolution.The beginning of the film shows sequential examples where Babylon '13 uses double exposure to produce an effect of ideological simultaneity, connecting the Maidan protesters to Kyiv's geography and to an ahistorical mythical space, represented above all by the Berehynia earth goddess. In the first still (Image 54.1), the ghostly figure of a revolutionary, implicitly one of the Heavenly Company murdered by Yanukovych's security forces, is superimposed onto the Maidan with the Berehynia column in the center.

In the next shot, costumed protesters themselves appear in the image of the Berehynia as they confront the security forces, their pure, white wings contrasting with the fires of the superimposed image of the burning Maidan (Image 54.2). In both cases, the earth goddess serves as the primary symbol of a Ukrainian

IMAGE 54.1 A still from *Heavenly Company*: a Maidan fighter is superimposed onto the Berehynia column.

IMAGE 54.2 A still from *Heavenly Company*: protesters dressed as Berehynia facing off against the Berkut riot police are superimposed onto the burning Maidan.

nationhood untainted by Imperial Russia or the USSR. With the help of double exposure, Babylon '13 conveys an image of divine transcendence in the act of revolution against the police state.

The remainder of *Heavenly Company* follows a more traditional documentary aesthetic, following the fast-paced action with frequent cutting among different vantage points, indicating that Babylon '13 used a variety of amateur footage from smartphones and digital cameras rather than professional equipment. The footage cuts between the confrontation on the Maidan with a funeral procession for the Heavenly Company and staged interviews with protesters and their family members to convey the message of martyred heroes. The audience is presented with distinct typologies of protesters—older men dressed as Cossacks, women in local folk costumes, young nationalists in military fatigues and steel helmets. This individuation of the recognizably Ukrainian protesters contrasts starkly to the gray and black mass of protesters in Loznitsa's *Maidan* or the multicultural European faces in Afineevsky's *Winter on Fire*. Toward the end of *Heavenly Company*, one middle-aged Maidan participant says to the camera with tear-filled eyes, "He's in the Heavenly Company. I believe they are protecting Ukraine." Like all the interview subjects in this film, he frames the Maidan in national terms. The audience sees ritualistic funeral processions and interviews conducted next to an apartment window shattered by a bullet, connecting the human participants with the everyday geography of the city. The city's identifiable historical spaces—the Dnipro River, St. Sophia, the Caves Monastery, not to mention the many monuments to the Second World War—remain absent from this postimperial, nationalist geography of Kyiv. The only urban landmark is the Berehynia column itself, which the filmmakers struggle to include in as many shots as possible, often employing a canted frame to connect the action with this object.

MAIDAN'S OBSERVATIONAL MODE

Sergei Loznitsa is the most experienced and established documentarian of the three filmmakers examined in this chapter, and has made several notable feature films. Although he spent his youth and early adulthood in Kyiv and was educated at the Russian Film Institute in Moscow, his career as a filmmaker took him to Berlin, where he has lived since 2001. *Maidan* was Loznitsa's first film about an openly Ukrainian theme, and until that time, most commentators understood him as a "Russian" filmmaker. Since 2014, Loznitsa has continued his interest in the current Ukrainian crisis with *Donbas* (2018) and in Ukrainian history with *Babi Yar: Context* (2021).

Unlike most mainstream documentaries, *Maidan* contains no narration or interviews, only short intertitles scattered throughout the film to provide some basic historical background. *Maidan* begins rather traditionally, with an image that each of the three documentaries share: an undifferentiated mass sings the Ukrainian national anthem in front of a temporary stage on the Maidan. Loznitsa reveals his unique intentions with the next shot, however, providing the viewer with a seemingly endless scene of protesters entering a building through a revolving door. In the next shot, we see protesters lounging around in a large room, talking quietly, sometimes singing, and often sleeping on makeshift bedding or in chairs. In another sequence, a marginally committed volunteer makes sandwiches for the Revolution while distracted by his smartphone. Despite the geographic rootedness of the Maidan, Loznitsa's *Maidan* takes us to an undifferentiated space of unnamed humans carrying on the daily life of the movement.

When leaders give speeches on the Maidan, we can barely hear their voices, and Loznitsa's camera is often pointed at the mundane moments of human actions during the Revolution: walking around, eating soup, building a fire, listening to boring speeches where speakers run out of things to say and stumble over their words. Our attention is constantly being diverted elsewhere, and sometimes nowhere. Most of the time, protesters simply wait for something to happen. Throughout these shots, Loznitsa's camera remains deliberately removed from the action. In Image 54.3, we see a typical shot from *Maidan*: compositionally, the framing is artless and in violation of standard rules of composition, largely because the object that grabs the viewer's attention is a pole that splits both the man in the military helmet, and the shot as a whole, in two. On the left edge of the frame, we see an advertisement for "Cossack Council" vodka, demonstrating the convergence of early modern Ukrainian nationalist history, remembered as a grand time when Cossack forebears made decisions collectively, in councils, with its late-capitalist representation. The shot becomes disconcerting in the way that it reorients our attention to everything and yet nothing. Later, when security forces begin clearing the square, the camera remains removed from the action, staying at the rear, pointed at protesters looking just as confused by this turn of events as we are in the audience.

IMAGE 54.3 A still from *Maidan*: Sergei Loznitsa's casual framing technique highlights the everyday life of the protest movement.

The absence of traditional scenes of action in Loznitsa's film is not intended as an insistence on objectivity, or as a means to allow the audience to "form its own judgement" about the Maidan, as Nowosad argued about Babylon '13's early shorts. After all, the film ends on a clear note of grief, highlighting the martyrdom of the Heavenly Company. We hear the crowd repeating the nationalistic mantra in unison—"Glory to the heroes!"—before the film ends. Instead, the observational mode here serves to broaden our understanding of the nature of revolution. In *Maidan*, revolution is a lived experience, rather than a series of decisive actions. The Revolution is an everyday fashion show, lunch, a social gathering, a place to sleep. In its refusal to conform to the typical documentary of political protest, the film implicitly reveals the mythmaking involved in the process of constructing a narrative. Loznitsa accomplishes two tasks in making this postimperial film. First, the film's observational mode works against the images of state-sponsored demonstrations emblematic of the Soviet era that were rooted geographically, temporally, and symbolically within a generically imperial space. And second, contrary to a long tradition of using observational or ethnographic cinematography to depict everyday life as exotic, Loznitsa took the exotic material of revolution and transformed it into the everyday.[3]

WINTER ON FIRE AND THE TRIUMPH OF THE LIBERAL NARRATIVE

Of these three films, none has become more globally significant than Evgeny Afineevsky's *Winter on Fire: Ukraine's Fight for Freedom*. Less well-known within international documentary circles than Loznitsa, or within the Ukrainian activist community than Babylon '13, Afineevsky has achieved recognition by collecting some of the best footage of the Maidan. He fits within a liberal framework of revolution already employed by such documentarians as Jehane Noujaim in her award-winning Netflix film *The Square* about the 2011 Egyptian Revolution. Within this liberal framework, individual stories of protest frame the action on the streets, and collective national symbols such as the Berehynia fade into the background without commentary by either the filmmaker or the human subjects within the film.

Winter on Fire presents the audience with a diverse array of photogenic representatives of the Revolution who not only explain what was happening, but also personalize a narrative of revolution. Thus, while *Heavenly Company* constructs a nationalist narrative, *Winter on Fire* constructs a liberal narrative of individuals—implicitly like *us*—fighting for freedom. These largely millennial heroes of the Revolution look at Facebook and speak about "European values." In line with this, Afineevsky presents the Maidan as a multicultural space, with Muslims, Jews, Catholics, Orthodox, Russian speakers, Ukrainian speakers, foreign residents, and citizens all working together. In comparison to *Maidan* and *Heavenly Company*, the action develops rapidly in *Winter on Fire*, and confrontations with the police are the central focus in the film. Image 54.4 combines the focus on mass action with attention to the individual's role.

IMAGE 54.4 A still from *Winter on Fire*: Afineevsky captures the psychological intensity of the Maidan.

This tightly framed close-up alludes to several themes in the film—the homemade shield as the primary tool of revolution, the small ribbon with the blue and yellow of the national flag (present but understated), and the smoke-filled chaos of the confrontation in the background. The film's primary focus, however, remains on the individual young protester's emotional response to the action, which we see in his eyes. Such scenes are entirely familiar to Western audiences from many other films about antigovernment protests. With its unambiguously happy ending, where a protest movement succeeds in overthrowing tyrannical state power, represented above all by squads of armored police, *Winter on Fire* conveys an inspiring story of revolutionary success, and it has galvanized antigovernment movements in Venezuela and Hong Kong.[4] The director himself, in fact, called the film a "manual for revolution . . . for others who may be oppressed."[5] The postimperial discourse of *Winter on Fire* presents a universalistic story of individuals who express personal desires and fears while fighting against monolithic state power.

Nonetheless, *Winter on Fire* shares with the other two films its unwillingness to explore ideological conflicts *within* the Maidan, and it refuses to distinguish between liberals and nationalists. Instead, we get the broad masses in Loznitsa's *Maidan*, national martyrs in *Heavenly Company*, and individual protesters in *Winter on Fire*. But nowhere do we get politics that goes beyond opposition to the existing authority—a politics that involves building a movement, defining goals, developing an ideology, and so on. Herein lies one of the central problems with making meaning or sustaining a movement from the Maidan in both film and history. The Maidan represented a kind of antipolitics that the filmmakers could not reconcile with the needs of building a postimperial, post-Yanukovych, Ukrainian national narrative.

NOTES

1. Babylon '13, "About Us," *Facebook*, https://www.facebook.com/pg/babylon13ua/about/?ref=page_internal (accessed May 22, 2020); Babylon '13, "About," *YouTube*, https://www.youtube.com/user/babylon13ua/about (accessed May 22, 2020).
2. Joanna Nowosad, "Babylon '13: Cinema of Civil Protest," *R/Evolutions: Global Trends and Regional Issues* 2, no. 1 (2014), 143, http://revjournal.org/wp-content/uploads/REV2/global_trends/10rev2_gt_nowosad.pdf (accessed May 22, 2020).
3. For an examination of early cinema's colonial gaze, see Martine Astier Loutfi, "Imperial Frame: Film Industry and Colonial Representation," in *Cinema, Colonialism, Postcolonialism: Perspectives from the French and Francophone Worlds*, edited by Dina Sherzer (Austin: University of Texas Press, 2010), 20.
4. Caroline Carter, "The Ukrainian Protest Film Gripping Hong Kong," *1843 Magazine*, October 15, 2019, https://www.1843magazine.com/dispatches/all-the-rage/the-ukrainian-protest-film-gripping-hong-kong (accessed May 24, 2020). For a more academic approach on *Winter on Fire* and theories of diffusion, see Emily Couch, "Summer on Fire: Hong Kong, Ukraine, & Discourses of Diffusion," *Emily Couch—Journalist and Writer*, August 24, 2019, https://emilycouchwriter.wordpress.com/2019/08/24/summer-on-fire-hong-kong-ukraine-discourses-of-diffusion/ (accessed May 24, 2020).
5. Christopher Miller, "'Winter on Fire' is an Oscar Nominee and a 'Manual for Revolution,' Says Director," *Mashable*, January 21, 2016, https://mashable.com/2016/01/21/ukraine-winter-on-fire-oscars/ (accessed May 24, 2020).

CHAPTER 55

THE POST-SOVIET BODY POLITIC: MEDIA, DIASPORA, AND PHOTOGRAPHS IN THE IMMORTAL REGIMENT

OLGA SHEVCHENKO

***REPRESENTATION* IS ONE** of those terms that push us to consider the connections between the political project of the modern state and the visual project of mass spectacle. How are the political and the visual dimensions of representation entangled? This chapter will look closely at the politics involved in visual representation at the annual commemorative ritual called the Immortal Regiment during the early years of its popularity, between 2015 and 2019.[1] The public processions that make up the Immortal Regiment flood the central thoroughfares of Russian cities and towns on May 9, known in Russia (as well as the rest of the post-Soviet space) as the day of the Soviet victory over the Nazi Germany (Image 55.1). What distinguishes these events—apart from their sheer scale—is that participants in the processions come to the streets to carry enlarged portraits of their veteran ancestors.[2] The first Immortal Regiment event was spontaneously organized in the city of Tomsk in 2012, but within three years, it became truly massive. In 2015, on the seventieth anniversary of the Victory, the control over this movement on both the local and federal level was seized by groups loyal to the Kremlin.[3]

As an example of political theater, the Immortal Regiment march is almost picture-perfect, and as such, it is regularly (one might say, obsessively) featured in Russian media both before and after May 9. What can we learn about the national and ethnic contours of a public, self-represented and self-constituted through visual imagery? In the case of a multiethnic federation with imperial aspirations, like today's Russia, this question lends itself to a geopolitical and global reading.

This chapter takes up two kinds of image production that evolved around the Immortal Regiment during its early years as a federal-level initiative: the depictions that abounded in state-sponsored media on the one hand, and the robust popular

ВТОРНИК, 10 МАЯ 2016 ГОДА

«Бессмертный полк» — новая традиция Дня Победы

Сотни тысяч людей во время шествия почтили память участников Великой Отечественной войны

Только в Москве на улицы вышли 600 тысяч неравнодушных граждан

Продолжение на стр. 03

Ревизоры Центробанка станут операторами

Анастасия Алексеевских

Центробанк расширил функционал своих представителей при проверках коммерческих банков. Уполномоченные ЦБ смогут

Схема приватизации «Башнефти» будет готова к августу

Ирина Кезик

Приватизация «Башнефти» должна состояться до конца 2016 года. По информации «Известий», схема продажи актива должна быть подготовлена

сле чего они будут обсуждаться в правительстве. Сроки подготовки критериев первый замглавы Минэнерго не уточнил.

Как сообщалось ранее, рассматриваются три варианта приватизации «Башнефти» —

«К 2021 году нужно переформатировать Госдуму»

Сопредседатель центрального штаба Общероссийского народного фронта, секретарь Общественной палаты АЛЕКСАНДР БРЕЧАЛОВ рассказал корреспонденту «Известий» Светлане Субботиной о выборах в Госдуму, на кого ОНФ делает ставку и как заставить чиновников на местах работать.

это происходит. Весь груз ответственности, проблем, критики у нас ложится на плечи президента. Президент вынужден решать вопросы, которые должны сниматься на начальном уровне — муниципалитетами, городскими, региональными властями.

— Да, по четыре часа идут «пря-

IMAGE 55.1 "The Immortal Regiment" on the front page of *Izvestiia*, May 10, 2016.

production of images that happened during and around the march on the ground. Let's start by looking at the photograph in Image 55.1. It is an aerial crowd shot taken from an elevated vantage point. It was made in Moscow in 2016, a year after the movement was coopted by Putin loyalists. That year, the Immortal Regiment reported over 600,000 participants in the city of Moscow alone, and 2 million participants across Russia, with marches also organized in forty countries around the world.[4]

This image was published on the front page of the national *Izvestiia* newspaper on May 10, 2016, under the heading "'The Immortal Regiment'—a New Victory Day Tradition." It features a composition that is repeated across countless digital and print media platforms that cover the event. Tightly packed human faces fill the frame, flanked on both sides by buildings and receding into the horizon. The aerial vantage point emphasizes the scale of mass participation, while the use of a telephoto lens visually compresses the crowd, making the participants look even more tightly packed than they likely were in reality. What is striking, and what differentiates these images from representations of other human multitudes on the streets, is the effect akin to photomontage. Depicting individuals holding up life-sized portraits of their veteran family members, these images visually merge together the living and the dead. While the portraits carried in the procession are all irreducibly individual, and intensely meaningful to each participant (these are their long-departed parents, grandparents, aunts, and uncles), in the aerial photographs we see an amalgamation composed of both the countless "engaged citizens" (as the *Izvestiia* caption characterizes the participants) *and* the deceased family members they are engaging with. This is an image of a trans-historical, intergenerational, and united collective body that has clear affinities to the tradition of visualizing the Soviet body politic as described by Erika Wolf in this volume (See Chapter 44).

The coverage of the Immortal Regiment in the media tended to emphasize the scale of each individual march, as well as the extensive reach of the initiative. No news program that aired on May 9 in Russia between 2015 and 2019 failed to include a segment about the Immortal Regiment in a given location, interspersed by the footage of similar marches filmed elsewhere. Every two to three hours, TV viewers would see news anchors, posed in front of a screen projecting the aerial footage of moving crowds, breathlessly recounting the list of cities and countries in which the marches were taking place, and tuning in to correspondents at different locations for individual updates (Image 55.2). The rapid sequence of multiple sites, all featuring ostensibly the same image of an endless "human river" of participants, sutured together a visual collage of the body politic that transcended location, and even national boundaries, serving as a visual expression of the *Russian World*—that is, a transnational space populated by Russians, broadly conceived. The notion of the Russian World received particular notoriety after Russia's annexation of Crimea in 2014, because the intervention into Ukraine was justified in the Russian media as a defense of the Russian-speaking minority there. The fact that the Immortal Regiment was harnessed in the interests of state-promoted patriotism, and received large amounts of state funding at the same time that Russia launched a hybrid war in Ukraine, is almost certainly not a coincidence. The initiative provided a visual expression to the claim that the reach of the Russian World was truly global, and in this way, both justified the intervention and implicitly staked out other potential areas of geopolitical interest.

IMAGE 55.2 A screenshot from news coverage of the Immortal Regiment procession on the news program *Vesti* on TV channel Russia 1, May 9, 2018.

These references to the supposed breadth of the Russian World coexisted with another significant feature in the media coverage of the marches—namely, the emphasis placed on the international nature of participation. The news cameras lingered on the visible ethnic diversity of the march participants, and local event organizers involved loyal diasporic organizations and encouraged the national dress and other attributes of ethnic difference among the participants. In Moscow, one could see individual participants wearing elements of national garb, as well as entire formations of participants from former Soviet republics, carrying national flags, playing national instruments, and sporting elements of traditional dress and headwear. To keep their ranks organized, and to maintain some distinctiveness from the surrounding marchers, such formations often carried banners with Victory Day symbols and messages in both Russian and their national language, further accentuating their status as a march-within-the-march.

This emphasis on ethnic difference followed the Soviet logic of *costumized* identity, described by Serguei Oushakine as a strategy of visual representation in which large collectives were depicted as both uniform (composed of more or less identical-looking bodies of generic citizens) and diverse (making use of national costumes to indicate the multiethnic character of the USSR).[5] As in the Soviet children's books described by Oushakine, the option of wearing ethnic dress did not seem to exist for the Russian-identified participants in the march, whom I never saw wearing folklorically inflected garb. When viewed from an elevated point, as they were in the aerial photographs discussed earlier, national formations within the procession were practically invisible. Yet they played a role in visualizing the broad appeal of the movement on the ground, drawing on the lasting resonance of the Soviet-era model of the USSR as a "family of nations."

Why did urban post-Soviet ethnic diasporas participate in the Immortal Regiment movement, and what could their perspective reveal about the visual politics of the march as a whole? For this, I turn to the experience of the Kyrgyz couple depicted in Image 55.3, whom I will call Karim and Aizhamal. This couple was among the several dozen Immortal Regiment participants I interviewed to get a bottom-up perspective on the Immortal Regiment movement, and they generously shared with me their photographs, thoughts, and memories of the 2017 procession in Moscow, when they marched as part of the Kyrgyz formation.

IMAGE 55.3 Digital photograph from the 2017 Immortal Regiment procession in Moscow.

The snapshot featured in Image 55.3 was taken with Karim's cellphone. At the time of our conversation, in the summer of 2018 and more than a year after the march, it was still on his cellphone, along with dozens of other snapshots from the same day. In this particular photo, Karim and Aizhamal are seen standing amongst their Kyrgyz compatriots, some of whom are dressed in full Kyrgyz traditional outfits, complete with embroidered robes and headdress. Others mix urban clothes with just one token element of national belonging (an iconic felt Kyrgyz hat in Karim's case) or none at all.

A similar mix of ethnic markers can be seen on the portraits held up by Karim and his wife. These portraits feature Aizhamal's grandfather (pictured twice: as a young soldier in Berlin during the final weeks of the war, and as an older man with a row of medals on his chest and an ornamental skullcap on his head) and Karim's parents (depicted in a recent photo that shows them in their status as clan elders). The latter placard features them wearing the same markers of ethnic belonging as the participants in the procession: a tall embroidered felt hat for the man, and an elaborate headdress paired with a silk white scarf with tassels for the woman.

Though featuring markers of ethnic difference, all three placards are visually united and symbolically tied to the people carrying them through the Moscow streets by the presence of the ribbon of St. George, the ubiquitous black-and-orange symbol of the Soviet victory in the war.[6] Featured on both the placards and chests of the participants of the march, the ribbon connects Karim, Aizhamal, and the other members of the Kyrgyz formation not only to their elders, but also to the hundreds of thousands of other marchers of all ethnicities on the street, as well as to *their* respective ancestors. In that way, it incorporates the Kyrgyz column into the procession as the descendants of members of the multinational entity, the Soviet people (*Sovetskii narod*).

The spectacle of ethnic diversity played an important role for Karim's experience of the march:

> Every nation wants to show off. We were just amazed: Azeris dance to their songs, Chechens dance, everyone walks past looking. The Kyrgyz also pass by and take photos of one another, cheering each other on.

But the appeal of this Soviet-style model of ethnic diversity for Karim and Aizhamal derived not just from its familiarity, but also from its contrast to how markers of ethnic difference were assessed, and often devalued, in their recent lived experience:

AIZHAMAL: We sometimes notice in the subway, in public places—the Russians look at us askance . . . it does happen . . . if we talk in our language, . . . they look like this . . . and think their different thoughts, and there [at the march] there is none of that, everyone is . . .

OLGA: No hostility?

KARIM: Yes.

AIZHAMAL: One family, and everything is with a smile.

In other words, Karim and Aizhamal suggested that the visual display of ethnic diversity in the old-fashioned Soviet mode at the march emphasized what Moscow's urban environment lacked—namely, respect for ethnic difference and a modicum of internationalism that they recalled from their late Soviet experience:

KARIM: We didn't use to have these divisions—you are Russian, you are some wrong color, or your eyes are slanted. We all studied together, sat at the same desk at school, Russians, and Georgians . . . We all served, some in Germany, some in Africa.

AIZHAMAL: I studied in Leningrad . . . the last years, when I was working on my diploma.

KARIM: We had a common . . . . Only now these divisions have begun . . . These slogans: Ukraine for the Ukrainians, Russia for the Russians, Kyrgyzstan for the Kyrgyz, and so on . . . . Everyone is fixated on that: why are you wearing a skull cap? These are today's mores . . .

AIZHAMAL: . . . and it used to make no difference. Whatever you want to wear.

In contrast to the routinized forms of everyday discrimination that marked their urban experience, the visual format of the processions appeared to bind the participants together. In the march, the portraits of the veterans were both individualized, through inscriptions of names and ranks, and homogenized, through repeated visual elements such as the St. George's ribbon and frame and compositional conventions, offering participants like Karim and Aizhamal a promise of visual democracy in which, for that one day, everyone was equal. For that particular moment and in that place, whether or not one was wearing a skull cap did not matter, and was not fraught with the threat of unwanted attention.

This promise was particularly portentous for the labor migrants, whose day-to-day lives were marked by subordination, disenfranchisement, and laboriously cultivated *in*visibility. This made for a sharp contrast to Victory Day, when the Immortal Regiment march offered Karim and his compatriots an opportunity to stake a visual claim to inclusion and membership in an idiom that was hard to ignore.

Victory Day gave members of migrant post-Soviet diasporas an opportunity to assert not only their equality, based on the equal share of sacrifices made by their grandparents during the war, but also something that would have been unspeakable during late socialism—namely, a claim to a special contribution to the Victory made by a specific national or ethnic group. The Kyrgyz formation, for example, placed special emphasis on the role of the Kyrgyz infantrymen during the battle of Moscow, putting the name of the division on the formation's banner. Karim drew my attention to it, saying with considerable pride:

> This division [Panfilovsky division no. 316] was formed in Kyrgyzstan, from there, it was the Central-Asian military district. It had Kazakhs, Kyrgyz, Tatars, and were it not for the Panfilovtsy, [Moscow would have perished]. The Volokolamsk highway . . . Our hero is there—Cholponbai Tuleberdiev, he blocked a machine gun with his body . . . His resting place is there, near Dubosekovo [*sic*] . . . and every year we go there, to the Dubosekovo village.

The unspoken message here was that the members of the Kyrgyz formation—as descendants of the soldiers who spilled their blood for Moscow in 1941—had a special claim to full franchise in the city. In this context, the act of carrying their fathers' portraits through the streets could be seen by Karim and his wife as an act of belated justice. This became a strong theme when we turned to a photograph taken at the Red Square, a highly charged symbolic space that Karim and Aizhamal remembered from childhood as the "center of the Soviet world":

AIZHAMAL: It's like a duty, I even talked to him out loud . . . look, Daddy, you are walking through Red Square on your own legs . . .

KARIM: I was filming myself as I walked in the metro—here I am, walking with Dad in the Moscow metro—and as I walked out—here we are, among the people . . .

OLGA: Like a video report?

KARIM: Yes, I shared the video with my family, and they were overjoyed as they watched. My sister was crying, it was all so touching . . .

The footage that Karim and Aizhamal filmed went straight to their native village in southern Kyrgyzstan. It is worth pondering the circuit of the images' mobility that is part and parcel of the Immortal Regiment as another way in which the circulation of visual images follows in the old tracks of empire, but that is perhaps material for a different chapter. For this one, let us consider the deep connections between political representation and visualization of large imagined communities. One aspect that made Immortal Regiment so popular, I suggest, is that it provided endless opportunities for imagemaking to represent, and thus constitute, a sovereign Russian nation. This is an invitation that made this event such a potent tool of political manipulation, as numerous scholars have observed.[7] But in doing so, it also offered a language for contestation, and an opportunity to, quite literally, "insert oneself into the picture" for those who seek inclusion, and thus stretch a little bit the boundaries of the post-Soviet body politic.

NOTES

1. In 2020, the Immortal Regiment took the form of a digital procession of images online because of the Covid-19 pandemic restrictions. While the processions have resumed from 2021, I have not been able to observe them. This chapter, thus, represents a snapshot of the scale, demographics and motivations that marked the event before 2020.
2. The cult of the Great Patriotic War, already prominent in the USSR, has grown in the last twenty years, becoming a key lynchpin of the Russian national identity. See Nina Tumarkin, *The Living and the Dead: The Rise and Fall of the Cult of World War II in Russia* (New York: Basic Books, 1994); and Boris Dubin, "Kollektivnaya pamiat o voine i natsional'naia identichnost v segodniashnei Rossii," in *Simvoly—Instituty—Issledovania*. (Saarbrücken: Lambert Academic Publishing, 2013).
3. On the emergence and eventual cooptation of the movement, see Julie Fedor, "Memory, Kinship, and the Mobilization of the Dead: The Russian State and the 'Immortal Regiment' Movement," in *War and Memory in Russia, Ukraine and Belarus*, edited by Julie Fedor, Markku Kangaspuro, Jussi Lassila, and Tatiana Zhurzhenko (Cham: Springer International Publishing, 2017), 307–345; and Mischa Gabowitsch, "Are Copycats Subversive? Strategy-31, the Russian Runs, the Immortal Regiment, and the

Transformative Potential of Non-Hierarchical Movements," *Problems of Post-Communism* 65, no. 5 (2018): 297–314.

4. Rostislav Ischenko, "Bessmertnyi polk zavoevyvaet zapadnyi mir," *RIA Novosti*, May 10, 2016, https://ria.ru/20160510/1430640572.html
5. Serguei Alex. Oushakine, "Machines, Nations, and Faciality," in *The Oxford Handbook of Communist Visual Cultures*, edited by Aga Skrodzka, Xiaoning Lu, and Katarzyna Marciniak (New York: Oxford University Press, 2020), 157–193.
6. As noted by Pål Kolstø, the meaning of the ribbon of St. George has morphed over the past decade from a symbol of Soviet victory to an expression of support for Putin's regime and its wars more broadly. See Pål Kolstø, "Symbol of the War — But Which One? The St. George Ribbon in Russian Nation-Building," *Slavonic and East European Review* 94, no. 4 (2016): 660-701.
7. See Fedor, "Memory, Kinship," 307–345; Gabowitsch, "Are Copycats Subversive," 297–314; and Maksim Hanukai, "Resurrection by Surrogation: Spectral Performance in Putin's Russia," *Slavic Review* 79, no. 4 (2020): 800–824.

CHAPTER 56

PHOTO ESSAY: PICTURING WARTIME (2022)

JOAN NEUBERGER

ON FEBRUARY 24, 2022, the Russian Federation invaded its neighbor, the sovereign nation of Ukraine. As I write, in May 2022, the war has been going on for 127 days. Russian President Vladimir Putin seems to have expected to take control of Ukraine in a matter of days, but Ukrainian resistance, backed by US and European weaponry, has been fierce and determined.

The Russian war on Ukraine began, in fact, in 2014, when Russia annexed Crimea and began fighting to seize control of the eastern Ukrainian regions of Luhansk and Donetsk, allegedly in support of local separatists. Although that conflict has claimed approximately 13,000 lives, it was largely ignored by the world outside Ukraine. In contrast, the February 2022 acceleration of that war was massive in scale and impossible to ignore. Russia targeted major cities, the entire eastern region of the country, and the majority of the Black Sea coast, and it has done so with ferocious, destructive violence. Putin's government has offered numerous justifications for the invasion, all related in some way to Russia's historical imperial power. Most prominently, Putin has argued that Ukraine was never a sovereign nation, but rather has always been, and should be, part of Russia. Putin and his media representatives have also argued that Ukraine is crawling with Nazis, who are committing "genocide" against Russians and Russian speakers there. These arguments resonate with many Russians, who take pride in the enduring memory of Soviet resistance to the Nazis in World War II, and who are eager to protect all those Russians abroad who make up what they call the Russian World. Yet not one of these and other rationalizations for invasion justifies the widespread, ruthless destruction and looting by Russian troops on Ukrainian territory, or the brutal attacks on civilians and their homes, hospitals, schools, theaters, and museums.

Throughout this book, we have asked whether visual images have agency: how they act on us, how they circulate, how they create and shape discourses. We have argued that images create their own power as much as they are created and disseminated by the powerful. When images are sent out into the world, they participate in dynamic networks of images, in a pictosphere. The art and photography produced in Ukraine, and circulated around the world since February 24, 2022, display the variety of ways that images "act" in such networks: how they travel, multiply, inform (and misinform), and shape opinions, even contradictory opinions. They show us how images are produced with an awareness of multiple audiences and geographies, and how they resonate differently in different societies and sectors of society. They reveal how states try to control, and also how they can lose control of, the images they produce. They also show the ways that people in duress—whether hiding or fleeing from the enemy or watching the war from afar—express their feelings or work through traumatic experiences. The power of these images has been magnified by their rapid and widespread circulation on the internet. In 2022, the Russian imperial pictosphere took on a global dimension.

What follows is a survey of that pictosphere as witnessed by an American historian of visual cultures and modern Russia, viewing the war and the images produced in connection with the war, in a variety of media, from the safety of the United States. Images of war take on different meanings when viewed from inside Ukraine or inside Russia or outside from afar: we are shaped differently by images depending on our position and perspective "amid."[1] Readers should also bear in mind that the war is on-going, so our perspectives are continually unfolding. In the weeks since I began writing, Sievierodonetsk was been razed to the ground (90 percent of its buildings destroyed); shelling has returned to Kyiv (more than once), continuing to target civilians; and G7 leaders found it necessary to pledge $4.5 billion to relieve global hunger caused by the war on Ukraine.[2]

In the early days of the war, international shock at the scale of Russia's invasion was reinforced by photographs of buildings reduced to rubble that only days before had been lively urban centers (Images 56.1 and 56.2). Since so many people had believed that Russia would not invade, or that it would stop at the boundaries of the Donbas in eastern Ukraine, photographs of Kyiv, Kharkiv, Mariupol, and other major cities in the center and the south looking like Aleppo, or Mosul, or even Dresden in 1945, played a major role in winning broad international support for Ukraine.

Photographs of people sheltering in basements and subway stations, and photographs of women and children with their suitcases and their pets crowded into railway stations and border checkpoints, amplified international sympathies (Images 56.3 and 56.4). (Americans and Europeans conveniently forgot the millions of other people seeking refuge on their borders in order to fast-track Ukrainian immigration.[3])

Within days, large protests condemning Russia's invasion took place all over Europe, the United States, parts of the Global South, as well as in Russia. In the weeks and months that followed, Ukraine's photogenic flag—a blue sky over a yellow wheat

IMAGE 56.1 Sergey Bobok, an apartment building damaged by Russian shelling in Kharkiv on March 8, 2022.

IMAGE 56.2 Fadel Senna, Trostyanets in northeastern Ukraine, recovering from Russian occupation.

field—sprang up on walls all over the world to express solidarity with Ukraine (Image 56.5). One of the first photographs to bring the human cost of the war to the attention of the world showed a woman with her two children and a family friend all lying dead on a street near Kyiv, killed as they tried to escape the carnage. That photo, which went viral, captured the lifeless bodies next to their pet dog trapped in its

IMAGE 56.3 Fadel Senna, families fleeing the fighting in the Donbas wait to board a train at Kramatorsk, April 5, 2022.

IMAGE 56.4 Sergey Bobok, families sheltering in a subway station in Kharkiv, April 2022.

green carrying case. At the University of Michigan, the figures of the fleeing family were painted in silhouette on a large rock near campus that was usually painted to celebrate team victories or wish someone a happy birthday (Image 56.6). Against a backdrop of the instantly recognizable blue and yellow stripes, the image needed no words to convey its tragic message.

IMAGE 56.5 Ukrainian flags in New York City. Composite of photographs by Anne Lounsbery.

IMAGE 56.6 Victims of war, painted in silhouette, against colors of the Ukrainian flag, Ann Arbor Michigan. Photograph by Valerie Kivelson.

In Russia, the letter "Z" has come to be associated with support for the war effort. It appeared on military vehicles, and then on walls and cars and t-shirts, but there is no authoritative explanation for why the Z was chosen. As a letter that doesn't exist in either the Russian or Ukrainian alphabet, the "Z" is what might be called an "empty signifier." A symbol with no predetermined meaning in local languages can take on entirely new meanings, imprecise and broadly resonant. In this case, the Z signals general patriotic support for Russia's war against Ukraine. The "empty signifier" seems an appropriate symbol for this war, which the Russian government insists is not a war, but rather a "special military operation."

The orange and black stripes of the Z, seen in a poster over a busy St. Petersburg street, further reinforces the association of the Z with Russia's military (Image 56.7). Orange and black stripes recall the military medal of St. George awarded by the Russian Empire and the Soviet Union, as well as the post-Soviet Russian Federation. But what once was associated with the all-Soviet victory over Nazi Germany has been monopolized by Russia and used as a sign of specifically Russian power in occupied territories. As a result, the Z and the St George's ribbon have been mobilized by both supporters and opponents of the war, both inside and outside of Russia, to convey their pro- and antiwar positions. In March, this antiwar graffiti was stenciled on a Petersburg street: "*Peterburg ne ziguet*" (Image 56.8). The verb *ziguet* is slang for making the one-armed Nazi salute, "Sieg Heil," but the Cyrillic "з" of the Russian word is replaced here with the Latin "z." This mash-up has the effect of linking the Russian

IMAGE 56.7 Pedestrians cross a street in front of a billboard in support of the Russian armed forces, with the symbol "Z" and the words "We don't abandon our own," St. Petersburg, March 7, 2022.

IMAGE 56.8 Anti-war graffiti stating Petersburg does not Seig Heil (give the Nazi salute).

war against Ukraine with the creeping fascism already on the rise in Russia before the invasion, and repudiating both.[4]

Visual images like this pointed but unobtrusive graffiti have played an important role in the opposition to the war within Russia. In the years since Putin's return to the presidency in 2012, the government has closed almost all independent media outlets, arrested and threatened protestors, and manipulated elections, in part by arresting opposition candidates. Openly protesting the war against Ukraine could lead to arrest, job loss, and other punitive measures after the passage of a law in March 2022 criminalizing "false information" or "discrediting" of the military.[5] The mass protests of February and early March 2022 were courageous but short-lived, and people in Russia sought more anonymous, veiled forms of protest. In the days before the invasion, the words "No to War" appeared in metro tunnels and on walls in many locations (Image 56.9). On Cosmonauts Day in April, the anniversary of Yuri Gagarin's record-breaking flight into space, rueful graffiti appeared on a statue of one of the few people universally revered in Russia, saying: "Yura, we fucked it all up" (Image 56.10). In May, a few weeks after horrific atrocities inflicted by Russian troops were discovered in the town of Bucha, a suburb of Kyiv, little stuffed animals were found on benches around Moscow, with the word *Bucha* written in blood-like red paint (Image 56.11). Russian media have countered the reports of atrocities in Bucha with assertions that the pro-Ukrainian accounts were "fake news," and that the photos were staged by "crisis actors" pretending to be dead. Yet another set of visual images—drone footage and journalists' photographs—countered this counterargument by connecting the killings with the Russian advance.[6] In this case, some of the same images took advantage of

IMAGE 56.9 A woman in Moscow walks past anti-war graffiti reading "Nyet Voine" or "Not to War," March 14, 2022.

IMAGE 56.10 Graffiti of despair on a bust of cosmonaut Yuri Gagarin.

IMAGE 56.11 Toys with the word *Bucha* painted in blood-red, Moscow, May 22, 2022.

the semantic malleability of the visual—its nonverbal openness to multiple meanings—to establish competing narratives.

In current conditions of war and censorship, it is difficult to tell how many people in Russia support the war against Ukraine, and how many oppose it; how many feel a sense of responsibility for causing such colossal suffering, and how many have responded positively to the Russian media's patriotic appeals and its focus on "denazification." Even if such numbers were obtainable, they wouldn't communicate the complexity of Russian responses to current events. Within Russia, widely circulated news stories about the Maidan revolution in Ukraine, the Russian incorporation of Crimea, and the long war in the Donbas together with their accompanying images have helped to shape a particular telling of the history of the past eight years. For example, the House of Trade Unions fire in Odesa on May 2, 2014, in which more than forty pro- and anti-Russian activists were killed, is understood by some in Russia not only as a human tragedy, but as an assault on Russians (with pro-Russian Ukrainians here recast as Russians) and, perhaps, on Russia itself (Image 56.12). Presented as such, this event and its fiery photographic documentation made a very strong, symbolic impression on some Russians, and became one of the motivators of anti-Ukrainian sentiment in Russia.[7] In contrast, interpretations of the House of Trade Unions fire are less definitive in Odesa itself, where residents have been debating the multiple and contradictory meanings that have adhered to the events of that day. The building remains untouched, surrounded by a metal fence, but for years Odesans been hanging texts and poems on the fence that reflect on and debate the

IMAGE 56.12 Fire in the House of Trade Unions in Odesa, May 2, 2014.

meaning of the violence that occurred during the Maidan demonstrations. Despite the variety of texts, some Odesans see all of the messages as pro-Russian.

In addition to news images, an abundance of Ukrainian art has also been flooding social media and circulating internationally. Many of these are paintings drawn from Ukrainian art history and are posted to introduce us to the overlooked richness of Ukrainian art traditions, but some are new, produced since the war started.

Mykola Honcharov is a Ukrainian artist who has been making some of the most powerful images denouncing the Russian invasion, including the earlier seizure of Crimea and incursions in the Donbas. One of the poster-style images that appeared on his Facebook page in 2022 is a reworking of one of the most well-known Christian icons, St. George Killing the Dragon, a creature who represents "the personification of Absolute Evil," as Galina Lyubimova put it in her essay in this volume (see Chapter 29) (Image 56.13). This image is popular in Eastern Orthodox as well as western Christian traditions dating back to the eleventh or twelfth century, and was adopted in numerous European countries as a sign of military strength. The image of

IMAGE 56.13 Mykola Honcharov, "St. George Killing the Dragon."

St. George vanquishing the dragon appeared in the Russian imperial crest and has long been recognized as a symbol of the might of the Russian dynasty and the Russian state. In Honcharov's version, though, the roles are reversed: with its orange and black stripes, the enemy to be vanquished is Russia. This simple inversion of a well-known image makes a visceral and indelible impression.

Honcharov's deceptively simple, two-dimensional poster-like images make equally powerful statements about Russian violence, Ukrainian courage and determination, and the terrible costs of the war. The annexation of Crimea was the stimulus for his image of a thief in the night, stealing what he illegitimately claims is "ours" (Image 56.14). In another image, the *matryoshka*, or nesting doll, universally associated with Russian craft and whimsicality is, shockingly, dripping blood from its mouth (Image 56.15).

Among the most striking works produced since February 2022 are the pairs of drawings posted by Zoya Cherkassky-Nnadi on her Instagram page.[8] Cherkassky-Nnadi is an Israeli artist, born in Kyiv, who is widely known for vivid drawings of her life

IMAGE 56.14 Mykola Honcharov, "Ours."

IMAGE 56.15 Mykola Honcharov, "Matryoshki."

IMAGE 56.16 Zoya Cherkassky-Nnadi, "On Line to Buy Bread, Before and After."

growing up in the Soviet Union. After the war started, she began juxtaposing those older images of her childhood in Kyiv with drawings of the same sites today. These stark comparisons of before and after the Russian invasion of Ukraine bring home the everyday impact of war in an immediate and devastating way. In one pairing, a depiction of people peacefully waiting in line to buy bread (with the bread store sign in Russian, typical of the Soviet period) is followed by a scene of bodies lying in a bloody pile in front of the same bread store, now signed in Ukrainian, and now also burning and surrounded by other bombed buildings (Image 56.16). An accordion player, a common sight in the courtyards before the war, now lies dead with his hands tied behind his back, like the victims in Bucha (Image 56.17). A mother and child who once enjoyed the warm summer air on their balcony now clutch each other in fear as tanks roll past burning buildings on the street below (Image 56.18). Memories of common Soviet experiences, drawn originally to capture the pleasures of everyday life, are brutally shattered in these juxtapositions in a way that is immediately palpable.

IMAGE 56.17 Zoya Cherkassky-Nnadi, "The Accordion Player, Before and After".

IMAGE 56.18 Zoya Cherkassky-Nnadi, "On the Balcony, Before and After."

IMAGE 56.19 Andrey Borodulin, the central district of Mariupol, May 18, 2022.

IMAGE 56.20 Sergei Supinsky, A man and his son walk past a mural by street artist Sasha Korban in Kyiv on June 14, 2022.

Although no longer in international headlines every day, the war continues. The lively city of Mariupol has been decimated (Image 56.19), as has the ancient city of Chernigiv, and the Donbas city of Sievierodonetsk. However, when Ukrainian forces pushed the Russian troops out of Kyiv and elsewhere in April, people in these Ukrainian cities showed remarkable signs of resilience, and spread tiny slivers of hope. The mural painter, Sasha Korban, painted an image of mending and unity, using the flag to convey his message (Image 56.20). Andrei Kurkov, a prolific writer and social media presence, began circulating images of regeneration on Twitter (@AKurkov) after the winter of despair. What could be more resonant with regeneration than a woman baking Easter bread in her oven, which was the only structure still standing in her village, (Image 56.21)? And the students of Kharkiv school No. 134 refused to abandon their long-made plans to celebrate their graduation, even if the school itself lay in rubble. Sixteen-year-old Valeria, resplendent in her bright red graduation dress, stands on the ruins of her school in Kharkiv (Image 56.22). None of these images of hope and resilience try to mask the trauma caused by the wreckage, or to conceal the

Gorenka, village near Kyiv that is present in my latest novel that was finished before the war. Gorenka is destroyed by Russia. But local old lady baked Easter cakes in the stove of her ruined house. I would love to send one such Easter Cake to Angela Merkel.

12:16 AM · 5/2/22 · Twitter Web App

IMAGE 56.21 Baking Easter bread, May 1, 2022.

The graduates of Kharkiv School 134 still decided to take photos in front of their school that was destroyed by Russians. There are 111 schools that are completely destroyed by Russia in Ukraine. This number will grow unless Ukrainian army can stop them.

3:36 AM · Jun 7, 2022 · Twitter Web App

IMAGE 56.22 "Valeria, Graduation, School No. 134," Kharkiv, June 7, 2022.

scale of destruction. The visual contrast adds to the poignancy and realism of the situations they depict.

This short survey of the wartime pictosphere is far from exhaustive.[9] Although sentiment in much of the world, especially the Global North, is largely pro-Ukrainian, demonstrations of support for Russia have appeared in the Central African Republic, Israel, Brazil, the United States, and elsewhere. Strict censorship makes the pictosphere within Russia itself differ in significant ways from the kaleidoscope of images I am collecting from the news, social media, and the now mostly self-exiled antiwar Russian media that I follow. In Russia, images of patriotic support are prevalent, and images of destruction are often minimized and called into question as "fake news."[10]

It is too soon to be able to analyze the choices that news agencies in various parts of the world make about which images to reproduce, or how those choices intersect with the decisions millions of people make daily about which images to post and repost on social media. We don't yet know how the control of the media in Russia is shaping the consequences of the military operation itself. But we can see that certain images have the power to capture the imagination on a mass scale, to advance arguments, to shape human perception, and to some extent, presumably, to guide policy. The circulation of images on Twitter, Instagram, Facebook, YouTube, and TikTok connects people all over the world in a particular pictosphere, and that form of dissemination is inseparable from the meanings we draw from each image. Patterns of circulation shape our interpretation of events and define the place that images hold in viewers' own visual imaginary. Honcharov's English texts and Kurkov's English tweets, for example, reinforce the sense that the making and circulating of these images is informed by a strong awareness of their multiple audiences. The formation of globally interconnected (or partially blocked) networks of images and their address to viewers in various locations and contexts show the dynamic pictosphere to be at the heart of the ways we picture and make sense of our worlds.

NOTES

1. Lesia Kulchynska, "Violence is an Image: Weaponization of the Visuality During the War in Ukraine *Institute of networked cultures*, Amsterdam University of Applied Sciences: October 26, 2022. https://networkcultures.org/tactical-media-room/2022/10/26/violence-is-an-image-weaponization-of-the-visuality-during-the-war-in-ukraine-2/?fbclid=IwAR0_cy13FmxZ5Yhfu4KewekSMuq1VXPdemkjemblFN7lD3JZPt3CwouG5GY
2. "Ukraine News: Mariupol's Mayor Describes Grim Russian Rule," *The New York Times*, June 24, 2022, Michael Crowley, Edward Wong, Marc Santora, Thomas Gibbons-Neff and Ivan Nechepurenko, https://www.nytimes.com/live/2022/06/24/world/russia-ukraine-war-news; "Ukraine Updates: Turkey Agrees to Allow Sweden and Finland to Join NATO," *The New York Times*, June 28, 2022, https://www.nytimes.com/live/2022/06/28/world/russia-ukraine-war-news

3. Adolfo Flores, "Ukrainians Are Getting Special Treatment At The US Border That Other Asylum-Seekers Fleeing Violence Aren't, Immigration Lawyers Say," https://www.buzzfeednews.com/article/adolfo-flores/ukrainians-us-mexico-border-treatment
4. Pyotr Sauer, "Why has the Letter Z Become the Symbol of War for Russia?" *The Guardian*, March 7, 2022, https://www.theguardian.com/world/2022/mar/07/why-has-the-letter-z-become-the-symbol-of-war-for-russia; Monetochka, "Mama, I Don't Sieg Heil," *YouTube*, posted February 24, 2020, https://www.youtube.com/watch?v=oxzaKk4CHnA (my thanks to Jason Cieply and Kevin Moss).
5. Anton Troianovski and Valeriya Safronova "Russia Takes Censorship to New Extremes, Stifling War Coverage," *The New York Times*, March 4, 2022, https://www.nytimes.com/2022/03/04/world/europe/russia-censorship-media-crackdown.html
6. Russian Foreign Minister Sergei Lavrov led the charge in calling the news of atrocities "fake news." See "Lavrov slams situation in Bucha as fake attack staged by West and Ukraine," Tass, Russian News Agency, April 4, 2022: https://tass.com/world/1432013. On drone footage as proof of atrocities, see "Bucha killings: Satellite image of bodies site contradicts Russian claims," BBC News, April 11, 2022: https://www.bbc.com/news/60981238
7. These events are still a source of controversy among historians. For one early attempt to contextualize and disentangle them, see Howard Amos, "'There was heroism and cruelty on both sides': the truth about one of Ukraine's deadliest days," *The Guardian*, April 30, 2015. https://www.theguardian.com/world/2015/apr/30/there-was-heroism-and-cruelty-on-both-sides-the-truth-behind-one-of-ukraines-deadliest-days. For a sustained examination of Russian positive and negative responses to the war, see Andrei Loshak's documentary *Razryv Sviazi* (*Broken Ties*), YouTube, posted June 19, 2022, https://www.youtube.com/watch?v=5qmQs2LbnaE
8. "'Before and After': An Artist Repaints Scenes of Her Ukrainian Childhood," *The Moscow Times*, April 18,2022,https://www.themoscowtimes.com/2022/04/18/before-and-after-an-artist-repaints-scenes-of-her-ukrainian-childhood-a77390
9. And in the months since I wrote this essay, numerous Ukrainian artists and art historians have been reflecting brilliantly on the role of art and artists in this war and in anti-colonial activism more generally. See, "Response of Ukrainian Artists to the War Started by the Russian Federation," https://ukrainer.net/illustrators-about-war-4/; See in addition, works by Katerynka Iakovlenko, Yevheniia Moliar, Oleksandra Osadcha, and Asia Bazdyrieva
10. "Polnaia rech' Putina v Luzhnikakh 19 marta 2022 na 8-letie vossoedineniia Kryma v Rossii," (Putin's Full Speech at Luzhniki Stadium, March 18, 2022, on the Eighth Anniversary of the Unification of Crimea with Russia)," *YouTube*, posted March 18, 2022, https://www.youtube.com/watch?v=X3tQg6yexpc

CREDITS

Frontispiece *Annushka, the Kalmyk*, by Ivan Argunov, circa 1767. © "Muzei-usad'ba Kuskovo."

PART I

PO1 The world map of Ibn Ḥawqal, Istanbul, Topkapı Sarayı Müzesi Kütüphanesi, A. 3346.

1.1a, 1.1b *Zlatnik* of Volodimer. National Museum of the History of Ukraine.

1.2 *Srebrenik* of Volodimer, type III. National Museum of the History of Ukraine.

1.3a, 1.3b *Nomisma histamenon* of Basil II and Constantine VIII. BZC.1948.17.3171 © Dumbarton Oaks, Byzantine Collection, Washington, DC.

2.1 The world map of Ibn Ḥawqal, Istanbul, Topkapı Sarayı Müzesi Kütüphanesi, A. 3346.

2.2 The world map of Ibn Ḥawqal with English translations.

3.1-3.2 Miniatures from the *Madrid Skylitzes* (Codex Matritensis Græcus vitr. 26-2), fol. 172r, bottom. National Library of Spain, Madrid. https://www.loc.gov/item/2021667859.

3.3 Mosaic. https://www.flickr.com/photos/jimforest/15305211541/in/photostream/.

3.4 Mosaic. https://www.flickr.com/photos/jimforest/15121632320/in/photostream/.

PART II

PO2 Miniature from *Litsevoi letopisnyi svod XVI veka. Rus' 1483–1491 ot V.Kh.*, bk. 16 (Moscow: AKTEON, 2022), l. 339, p. 457. Also, https://runivers.ru/upload/iblock/8ff/LLS16.pdf, p. 462. By kind permission of AKTEON.

4.1 Detail. *Nova Absolutaque Russiae Moscoviae et Tartariae descriptio*. With permission of Wrocław University Library, Wrocław, Poland.

5.1 Miniature from *Litsevoi letopisnyi svod XVI veka. Rus' 1483–1491 ot V.Kh.*, bk. 16 (Moscow: AKTEON, 2022), l. 339, p. 457. Also, https://runivers.ru/upload/iblock/8ff/LLS16.pdf, p. 462. By kind permission of AKTEON.

5.2 Miniature from *Tale of the Battle of Mamai*, Barsovskoe sobranie № 1798, GIM 48987/2220 ГК 19075513 Aleksandriia. Skazanie o donskom boe, 1680s.

5.3 Miniature from "Zhitie Evfrosinii Suzdal'skoi," Gosudarstvennyi Vladimiro-Suzdal'skii istoriko-arkhitekturnyi i khudozhestvennyi muzei-zapovednik (No. B-29600/1482-KP-832).

5.4 Icon detail. By permission of Gosudarstvennoe biudzhetnoe uchrezhdenie kul'tury Arkhangelskoi oblasti "Sol'vychegodskii istoriko-khudozhestvennyi muzei."

6.1 Tommaso Dolabella, *Stanisław Żółkiewski Brings the Vaptured Shuisky kings to King Sigismund and Prince Władysław at the 1611 Sejm* (after 1611). Lviv Historical Museum. https://commons.wikimedia.org/wiki/File:Dolabella_Shuysky_Czars_before_Sigismund_III.png
6.2 Sigismund III column. https://commons.wikimedia.org/wiki/File:Warszawa_-_Zamek_Kr%C3%B3lewski.jpg.
7.1 Lazar Baranovych, *Mech dukhovnyi* (Kyiv, 1666), Frontispiece. Courtesy of the Russian State Library (Moscow). https://dlib.rsl.ru/viewer/01004085062#?page=7.
7.2 *Bibliia* (Moscow, 1663). Frontispiece. Courtesy of the Russian State Library (Moscow). https://dlib.rsl.ru/viewer/01003345095#?page=3.
7.3 *Mech dukhovnyi*, Title page. Courtesy of the Russian State Library (Moscow). https://dlib.rsl.ru/viewer/01004085062#?page=5.
8.1 Semën Ul'ianovich Remezov (1642–c. 1720), *Khorograficheskaya kniga* [chorographical sketch-book of Siberia]. MS Russ 72 (6). Houghton Library, Harvard University, Cambridge, Mass, f. 116. https://nrs.harvard.edu/urn-3:FHCL.HOUGH:4435676.
8.2 Remezov, *Khorograficheskaia kniga*, f. 152. https://nrs.harvard.edu/urn-3:FHCL.HOUGH:4435676.
8.3 *Remezovskaia letopis': istoriia sibirskaia; letopis' sibirskaia kratkaia kungurskaia faks. izd., issl., tekst i per./Podgotovka izd., tekst, spr. app. E. Dergacheva-Skop*, t. 1 (Tobolsk: Fond Vozrozhdenie Tobol'ska, 2006), chapter 15. By permission of the Russian Academy of Sciences Library (BAN 16.16.5).
9.1 *Remezovskaia letopis'*, chapter 138. By permission of the Russian Academy of Sciences Library (BAN 16.16.5).
9.2 Innokentii Gizel, *Synopsis* (Kyiv, 1680 edition).
9.3, *Remezovskaia letopis'*, chapter 151. By permission of the Russian Academy of Sciences Library (BAN 16.16.5).

PART III

PO3 Father Hyacinth (Iakinf), *Self-Portrait*, Institut Vostochnykh Rukopisei, RAN, "Pervyi Al'bom," book. no.1, p. 74.
10.1 Sir Godfrey Kneller, *Petrus Alexeewitz Magnus Dominus Tzar et Magnus Dux Moscoviae* (1698). Image courtesy: Royal Collection Trust/© Her Majesty Queen Elizabeth II 2021.
10.2 Frontispiece, *Symbola et emblemata* (Amsterdam, 1705). Image courtesy: Getty Research Institute, Los Angeles (2825-020).
10.3 Title page, *Symbola et emblemata* (Amsterdam, 1705). Image courtesy: Getty Research Institute, Los Angeles (2825-020).
11.1 Sketch of Great Wall. Russian State Archive of Ancient Documents (RGADA), Moscow, f. 199, op. 1, d. 349, ch. 2, ll. 560b-57 (1736).
11.2 Sketch of a Buddhist shrine. Russian State Archive of Ancient Documents (RGADA), Moscow, f. 199, op. 1, d. 349, ch. 2, l. 320b. (1736).
11.3 3. A. M. Legashov, *Chinese Town*, 1864.
12.1 "General Map of the Russian Empire," in *Atlas of the Russian Empire* [*Atlas Rossiiskii, sostoiashchii iz deviatnadtsati spetsial'nykh kart predstavliaiushchikh Vserossiiskuiu Imperiiu s pogranichnymi zemliami, sochinennoi po pravilam Geograficheskim i noveishim observatsiiam, s prilozhennoi pritom general'noi kartoi velikoi sei Imperii, staraniem i trudami Imperatorskoi akademii nauk* (St. Petersburg: Akademiia nauk, 1745)].
13.1 Engraving from G. F. Müller, *Opisanie zhivushchikh v Kazanskoi gubernii iazycheskikh narodov*, (St. Petersburg, 1791).
13.2 Photo: Hans Thorwid, Nationalmuseum, Stockholm, Inventory Number THC 3505.
13.3 Illustration for the French translation of J. G. Gmelin's *Reise durch Siberie* in *Continuation de L'Histoire générale des voyages ou collection Nouvelles*. T. 18 (Paris: Chez Rozet, 1768).
13.4 Illustration from J. G. Georgi, *Opisanie vsekh obitaiushchikh v rossiiskom gosudarstve narodov*. 2nd ed. (St. Petersburg, 1799).
14.1 *Annushka, the Kalmyk*, by Ivan Argunov, c. 1767. © "Muzei-usad'ba Kuskovo."
15.1 Vigilius Eriksen, *Catherine II Astride Brilliant*, 1762.
15.2 Mikhail Shibanov, *Catherine the Great in Travelling Costume*, 1787. Royal Collection Trust/All Rights Reserved.
16.1 Leontii Stanishchevskii, *Portrait of Aleksei Turchaninov*, oil on canvas, 1777, Ekaterinburg Museum of Fine Arts, Ekaterinburg, Russia.
16.2 Fedor Cherniavskii, *View of the Zlatoust Plant, the Armory Factory, and the Village*, gouache on paper, 1818, State Russian Museum, St. Petersburg, Russia.
17.1 Father Hyacinth (Iakinf), *Self-Portrait*, Institut Vostochnykh Rukopisei, RAN, "Pervyi Al'bom," book. 1, p.74.

18.1 Illustration from *Opisanie sviashneishago koronovaniia . . . imperatora Aleksandra Vtorago i imperatritsy Marii Aleksandrovny vsei Rossia*, (St. Petersburg?, 1856), Slavic and Baltic Collection. New York Public Library.

18.2 Illustration from Coronation Album of Alexander II. *Opisanie sviashchenneishago koronovaniia . . . imperatora Aleksandra Vtorago i imperatritsy Marii Aleksandrovny vsei* Rossia, (St. Petersburg?, 1856), Slavic and Baltic Collection. New York Public Library.

18.3 Deputies of "Asiatic peoples under the power of Russia." Coronation Album of Nicholas II, *Koronatsionnyi sbornik: Koronovanie v Moskve, 14 maia 1896*. New York Public Library.

19.1 Chokan Valikhanov. *Uch aiach. Three Women*. Pencil. 1856. Published in Ch. Ch. Valikhanov, "Graficheskoe nasledie," in *Sobranie sochinenii v piati tomakh*. Tom 5. (Alma-Ata: Izdatel'stvo Akademii Nauk Kazakhskoi SSR, 1972), 96.

19.2 Valikhanov, *Issyk-Kyl' Kyrgyz Women*. Pencil. 1856. Published in his "Graficheskoe nasledie," 94.

19.3 Valikhanov, *Nomadic Travels of the Kyrgyz from Issyk-Kul'*. Pen Drawing. 1856. Published in his "Graficheskoe nasledie," 97.

20.1 Charles Borchardt, *Portrait of Mari Weinberg*, 1866, photograph, Eesti Ajaloomuuseum, Tallinn.

20.2 Johannes Behse, *Lydia Koidula in Folk Costume*, 1866, photograph. Lydia Koidula, täisportree., CRJM F TR I 433 F 469, Carl Robert Jakobsoni Talumuuseum, Kurgjal. http://www.muis.ee/en_GB/museaalview/1832077.

20.3 Carl Timoleon von Neff, *The Chicken Feeder*, 1839, oil on canvas, Eesti Kunstimuuseum, Tallinn.

21.1 Vasily Vereshchagin, *After Victory*, 1868: *Vasily Vereshchagin*. Moscow: Gosudarstvennaia Tretiakovskaia Galereia, 2018. P.114.

21.2 Nikolai Karazin, "Execution of Criminals in Bukhara," *Vsemirnaia Illiustratsiia*, January 29, 1872, vol. VII, no. 161, p. 84.

21.3 Nikolai Karazin, "Exhibition of War Captives' Heads," *Vsemirnaia Illiustratsiia*, January 29, 1872, vol. VII, no. 161, p. 85.

22.1 Ilya Repin, *The Cautious One* (*Muzhichok iz robkikh*), 1877 (Nizhnii Novgorod Art Museum).

22.2 Ilya Repin, *Barge Haulers on the Volga* (*Burlaki*), 1873 (State Russian Museum, St. Petersburg).

22.3 Ilya Repin, *Procession of the Cross in Kursk Province*, 1883 (State Tretyakov Gallery, Moscow).

23.1 View purportedly of Tyumen from James W. Buel, *Russian Nihilism and Exile Life in Siberia* (1883).

23.2 Illustration from Harry De Windt's *Siberia As It Is* (1892).

23.3 Illustration from George Kennan's *Siberia and the Exile System* (1891).

24.1 Vasily Polenov, *The Darial Gorge*, 1891, watercolor on paper, 14.2 × 20.3 cm. Federal State Cultural Establishment Artistic and Literary Museum-Reserve Abramtsevo, Russia.

24.2 Mikhail Vrubel, *Demon and Tamara*, 1890–1891, watercolor and gouache on paper, 96 × 65 cm, State Tretyakov Gallery, Moscow, Russia. Photo Credit: HIP/Art Resource, NY.

24.3 Mikhail Vrubel, *The Dance of Tamara*, 1890-1891, watercolor and gouache on paper, 50 × 34 cm, State Tretyakov Gallery, Moscow, Russia. Photo Credit: Scala/Art Resource, NY.

25.1 Marie-Félicité Brosset, "The Main Gate of Ani," lithograph, from *Les Ruines d'Ani. Atlas Général* (St.-Pétersbourg: L'Académie Impériale des Sciences, 1861), 27.

25.2 Photogravure of the Safarskii Monastery, in Gr. P. S. Uvarova, ed., *Materialy po arkheologii Kavkaza*, vyp. 4 (Moscow: Tip. A. I. Mamontova i Ko., 1894), 80.

25.3 Photograph from N. Ia. Marr, *O raskopkakh i rabotakh v Ani letom 1906* (St. Petersburg, 1907), tabl. 13.

26.1 "Nerchinsk Hard Labor Type. Chained to a Wheelbarrow." Fotografiia A. Kuznetsova, Chita, no date. (Author's collection.)

27.1 Vasily Surikov, *Yermak's Conquest of Siberia*, 1895. State Russian Museum, St. Petersburg.

27.2 Vasily Surikov, *Study for Yermak: Head of a Khakassian*, 1895. State Russian Museum, St. Petersburg.

27.3 Vasily Surikov, *Yermak's Conquest of Siberia*. Sketch of the composition, 1891. State Russian Museum, St. Petersburg.

28.1 "Novaya Zemlya. The Sailboat 'Dream. (Mechta).'" Magic lantern slide, made in 1915 in the Polytechnic Museum from a painting by A. Borisov. KP 18589/80, PM, Moscow.

28.2 "Novaya Zemlya. Drinking tea with a Samoyed on Novaia Zemlia." Magic lantern slide, made in 1915 in the Polytechnic Museum from a painting by A. Borisov. KP 18589/83, PM, Moscow.

29.1 Archival photograph of a peasant painting with the image of Yermak striking the enemy. Russian Ethnographic Museum, St. Petersburg.

29.2 Ivan Krest'iannikov, Icon of Savior the Almighty. Late nineteenth to early twentieth century (Siberian icon: album. Omsk: Irtysh-92, 1999).

29.3 Icon of St. George. Novgorod school. 1130–1140 (State Tretyakov Gallery, Moscow).

29.4 V. V. Vasnetsov. *Bogatyri*. 1898 (State Tretyakov Gallery, Moscow).

30.1 Sergei Prokudin-Gorskii, "From Nature." Process and printing by S. M. Prokudin-Gorskii. *Fotograf-liubitel'* (*Amateur Photographer*), 1906.

30.2 Sergei Prokudin-Gorskii, Greek women workers harvesting tea. Digital color composite from digital file from glass negative, c. 1905–1915. Library of Congress, Prints & Photographs Division, Prokudin-Gorskii Collection, reproduction number LC-DIG-prokc-21522.

30.3 Side-by-side juxtapositions of *Bol'shoe Chertovo Gorodishche* by "S." From the "Open Research Project on the Heritage of Sergei Prokudin-Gorsky." http://prokudin-gorskiy.ru/group.php?ImageID=2515&mode=2.

PART IV

PO4 "Celebrating the destruction of rebellion," *Calamity* (*Khat'abala*), October 14, 1906, issue no. 18. Courtesy of the National Library of Armenia.

31.1 "Celebrating the destruction of rebellion," *Calamity* (*Khat'abala*), October 14, 1906, issue no. 18. Courtesy of the National Library of Armenia.

31.2 "'Haji, get up and go be Russian.'" *Molla Näsräddin*, April 14, 1906, issue no. 2. Courtesy of the National Parliamentary Library of Georgia.

31.3 "Congress of priests and press representatives," *The Devil's Whip*, January 1, 1908, issue no. 14. Courtesy of the National Parliamentary Library of Georgia.

32.1 Postcard written by Stalin to Mikheil Monaselidze, addressed in Russian, with text in Georgian. Reproduced with the permission of the State Archive of the Russian Federation.

32.2 Postcard depicting the painting. *The Attack* (*Hyökkäys*) by Eetu Isto, 1899, Used under Creative Commons License.

33.1 D. Moor, "Be on Guard!" Political poster, 1921. Manuscripts and Archives Division, The New York Public Library.

33.2 Anonymous poster: "Look! The riches of the Soviet Republics await the exertions of labor!" Political poster, 1921. Rare Books Division, The New York Public Library.

34.1 Konstantin Chebotarev, *Red Army*. 1917. Oil on cardboard. The State Museum of Fine Arts of the Republic of Tatarstan, Kazan.

34.2 Konstantin Chebotarev, *Breakfast in Suuk-Su*. 1918. State Russian Museum, St. Petersburg.

34.3 Unknown artist. *Tatar Shamail on Glass*. Beginning of the twentieth century. The State Museum of Fine Arts of the Republic of Tatarstan, Kazan.

PART V

PO5 Maria Nesterova [aka Maria Nesterova-Berzina], untitled poster (1926–1927). Lithograph on paper, 71.4 × 89.8 cm. Text in Uzbek (Arabic script). State Archive of the Russian Federation (GARF), Moscow, document number F. P-3316, O. 48, D. 85, L. 14. Reproduced with the permission of the State Archive of the Russian Federation.

35.1 Maria Nesterova [aka Maria Nesterova-Berzina], untitled poster (1926–1927). Lithograph on paper, 71.4 × 89.8 cm. Text in Uzbek (Arabic script). State Archive of the Russian Federation (GARF), Moscow, document number F. P-3316, O. 48, D. 85, L. 14. Reproduced with the permission of the State Archive of the Russian Federation.

35.2 Unknown artist, *Mount Ararat* (c. 1900–1920). Lithograph on paper, 52 × 69.5 cm. Mardjani Foundation, Moscow, catalog number Sh. 101. Reproduced with permission of the Mardjani Foundation.

35.3 Unknown artist, *The Names of the Four Righteous Caliphs* (1908). Lithograph on paper, 55.4 × 74 cm. Mardjani Foundation, Moscow, catalog number Sh. 93. Reproduced with permission of the Mardjani Foundation.

36.1 A still from *Tungus from the Khenychar*, Studio Kinosibir, 1929.

37.1 A still from *Roof of the World*, 1928.

37.2 A still from *At the Foothills of Death*, 1928.

37.3 A still from *At the Foothills of Death*, 1928.

38.1 Vazhia. A still from *Eliso*. From the collections of Gosfil'mofond Russia.

38.2 The milk separator as peace-offering. A still from *The Last Crusaders* (1933). From the collections of Gosfil'mofond Russia.
38.3 The Caucasus as Romantic vision. A still from *The Last Crusaders* (1933). From the collections of Gosfil'mofond Russia.
38.4 The milk separator between past and future. A still from *The Last Crusaders* (1933). From the collections of Gosfil'mofond Russia.
39.1 Georgii Zel'manovich, *Cotton Spinner, Uzbekistan*, between 1926 and 1928. Bodo von Dewitz, Sowjetische Fotografien 1918-1941, Göttingen Steidl Verlag, 2009, p. 180. The Daniela Mrázkowá collection, Museum Ludwig Köln.
39.2 Eleazar Langman, *Camel Caravan, Kazakhstan*, 1934/1935.
39.3 Maks Al'pert, *Kyrgyz Riders, Kyrgyzstan*, 1937. *USSR in Construction*, no. 3, 1938.
40.1-2. V. V. Konovalov, ed., "Political Map of Europe," 1:3.5 million, GUGSK NKVD SSSR, February 1938. Source: Private collection.
40.3 Alexander Ustinov, "Political Instructor G. S. Aksakalov conducts political training with young soldiers." Photograph, November 1940. Source: Archive of Alexander Ustinov. Image courtesy of Fedor Derevianskii.
41.1 Man holding a copy of *Birobidzhaner shtern* (*The Birobidzhan Star*), 1931. Personal collection of the author.
41.2 Soviet propaganda poster in Yiddish (1931). "The pig is our main machine for producing meat in the near future." Blavatnik Archive Foundation, 2021. https://blavatnikarchive.org/manifest/mv?manifest=22965.
41.3 Soviet propaganda poster in Russian "Let's turn the Jewish Autonomous Region into a flourishing area of the Far-Eastern Territory" (1936). Blavatnik Archive Foundation, 2021. https://www.blavatnikarchive.org/manifest/mv?manifest=2296642: 1.
42.1 Letters to O'g'ulxon with newspaper photographs attached. AAN RUz, f. 54, op. 1, d. 21, li. 99 and 118. Courtesy of the Arkhiv Akademii Nauk Respubliki Uzbekistana.
42.2 Postcard with picture of the Moscow Kremlin, AAN RUz, f. 54, op. 1, d. 21, li. 96. Courtesy of the Arkhiv Akademii Nauk Respubliki Uzbekistana. My thanks to Christopher Fort for help translating this text.
43.1 Jadej wada. N'urt'el p'el'a. G. Prokofjew padnas'. [*New Word: A Primer in Nenets Language*. Compiled by G. Prokofiev]. Moscow: Uchpedgiz. 1932. Pp. 10 and 26.
43.2 Comparison of illustrations in earlier and later primers, Nanai 1936 and 1956. Nanai 1936: Sunik O. P. Bukwar: Bichawa aloseori dansa [*A Primer: Book to Learn to Write*]. Moscow and Leningrad: Uchpedgiz, 1936. Pp. 50–51; Nanai 1956: Sunki O. P. Nanai tepch. shk. belechiuri kl. [Nanai primer for preparatory grade]. Leningrad: Uchpedgiz. 1956. Pp. 18–19.
43.3 Illustrations from late Soviet primers for Saami and Nentsi. Antonova A. A. Bukvar' dlia podgotovitel'nogo klassa saamskoi shkoly [*A Primer for the preparatory grade of Saami school*]. Leningrad: Prosveshcheniie: Leningradskoe otdelenie. 1982. Pp. 24–25; Rozhim A. I. Nenetsa bukvar' [*Nenets Primer*]. 4th ed. Leningrad: Prosveshcheniie: Leningradskoe otdelenie. 1986. Pp 14–15.44: 1.
44.1 Boris Berezovskii and Mikhail Solovyov, *Under the Leadership of the Great Stalin – Forward to Communism!* 1951. Poster, 77 × 115 cm. Reprinted with permission from The Ne boltai! Collection.
44.2 *Augustus of Prima Porta*, first century. White marble, 204 cm high. Vatican Museums. Photograph by Till Niermann, Wikimedia Commons (CC).
44.3 Frontispiece for Thomas Hobbes, *Leviathan*, 1651. Engraving by Abraham Bosse. The British Library.
44.4 El Lissitzky, "Article 126," *SSSR na stroike* (*USSR in Construction*), 1937, no. 9–12. Photomontage spread, 42 × 60 cm. Reprinted with permission from The Ne boltai! Collection
44.5 Boris Berezovskii, *It Is the Responsibility of Every Citizen to Complete the Census*, 1959. Poster, 88 × 58 cm. Reprinted with permission from The Ne boltai! Collection.
45.1 Boris Efimov, "Clamping Down on Cold War Enemies." *Izvestiia*, January 27, 1965, front page caricature. Reprinted with permission from The Ne boltai! Collection.
45.2 Boris Efimov, "A Polaris Missile Walks into a Bar." Reprinted with permission from The Ne boltai! Collection.
45.3 Correcting Cold War cartoons. A concerned reader of *Izvestiia* marked the flaws on Efimov's 1965 caricature and sent it back to the cartoonist along with a letter

further explaining the cartoon's problems. Reprinted with permission from The Ne boltai! Collection.

45.4 Boris Efimov, "Hands Off Czechoslovakia." Reprinted with permission from The Ne boltai! Collection.

46.1-4 Stills from *Sakhalin Island* (1954), directed by El'dar Riazanov and Vasilii Katanyan. Reproduced with permission of the Russian State Archive of Cinematic-Photographic Documents.

47.1 A woman wearing a *surpan* of the Vir'ial (upper) group of the Chuvash. Early twentieth century.

47.2 *Surpans* of the Anatri (lower) group of the Chuvash. Late nineteenth century.

47.3 Chuvash artist and designer E. I. Efremova in her studio.

48.1 Niko Pirosmani, *The Feast of Tbilisi Merchants with a Gramophone*. Undated, probably 1900s–1910s. Wikimedia Commons.

48.2 Aragvi restaurant, Moscow, 1965. Central State Archive of the City of Moscow, Division for the Preservation of Audio-Visual Documents.

48.3 Label for the Georgian wine Kindzmarauli, bottled in Leningrad in the 1980s. Wikimedia Commons.

49.1 T Noorits, "Madonna-85," in *Zhenshchina v fotoiskusstve* (Women in Photographic Art), exhibition catalog, cover, 1986. Used with permission of The National Archives of Estonia.

49.2 Y. Lun'kova, "Motherhood," in *Zhenshchina v fotoiskusstve* (Women in Photographic Art), exhibition catalog. Used with permission of The National Archives of Estonia.

49.3 A. Tenno. "No. 17," in *Zhenshchina v fotoiskusstve* (*Women in Photographic Art*), exhibition catalog. Used with permission of The National Archives of Estonia.

PART VI

PO6 The Demolition of the "Glory Monument," in 2021. Photograph by Halyna Tereshchuk for radiosvoboda.com (RFE/RL). https://www.radiosvoboda.org/a/news-lviv-demontazh-skulptury/31374203.html?fbclid=IwAR1ugeiEfqlt1gm09PLQGdL082wsd6rPjzSRFUMtCE_oIS5RnCKCKwA5BIo. Copyright © 2021 RFE/RL, Inc. Reprinted with the permission of Radio Free Europe/Radio Liberty, 1201 Connecticut Ave NW, Ste 400, Washington, DC 20036.

50.1 "Sviatoslav's Last Battle." Diorama by Nikolai Ovechkin.

50.2 A miniature from the fifteenth-century *Radziwill Chronicle*.

50.3 Wilhelm Hauschild. *Siegfried Kills the Dragon*. 1880.

51.1 Page from the 1672 *Tituliarnik* with the emblem of the Tsardom of Siberia.

51.2 Coin with the Siberian Sables minted in Siberia in the late eighteenth century. Used with permission from Photogenica

51.3 Monument in Novosibirsk. Used with permission from Photogenica.

52.1 "The Bronze Soldier." Photograph by Liilia Moroz, Wikipedia.

52.2 "Monument to the War Glory of the Soviet Armed Forces," in Lviv, Ukraine, 2013. Reproduced with permission of the photographer, Donald G. Hukle.

52.3 The Demolition of the "Glory Monument," in 2021. Photograph by Halyna Tereshchuk for radiosvoboda.com (RFE/RL). https://www.radiosvoboda.org/a/news-lviv-demontazh-skulptury/31374203.html?fbclid=IwAR1ugeiEfqlt1gm09PLQGdL082wsd6rPjzSR-FUMtCE_oIS5RnCKCKwA5BIo. Copyright © 2021 RFE/RL, Inc. Reprinted with the permission of Radio Free Europe/Radio Liberty, 1201 Connecticut Ave NW, Ste 400, Washington, DC 20036.

53.1 "Crimea in My Heart." Photo by Sasha Mordovets/Getty Images. Vladimir Putin celebrating the annexation of Crimea, March 18, 2014.

53.2 Internet meme juxtaposing Vladimir Putin with Catherine the Great. https://antimaidan.ru/photo/282

53.3a, 53.3b Vladimir Putin before and during his plunge into Lake Seliger, January 19, 2018. Photo by Alexei Druzhinin; reproduced with permission of Sputnik Images.

54.1-2 Stills from *Heavenly Company*, by the documentary collective Babylon '13.

54.3 A still from *Maidan* directed by Sergei Loznitsa.

54.4 A still from *Winter on Fire*, directed by Evgeny Afineevsky,

55.1 "The Immortal Regiment" on the front page of *Izvestiia*, May 10, 2016.

55.2 A screenshot from the news coverage of the Immortal Regiment procession in the news program *Vesti* on TV channel Russia 1, May 9, 2018.

55.3 Digital photograph from the 2017 Immortal Regiment procession in Moscow. Personal collection of Karim and Aizhamal K., used with permission.
56.1 Sergey Bobok, an apartment building damaged by Russian shelling in Kharkiv on March 8, 2022. Getty Images.
56.2 Fadel Senna, Trostyanets in northeastern Ukraine, after Ukrainian forces liberated the city from Russian occupation, March 29, 2022. Getty Images.
56.3 Fadel Senna, families fleeing the Donbas, April 5, 2022. Getty Images
56.4 Sergey Bobok, families sheltering in a subway station in Kharkiv, April 2022. Getty Images.
56.5 Ukrainian flags in New York City. Photographs by Anne Lounsbery.
56.6 Victims of war, painted in silhouette, against colors of Ukrainian flag, Ann Arbor, Michigan. Photo by Valerie Kivelson
56.7 Billboard in support of the Russian armed forces, St. Petersburg, March 7, 2022. Getty Images.
56.8 Anti-war graffiti, St. Petersburg.
56.9 Anti-war graffiti reading *"Nyet Voine,"* or "No to War.": Getty Images Europe
56.10 Anti-war graffiti of despair on a bust of cosmonaut Yuri Gargarin.
56.11 Toys with the word *Bucha* painted in blood-red, Moscow. May 22, 2022.
56.12 Fire in the House of Trade Unions in Odesa, May 2, 2014. [Source: theguardian.com, photo: Stringer/ Reuters.]
56.13 Mykola Honcharov, "St. George Killing the Dragon." Used with permission.
56.14 Mykola Honcharov, "Ours." Used with permission.
56.15 Mykola Honcharov, "Matryoshki." Used with permission.
56.16 Zoya Cherkassky-Nnadi, "On Line to Buy Bread: Before and After."
56.17 Zoya Cherkassky-Nnadi, "The Accordion Player."
56.18 Zoya Cherkassky-Nnadi, "On the Balcony, Before and After."
56.19 Andrey Borodulin, the central district of Mariupol, May 18, 2022. Getty Images.
56.20 Mural by Sasha Korban, Photo by Sergei Supinsky / AFP
56.21 Baking Easter bread, May 1, 2022. Twitter. Used with permission.
56.22 "Valeria, Graduation, School No. 134," Kharkiv, June 7, 2022. Twitter. Used with permission.

INDEX

Images and maps are indicated by italic page numbers.

N

Y

Z